Weak Knowledge: Forms,
Functions, and Dynamics

Schwächediskurse und Ressourcenregime

Discourses of Weakness & Resource Regimes

Edited by Iwo Amelung, Moritz Epple, Hartmut Leppin
and Susanne Schröter

Volume 4

Moritz Epple, Annette Imhausen and *Falk Müller* teach history of science at Goethe
University Frankfurt/Main and have directed research projects within Frankfurt's
Collaborative Research Center "Discourses of Weakness and Resource Regimes."

Moritz Epple, Annette Imhausen, Falk Müller (eds.)

Weak Knowledge: Forms, Functions, and Dynamics

Campus Verlag
Frankfurt/New York

ISBN 978-3-593-50977-8 Print
ISBN 978-3-593-44029-3 E-Book (PDF)

Cover design: Campus Verlag GmbH, Frankfurt-on-Main
Printing office and bookbinder: Beltz Grafische Betriebe GmbH, Bad Langensalza
Printed on acid free paper
Printed in Germany

For further information:
www.campus.de
www.press.uchicago.edu

Contents

Climate and Environment

Medical Knowledge

Preface

The present volume collects contributions to a conference held in Frankfurt/Main on 2-4 July 2017, contributions which have been re-worked after intense exchanges both during and following the conference. They pursue a common objective: to re-evaluate and challenge historiographical conceptions of the epistemic, social, cultural and practical strength, the robustness, of scientific knowledge. Whether we look at ancient or modern, at metropolitan or peripheral knowledge, whether we consider medical or mathematical knowledge, the empirical material of all but the most superficial studies of an episode in the history of science will reveal that, in its own period, and from the perspective of those involved, the bodies of knowledge involved were often quite different in nature from what textbook epistemology tells us. Justifications of knowledge claims may have been – and often were – found to be lacking, the practical uses of the knowledge in question may have provided formidable obstacles or were entirely missing, the cultural embedding of a given body of knowledge may have been difficult, and/or the social or institutional support for it may have been less than what some actors had hoped for.

While this does not come as a surprise for any serious historian of science, the question of what this observation *implies* for an analysis of scientific knowledge and its historical dynamics has less often been posed. What kinds of deficiencies in knowledge were articulated, when, and by whom? What is the role that such articulations of deficiencies played in the dynamics of knowledge? Were they intended as criticisms of knowledge claims that certain actors hoped to reject, or were they admissions of weaknesses by those producing and defending new bodies of knowledge, intended to help in improving this knowledge? Questions such as these are asked by the contributors to this volume. Taken together, their contributions show that there is a wide variety of possible answers – depending on the particular episodes studied, and on the specific interest that the authors bring to their materials.

In times of mounting criticism of scientific research on the part of political actors interested in undermining, or even denying, scientific evidence altogether, at least in certain fields such as climatology or medicine, it is important to clarify what a historical analysis of the weaknesses of knowledge advocated here does strive for, and what it does not. By discussing the wide variety of articulations of perceived weaknesses in scientific knowledge, be they epistemic, social, or practical in nature, this collection certainly does not intend to lend a hand to any form of science denialism. Quite the opposite. We hope to contribute to a better understanding of the fluidity and even fragility of scientific endeavours in the historical situations in which they are undertaken, and of the intellectual and social processes by which they are formed. Even a knowledge fraught with, and aware of, deficiencies of many kinds, may be the best guide to reasonable and responsible action in a complicated world.

The contributions in this volume are grouped in four sets. The first three chapters discuss general perspectives on our topic. Moritz Epple begins by outlining a framework for a historical epistemology of weak knowledge. He is followed by an essay in which Anne Marcovich and Terry Shinn sketch their understanding of weaknesses, in what they have proposed to call science research regimes in earlier work. Andy Pickering, in turn, challenges our conceptions of the role – and strength or weakness – of knowledge in action, by offering new reflections on, and examples of, what he has termed dances of agency.

These reflections are followed by historical case studies. In the first group, Daryn Lehoux discusses the status of uncertain knowledge in ancient astrology, Laurence Totelin takes a look at the role of weak actors in Graeco-Roman pharmacology, and Orna Harari discusses the attempts of metaphysicians in Late Antiquity to claim the status of an exact science for their field. A comment by Annette Imhausen closes this group. The second group of case studies addresses modern bodies of knowledge that have been considered as weak. Sven Dupré discusses the ways in which "failures" were addressed in early modern artisanal knowledge. Rivka Feldhay offers an analysis of historical knowledge claims in Dostoevesky's novels and asks how historical knowledge, or experience, in literary writing compares to that of historians. In her chapter on narratives and theories in economics in the 1920s, Monika Wulz discusses another literary tool with a precarious relation to scientific knowledge: the role of fictions. An area of physical knowledge whose status with respect to the established hierarchy of scientific disciplines was – at least initially – perceived as weak is discussed in Falk Müller's chapter on industrial physics in Germany. This group is closed with a joint contribution by participants of a pre-conference workshop for young scholars exploring the analysis of weak knowledge in yet other fields, including early modern literature and meteorology, recent child psychiatry, and educational sociology, while also taking up general reflections on Chinese "science" and Latourian science studies.

In the third set, Dominique Pestre, Matthias Heymann, and Richard Staley address articulations of weaknesses in bodies of knowledge relating to climate and the environment. In their contributions, we can, in particular, follow the motives of such articulations from the inner workings of climate research (as in Heymann's discussion of computer-based climate modelling) to the political and economic attacks on it (as in Pestre's look at environmental knowledge and regulation, or in Staley's account of self-proclaimed "heretics" in climate science)."

The fourth and final set of contributions is devoted to medical knowledge, and thus to another field of knowledge in which claims of inherent weaknesses formed part and parcel of the field's tradition and were re-negotiated in each historical period. Suman Seth looks at the contested role of medical knowledge in late eighteenth-century abolitionist debates. José Brunner takes us to the courtrooms of Victorian England and the medical discourse on "nervous shock" in the context of railway accidents. John Harley Warner, in turn, analyses the co-emergence of a weaker, more personal form of medical knowledge with modern scientific medicine in the USA in the decades around 1900. The latter, and the specific discourses of weakness in the later rise of "evidence-based medicine", are the subject of Cornelius Borck's contribution. The four chapters in this set are then commented upon by Mitchell Ash.

As readers will find, several threads connect the contributions in this volume. One of these concerns the epistemology of various bodies of knowledge perceived to be weak, across the periods explored. A second is, clearly, the social and political status of such bodies of knowledge, or, in other cases, the social and political status of claims that a certain form of knowledge is weak. Finally, one recurring theme here is the practical relevance of knowledge and the role this plays in perceptions of its strength or weakness. Throughout, we find that an analysis of such perceptions of weakness, and of the discourses in which such perceptions were articulated, provides ample material for historical analysis, an analysis, we hope, that can deepen our understanding of both the significance and the fragility of knowledge in the "mangle of practice" (to borrow Andy Pickering's term).

*

The conference upon which this collection is based was funded by Frankfurt's Collaborative Research Centre (CRC - Sonderforschungsbereich) 1095 Discourses of Weakness and Resource Regimes, in turn funded by the German Science Foundation (DFG). We thank our CRC speaker, Iwo Amelung, and its manager, Mi Anh Duong, for generously supporting the conference. We are grateful for further financial support from Goethe University of Frankfurt/Main and the Vereinigung der Freunde und Förderer der Goethe Universität.

Neither the conference nor the research performed in our group would have been possible without the work of our doctoral students, Theresa Dittmer, Nadine Eikelschulte, Lukas Jäger, and Linda Richter. They, and Martin Herrnstadt, at the time working with a Minerva fellowship at the Cohn Institute for the History and Philosophy of Science and Ideas at Tel Aviv University, also made it possible to organise the highly successful pre-conference workshop, bringing together doctoral students and post-docs from Israel and Germany. We are extremely grateful to all organisational support given by our secretaries, Susanne Bernhart and Judith Delombre, student helpers, Leo Kaiser and Nelli Kisser, and our local magician Convin Splettsen (whose magical knowledge is definitely *not* weak). The manuscript of this volume has been prepared for the press by Chris Engert in Florence, whose careful language editing improved all contributions, and Nelli Kisser, whose diligent work accompanied all stages of the production process from its early beginnings until the final layout.

We also need to thank two speakers whose important contributions to the conference could not be included in the present collection, Katharine Anderson and Eleanor Robson. Finally, one of the editors, Moritz Epple, wishes to thank Hans-Jörg Rheinberger for choosing *fumaria officinalis* as the subject of his first poem, opening this collection. This is a surprising coincidence, involving weak medical knowledge of a very personal relevance.

Frankfurt am Main, July 2019
Moritz Epple, Annette Imhausen, and Falk Müller

Schwaches Wissen I
Erdrauch

Hans-Jörg Rheinberger

Den Erdrauch
bekam Carl von Linné
aus Sibirien geschickt.
Es war ein Versehen.
Als die Samen aufgingen
im Garten von Hammarby
war die Enttäuschung
des Naturforschers groß.
Er sah nicht
die Herzblume wachsen
über die er gelesen hatte
in der Dissertation
jenes russischen Studenten
und die er
hatte mustern wollen
mit eigenen Augen.
Doch die Fumarie
wuchs prächtig
an der Mauer seines Hauses
und breitete sich
ohne sein Zutun aus
über Uppsala und Umgebung.

Von dort

nahm sie ihren Weg

durch ganz Europa.

Vom Altai bis nach Schweden

hatte die Post

ihren Samen getragen.

Der Rest war das Werk

der Ameisen

denen der Anhang

ihrer Nüsse schmeckt.

Hätte er das alles gewusst

er wäre vorsichtiger

mit ihr umgegangen.

Und schließlich:

Wie so viele Pflanzen

aus seinem System ist sie

auch theoretisch gewandert.

Sie hat die Gattung gewechselt

und gehört heute

zu den Corydalien.

Schwaches Wissen II
Der unsichtbare Begleiter

Hans-Jörg Rheinberger

Südafrika

war das Ziel ihrer Reisen.

Auf getrennten Wegen

kamen die beiden Schüler Linnés

ans Kap der Guten Hoffnung.

Carl Peter Thunberg

wandte sich

dem Landesinneren zu

bevor er

in holländische Dienste trat

um Java und Japan zu bereisen.

Anders Sparrman

schloss sich am Kap

der Zweiten Cookschen Weltreise an

bevor auch er, zurück

aus dem pazifischen Archipel

sich mit der Südspitze Afrikas

vertraut machte.

Aber vergessen wir nicht:

Ohne den jungen

Daniel Ferdinand Immelman

den gebürtigen Kapstädter

den kundigen Führer
wären beide
nicht weit gekommen.
Wenn wir den zwei
Naturforschern heute
in ihren Werken begegnen
und ihr Wissen bewundern:
Denken wir auch an ihn
den unsichtbaren Reisenden
er hat ihnen
den Weg gewiesen.

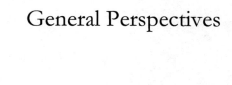

General Perspectives

The *Theaetetus* Problem: Some Remarks Concerning a History of Weak Knowledge

Moritz Epple

Abstract

In philosophy and history of science, knowledge and science have long been viewed as a cultural resource of remarkable epistemic, social, and practical strength. However, many recent studies indicate that, both in the period of their emergence and in many other historical circumstances, bodies of knowledge have been epistemically deficient, socially marginal, culturally fragile, and/or weak in other respects. This may be the case even when the knowledge in question is a highly desired resource within a given historical formation. The chapter outlines an analytic framework for investigating the forms, functions, and dynamics of weak bodies of knowledge.

1. History of science as a historiography of strength?

The beginnings of the historiography of science in early modern Europe were informed by a historical narrative in which science – as a body of knowledge, as a cultural tradition, or as a web of institutions – was placed in a position of epistemic, cultural, and, eventually, social, strength. As is well known, for eighteenth century historians of the exact sciences, such as Jean-Étienne Montucla and others, the progress of the exact sciences, and of astronomy in particular, served as an exemplar for the progress of reason and of the human mind.[1] Others, including Jean D'Alembert in his *Discours préliminaire* (1751) to the *Encyclopédie* co-edited by Denis Diderot and himself, and later Nicolas de Condorcet in his *Esquisse d'un*

---

1 Montucla 1758. Among the histories of astronomy of the period, one should mention Pierre Estève's *Histoire générale et particulière de l'astronomie* (1755); Jean Sylvain Bailly's contested writings; and, one generation later, Jean Baptiste Joseph Delambre's *Histoire de l'astronomie moderne*, in several volumes (1817–1827). This narrative was not new in the eighteenth century. An early praise of astronomy as a result of long-term epistemic progress was given by Johannes Kepler in his *Apologia pro Tychone contra Ursum*, see Jardine 1988.

tableau historique des progrès de l'esprit humain (published posthumously in 1795[2]), went a step further and declared the progress of knowledge to be a crucial factor in, and a measuring rod for, social progress in general.[3] States in which attention was given to the advancement of knowledge were considered to be far superior to those deplorable kingdoms in which ignorance reigned. When, several decades earlier, Voltaire had declared in his *Lettres sur les Anglais* of 1734 that a scientist such as Isaac Newton, and not a violent political leader, was the greatest human being of all times, he did not trigger laughter, but – in co-operation with a group of like-minded intellectuals and patrons – a Newtonian fashion which, in some senses, continues to this day.[4]

In those "modern" societies which have formed since that time, and in particular, in the European nation states of the nineteenth century, and all those later states that were based upon this model, the sciences were organised as a strong arrangement of institutions from elementary schooling to high-prestige research, which profoundly shaped both social and technological life. The main product of this institutional arrangement – *knowledge* – thereby acquired a strong and constitutive role in such societies. Historians have been tempted to speak of societies which were modelled on these states as "knowledge societies". Scientific and political discourses which aim at stabilising and extending this position of strength, and historical discourses contributing to a politics of memory which celebrates the sciences as a unique modern achievement, are so widespread that they are hard to survey. Even certain recent and sophisticated forms of professional history of science are still feeding upon this narrative of strength.[5]

The narrative is mirrored, and, to some extent, pre-figured, in the philosophical tradition that has addressed the topic of knowledge since antiquity. One *locus classicus* of this tradition is Plato's dialogue *Theaetetus*, which offers the philosophical definition of knowledge that probably remains its most widely-discussed definition in philosophical circles, and, according to which, knowledge is a belief (gr. *doxa*) endowed with two additional features providing strength, i.e., *truth* or *correctness* (gr. *orthe doxa*), and a *justification* (gr. *logos*) for the truth of the given belief. The argument of Plato's dialogue consists in a graded criticism of *deficient* forms of knowledge or beliefs: pure sense perception, belief without a truth-check, and correct belief without justification. Plato's text is radical and consistent in its re-

---

2 The *Esquisse*, written shortly before Condorcet's death, summarises the drafts and fragments on which Condorcet had worked for years; see de Condorcet [1772–1794] 2004.
3 For an illuminating discussion of the idea of progress and its decline, see Canguilhem 1987.
4 Compare, among others, Shank 2008.
5 This is even the case in varieties of the history of (scientific) knowledge, such as the literature on the "science question in feminism" or on "colonial science". When "modern" or "Western" science is characterised as being an instrument of male or colonial domination, the assumption rests in place that this instrument is powerful and can serve its purpose on the grounds of this strength.

fusal even to call such deficient forms of believing "knowledge". And while modern philosophical interpreters differ widely with respect to the specific meaning to be given to the individual elements of the conception of knowledge offered by the *Theaetetus*, there is widespread agreement that the conception's general structure should be defended.

2. The *Theaetetus* problem

From these and similar theoretical approaches to knowledge, a problem emerges for the historian of science, which I will call the *Theaetetus* problem: Can, and, if so, should the history of science be based upon such a demanding and openly normative conception of knowledge (independently of whatever specific version one might prefer)? Some care is needed to frame the *Theatetus* problem in the right way, and to clarify what it entails and what it does not. Among other things, it needs to be distinguished both from standard philosophical arguments about the interpretation and validity of Plato's conception of knowledge, and from the quest for a sociological approach to knowledge.

First of all, if we consider a text such as Plato's *Theaetetus* as a historical trace, and if we understand the conception of knowledge described in it as a time-dependent, situated conception with its specific ancient Greek motives and functions, the *Theaetetos* problem disappears, of course. Few historians of science would feel bound today by the specific normativity ascribed to the knowledge described, for example, in Plato's curriculum in his *Republic*. Quite obviously, the Athenian philosophers searched for a normative conception of knowledge, and they did so for interesting and complex reasons.[6] A famous Greek parallel to the *Theaetetus* can be found in Aristotle's opening of book *A* of his *Metaphysics*, which sought to characterise *episteme* as a particularly demanding form of knowledge, superior to other forms of knowing, such as artisanal knowledge or medical experience.[7] Some of the essays in this volume will touch upon related issues in ancient science.

Now, we may go through history and look for comparable articulations of strong, normative conceptions of knowledge, be they philosophical, historiographical, or expressed by scientists of any kind, and we will, of course, find many instances. Let me just mention the prefaces to Kant's *Critique of Pure Reason*, in

---

6 See, for instance, the discussion by Lloyd 1979.

7 This demanding notion of *episteme* is further developed in Aristotle's methodological writings, in particular in his *Posterior Analytics*. Wolfgang Detel has argued that, also in these considerations, a central role is played by a reflection on the deficiencies of human cognitive capabilities; see his introduction to Aristoteles' *Zweite Analytik/Analytica Posteriora* (2011).

which (in the preface to the second edition) he repeatedly suggested that the "*sichere Gang*" – a literal translation would be the *secure gait* – of cumulative progress in a given body of knowledge was the characteristic feature of scientific knowledge (in his view, this secure gait had not yet been attained in metaphysics nor in several domains of knowledge about nature). In other places, Kant famously mentioned *mathematics* as the essential ingredient of true scientific knowledge. ("*Ich behaupte aber, dass in jeder besonderen Naturlehre nur so viel eigentliche Wissenschaft angetroffen werden könne, als darin* Mathematik *anzutreffen ist.*" (Kant 1786, A VIII) Or let us recall the conceptions of science and knowledge advanced by the various forms of positivism of the nineteenth century French or twentieth century Viennese variety, or finally, the many and diverse conceptions of knowledge which, while being only half-way articulated or fully implicit, were endorsed by scientists at different times and places in their actual practice.

In a certain sense, different philosophical interpretations of, and reactions to, the *Theaetetus* provide very similar additional material for a history of the conceptions of knowledge. Some of these have been simple variations of the list of criteria for knowledge given by Plato, such as Alwin Goldman's proposal to denote mere true belief (disregarding justification) as "weak knowledge" (Goldman 1999). Others have aimed for a re-interpretation of one or several of these criteria, in particular, trying to give modified accounts of what it means to justify a given belief. Similarly, any later philosophical framing of the idea of knowledge has found its variety of modern interpretations. However, as will be seen shortly, such proposals do not resolve the problem posed here.

Indeed, we cannot easily make the *Theaetetus* problem disappear in a historicist or philosophical way by pointing to a plurality of different notions of (scientific) knowledge. The history of science, and the history of knowledge more generally speaking, cannot escape the question of *which* conception of knowledge should be chosen as the basis of its historiography, for the simple reason that it needs to decide what should be included within its domain, and what should remain outside. Clearly, this question has been asked before, and here, finally, we need to address the traditions of a sociology of knowledge which have called for a radical reframing of the notion of (scientific) knowledge for several decades. The Edinburgh approach, in particular, has asked us to treat the belief systems of different historical and/or social origin(s) in an *impartial* and *symmetric* fashion, methodically avoiding allowing the "truth" or "falsity" of beliefs enter any explanation of why a belief system has been endorsed as knowledge in a particular social configuration, and considering "justifications" to be social phenomena that *require* (sociological) explanation, rather than *providing* it for the knowledge in question (Bloor 1991, Chapter 1).

However, truth and falsity and the validity of justifications are not the only topics raised by the *Theaetetus* problem. Rather, it brings to the fore the problem of a gradation, or a hierarchy of more or less *deficient* forms of what is – in one way or the other – considered to be knowledge. This feature is shared by most, if not all, conceptions of knowledge that we can identify in the historical record. Indeed, even in the *strong programme*'s approach to knowledge, a closer look reveals a gradation of, more or less, deficient forms of knowing. Let me quote from David Bloor's famous passages exposing the *strong programme* in his *Knowledge and Social Imagery*:

> Of course knowledge must be distinguished from mere belief. This can be done by reserving the word 'knowledge' for what is collectively endorsed, leaving the individual and idiosyncratic to count as mere belief. (Bloor 1991, 5)

Thus, and quite consistently in Bloor's programme, it is the *degree of collective recognition* of a given belief that decides about its status in the hierarchy of knowledge. The *Theaetetus* problem thus re-appears in modified form: Can and, if so, should a historical sociology of (scientific) knowledge accept the restriction implied by Bloor to study beliefs endorsed by (large) collectives, or, in other words, to knowledge which has at least *some* strength in social respect?

Similar arguments can be made with respect to proposals such as the one made by Helga Nowotny and her co-authors to distinguish "epistemically robust" knowledge from "socially robust knowledge" (Nowotny et al. 2001), or any other recent approach to the sociology of knowledge. What all such approaches offer are alternative versions of a *gradation* between stronger and weaker forms of knowing, framed in a specific – here, sociological – way. For Nowotny, to provide social robustness to modern expert knowledge is a *normative* stance, intended to strengthen the democratic legitimacy – and social efficacy – both of certain bodies of knowledge and of the procedures by means of which they are obtained, and it was crucial in her analysis that some bodies of knowledge did *not* possess the robustness for which she asked.

The *Theaetetus* problem, therefore, lies deeper than the transition from a traditional epistemological conception of knowledge to a historicist or to a sociological one. It is one task to distance oneself as a historian from normative conceptions of knowledge framed in particular historical situations, and to transform them from unreflected starting-points of historiography into objects of historical study in their own right. (In this move, I fully agree with the sociology of scientific knowledge and historicist methodologies.) But it is *another* task to bring to light the various scales of differences articulated *within* such normative conceptions, between knowledge in the full sense, and forms of knowing that were or are considered more or less deficient from the point of view of any such conception. Not only texts such as the *Theaetetus* or the beginning of Aristotle's *Metaphysics*, but also many non-reflexive documents of the history of science, and even Bloor's distinction between "knowledge" and "mere belief" or Nowotny et al.'s degrees of social robustness, indicate that, together with every conception of knowledge, there usually comes *a gradation and hierarchy of forms of knowledge perceived to be stronger or weaker, or more or less deficient,* which deserves the attention of historians.

The essential question to be asked here is: Does an ambitious conception of knowledge – be it that of the Athenian philosophers, Bloor's or any other – indeed apply to the empirical material in the archive of past scientific activity?[8] To all who have dealt with – at least mildly – complex episodes in the history of science, the answer should be obvious: no, it does not. Against the backdrop of a rigid Platonic conception of knowledge, a large part of what has been passed down as knowledge from earlier times, i.e., a large part of the empirical material of history of science, would have to be sacrificed. On the other hand, also knowledge that was initially only shared by one or very few individuals and that circulated only in very small groups, or knowledge that could not be considered to be justified, reliable, or socially robust, has been, and will be, of interest to the history of science in many cases.

Let us rephrase these considerations in slightly more formal terms. Let A be any characterisation of knowledge that appears in history (whether it be articulated explicitly or shared implicitly by knowledge actors at a particular time and in a particular place, or any of its modern interpretations). Then, we call a fragment or a body of knowledge A-*weak*, if – and only if – it appears to be deficient from the perspective of A.[9]

This *relative* characterisation of the weakness of fragments or bodies of knowledge encompasses rather different cases. A certain knowledge can be *Plato-weak* or *Bloor-weak*, it can be weak in the sense of the Vienna circle, or in the sense of present climatology. Moreover, the status of a fragment or body of knowledge as "weak" or "strong" in this sense is never given once and for all, but may change whenever the guiding conception of knowledge within a certain area of knowledge changes over time, or from place to place, or between different groups of actors. A fragment of knowledge may appear to be weak from a *contemporary* or from a *later* perspective, or it may appear to be weak from the standpoint of one conception of knowledge while *at the same time* it appears to be strong from a competing perspective. A well-known example of the latter situation would be any experimental knowledge gained from a seventeenth century vacuum pump, evaluated either from a Boylean or, conversely, from a Hobbesian, conception of knowledge.[10] Even within one and the same conception of knowledge A, a frag-

---

8 We may take the notion of the "archive" here in a wide, Foucauldian sense.

9 My thanks to Kärin Nickelsen for a discussion that made me aware of the usefulness of this clarification.

10 This is one of the main conclusions to be drawn from Schaffer and Shapin's analysis of the controversy; see Schaffer and Shapin 1985.

ment of knowledge may appear to be A-weak in one respect, while appearing to be strong in another.

Our central conjecture is that – in stark contrast to the traditional narrative of strength – a very large, and probably the largest, part of knowledge passed down in the history of science has appeared to be weak at least from the perspective of *some* historically relevant conceptions of knowledge. The *Theaetetus* problem, in its most general form, then, consists in studying this conjecture and its potential implications for understanding the dynamics of (scientific) knowledge.

For the history of science and the history of knowledge, the Platonic way out of this situation is blocked.[11] For several reasons, historians cannot accept the Platonic stance to reserve the term "knowledge" only for its non-deficient forms, be it in its original Platonic version or in any of its later re-interpretations or alternatives. For one, such a move would fly in the face of the firm conviction of most historical individuals whom we encounter in the history of science and who, as a rule, have defended their beliefs emphatically as knowledge – perfectly independent of all criticism addressed at their knowledge claims by contemporary or later critics, or by today's epistemologists. Moreover, we cannot undo the essential relativisation of the notion of knowledge and the corresponding historical relativisation of any scale or gradation of deficient forms of knowledge which we find in the historical archive. If we did so, we would, in fact, render invisible the historical variety and variation of such gradations, which a historical study of weak knowledge aims to uncover.

It should be clear from the previous remarks that the *Theaetetus* problem is not limited to what we are presently used to calling science. Not only does "science" – in whichever form it is defended at a given time and in a given place – denounce other bodies of knowledge not considered to be science, but even within such alternative bodies of knowledge or belief(s) the question of a gradation of weaker and stronger forms recurs both internally and externally – as, for instance, is the case when, in the agricultural literature of the eighteenth century, the weakness of the contemporary physicist's knowledge about weather was pointed out, or when, in modern alternative medicine, the knowledge claims of "school medicine" are attacked in the name of an alternative experience of health.

---

11 On some interpretations, even Plato refuses to take this road, since he ends the *Theaetetus* in an *aporia*. Even the definition of knowledge as true belief with justification is rejected by Socrates, which leaves two possibilities: either knowledge is an even higher, but indefinable form of insight, or we are left with a multitude of deficient forms of knowledge, without ever being able to obtain knowledge in its fullest and purest form. This would resonate with the claim in Aristotle's *Ethics* that true *theoria* is reserved for gods.

3. Some examples

In order to illustrate the scope of our central conjecture, it will help to mention briefly some examples and types of weak knowledge. Since the present collection brings to the fore a wide range of very different material, a general remark and a very small set of examples shall suffice. This will, at the same time, provide occasion to introduce a number of additional terms and tools for a historical analysis of weak knowledge.

The general remark is that the examples for weak knowledge are not limited to a few cases of knowledge claims rejected by the various scientific mainstreams of different periods and cultures, such as, for instance, astrology or alchemy in the modern period, or certain forms of divination in antiquity, or alternative medicine in the present. Quite the opposite: they include entire bodies of knowledge which came to great historical fame, such as large parts of medical knowledge in different periods, and, in particular, knowledge about the causes of diseases, or knowledge about living beings and their internal and external function, or contested experimental knowledge, both early and late modern cosmological knowledge, and so forth. Moreover, one might want to include entire bodies of unwritten knowledge, and/or "tacit" knowledge, among the forms of weak knowledge in the sense outlined here.

Let me, therefore, take my specific examples of weak knowledge from a tradition that has long and often been regarded as being closest to a strong ideal of knowledge, i.e., from the mathematical sciences. Even here, examples abound of knowledge that was, or is, considered weak from at least some perspectives. All the following examples are well-known. They are used here to underline certain features of diagnoses or articulations of weaknesses in fragments or bodies of knowledge that are of a more general relevance for other cases as well.

To begin with, we may consider almost every statement made in the context of seventeenth century infinitesimal mathematics as a case of weak knowledge. This is not only true from the perspective of later conceptions of mathematical rigour. Even at the time, many of the statements of infinitesimal mathematics were contested in heated debates about the validity or viability of the many proposed "methods". Here, we may think of René Descartes' criticism of Pierre de Fermat's claims, of the debate about Bonaventura Cavalieri's method, or of George Berkeley's fervent attack against the missing proofs and inconsistent arguments of Isaac Newton's fluxional method and Gottfried Leibniz's infinitesimal calculus.[12] The latter attack not only shows a theologian trying to combat disciplinary and ideological competition from mathematicians within the field of seventeenth century learning. It was equally cogent on an epistemic level – so

---

12 From the large literature on early infinitesimal methods, see, for example, Baron 1969; Giusti 1980; Anderson 1985; Mancosu 1996; Cifoletti 1990.

much so that the Newtonians saw the necessity to compensate for the weakness of their knowledge claims by means of sophisticated supplementary work.[13]

In such cases, we find what we will term a *contemporary discourse of weakness*, which can be analysed historically. Taking Berkeley's attacks on the Newtonians as an example, we find that such a discourse consists of articulations or diagnoses of specific weaknesses in a given body of knowledge, or in a set of knowledge claims, which may range from epistemic to social aspects, often combined in ways which aim at increasing the force of an ascription of weakness, for instance, when Berkeley adds the moral insult of being untrustworthy to the epistemic injury of pointing out what he sees as logical contradictions in the calculus of fluxions or in infinitesimal analysis.

When the weaknesses of infinitesimal mathematics were again, albeit very differently, criticised in the context of the so-called "revolution of rigour" during the nineteenth century,[14] and then again from the perspective of twentieth century formal mathematics, we are confronted with two different *retrospective discourses of weakness* concerning this body of knowledge. In other words, the perception, articulation and problematisation of weaknesses in a given body of knowledge may itself have a history. In this, as in similar cases, this history was closely intertwined with the history of the *knowledge culture* shaping the field or discipline of which the given body of knowledge was a part, mathematics in this case.

A second example, equally well-known in the historiography of mathematics, makes it clear that not only can the specific perception or articulation of an epistemic weakness shift over time, but, in fact, a certain body of knowledge that has been considered to be exceptionally strong for centuries can suddenly appear to be weak – a change, which was again coupled to a deep change in knowledge culture. Such was the case with geometric knowledge in Euclid's *Elements*. In the first proposition in the first book of the *Elements*, it is shown that an equilateral triangle can be constructed on any given line segment. The argument runs as follows: Let AB be the given segment, then let a circle be drawn about A with radius AB, and another circle about B with the same radius. Then, Euclid assumes, there will be a point where the circles intersect. Let it be denoted by C and let the lines AC and BC be drawn (the interested reader will easily provide a diagram illustrating the construction). Then ABC is the equilateral triangle sought, as Euclid does not fail to prove after the construction with recourse to the definitions, postulates and axioms stated at the beginning of the *Elements*. In his *Vorlesungen über neuere Geometrie* of 1882, the Gießen mathematician Moritz

---

13 See Jesseph 1993; in particular, the discussion of Colin Maclaurin's extensive efforts to defend Newton's fluxional calculus against Berkeley's criticism by reworking it in a synthetic style.

14 The term "revolution of rigour" seems to have been coined by Imre Lakatos; see the contributions in Gillies 1992.

Pasch was to declare this proof to be insufficient, since none of Euclid's postulates and axioms guaranteed that the two circles *did* indeed have a point in common (Pasch 1882, 44–45). Euclid had passed over this issue (and several others) without any comment. Thus, even the simplest, first proposition in this exemplar of a demonstrative science was, in Pasch's eyes, lacking proof. The intended implication was clear: in its traditional form, Euclid's *Elements* were insufficient as a foundation of geometrical knowledge. For centuries, the point raised by Pasch had *not* been questioned at all.

What does this example imply? We could, in fact, say that here the Platonic conception of knowledge was mobilised against a long-standing paradigm of true knowledge. For Pasch, it was not the truth, but, indeed, the lack of justification that made Euclid I.1 a weak knowledge claim. But, in order to evaluate this ascription of weakness historically, we must understand the requirement of proof, or justification, in Pasch's specifically *modern* sense, and *not* in the traditional form of Euclidean proof. We are thus again confronted with a change in the guiding conception of knowledge. This particular change was connected with the changing role of intuition as a faculty of the mind capable of justifying mathematical knowledge, a capability first partially – and then entirely – rejected in mathematical culture after the mid-nineteenth century, a change that would have deep and far-reaching consequences in the twentieth century.[15] Pasch's diagnosis of an epistemic weakness in Euclid (and we can find a large number of similar examples in the mathematics of this period) thus had a *dynamising function*: his aim was to argue for a complete re-structuring of geometry (and, of course, he believed he had the key for this re-structuring in his hands). This connection between *ascriptions of weakness* and *knowledge dynamics* is one of the points of our approach.

My last example is taken from nineteenth century geometry as well. Let us briefly recall the first systems of so-called non-Euclidean geometry before, say, the year 1868.[16] Both from a later *and* from a contemporary perspective, the systems proposed by Janos Bolyai, Nikolai Lobachevsky and a few other geometers in the late 1820s were considered to be epistemically weak. It was unclear whether, and in what sense, they could be considered to be consistent, demonstrated, or true, in the sense that they accurately described the structure of phys-

---

15 Pasch's argument provides an interesting example of a retrospective ascription of weakness, since his criticism revolves about an issue which had been addressed, in general form, already in ancient Greece, when Plato discussed geometrical practices of drawing which, in his view, mixed up sensual perception with knowledge; see his *Republic*, 510. A critique of intuition as a basis for mathematical knowledge is a recurring motive of discourses of epistemic weakness; see Hahn 1993, and, taking its cue from this article, Volkert 1986.

16 In 1868, three texts were published which changed the status of this new mathematical speciality: Bernhard Riemann's still unpublished inaugural lecture, held in Göttingen in 1854, entitled *Über die Hypothesen, welche der Geometrie zu Grunde liegen*, Hermann von Helmholtz's essay entitled *Ueber die Thatsachen, welche der Geometrie zum Grunde liegen*, and the contribution by Eugenio Beltrami mentioned above. See, e.g., Gray 1989.

ical space, and so forth. However, even more important for the present discussion may be the fact that the beliefs of their authors were not endorsed collectively, not even within a small, conspired thought collective. In other words, their knowledge was, in this period, *Bloor-weak*. It disappeared in a flood of widely-shared belief in the truth of traditional Euclidean geometry, as is easily shown by bibliometric means, and as was acutely felt by the early non-Euclideans.[17]

Again, we find a mobilising function of this diagnosis of social weakness. Around 1868, it motivated a number of new approaches to the topic, not least the essay by the Italian Eugenio Beltrami with the telling title *Saggio di interpretazione della geometria non-euclidea*, published in 1868. In this essay, Beltrami – well aware of the social weakness of the new geometry – sought to develop a new mathematical *interpretation*, in the precise sense given to this word by the author, of the new geometrical ideas within the framework of traditional geometry. He succeeded, but had to pay a price which may not even have been clear to Beltrami himself. In his interpretation, a kind of negatively curved surfaces made their appearance which could no longer be fully represented in space as it was conceived by geometrical tradition. In order to surmount the widely-shared disbelief in non-Euclidean geometry, Beltrami (and others following him) opened up an epistemic fissure in the contemporary web of geometric thought which would gradually widen and eventually transform what Gaston Bachelard termed the *esprit scientifique* within geometry.[18]

All three types of example point to different situations in which contemporary or retrospective diagnoses of weakness of a fragment or body of knowledge, and different dimensions of weakness, have played a role, and they point to different dynamic functions that such articulations of deficiencies could have in the production of knowledge.

4. Dimensions of weakness in (situated) knowledge

It is thus time to turn the tables on the forms, functions and dynamics of weak knowledge. Let us systematically ask about the historical roles of fragments and bodies of knowledge – including scientific knowledge – that have been perceived or criticised as weak from the perspective of one or several strong conceptions of knowledge, including the perspectives of various philosophies, historiographies, or non-reflexive discourses of scientists.

In our group in Frankfurt's *Sonderforschungsbereich 1095*, we are trying to make some inroads into this topic both from a systematic point of view, and based

---

17 See the bibliography given in Stäckel and Engel 1895.
18 See Bachelard 1934, Chapter 1.

upon a (small) number of empirical studies on different episodes from both ancient and modern contexts. Throughout, we take as our starting-point the conviction that knowledge – at least in so far as we can trace it historically – is never
given *per se* but is always given in situated form, for specific knowledge actors in
specific historical constellations. Even if 12x12 may always be 144 (a question
that, in contrast to the strong programme and some other forms of epistemology,
we do not want to discuss), knowledge about this relation is neither given trans-
historically nor ubiquitously. Rather, it is always present in a concrete form,
phrased in a specific language, bound to specific circumstances and individuals
(producers, distributors, and consumers of knowledge), it is carried by varying
forms of material support, culturally interpreted, endowed with social functions,
and so forth.

It is surely superfluous to recall these things here. However, it may be worthwhile to point out that the notion of "situatedness" itself is not entirely clear when
applied to knowledge. What, indeed, are the features of a historical or social constellation in which a fragment or body of knowledge may be perceived by a group
of actors as strong or weak? One of our sub-projects, presently pursued by Lukas
Jäger, looks at the various meanings given to the idea of "situatedness" in the
tradition of the sociology of knowledge, in order to explore relevant dimensions
in which knowledge can be considered as being historically situated.[19] One of the
relevant traditions has tied the notion of "situation" or "constellation" to various
versions of a description of social position, ranging from Marxist class position,[20]
to Karl Mannheim's analysis of "social layers" and Edgar Zilsel's distinction of
different professional groups as bearers of a specific experience and knowledge
(humanists, university scholars, artisans). A second line of thought has considered
the human body in its individual development as a site of "personal" knowledge
(the main author here is Michael Polanyi, of course, but one may also point to a
variety of accounts drawing on psychoanalysis, including Gaston Bachelard's pertinent writings), and there are a number of combinations of these two traditions
outlined, for example, by Norbert Elias and, in particular, by Donna Haraway's
more recent defence of "situated knowledges".[21]

For our purposes, it is not necessary to limit the analysis to one of these different perspectives in which some given knowledge may be "situated", just as it
would be beside the point to opt for one specific conception of knowledge. Rather, we can conceive of "situatedness" in any and all of these dimensions, depending on the specific needs of understanding for a given historical constella-

---

19 For a full account of Lukas Jäger's study, I must point the interested reader to his Ph.D. dissertation, in preparation.

20 The point of reference for this view in the early twentieth century debates was Lukács 1923.

21 Yet another approach to situated knowledge, emphasising the intertwining of human and non-
human elements in what he terms "dances of agency" has been proposed by Andy Pickering.
See his contribution to the present volume.

tion. Within such constellations, knowledge may have been perceived or have appeared to be weak. Any diagnosis, or ascription of weakness to a given fragment or body of knowledge is therefore doubly relative: both with respect to a specific standard of knowledge against which it is evaluated, and with respect to the specific situation *in* which it is evaluated.

As indicated in the previous section, such a qualification can either be a contemporary ascription by historical actors, or a retrospective ascription by later actors at different times (including, in fact, ourselves as historians and knowledge actors in our own present). Accordingly, when we are dealing with discourses about the weakness of a fragment or body of knowledge, we need to distinguish between contemporary or retrospective discourses of weakness. Plato's critique of sense perception or his critique of beliefs without justification was a form of ancient Greek discourse on the weakness of certain forms of knowledge. Similarly, Aristotle's remark that medical experience fell short of what he termed *episteme* contributed to that discourse. George Berkeley's criticism of infinitesimal methods, in turn, contributed to a comparative form of a discourse of weakness: Theological argument, he claimed, was logically more rigorous than Newtonian or Leibnizian analysis (shaky and inconsistent in his view), an argument that was intended to raise concerns both on the epistemic level and on the social level of disciplinary power. And so forth.

Looked at in this way, the archive of the history of science contains a wealth of materials from which an analysis of weak forms of knowledge, of the pertinent articulations and discourses of weakness, and the historical changes connected with them may begin. This volume brings to the fore a wide range of such materials from different periods and different scientific fields. Based upon a survey of such materials, focusing on contemporary and retrospective forms of ascriptions and discourses of weakness, and based upon a survey of the various explicit or implicit conceptions of knowledge operative within them, we may hope to develop a more systematic understanding of the possible dimensions of weakness or strength in knowledge – not in the sense of an ultimate, all-encompassing scale on which we can measure the strength and weakness of knowledge, but in the sense of finding recurring patterns in discourses on the weakness of certain fragments or bodies of knowledge in our empirical material.

In our Frankfurt group, we have found it useful to frame analytic descriptions of historical episodes, in which weak knowledge played a role, according to the following preliminary grid of three dimensions of weakness. In each of these three dimensions, and a number of sub-dimensions, weaknesses of knowledge have repeatedly been addressed by historical actors:

1. The dimension of *epistemic weakness*:

a. knowledge with weak rational anchoring (e.g., missing proof or stringent argument, lack of precise vocabulary, ...);
b. knowledge with weak empirical anchoring (e.g., based upon problematic forms observation or experiment, ...).

2. The dimension of *social* and/or *cultural weakness*:

a. knowledge supported only by few, or by socially weak, knowledge actors;
b. knowledge with weak institutional anchoring;
c. knowledge with weak cultural embedding.

3. The dimension of *practical weakness*:

a. knowledge that lacks usefulness in specific (technical or social) practices;
b. knowledge that lacks embedding in larger technologies pervading society.

We expect this grid to be transformed by further historical work. In particular, the sub-dimensions listed above may prove to be insufficient, or not detailed enough to encompass all interesting forms and dynamics of weak knowledge. However, a brief look at one of the case studies carried out by a member of our group may illustrate that in historical episodes of some complexity all dimensions outlined in the grid do indeed arise and pose interesting challenges for historical investigation.

Linda Richter's study of knowledge about the weather in German-speaking literature between 1750 and 1850 provides ample material for a history of weak knowledge.[22] Drawing on an analysis of the corpus of writings on meteorological subjects compiled by Gustav Hellmann in the late nineteenth century, Richter distinguishes three main bodies of knowledge related to the weather: a body of *physical* knowledge aiming at establishing causes and laws of the weather; a body of *semiotic* knowledge giving rules for interpreting a wide variety of natural or artificial signs pointing to the weather that was, is, or will be; and a body of *organic* knowledge taking the weather to be either related to living beings or even a form of life of its own. In each of these bodies of knowledge, perceptions and mutual ascriptions of weaknesses to individual fragments of knowledge abounded.

For instance, when, in 1837, Heinrich Wilhelm Dove claimed to have found a "fundamental law" of the rotation of winds, others – such as James D. Forbes – were quick to point out that neither the observational basis nor a theoretical

---

22 For a full account, see Richter 2019. For other studies of meteorology before the advent of national meteorological institutions, from a number of related but different perspectives, see Janković 2000; Anderson 2005; Golinski 2007; Locher 2008.

argument warranted speaking of a "law" in this case.[23] Similarly, the claims made in the French officer Denis-Bernard Quatremère d'Isjonval's *Aranéologie* of 1798 of being able to draw inferences from the behaviour of spiders to the weather of the next two weeks or so were considered to be empirically weak – which did not prevent many scholars of the time from keeping spiders in their offices in order to observe any possible relation between their agility or the shape of their webs, and the local weather.

To turn to the social dimension: when physicists of the time admitted that their knowledge about the weather to come was surpassed by the experience of farmers, there was an interesting trade-off between the epistemic weakness perceived by the physicists in their own knowledge and the weakness that they perceived in the knowledge claimed by their competitors of lower social status (and hence, they assumed, lower reliability).[24] An institutional weakness, on the other hand, was both admitted and deplored in virtually all efforts to make sustained weather observations prior to the existence of standardised, institutionally supported observational procedures, even in those efforts that provided a certain amount of collected observational data over a certain span of time and space. For an example of a body of knowledge with a weak cultural embedding, Richter points to the tradition of botanical or floral calendars, advocated by Carl Linnaeus and some of his followers, such as Linnaeus' student Alexander Malachias Berger and the Silesian landowner Heinrich Graf von Mattuschka: while the idea of measuring the "botanical" progress of the year by means of a suitable sequence of flowerings of plants (which would naturally adapt to the variations of the weather) may have been both valuable and attractive to a few, it never found broader cultural support in the period considered.[25]

That the practical dimension of weakness was relevant in knowledge about the weather is obvious and expected. Here we find, on the one hand, the admission of the limited practicability of written (and, at times, printed and sold) rules intended to determine the local weather tomorrow from instrumental observations at one's house (a vision endorsed, for example, in Michael Adelbulner's collection of essays entitled *Kurze Beschreibung der Barometer und Thermometer, auch anderer zur Meteorologie gehörigen Instrumenten, nebst einer Anweisung, wie dieselben zum*

---

23 Dove 1837, iii. Forbes's criticism (1841) can be found in his *Supplementary Report on Meteorology*, 108.

24 See, for example, de Saussure 1783, 489–491.

25 Benjamin Stillingfleet translated Berger's text into English and published it in his *Miscellaneus Tracts Relating to Natural History, Husbandry, and Physick: To which is Added the Calendar of Flora* (1762), 229–327. Mattuschka's proposal was published as *Anzeige der Beobachtungen, welche dienen können, einen für Landwirthesehrnützlichen Naturkalenderzuverfassen; entworfen für die patriotische Gesellschaft in Schlesien* (1775).

Vergnügen der Liebhaber, und zum Vortheil des Publici gebraucht werden sollen of 1768).[26] On the other hand, we may consider the impracticability of processing even small amounts of the large avalanches of printed numbers from weather observations in journals such as the *Ephemerides Societatis Meteorologicae Palatinae* or the later, short-lived *Annalen für Meteorologie, Erdmagnetismus und verwandte Gegenstände* within a (non-existing) national system of weather forecasting at the time.

It may be helpful to emphasise two aspects of the analytic grid just proposed. First, the grid allows us to study, in any given episode in the history of knowledge, the mutual dependence, or, in fact, independence, of these dimensions of weakness. One might be tempted to ask whether the table is intended to show that epistemic strength is often, or always, coupled with social or cultural, as well as practical weakness, or whether there is a pattern of intrinsic historical development that ends up with such a coupling. To this question, a historian's reply should be: whether or not such couplings exist in a given episode is a matter of empirical investigation, and not a matter to be decided *a priori*. Indeed, the distinction between the different dimensions of potential weakness is meant to open up a space for such investigations, rather than close it by any form of pre-emptive epistemology. And, indeed, case studies such as Linda Richter's indicate that, for extended periods, the perceived weaknesses of a given area of knowledge in the three dimensions may be independent from each other.

Second, the question needs to be raised of what the status of this table is with respect to the distinction between contemporary and retrospective ascriptions of weakness. Is this a pattern that was active in any past discourse on the weakness of knowledge? Or is this just an analytic device based upon our own pre-conceptions that will eventually need to be replaced by a very different one? To this, I would answer that it is a bit, and neither, of both. At this point, the proposed grid may be understood as an abstraction from a variety that we find in history, i.e., as a pattern of which instances can be found in rather diverse concrete forms in our empirical material. Nonetheless, the abstraction may have some value since it points to recurring aspects in a wide variety of historical episodes and situations.

5. The *Theaetetus* trap and the dynamics of weak knowledge

Since any of the dimensions of potential weakness in knowledge is obviously related to a corresponding, complementary dimension of strength, it might, at first

---

26 Adelbulner was an astronomer in Nürnberg and editor of a journal *Merkwürdige Himmelsbegebenheiten*, in which the material of this monograph originally appeared. Adelbulner's monograph went through three editions: Nürnberg 1768, Frankfurt/Main and Leipzig 1776, and again in 1781.

sight, appear that, in the end, our list amounts to no more than an enumeration of all potential deficiencies (epistemic, social, cultural, practical) that proper knowledge has to overcome. And that a historiography of weak knowledge, in the end, might offer nothing but a mere contribution to a historiography of the heroic overcoming of all these deficiencies, and the deserved failure of all bodies of knowledge that remain weak.

This, however, would be a misunderstanding. It would mean falling into what may be called the *Theaetetus* trap in the historiography of science. The point of a historical analysis of articulations of weaknesses and deficiencies in knowledge is not to prepare for the ultimate, total conception or historiography of strong, epistemically, socially and practically robust knowledge, or to consider any belief or knowledge which fails to fulfil these criteria just as a preliminary stage or a deficient form of such ultimate knowledge.

On the contrary, the analysis of weaknesses in knowledge must remain based upon the doubly relative notion of weakness introduced above, and its objective is to understand the historical role both of diagnoses and discourses of weaknesses in fragments or bodies of knowledge in specific historical constellations, and of the knowledge so described. All ascriptions of weakness, in any of its dimensions, are to be understood as historically constituted, situated perceptions or constructions within a framework of changing conceptions of what constitutes "proper" knowledge (i.e., knowledge without deficiencies), not as objective properties of given fragments or bodies of knowledge. And, to repeat our central conjecture, in a very large class of historical situations, the amount of knowledge that was perceived as weak in an epistemic or social or practical sense outweighed the fragments of knowledge accepted as being strong in *all* these dimensions by far. This alone requires us to revise the traditional narrative of strength in the history of science, and to avoid the trap of an assumed teleology. It may also allow us to trace, at least in certain cases, the surprisingly strong performance of bodies of knowledge otherwise thought to be weak. In Richter's study of meteorology, the *semiotic* body of knowledge about the weather proves to be a case in point: even the physicists of the period were forced to admit that, despite its epistemic weakness, and despite the comparatively low social position of some of its proponents, a semiotic approach to weather prediction had more to offer to the interested "public" than their own physical hypotheses on the course of the weather.

Perhaps, the most important aim in an analysis of weak knowledge is to understand what the *functions* of these relative weaknesses have been in the dynamics of knowledge in culture at large, and in society (or, if you prefer, in society/nature). Articulations of weaknesses in knowledge are not only made by the bearers of such knowledge, but also by actors and groups that make use of, or provide patronage for, or offer competing cultural resources to, the knowledge in question. A general hypothesis in our *Sonderforschungsbereich* in Frankfurt is that perceptions and discourses of weakness in historical formations (of all kinds, not just when they concern and involve knowledge) are related to change, to historical transformations in specific ways. From this perspective, the question to ask is: How were, and are, (the perceptions and articulations of) weaknesses in knowledge functionally related to historical change? In which domains? In what ways? Let me conclude, therefore, with a few remarks on knowledge dynamics within the sciences, followed by a look at dynamics within society and culture.

(1) We have learned to appreciate that virtually all *new* scientific knowledge is weak at least for a certain period. In the phase of its emergence it is often volatile and precarious, difficult to stabilise, to communicate, or to justify, it can be tied to actors who are marginal in the scientific communities of their day, it often lacks practical relevance, and so forth. The historiography of *knowledge in the making*, as has been advocated by many, from Latour and Woolgar's *Laboratory Life*, to the more recent efforts of Hans-Jörg Rheinberger and his group in studying the history of experimental systems and *Wissen im Entwurf* has pointed to many aspects of the dynamic role of weak knowledge in the very core of scientific practice.[27]

(2) Second, we can take another look at the historiography of *controversies* about knowledge, especially those in which the *weakness* of knowledge claims was thematic (rather than priority issues or the like). Several famous cases quickly come to mind; the reader may choose her or his favourite example.[28] In such controversies, we are not only faced with the social dimension of knowledge claims, but often the epistemic and practical dimensions that are also involved. We could say that, in controversies of this kind, the weakness of the knowledge in question is a condition of possibility for the controversy itself. Since situations of controversy are highly dynamic, we again find a rather general, dynamic role of weaknesses of knowledge.

(3) To move to the role of knowledge in society at large, here, it is particularly interesting to follow those lines of thought that view knowledge as a resource of social and material practices and configurations. Just like a precious metal in ore that is hard to mine, knowledge can be scarce, or difficult to exploit, as it were, in a given social constellation. Examples of this kind are often found in historical situations in which a need for knowledge (or rather, a limitation of available knowledge) is explicitly articulated by actors other than the producers of such knowledge. A well-known case in point would be the group behind the 1714 *Longitude Act*, bringing together the military, politicians, and scientists asking for

---

27 Latour and Woolgar 1979; for the publications of the group around Rheinberger, see for example: http://knowledge-in-the-making.mpiwg-berlin.mpg.de/knowledgeInTheMaking/de/index.html, last accessed 23 March 2019.

28 Famous early modern examples would be the controversies about solar spots, about comets, and even the controversies about the system of the world. In all these controversies, the weaknesses of the opponent's knowledge claims were fervently attacked.

better methods for navigation. In such cases, we find a discourse of weakness or scarcity of knowledge reaching beyond the ivory towers of science, usually revolving around the practical weakness of the bodies of knowledge already at hand, and, more often than not, (and indeed in the case of navigation) this practical weakness is not easily or quickly overcome. A similar situation obtained in eighteenth and nineteenth century meteorology with respect to the practical desire for weather prediction, be it in the context of maritime transportation or agriculture. Whatever theoretical progresses towards a dynamical meteorology may have been achieved during the nineteenth century, they did not satisfy the needs for predictive knowledge articulated in seafaring or storm-ridden nations. And when Vilhelm Bjerknes eventually offered his differential equations for calculating the weather, they remained difficult to exploit (numerically, based upon sound observational experience, and technically) for quite some time.

More recent examples of this kind come to mind when looking at the decision by national governments to invest in the sciences related to aviation from the early twentieth century (in fact, including meteorology as a resource for aviation during World War I), or at medical knowledge required to treat health issues that are perceived to be of major social relevance. In these and similar cases, one finds broad discourses in which the weakness of certain bodies of knowledge is articulated along with other weaknesses of a social constellation, be it a state, an industry, or a smaller social unit. The dynamic role of discourses of weakness of this kind may (and is often hoped to) be a mobilisation of other resources, and, in particular, resources for the production of knowledge in the areas concerned. In other words, we find a constellation of the kind Mitchell Ash has described as one in which knowledge production and other social practices become resources for each other (Ash 2002 and 2016).

(4) A fourth, highly dynamical field in which the weaknesses of knowledge play a key role is that of the cultural *migration of knowledge*. This is true on many levels, and, again, it is easy to think of relevant examples.[29] Among other issues, there arises the crucial issue of *translation*, both in the literal sense that the receiving language may be unable to render (or interpret) knowledge expressed in the foreign language, and, in the more general sense, that the *cultural framing* of the knowledge in migration may be difficult or impossible to transfer from the place of origin to the place of reception. In all these respects, foreign knowledge may be perceived (and criticised) as being weak, engendering a dynamics of knowledge that may or may not transform the knowledge culture of the receiving side. And, not least, there is the problem, known only too well in our own period: migrants

---

29 A research group addressing this issue, and, in particular, migrating knowledge between late antiquity, classical Islam, and late medieval Europe is directed by Rivka Feldhay, see: http://mhc.tau.ac.il/en/category/migrating-knowledge, last accessed 30 June 2018; see, also, Feldhay and Ragep 2017; Schiebinger 2017, and a growing body of further literature.

and travellers are often not in strong social positions, hence the knowledge that they might bring is often *socially weak*, at least initially.

In all these and many other situations, the dynamic aspects of weak knowledge, and of articulations and discourses of weakness in knowledge, are obvious. This does not just concern the internal dynamics of knowledge but also the functions and transformative roles of knowledge in society and culture, and, in the last consequence – looking at the material practice of both – even in nature, as it is transformed by knowledge-based action.[30] In the perspective taken in the previous remarks, both scientific and non-scientific knowledge are often, if not in most cases, encountered as a precarious, unstable, and sometimes scarce resource of social and material practice. They are ingredients of *assemblages* that go far beyond their epistemic dimension. The dynamic roles of their weaknesses, perceived and articulated in many different ways, are varied and complex – be it in situations in which knowledge is employed for the securing and advancement of social formations and power structures, such as the modern state, or in situations in which weak and marginal actors are looking for knowledge-based alternatives to the hegemonic structures of their *Lebenswelt*.

References

Adelbulner, Michael (1768): *Kurze Beschreibung der Barometer und Thermometer, auch anderer zur Meteorologie gehörigen Instrumenten, nebst einer Anweisung, wie dieselben zum Vergnügen der Liebhaber, und zum Vortheil des Publici gebraucht werden sollen.* Nürnberg: Joseph Fleischmann.

Anderson, Katharine (2005): *Predicting the Weather: Victorians and the Science of Meteorology.* Chicago IL: University of Chicago Press.

Anderson, Kirsti (1985): "Cavalieri's Method of Indivisibles." *Archive for the History of Exact Sciences,* 31 (4): 291–367.

Aristoteles (2011): *Zweite Analytik / Analytica Posteriora.* Greek and German, ed. by Wolfgang Detel. Hamburg: Meiner.

Ash, Mitchell G. (2002): "Wissenschaft und Politikals Ressourcen füreinander." In: Rüdiger vom Bruch and Brigitte Kaderas (Eds.): *Wissenschaften und Wissenschaftspolitik: Bestandsaufnahmen zu Formationen, Brüchen und Kontinuitäten im Deutschland des 20. Jahrhunderts,* 32–51. Stuttgart: Steiner.

Ash, Mitchell G. (2016): "Reflexionen zum Ressourcenansatz." In: Sören Flachowsky et al. (Eds.): *Ressourcenmobilisierung: Wissenschaftspolitik und Forschungspraxis im NS-Herrschaftssystem,* 535–553. Göttingen: Wallstein.

Bachelard, Gaston (1934): *Le nouvel esprit scientifique.* Paris: Felix Alcan.

Baron, Margaret E. (1969): *The Origins of Infinitesimal Calculus.* Oxford: Pergamon.

---

30 Here, we may again refer to Andy Pickering's contribution in the present volume.

Bloor, David (1991): *Knowledge and Social Imagery*. 2nd edn. Chicago IL: Chicago University Press.

Canguilhem, Georges (1987): "La décadence de l'idée de progrès." *Revue de métaphysique et de morale*, 92: 437–454.

Cifoletti, Giovanna (1990): *La méthode de Fermat: Son statut et sa diffusion.* Cahiers d'histoire et de philosophie des sciences, nouvelle série 33, Paris: Société française d'histoire des sciences et des techniques.

de Condorcet, Nicolas (2004): *Tableau historique des progrès de l'esprit humain: Projets, Esquisse, Fragments et Notes (1772–1794).* Edited by Jean-Pierre Schandeler and Pierre Crépel. Paris: Institut National d'Études Demographiques.

Delambre, Jean Baptiste Joseph (1817–1827): *Histoire de l'astronomie, in several volumes.* Paris: Courcier.

Dove, Heinrich Wilhelm (1837): *Meteorologische Untersuchungen.* Berlin: Sander.

Estève, Pierre (1755): *Histoire générale et particulière de l'astronomie.* Paris: Jombert.

Feldhay, Rivka, and F. Jamil Ragep (Eds.) (2017): *Before Copernicus: The Cultures and Contexts of Scientific Learning in the Fifteenth Century.* Montreal: McGill-Queen's University Press.

Forbes, James D. (1841): "Supplementary Report on Meteorology." In: *Report of the Tenth Meeting of the British Association for the Advancement of Science held at Glasgow in August 1840. London 1841*, 37–156.

Gillies, Donald (Ed.) (1992): *Revolutions in Mathematics.* Oxford: The Clarendon Press.

Giusti, Enrico (1980): *Bonaventura Cavalieri and the Theory of Indivisibles.* Rome: Edizioni Cremonese.

Goldman, Alvin I. (1999): *Knowledge in a Social World.* Oxford: Oxford University Press.

Golinski, Jan (2007): *British Weather and the Climate of Enlightenment.* Chicago IL: University of Chicago Press.

Gray, Jeremy J. (1989): *Ideas of Space: Euclidean, Non-Euclidean, and Relativistic.* 2nd edn. Oxford: Clarendon Press.

Hahn, Hans (1933): "Die Krise der Anschauung." In: *Krise und Neuaufbau in den exakten Wissenschaften.* Fünf Wiener Vorträge, 1. Zyklus, Leipzig/Vienna: Deuticke.

Janković, Vladimir (2000): *Reading the Skies: A Cultural History of English Weather, 1650–1820.* Chicago IL: University of Chicago Press.

Jardine, Nicholas (1988): *The Birth of History and Philosophy of Science: Kepler's "A Defence of Tycho against Ursus" with Essays on its Provenance and Significance.* Cambridge: Cambridge University Press.

Jesseph, Douglas M. (1993): *Berkeley's Philosophy of Mathematics.* Chicago IL: Chicago Univerity Press.

Kant, Immanuel (1786): *Metaphysische Anfangsgründe der Naturwissenschaft.* Riga: Hartknoch.

Latour, Bruno, and Steve Woolgar (1979): *Laboratory Life: The Social Construction of Scientific Facts.* Beverly Hills CA: SAGE Publications.

Lloyd, Geoffrey E.R. (1979): *Magic, Reason and Experience: Studies in the Origin and Development of Greek Science.* Cambridge: Cambridge University Press.

Locher, Fabien (2008): *Le Savant et la tempête: Étudier l'atmosphère et prévoir le temps au XIXe siècle.* Rennes: Presses Universitaires.

Lukács, Georg (1923): *Geschichte und Klassenbewusstsein: Studien über marxistische Dialektik.* Berlin: Malik.

Mancosu, Paolo (1996): *Philosophy of Mathematics and Mathematical Practice in the Seventeenth Century.* Oxford: Oxford University Press.

von Mattuschka, Heinrich Graf (1775): *Anzeige der Beobachtungen, welche dienen können, einen für Landwirthe sehr nützlichen Naturkalender zu verfassen; entworfen für die patriotische Gesellschaft in Schlesien.* Sagan: Lauh.

Montucla, Jean-Étienne (1758): *Histoire des mathematiques.* 2 vols., Paris: Jombert.

Nowotny, Helga, et al. (2001): *Re-Thinking Science: Knowledge and the Public in an Age of Uncertainty.* Oxford: Folity Press.

Pasch, Moritz (1882): *Vorlesungen über neuere Geometrie.* Leipzig: Teubner.

Richter, Linda (2019): *Semiotik, Physik, Organik: Eine Geschichte des Wissens vom Wetter, 1750–1850.* Frankfurt/New York: Campus.

de Saussure, Horace-Bénédict (1783): *Essais sur l'hygrométrie.* Neuchâtel: Fauché.

Schiebinger, Londa (2017): *Secret Cures of Slaves: People, Plants, and Medicine in the Eighteenth-Century Atlantic World.* Stanford CA: Stanford University Press.

Shank, J. B. (2008): *The Newton Wars and the Beginning of the French Enlightenment.* Chicago IL: University of Chicago Press.

Shapin, Steven, and Simon Schaffer (1985): *Leviathan and the Air-Pump: Hobbes, Boyle, and the Experimental Life.* Princeton NJ: Princeton University Press.

Stäckel, Paul, and Friedrich Engel (1895): *Die Theorie der Parallellinien von Euklid bis auf Gauss.* Leipzig: Teubner.

Stillingfleet, Benjamin (1762): *Miscellaneous Tracts Relating to Natural History, Husbandry, and Physick: To which is Added the Calendar of Flora.* 2nd. edn., London: Dodsley.

Volkert, Klaus (1986): *Die Krise der Anschauung: Eine Studie zu formalen und heuristischen Verfahren in der Mathematik seit 1850.* Göttingen: Vandenhoeck & Ruprecht.

Science Research Regimes: From Strength to Weakness – The Polycentric Regime

Anne Marcovich and Terry Shinn

Abstract

In this chapter, we discuss the properties of weakening and weakness in the framework of our larger research programme on a comparative historical sociology of science research regimes. We study the evolution and transformation of scientific research regimes through four intellectual and institutional dimensions – boundary, authority, community, and circulation, and their interlacing. Our study of weakness revolves around a historical paradox in which weakness constitutes an essential component of regime dynamics, survival and even success. We will see that, in the regime studied here (the "polycentric regime" from the Renaissance to the eighteenth century), the weakness of some of its components proves essential to its operation. By contrast, the strengthening of this component eventually eroded and even nullified the regime. Here, one observes a crucial paradox between weakness and strength. Astonishingly, in this regime, the weakness of the dimension of the boundary constitutes its power.

Introduction

In this chapter, we discuss the properties of weakening and weakness in the framework of our larger research programme on a comparative historical sociology of science research regimes. Our study of weakness revolves around a historical paradox in which weakness constitutes an essential component of regime dynamics, survival, and even success. We will see that, in the regime studied here (the "polycentric regime"), the weakness of some of its components proves essential to its operation. By contrast, the strengthening of this component eventually eroded and even nullified the regime. Here, one observes a crucial paradox between weakness and strength.

This essay opens with a definition of the term "science research regime". We then introduce the four underlying dimensions that are, in our framework, constitutive of all regimes (boundary, authority, community, and circulation). These dimensions are omnipresent independently of the provenance and trajectory of all science regimes. However, the substance and thrust of the selective inter-weavings of their dimensions are regime specific. In effect, the content of different research regimes evolves around the particularities of the interacting links between the dimensions. In this text, we will speak principally of the "polycentric research regime" (which stretched from the early seventeenth century to the early mid-nineteenth century) and the architecture and substance of its progressive weakening.

Section 1 of this chapter proposes a definition of "science research regime", and presents our four architectural dimensions of "boundary", "authority", "community", and "circulation", and furthermore evokes configurations of dimension interactions. Section 2 introduces the hierarchy and selective affinities of these dimensions in the polycentric science research regime. This is accompanied by extensive historical information. Section 3 identifies the structural dimensions and relations that were involved in the processes of the weakening of polycentric science. Finally, Section 4 examines the pattern of our four dimensions for two additional regimes with particular attention to the properties of weakness.

1. Definition, structure and methodology

The term "regime" is prolific in the sociology of many activities (politics, economics, science policy, etc.), but it is only infrequently used with reference to science studies. For example, some scholarly work concerned with standarisation (Jaspers et al. 2013) mobilises the term "regime". However, investigation demonstrates that this is unrelated to science and not easily transferable into our historical sociology of science. The same observation can be made in the case of the work by Geneviève Teil on objectivity (2012). The authors consider the question by examining the dispute between scientists and vintners on the issue of *terroir*. The term "regime" proves to be unenlightening with regard to the organisation of knowledge. "Regime-related" studies, such as these, flourish *ad infinitum*.

There nevertheless do exist a few regime-related analyses which focus directly on scientific research. Indeed, the work of Gibbons et al. that concerns mode 1 and mode 2 science, intermittently engages the language of regime (Gibbons et al. 1994). The mode 1 regime refers to self-defined, inward-looking scientific production and organisation. This constitutes a historical organisation of science. By contrast, mode 2 is understood as development of a strong interlocking relationship between science and industry in particular (in effect, with society at large). This work that introduces the term "regime" neglects to identify its components and operations. The term "regime" principally serves as a flag for mode

1 and mode 2 (Shinn 2002). For its part, the Triple Helix, as understood in terms of regimes, refers to the coupling of science, state, and industry.[1] Its apparent regime-like cast may be understood as a discontinuity with earlier science in which the state and industry were less implicated in the organisation and direction of academic research.

More specifically, how is one to understand the sense of regime as applied to science? Our purpose is to mobilise "scientific research regimes" as a device for the exploration of the structures and dynamics of stability and transformation or weakening in scientific research. But what do we mean by "scientific research regime"? A science research regime is defined as a historically, empirically identifiable, set of four dimensions – boundary, authority, circulation, and community – whose particular expression, and the singular product of their specific interaction, determine a differentiated intellectual and organisational profile. Equally important, it permits greater understanding of the factors and forces that stimulate transformation in science, including some forces of weakening and strengthening. What configurations of our four dimensions and their interactions serve to weaken a regime, and alternatively what forms of architecture prove to be empowering? In a word, the regime perspective provides a key for the examination of mechanisms of both conservatism and change in the intellectual and social architecture and dynamics of research.

As signalled above, the structures and dynamics of science research regimes revolve around the relations that exist between the four dimensions (boundary, authority, community, and circulation). In our work, boundary refers to issues of differentiation and of degree of freedom.[2] Boundary evokes language of height, width, density, impenetrability and, eventually, the immovability of barrier. It can thus be penetrable, resistant, or impenetrable! It introduces issues of exclusion and inclusion. Boundary evokes issues of territory and space, as well as differentiation, margin of freedom, and severity of constraint (Forman 2012). The dimension of authority is a second essential element to our regime perspective. It is a marker of intellectual legitimacy and the capacity to mobilise symbolic and material resources.[3] It deals with intellectual reputation, and refers to the power of control and attraction (Biagioli and Galison 2014). It is also indissociable from matters of institutional and intellectual autonomy (Whitley 2000). Authority is similarly linked to the capacity to mobilise and allocate resources, and to confer favour and entitlement.

The third dimension of scientific research regimes is that of community. Community is associated with partnership, and its opposite, discrimination.[4] It

---

1 Etzkowitz and Leydesdorff 2008; Campbell and Pedersen 2001.
2 Luhmann 1993; Abbott 1995; Marcovich and Shinn 2011.
3 Friedman 1990; Bruffee 1999; Sassen 2006.
4 Crane 1972; Giddens 1991; Elias 1997.

revolves around degree of connectivity. Communities can be expansive or ostracising: they can be dynamic or alternatively quiescent and closed. In our work, it is particularly explored in terms of objective, scale, homogeneity, stability, and institutional objectives and environment. Here, the matter of communication falls under the heading of community. Communication today comprises a major field of science studies, as witnessed by the huge quantity of research on citation counts. Indeed, communication studies constitute a field in its own right. In our exploration, communication operates in conjunction either with differentiation (boundary) or circulation.

The fourth science research regime dimension – circulation – deals with diffusion of ideas and with strategic moves of scientists.[5] Circulation is synonymous with displacement, and it is analysed here in terms of frequency, distance, motivation, benefits and strategy. It thus deals with the cognitive domain (intellectual mobility), institution (transfer), professional function (education, finalised or economic-related research, administration), geographic location. Circulation can, in part, be understood as the complexity of the forces between centripetal and centrifugal dynamics. The metrics of some regimes is open to circulation, while others prove to be closed. The four above-introduced dimensions provide standardised machinery for description of the multiple geometries of science research regimes, and they offer a methodology for comparing them. Later in this chapter, we will set out to determine which dimensions are the more likely ones in situations of science research regime weakening.

In our work, reflection related to weakness directs attention towards three related poles. First, weakness may signify formerly coherent and effective internal structures or practices situated within a hitherto relatively smoothly operating system which had heretofore offered opportunities for established and new vistas, but that no longer prove sufficiently advantageous. Something has gone wrong or is broken. Second, weakness alternatively evokes the notion of reduced relevance, in which the potential of relevance is connected to internal erosion or to the introduction of more powerful dynamics or structures, or to alternative demand. Third, weakness can be largely context contingent. What has been "strong" can become "irrelevant". In this reading, weak rhymes with inadequate. These expressions of weakness are the empirical product of our reading of the polycentric research regime: detailed familiarity with the structures and dynamics of additional research regimes (disciplinary, transverse research technology) will probably extend and enrich the conceptual grasp of "weakness" in science research.

Regime dynamics are such that all dimensions are inter-dependant. This interdependence enforces the significance and impact of each dimension, which implies that the modification of one dimension produces modifications in the oth-

---

5 Bourdieu 2002; Gaillard and Gaillard 1999; Marcovich 2001.

ers. This is analogous to how the deformation of one part of a drapery necessarily recasts the architecture of the whole. The relative position and interactions of dimensions with reference to proximity and reciprocal impact proves central to the understanding of the workings of regimes. First, the specific impact of a particular dimension of a regime is established by hierarchic relationships with the other dimensions. Some regimes exhibit an acute hierarchy of dimensions, while others are patterned more horizontally. The configuration of the dimensions reveals much about the distribution of their power and their consequent influence. Second, linkage between dimensions takes the form of "selective affinity": dimensions may stand as singles, or alternatively as pairs or even triplets. Selective affinity, coupled to hierarchy, comprises the analytical architecture for the intelligibility of each regime, and the configurations and processes of its weakening.

2. The polycentric research regime and dynamics of weakness

Grounded in the empirical historical expressions of the hierarchies and the elective affinities of our four above-discussed dimensions as articulated in the now to be discussed polycentric science research regime, we will here identify and analyse a specific instance and form of weakening. The polycentric regime extends from the end of the Renaissance right through the early decades of the nineteenth century (Crosland 1967). It is sometimes referred to as the early modern period in the history of science. In the polycentric research regime, the pairing of community and authority is paramount – here there exists a pronounced "selective affinity". It stands at the summit of a two-tier hierarchy. A second pairing consisting of circulation and boundary is subsidiary to community and authority. Counter-intuitively, boundary and circulation are mutually re-enforcing here. But what lies behind the primacy of the community-authority doublet of the polycentric regime? What strongly connects the boundary-circulation selective affinity? And why is this hierarchic relationship between the community-authority on an upper level *versus* the circulation-boundary on a subordinate level?

The polycentric regime is characterised by the development of a huge quantity of communities, and indeed communities of different sorts. First of all, in the continuity of the scholastic institutions, universities persisted as a reference in terms of traditional scholarship, employment, teaching, and, to some degree, new knowledge (Gascoigne 1990). Scores of universities were scattered across Italy, France, the Lowlands (Holland) and lands of Germany, across Eastern Europe, Scandinavia, the British Isles and the Iberian Peninsula! Of utmost importance, each university was notably autonomous during the centuries in question. Historical convention did colour instruction and administration; but a huge variety and disarray prevailed. In effect, university policy and practice enjoyed a good measure of practical autonomy – in the main, a form of curtailed variation prospered. The university community was itself divided into two sub-communities, Protestant and Catholics.[6] The Catholic University was, for its part, linked to the Jesuit order, which had, as one of its functions, the extension of knowledge (see the *Collegio Romano*) (Lattis 2010). The differentiated Protestant University community extended from the central German States to Eastern and Northern Europe. The relations between the Catholic and Protestant universities were exclusionary. The trajectory of Renier de Graaf (1641–1673) exemplifies the divergence and hostility between the two communities. In view of his intellectual reputation (he discovered the follicles which carry his name), de Graaf would have had a chair in the prestigious University of Leiden, had he not been Catholic (Cook 1992).

Princely courts constituted a second, entirely different species of community across the seventeenth and eighteenth centuries. They acted as a gravitational field which sometimes sponsored scholars and often attracted visiting *savants* from far and wide who met in this temporary shelter. The work of Galileo Galilei (1564–1642) on the laws of movement was encouraged and sustained by the Court of Florence (Biagioli 1993). Otto von Guericke (1602–1686) found legitimacy for his contribution to development of the air pump and for his research on air pressure at the Court of Brandenburg (Conlon 2011); Johannes Kepler's (1571–1630) activities were enthusiastically promoted by the Dresden Court (Dupré and Korey 2009). It is important to note that men circulated between these courts, thereby constituting a peripatetic community which exhibited a characteristic species of credentials, work procedures and landscape of output.

With reference to the further development of a polycentric architecture of a research community, key initiatives transpired in the 1660s with the creation of the *London Royal Society* and of the *Académie Royale des Sciences de Paris*. Particularly with reference to the latter, science as a community became identified with the state. This marked a transformation of geographic legitimacy, greater access to material resources, and not least of all, the acquisition of enhanced status for research activities. This significantly altered the physiognomy of the field of research. In addition to the London and Paris academies, the Berlin Academy was set up in 1700, the Saint Petersburg Academy in 1724 and the Swedish Academy in Uppsala in 1739. The scale of the operation and reputation of such institutions importantly impacted the organisation of science as community. Inside the community, science took a turn towards professionalisation. The members of the Paris Academy received an annual salary which permitted them to engage in scientific research upon a full time basis – the research function was born. In a somewhat parallel logic, the magnitude and spread of research community was

---

6 Kittelson and Transue 1984; Lindberg and Westman 1990; Porter and Teich 1992.

enhanced through an explosive increase in the number of already existing or new local municipal science societies.[7] In his book, James McClellan (1985) documents up to sixty municipal societies in France during the seventeenth and eighteenth centuries. Each one of these institutional constellations constituted a different world in itself. Notwithstanding this, scholars could, in large part, relate to the whole. The above-cited rich documentation undeniably establishes the primacy of the "community" dimension in the polycentric research regime. The power of these dispersed, heterogeneous and even sometimes counterpoised communities constitutes one of the weaknesses that contributed to the erosion of the polycentric regime.

The activities of communication are integral to our dimension of community: this interlocking proved most visible and powerful in the dynamics of "networking" – so central to researcher intercourse and collective association between *circa* 1600 and about 1825. In the polycentric regime, networking could take the form of personal encounters between scientists travelling to meet one another. It could alternatively consist of chains of written correspondence. Correspondence networks do indeed comprise one key landmark of the polycentric community-communication dimension. This is nowhere better illustrated than in the case of Marin Mersenne (1588–1648) (Lenoble 1943). For some of the members of this vast and systematic network stretching across the length and breadth of Europe, the quantity and the regularity of epistolary exchanges allowed members to learn about one another's work, to criticise and to move forward intellectually. This community corresponds to the definition of "intelligencing" (Grosslight 2013), where the purpose is the transmission, discussion and querying, as well as injection of new ideas. Here, one can observe what will be discussed below, the supremacy of circulation over boundary. The magnitude and heterogeneity of these communities resulted in many wide-open spaces accompanied by autonomy and diversity which authorised and even encouraged fragmentation of all sorts. In such an environment, the nucleation of well-defined scientific fields and intellectual consensus was not easy. Acute freedom came at the cost of consensus.

In the light of the above-introduced concept of "selective affinity" between dimensions, our dimension of community connects strongly with the dimension of authority (Shapin and Schaffer 2011). It is community that provides the context of authority, setting the rules of the research procedures and the evaluation of results, and distributing the rewards. The power of community entailed the adjudication of admissibility and inadmissibility. Emblematic of this, the Paris Academy of Science barred access to Cartesians and Jesuits – and thus denied the legitimacy of such thinking.[8] The French University system similarly functioned as an institution that exercised authority. It should be recalled that it was not until

---

7 Hahn 1971; Stroup 1990.
8 Hahn 1971; Brockliss 1987; Gascoigne 1990.

the 1730s that it became possible for students to submit a dissertation that defended the stance of Isaac Newton (1643–1727) with reference to gravitation (Guerlac 1981). In the same vein, it was only about a decade earlier that the French Universities accepted the thinking of René Descartes (1596–1650) and hence conferred authority on it. In the case of England, the intellectual and personal authority of Isaac Newton and Robert Boyle (1627–1691) proved so acute that they could bar access to opponents and smooth the way to clients to the community of the Royal Society. A measure of Guericke's authority derived from the approval of the Prince of Brandenburg. One sees here that community frames the jurisdiction of authority.

We have described above community and authority as the strong pairing in the polycentric quadrangle of dimensions. Boundary and circulation constitute the other, and subordinate selective affinity doublet in the hierarchy. This dynamics underpins the key capacity in this regime concerned with margins of manoeuvre. At first sight, the two dimensions of boundary and circulation may appear to be antinomic. However, at this moment of history, the confines of boundary were still heterogeneous, feeble and even contradictory. This offered space for multiple degrees and expressions of circulation. As stated above, boundary refers to issues of differentiation, degrees of freedom, and permeability. Boundaries were frequently institutionally and doctrinally (for example, cartesianism *versus* newtonianism) exclusionary. Yet, at the same time, with reference to research fields, boundaries were extremely low, porous and blurred. For an individual practitioner, low and fluid boundaries authorised engagement in plural research domains, and indeed many scientists accumulated authority in multiple areas. This is truly the acme of intellectual polycentricity. Among others, René Descartes engaged in the plural fields of optics, mechanics, geometry, algebra, and, of course, philosophy and metaphysics (Dear 2008). For his part, Isaac Newton conducted research in the domains of mathematics, optics, mechanics, acoustics and chemistry (Westfall 1981). Christian Huygens (1629–1695) likewise traversed many boundaries (mathematics, optics, acoustics, astronomy …) (Yoder 1988). In his work, Blaise Pascal (1623–1662) pursued investigations in mathematics, hydrostatic, mechanics, etc. (Adamson 1995). In the closing decades of the polycentric research regime, the output of Jean-Baptiste Biot (1774–1862) ranged hugely (Crosland 1967), focusing on mathematics, optics, chemistry, and meteorology. It is not only the great names in science who were engaged in plural topics and hence traversed many boundaries. A "secondary" figure such as Robert Hooke (1635–1703) exemplifies the magnitudes of topics effectively investigated by a scientist who enjoyed a much lower level of scientific authority. Officially, he was a mere workman for instruments and the preparation of experiments for the great men of the Royal Society (Newton, Boyle …). Nevertheless, very much working on his own, Robert Hooke contributed importantly to astronomy, microscopy, mathematics, mechanics, and other fields. His book entitled *Micrography* (1665) encountered considerable success (Westfall 1981).

Up to the beginning of the nineteenth century, many who contributed to the mathematical and physical sciences were first trained in medicine (Crosland 1967). These low and porous boundaries between fields were so rooted in the scientific activity of this regime that institutions which were usually rigid towards demarcation could sometimes also prove astonishingly permeable regarding intellectual boundaries. For example, the Paris Academy of Sciences in 1798 offered a prize in "physics" for the best paper on "the comparison of the nature, form and uses of the liver in the various classes of animals" (Heilbron 1982)! The inclusion of the topic revolving around anatomy and physiology in a competition designated as lying in physics, points to an extremely flexible, "almost laughable", understanding of boundary! The pages of the *Journal de Physique, de Chimie, d'Histoire Naturelle et des Arts*, of the *Transactions of the London Royal Society*, and of *Acta Eruditorum* were open to a haphazard mix of research fields. Briefly stated, the focus of scientist investigation was largely unaffected by the constraints of a question or a domain; and the journals that circulated findings exhibited no penchant for selective focus of topic. To repeat the above observation, boundary was on the whole inoperable for most aspects of science activity throughout the polycentric research regime's workings. What a testimony to the absence of intellectual boundaries!

In a word, in the intellectual realm, boundaries were hugely abundant yet amazingly low and easy to traverse. Indeed, as concerns the ensuing weakening of the polycentric regime, it would be a transformation in the composition and operation of the intellectual (but also institutional) boundary that would ultimately weaken the regime. At the same time, as has been established in the preceding paragraphs concerned with community, institutional boundaries were elevated. This high/low configuration generated a mix of intellectual mobility, institutional predictability and possibilities to develop strategic opportunities. This tangled and unruly landscape of boundaries persisted right across the seventeenth and eighteenth centuries – through the early modern period and the Enlightenment; and it only began to dissipate in the nineteenth century under the changed rules of the disciplinary regime's transformations in the content of the dimensions and their interactions.

The pliancy of boundary found its complement in the dimension of circulation which suffuses the polycentric regime. In the case of the centuries discussed here, "poly" frequently signified the passage from one intellectual domain or institution to another. Such circulation was often repeated numerous times in the course of a practitioner's life. Circulation is about exchanges between *savants* and institutions; and as seen above, communication at large is predicated on its logic. Circulation is a particularly complex and paradoxical dimension in this research regime. It was abundant in the volume of circulating entities (quantity, frequency, and distance), in the movement of practitioners across intellectual, organisational and geographic boundaries. The occupancy of plural spaces of polycentric regime scientists – be it with reference to boundary, authority or community – has been documented above.

This ensemble is no better illustrated than in the case of Isaac Beeckman (1588–1637) (Cook 1992), who was first schooled in Middelburg (Lowlands), and then moved to Leiden where he learnt mathematics. In his early years, he was associated with artisanal work and then with activities in connection with conduits, pumps and pumping. Beeckman also moved to meteorological investigations. The young *savant* then travelled to Caen (France) for medical training (1618); on his return to the Lowlands, Beeckman met the young René Descartes with whom he shared multiple interests including geometry, acoustics, hydrostatics and falling bodies, etc... Beeckman obtained a teaching post in Rotterdam from 1620 to 1627, and then moved to Dordrecht where he held the position of rector from 1627 to 1637.

Throughout the polycentric regime, geographic circulation and circulation of research instrumentation were also central to the development of knowledge and to personal and institutional interactions. The polycentric regime witnessed a multiplication in variety and quantity of research instruments. These instruments include devices such as the compass, the thermometer, the electrometer, the microscope, the air pump... These and like instruments circulated widely, as sometimes did the practitioners who used them (Feldman 1990). The recruitment of these different machines designed to address a specific question, served as a common denominator capable of producing convergence in an otherwise scattered population of scientists. On another register, it could even function as a node of homogenisation in rules of measurement. The consensus and relevance of an instrument in a specific domain functioned as a vehicle which guaranteed the circulation of ideas and people within a sphere. The operation of a category of apparatus and its metrology simultaneously served as a boundary. In summary, instrumentation acted as a pivot that strongly combines circulation and boundary, here essentially porous and low. Weak boundaries constitute a paramount strength of the polycentric regime.

As seen above, the quantity and extensiveness of pliancy and movement afforded in the infinity of combinatorials of the minimalist boundary and vigorous circulation precipitated both a multitude of paths and possibilities, and ultimately a cognitive and institutional landscape which had relatively few markers and rallying-points. The power of polycentricity resided for a long time in the promotion and legitimation of plurality and mobility; however, at one juncture, plural began to prove costly. Undirected and unorganised spaces for the formulation and development of questions and the distribution of information dominated in a regime marked by a minimal boundary. In Section 3 below, we address the complex dynamic of processes of "weakening" in the polycentric science research regime in which a former asset evolves into a liability!

It is essential to understand that the "inferior" position of boundary in the polycentric regime is conditioned by the power exercised by the coupling of the two dominant dimensions of community and authority. It should be recalled that the substance of all regimes depends on affinities and hierarchies of dimensions. In the polycentric regime, the power of the pairing of the two dimensions of authority and community proved to be so assertive that weakness in the dimension of boundary was an inescapable consequence. We point out here that the weakness of boundary was not necessarily a consequence of its qualities, but more so a product of its relative position in the quadrangle of dimensions.

3. Processes of weakening – from asset to liability

Now, in Section 3, we will indicate the historical composition, unfolding, and outcome of this boundary-based weakening in the polycentric research regime. We will mobilise the periodicals which were published during this period and show how the topics switched from multiple orientations towards more defined and de-limited research fields. In Section 2, we demonstrated the massive development of science during the polycentric regime. Older established science institutions multiplied and flourished. Natural philosophers generated mammoth quantities of learning in extant domains and marched forward as they discovered hitherto unknown domains. Scholars circulated among fields and across borders. An individual often belonged to several communities and exercised authority in plural intellectual and institutional quarters and fields. This map of science within the polycentric regime was importantly linked to the structures and operations of boundary. Paradoxically, the essence of polycentric science boundaries was their minimal operation. The weakness of boundaries offered an environment in which practitioners could spread their wings. There indeed existed many boundaries, but so low, permeable, mobile and forgiving that they seldom constituted impediments. The weakness of boundaries spells the strength of the regime.

This minimalist environment that so very much underpinned and enriched the polycentric regime for two centuries began at one moment to mark the regime's weakening. This weakening became visible along three major lines: first, constant intellectual fluidity – as scholars shifted from theme to theme and question to question – spelled fragmentation. Knowledge grew, but in an environment that lacked architectural structure. Second, in line with this, for a very long time, there was little possibility for the development of strongly associated collective work.[9] Collective effort entails some sort of boundary! The key grounds for the growth of polycentric work came to constitute a central weakness that condemned the future of the regime. The asset became a liability. Third, the plurality born of the possibility of infinite freedom of movement meant that, until late into the eighteenth century, the task of establishing stable, powerful and standardised institutions for the diffusion of established learning found the going difficult. Indeed, the reproduction of new learning requires intellectual and institutional boundaries (Helmholtz [1862] 1995). Fourth, as the volume of polycentric learning expanded and the pace of discovery quickened, a regime in which boundaries were not paramount meant that routine and standardised reporting and the circulation of results was haphazard! Some of the expansive and fluid traits of such centrality to polycentricity gradually emerged as internal weaknesses. What had once stood proudly as commanding strengths (boundarylessness) now became conditions that had to be re-fashioned or deleted.

The former intellectual benefit associated with low boundaries and easy circulation between domains clearly became an impediment to learning in the eighteenth century. This is best seen in the number and logic of research related journals. Four journals punctuated the latter half of the seventeenth century: the *Philosophical Transactions of the Royal Society of London* (launched in 1665), the *Journal des Sçavans* (1665); *Acta Eruditorum* (1682); the *Memoirs de l'Académie Royale des Sciences* (1699). The remarkable historian of science, Robert Mortimer Gascoigne, who carefully documented the historical landscape of science publications from 1665 to 1900, classifies all of these journals as general science periodicals (Gascoigne 1985). This category of journal published pieces on any and all knowledge topics with little attention to grouping or classification. The concept of intellectual boundary was virtually absent. Bits of knowledge were treated as fragments – as disconnected. One observes few attempts to develop relations, draw lines or make comparisons between contributions. If one were to speak epistemologically, no identifiable domain emerged. This unbounded system of general science journals extended deep into the eighteenth century. Examples of such periodicals include the *Journal de Physique, de Chimie, d'Histoire Naturelle et des Arts* founded by Rozier in 1771. Many journals of the same ilk grew up in the Germanies (*Der Naturforscher*, 1774) and in Great Britain (*A Journal of Natural Philosophy, Chemistry and the Arts*, 1797) in the same period. Generalist journals were very broad in scope, frequently containing articles on astronomy, mathematics, botany, geology, medicine, meteorology, optics, mechanics, etc. […]. The expression of "let a hundred flowers bloom" that circulated in communist China in the 1960s could be applied to the intellectual orientation of general science journals. In a word, the high porosity and low measure of cognitive boundaries encouraged the de-

---

9 With the remarkable exception of the organization and work conducted at the Paris *Académie des Sciences* (Hahn 1971).

velopment of many directions of learning, while, at the same time, co-ordinated orientation, concentration and linkage logically were lacking. The movement that would later progressively weaken the predominance of general periodicals would prove concomitant with the weakening of the intellectually pluralist community.

By the end of the eighteenth century, some timid changes appeared. Journals which we call hybrid with more restricted topics were founded. Hybrid journals may be seen as marking a transformation in the composition and status of the intellectual boundaries of the polycentric research regime. The transformation in the status of the boundary has the effect that one begins to observe a slight exclusionary drift. Hybrid is more exclusionary (boundary rich) than the general journal class through its limitation of the topics covered, and it tries to associate fields to a certain degree. It should be noted in particular that, in this new category of journals, theology, philosophy, history, and philology were excluded; more interestingly, mathematics was not included in these hybrid periodicals, which may be interpreted as indicating that it already enjoyed a differentiated and particularly elevated status. On the other hand, the aforementioned domains of medicine, botany and meteorology were retained. One domain was particularly privileged, that of chemistry (Gascoigne 1985). As indicated in the journal titles, this is visible in the case of *"Chemisches Journal für die Freunde der Naturlehre"* founded by Lorenz Crell in 1778, the *"Annales de Chimie"* founded by Louis-Bernard Guyton de Morveau, Antoine Laurent Lavoisier, Gaspard Monge, Claude-Louis Berthollet and Antoine François Froucroy in 1789, and the *"Allgemeines Journal der Chemie"*, edited by Alexander Nicolaus Scherer in 1798. In the 1790s and the early nineteenth century a good deal of chemistry was equally included in the *Journal der Physik* (1795), later the *Annalen der Physik und Chemie* (1824). One can make the same point with the *Mémoires de Physique et de Chimie de la Société d'Arcueil* (1807) (Crosland 1967).

The paradox of "weak/strong" with reference to boundary climaxes in the category of journals designated by Gascoigne as individual science periodicals. Throughout the polycentric research regime, boundaries had been central to the dynamics of the regime because they were weak, and their weakness was essential for the measure of liberty enjoyed by practitioners. Strong boundaries would have circumscribed the range of fields in which they worked. The fact that boundaries, at the beginning of the nineteenth century, were becoming tall and impermeable constituted the pre-condition for the definition and autonomy of a specific discipline. This was the very substance that was soon to emerge as differentiated disciplinary journals.

The *"Astronomische Nachrichten"*, founded in 1820, immediately became the mainstay of German astronomy, a position it continued to enjoy through the century and beyond. The *"Botanische Zeitung"*, created in 1843 is another expression of a disciplinary boundary. The journal founded by Justus Liebig in 1832,

"*Annalen der Chemie und Pharmacie*", is one of the numerous testimonies to the growth of chemistry as a lighthouse of disciplinarity. The *Journal de Physiologie Expérimentale et Pathologique*, founded in 1821, also demonstrates the centrality of speciality in scientific knowledge. What could differ more from the plural and very mixed cognitive spheres that were characteristic of weak boundary polycentricity? In polycentricity, weak boundaries meant vitality of the regime. Boundaries could afford to be weak because there were strong communities which were intellectually enriched and institutionally empowered by the presence of multifield scholars possessing authority.

During the nineteenth century, the development of science was such that the referent on which a scientist could rely was more and more confined to the boundaries of his speciality (in effect, his discipline). The boundary-driven logic of "individual" science journals (in the language of Gascoigne) became re-inforced in the broader framework of specialised science societies. Societies came to constitute a major institutional and professional focus for many practitioners. The *Geological Society*, based in London, was created in 1807, the *Royal Astronomical Society*, also in London, followed in 1820. As indicated above, chemistry operated as an encompassing intellectual boundary which was translated into many community bodies expressed as professional societies – among them, the *American Association for the Advancement of Science* (with its section devoted to chemistry), founded in 1848, the *Société Chimique de Paris*, which was established in 1857. Professional science societies also developed in innumerable additional scientific domains – mineralogy, botanics, physiology, etc. The tall and tight boundaries of these scientific communities strongly contrast with the loose and permeable boundaries which fostered the plurality of the individual's research fields and their enriching capacity to circulate between them during the polycentric regime. Let us repeat, the force of the polycentric regime resided precisely in the *weakness* of its boundaries. Here, weakness constituted an essential strength. The subsequent strengthening of boundaries undermined polycentrism and came to constitute the power of the following disciplinary regime – now to be discussed.

4. Brief remarks on two additional science research regimes: The disciplinary regime and the transverse research technology regime

The chronology of the disciplinary regime extends from the early nineteenth century right up to today. In this regime, we suggest that the pairing of "boundary-authority" is dominant over a second pairing, that of "community-circulation". This regime is rooted in the segmentation and differentiation transformations of the nineteenth century that mark disciplinary science both intellectually and organisationally. This is beautifully illustrated by the work of Kathryn Olesko (1991), of Myles Jackson (2000), and of Friedrich Steinle (1995). For her part, Olesko documents the formative and homogenising impact of the Berlin ministry-based demands and regimentation over the shaping of an emergent discipline, mathematical physics. Here, authority and boundary are paramount. In the disciplinary regime, it is supposed that authority is reserved to the space defined by boundary (Ben-David and Collins 1966). Here, communities are set by the boundaries of the disciplines (Bechtel 1986). Circulation is restrained within the walls of a community. Here, boundary proves paramount and is of foremost importance for this regime. One may ask whether this "paramount" is sometimes not so acute as to become stifling. The subsequent emergence of "interdisciplinarity" may be interpreted as a kick-back consequence of the rigidity and of the strangling imposed by the censorship of boundaries. In interdisciplinarity, the paramount pairing of our dimensions would lean towards circulation and community. Here, we imply that, in the long run, the interpenetration of boundary and authority may constitute a weakness in the constitution and operation of disciplinarity.

The geography of relations between dimensions proves quite different in the case of the transverse research technology regime. Here, circulation seems paramount, and authority is rooted in minimal boundaries and easy boundary crossing. The pairing of circulation and authority is dominant. In the transverse research technology regime, circulation appears as the leading dimension. Instruments and methodologies readily flow across boundaries, passing unimpeded from one domain or discipline to another. The community in which one exercises authority is remarkably extensive but nonetheless confined to the application of the device. Examples of research technology include the Ultra-centrifuge (Joerges and Shinn 2001), the Fourier Transform Spectroscope (Shinn 2008), the Electron Microscope (Lettkemann 2017), the Scanning Tunnelling Microscope[10] and Magnetic Nuclear Resonance (Hentschel 2015). The dimension of authority is entirely contingent on circulation. No institutional authority supervises the functioning of scientific work in the transverse regime. In this regime, power is generated by the universal applicability and presence of a technology or metrology in the largest possible number of domains. Here, community is synonymous with an instrument and not a specific cognitive or institutional niche. This regime came into its own in the latter third of the nineteenth century, and it continues to develop (Shinn 2001 and 2002). To repeat, one observes that this regime seems to concern mainly scientific instruments or methodology principally in physics. Three powerful generic instrumentation journals signal the origins and growth of the research technology regime – namely, the *Zeitschrift für Instrumentenkunde* (1879), "Re-

---

10 Mody 2011; Marcovich and Shinn 2014.

view of Scientific Instruments" (1930), and *"Nuclear Instruments"* (1957). This regime would be weakened by intra-disciplinary, exclusively self-regarding initiatives in instrument developments in which broader diffusion was technically unlikely. Stated differently, hyper-instrument specialisation. It could also conceivably be weakened by a collapse of the specific form of recognition attached to instrumentation work. This could perhaps arise if the work associated with the invention and application of generic instruments became so specialised and fragmented that individual authority would not occur. This would certainly prove poisonous to the regime.

Conclusion

Our understanding of weakness in science is based upon our studies of science research regimes. In this perspective, it revolves around our four dimensions of boundary, authority, community, and circulation. In this framework, weakening refers to the relative impact of a regime dimension with reference to its other dimensions. Change in the weakness or strength of any dimension must be understood as relativistic and contextual. Strength and weakness do not function as inherent attributes. They are entirely historical. This is nowhere clearer than in the dance between weakness and strength in the overlapping histories of the polycentric and disciplinary regimes.

In the metamorphosis of the polycentric regime towards the disciplinary regime, the boundary dimension experienced a double transformation. It switched status as it moved from a secondary pairing to a primary one and connected with the dimension of authority *versus* circulation (which had been the pairing in the polycentric regime). As stated above, in the disciplinary regime, the lead pairing is boundary-authority, and the subsidiary pairing is the association of community and circulation. Here, the content/action of boundary changed from openness to closure. It is not some essential quality of boundary that mutated, but rather modifications in the context in which it developed. Let us repeat, strength and weakness must be understood in relativistic *versus* absolutist/essentialist terms. In view of this, one might profitably examine weakness through dynamics of interactive forces, and more specifically through the lens of selective affinities between the dimensions and transformations from one pairing to another. Re-evoking an image expressed above, the interlacing of dimensions in regimes may be depicted as a cloth in which the introduction of a wrinkle anywhere generates deformation throughout the structure of the drapery.

References

Abbott, Andrew (1995): "Things of Boundaries." *Social Research*, 62 (4): 857–882.

Adamson, Donald (1995): *Blaise Pascal: Mathematician, Physicist, and Thinker about God*. London-New York: Macmillan.

Bechtel, William (Ed.) (1986): *Integrating Science*. Dordrecht: Martinus Nijhoff Publishers.

Ben-David, Joseph, and Randall Collins (1966): "Social Factors in the Origins of a New Science: The Case of Psychology." *American Sociological Review*, 31 (4): 451–465.

Biagioli, Mario (1993): *Galileo, Courtier: The Practice of Science in the Culture of Absolutism*. Chicago IL: University of Chicago Press.

Biagioli, Mario, and Peter Galison (2014): *Scientific Authorship: Credit and Intellectual Property in Science*. London: Routledge.

Bourdieu, Pierre (2002): "Les conditions sociales de la circulation internationale des idées." *Actes de la recherche en sciences sociales*, 5: 3–8.

Bruffee, Kenneth A. (1999): *Collaborative Learning: Higher Education, Interdependence, and the Authority of Knowledge*. Baltimore MD: Johns Hopkins University Press.

Brockliss, Laurence W.B. (1987): *French Higher Education in the Seventeenth and Eighteenth Centuries. A Cultural History*. Oxford: Clarendon Press.

Campbell, John L., and Ove K. Pedersen (2011): "Knowledge Regimes and Comparative Political Economy." In: Daniel Béland and Robert Henry Cox (Eds.): *Ideas and Politics in Social Science Research*, 167–191. Oxford: Oxford University Press.

Conlon, Thomas E. (2011): *Thinking about Nothing: Otto Von Guericke and the Magdeburg Experiments on the Vacuum*. Morrisville NC: Lulu Press.

Cook, Harold John (1992): "The New Philosophy in the Low Countries." In: Roy Porter and Mikuláš Teich (Eds.): *The Scientific Revolution in National Context*, 115-149. Cambridge: Cambridge University Press.

Crane, Diana (1972): *Invisible Colleges: Diffusion of Knowledge in Scientific Communities*. Chicago IL: University of Chicago Press.

Crosland, Maurice P. (1967): *The Society of Arcueil. A View of French Science at the Time of Napoleon I*. London: Heinemann.

Dear, Peter (2008): *Revolutionizing the Sciences: European Knowledge and its Ambitions, 1500–1700*. Basingstoke: Palgrave Macmillan.

Dupré, Sven, and Michael Korey (2009): "Inside the Kunstkammer: The Circulation of Optical Knowledge and Instruments at the Dresden Court." *Studies in History and Philosophy of Science*, Part A 40 (4): 405–420.

Elias, Norbert (1997): *Logiques de l'exclusion: enquête sociologique au coeur des problèmes d'une communauté*. Paris: Fayard.

Etzkowitz, Henry, and Loet Leydesdorff (2008): *The Triple Helix: University-Industry-Government Innovation in Action*. London: Routledge.

Feldman, Theodore S. (1990): "Late Enlightenment Meteorology." In: Tore Frangsmyr et al. (Eds.): *The Quantifying Spirit in the Eighteenth Century*. Berkeley CA: University of California Press.

Forman, Paul (2012): "On the Historical Forms of Knowledge Production and Curation: Modernity Entailed Disciplinarity, Postmodernity Entails Antidisciplinarity." *Osiris*, 27 (1): 56–97.

Frangsmyr, Tore, et al. (Eds.) (1990): *The Quantifying Spirit in the Eighteenth Century*. Berkeley CA: University of California Press.

Friedman, Richard B. (1990): "On the Concept of Authority in Political Philosophy." In: Joseph Raz (Ed.): *Authority*, 56–91. New York: New York University Press.

Gaillard, Anne-Marie, and Jacques Gaillard (1999): "Les enjeux des migrations scientifiques internationales: de la quête du savoir à la circulation des compétences." *Documentation IRD*.

Gascoigne, Robert Mortimer (1985): *A Historical Catalogue of Scientific Periodicals, 1665–1900: With a Survey of their Development*. New York-London: Garland.

Gascoigne, John (1990): "A Reappraisal of the Role of the Universities in the Scientific Revolution." In: David C. Lindberg and Robert S. Westman (Eds.): *Reappraisals of the Scientific Revolution*, 207–261. Cambridge: Cambridge University Press.

Gibbons, Michael, et al. (1994): *The New Production of Knowledge. The Dynamics of Science and Research in Contemporary Societies*. London: SAGE Publications.

Giddens, Anthony (1991): *Modernity and Self-identity: Self and Society in the Late Modern Age*. Stanford CA: Stanford University Press.

Grosslight, Justin (2013): "Small Skills, Big Networks: Marin Mersenne as Mathematical Intelligencer." *History of Science*, 51 (172): 337.

Guerlac, Henry (1981): *Newton on the Continent*. Ithaca NY: Cornell University Press.

Hahn, Roger (1971): *The Anatomy of a Scientific Institution: The Paris Academy of Sciences, 1666–1803*. Berkeley CA: University of California Press.

Heilbron, John L. (1982): *Elements of Early Modern Physics*. Berkeley CA: University of California Press.

Heilbron, W. Johan (2004): *A Regime of Disciplines: Toward a Historical Sociology of Disciplinary Knowledge. The Dialogical Turn: New Roles for Sociology in the Postdisciplinary Age*. Lanham MD: Rowman & Littlefield.

Helmholtz, Hermann von ([1862] 1995): "On the Relation of Natural Science to Science in General." In: Hermann von Helmholtz, *Science and Culture: Popular and Philosophical Essays*, 76–95. Edited by David Cahan. Chicago IL: University of Chicago Press.

Hentschel, Klaus (2015): "Periodization of Research Technologies and of the Emergence of Genericity." *Studies in the History and Philosophy of Modern Physics*, 52 (Part B): 223–233.

Jackson, Myles W. (2000): *Spectrum of Belief: Joseph von Fraunhofer and the Craft of Precision Optics*. Cambridge MA: The MIT Press.

Jaspers, Patricia, et al. (2013): "Ethical review: Standardizing Procedures and Local Shaping of Ethical Review Practices." *Social Science & Medicine*, 98: 311–318.

Joerges, Bernward, and Terry Shinn (Eds.) (2001): *Instrumentation between Science, State and Industry*. Dordrecht: Kluwer Academic Publishers.

Kittelson, James M., and Pamela J. Transue (1984): *Rebirth, Reform, and Resilience: Universities in Transition, 1300–1700*. Columbus OH: The Ohio State University Press.

Lattis, James M. (2010): *Between Copernicus and Galileo: Christoph Clavius and the Collapse of Ptolemaic Cosmology*. Chicago IL: University of Chicago Press.

Lenoble, Robert (1943): *Mersenne*. Paris: J. Vrin.

Lettkemann, Eric (2017): "Nomads and Settlers in the Research-technology Regime: The Case of Transmission Electron Microscopy." *Social Science Information*, 56 (3): 393–415.

Lindberg, David C., and Robert S. Westman (1990): *Reappraisals of the Scientific Revolution*. Cambridge: Cambridge University Press.

Luhmann, Niklas (1993): *Communication and Social Order: Risk: A Sociological Theory*. Piscataway NJ: Transaction Publishers.

Marcovich, Anne (2001): *A Quoi Rêvent les Sociétés?* Paris: Odile Jacob.

Marcovich, Anne, and Terry Shinn (2011). "Where is Disciplinarity Going? Meeting on the Borderland." *Social Science Information*, 50 (3–4): 582–606.

Marcovich, Anne, and Terry Shinn (2014): *Toward a New Dimension: Exploring the Nanoscale.* Oxford: Oxford University Press.

McClellan, James E. (1985): *Science Reorganized: Scientific Societies in the Eighteenth Century.* New York: Columbia University Press.

Mody, Cyrus C.M. (2011): *Instrumental Community: Probe Microscopy and the Path to Nanotechnology.* Cambridge MA: The MIT Press.

Olesko, Kathryn M. (1991): *Physics as a Calling: Discipline and Practice in the Königsberg Seminar for Physics.* Ithaca NY: Cornell University Press.

Porter, Roy, and Mikuláš Teich (1992): *The Scientific Revolution in National Context.* Cambridge: Cambridge University Press.

Sassen, Saskia (2006): *Territory, Authority, Rights: From Medieval to Global Assemblages.* 4 edn. Princeton NJ: Princeton University Press.

Shinn, Terry (2001): "The Research-technology Matrix: German Origins, 1860–1900." In: Bernward Joerges and Terry Shinn (Eds.): *Instrumentation between Science, State and Industry*, 29–36. Dordrecht: Kluwer Academic Publishers.

Shinn, Terry (2001): "Strange Cooperations: The U.S. Research-technology Perspective, 1900–1955." In: Bernward Joerges and Terry Shinn (Eds.): *Instrumentation between Science, State and Industry*, 69–97. Dordrecht: Kluwer Academic Publishers.

Shinn, Terry (2002): "The Triple Helix and New Production of Knowledge: Prepackaged Thinking on Science and Technology." *Social Studies of Science*, 32 (4): 599–614.

Shinn, Terry (2008): "Fourier Transform Spectroscopy." In: Terry Shinn, *Research-Technology and Cultural Change: Instrumentation, Genericity, Transversality.* Oxford: The Bardwell Press.

Shapin, Steven, and Simon Schaffer (2011): *Leviathan and the Air-Pump: Hobbes, Boyle, and the Experimental Life.* Princeton NJ: Princeton University Press.

Steinle, Friedrich (1995): "Looking for a 'Simple Case': Faraday and Electromagnetic Rotation." *History of Science*, 33 (2): 179–202.

Stroup, Alice (1990): *A Company of Scientists: Botany, Patronage, and Community at the Seventeenth-century Parisian Royal Academy of Sciences.* Vol. 8. Berkeley CA: University of California Press.

Teil, Geneviève (2012): "No such Thing as Terroir? Objectivities and the Regimes of Existence of Objects." *Science, Technology & Human Values*, 37 (5): 478–505.

Westfall, Richard S. (1981): *Never at Rest: A Biography of Isaac Newton.* Cambridge: Cambridge University Press.

Whitley, Richard (2000): *The Intellectual and Social Organization of the Sciences.* Oxford: Oxford University Press on Demand.

Yoder, Joella G. (1988): *Unrolling Time: Christian Huygens and the Mathematization of Nature.* Cambridge: Cambridge University Press

Poiesis in Action:
Doing without Knowledge

Andrew Pickering

Abstract

In his essay "The Question Concerning Technology", Martin Heidegger characterised our usual way of being in the world as enframing, a dominating stance
backed up by modern scientific knowledge. He also invoked an alternative stance
to enframing that he called *poiesis*, though without giving any convincing examples. This essay tries to put some flesh on the notion of *poiesis* by understanding
it as a primarily performative (rather than cognitive) mode of being that foregrounds experimental dances of human and non-human agency. Three examples
focus on our relations with the environment and nature: erosion control, the
adaptive management of waterflows in the Grand Canyon, and a form of "natural
farming" developed in Japan by Masanobu Fukuoka. A key distinction in the
analysis is that between experimentation in the wild – directly on the object of
concern – and scientific experimentation in the laboratory, which entails a detour
away from the thing itself aimed at providing de-contextualised and transportable
knowledge. The essay concludes by reframing the argument in terms of traditional Chinese philosophy, especially notions of *shi*, *wu wei* and the *Tao* – the propensity of things, not-doing and the Way.[1]

The phrase "weak knowledge" points to the possibility of other ways of knowing
the world, ways which are somehow different from the "strong" knowledge of
modern sciences such as physics. That some such alternative to science does or
should exist is a theme that runs through the philosophy of science. Martin
Heidegger (1977) associated science with a mode of being he called enframing
(*Gestell*), and he gestured towards another way which he called *poiesis*. Max Weber
distinguished between two forms of rationality: instrumental/formal (scientific)

---

1 Acknowledgements: For useful comments on earlier versions of this essay, I thank Louise
Amoore, Moritz Epple, Judith Farquhar, Regenia Gagnier, Malcolm Nicholson, Tom Smith,
participants at a seminar at Durham University organised by Ernesto Schwartz-Marin, and participants at the Frankfurt conference on weak knowledge where the paper which resulted in this
chapter was first presented. I also thank Lisa Asplen for introducing me to the Glen Canyon
AMP many years ago, and Tom Smith for more recently introducing me to Fukuoka's work.

and substantive/value (having to do with ends in themselves) (Rice 2013, 414). Herbert Marcuse (1964, 167) discussed "two contrasting rationalities".[2] Deleuze and Guattari (1987, 367–74) spoke of "royal" versus "nomad science".

Many authors have thus argued, or at least hoped, for some alternative to modern science, but the substance of that alternative remains obscure. Martin Heidegger (1997) evoked the arts of ancient Greece to exemplify *poiesis*, which does not take us far in the present; Gilles Deleuze and Félix Guattari's distinctions are opaque; Herbert Marcuse had nothing concrete to say. So here I want to clarify my own sense of what this alternative to the strong knowledge of science is. I suspect that the nature of *poiesis* remains obscure and puzzling, not because it is puzzling in itself but because it is not *any* kind of knowledge.

My argument here is that, to get to grips with *poiesis* – let's call it that – we need to think first about performance, about doing things in the world, rather than about knowledge per se. More particularly, I want to think of *poiesis* as the deliberate *staging* of what I call *dances of agency* (Pickering 1995) as a way of coming to terms with complex and emergent systems that resist domination through knowledge.[3] Hence, the idea that we can "do without knowledge". We could say that these dances stand in for knowledge, or that, conversely, scientific knowledge functions as a shortcut that eliminates them by (apparently) enabling us to see and design the future. I do not deny, however, that some knowledge intertwines with these dances, and attention to this leads to a further strong/weak knowledge distinction, now between strong laboratory-based scientific knowledge and a weaker situated knowledge that emerges from what I call experimentation in the wild.

To be clear, then, the examples to follow try to develop a performative account of *poiesis*, understood as another way to relate to the world, one that is different from one centred on strong scientific knowledge. I focus on our rela-

---

2 Habermas 1970, 85–86, dismisses Marcuse's line of thought while putting him in a long philosophical lineage: "In several passages Marcuse is tempted to pursue this idea of a New Science in connection with the promise, familiar in Jewish and Protestant mysticism, of the 'resurrection of fallen nature.' This theme, well-known for having penetrated Schelling's (and Baader's) philosophy via Swabian Pietism, returns in Marx's *Paris Manuscripts*, today constitutes the central thought of Bloch's philosophy, and in reflected forms, also directs the more secret hopes of Walter Benjamin, Max Horkheimer, and Theodor W. Adorno."

3 My general argument is that "dances of agency" are to be found everywhere, and I first documented and analysed them within scientific research itself (Pickering 1995, see also, for example, Kohler 1994, and Rheinberger 1997). Subsequently, I have come to see the dances in science as having a peculiar structure in that they aim to produce a detachable product, such as objective knowledge or a free-standing machine or instrument (see Pickering 2009b, and 2017, on "islands of stability"). Science, I want to say, foregrounds these products and backgrounds the dances that lead up to and away from them. It is, for instance, very difficult to find descriptions by scientists of these dances; the scientific research literature is devoted exclusively to the products. So here I want to focus on practices that make a gestalt switch and foreground dances of agency without aiming at detachable products.

tions with nature and the environment, and the examples concern a traditional approach to erosion control, the adaptive management of dams, and a form of agriculture known as "natural farming" or "permaculture".[4] At the end, I briefly re-formulate what has been said in terms of traditional Chinese philosophy.

*

My first example is taken from James Scott's book, *Seeing like a State* (1998, 327), in which he makes a Heidegger-style contrast between two forms of knowledge. Like Heidegger, Scott is critical of unsituated, universalising, modern scientific knowledge because, he argues, it is prone to lead to disaster when implemented in practice (that is the thrust of his book). Against this, he poses another kind of knowledge which he calls *metis*, situated, revisable knowledge somehow tuned into its specific domain of application.[5] His nicest example of *metis* in action is drawn from a traditional Japanese approach to forest management:

Erosion control in Japan is like a game of chess. The forest engineer, after studying his eroding valley, makes his first move, locating and building one or more check dams. He waits to see what nature's response is. This determines the forest engineer's next move, which may be another dam or two, an increase in the former dam, or the construction of side retaining walls. Another pause for observation, the next move is made, and so on, until erosion is checkmated. The operations of natural forces, such as sedimentation and revegetation, are guided and used to the best advantage to keep down costs and to obtain practical results.

What, then, is *metis*? Should it really be considered a form of knowledge at all? Certainly, some knowledge enters into the process that Scott describes. One needs some conception of "erosion" and why it is a problem, some empirical observations to show that this valley is eroding, some ideas on how water flows past barriers, and how plant life can spring back on the eroded terrain. But noth-

---

4 For examples drawn from the history of cybernetics, see Pickering 2009b, and 2010. For an earlier discussion of our relations with the environment, see Pickering 2008, and 2013. The interest in alternative sciences is usually motivated by a critique of modern science and technology that focuses on its relation to control and especially social control. I do not seek to develop that argument here, but instead stress the potential for disaster that seems to be integral to science-based practices.

5 Scott takes it for granted that *metis* is some sort of knowledge: "I attempt to conceptualize the nature of practical knowledge and to contrast it with more formal, deductive, epistemic knowledge. The term *metis* ... denotes the knowledge that can come only from practical experience." (1998, 6); "Metis, with the premium it places on practical knowledge, experience, and stochastic reasoning, is of course not merely the now-superseded precursor of scientific knowledge. It is the mode of reasoning most appropriate to complex material and social tasks where the uncertainties are so daunting that we must trust our (experienced) intuition." (1998, 327).

ing in this catalogue helps us to see what is special about *metis*. These are simply bits of everyday knowledge, some of which might be elevated to the sort of generalised science and engineering that Scott criticises. What makes Scott's story distinctive, it seems to me, is not knowledge at all. It is, instead, the deliberate staging of interlinked human and non-human performances that I call a dance of agency – here, the extended process of building dams and walls, seeing what the valley does in response to that, responding to the latter with revised engineering works, and so on.

And this is the central point that I want to make. At the opposite extreme from strong, scientific knowledge, one can find not so much weak knowledge, but the non-cognitive, performative dances of agency which Scott associates with *metis*, and which I am identifying with *poiesis*. If you want to know what *poiesis* is – and what a poetic mode of engagement with the environment looks like – think about this simple example. And we can note that *metis/poiesis* can be enough. In Scott's little example, nature ends up "checkmated", and the human engineer accomplishes his or her ends. This is my sense of "doing without knowledge". I think that this process is central to our being in the world, but it is hard to see in more familiar discourses that privilege epistemology, which is why I want to focus on it here.

Two points are worth thinking about here before moving on. First, though I want to emphasise the performative aspect of *poiesis*, I have already mentioned the strands of knowledge that can enter into this mode of being. We should therefore see it as a hybrid assemblage of mangle-ish performance and knowledge, but within a *gestalt* defined by a focus on the former. Performance defines the centre of gravity of this assemblage, we could say.

Second, it might be instructive to go further into the contrast between the characteristic modes of poetic and scientific action. On the one hand, we have deliberately staged dances of agency, but what form of practice hangs together with strong knowledge and modern science? It is, in fact, the latter that especially concerns Scott, and his case studies are of projects in which scientific knowledge functions, so to speak, as a shortcut to the future. He is interested, for example, in large-scale transformations of agriculture designed in advance upon the basis of the best scientific input. One calculates the most efficient use of land and then re-organises farming to fit. The shortcut, then, is the elimination of painstaking poetic dances of agency in favour of disembodied computation.[6]

---

6 We could say that making this shortcut is the point of scientific knowledge. The contrast is with the sort of local knowledge that I associate here and below with poetic explorations of the environment. I should perhaps emphasise that it is the use of scientific knowledge as a finished product that is at issue here. As stated in note 3 above, scientific research, which includes the process of producing knowledge, is itself poetic; Pickering 1995.

So here, the contrast between poetic and scientific forms of action is that the former is centred on a temporally extended process of finding out how some object will behave in specific circumstances, while the latter already knows that, or pretends to know it, upon the basis of scientific knowledge and rational calculation. These are evidently very different paradigms for action in the world (Pickering 2009a), and Scott's goal is, in fact, to emphasise the dangers inherent in the rational scientific approach by exploring how, to quote his subtitle, "certain schemes to improve the human condition have failed". One way to think about this is in terms of emergence and becoming (Pickering 1995). The scientific stance blocks out any awareness of emergence – meaning unpredictable surprise – until it is too late, and a disaster such as famine has already happened. *Metis* as *poiesis*, instead, is deliberately alive to emergence, and traces out emergent properties in its dances of agency. Heidegger (1977) described enframing as the "supreme danger", and this veiling of emergence by science might be a key aspect of that.

*

My second example also has to do with water and environmental engineering, but moves from the past to the present and from the micro to the macro. It concerns the construction and operation of dams, in particular, the Glen Canyon Dam on the Colorado River, completed in 1963 upstream of the Grand Canyon in the US. Like all such constructions, this dam set in motion many unexpected downstream physical and biological transformations. Sandbanks eroded; native species of plants and fish became endangered; alien species started to move in. What interests me here is the programme of so-called *adaptive management* that was introduced to address these changes. And the key point that I want to emphasise is that adaptive management is isomorphous with our previous example of erosion control, albeit on a different scale. It can stand as another instance of *poiesis* in action, now written very large.[7] Its core, again, as I will sketch out briefly (following the work of Lisa Asplen and James Rice), is not articulated knowledge but another deliberate, iterative and performative dance of agency, orchestrated now between the dam operators and the downstream ecosystem.

The model for the Glen Canyon Dam Adaptive Management Program or AMP for short, was an artificial flood that happened in 1983. In that year, Lake Powell, upstream of the dam, was in danger of overflowing, and, as an emergency measure, vast quantities of water were released through the dam. And it was noticed that that this had beneficial downstream effects: "Depleted beaches were replenished, exotic vegetation was killed along the riverbanks, and previously de-

---

7 Given the difference in scale, it would be hard to describe operations on the Colorado as *metis* on Scott's description.

graded animal habitats were re-created." (Asplen 2008, 172) Here, then, we have the first moves in another dance of human and non-human agency: the release of abnormally large flows of water from Lake Powell, followed by material reconfigurations emerging below the dam. And at the heart of the AMP that followed was a succession of deliberate artificial floods, known as High Flow Experiments (HFEs), modelled on this first one, each aiming to learn from the upshot of the others in terms of operating conditions and downstream modifications.[8]

To date, seven HFEs have been conducted on the Colorado, and we should note that, in this case, unlike Scott's example, nature has not been "checkmated". Early experiments looked promising. The first HFE, in 1996, initially appeared to be a success and "increasing sedimentation was readily apparent. ... What we found was really quite extraordinary. The success of the event exceeds ... even our most optimistic hopes of our staff of scientists" (Rice: 418–19). But the optimism soon evaporated. Sandbanks that had been built up during floods were quickly eroded again; invasive species turned out to be hiding in the mud and soon re-appeared; the population of humpback chub (*gila cypha*), an endangered species, continued to decline.[9]

After two HFEs [1996 and 2004] and nearly 10 years of adaptive management, the ecological conditions below the Glen Canyon Dam exhibited little sustained improvement [...]. Long-term increase in sedimentation had not been achieved, the presence of humpback chub continued to decline even as nonnative trout were thriving, and nonnative vegetation, particularly tamarisk, remained entrenched along the Colorado River corridor. (Rice 2013, 420)

Clearly, staging dances of agency is no magic bullet. But, "Arguably, a great deal of insight into the interplay of controlled flooding and ecological response was gleaned after two HFE's", and it is interesting to reflect on this. The basic insight derived from the 1983 flood was simply that flooding was, to some extent, performatively effective in modifying the downstream ecosystem. Later developments were progressively understood in terms of sediment deposition. The Glen Canyon Dam slowed the Colorado down, encouraging it to deposit most of its sediment above the dam, and the conviction arose that it was a lack of sediment that was at the heart of the problems downstream. The solution to this was then thought to be better use of the sediment carried by two other rivers, the Little Colorado and the Paria, that joined the Colorado below the dam. Thus, the spring

---

8 The AMP also included modifications to ramping rates for electricity production but I omit these details here.

9 The time-dependence of the river's response marks this example off from others that I have written about, where the contours of each move in dances of agency were more or less immediately apparent. In my study of the history of the bubble chamber, for example, Donald Glaser simply set up the apparatus and filmed what it did, with no idea that its performance would change over time; Pickering 1995, Ch. 2.

2008 HFE "was precipitated by flooding on the Paria River and an estimated sediment inflow to the Colorado 3 times greater than observed before the 2004 HFE". The hope was that re-distribution of the sediment from the Paria river would restore the downstream ecology. "There was evidence of re-deposition of sediment [but] six months later, however, a majority of new sedimentation was lost to erosion, and [again] nonnative [...] vegetation was temporarily buried rather than scoured from the Grand Canyon. Researchers now suspect that too much time had passed between sediment inflow and the 2008 HFE such that a substantial proportion was lost under normal operating conditions", and later HFEs were accordingly planned to be "triggered" by large sediment inflows (Rice 2013, 420, 422).[10]

This is as far as I can take the story of the AMP. Like Scott's account of forest management techniques, it exemplifies my interpretation of *poiesis* as the foregrounding and intentional staging of dances of human and non-human agency. Though not permanently effective, the emergent emphasis on sedimentation and the triggering of flows points towards what I think of as a *choreography of agency*, an intertwining and reciprocal tuning of the performances of the dam operators and the Little Colorado and Paria (rivers) that might be able to maintain the downstream ecosystem in a favourable state of dynamic equilibrium. We can examine this sort of choreography in more detail in my third example, but, before that, the AMP invites some further reflections on science and enframing as the contrast class to *poiesis*.

*

First, I need to qualify my remarks on "doing without knowledge". The cluster of ideas around sedimentation clearly counts as some sort of knowledge emerging from the adaptive management program, and, again, we should think of the AMP as a hybrid performance/knowledge assemblage – with its centre of gravity again in the realm of performance, not knowledge. But it is worth clarifying what sort of knowledge is involved here, and it helps now to think of an ambiguity in the word "experiment". *Scientific* experiment takes place in the lab. It entails a *detour* away from the thing itself – in this case, the Colorado River – with the object of stripping away the particulars and producing universal and unsituated knowledge that can then be transported back to *any* particular situation. And, in contrast to

10 See Rice on the 2008 HFE. On the AMP and the 2008 HFE, see, also, Melis et al. 2012. There is plenty of information on subsequent HFEs available on the web. Grams et al. 2015, 5, report that "resource managers ... consider the 2012–2014 results encouraging". The current wisdom is that there should be relatively frequent artificial floods timed to coincide with major sediment inputs from the Paria and Little Colorado rivers. A more radical and expensive proposal is a pipeline to transport sedimentary material downstream of the Glen Canyon Dam.

this, we should see the knowledge of the importance of sedimentation generated in the AMP as the product of what I would call *experimentation in the wild* – experiment directly on the Colorado River itself, with no detour away from the river and through the lab.[11] The detour through the lab, away from and back to objects in the world, thus marks off science from the sort of knowledge that goes with *poiesis*. Putting this another way, we can note that, while the entire point of the trip through the lab is to produce universal and transportable knowledge, the sort of knowledge produced in experimentation in the wild is ancillary to something else, namely, the dance of agency from which it emerges. And we could put this more strongly by saying that the poetic dance of agency is the *object* of adaptive management. The aim is to find a performative solution to downstream ecological transformations, *not* to produce knowledge.[12]

One last point deserves some attention before we leave the Colorado. I take the AMP to be an exemplar of *poiesis*, but what exactly does enframing, as the Heideggerian contrast class, look like? Heidegger's idea was that enframing is a "challenging forth" in which the world is made to appear as "standing reserve", and his example is, as it happens, a hydro-electric dam on the Rhine River. But what does this "challenging forth" consist of? In our example, we need to look *upstream* from the Glen Canyon Dam (rather than downstream, as we have been.) Upstream we find, not deliberately staged exploratory dances of agency, but a pre-formed scientific-engineering design being imposed on nature come what may. Some simple maths and science, plus some engineering lore, enables engineers to calculate in advance just where and how high the dam needs to be in

---

11 The aim of the detour is to create de-localised knowledge that can be moved anywhere; experimentation in the wild yields knowledge that does not need to move because it is immediately about the object of interest. For more on these contrasting senses of "experiment" in the context of art, see Pickering 2016. Many of Latour's classic studies focus on the detour through the lab (or some "centre of calculation"): on Pasteur, Latour 1983; on Lapérouse and Sakhalin Island, Latour 1987, Chapter 6; on the "pédofil", Latour 1995. A political critique of Latour would be that he cannot seem to imagine a way of going on that does not involve this detour; Pickering 2009. On "wild experiments", see, also, Lorimer and Driessen 2014.

12 This is not to say that there has been no real science involved in the AMP. There is plenty, with scientists computing flow rates and sedimentation rates and trying to predict the effects of future HFEs. Sometimes the predictions have proved to be right; others wrong. Speaking of the 1996 HFE, Asplen 2008, 174–175, notes: "The results turned out to be a mixed bag of expected and unexpected outcomes based on the scientific models that informed the design of the flood." The progress of the flood down the river and the removal of constrictions were correctly anticipated. The erosion that followed the buildup of sandbars, in contrast, was not: "One group was so surprised by this behavior that they ended up 'watch[ing] as $70,000 worth of borrowed equipment was first buried, then excavated and finally carried away'." In the end, sandbars have become the central focus of the AMP. They are valued as a physical feature, visually but also as campgrounds. At the same time they maintain the ecosystems in which native species can flourish. There is clearly a nonlinear relation between the topology of the sandbars and water flows and, in effect, the aim of the AMP is to explore and find a good operating point on a curve linking flows and sandbars.

order to contain so much water, generate so much electricity, and so on. Heidegger's idea was that science *sets nature up* for enframing, and we can see how that works here. The calculation of volumes, pressures, energy generation, etc., leaves nature defenceless to exploitation.

As in the previous example, we can also think here about *emergence*, the appearance of brute novelty in the world. As I suggested above, *poiesis* actively explores emergence in deliberate dances of agency. Scientific knowledge, in contrast, hides or *denies emergence*. It is, in a way, a shortcut to the future. From the perspective of science, there is nothing left to find out in dam design or enframing in general. This observation is at the heart of the contrast between *poiesis* and enframing, as I conceive them.

At the same time, it is worth noting that science is not enough in projects of enframing. No list of equations will ever build the Glen Canyon Dam. To do that, you also need entire industries devoted to civil engineering, re-configuring the land, making and pouring concrete and whatever. So, enframing is not just, or necessarily, *scientific knowledge*. It has a massive, material component that is also imposed on nature.

And the other point to note is, that, if scientific knowledge acts to make emergence hard even to imagine, it does not get rid of it. Dams do not, in fact, always work as designed. There are very many historical instances of dam failures and downstream disasters. In the first artificial flood on the Colorado River, some of the excess water was discharged through purpose-built spillways – which immediately began to degrade dangerously and have never been put to use again. In the mode of enframing, then, emergence returns as unexpected accidents, disasters and catastrophes, and we could see this as one of the dark sides of enframing. This, of course, is precisely James Scott's argument in *Seeing like a State*, and another reason to be interested in *poiesis* as another way to be.[13]

*

---

13 Heidegger 1977, called enframing the "supreme danger". For a catalogue of disastrous dam failures, see Perrow 1984, Chapter 7. For just one account of hundreds of deaths following the collapse of a dam in Pennsylvania a century ago, see www.nytimes.com/learning/ general/onthisday/big/0531.html#article. The tide of poisonous red sludge that escaped from an alumina reservoir in Hungary in 2010 sticks in my mind for some reason: www.voxeurop.eu/en/content/article/356951-hungarys-red-tide. Schivelbusch 1986 conceptualises the increasing perils of technological domination in terms of the "falling height" of the systems in question, and dams illustrate his point nicely. For a film about the first artificial flood on the Colorado, see https://www.youtube.com/watch?v=VPcrccxcNsI. The provocatively mis-spelt subtitle (or perhaps a play on words) of the movie is *Glen Canyon Damn Nearly Busts!* For a recent example of another spillway near-disaster, see Nagourney and Fountain 2017.

My third and last example is what is known as "natural farming" (or "permaculture"), which was pioneered in Japan by Masanobu Fukuoka (1913–2008) (Fukuoka 1978) (and brought to my attention by a very insightful essay by Thomas
Smith, no date).[14] Natural farming is very different from both traditional agriculture and post-war techno-scientific agriculture. Its most striking feature is its "do
nothing" stance. In contrast to conventional farming, the land is not ploughed or
worked over in any way, no weeding is done and no flooding (as is usually the
case in rice farming), no chemicals are used, either as fertiliser or pesticide. The
basic activities of natural farming are simply scattering seed, harvesting the crop
(alternately rice and barley growing, in turn, in the same field in autumn and
spring) and mulching the ground with the straw left over from threshing. The key
trick is timing. If the mulch is spread at the right time, it hinders weeds and fosters
the next crop. Using simple methods like these, Fukuoka reports crop yields comparable, if not greater, than labour-intensive or chemical-dependent forms of
farming.[15]

What can we say about natural farming? First – thinking of other ways to be
– it is so different that I find it shocking. I am used to seeing farmers ploughing
their land every year, and the possibility that you can farm without ploughing
never crossed my mind until I read Fukuoka (1978). Second, we can ask where
natural farming came from. According to Fukuoka (1978, 7–12), it began in 1938
with a spontaneous philosophical revelation that we (humanity) are *doing too much*,
setting ourselves outside nature as its masters. This is Heideggerian enframing,
and Fukuoka thought that it must be possible to get out of it, to remain in – or
at least closer to – nature, and take part in the natural flow of events, instead of
ordering them around – *poiesis*.[16]

He set out to test this idea in the case of farming, working initially on his
father's land, and what followed was another poetic and performative dance of
agency isomorphic with our previous examples. His first thought was simply to
let his father's orchards go – not to look after them at all. This failed completely

---

14 Smith's essay covers a broad sweep of "permaculture", which, he states, began in Australia. I
   find it better here to concentrate on Fukuoka's extensive account of his form of natural farming.

15 "So the order of planting in this field is like this: in early October clover is broadcast among the
   rice; winter grain then follows in the middle of the month. In early November, the rice is har-
   vested, and then the next year's rice seed is sown and straw laid across the field. ... In caring for
   a quarter-acre field, one or two people can do all the work in a matter of a few days. It seems
   unlikely that there could be a simpler way of raising grain" (Fukuoka 1978, 3). Fukuoka also
   discusses fruit and vegetable farming at length but I will focus largely on rice and winter crops
   here.

16 On the idea that mastery in farming requires more rather than less human labour, see, also,
   Dawn Coppin's studies of mega-hog farms: Coppin 2002, 2003, 2008.

– all the trees died (Fukuoka 1978, 13).[17] He then took a more active role, looking for ways to approach his goal progressively, rather than in a single leap. He tried planting white clover as groundcover that would enrich the soil while inhibiting (but not eradicating) weeds. This worked. Reasoning that one had to return as much goodness as possible to the land each year, Fukuoka re-distributed all the straw that remained after threshing each crop. This ran into difficulties. Looking more closely, it seemed the problem was that he had thrown the mulch onto the land in clumps (Korn 2012, 8) or distributed it too carefully and geometrically (Korn 2012, 48). Either way, the mulch was inhibiting the germination of the crops. And, trying it another way, he discovered that mulching was a success if he simply broadcast the straw randomly across the land (Korn 2012, 48).[18]

After many more twists and turns, Fukuoka finally arrived at the mature form of natural farming.[19] He had learned how to obtain good yields of crops with a minimum of effort, while dispensing with otherwise definitive elements of farming, such as ploughing, weeding, the use of fertilisers and pesticides, and much hard labour. I want now to examine what this stabilised form of natural farming looks like, and I want especially to get at its poetic quality, in contrast to conventional agriculture.[20]

---

17 "From that point on the question, 'What is the natural pattern?' was always in my mind. In the process of arriving at the answer I wiped out another 400 trees, Finally I felt I could say with certainty, 'This is the natural pattern'." (1978, 16).

18 "Fukuoka also implies that our fixation on control over nature has led us to assume visual order - the straight weeded rows of uniform fields - is superior farming" (Lappé 2009, Introduction, x). This sort of visual order is precisely the target of Scott 1998, as signalled in the title: *Seeing like a State.*

19 In the early days, he found it necessary to control insects with a naturally prepared insecticide (pyrethrum) but as his fields developed he found he could dispense with that too. He occasionally sprays his trees with an emulsion of machine oil against "scale" (1978, 34) (see below). On his account, sparrows have been an enormous problem, pecking up the seed as quickly as he threw it across the ground. "I tried scarecrows and nets and strings of rattling cans, but nothing seemed to work very well. Or if one of these methods happened to work, its effectiveness did not last more than a year or two" (1978, 52). The solution to that proved to be a new chore - coating the seeds in mud pellets before sowing them (1978, 44–45, 51). Fukuoka found that if he let ducks wander around on his fields, their droppings would help the mulch decompose more quickly. Then a new road divided his fields from the ducks' houses and Fukuoka had to take over, lightly covering the mulch with duck or chicken droppings (37). At one point, he rented some land from a neighbour and obtained a good crop using his usual approach, except in one corner where the "plants came up too thickly and were attacked by blast disease". When asked, his neighbour stated he put all his chicken droppings there, from which Fukuoka learned something about over-feeding his crops (37). "I once thought there would be nothing wrong with putting ashes from the fireplace onto the fields [as he did in his kitchen garden]. The result was astounding. Two or three days later the field was completely bare of spiders. The ashes had caused the strands of web to disintegrate. How many thousands of spiders fell victim to a single handful of this apparently harmless ash?" (28).

20 So far we have been looking at examples of exploratory transformative processes; now we can examine an example of their end-state, a stabilised practice. (The equivalent for the Colorado

If we followed James Scott, we would have to say that, like Scott's forest engineer, in natural farming, Fukuoka checkmated the soil and plants. But this metaphor turns out to be misleading. It invites images of pinning down an opponent, imposing one's will on them – that is to say, enframing – so it is important to note that, in natural farming, Fukuoka appears more as a *responsive partner* than as a dominating other. Thus, beyond repetitive operations such as sowing and reaping, in natural farming, the farmer has to be attentive to nature in order to determine the *timing* of operations. Fukuoka (1978, 38) outlines how "Timing the seeding in such a way that there is no interval between succeeding crops gives the grain a great advantage over the weeds". Likewise, "The important thing is knowing the right time to plant. For spring vegetables the right time is when the winter weeds are dying back and just before the summer weeds have sprouted. For the fall sowing, seeds should be tossed out when the summer grasses are fading away and winter weeds have not yet appeared. It is best wait for a rain which is likely to last for several days."[21]

In this respect, then, the farmer is, so to speak, *in the same plane* (Pickering 1995) as the plants and the earth, responding to developments there in actions which return directly to the land with no detour, and this is the basic sense in which natural farming exemplifies *poiesis*, now as an established practice, rather than as a process of finding out. The contrast might be with a dam that stands firm – unresponsive and unchanging – and simply imposes its will on a river, or with chemical farming which imposes a fixed regime of ploughing, fertiliser, herbicides and pesticides on the land, come what may.[22] In Heidegger's terms, the dam and chemical farming are examples of enframing, not in the plane but standing dualistically above nature and inflexibly imposing conditions on it.[23]

River would be a regularised operating mode of the Glen Canyon Dam that indeed restored the downstream ecosystem to something like its pre-dam configuration.) The argument is that objects and established practices can also have a poetic quality, in as much as *poiesis* (as a process) lacks the technoscientific telos of a detached product.

21 Fukuoka 1978, 66–67. One of the lessons of the Glen Canyon AMP is again the need to pay attention to the timing of artificial floods in relation to the behaviour of the Little Colorado and Paria Rivers, as a way of tilting the balance towards sandbar formation. This timing of operations in relation to worldly performances also appears in Scott's chapter on *metis* (1998, 311): European settlers in the New World "were told by Squanto ... to plant corn when the oak leaves were the size of a squirrel's ear".

22 Of course, conventional farming has some sensitivity to conditions on the ground - it is weather dependent, for example. But this is ancillary to the schema of ploughing, etc., just listed - the weather just gets in the way. In natural farming, in contrast, the dynamic coupling to the land is more or less all there is.

23 Note that the contrast is performative, not cognitive: these are different patterns of action in the world. We can think again here about different gestalt patterns. Natural farming thematises the dance of agency between the farmer, land and crops, while chemical farming backgrounds it. It might help here to think about a contrast which I made in Pickering 2010 between two modes of adaptation. In symmetric adaptation all of the elements involved are free to adapt to

Having made this basic contrast, I want to explore it further from various angles.

1) In natural farming, one has the image of *loops closing*, in which each step in dances of agency sets up the conditions for the next: the winter crop nurtures the rice crop which is waiting in the wings, while slowing down the weeds, and *vice versa*. This process could be described as a circular and regularised *choreography* of agency. And, indeed, as in the previous examples, we could think of Fukuoka's path to natural farming as performative experimentation oriented to *finding* just such a circular arrangement of agencies, including his own. And if laboratory experimentation aims to produce unsituated *knowledge*, in the cases discussed here, experimentation in the wild aims, instead, at this performative choreography. The characteristic destination of the poetic process is a regular choreography of agency, not knowledge.[24]

I could add that this is one of several points of intersection between natural farming and cybernetics. The idea of loops closing on themselves evokes the image of Ourobouros, the mystical snake that eats its own tail, which Heinz von Foerster (2014) adopted as the logo of cybernetics – though he was thinking about eigenstates of mathematical systems, not worldly performances.[25]

2) We could see loops closing as a sort of *lock-in*, a situation to be dynamically maintained, not anything fixed. We could also see loops which *fail* to close as a different sort of lock-in, as continually calling for new responses in dances of agency that threaten to get out of hand. I have talked elsewhere about the US Army Corps of Engineers trying to manage the Mississippi River in just these terms, forever building flood defences and control structures that the river sooner or later overflows or destroys (Pickering 2008). In the present context, we could think of weeds becoming resistant to pesticides, say, and thus calling for more or

---

the behaviours of each other. In asymmetric adaptation, one element stands firm and the others have to adapt to that. Natural farming is then symmetric adaptation, in which the farmer responds to the performance of the land and vice versa. Dams and chemical farming stand for the asymmetric alternative. In Pickering 2010, I showed that symmetric and asymmetric practices and products look very different in all sorts of fields of endeavour, with specific reference to cybernetics.

24 Nor indeed a free-standing, detachable, device or machine such as the bubble chamber, one of my original examples of the mangle of practice in action.

25 This circular choreography of agency is also reminiscent of Maturana and Varela's conception of *autopoiesis*. We could wonder again here about the contrast with chemical agriculture. Can one find there a comparable closing of the loops? Not if one focusses on the farm alone - continual inputs of chemicals are required from outside. But what if one expands one's view of the farm to include chemical factories, etc - do the loops close then? Not really. This expansion would have eventually to include sources of raw materials, such as oil wells, which would leave us with an image of progressive depletion rather than circular replenishment. So this linear depletion versus circular replenishment contrast might be another characteristic demarcation between enframing and *poiesis*. We could also think about the "performative excess" (Pickering 2017) associated with chemical farming. The run-off of chemicals and the consequent ecological effects are another aspect of loops which do not close.

better pesticides.[26] In the mode of enframing, the basic image is thus one of the dance of agency as an *arms race*.

Fukuoka himself analyses the difficulty of moving from conventional to natural farming in just these terms. Once the chemical dance of agency has been set in motion, the soil becomes depleted and *has* to be enriched by fertiliser, and so on. To refuse to add fertiliser in such circumstances is simply to invite disaster – as Fukuoka did, when he left his father's orchards untended.[27]

3) We can take this line of thought one step further by thinking about pests and pesticide use. As one would expect, Fukuoka is basically against chemical responses to pests and diseases, and centrally at issue here is a vision of an ecological great chain of being, in which the existence of endlessly reverberating dances of agency makes the efficacy of the targeted interventions suspect.[28] Fukuoka discusses, for example, attempts to protect pines from an outbreak of weevils by spraying pesticide from helicopters:

---

26 Fukuoka 1978, 35, gives a very abbreviated example of this process: "When the soil is cultivated the natural environment is altered beyond recognition. The repercussions of such acts have caused the farmer nightmares for countless generations. For example, when a natural area is brought under the plow very strong weeds such as crabgrass and docks sometimes come to dominate the vegetation. When these weeds take hold, the farmer is faced with a nearly impossible task of weeding each year. Very often, the land is abandoned."

27 "The reason that man's improved techniques seem to be necessary is that the natural balance has been so badly upset beforehand by those same techniques that the land has become dependent on them ... Look over at the neighbour's field ... The weeds have all been wiped out by herbicides and cultivation. The soil animals and insects have been exterminated by poison. The soil has been burned clean of organic matter and microorganisms by chemical fertilizers. In the summer you see farmers at work in the fields, wearing gas masks and long rubber gloves. These rice fields, which have been farmed continuously for over 1,500 years, have now been laid waste by the exploitive farming practices of a single generation" (Fukuoka 1978, 15, 33). And hence the difficulty of getting out of real arms races: the old one around nuclear weapons, the newer one against "terror", etc., etc. For Fukuoka, this is not just a point about farming. To move away from nature in any sort of activity, according to him, is to become embroiled in one of these arms races. I doubt whether he made many friends by suggesting that schooling has this quality (16–17): "To the extent that trees deviate from their natural form pruning and insect extermination become necessary, to the extent that human society separates itself from a life close to nature, schooling becomes necessary. In nature formal schooling has no function." Perhaps he could have asked himself whether there could be a "natural education" to mirror natural farming; see Glanville 2002.

28 "Methods of insect control which ignore the relationships among the insects themselves are truly useless. Research on spiders and leaf-hoppers must also consider the relation between frogs and spiders. When things have reached this point, a frog professor will also be needed. Experts on spiders and leaf-hoppers, another on rice, and another expert on water management will all have to join the gathering. Furthermore, there are four or five kinds of spiders in these fields ..." And, of course, not everything about individual species is known even by the relevant scientists: "The phenomenon of these great swarms of spiders, which appear in the rice fields in the autumn and like escape artists vanish overnight, is still not understood. No one knows where they come from, how they survive the winter, or where they go when they disappear" (Fukuoka 1978, 28).

I do not deny that this is effective in the short run, but I know there must be another way. Weevil blights, according to the latest research, are not a direct infestation, but follow upon the action of mediating nematodes. The nematodes breed within the trunk, block the transport of water and nutrients, and eventually cause the pine to wither and die. The ultimate cause, of course, is not yet clearly understood. Nematodes feed on a fungus within the tree's trunk. Why did this fungus begin to spread so prolifically within the tree? Did the fungus begin to multiply after the nematode had already appeared? Or did the nematode appear because the fungus was already present? [...] Furthermore, there is another microbe about which very little is known, which always accompanies the fungus, and a virus which is toxic to the fungus. Effect following effect in every direction, the only thing that can be said with certainty is that pine trees *are* withering in unusual numbers. (Fukuoka 1978, 39–40)

You can eradicate the weevils but this just leaves the nematodes, funguses and viruses to do their thing, whatever that will emergently turn out to be.[29]

Fukuoka's position is that natural farming encourages a diverse and resilient ecosystem to flourish, in which the different elements keep each other, including "pests", in check.[30] And this is his basic claim: with little assistance, naturally farmed land is quite (not totally) resistant to pests and diseases because of its ecological diversity, in which prey and predators quickly come into equilibrium.[31] The dance of agency more or less choreographs itself. Again, we have the image of performative and poetic loops that close on themselves, in comparison with the open-ended arms races of pesticides and herbicides.

(4) We can return to questions of weak and strong knowledge here. Fukuoka does not question the validity of "strong" scientific accounts of individual elements of ecosystems.[32] His idea, though, is that this knowledge describes just some elements in an endless web which, in total, always exceeds our knowledge of it. "People cannot know what the true cause of the pine blight is, nor can they

---

29 Fukuoka 1978 40, continues: "If the situation is meddled with unknowingly, that only sows the seeds for the next great catastrophe." Another resonance with the history of cybernetics is evident here: see Ashby's discussion of "stabilizing the stabilizer" with the postwar British economy as his example (Ashby 1945; Pickering 2010, 147). Think also of Bateson's (2000), idea that attempting to control an ecosystem is like trying to reverse a truck with two trailers.

30 "I think that everyone knows that since the most common orchard 'pests', ruby scale and horned wax scale, have natural enemies, there is no need to apply insecticide to keep them under control. At one time the insecticide Fusol was used in Japan. The natural predators were completely exterminated [along with the pests], and the resulting problems still survive in many prefectures. ... Most farmers have come to realize that it is undesirable to eliminate predators because in the long run greater insect damage will result. ... If ... the insect communities are left to achieve their natural balance after [spraying with a solution of machine oil which is relatively harmless to the predators], the problem will generally take care of itself. This will not work if an organic phosphorous pesticide has already been used in June or July since the predators are also killed by this chemical" (Fukuoka 1978, 59–60).

31 On the vulnerability of monocultures, see Tsing 2012.

32 Fukuoka was himself a laboratory scientist before the revelation that led him to natural farming (1978, 4–10).

know the ultimate consequences of their 'remedy'." (Fukuoka 1978, 40–41) Almost paradoxically, then, when scientific knowledge is assembled into a complex whole, it becomes weak and loses its predictive force.[33] There are interesting parallels here to contemporary sciences of complexity and the notions of unpredictability and emergence that go along with them.

(5) We can end this section by thinking again about enframing and science. Fukuoka's critique is directed at traditional farming, which goes back thousands of years, as well as to post-war chemical farming. So where does this leave traditional farming in relation to Heidegger's *schema*? If natural farming counts as *poiesis*, perhaps traditional farming is enframing.[34] But how should we conceptualise that? On the one hand, I suppose, traditional farming consists of imposing on nature a relatively rigid procedure (of ploughing, fertilising, weeding, flooding) isomorphous to the engineering work of building a dam mentioned in the previous section. Tradition here, rather than science, acts as the shortcut that backgrounds dances of agency. From a different angle, we could also say that traditional farming is enframing in as much as it maintains a system (the land and the crops) *far from equilibrium*. Natural farming, instead, orchestrates the equilibrium condition itself.[35]

What, then, of post-war technoscientific agriculture? It must also count as enframing. But how does science fit into the story? Heidegger said that science sets the world up for enframing, and it is pretty clear how that goes in calculations around dam-building. But less so here. Farmers do not calculate how to grow this year's crop. Instead, it seems to me that science enters the story of agriculture through another kind of detour through the lab, not, this time, a detour oriented to the production of unsituated knowledge, but, instead, to the production of novel *materials* – new and improved pesticides, fertilisers, genetically-modified seeds – that themselves circulate back as ingredients and accelerants in "arms races" with nature. This scientific detour through the lab once more marks the difference between enframing and *poiesis*.[36]

---

33 This is also basically Perrow's (1984) point about "normal accidents". Of course, it is Bateson's (2000) basic ontological point about the impossibility of reversing a truck with two trailers.

34 Heidegger (1977) has windmills on the good, non-enframing, side, though he does not invoke them as examples of *poiesis*.

35 We could also think here of the contrast between two technological paradigms in computing that I drew in Pickering 2009. Conventional computing depends on reconfiguring matter (silicon chips) more or less down to the atomic scale. This is engineering in the mode of enframing, which parallels the re-configuration of the soil (ploughing, etc.) in traditional farming. Biological computing, in contrast, seeks to latch onto and entrain the liveliness of naturally occurring systems, and the analogy to natural farming is clear.

36 On this kind of detour in the establishment of the synthetic dye industry, see Pickering 2005, and, in farming, see Coppin 2002, 2003, and 2008. Justus von Liebig (1803–1873) was a key figure in both the history of scientific farming and organic chemistry.

*

The spirit of technology without theoretical science seems ...
to be found within Taoist philosophy itself.
Joseph Needham

Putting 'doing nothing' into practice is the one thing the farmer
should strive to accomplish. Lao Tzu ... would certainly
practice natural farming.
Masanobu Fukuoka

I have been trying to conjure up an understanding of *poiesis* as a performative stance in the world that foregrounds and choreographs dances of human and non-human agency. The contrast is with the stance of enframing which backgrounds agency and performance and foregrounds, instead, established tradition, strong knowledge and scientific detours through the lab. I want to end by briefly changing perspective and moving eastwards. I suspect that it is not a coincidence that two of my examples come from Japan. Probably, the easiest way to approach the subject matter of this essay would have been to begin not with Heidegger but with traditional eastern philosophy, which, it seems to me, is all about *poiesis* as a mode of being in the world.

Take the Chinese concept of *shi*. François Jullien (1999) translates *shi* as the "propensity of things" – the disposition of things to act in specific ways. From the present perspective, the attractive feature of *shi* is that it refers directly to performance. And, in Chinese thought, *shi* has immediate implications for human performance: human action is proper and effective if it is in tune with the *shi* of the situation in which it takes place. From one angle, of course, just what *shi* is itself remains foggy. How are we to know the *shi* that we are dealing with? One answer is a sort of inner non-cognitive mastery based upon long experience. But my examples help us to come at the question differently. All of the examples are about actively *finding out* and taking advantage of what the *shi* of particular constellations is. In my first example, the forest engineer explores the *shi* of water, vegetation, and so on, discovering how they will perform when configured this way or that. The Glen Canyon Dam story has just the same form, messing around with water flows, hoping to find a propensity to restore downstream sandbanks and ecologies. Fukuoka explored the *shi* of different arrangements of plants and land, finally finding a simple constellation of *shi*s that fed into one another in a circular pattern.

All very simple. If we already had the concept of *shi*, I could have told these stories very directly. Conversely, one virtue of the stories is that they help us westerners to grasp the meaning of "*shi*" and what it means to act in accordance with it – which is what I have been referring to as *poiesis*. The hard thing to understand from this angle would then be the twists and turns and detours back and forth of enframing (including modern scientific knowledge and instrumentation, and the detour through the lab). Which is as much as to say that starting from a *shi*-ontology would be an excellent way to bring our dominant patterns of thinking and acting into focus – to problematise what we usually take for granted, science and engineering.

And from *shi* it is easy to move to the *Tao*. The Tao, the Way, is impossible to define, but the familiar Taoist idea of going with the flow is not misleading, and it is evident that our three examples all illustrate what this could mean. Following the Way, acting in accordance with *shi*, and *poiesis* mean much the same as far as I can make out. And, as before, we can turn this around and say that our examples help us to understand what the Way is – a performative attribute of humans and situations, always waiting to be explored – and hence necessarily foggy in terms of knowledge. If you want to make sense of "*wu wei*" – often translated as notdoing – a key concept of Taoism – just look at Fukuoka's minimalist approach to farming. *Wu wei* is not literally "doing nothing" – as when Fukuoka abandoned his father's orchards. It is more like gracefully inserting oneself into the flow of agency and becoming.[37] Enframing is the oafish contrast-class: it is our way – wrestling the other into submission.[38]

---

37 Scott 1998, 424, note 12, also invokes the Tao in his chapter on metis. Another example to think about here would be the ancient Dujiangyan control structure on the Min River in China. The structure directs water flows in different directions depending on flow rates at different times in the year, thus supporting irrigation while controlling flooding. Various human interventions and annual maintenance activities accompany these variations. The whole assemblage is much like natural farming's choreography of agencies, though more complex. One can even trace out the evolution of the control structures: different positioning of the "fish mouth"; other structures (including the iron turtle) lost in floods; various additions and changes in materials. Temples connect heaven and earth. Zhang et al. 2013, offer a useful and relatively comprehensive technical description of Dujiangyan's components and functioning; I thank James Hevia for drawing this paper to my attention. Needham (1971, 288–96) is another valuable and simpler description (under the headings of Kuanhsien and Tu-Chiang Yen). Needham (234–35) discusses what he calls Taoist hydraulics, for which "wu wei was the best watchword". Opposing this was a Confucian approach to engineering which favoured building dykes to contain rivers, in just the same way as the US Army Corps of Engineers has attempted to control the Mississippi (see Needham 1971, 249; Pickering 2008 and 2013). Needham (1971, 249–50) discusses Dujiangyan as an exemplar of Taoist water engineering. We could also take *wu wei* more literally as doing nothing, as in my discussion of the Exe valley (Pickering 2013) and on a much grander scale in the Room for the River project re-configuring the Rhine, including repositioning dykes: for example, www.ruimtevoorderivier.nl/english.

38 For a vivid and amusing evocation of this contrast, see Westwell 2014.

I began with unclear speculations about other ways of knowing the world: Heidegger and *poiesis*, Deleuze and Guattari and nomad science, Scott and *metis*, Marcuse and what Jürgen Habermas has called New Science. My argument is that one can blow away the fog and trace out the shape of something like *poiesis*, but, to do so, we need to focus first on performance, not knowledge. This other way is not primarily cognitive at all. And this last section, perhaps, shows that what is required is difficult because it entails something of a *gestalt shift* – away from the modern preoccupation with knowledge and representation, and towards understandings of performance proper to ancient non-western philosophy. To understand our own dominant forms of knowledge and practice, as well as alternatives to them – to put them in their place – perhaps we should start with the Tao.[39]

References

Ashby, W.R. (1945): "Effect of Controls on Stability." *Nature*, 155: 242–43.

Asplen, Lisa (2008): "Going with the Flow: Living the Mangle in Environmental Management Practice." In: Andrew Pickering and Keith Guzik (Eds.): *The Mangle in Practice: Science, Society and Becoming*. Durham NC: Duke University Press, 163-84.

Bateson, Gregory (2000): *Steps to an Ecology of Mind*. 2nd ed. Chicago IL: University of Chicago Press.

Coppin, Dawn Michelle (2002): "Capitalist Pigs: Large-Scale Swine Facilities and the Mutual Construction of Nature and Society." Ph.D. dissertation. University of Illinois at Urbana-Champaign, unpublished.

Coppin, Dawn Michelle (2003): "Foucauldian Hog Futures: The Birth of Mega-Hog Farms." *Sociological Quarterly* 44 (4): 597–616.

Coppin, Dawn Michelle (2008): "Crate and Mangle: Questions of Agency in Confinement Livestock Facilities." In: Andrew Pickering and Keith Guzik (Eds.): *The Mangle in Practice: Science, Society and Becoming*, 46–66. Durham NC: Duke University Press.

Deleuze, Gilles, and Félix Guattari (1987): *A Thousand Plateaus: Capitalism and Schizophrenia*. Minneapolis MN: University of Minnesota Press.

Fukuoka, Masanobu (1978): *The One-Straw Revolution: An Introduction to Natural Farming*. New York: New York Review Books.

Gond, Jean-Pascal, et al. (2016): "What do we Mean by Performativity in Organizational and Management Theory? The Uses and Abuses of Performativity." *International Journal of Management Reviews*, 18 (4): 440–63.

---

39 I find it interesting that Fukuoka's book can be crudely divided into two parts. The first is largely about performance and natural farming. That is the part I have discussed here and that easily connects to *shi* and the *Tao*. The second part (which begins with Section IV, 121) moves into the Buddhist critique of the discriminating mind. In my experience, western readers latch onto the latter, precisely because it is about knowledge, our favourite topic. Krueger 2009 swims against the tide and foregrounds nicely the performative, non-cognitive, non-representational aspects of the Tao and western pragmatism.

Glanville, Ranulph (2002): "A (Cybernetic) Musing: Some Examples of Cybernetically Informed Educational Practice." *Cybernetics & Human Knowing*, 9: 117–26.

Grams, Paul, et al. (2015): "Building Sandbars in the Grand Canyon." *EOS: Earth and Space Science News*, 96 (11): 12–16. Available at: https://eos.org/features/building-sandbars-in-the-grand-canyon, last accessed 3 June 2015.

Habermas, Jürgen (1970): "Technology and Society as 'Ideology'." In: Jürgen Habermas (1971): *Toward a Rational Society: Student Protest, Science, and Politics*, 81–122. Boston MA: Beacon Press.

Heidegger, Martin (1977): "The Question Concerning Technology." In: *The Question Concerning Technology and Other Essays*, 3–35. Transl. W. Lovitt, New York: Harper & Row.

Jullien, François (1999): *The Propensity of Things: Toward a History of Efficacy in China*. New York: Zone Books.

Kohler, Robert E. (1994): *Lords of the Fly: Drosophila Genetics and the Experimental Life*. Chicago IL: University of Chicago Press.

Korn, Larry (2012): "Masanobu Fukuoka and Natural Farming." *Final Straw*, available at: www.finalstraw.org/masanobu-fukuoka-and-natural-farming, last accessed January 2019.

Krueger, Joel (2009): "Knowing through the Body: The *Daodejing* and Dewey." *Journal of Chinese Philosophy*, 36 (1): 31–52.

Lappé, Frances M. ([1978] 2009): "Introduction." In: Masanobu Fukuoka: . *The One-Straw Revolution: An Introduction to Natural Farming*, vii–x. New York: New York Review Books.

Latour, Bruno (1983): "Give me a Laboratory and I will Raise the World." In: Karin Knorr-Cetina and Michael Mulkay (Eds): *Science Observed: Perspectives on the Social Study of Science*, 141–170. Beverly Hills CA: SAGE Publications.

Latour, Bruno (1987): *Science in Action: How to Follow Scientists and Engineers through Society*. Cambridge MA: Harvard University Press.

Latour, Bruno (1995): "The 'Pédofil' of Boa Vista: A Photo-Philosophical Montage." *Common Knowledge*, 4 (1): 144–187.

Lorimer, Jamie, and Clemens Driessen (2014): "Wild Experiments at the Oostvardersplassen: Rethinking Environmentalism in the Anthropocene." *Transactions of the Institute of British Geographers*, 39 (2): 169–181.

Marcuse, Herbert (1964): *One-Dimensional Man: Studies in the Ideology of Advanced Industrial Society*. Boston MA: Beacon Press.

Melis, Theodore S., et al. (2012): "Abiotic and Biotic Responses of the Colorado River to Controlled Floods at Glen Canyon Dam, Arizona, USA. *River Research and Applications*, 28 (6): 764–776. Special issue on Dam Operations for Sustainable Regulated River Management.

Nagourney, Adam, and Henry Fountain (2017): "Oroville is a Warning for California Dams, as Climate Change Adds Stress." *New York Times*, 14 February 2017.

Needham, Joseph (1956): *Science and Civilisation in China*. Vol 2: *History of Scientific Thought*. Cambridge: Cambridge University Press.

Needham, Joseph (1971): *Science and Civilisation in China, Vol 4: Physics and Physical Technology, Part III, Civil Engineering and Nautics*. Cambridge: Cambridge University Press.

Perrow, Charles (1984): *Normal Accidents: Living with High-Risk Technologies*. New York: Basic Books.

Pickering, Andrew (1995): *The Mangle of Practice: Time, Agency, and Science*. Chicago IL: University of Chicago Press.

Pickering, Andrew (2005): "Decentring Sociology: Synthetic Dyes and Social Theory." *Perspectives on Science*, 13 (3): 352–405.

Pickering, Andrew (2008): "New Ontologies." In: Andrew Pickering and Keith Guzik (Eds.): *The Mangle in Practice: Science, Society and Becoming*, 1–14. Durham NC: Duke University Press.

Pickering, Andrew (2009a): "Beyond Design: Cybernetics, Biological Computers and Hylozoism." *Synthese*, 168 (3): 469–91.

Pickering. Andrew (2009b): "The Politics of Theory: Producing another World, with some Thoughts on Latour." *Journal of Cultural Economy*, 2 (1–2): 199–214.

Pickering. Andrew (2010): *The Cybernetic Brain: Sketches of Another Future*. Chicago IL: University of Chicago Press.

Pickering, Andrew (2013): "Being in an Environment: A Performative Perspective." *Natures Sciences Sociétés*, 21 (1): 77–83.

Pickering, Andrew (2016): "Art, Science and Experiment." *MaHKUscript: Journal of Fine Art Research*, 11 (2): 1–6.

Pickering, Andrew (2017): "In Our Place: Performance, Dualism, and Islands of Stability." *Common Knowledge*, 23 (3): 381–95.

Rheinberger, Hans-Jörg (1997): *Toward a History of Epistemic Things: Synthesising Proteins in the Laboratory*. Stanford CA: Stanford University Press.

Rice, James (2013): "Controlled Flooding in the Grand Canyon: Drifting Between Instrumental and Ecological Rationality in Water Management." *Organization and Environment*, 26 (4): 412–30.

Schivelbusch, Wolfgang (1986): *The Railway Journey: The Industrialization of Time and Space in the Nineteenth Century*. Berkeley CA: University of California Press.

Scott, James C. (1998): *Seeing like a State: How Certain Schemes to Improve the Human Condition have Failed*. New Haven CT: Yale University Press.

Smith, Thomas (no date): "Self-So and Self-Sow: An Exploration of the Parallels between Permaculture and Daoism." Masters essay, unpublished, University of Cork.

Tsing, Anna (2012): "Unruly Edges: Mushrooms as Companion Species: For Donna Haraway." *Environmental Humanities*, 1 (1): 141–154.

von Foerster, Heinz (2014): *The Beginning of Heaven and Earth has No Name: Seven Days with Second-Order Cybernetics*. Edited by Albert Müller. New York: Fordham University Press.

Westwell, Brett (2014): *Cyborg Studies*. Unpublished essay, Exeter University.

White, Lynn (1962): *Medieval Technology and Social Change*. Oxford: Oxford University Press.

Wise, M. Norton, and David C. Brock (1998): "The Culture of Quantum Chaos." *Studies in the History and Philosophy of Modern Physics*, 29 (3): 369–389.

Zhang, Shanghong, et al. (2013): "Hydraulic Principles of the 2,268-Year-Old Dujiangyan Project in China." *Journal of Hydraulic Engineering*, 139 (5): 538–46

Historical Cases

On Certain Uncertainties in Ancient Astrology

Daryn Lehoux

neque enim esset eius vera substantia,
nisi contra eam tantis
argumentorum viribus niterentur.

Nor would there be any true foundation
to astrology without its opponents struggling
with such force of argument against it.

Firmicus Maternus

Abstract

In his monumental synthesis of ancient astrology, the *Anthology*, Vettius Valens introduces a number of case studies as empirical evidence for the astrological theories, forces, and relationships at play in the universe. He also lambastes rival practitioners who, he says, are bringing the discipline of astrology into disrepute by providing incorrect predictions. This essay aims to unpack the epistemology that underlies Valens' sophisticated text, in order to understand how Valens saw and characterised the foundations of his own knowledge, a disciplinary knowledge of the cosmos that he thought should have permitted an accurate foreknowledge about the fate that awaited individual human beings, but that in fact often hit up against outcomes that were inconsistent with the predictions. By comparing Valens' strategies for corralling and explaining variability with both other astrologers (Ptolemy, Firmicus Maternus) and with critics of astrology (Sextus), we will see how the problems of prediction could still be incorporated into an epistemological framework that, in theory at least, promised certainty.

Introduction

Like many scientific theories today, ancient theories about nature were often contentious and debated, both within and without the community of people working and writing in their field. Some subjects, such as physics, saw rival schools developing their own competing systems, starting from different basic assumptions about matter and the cosmos, and building elaborate constructions on those foundations. The competing schools challenged each other's arguments, and we can see much cross-fertilisation in the interplay, as each side sought to buttress their own theory against the objections of the other. Something similar is true for ancient astrology, but here we see some interesting variations in how the interaction plays out.

Coinciding with the rise of the Hellenistic schools of philosophy under the Roman empire, the rise in popularity of astrology was in (large?) part tied to its taking sides in one of the great ancient debates in physics, that between Epicurean atomism and, well, pretty much everyone else. The story of how we can talk about the category of "pretty much everyone else" is complex and my wording it in this way may be a little provocative, but, if we keep in mind the broad consensus on cosmology and theology that generally held between the schools of Stoicism, Middle Platonism, and the Peripatetics – the universe is meaningful, rationally ordered, and causally non-random – we can see the basic common ground against which Epicureans found themselves positioned.[1]

Stoicism, the most widely popular of these Hellenistic schools held the cosmos to be a single unified body, animated and physically permeated throughout by a divine mind. An air-like substance called *pneuma* was thought to hold everything together and unite all things in the cosmos, opening an easy explanatory channel for astrology, with its stellar influences radiating down to us here on earth. A second, more contentious aspect of Stoicism also fed into the debates in (and about) astrology, in the shape of the Stoic belief in pre-determination. Stoic pre-determination worked because of their insistence that physical causes and their effects were linked non-randomly. If two bodies acting on one another do so in perfectly law-like ways, then one cause can only have one effect. That cause, though, is itself an effect of other causes, themselves again the effects of others, in an unbroken chain all the way back to the beginning of the cosmos.[2] This necessitates a strict nomological determinism, and a cosmos in which Laplace's

---

1 To be sure, the Platonists of the day were often sceptics, but sceptics of a particular stripe that allowed themselves to hold the best arguments posed by others to be what we might call provisionally true. Cicero's (provisional) acceptance of a broad range of Stoic theories in physics and ethics is a good example. For my more complete arguments on what I call the "concentric schools", see Lehoux 2012; see. also, Dillon and Long 1988.

2 In wording it in this way, I admit that I am not being perfectly true to one of the more unusual technical details of Stoic causal theory, where causes are bodies but "effects" are predicates. Drawing out this distinction would be rather unhelpful for my current purposes and I am instead using "effect" in its everyday sense just to make a minor point. On Stoic causal theory, see, for example, Frede 2008; Hankinson 1999a; Bobzien 1998. On determinism, see, for example, those same three references, plus Hankinson 1999b.

demon would have felt perfectly at home, and in which astrology could find a very comfortable reception indeed.

Having said that, though, we should note that the debates around the validity of astrology were not necessarily always school-specific in the same way as debates around, say, the nature of sound or the shape of the earth. True, we see the Stoicizing Manilius take on Epicureanism directly in his great astrological poem, but, in many instances, objections to astrology transcend or even ignore specific school doctrines, focusing instead on problems of data, logical consistency, and plausibility (although also often packaging themselves in larger attacks on pre-determinism). At the same time, it bears noting that these attacks on, and defences of, astrology differed in important ways from the attacks and defences of, for example, modern-day climate science or vaccines.[3] In the modern context, the authority of climate science is rooted in a scientific consensus around the authority of a collected body of evidence.[4] Ancient astrologers also often pointed to efficacy and experience as evidence for their discipline, but the larger epistemological authority often came from what astrologers called the "divine" nature of the subject, sometimes going so far as to claim that god himself passes astrological knowledge on to practitioners. This divine origin, I will argue, creates a difficult tension within astrology, where its authors oscillate between confidence in the discipline's foundations, and clear awareness of the discipline's vulnerability to attack.

Our evidence for opposition to astrology comes in two forms: on the one hand, from actual attacks on astrology, such as we find in Aulus Gellius, Sextus Empiricus, and Cicero, for example, and, on the other hand, from defences of astrology, where we can see astrologers who are acutely aware of the weaknesses in their discipline and who work to buttress their theory from obvious, known lines of attack. Many of the arguments that astrologers were faced with appear in multiple sources. Of these standard objections, I have already mentioned the rejection of determinism, easily re-purposed for astrology (which was largely seen as entailing strict pre-determination – we shall see that this was not, in fact, always a concomitant, but it was admittedly a common one). There was also the problem of twins: how could two people born at the same time have differing lifespans? There was the problem of accuracy: How sensitive is the system when it claims to capture a snapshot of the rapidly whirring heavens? There were questions of empiricism: How far back in time must we suppose astrology to go for it to claim that some configuration of the stars has been previously observed? What good would astrological foreknowledge be, anyway? If we could not avoid the fates

---

3 See, for example, Michaels and Monforton 2005; Michaels 2008.

4 It also differs in that modern climate science will, one assumes, turn out to have been generally correct, whereas, in the case of the ancient astrologers, it is the sceptics who prevailed in the long run.

predicted, what is the use in knowing about them? Does astrology apply to animals? (As Aulus Gellius memorably put it: Does it apply to *sponges*??)[5]

In what follows, a number of these common arguments will be re-visited, but
I want to single out two of them for a little more detailed study to see how subtle
the objections and responses could sometimes be, and to use them as representatives of the call-and-response at the heart of astrological epistemology. Let us
begin with a look at the stronger claims for astrology's epistemological foundation and proceed to its handling of objections in the light of these claims. At the
end of the chapter, we will see how Ptolemy offers a nuanced understanding of
astrological causation that neatly side-steps the range of objections, albeit at a cost
that many other astrologers would find too high.

God-givenness

A number of astrological authors reflect on the divine nature of their discipline,
each parsing it out in subtly different ways. Manilius makes one of the strongest
such assertions when he says that god himself gave astrologers their discipline,
acting directly on their minds to inscribe knowledge directly therein:

[sacerdotibus] [...] ipsa potentis
numinis accendit castam praesentia mentem,
inque deum deus ipse tulit patuitque ministris.
hi tantum movere decus primique per artem
sideribus videre vagis pendentia fata.

The presence itself of powerful divinity kindled a pure mind for [the priests], and god
himself brought them to god and revealed himself to his servants. These people began
our honoured study, and by that art were the first to see the fates that dangle from the
wandering stars.[6]

He goes on to say that god reveals his face and body (seen as the heavenly vault)
to people, and that he literally *impresses* himself on them, *ipsum inculcat*, "so that he
may be clearly known, and to teach those who look [on him] how he proceeds,
and to compel them to direct their attention to his laws", *ut bene cognosci possit
doceatque videntis, | qualis eat, cogatque suas attendere leges.*[7] This theme of the divine
source for astrological knowledge recurs throughout the poem, and is situated, as
in this last passage, in a Stoicizing context that sees an important oneness of cosmos, god, and humanity. This is beautifully captured in a sentence that Goold
called "two of the poet's finest lines", later inscribed – in what is perhaps the

---

5 Aulus Gellius, *Attic nights*, 14.1.31.
6 Manilius, *Astronomica*, 1.48–52.
7 Manilius, *Astronomica*, 4.918–19.

perfect metonym for the entire romantic movement – by Goethe in a visitor's book after having climbed the highest peak of the Harz mountains: *quis caelum posset nisi caeli munere nosse, | et reperire deum, nisi qui pars ipse deorum est?*[8] "Who can know heaven except by the gift of heaven, or know god except one who is part of divinity?"

This direct action by god on the minds of astrologers implies the strongest possible epistemological foundation for the discipline, but it does require a previous buy-in: if an opponent does not already believe in astrology, "god gave it to us" is not particularly convincing. Having said that, though, there are two things to be pointed out. First, my current concern in this chapter is not with how astrologers tried to persuade others of the veracity of their discipline, so much as with the related question of how astrologers handled, within their own systems, the challenges posed by what we might call "messy data" (predictions do not always come true), as well as by what outside opponents saw as contradictions entailed in the theoretical foundations of the discipline. Secondly, "god gave it to us" may not convince a sceptic, but it *does* do some work within the larger intellectual context of what I have called the "concentric" philosophical schools of the day,[9] which saw the cosmos as divinely ordered, profoundly interconnected, and rational, and which held *sympathy* and *antipathy* to be physical forces explaining multiple causal relationships.

To be sure, Manilius does also mention the true predictions of the astrologers as a further basis for belief. As part of the same argument that gave us Goethe's two-line ode to the majesty of the Brocken, above, Manilius adds:

ipsa fides operi faciet pondusque fidemque;
nam neque decipitur ratio nec decipit umquam.
rite sequenda via est ac veris credita causis,
eventusque datur qualis praedicitur ante.
quod Fortuna ratum faciat, quis dicere falsum
audeat et tantae suffragia vincere sortis.

The very reliability of the work and its importance will bring about faith [in it], for the system is neither deceived nor does it ever deceive. It is a road to be followed devoutly on the grounds of its truth, the outcome delivered just as [it was] predicted earlier. Who would dare to call what Fate has calculated false, or to overthrow the vote of so great an elector?[10]

---

8 Manilius, *Astronomica*, 2.115–16. Compare also passages such as 4.920, 2.82–3, among many others. The Goold quote and Goethe story are on p. xv of Goold's Loeb translation (= Manilius, *Astronomica*).

9 I.e., Stoicism and the Stoic-influenced versions of Platonism and even to some extent Aristotelianism that were so prominent in the Roman period. See Lehoux 2012, Chapter 8.

10 Manilius, *Astronomica*, 2.130–35. See Firmicus Maternus, *Mathesis*, 1.3.1. The word phrase, *tantae sortis*, actually means "so great a lot", either in the literal sense of a lot cast for decision-making,

Fate, for Manilius, is closely tied to a heavenly machine inevitably clicking out its pre-calculated motions. The knowledge of this complex system is guaranteed by, and indeed inculcated in us directly by, a divinity.

The great fourth-century astrologer Firmicus Maternus likewise says that the divinity "shows and reveals itself" to the mind, linking the mind to divinity through something very like the Platonic origin story, where the soul breaks away from the divine heavens to come down to earth and occupy a person's body for a while: *cui se tota natura divinitatis et ostendit et prodidit, nisi animo qui, ex caelesti igne profectus, ad regimen et ad gubernationem terrenae fragilitatis immissus est,* "to whom does the whole nature of divinity show and reveal itself if not to the mind which, having departed from the celestial fire, is sent as guide and governor of our earthly fragility".[11] But note: these last two words mark an important qualification for Firmicus, one that can help explain why, if astrology is god-given, it can still make mistakes. The answer is that astrology is a difficult discipline to master, precisely because this soul of ours – divine though it be – is unfortunately enclosed in a shell of earthly flesh.

divinitas enim eius, quae sempiterna agitatione sustentatur, si in terreno corpore fuerit inclusa, iacturam quamdam divinitatis suae patitur temporalem, cum vis eius atque substantia coniunctione et societate terreni corporis et assidua dissolutione mortalitatis hebetatur. unde fit ut omnia quae ad investigationem divinarum artium pertinent difficili semper nobis cognitione tradantur.

[The soul's] divinity, which is sustained by an eternal motion, once it has become shut up inside an earthly body, suffers a kind of temporary diminution in its divinity because its power and substance are dulled by the connection and earthly association of the body, and by the constant wear and tear of mortality. Whence it is that all matters pertaining to the investigation of divine subjects are always surrendered to us [only] with difficult study.[12]

He then gives a hypothetical re-construction of the development of astrology, where one person figured out the theory, one how to calculate motions, one what the aspects were, gradually building up the knowledge base in an ongoing process of accumulation, generation after generation passing on what each had learned.

Vettius Valens had earlier painted an (if anything) even more vivid picture of a discipline in progress than Firmicus. He tells us repeatedly of his own process of learning and discovery, in places going back and telling us that he has improved on his or another astrologer's earlier technique. In one of his many discussions of the calculations for the length of a person's life, he tells us not only that he seeks improvement in the theory, but also improvement in clarity (a desideratum he comes back to throughout his work). He says:

---

or in the figurative sense of one's lot in life. I'm translating it here in the more literal sense, but the double meaning may be relevant.

11 Firmicus Maternus, *Mathesis*, 1.4.4.
12 Firmicus Maternus, *Mathesis*, 1.4.2.

εὗρον δὲ καὶ ταύτην τὴν αἵρεσιν περὶ χρόνων ζωῆς ὑπὸ μὲν τῶν ἀρχαίων ἀναπεπλεγμένην ποικίλως, αὐτὸς δὲ διὰ πείρας ἀναζητήσας διέκρινα καὶ οἴομαι μᾶλλον τοῖς πλείστοις ἀρέσκειν.

I have found this system for the length of life to be obscurely elaborated by the ancients, but through investigative trials I myself figured it out and I think [my method] better for most readers.[13]

At these moments he is often quick to thank the deity. After telling us again that older writers on a certain topic were unhelpfully obscure (and, in the event, wrong), he narrates his arduous quest to find the truth, only to be misled – and overcharged – by greedy teachers in Egypt. He continues:

καὶ δὴ πολὺν μὲν χρόνον ἀνιαρῶς διήγομεν, καὶ ἐπιλύπως τὰς μεταβολὰς τῶν τόπων ποιούμενοι, τοῖς περὶ τὰ τοιαῦτα ἐσπουδακόσι συμμίσγοντες, διάπειραν ἐλαμβάνομεν, μέχρις οὗ τὸ δαιμόνιον βουληθὲν διά τινος προνοίας τὴν παράδοσιν ἔν τινι τόπῳ πεποίηται διά τινος φιλομαθοῦς ἀνδρός. ἀρχὴν οὖν λαβόμενοι καὶ πολὺν πόνον εἰσενεγκάμενοι κατελαβόμεθα τοῦ σκοποῦ ὃν καὶ ἐκτησάμεθα ἐπεισενεγκάμενοι καὶ αὐτοὶ πολλὰς δυνάμεων εὐχρηστίας. ἐκ γὰρ τῆς καθημερινῆς τριβῆς καὶ πολυάνδρου συμβολῆς καὶ τῆς τῶν παθῶν αὐτοψίας ἱερὰν μὲν καὶ ἀθάνατον τὴν θεωρίαν ἐκρίναμεν, ἄφθονον δὲ τὴν μετάδοσιν ποιησόμεθα.

Moreover we spent a great deal of time in grievous difficulty and, painfully making the changes to [the theory of] the places and working with [other] students eager about these things, we found the crucial proof: eventually god in his will and through a certain foresight gave instruction with respect to a particular place, through the instrument of a certain learned man.[14] Taking this beginning and contributing much labour we achieved our aim, procured by further introducing many useful techniques ourselves. For by daily work, coming together with many others and by our own observations of events, we have discovered the sacred and eternal system and passed it on ungrudgingly.[15]

This picture of the divinely guided seeker, working slavishly to find answers and thankful to the deity for guidance when those answers come, recurs again and again in the *Anthology*, and it is closely associated with Valens' continual presentation of the uncovering of astrological knowledge as a continual work in progress. At several points, he describes, in almost reverential tones, how these moments stir in him an ecstasy. On one occasion, for example, apologising for occasionally repeating himself, he says that he had returned to these subjects with new material:

ἃ μὲν γὰρ ἐντυγχάνων τοῖς προγεγονόσι συνέτασσον διὰ τὸ τῆς ἐπιθυμίας καὶ εὑρέσεως αἰφνίδιον (ἐνθουσιᾷ γὰρ ὁ συγγράφων, μάλιστα δὲ περὶ τούτων, καὶ θεῷ προσομιλεῖν δοκεῖ).

---

13 Vettius Valens, *Anthologia*, 3.11.1.
14 There is a curious repetition of the Greek indefinite pronoun, τις, in this sentence, it being appended to the foresight, the place for which god gave instruction, and the learned man. It gives the whole sentence a kind of loose, "happenstancy" feel.
15 Vettius Valens, *Anthologia*, 4.11.7–9.

encountering some things I added them to the already-written part in the suddenness of excitement and discovery (this author has been in ecstasy, especially at such moments, when he seems to be in the presence of god).[16]

This is a nice snapshot of the thrill of discovery, and Valens returns to the presence-of-god theme again and again in the work, saying that it further inspires him to moral purity, and that this converse with the deity gives him a share of immortality.[17] How important he sees the work and how acutely aware he is that it is unfinished, is underscored by a reflection he makes on his own looming mortality and how little time there is left to finish what he started.[18]

Finally, we see Valens use the divine revelation of astrology to side-step one of the standard sceptical arguments, that foreknowledge of what is fated is useless: God would not have given us astrology if he had not wanted to and (this is implied) thought it useful.[19]

Objections 1: The twin problem

As I mentioned earlier, the idea that twins sometimes died years apart was a common objection to astrology. One of the canonical examples, because it was so dramatic and its characters so famous, involved the emperor Commodus, who was born the younger of a pair of twins. But the older brother, Antoninus, died at only four years of age, while Commodus lived to become emperor (eventually being assassinated at the age of 31). As the anonymous *Augustan History* put it:

cum autem peperisset Commodum atque Antoninum, Antoninus quadrimus elatus est, quem parem astrorum cursu Commodo mathematici promittebant.

but after [Faustina] had given birth to Commodus and Antoninus, Antoninus, whom the astrologers were predicting to be equal to Commodus with respect to stellar influence, only lived to be four years old.[20]

Similar stories abound.[21]

---

16 Vettius Valens, *Anthologia*, 6.1.19. Two minor notes on my translation: I have used the English present perfect tense ("has been in ecstasy") to render a Greek imperfect in order to maintain the implied repetition of his ecstatic feeling, and I have used "especially at such moments" for a Greek phrase that literally says "especially about these things", which I find a little awkward in English.

17 Vettius Valens, *Anthologia*, 5.6.16, 6.1.15, 6.6.1, 7.4.7, 9.9.12.

18 Vettius Valens, *Anthologia*, 6.8.1.

19 Vettius Valens, *Anthologia*, 7.4.2.

20 *Historia Augusta*, Commodus, 1.4.

21 Cicero (who predated Commodus and Antoninus by two centuries) offers us a similar, if less dramatic, example in the twin (mythical?) Spartan kings Procles and Eurysthenes, one of whom outlived the other by a year (*De divinatione*, 2.90–91).

It will be worth noting an important distinction at this point. Notice where the criticism in the *Augustan History* version of the twins story is directed. It is not saying explicitly that there is no such thing as astrological influence, but instead calls out the astrologers for their incorrect predictions: "Antoninus, whom the astrologers were predicting to be equal to Commodus." The idea that astrologers are all, or mostly, unreliable is one claim. The idea that the stars do not affect our destinies is another, and we will do well to keep the distinction in mind, as one is an objection to the science in principle, the other to the science as practised.

And not all twin objections are precisely the same. Augustine, for example, gives us an interesting argument that, at first glance, looks similar to the usual twins narrative, but turns out to have interesting differences from the generally circulated one. He recounts to us, at some length, a tale told to him by his friend Firminus, whose father had been keenly obsessed with astrology, to the point of making charts even for his barn animals. The father used to compare notes with a friend of his who was equally obsessed with the discipline, who also made charts *etiam canum*, "even for his dogs".[22] When Firminus' mother went into labour with him, Firminus' father, knowing that his astrologer-friend had a female slave that was likewise in the last stages of pregnancy, took pains to note carefully the time and to send notice to his friend, who by coincidence was putting together careful notes and messages at his own house for his slave:

atque ita factum esse, ut cum iste coniugis, ille autem ancillae dies et horas minutioresque horarum articulos cautissima observatione numerarent, enixae essent ambae simul; ita ut easdem constellationes usque ad easdem minutias utrique nascenti facere cogerentur, iste filio, ille servulo [...] atque ita qui ab alterutro missi sunt, tam ex paribus domorum intervallis sibi obviam factos esse dicebat, ut aliam positionem siderum aliasque particulas momentorum neuter eorum notare sineretur.

And so it was, that with the most exact observation they each reckoned the days and the hours and even the smallest fractions of the hours, the one for his wife, the other for his slave, and both the women gave birth at the same time, such that they had to assign the same constellations, even to the minutest detail, to each of the nativities, the one to his son, the other to his little slave [...]. And thus messengers were sent, each to the other, and he said they met each other halfway between the houses, such that neither of them could allow any variation in the position of the stars or any other details concerning the timings [between the births].[23]

And yet, Augustine continues, the two children had two very different lives. Indeed, we can see him emphasising the difference at every point in the story above: *coniungis* | *ancillae*, "for his wife" / "for his servant"; *filio* | *servulo*, "to his son" / "to his little slave". Firminus was born to wealth, invested wisely, and became a notable citizen, whereas the *servulus*, who Firminus apparently continued to know throughout his life, never rose above his baleful station.

---

22 Augustine, *Confessions*, 7.6.
23 Augustine, *Confessions*, 7.6.

What separates this from the usual narrative about twins, apart from the sheer charm of the story, is twofold. On the one hand, it attempts to get around the possible objection that twins are not *really* born at the same time, only approximately so. On the other hand – and this is, in many ways, the more interesting aspect – is the way in which it invokes socioeconomic differences, rather than differences in the length of life. Twins, after all, are necessarily born into identical socioeconomic classes and circumstances, and so the lengths of their lives are going to be perhaps the most obvious difference in their fates that one could latch on to (that the difference is suitably dramatic surely does not hurt, either). But, in Augustine's story, we see the primary difference being the economic and political fates of the two men, the one rising to wealth, distinction, and honour, the other grovelling in lifelong servitude. Add to this, the sheer vibrancy of Augustine's telling, putting the words in the mouth of the very friend, Firminus, to whom the story applied, and we have here a compelling disproof of astrology for Augustine's reader.

Augustine's story is, however, still not bullet-proof, and this is the case on a couple of fronts. An astrologer could object that any astrologer would know that the chart of a slave should simply be read differently than the chart of a wealthy landowner. Aspects and positions can often mean more than one thing, and some of those things are going to be relevant in different ways for natives with different stations in life.

The second, perhaps more compelling, defence against Augustine's story is that Augustine's "exact same time" cannot really be the *exact* same time. The heavens move so swiftly that even minor variations in birth times can lead to very different outcomes. As Valens put it:

δυνατὸν μὲν οὖν καὶ ἐν τῷ αὐτῷ μέρει τῆς ὥρας διδύμους γεννᾶσθαι, ἡ δὲ τῆς ὥρας ὀξυρροπία παραλλάξασα τὴν μοῖραν ἀνεικάστους τοὺς χρόνους εἰργάσατο· καὶ ἀπὸ ἐλαχίστου συνδέσμου εἰς μείζονα περιγράψασα πολυχρόνιον ἐποίησεν ἢ ἀπὸ μείζονος εἰς ἐλάχιστον ὀλιγοχρόνιον τὸν ἕτερον.

although it is possible for twins to be born in the same fraction of an hour, the rapid tipping of the scales of time, having changed the degree makes the [exact] moments ungraspable,[24] and a very minor conjunction leading to a greater [span] makes a long-lived [twin], and a wider [conjunction] causing a lesser [span], the other is short-lived.[25]

As he puts it elsewhere:

χρὴ συλλογίζεσθαι τὰς τῶν ὀλιγοχρονίων καὶ πολυχρονίων γενέσεις καὶ τὰς τῶν διδύμων. πολλάκις γὰρ περὶ μὲν τὸ πρῶτον τεχθὲν ὁρίου κακοποιοῦ τῆς ἀφέσεως κυριεύσαντος ἢ καὶ τοῦ οἰκοδεσπότου παραπεσόντος, ὀλιγοχρονιότης ἐγένετο, περὶ δ' ἕτερον ἐναλλαγέντος τοῦ ὁρίου ἢ καὶ τοῦ οἰκοδεσπότου, πολυχρονιότης καὶ βίου ὑπόστασις παρηκολούθησεν, ὅθεν μιᾶς καὶ δευτέρας μοίρας πολλάκις ἡ παραλλαγὴ μεγίστην δύναμιν ἐνδείκνυται.

---

24 Elsewhere he tells us that only the gods can achieve perfect accuracy (9.12.11).
25 Vettius Valens, *Anthologia*, 8.4.9.

It is necessary to consider the nativities of short- and long-lived individuals and those of twins. For often, concerning the first-born, when a malefic term rules the vital quadrant or the house-ruler is badly placed, it is born short-lived, while the other, if the term or the house-ruler changes, is born long-lived and a solidity of life attends [him]. This difference shows what a great power one or two degrees [has].[26]

Then, again, in book nine, he re-iterates how great a difference even a "fraction of an hour" can make to length of life calculation.[27] Similarly, back at 8.7, he offers us several concrete examples of how sensitive the mechanism for these length-of-life calculations can be. Although he is not discussing twins specifically, he points out that, at certain points in the determination, very minor changes in the relevant variables can cause significant changes in the expected length of life. In one case, for example, the prediction of a life of 104 years will, with only a slight shift, invert to an expected span of only six years.

Favorinus, the great second-century rhetorician and a contemporary of Valens, very cleverly points out that this puts the astrologer in a dilemma: either the astrologer accepts that the heavens change too quickly to be graspable, or else slowly enough that the fates of twins pose a serious problem, along the lines that we have already seen. Favorinus' argument is quoted by Aulus Gellius as follows: "I would like, Favorinus said, for [astrologers] to explain to me,"

id velim etiam, inquit, ut respondeant: si tam parvum atque rapidum est momentum temporis, in quo homo nascens fatum accipit, ut in eodem illo puncto sub eodem circulo caeli plures simul ad eandem competentiam nasci non queant, et si idcirco gemini quoque non eadem vitae sorte sunt, quoniam non eodem temporis puncto editi sunt – peto, inquit, respondeant, cursum illum temporis transvolantis, qui vix cogitatione animi comprehendi potest [...] cum in tam praecipiti dierum noctiumque vertigine minima momenta ingentes facere dicant mutationes.

[how] if the movement of time, in which the person born receives his fate, is so minute and rapid that in that exact moment others cannot be born under the same zodiac with the same aspect[s], and if on that account not even twins have the same fate since they are not born at the exact same time – I beg them to tell me, he said, how it is at all possible to arrest the trajectory of fly-by time with a deliberation of the mind [...] when they say that in such a headlong whirling of days and nights the tiniest moments make such huge differences.[28]

Gellius presents this as a (rough?) quotation from Favorinus, one taken from notes that Gellius had made in haste after the original declamation had ended.[29] Whatever the original Greek of the oration had been, Gellius' Latin, as presented here, is nicely polished and the argument is both philosophically and rhetorically quite clever. Moreover, the phrase I have translated as "how [is it] at all possible

---

26 Vettius Valens, *Anthologia*, 3.7.14–15.
27 Vettius Valens, *Anthologia*, 9.8.30.
28 Quoted in Aulus Gellius, *Attic Nights*, 14.1.26.
29 Aulus Gellius, *Attic Nights*, 14.1.2. He adds that his recollection follows Favorinus "generally", *ferme*.

to arrest the trajectory of fly-by time", *cursum illum temporis transvolantis, qui ... comprehendi potest*, very nicely mirrors our earlier passage from Valens, "the rapid tipping of the scales of time ... makes the [exact] moments ungraspable", "ἡ δὲ τῆς ὥρας ὀξυρροπία [...] ἀνεικάστους τοὺς χρόνους εἰργάσατο".[30] It bears noting, though, that Valens' wording is unusual: the word ἀνείκαστος (my "ungraspable") is a fairly rare word outside of Byzantine theological texts,[31] while the noun he uses for my "rapid tipping of the scales", "ὀξυρροπία", is a *hapax legomenon* – this is its only appearance in ancient Greek.[32] This makes the phrase highly memorable. Now, there is nothing to suggest conclusively that Favorinus is trying to capture either of these two unusual words specifically (although keeping in mind that we are reading a Latin translation of a recollection) or that either Favorinus or Gellius had read Valens directly, but the parallels are striking all the same, and it makes Favorinus' argument that much more pointed. If the differences in outcomes can vary so quickly that the same fate can apply to no two babies, no matter how near-simultaneous their births, we are left with such minute differences in aspects and configurations as to be analytically meaningless.

So how do the astrologers respond to this problem? Valens and Firmicus both offer us interesting possible ways out of the dilemma, Valens' having to do with how we manage reports of the timing of twin births, and Firmicus' having to do with the chart at conception, rather than birth. For Valens, the birth of twins seems to have been subject to a curious temporal schematisation, where he tells us how to manipulate mathematically the reports that the astrologer is given of the times for each twin's birth.[33] The details are a little confusing, not least because there seems to be considerable textual corruption affecting this section. What Valens seems to be working towards may be a solution to the combined problems of time-keeping in antiquity and the testimonial basis of the information, coupled with a certain kind of "artificiality" or complex schematisation sometimes demanded by astrology in Valens' work.[34] If we are told only that the twins were born "in the first hour of the day", we are, he says, to assume that one was born in the first quarter of that hour and the other in the last quarter. Indeed, he adds at this point that it is "even possible for both to have been born in the same quarter of an hour, or for one to have followed the other [immediately]", δυνατὸν δέ ἐστι καὶ ἀμφοτέρους ἐν τῷ αὐτῷ μέρει τῷ δ΄ γεγενῆσθαι καὶ ἕτερον ἑτέρῳ

---

30 Vettius Valens, *Anthologia*, 8.4.9.

31 Plus two recensions of the *Alexander Romance*.

32 The *Thesaurus Linguae Graecae* lists just one later instance, in the thirteenth-century hagiographer Theodosius Gudeles. The adjective upon which the noun is based is not particularly common itself.

33 Vettius Valens, *Anthologia*, 8.4.

34 I am thinking of things like the length-of-life calculation at Vettius Valens, *Anthologia*, 8.5, for example, or the calculation of the date of conception from the previous new moon rather than from the actual date at 6.9.

ἀκολουθῆσαι.[35] We are still, it seems, to employ the first-quarter/last-quarter split for the purposes of their charts. If we are told one twin was born at the beginning of the second hour and the other in the third, assume for the purposes of their charts that the later twin was born at 2:30. Similarly for hour five (assume 4:30), seven (assume 6:30), and so on, until 12:00, at which point we do not change the reported time. He then gives very different formulae for the case in which the first twin was born late in the first or second hour and the second twin said to be an hour later. The whole passage is more than a little obscure. Nevertheless, it seems to be an attempt, at least, to impose a rational structure on the timing for the sake of the charts. If one were to object that schematising the charts like this does a disservice to the real times at which the twins were born, I suspect the answer would be that this technique is what is known to produce the most relia-ble, truest, charts, and what is truth-conducive must be correct.

Firmicus, by contrast, offers us a way of finding a kind of combination chart that explains the differences by casting a chart from what seems to be the mo-ment of conception or possibly the chart of one of the parents. He doesn't go into a great deal of detail, unfortunately, nor does he tell us how generalizable the method might be, but he offers the following to explain differing lengths of life in twins, at least:

illud sane observandum est, ne quem horum malivola stella superior effecta respiciat. nam si unum eorum respexerit, de geminis quicumque prior conceptus fuerit, aut in partu morietur, aut ante tempus eicietur.

it should be carefully noted: let not a maleficent planet standing above be in aspect to [Jupiter or Mercury].[36] For if it is in aspect to one of them, whichever of the twins was conceived first will either die at birth or be born prematurely.[37]

What it shows is that we can calculate from this single chart, whatever it repre-sents, that one twin will have a very different fate than the other. Notice, too, that he thinks there to be a (negligible?) time difference in the moments of conception of each twin, where the malefic aspect affects only the *prior conceptus*, the first-conceived, which need not necessarily be the first-born. As I said above, this seems to be a chart done either for one of the parents or for the date of concep-tion. We know from Valens that one could use the latitude of the moon at birth to calculate the position of the moon at the moment of conception, but that is not quite the same thing as what we are looking at in Firmicus.[38] In the same passage, Firmicus tells us that a certain aspect means that *gemini nascentur*, "twins

---

35 Vettius Valens, *Anthologia*, 8.4.2.

36 In astrology, planets are said to be "in aspect to" each other when they are in one of several significant geometrical relationships to each other, such as trine, square, conjunct, etc. Such relationships can either re-inforce or cancel out the effects of one or both planets, depending on the details.

37 Firmicus Maternus, *Mathesis*, 7.3.2.

38 Vettius Valens, *Anthologia*, 6.9.

will be born", in the future tense, implying that the chart is based upon something other than the birth of the twins themselves. It is certainly possible that this is taken from a parent's chart, as he elsewhere tells us that a certain chart means *aut gemina est genitura aut qui sic natus fuerit geminos habebit filios*,[39] "either it is a twin birth or the one with this chart will have twin children". He also, in the same chapter, tells us how to determine in advance what the sex(es) of the twins will be, whether both will live or die, and even whether we should be expecting triplets or quintuplets. Clearly, there is no problem with deducing details about future children from *some* earlier chart, be it of conception or of the parent.

Objections 2: Fate

The idea that we can predict something about the birth of children from the charts of a parent is a perfectly comfortable one in ancient astrology, where every practitioner agrees that the motions of the heavens are eternally non-random, governed by discovered or discoverable mathematical laws and ticking away from the past into the future in a predictable way. This would seem to mean that, if you believe human destinies to be influenced by these predictable motions, you are committed to the proposition that all future events in the cosmos are, at least in theory, predictable from any given chart at any given time.

This was pointed out forcefully by Favorinus in his critique. He begins by asking how astrologers can handle the fact that differing configurations of the stars presided over an infant's conception and its birth – shouldn't that give two different readings? This may not look directly connected to the question of fate at first, but Favorinus takes things farther back still: If the planets cause the individual's fate, and the motions of the planets are law-like and inevitable for all time, shouldn't the charts of the parents portend the fates of their children, even though the parents' and the children's charts are very different? And shouldn't we be able to take this back in time *supra longe, atque longe per infinitum ... primo caeli atque mundi exordio*,[40] "farther, even as far back as infinity ... to the first stirrings of heaven and earth"?

Now, one of the fairly common tropes of ancient astrology is the idea of a *thema mundi*, a horoscope for the cosmos itself. Tying in nicely with the Stoic idea of a cyclic conflagration and re-birth of the cosmos, the idea was that the cosmos must have had a determinate beginning in time. Firmicus gives the chart for the cosmos an ancient Egyptian pedigree, and describes for his reader the positions of the planets at the beginning of the world. Highly schematic (every planet is at

---

39 Firmicus Maternus, *Mathesis*, 7.3.1.
40 Aulus Gellius, *Attic Nights*, 14.1.20.

15° of its "zodiacal house", and with both Venus and Mercury at impossible dis-
tances from the sun),[41] the chart was, on Firmicus' telling, "devised"[42] by ancient
astrologers to represent the beginning of the world (no-one was there to record
the actual event, after all), by means of "a divine exposition of inference", *divina
coniecturae interpretatione*.[43] And the idea was that the *thema mundi* should be compatible with all future predictions:

*secundum hanc itaque genituram et secundum has conditiones stellarum et secundum testimonia quae huic
geniturae perhibent, et secundum istas rationes etiam hominum volunt fata disponi [...] prorsus ut nihil
ab ista mundi genitura in singulis hominum genituris alienum esse videatur.*

And so, according to this chart, according to these positions of the stars, according to the
testimony that bears witness to this chart, and according to these laws [the great early
astrologers Nechepso and Petosiris] want even the fates of men to be construed [...] such
that nothing, certainly, from this *thema mundi* should appear to contradict the charts of
individual men.[44]

That may all be well and good, objects Favorinus, but it presents us with a problem. For it is one thing to think that a chart purportedly explaining "the kind of
thing the world is" more or less fits in with the chart of an individual person living
in that world, but it is entirely another thing to think that every chart of every
person must be entailed by the chart at the beginning of the universe. Worse, if
everything is just a clockwork unfolding of the universe's initial conditions, it
would seem therefore to follow that the chart of every person should then entail
the chart of every other person. Favorinus, in the event, limits his argument to
the charts of one's ancestors all entailing one's own and each other's charts down
the family line, but the point would seem to be generalisable.[45] Referring to the
configuration of the stars at "the first stirrings of heaven and earth", Gellius continues with Favorinus' account:

*quo autem, inquit, pacto credi potest, uniusquiuscumque stellarum formae et positionis sortem atque for-
tunam uni omnino homini certam destinatamque esse eamque formam post longissima saeculorum spatia
restitui, si vitae fortunarumque eiusdem hominis indicia in tam brevibus intervallis per singulos maiorum
eius gradus perque infinitum successionum ordinem tam saepe ac tam multipliciter eadem ipsa, non eadem
stellarum facie denotantur?*

---

41 The sun and moon each have one house (Leo and Cancer, respectively) but the other planets
   each have two. For the *thema mundi*, they are assigned to just one of their two signs. Mercury is
   at 30° from the sun (a little over 2° from what is possible) and Venus at 60° (approximately 14°
   too far).

42 He says that the wise men of old *finxerunt*, "devised", it – *finxi* is the perfect tense form of the
   verb *fingo*, which will be familiar to historians of science from Newton's famous formulation
   hypotheses non fingo.

43 3.1.15.

44 Firmicus Maternus, *Mathesis*, 3.1.2.

45 I thank Cristian Tolsa for a fruitful discussion on this section.

But on what grounds, [Favorinus] said, is it possible to believe that the lot and fortune from an arbitrary configuration and position of stars [a long time ago] is also the fixed destiny of one single man [now] and that the [original] configuration comes back to life[46] after this incredible length of time, in so far as the significations of this man's life and fortunes, so repeatedly and so variously the same (in the very brief spans of time through the individual steps that are his ancestors as well as across the countless series of generations), are not marked by that same arrangement of the stars?[47]

The passage is terse and difficult, to be sure, but Gellius situates it in the middle of a longer argument that makes its force clearer. Starting, he is saying, from some random and arbitrary ancestor's chart as far back in time as we want to go – if that chart truly entails this-man-here's fate, then it must have done so all along, and done so consistently ("so repeatedly the same") through all the countless intervening generations, each with its own chart (again, entailed by the original), diverse as those must be ("so variously the same"). And here we hit the wall. For somehow, this-man-here's chart must have also been carried in entailment by each of those intervening charts, none of which was the same as the original,

---

46 The verb, *restitui*, is usually translated as something like "repeated", but I take the overall argument beginning at 14.1.19 to force something a little less literal than an actual repetition of the same heavenly configuration (i.e., an actual return of the "great year", which, in any case, Favorinus has told us a little earlier would involve so much time as to be meaningless [14.1.18]). The argument here has nothing to do with the great year and everything to do with a previous and different signification carrying across time to instantiate itself in a man now. In an interesting passage from his commentary on Manilius, Scaliger seems to agree with my reading, in so far as he replaces *eamque formam restitui* with *eamque formaturam restitui*, i.e., "with this same act of shaping being brought back". (Scaliger 1579, 239) He specifically mentions and emends the Gellius passage while commenting on Maniulius' *in [...] variasque figuras dispositum genus est hominum*, "the human race is made with different features" at Manilius, 4.711–12. He equates the *figurae* in this passage with Gellius' substituted *formatura*, which on this reading must refer to the effect of the stars in humans rather than to the arrangement of the stars and planets (it may be worth noting that Scaliger's Greek translation of *formatura*, μόρφωσις, is used by Valens to talk about the *product* of the mixing of colours by painters in an analogy to how the mixing of the effects of different stars can mould humans [Vettius Valens, *Anthologia*, 6.3]). As for his source, Scaliger says: *sic restituimus ex manu scripta lectione*; "I have restored this from a manuscript reading." (I wonder if his use of *restituimus* is a little light humour, playing on the *restitui* in Gellius.) I think Scaliger's substitution of *formatura* for *forma* seems to be motivated by concerns similar to my own. He clearly sees something at issue, as he even goes so far as to translate the relevant passage into Greek (hypothetically re-constructing Favorinus' original, I think), as τοιαύτην μόρφωσιν ἀποκαθίστασθαι, "the same act of shaping being brought back". Having said that, though, I also note that (a) no other edition of Gellius that I can find mentions an alternate MS reading, and (b) something made Scaliger omit the whole section from his revised 1600 commentary, so, for one reason or another, he seems to have had a change of heart. Finally, *contra* my reading, see *eamque formam [...] restitui* is translated as "the same form [...] should again appear" (Beloe 1795), "the same position [...] is restored" (Rolfe 1927), "diese Aufstellung [...] sich wiederhold" (Weiss 1875), "cette configuration est rétablie" (Marache 1989), etc.

47 Aulus Gellius, *Attic Nights*, 14.1.21.

none of which was the same as this-man-here's, and none of which was the same as any of the others:

quod si fieri potest eaque diversitas atque varietas admittitur per omnis antiquitatis gradus ad significanda eorum hominum qui post nascentur exordia imparilitas haec turbat observationem omnisque ratio disciplinae confunditur.

But if this can happen, and, across the stages of the whole of antiquity, this diversity and variation is admitted in the births being signified of those men who are born after, this incongruity[48] throws observation up in the air and confounds the rational basis of the whole discipline.[49]

There is simply no way to make sense of the variation from chart to chart as all being serially necessitated by the original chart we started with, and at the same time serially necessitated by each other.

Even worse than this multiple-entailment problem, fate may even be construed to rob humans of their moral culpability. This was a common ancient objection to Stoicism, and it was clearly applied to astrology as well. Firmicus – a vocal proponent of the rigorous inescapability of fate – calls it "the most powerful and forcefully levelled argument" against astrology *(potentissima et vehementer contra nos posita peroratio)*.[50] As he formulates the objection, he cuts to the heart of the Roman self-image: justice, trust, piety – if all was ruled by fate, these core virtues would be entirely due to the stars, rather than human moral attainment. Farmers would not have to call upon the gods when planting their "line of olive trees in their individual, ordered battle-ranks", *olivam in aciem distinctis componis ordinibus.*[51] Even the very *deliberation of justice* would be accounted to the stars:

tu qui promulgas leges ac iura sancis, tolle scita, refige tabulas et istis nos severissimis animadversionibus libera: illum sacrilegum Mercurius, ut mathematici volunt, illum adulterum Venus fecit; illum ad neces hominum Martis sidus armavit, illum mutare tabularum fidem, illum venena miscere.

You, who publish laws and establish rights, take back your ordinances and tear down your decrees. Free us from those terrible punishments, for it was Mercury who made this man sacrilegious, Venus made that one adulterous. It was Mars whose sword equipped this one for homicide, that one for forgery of public records, this other for mixing poison.[52]

While Firmicus never quite answers this objection directly, his general approach to the idea of fate shows that he thinks it a moot point, much like the standard answer given by Stoics. A story is told about this in connection with Zeno of

---

48 *imparilitas* is parsed at Gellius' *Attic Nights*, 5.20.1 as being the older Latin word to describe a grammatical error. For what it is worth, Charles Knapp (1893) points out that in their entry for this word, Lewis and Short's *A Latin Dictionary* incorrectly attributes this use in Gellius to Nigidius Figulus rather than to Favorinus.

49 Aulus Gellius, *Attic Nights*, 14.1.22.

50 Firmicus Maternus, *Mathesis*, 1.2.5.

51 Firmicus Maternus, *Mathesis*, 1.2.9.

52 Firmicus Maternus, *Mathesis*, 1.2.10.

Citium, the founder of Stoicism. Zeno, it is said, was once flogging his slave for stealing, in the midst of which the slave (sarcastically) pleaded that he should not be held accountable because it was fated for him to steal, to which Zeno rejoined: "yes, and to be flayed, too."[53]

Ptolemy's solution

In the end, it is Ptolemy who offers us the cleanest way out of these difficulties, but – and this is no small *caveat* – he is forced by these objections and others to abandon the hard connection between the stars and human destinies, opting, instead, for a multi-tiered system of indirect causation. The overall thrust of his argument is that because astrology deals with the *physical* effects of the stars, which is to say, because it deals with material causes and effects, rather than being rooted in pure mathematical deduction, there is an inherent uncertainty in its predictions. Matter is simply too fickle to offer us complete certainty no matter how we examine it. Add to this the complexity of the heavenly system that astrology studies, the myriad positions and minute interrelations between planets, signs, and the horizon, and we see ample room for simple human error or even ignorance – we cannot have figured the whole thing out yet, not quite, at any rate. Finally, in so far as our knowledge base in astrology is ultimately and only empirical, Ptolemy points out that the study of the heavens is not old enough for human cultures to have observed every cosmic configuration that there may be – this sky tonight, these planets arranged just this way at just this time of birth, have not been previously encountered, or at least not exactly and not in every detail. He then alludes to the idea of the astrological "great year", that time after which all the stars and planets whizzing around in their regular orbits will return to some prior configuration that they had had once upon a time, and the whole complicated dance will start anew, with their subsequent configurations necessarily mirroring their previous ones, one after another after another.

ἔτι καὶ τοῖς παλαιοῖς τῶν πλανωμένων συσχηματισμοῖς, ἀφ' ὧν ἐφαρμόζομεν τοῖς ὡσαύτως ἔχουσι τῶν νῦν τὰς ὑπὸ τῶν προγενεστέρων ἐπ' ἐκείνων παρατετηρημένας προτελέσεις, παρόμοιοι μὲν δύνανται γίνεσθαι μᾶλλον ἢ ἧττον καὶ οὗτοι διὰ μακρῶν περιόδων, ἀπαράλλακτοι δὲ οὐδαμῶς, τῆς πάντων ἐν τῷ οὐρανῷ μετὰ τῆς γῆς κατὰ τὸ ἀκριβὲς συναποκαταστάσεως [...] ἢ μηδόλως ἢ μὴ κατά γε τὸν αἰσθητὸν ἀνθρώπῳ χρόνον ἀπαρτιζομένης.

And moreover, with regard to the ancient configurations of the planets according to which we apply the predictions carefully recorded by our forebears in their own day to the configurations that the planets have now, they may be similar (more or less and at great inter-

---

53 Diogenes Laertius, *Lives of Eminent Philosophers*, 7.23.

vals) but they are never *exactly* so, with the realignment[54] of all the planets in the sky and with the earth never fitting precisely, if we are being accurate, or at least never in a time span perceptible by humans.[55]

Since, Ptolemy is saying, astrology is empirical and works from past observations of the conjunction of heavenly configurations and their earthly consequents, we are stuck with the fact that those heavenly configurations do not repeat precisely in a manageable period of time. There *may* be a great year, but it would have to be very, very long, and so the configuration of the planets for today's nativity only approximates, more or less, the observed historical configuration that forms the basis for my prediction of this person's fate.

Ptolemy further contextualises the epistemological situation of astrology by analogy, using a series of gradations beginning with the farmer or sailor who is able to predict generalities about the weather and the seasons from the positions of the sun and moon, plus the phases of the fixed stars. These rustics make mistakes, though, because they are (a) imprecise in their observations, and (b) ignorant of the non-negligible effects of the planets on the atmosphere. The astrologer, by contrast, can take into account the planetary influences, and measure the various positions more accurately, but even then they can only predict with so much accuracy. Part of this is the problem of empiricism that we just flagged: past correspondences are only approximate models, and part of it seems to be just a problem of the uncertainty of physics. Moreover, for Ptolemy, the astrological influences of the stars on humans are never quite direct. Instead, the effects of the stars work *via* an intermediary, the atmosphere, whose qualities are influenced by the heavenly bodies. It is this atmosphere which, in turn, influences human character and destiny. Even if we did have perfect knowledge of astral positions and causation, he says, we would still only know so much. Specifically, what the astrologer would know is the ἰδιοτροπία, the "peculiar quality" of the atmosphere, which he unpacks as knowing whether it would be – and this is as specific as he gets here – "warmer or wetter", for example (θερμότερον ἢ ὑγρότερον).[56] Based upon this, the competent practitioner could then discern:

τήν τε καθόλου ποιότητα τῆς [τοῦ ἀνθρώπου] ἰδιοσυγκρασίας ἀπὸ τοῦ κατὰ τὴν σύστασιν περιέχοντος [...] οἷον ὅτι τὸ μὲν σῶμα τοιόσδε, τὴν δὲ ψυχὴν τοιόσδε, καὶ τὰ κατὰ καιροὺς συμπτώματα.

---

54 The word συναποκατάστασις is a relatively rare quadruple compound, used only in this astronomical context of the great year.

55 Ptolemy, *Tetrabiblos*, I.2.15–16.

56 Ptolemy, *Tetrabiblos*, I.2.10–11.

the general quality of [a man's] particular temperament[57] from the composition of the atmosphere, [facts like]: his body is of such a sort, or his soul is of this type, and sometimes [he can predict] things that will befall him.[58]

To be sure, Ptolemy seems to be arguing a minimal case here and it is clear from the rest of his book that he thinks a good deal more than occasional life events are astrologically predictable, but I think the caution that he exhibits in this passage is indicative of his attitude to the larger epistemic situation and the kinds of certainty of which astrology is capable.

This is an effective end-run around the kinds of objections which we have been looking at, but one that sacrifices – clearly in the light of just these kinds of objections – the certainty that astrology can provide, the strong causal link between the heavens and humans, and even the epistemological foundations of the discipline. Where our other astrologers were nearly unanimous in calling on a divine foundation, one way or another, for astrology, and bringing in empiricism only as a corollary of that divine foundation, Ptolemy makes a clear distinction between the divine and fore-ordained motions of the planets, and the mutable fates down here on earth. Indeed, if we do a word-search for *divinity* and related terms in the *Tetrabiblos*, we find this remarkable passage driving home the contrast most forcefully:

ἔπειθ᾽ ὅτι μηδ᾽ οὕτως ἕκαστα χρὴ νομίζειν τοῖς ἀνθρώποις ἀπὸ τῆς ἄνωθεν αἰτίας παρακολουθεῖν, ὥσπερ ἐξ ἀρχῆς ἀπό τινος ἀλύτου καὶ θείου προστάγματος καθ᾽ ἕνα ἕκαστον νενομοθετημένα [...] ἀλλ᾽ ὡς μὲν τῆς τῶν οὐρανίων κινήσεως καθ᾽ εἱμαρμένην θείαν καὶ ἀμετάπτωτον ἐξ αἰῶνος ἀποτελουμένης, τῆς δὲ τῶν ἐπιγείων ἀλλοιώσεως καθ᾽ εἱμαρμένην φυσικὴν καὶ μεταπτώτην τὰς πρώτας αἰτίας ἄνωθεν λαμβανούσης κατὰ συμβεβηκὸς καὶ κατ᾽ ἐπακολούθησιν.

Furthermore, we must not think that every specific event happens to people because of some cause raining down from above, as though it were written into law for each individual from the beginning by some unbreakable and divine command [...] but rather that the motions of the heavenly bodies are unfolded according to a divine and unchangeable fate from the beginning, whereas change in earthly things takes its first cause from on high [but is unfolded] according to a natural and changeable fate, happening as it might and according to [its own] causal sequence.[59]

---

57 The noun ἰδιοσυγκρασία, which gives us the English *idiosyncrasy*, is in fact quite rare in Greek, turning up only in Ptolemy and Galen (Hephaestion quotes it from Ptolemy, and it shows up once in a pseudo-Galenic text, the *Definitiones medicae*, but both contexts are clearly derivative). Galen equates it with the nature (φύσις) of the patient and adds that ὀνομάζουσι δέ, οἶμαι, τοῦτο πολλοὶ τῶν ἰατρῶν ἰδιοσυγκρασίαν, καὶ πάντες ἀκατάληπτον ὁμολογοῦσιν ὑπάρχειν, "many doctors, I think, call this the *idiosyncrasy*, and all agree that it is incomprehensible." (Galen, *Method of Medicine*, 209K)

58 Ptolemy, *Tetrabiblos* I.2.11.

59 Ptolemy, *Tetrabiblos* 1.3.6–7.

Astronomy is divine; astrology is derivative.[60] This significantly weakens the epistemological position of astrology, but with the virtue that it renders it noticeably less vulnerable to attack from its opponents.

This is not, it bears saying, the standard line of approach taken by our other astrologers. Where they had case-by-case answers to particular challenges, as we have seen, Ptolemy opts instead to re-work thoughtfully the entire grounding of the discipline in a way that would certainly have been unsatisfying for a Valens, a Firmicus, or a Manilius. To be sure, it solves many of the epistemological problems that beset all of them, but, they would reply, it does so at far too great a cost.

References

Primary Sources

Augustine:

S. Aureli Augustini Confessionum libri XIII, edited by M. Skutella, H. Juergens and W. Schaub. Leipzig: B. G. Teubner, 1981.

Cicero:

M. Tulli Ciceronis De divinatione, De fato, Timaeus, edited by W. Ax. Leipzig: B. G. Teubner, 1977.

Galen:

Galen, Method of Medicine, edited and translated by Ian Johnston and G. H. R. Horsley. Cambridge MA: Harvard University Press, 2011.

Aulus Gellius:

The Attic Nights of Aulus Gellius, translated by William Beloe. London: J. Johnson, 1795.
Die attischen Nächte des Aulus Gellius, translated by Fritz Weiss. Leipzig: Fues's Verlag (R. Reisland) 1875.
Aulus Gellius, Attic Nights, 3 vols., with an English translation by John C. Rolfe. Cambridge, MA: Harvard University Press, 1927.
Aulu-Gelle, Les nuits attiques, edited and translated by René Marache. Paris: Les Belles Lettres, 1989.

Historia Augusta:

Scriptores Historiae Augustae, edited by E. H. Hohl. Leipzig: B. G. Teubner, 1971.

Diogenes Laertius:

Diogenes Laertius: Vitae philosophorum, edited by M. Marcovich. Leipzig: B. G. Teubner, 1999.

---

60 I develop this idea somewhat differently in Chapter 7 of Lehoux 2012.

Manilius:

Manili Astronomicωn [sic] libri quinque. Iosephus Scaliger Iul. Caes. F. recensuit, ac pristino ordini suo restituit; eiusdem Ios. Scaligeri commentarius in eosdem libros et castigationum explications. Paris: Mamertum Patissonium typographum regium, in officina Roberti Stephani, 1579.

Manilius, Astronomica, with an English translation by G. P. Goold. Cambridge MA: Harvard University Press, 1977.

Firmicus Maternus:

Firmicus Maternus: Mathesis, edited and translated by P. Monat. Paris: Les Belles Lettres, 2002.

Ptolemy:

Ptolemaeus: Apotelesmatika, edited by F. Boll and A. Boer. Leipzig: B. G. Teubner, 1954.

Vettius Valens:

Vettii Valentis Antiocheni Anthologiarum Libri Novem, edidit David Pingree. Stuttgart: Teubner, 1986.

Secondary Literature

Algra, Keimpe, et al. (Eds.) (1999): *The Cambridge History of Hellenistic Philosophy.* Cambridge: Cambridge University Press.

Beloe, William (1795): s.v. Aulus Gellius in Primary Sources.

Bobzien, Susanne (1998): *Determinism and Freedom in Stoic Philosophy.* Oxford: Oxford University Press.

Dillon, John M., and Anthony A. Long, (Eds.) (1988): *The Question of Eclecticism: Studies in Later Greek Philosophy.* Berkeley CA: University of California Press.

Frede, Dorothea (2003): "Stoic Determinism." In: B. Inwood (Ed.): *The Cambridge Companion to the Stoics,* 179–205. Cambridge: Cambridge University Press.

Hankinson, Robert J. (1999a): "Explanation and Causation." In: Algra et al. (Eds.): *The Cambridge History of Hellenistic Philosophy,* 479–512. Cambridge: Cambridge University Press.

Hankinson, Robert J. (1999b): "Determinism and Indeterminism." In: Algra et al. (Eds.): *The Cambridge History of Hellenistic Philosophy,* 513–541. Cambridge: Cambridge University Press.

Knapp, Charles (1893): "Corrections and Additions to Lewis and Short in Connection with Aulus Gellius." *American Journal of Philology,* 14 (2): 216–225.

Lehoux, Daryn (2012): *What Did the Romans Know? An Inquiry into Science and Worldmaking.* Chicago IL: University of Chicago Press.

Marache, René (1989): s.v. Aulus Gellius in Primary Sources.

Michaels, David (2008): "Manufactured Uncertainty." In: Robert N. Proctor and Londa Schiebinger: *Agnotology: The Making and Unmaking of Ignorance,* 90–107. Stanford CA: Stanford University Press.

Michaels, David, and Celeste Monforton (2005): "Manufacturing Uncertainty: Contested Science and the Protection of the Public's Health and Environment." *American Journal of Public Health*, 95 (S1): S39–S48.

Rolfe, John C. (1927): s.v. Aulus Gellius in Primary Sources.

Scaliger, Joseph (1579): s.v. Manilius in Primary Sources.

Weiss, Fritz (1875): s.v. Aulus Gellius in Primary Sources.

A Little Old Lady Told Me: Appropriation of Weak Actors' Knowledge in Graeco-Roman Pharmacology

Laurence Totelin

Abstract

Ancient pharmacological texts in Greek and Latin incorporate material from all strata of society: from peasants, peddlers, herbalists, learned physicians, and rulers. This chapter investigates some of the material attributed to the weakest social actors: slaves, people of the lower classes, and women. It examines the methods through which learned authors collected this material by examining some of the anecdotes they give us of their encounters with weak agents. We will see that these anecdotes are often included for entertainment purposes, and may therefore further diminish the authority of already weak agents. Second, it looks at the ways in which learned authors distanced themselves from these socially weak agents, and in particular at the erasing of these agents' personal names. Indeed, these agents are rarely identified by their name, but rather by some general reference to their ethnicity, status, and/or profession. It concludes with some reflection on literacy and orality in classical antiquity. Many weak actors – but not all – would have transmitted their knowledge orally rather than in writing. Thus, while learned authors shamelessly appropriated for themselves weak actors' pharmacological and botanical knowledge, they paradoxically lent them a voice by preserving some of this knowledge in writing.

1. Introduction

The history of weak actors in Graeco-Roman pharmacology can only be accessed through anecdotes, stories told by élite literate authors. I therefore start with such an anecdote, which is preserved in the *Compound Remedies* of Scribonius Largus,[1] a medical author of the first century CE:

---

1 Baldwin 1992; Sconocchia 1993; Nutton 1995.

Hoc medicamento muliercula quaedam ex Africa Romae multos remediavit. Postea nos per magnam curam compositionem accepimus, id est pretio dato, quod desideraverat, aliquot non ignotos sanavimus, quorum nomina supervacuum est referre, constat autem medicamentum ex his rebus: cervi cornua sumuntur, dum tenera sunt [...] furnace uruntur, donec in cinerem candidissimum redigantur, atque ita in vaso vitreo mundo reponuntur, cum dolorem habuit aliquis, [...] summuntur ex cornibus coclearia tria cumulata satis ampla, quibus miscentur piperis albi grana novem trita et myrrhae exiguum, quod odorem tantummodo praestare posit.

A certain little woman [*muliercula*] from Africa cured many in Rome with the following medicament. Thereafter, we obtained this recipe by means of great effort (that is, having paid for it, as she wished) and we cured many people, who are not unknown, but whose name it is unnecessary to record. This medicine is constituted of these ingredients: take deer horns when they are quite soft [...] put them in the oven until they have been turned into the whitest ashes and place them in a clean glass vase. When someone has a pain, take three spoons, well filled with the horn, to which are mixed nine crushed grains of white pepper, and a little myrrh, enough to provide the smell.[2]

Scribonius Largus believed this remedy to be efficacious; if not, he would not have made the effort he did to obtain it, he would not have paid a price for it. Whether Scribonius himself met the "little woman" or heard about her miraculous cure and asked someone else to purchase it for him, we do not know. In any case, this woman is left anonymous in Scribonius' story; she does not have a personal name. Instead, she is identified by her geographical origin (she is African, that is, she probably comes from the Roman province of Africa), by her place of residence (Rome), and by her gender. "*Muliercula*" is a rather dismissive term, which normally referred to a woman of the lower classes, and which may indicate that she was a prostitute.[3] Clearly, these elements of identification were sufficient in Scribonius' eyes; her name was not deemed worthy of being recorded – it would have been superfluous. This attribution of the remedy to the African *muliercula* is only one step removed from anonymity: Scribonius acknowledged that he had obtained a medicament from a woman of a lower stratum of society, but he did not judge it necessary to identify her by her personal name.

On the other hand, the famous people whom the pharmacologist went on to cure with this medicine are left anonymous, in what appears to be a wish to protect their identity. In contrast to the little woman, Scribonius' clients were from the highest classes of Roman society.

It is also worth mentioning that Scribonius did not tell us how the African lady obtained her expertise in curing diseases – we do not know whether she was a "professional" healer or not.[4] In his account, Scribonius tried to give central

---

2 Scribonius Largus, *Compositiones*, 122. Unless stated otherwise, all translations are mine.

3 Adams 1983; Santoro L'Hoir 1992, 40.

4 The notion of "profession" in relation to ancient healing is famously complex. There were no official licences to practice healing. It was not uncommon for people to be healers in addition to their normal occupations (see, for instance, the story of the hostess in a wine shop who left

place to the remedy in his account, and to leave its inventor, an obscure little woman, at the margins.

The same recipe is found in the ninth book of Galen's *Composition of Medicines according to Places*:

Πακκίου Ἀντιόχου, τῆς ὅλης ἀπαλλάττει διαθέσεως. Κέρατος ἐλαφείου νεοβλάστου, μαλακωτάτου κεκαυμένου ὥστε λευκὸν εἶναι, κοχλιάρια γ΄. μείζονα τῷ μεγέθει, πεπέρεως λευκοῦ κόκκοι ι΄ ἢ θ΄. σμύρνης ὀλίγον ὀσμῆς χάριν, ἅπαντα τρίβεται [...].

[The remedy] of Paccius Antiochus, which relieves from the entire affliction: soft deer horn, slowly burnt until it becomes white, three spoons full, quite large in size; white pepper, 9 or 10 grains; a little myrrh for the smell; crush all [...].[5]

Galen, however, attributed the medication to a certain Paccius Antiochus. Paccius Antiochus was an older contemporary of Scribonius, and Scribonius mentioned him three times in the *Compound Remedies*.[6] Paccius was a physician who had studied with an established medical authority (Philonides Catinensis),[7] and who had written works on pharmacology.[8] The attribution of the remedy with deer horn to Paccius Antiochus is probably the result of the conflation of pieces of information found in the works of Scribonius by Galen's source (Andromachus, a first century CE pharmacologist).[9] The remedy certainly benefited in the process: it lost its connections with an obscure woman, whose expertise in medicine could not be established, to become the creation of an honourable physician.

This anecdote is an excellent introduction to the role of "weak actors" in ancient pharmacology. While I have often felt uncomfortable with the notion of popular medicine and science (how does one define "popular"?),[10] and even more so with the notion of folkloric medicine and science ("folk" being a synonym of "people", but with further negative connotations[11]), I feel somewhat more comfortable with the notion of "weak actors", or perhaps to be more accurate "wea-

---

her clients to assist a kinswoman in childbirth: Eunapius, *Lives of the Philosophers*: 463). Scribonius Largus uses the Latin word *professio* in the preface to his *Compound Remedies*, in which he appears to allude to the Hippocratic Oath and the ethical principles outlined therein (see Hamilton 1986).

5 Galen, *Opera Omnia*: 13.284–5. (It is customary in references to Galenic texts to list the relevant volume (here 13) and the page (here 284–5) of Kühn's edition.)

6 Scribonius Largus, *Compositiones*: 97, 156, and 220.

7 See Scribonius Largus, *Compositiones*: 97.

8 See Scarborough 2008a.

9 See Touwaide 2008. Galen's pharmacological works are collections of extracts from older authors (see Fabricius 1972). Although Galen mentions Scribonius Largus (in particular, in the recipe that precedes that which interests us, Galen, *Opera Omnia*: 13.284), it is quite likely that his knowledge was second-hand, mediated through the writings of one of his main sources, Andromachus the Younger. Andromachus is mentioned a little earlier in this chapter of Galen's *Compositions of Medicines according to Places* (Galen, *Opera Omnia*: 13.276).

10 See the collection of essays edited by Harris (2016).

11 The phrase "folk medicine" is used in a positive sense by Scarborough 1987.

kened actors". Weakness is only ever relative: the "little woman" in our story may have been quite a powerful healer in the circles in which she operated; however, Scribonius deliberately weakened her by denying her a full identity and by using a dismissive term to call her: *muliercula*, a little old lady.

In this chapter, I will examine some of the ways in which Greek and Roman pharmacological authors deliberately weakened actors other than themselves. In other words, I will be looking at some of the means of constructing otherness.[12] The correlate question is, of course, that of authority, because, by weakening other actors, ancient pharmacological authors augmented their own authority. Since ancient medical writings constitute our largest source for Graeco-Roman pharmacology, it is crucial to understand the ways in which their authors distorted our views of a business that provided a living for numerous people, from root cutters to market peddlers, in what Vivian Nutton (1992) has called "the medical market place". I will focus here on authors who were active in the first and second centuries CE, that is, during the two first centuries of the Roman Empire.

2. My profession and yours

An effective method to construct an "other" is to talk of a group of people as an indistinct mass, without acknowledging the possibility for individuality within the group. Ancient pharmacological authors regularly used this technique, "lumping together" the members of a group, be it professional, regional or ethnic. I will examine all such groups, starting with professional groups, or, perhaps more accurately for the ancient world, trade or craft groups.[13]

Assertions that root cutters, drug sellers, midwives, or retail dealers did something in a specific way occur frequently in ancient pharmacological writings. These assertions create the – certainly wrong – impression that these trade groups had uniform practices, rather than the multitude that must have existed, practices that were often grounded in the transmission of knowledge along family lines and which may have included an element of secrecy.[14]

Soranus (a prominent physician of the first century CE belonging to the Methodist sect) (Hanson and Green, 1994), provides us with a particularly good example of this method, when he reports some of the (not-so-recommendable) practices of wet nurses when treating tonsillitis in children:

---

12 The notions of "othering" and "otherness" are often used by classicists in relation to "barbarians". See the articles edited by Almagor and Skinner 2013.

13 See note 4 above.

14 Long 2001, Chapter 3.

Φλεγμηνάντων δὲ τῶν παρισθμίων ἡ μ ε ῖ ς μὲν τοῖς αὐτοῖς χρώμεθα παρενστάζοντες μελίκρατον καὶ πτισάνης χυλόν· αἱ τροφοὶ δὲ κυμίνῳ πεφρυγμένῳ δι' ὕδατος καταπλάσσουσι τὸν ἀνθερεῶνα, τὰ δὲ παρίσθμια παρατρίβουσιν ἅλατι καὶ παλαιῷ ἐλαίῳ, καὶ διὰ μιᾶς χειρὸς ἑκατέρων ἐπιλαμβανόμεναι τῶν σκελῶν ἐπὶ κεφαλὴν σχηματίζουσι τὸ βρέφος μεταξὺ θύρας καὶ τῷ βρέγματι προσάπτονται τοῦ τῆς στέγης <ὑπὸ> ποσὶν ὁδοῦ, καὶ τοῦτο ποιοῦσιν ἑπτάκις.

When the tonsils are inflamed, we use the same remedies and drop [into the mouth] honey water and barley juice. The wet nurses, however, apply to the throat a cataplasm of roasted cumin mixed with water; they rub the tonsils with salt and old oil, and grabbing both legs with one hand, they place the infant head downwards in the doorway and make her forehead touch the threshold of the house; and this they repeat seven times.[15]

Soranus strongly opposed his own – sound – pharmacological practice to those of the wet nurses.[16] He assimilated all wet nurses into one single category; he did not acknowledge the fact that there were probably as many remedies for tonsillitis in children as there were wet nurses. Soranus' text conveys the impression that the remedies which he mentions are common practice, when they might, in fact, have been rare and marginal.

Naturally, the professional groups most often mentioned by pharmacological writers are those involved in the handling and trade of medicinal substances, and particularly of plants: the root cutters, herbalists, and drug sellers.[17] While authors such as Galen, Pliny the Elder (24–79 CE) (Murphy 2004), and Dioscorides (first century CE) (Riddle 1985), mentioned these groups as their sources, they did so rather reluctantly, and generally gave them a very bad press. They often accused them of superstition, criticising the rituals surrounding the gathering of herbs, and the fantastical stories that they circulated about the magical power of plants and the mysterious animals protecting them.[18] Pharmacological writers also accused plant handlers of dishonesty. For instance, Pliny accused herbalists in the following words:

Scelus herbariorum aperietur et in hac mentione: partem eius servant et quarundam aliarum herbarum, sicuti plantaginis, et si parum mercedis tulisse se arbitrantur rursusque opus quaerunt, partem eam, quam servavere, eodem loco infodiunt, credo, ut vitia, quae sanaverint, faciant rebellare. saliuncae radix in vino decocta sistit vomitiones, conroborat stomachum.

The wickedness of the herbalists is apparent also in this instance: they keep a part of it [an iris] and of some other plants, such as plantain. If they consider their pay too little and look for further work, then, they bury in the same place the part they have kept, they do so I believe in order that the ailments they have cured would break out again.[19]

---

15 Soranus, *Diseases of Women*. 2.50.
16 On wet nurses in Rome, see Bradley 1986; Joshel 1986.
17 Korpela 1995; Boudon-Millot 2003; Samama 2006; Totelin 2016a.
18 Ducourthial 2003; Hardy and Totelin 2016, 43–49.
19 Pliny, *Natural History*. 21.144; see Hardy and Totelin 2016, 44.

If we are to believe our preserved pharmacological authors, plant handlers also commonly adulterated the plants which they sold in order to make higher profits. Even Galen's compliment to the herbalists of Crete, who rarely adulterated plants, is somewhat back-handed:

Διὰ γὰρ τὸ πλῆθος τῶν γενομένων βοτανῶν ἐν τῇ νήσῳ οὐ πάνυ τι πανουργεῖν ἐπιχειροῦσιν οἱ κατ' αὐτὴν βοτανικοί, οὐ μὴν οὐδ' ἡ καινουργία μεγάλη, καθάπερ ἐπ' ἄλλων, ἀλλ' ἀντὶ τοῦ χυλὸν ἀψινθίου μόνου ποιήσασθαι πρασίου μιγνύουσιν, ἤ τι τοιοῦτον παραποιοῦσι μικρόν, ὥστε τοὺς ἐν Ῥώμῃ μυροπώλας ὠνουμένους καθ' ἕκαστον ἔτος τὰ πλήρη τῶν φαρμάκων ἀγγεῖα τὰ πλεκτά, πρῶτον μὲν ἕκαστον αὐτὸν διδάσκεσθαι γνωρίζειν, εἰ καὶ μὴ πρότερον ἑορακώς τις εἴη.

Because of the abundance of plants on the island [of Crete], its herbalists hardly try to adulterate drugs, which is unlike the great manufacture [of forged drugs] occurring elsewhere. However, instead of [selling] the pure juice of wormwood, they mix it with horehound, or they adulterate it slightly, so that the perfume sellers in Rome who, every year, buy the *plekta* vessels filled with drugs, must learn to recognise whether something has been altered.[20]

In this passage, Galen ascribed some skill to the perfume sellers of Rome: they could recognise what is adulterated.[21] In fact, Galen even acknowledged that there was skill in the art of adulteration:

Ἔνιαμὲν γὰρ παραποιοῦσιν οἱ καπηλεύοντες οὕτω σαφῶς, ὡς καὶ τοὺς τριβακωτάτους ἐν αὐτοῖς λανθάνειν.

For the retail dealers forge some products so skilfully that it escapes the notice even of those who know them [the drugs] well.[22]

Galen offered his solution to all these issues: use trustworthy friends, or go and gather the drugs oneself:

Ἐφ' ὧν κάλλιστόν ἐστιν αὐτῶν ἐκ πολλοῦ παρεσκευάσθαι διὰ φίλον ἀνόθευτον ἐκ τοῦ χωρίου, καθ' ὃ κάλλιστον γεννᾶται, πορίζεσθαι τὸ φάρμακον, ἢ ἅπαξ πορευθέντα παρασκευάσασθαι τὰ διαμεῖναι δυνάμενα πρὸς ὅλον τὸν βίον, ὁποῖα σχεδὸν ἅπαντά ἐστι τὰ μεταλλικὰ καλούμενα.

Hence, it is best to have the drugs brought, through a trustworthy friend, from the region where they occur in their best state, or simply to go there oneself and to procure the products that will last for the rest of one's life, as is particularly the case of the so-called metallic drugs.[23]

Galen then went on to explain how he obtained drugs from a friend in Cyprus, an associate of the governor of the mines. Elsewhere, Galen presented himself as a roving pharmacologist, criss-crossing the Mediterranean world in search of un-

---

20 Galen, *On Antidotes*. 1.1, (Galen, *Opera Omnia*. 14.10). A little earlier, Galen explained that the *plekta* vessels were plaited from agnus castus: *On Antidotes*. 1.2 (Galen, *Opera Omnia*. 14.9).

21 Galen at times uses the words *pharmakopōlai* (drug sellers) and *muropōlai* (perfume sellers) as almost synonymous.

22 Galen, *On Antidotes*. 1.1 (Galen, *Opera Omnia*. 14.7).

23 Galen, *On Antidotes*. 1.1 (Galen, *Opera Omnia*. 14.7).

adulterated drugs.[24] Not everyone, however, had the wealth necessary to do this. Besides, money could only take one so far in the ancient world: even Galen never travelled to Eastern Asia to get cinnamon, or to southern Arabia to collect frankincense.[25]

Ancient pharmacological authors such as Galen, quite understandably, presented a picture of themselves in full control of their field. The reality, however, is that even élite pharmacologists could not control all aspects of the preparation of certain remedies, and in particular of the multi-ingredient antidotes that were so in fashion in the first few centuries of the Common Era. They had to rely on a large amount of people: herb gatherers, traders, and sailors. It was, of course, easier for ancient writers to "lump" all these people into simple, closed-up categories, especially if they could deflect any blame onto them. It is important not to put too much trust in our preserved authors when they present these other people as unskilled, dishonest, greedy and marginal. There are two reasons for this.

First, within these seemingly uniform categories, there was most certainly a lot of variety: in practice, in wealth, and in recognition. We know that some people within these categories attained levels of wealth sufficient for their families to honour them with relatively elaborate funeral monuments (Korpela 1995). However, wealth can be acquired through dishonest means, which is precisely what an author such as Galen would have said. What Galen did not quite acknowledge, however, is that the people in these categories which he so criticised were trusted and became minor celebrities. Despite accusing drug-sellers and other tradespeople of ineptitude, he recorded recipes attributed to characters such as Pharnakes the root cutter, Antonius the root cutter (perhaps the same person as Antonius Musa, who was a famous physician), or Chariton the crowd-gatherer.[26] When Galen recorded these people's remedies, he did so without suggesting that they were dangerous or ineffective; in the same way as the *muliercula*'s recipe, they were deemed to be useful and efficacious.

---

24 See Totelin 2016b for the story of Galen travelling to the island of Lemnos to find its medicinal earth.

25 In the same treatise, Galen discussed how stocks of imperial cinnamon had taken a hit when the emperor Commodus sold the stocks of his father, Marcus Aurelius: Galen, *On Antidotes*: 13 (Galen, *Opera Omnia*: 14.65). In another treatise, *Avoiding Distress*, Galen deplored the loss of large personal stocks of cinnamon in the great fire of Rome in 192 (Chapter 6). There are debates as to the identification of the plant called *kinnamōmon* in Greek is debated, but I would argue that the Greeks and Romans had access to true cinnamon, which grows in Sri Lanka (see Amigues 1996 for insights into the question).

26 Pharnakes: Galen, *Composition of Medicines according to Places*: 8.7 (Galen, *Opera Omnia*: 13.204). Antonius: Galen, *Composition of Medicines according to Places*: 2.1 (Galen, *Opera Omnia*: 12.557) and 2.2 (Galen, *Opera Omnia*: 12.580); see also Keyser 2008; Totelin 2010. Antonius Musa cured the Emperor Augustus from a bilious illness with a cold regimen in 23 BCE; see Michler 1993; Scarborough 2008b. Chariton: Galen, *On Antidotes*: 2.13 (Galen, *Opera Omnia*: 14.180).

The second reason why we must not trust our sources too much when they portray pharmacological actors in a negative light is the natural inclination people have to place themselves at the centre of their own narratives. It was only natural for Galen, Soranus and Scribonius Largus to depict their practices as central, and that of others as marginal. We should be careful not to fall into the trap that they have set for us. Véronique Boudon-Millot, in an excellent article, argues that such people are at "the margins of rational medicine" (Boudon-Millot 2003). The position of the "margins", however, depends on where one stands. To Galen, an extremely wealthy and educated physician, a small drug-trader in a shady part of Rome might have appeared very marginal indeed; but Galen is not representative of the population of the ancient world, of people who often had no access to doctors, or, when they did, had to rely on rough and ready remedies. I now turn to this topic, and to the contrasts that ancient élite pharmacological doctors drew between city and country, and between their country and foreign ones.

3. Country and city; home and away

In the tenth book on *Simple Drugs*, Galen told the story of an anonymous doctor from Mysia who used dung to cure his patients, peasants affected with dropsy:

Περὶ βοείας κόπρου [...] Τοὺς ὑδερικοὺς δέ τις ἐν Μυσίᾳ τῇ ἐν Ἑλλησπόντῳ βολβίτῳ καταχρίων ἐν ἡλίῳ κατέκλινε φαρμάκων ἔμπειρος ἰατρός. Ὁ δ᾽ αὐτὸς οὗτος ἐπετίθει καὶ τοῖς φλεγμαίνουσι μέρεσι τῶν ἀγροίκων ὑγρὰν λαμβάνων ἦρος, ὅτε νέμονται τὴν πόαν οἱ βόες [...] Εἰδέναι μέντοι χρὴ πάντα τὰ τοιαῦτα φάρμακα σκληροῖς σώμασιν ἀγροίκων ἀνθρώπων ἁρμόττειν, σκαπανέων τε καὶ θεριστῶν καὶ τῶν ἰσχυρὸν οὕτως ἔργον διαπραττομένων, εφ᾽ ᾧ καὶ πρὸς χοιράδας ὁ κατὰ τὴν Μυσίαν ἰατρὸς ἐχρῆτο.

Concerning bull dung [...] A certain doctor in Mysia, in the Hellespont, an expert in drugs, smeared his dropsical patients with dung and made them recline in the sun. The same man also applied dung to the inflamed parts of country people, taking it moist, when the bulls were grazing on grass [...] It is, however, necessary to know that all these types of remedies [sc. dung and other similar remedies] are good for the hardened bodies of country people, diggers, harvesters and those accomplishing this type of heavy work, in which case (and against scrofulous swellings) the doctor from Mysia used the dung.[27]

This anecdote is situated in the Hellespont, far away from Rome and Alexandria, which were the main centres of the drug trade in Galen's time. There, a physician used bull dung – a rather unsavoury remedy – to cure patients affected with dropsy.[28] The purpose of this anecdote is ambivalent. On the one hand, it gave credit to the medication; Galen did not deny the fact that bull dung was effective. On the other hand, it allowed Galen to distance himself from this type of treat-

---

27 Galen, *Mixing and Powers of Simple Drugs*: 10.23 (Galen, *Opera Omnia*: 12.300–1).
28 On the episode, see Debru 1996; Gourevitch 2016, 256–259.

ment: it was only suitable for countrymen whose bodies had been hardened by physical work. In other words, it was not appropriate for most of Galen's clientele: wealthy city dwellers. The doctor of this anecdote is presented as an expert in drugs (he has *empeiria*); however, because he was a country physician whose patients were composed mainly of rustics, Galen did not deem it necessary to record his name.

While the country people in Galen's stories still had access to a doctor, clearly not all people in the countryside had that chance. Ancient authors at times indicated that country people treated themselves. For instance, after offering a list of remedies to cure toothache, the encyclopaedist Celsus added:

Haec medicis accepta sunt. Sed agrestium experimento cognitum est, cum dens dolet, herbam mentastrum cum suis radicibus evelli debere, et in pelvem coici, supraque aquam infundi, collocarique iuxta sedentem hominem undique veste contectum; tum in pelvem candentes silices demitti, sic ut aqua tegantur; hominemque eum hiante ore vaporem excipere, ut supra dictum est, undique inclusum.

These are recognised by physicians. But country people have found out by experience that, when a tooth aches, one must pull out catmint with its roots, put it in a pot, pour water over it, and place it beside the man as he sits covered by his clothes; then throw hot stones in the pot, so that the water covers them; the man inhales the vapour with his open mouth; as said above, he is completely covered over.[29]

Celsus contrasted the physicians (*medici*) with the country people (*agrestes*), but did not judge either negatively.[30] Celsus did not romanticise country remedies, he simply acknowledged, as Galen did, that different circumstances might call for different medicines.

The main characteristic of the country people's remedies for toothache and dropsy is simplicity, a characteristic that typifies most (if not all) country cures reported by our pharmacological authors – they contain ingredients that were widely available and usually inexpensive. For instance, one could contrast a simple five-ingredient "country man's antidote against viper venom" to the famous antidote allegedly created by King Mithradates VI, an antidote which included at least forty ingredients, most of which were rare and/or expensive.[31] All the ingredients of the first recipe are easy to find around the Mediterranean, and they are cheap.

---

29 Celsus, *De Medicina* 6.9.7; translation: W.G. Spencer.
30 There is debate as to whether Celsus was trained as a physician; see Schulze 1999 and 2001.
31 Antidote of the country man: Galen, *On Antidotes* 2.13 (Galen, *Opera Omnia* 14.184): Ἡ τοῦ ἀγροίκου ἐχιοδήκτου. Τριφύλλου, στάχυος, ὀρόβου ἠλεσμένου, πηγάνου ἀγρίου σπέρματος, ἀριστολοχίας στρογγύλης, ἀνὰ <η΄. οἴνῳ διαλύσας ἀνάπλαττε τροχίσκους, καὶ δίδου α΄. μετ' οἴνου κυάθων γ΄. δὶς καὶ τρὶς τῆς ἡμέρας. Translation: "Antidote of the countryman against viper bites: clover, corn, ground bitter vetch, seed of wild rue, round birthwort, of each 8 obols; dilute into wine; and make pastilles. Give one pastille with three *kyathoi* of wine, two or three times per day." For Mithradates' antidote, of which several recipes are preserved, see Totelin 2004.

There was, in antiquity, a literary genre that specialised in the transmission of simple recipes based upon ingredients that were easily procured: the *Euporista* (literally, the easy-to-procure remedies).[32] Yet, even the *Euporista* treatises were not available to everyone. As Celsus noted, literacy was not widespread in the ancient world:

Si levata tussis est, leni lectione uti, iamque et acres cibos et vinum meracius adsumere. Quae ita a medicis praecipiuntur, ut tamen sine his rusticos nostros epota ex aqua herba trixago satis adiuvet.

If the cough has been relieved, the patient should read a little out loud, and then take both sharp food and undiluted wine. Though such are what medical practitioners prescribe, our country people, lacking these remedies, still find help enough in a draught of germander.[33]

"Country" practices, of course, vary from one region to the next (and from one household to the next, but there is little hope of recovering this microlevel for the ancient world). Ancient authors were aware of this cultural variety, and recorded plant knowledge and remedies that they attributed to various ethnic groups. Thus, they acknowledged variety within the Italian peninsula and the Greek world, attributing special pharmacological knowledge to the Marsi, a people from central Italy renowned for its cures for serpent bites by charms and herbal remedies, and to the Thessalians, whose women specialised in the preparation of love philtres.[34] Medical authors also attributed numerous recipes to the Egyptians, the Spanish, the Libyans, the Indians and various other ethnic groups (see Totelin 2016b for references). These attributions are never neutral and carry with them a host of ethnic prejudices, be they benevolent or negative. Let us take one example among many: a recipe for an "Egyptian" grey plaster attributed by Galen to Andromachus, the pharmacologist active in the first century CE.

Φαιὰ Αἰγυπτία Ἀνδρομάχου. Ὁ μὲν γὰρ Ἀνδρόμαχος οὕτως ἔγραψε κατὰ λέξιν. φαιὰ Αἰγυπτία λιθαργύρου <μδ΄. κίκεως κο. στ΄. κηροῦ <ρμδ΄. ἀμμωνιακοῦ θυμιάματος <οβ΄. τερμινθίνης <λστ΄. ἐρίων κεκαυμένων <ιη΄. λεπίδος στομώματος <η΄. λεπίδος χαλκοῦ <η΄. ἀριστολοχίας <η΄. λιβάνου <η΄. ἔνιοι δὲ σμύρνης <δ΄. ὀποπάνακος <β΄. θαλάσσης <ν΄. εἰς ἐμβροχὴν κηροῦ.

Grey [plaster] of Andromachus. Andromachus wrote this recipe in these exact words. Grey Egyptian: litharge, 44 drachmas; castor oil, 6 *kotylai*; wax, 144 drachmas; gum-am-

---

32 Oribasius (fourth century CE) dedicated a work in four books on *euporista* to Eunapius (Oribasius, *Synopsis at Eustathium*, 315–498). Three books attributed to Galen (but not by him) are preserved in the Galenic Corpus: Galen, *Opera Omnia*: 14.311–581. Galen himself wrote a book of *euporista*, but it is lost (see Galen, *On the Properties of Foodstuffs*: 2.46 (Galen, *Opera Omnia*: 6.634). Other works on *euporista* are also lost: see, for instance, Apollonius' *Euporista*, mentioned by Galen, *On the Composition of Medicines according to Places*: 1.8 (Galen, *Opera Omnia*: 12.475).

33 Celsus, *De Medicina*: 4.13.3; translation: W.G. Spencer. On the difficulty of determining levels of literacy in the ancient world, Harris 1991, remains important. For a different approach to the topic, see Woolf 2015.

34 For references to the Marsi, see, for example, Pliny, *Natural History*: 25.11 and 86; see Jones-Lewis 2012. For references to the Thessalian women, see, for example, Dioscorides, *Materia Medica*: 3.126 and 4.131; see Phillips 2002.

moniac to be used for embalming, 72 drachmas; turpentine, 36 drachmas; burnt wool, 18 drachmas; steel debris, 8 drachmas; copper debris, 8 drachmas; birthwort, 8 drachmas; frankincense, 8 drachmas (some say: myrrh, 4); opopanax gum, 2 drachmas; sea-water, 50 drachmas; mix into an embrocation of wax.[35]

It is entirely unclear what makes this recipe "Egyptian", beyond the fact that it includes castor oil and two types of gums (gum ammoniac and opopanax), which were ingredients associated with North Africa or Egypt in the ancient world.[36] We get an overly-romantic view of Egypt and its medicine here, one that is centred around expensive gums – Egypt was associated with scented products in the Greek and Roman imagination.[37]

Elsewhere, Galen associated Egyptian medicine with superstitious practices that were best avoided, even though they had proved very attractive to other Greek-writing authors.[38] Clearly, it would be impossible to re-construct the medical practices of regions such as Roman Egypt or Spain from the recipes supposedly produced there.

At times, ancient authors travelled to regions wherefrom they allegedly obtained foreign remedies. In other cases, as in that of the *muliercula*'s remedy with which I opened this chapter, they acquired a recipe from a foreigner whose medical practice may well have undergone a process of hybridisation.

4. Conclusion

In this chapter, I have examined some of the techniques used by ancient pharmacological actors for "othering" their sources: denying them full identity, and subsuming them into broad, vague categories. In some cases, these techniques were intentionally critical: one cannot read the "lumping" of most drug retailers into the dishonest category in a positive light. This was a deliberate way for pharmacological authors to distance themselves from their sources, and to deflect the blame onto them should anything go wrong in the process of drug making and taking. These authors constructed their own authority by slandering and weaken-

---

35 Galen, *Composition of Medicines according to Types*: 6.8 (Galen, *Opera Omnia*: 13.890–891).

36 The word, κίκι, castor oil, is almost certainly a word borrowed from the Egyptian; see Fournet 1989, 60–61. Dioscorides informs us that gum ammoniac is the sap of a giant fennel growing near Cyrene (Roman Libya) (*Materia Medica*: 3.84); and that the plant from which the gum opopanax is extracted grows in Cyrene, as well as in Boeotia, Arcadia and Macedonia (*Materia Medica* 3.48).

37 See Totelin 2016b for references.

38 See, for instance, *Mixing and Powers of Simple Drugs*, preface (Galen, *Opera Omnia*: 11.792), in which Galen accused the author Pamphilus (first century CE) of being attracted by "silly Egyptian magical tricks"; see Boudon-Millot 2003, 119.

ing people who had crucial roles to play in the ancient drug business. Because these actors left no, or very little, written record, it is particularly difficult to recover their practices, and it can be very tempting to trust those authors who deliberately presented them in a bad light.

Nor should we put too much trust in ancient pharmacological authors when they offer us foreign or regional remedies. While they were not necessarily critical towards local practices, they certainly presented them in a manner that lacked nuance. It is also possible that many "foreign" recipes came to Rome, Alexandria, Pergamum and other important urban centres of the Roman Empire together with slaves, who are among the weakest historical agents.

Finally, ancient pharmacological authors half-anonymised their sources. The intent may not have been malicious: these authors might have felt that an informant's name would be of little interest to their readers. Yet, depriving people of their names weakens them: identifying someone by their gender, job, or ethnicity is a form of reification.

Behind this deliberate weakening of actors, there was certainly a certain epistemic weakness in ancient pharmacology. Authors such as Galen recognised that it is difficult to explain why a drug, especially a compound one, works in the way in which it does.[39] Pharmacology was an empirical science in which a sufficient number of claims that a drug was effective was taken to mean that the drug was effective, as expressed in Celsus' suggestion that peasants had discovered the efficacy of catmint in the treatment of toothaches through experience. Anyone with – or even without – experience in healing could discover a new effective drug. The role of the élite author was to give them a written format. Thus, paradoxically, by weakening and sometimes silencing many sources, they also gave written expression to their knowledge and expertise.

References

Primary Sources

Aulus Cornelius Celsus:

Celsus. De Medicina. Vol. 2. With an English Translation by W. G. Spencer. London: William Heinemann, 1938.

Pedanius Dioscorides:

Pedanii Dioscuridi Anazarbei De materia medica libri quinque. Edidit M. Wellmann. Volumen II quo continentur libri III et IV. Berlin: Weidmann, 1906.

---

39 On this issue, see van der Eijk 1997; Vogt 2008.

Eunapius:

Philostratus. Lives of the Sophists. Eunapius. Lives of the Philosophers and Sophists. With an English Translation by W. C. Wright. London: William Heinemann, 1921.

Galen:

Claudii Galeni opera omnia. Edidit Karl G. Kühn. 20 Vols. Berlin and Leipzig: C. Cnobloch, 1821–1833.
Galien. Œuvres. Tome IV. Ne pas se chagriner. Texte établi et traduit par V. Boudon-Millot et J. Jouanna, avec la contribution d'A. Pietrobelli. Paris: Les Belles Lettres, 2010.
On Theriac to Piso. Attributed to Galen: A Critical Edition with Translation and Commentary by Robert Leigh. Leiden: Brill, 2015.

Oribasius:

Oribasii Synopsis at Eustathium. Libri ad Eunapium. Edidit Ioannes Raeder. Leipzig and Berlin: Teubner, 1926.

Pliny:

Pliny. Natural History. Books XII–XVI. With an English Translation by H. Rackham. Revised edition. Cambridge MA-London: Harvard University Press, 1968.

Scribonius Largus:

Scribonii Largi Compositiones. Edidit Sergio Sconocchia. Leipzig: Teubner, 1983.

Soranus of Ephesus:

Soranos d'Éphèse. Maladies des femmes. Tome 2, Livre II. Texte établi, traduit et commenté par Paul Burguière, Danielle Gourevitch et Yves Malinas. Paris: Les Belles Lettres, 1990.

Secondary Literature

Adams, J.N. (1983): "Words for 'Prostitute' in Latin." *Rheinisches Museum für Philologie*, 126 (3/4): 321–58.
Almagor, Eran, and Joseph Skinner (Eds.) (2013): *Ancient Ethnography: New Approaches.* London: Bloomsbury.
Amigues, Suzanne (1996): "Un cinnamome fantomatique." *Topoi. Orient-Occident*, 6 (2): 657–64.
Baldwin, Barry (1992): "The Career and Work of Scribonius Largus." *Rheinisches Museum für Philologie*, 135 (1): 74–82.
Boudon-Millot, Véronique (2003): "Aux marges de la médecine rationnelle: médecins et charlatans à Rome au temps de Galien (IIe s. de notre ère)." *Revue des Études Grecques*, 116 (1): 109–31.
Bradley, Keith R. (1986): "Wet-Nursing at Rome: A Study in Social Relations." In: Beryl Rawson (Ed.): *The Family in Ancient Rome: New Perspectives*, 201–29. Ithaca NY: Cornell University Press.

Debru, Armelle (1996): "The Gardener and the Lady: Therapeutics and Society in the Age of Galen." In: Regine Pötzsch (Ed.): *The Pharmacy: Windows on History*, 23–33. Basel: Editiones Roche.

Ducourthial, Guy (2003): *Flore magique et astrologique de l'antiquité*. Paris: Belin.

Eijk, Philip J. van der (1997): "Galen's Use of the Concept of 'Qualified Experience' in his Dietetic and Pharmacological Works." In: Armelle Debru (Ed.): *Galen on Pharmacology, Philosophy, History of Medicine*, 35–57. Leiden-Boston MA: Brill.

Fabricius, Cajus (1972): *Galens Exzerpte aus älteren Pharmakologen*. Berlin-New York: Walter de Gruyter.

Fournet, Jean-Luc (1989): "Les emprunts du grec à l'égyptien." *Bulletin de la Société de Linguistique de Paris*, 84 (1): 55–80.

Gourevitch, Danielle (2016): "Popular Medicines and Practices in Galen." In: William V. Harris (Ed.): *Popular Medicine in Graeco-Roman Antiquity: Explorations*, 251–71. Leiden: Brill.

Hamilton, J.S. (1986): "Scribonius Largus on the Medical Profession." *Bulletin of the History of Medicine*, 60 (2): 209–16.

Hanson, Ann E., and Monica H. Green (1994): "Soranus of Ephesus: *Methodicorum Princeps*." In: Wolfgang Haase and Hildegard Temporini (Eds): *Aufstieg und Niedergang der römischen Welt: Geschichte und Kultur Roms im Spiegel der neueren Forschung. Teil 2 Principat. Bd.36 Philosophie, Wissenschaften, Technik. Tbd.7 Philosophie (systematische Themen; indirekte Überlieferungen; Allgemeines; Nachträge)*, 968–1075. Berlin-New York: Walter de Gruyter.

Hardy, Gavin, and Laurence Totelin (2016): *Ancient Botany*. London-New York: Routledge.

Harris, William V. (1991): *Ancient Literacy*. Cambridge MA-London: Harvard University Press.

Harris, William V. (Ed.) (2016): *Popular Medicine in Graeco-Roman Antiquity: Explorations*. Leiden-Boston MA: Brill.

Jones-Lewis, Molly Ayn (2012): "Poison: Nature's Argument for the Roman Empire in Pliny the Elder's *Naturalis Historia*." *Classical World*, 106 (1): 51–74.

Joshel, Sandra R. (1986): "Nurturing the Master's Child: Slavery and the Roman Child-Nurse." *Signs*, 12 (1): 3–22.

Keyser, Paul T. (2008): "Antonius 'Root-Cutter'." In: Paul T. Keyser and Georgia L. Irby-Massie (Eds.): *The Encyclopedia of Ancient Natural Scientists: The Greek Tradition and its many Heirs*, 101. London-New York: Routledge.

Korpela, Jukka (1995): "Aromatarii, pharmacopolae, thurarii et ceteri: Zur Sozialgeschichte Roms." In: Philip J. van der Eijk et al. (Eds.): *Ancient Medicine in its Socio-Cultural Context: Papers Read at the Congress held at Leiden University, 13–15 April 1992*, 101–118. Amsterdam and Atlanta: Rodopi.

Long, Pamela O. (2001): *Openness, Secrecy, Authorship: Technical Arts and the Culture of Knowledge from Antiquity to the Renaissance*. Baltimore MD-London: The Johns Hopkins Press.

Michler, M. (1993): "Principis medicus: Antonius Musa." In: Wolfgang Haase and Hildegard Temporini: *Aufstieg und Niedergang der römischen Welt: Geschichte und Kultur Roms im Spiegel der neueren Forschung. Teil 2 Principat. Bd.37, Philosophie, Wissenschaften, Technik. 1. Teilbd, Wissenschaften (Medizin und Biologie)*, 757–785. Berlin-New York: Walter de Gruyter.

Murphy, Trevor (2004): *Pliny the Elder's Natural History: The Empire in the Encylopaedia*. Oxford-New York: Oxford University Press.

Nutton, Vivian (1992): "Healers in the Market Place: Towards a Social History of Graeco-Roman Medicine." In: Andrew Wear (Ed.): *Medicine in Society: Historical Essays*. Cambridge: Cambridge University Press: 15–58.

Nutton, Vivian (1995): "Scribonius Largus, the Unknown Pharmacologist." *Pharmacological Historian*, 25 (1): 5–8.

Phillips, O. (2002): "The Witches' Thessaly." In: Paul Minecki and Marvin Meyer (Eds.): *Magic and Ritual in the Ancient World*, 378–85. Leiden: Brill.

Riddle, John M. (1985): *Dioscorides on Pharmacy and Medicine*. Austin TX: University of Texas Press.

Samama, Evelyne (2006): "*Thaumatopoioi pharmakopôlai*: la singulière image des préparateurs et vendeurs de remèdes dans les textes grecs." In: Franck Collard and Evelyne Samama (Eds.): *Pharmacopoles et apothicaires. Les "pharmaciens" de l'Antiquité au Grand Siècle*, 7–27. Paris: L'Harmattan.

Santoro L'Hoir, Francesca (1992): *The Rhetoric of Gender Terms 'Man', 'Woman', and the Portrayal of Character in Latin Prose*. Leiden: Brill.

Scarborough, John (1987): "Adaptation of Folk Medicines in the Formal Materia Medica of Classical Antiquity." In: John Scarborough (Ed.): *Folklore and Folk Medicine*, 21–32. Madison WI: American Institute of the History of Pharmacy.

Scarborough, John (2008a): "Antiokhos, Paccius." In: Paul T. Keyser and Georgia L. Irby-Massie (Eds.): *The Encyclopedia of Ancient Natural Scientists: The Greek Tradition and its Many Heirs*, 95. London-New York: Routledge.

Scarborough, John (2008b): "Antonius Musa." In: Paul T. Keyser and Georgia L. Irby-Massie (Eds.): *The Encyclopedia of Ancient Natural Scientists: The Greek Tradition and its Many Heirs*, 101. London-New York: Routledge.

Schulze, Christian (1999): *Aulus Cornelius Celsus: Arzt oder Laie? Autor, Konzept und Adressaten der De Medicina libri octo*. Trier: Wissenschaftlicher Verlag.

Schulze, Christian (2001): *Celsus*. Hildesheim-Zurich-New York: Georg Olm Verlag.

Sconocchia, Sergio (1993): "L'opera di Scribonio Largo e la letteratura medica latine del 1 sec. d.C." In: Wolfgang Haase and Hildegard Temporini (Eds.): *Aufstieg und Niedergang der römischen Welt: Geschichte und Kultur Roms im Spiegel der neueren Forschung. Teil 2 Principat. Bd.37, Philosophie, Wissenschaften, Technik. 1. Teilbd, Wissenschaften (Medizin und Biologie)*, 843–922. Berlin-New York: Walter de Gruyter.

Totelin, Laurence M.V. (2004): "Mithradates' Antidote: A Pharmacological Ghost." *Early Science and Medicine*, 9 (1): 1–19.

Totelin, Laurence M.V. (2010): "A Recipe for a Headache: Translating and Interpreting Ancient Greek and Roman Remedies." In: Annette Imhausen and Tanja Pommerening (Eds.): *Writings of Early Scholars in the Ancient Near East, Egypt and Greece: Zur Übersetzbarkeit von Wissenschaftssprachen des Altertums*, 219–37. Berlin-New York: Walter de Gruyter.

Totelin, Laurence M.V. (2016a): "Pharmakopolai: A Re-Evaluation of the Sources." In: William V. Harris (Ed.): *Popular Medicine in Graeco-Roman Antiquity: Explorations*, 65–85. Leiden-Boston MA: Brill.

Totelin, Laurence M.V. (2016b): "The World in a Pill: Local Specialties and Global Remedies in the Graeco-Roman World." In: Rebecca Futo Kennedy et al. (Eds.): *The

Routledge Handbook of Identity and the Environment in the Classical and Medieval World, 151–70. London-New York: Routledge.

Touwaide, Alain (2008): "Andromakhos of Crete (Younger)." In: Paul T. Keyser and Georgia L. Irby-Massie (Eds.): *The Encyclopedia of Ancient Natural Scientists: The Greek Tradition and its Many Heirs*, 79–80. London -New York: Routledge.

Vogt, Sabine (2008): "Drugs and Pharmacology." In: Jim Hankinson (Ed.): *The Cambridge Companion to Galen*, 304–22. Cambridge: Cambridge University Press.

Woolf, Greg (2015): "Ancient Illiteracy?" *Bulletin of the Institute of Classical Studies*, 58 (2): 31–42.

Metaphysics and the Principles of the Demonstrative Sciences: Weak and Strong Knowledge in the Late-Antique Commentary Tradition

Orna Harari

Abstract

In this essay, I examine the implications of the idea that metaphysics is a demonstrative science for late-antique interpretations of Aristotle's account of the principles of demonstration, thereby bringing to light two formulations of the distinction between weak and strong knowledge: One that rests on the distinction between disputable and indisputable knowledge, and the other that rests on the distinction between relative and absolute knowledge. In so doing, I address the question of why the idea that metaphysics is a demonstrative science has consequences for the epistemic worth of the other sciences and show that philosophical considerations alone fail to answer it satisfactorily. In view of this conclusion, I turn to scientific texts from the second and third centuries AD and suggest that this consequence can be better understood as a response to scientists' attempts to appropriate the subject matter of metaphysics. Next, I discuss the different attempts of philosophers to counter this approach and show that they led to weakening the other sciences' epistemic worth in a way that inadvertently cast doubt on the possibility of attaining strong knowledge by demonstrative methods.

1. Introduction

The Elements of Theology, written by the fifth century AD Neoplatonic Philosopher, Proclus, manifests in its form his understanding of the epistemic worth of the primary branch of philosophy, called theology, first philosophy, or metaphysics. Here, Proclus does not address this subject in an exploratory or dialectical way, as Plato and Aristotle did, but adopts a deductive method that resembles Euclid's *Elements*, presenting chains of demonstrations that prove in a descending order of logical priority the principal doctrines of his metaphysics. Placed in the context of Proclus' methodology of science, the *Elements of Theology* is more than an understandable attempt to strengthen metaphysical knowledge by using the method employed in the most rigorous and certain science, i.e., geometry. It involves a significant modification of Aristotle's account of the principles of demonstration that weakens the epistemic worth of the other sciences, by regarding them as resting not on indemonstrable principles, as Aristotle holds, but on evident propositions that scientists assume without demonstration.

In what follows, I examine this consequence of the idea that metaphysics is a demonstrative science, thereby bringing to light two formulations of the distinction between weak and strong knowledge: one that rests on the distinction between disputable and indisputable knowledge, and the other that rests on the distinction between relative and absolute knowledge. In so doing, I address the question of why the idea that metaphysics is a demonstrative science has consequences for the epistemic worth of the other sciences, and show that philosophical considerations alone fail to answer it satisfactorily. In view of this conclusion, I turn to scientific texts from the second and third centuries AD and suggest that this consequence can be better understood as a response to scientists' attempts to appropriate the subject matter of metaphysics. Next, I discuss the philosophers' attempts to counter this approach and show that they led to a weakening of the other sciences' epistemic worth in a way that inadvertently cast doubt on the possibility of attaining strong knowledge by demonstrative methods.

2. Alexander of Aphrodisias on metaphysics as a demonstrative science

Although the *Elements of Theology* is an exceptional work, its underlying assumption that metaphysics is a demonstrative science predates Proclus. It is mentioned in the earliest extant commentary on any of Aristotle's works, Aspasius' commentary on the *Nicomachean Ethics* dated to the mid-second century AD[1] and more elaborately presented in Alexander of Aphrodisias' commentary on Aristotle's *Metaphysics* written in the third century AD, which is, as Dominic O'Meara has shown, the source of Proclus' and his teacher Syrianus' view that metaphysics is a demonstrative science (O'Meara 2012, 41–46). In the latter work, this view appears in two contexts that suggest that the science that Alexander regards as demonstrative is a universal science that studies being in general, and demonstrates the attributes that all things have in common. In the first context, Alexander clarifies Aristotle's claim in *Metaphysics* IV.1, that there is a certain science

---

1 Aspasius, *In ethica Nicomachea* 37.20–21.

(ἐπιστήμη τις), distinct from the specific sciences, which studies one part of being (for example, mathematics), that generally examines (θεωρεῖ) being as being, and its essential attributes (1003a21–22):

He first assumes that there is a certain science about being as being, that is to say, a theoretical (θεωρητική) [science] of being as being and a demonstrative (ἀποδεικτική) [science] of its essential attributes. For any science of anything whatsoever is a demonstrative [science] of the essential attributes that hold for this thing.[2]

In the second passage, he comments on a passage from *Metaphysics* IV.2, in which Aristotle supports his claim that it is the task of the philosopher to study all things, by pointing out that dialectic, too, discusses all things and shares with philosophy its subject matter (1004b19–23):

He says that philosophy differs from dialectic in the manner of [exercising] the faculty [of reasoning]. For both deal with being and its attributes and both are syllogistic, but philosophy has the syllogistic power of demonstrating truths, whereas dialectic is tentative (πειραστική) with regard to truths and syllogistic with regard to reputable opinion. For this reason, the dialectician argues for both sides of an issue and is tentative about the very things about which the philosopher has demonstration and knowledge.[3]

In the first passage above, Alexander does not simply state that the science of being as being is demonstrative, but distinguishes this science's treatment of its subject matter from its treatment of its attributes, saying that it is *theoretical* of being as being and *demonstrative* of its attributes. This distinction also features in the second passage above in which Alexander understands Aristotle's claim that philosophy and dialectic share the same subject as implying that they both deal with being and its attributes. Alexander's stress on this distinction reveals the textual basis upon which his construal of metaphysics as a demonstrative science rests.

The distinction between the theoretical and the demonstrative branches of a science serves Alexander in solving the fourth aporia found in *Metaphysics* III.2, which turns on the question of whether wisdom (σοφία) is a science that studies only substances, or their attributes, too. This question leads to aporia because an affirmative answer entails that this science is demonstrative and that substance, in the sense of the essence (i.e., the definition) of a thing, can be demonstrated, whereas a negative answer leaves us with the question, which Aristotle deems very difficult (παγχάλεπος), of what science studies the attributes of substances (997a25–34). Alexander's distinction between the theoretical and the demonstrative branches of one science solves this aporia, by showing that the assumption that one science studies both substances and their attributes does not entail that substances can be demonstrated because one science can study substances and

---

2 Alexander, *In metaphysica* 239.6–9. All translations are mine.
3 Alexander, *In metaphysica* 260.1–7.

attributes through different methods: it defines substances, and demonstrates their attributes.[4]

Later, in his commentary on this aporia, Alexander uses this distinction in addressing a different problem, i.e., whether sciences whose objects are substances are demonstrative. Here, Alexander argues first that, by taking geometry as an example (977a27–30), Aristotle almost solves the aporia,[5] and then he outlines the full solution. He points out that the distinction between the theoretical and demonstrative branches is found not only in the mathematical sciences whose objects are abstractions, but also in physics whose objects are substances (for example, the cosmos and the sun), and concludes that, if the objects of metaphysics, i.e., primary substances, have a certain accident, the person who studies them will also demonstrate their attributes.[6]

In the light of this interpretation, Alexander's view that metaphysics is a demonstrative science rests on three exegetical assumptions: (1) The fourth aporia turns on the question of whether metaphysics is a demonstrative science; (2) an affirmative answer to this question depends on whether its objects have attributes; and (3) the objects of metaphysics are the primary substances, i.e., the eternal, incorporeal, and unmoved substances.[7] These assumptions entail that, if the primary substances have attributes, the science that studies them is demonstrative, but they do not entail the conclusion that Alexander draws in the above passages, i.e., the science of being as being that shares its subject matter with dialectic is demonstrative, because this universal science does not study the attributes of a specific class of objects, but the attributes that all beings have in common such as one, other, same, prior and posterior, and whole and part.[8] To draw this conclusion, Alexander has to justify his contention in the first passage above that any science of any subject whatsoever is demonstrative, by showing not only that the science of primary substances is demonstrative, but also that a universal science that studies all beings is demonstrative. However, this conclusion is unwarranted on Alexander's own understanding of Aristotle's account of metaphysics as a science.[9]

According to the *Posterior Analytics* I.7, any demonstrative science must have three components: (1) a conclusion; (2) the axioms through which it is proved;

4 Alexander, *In metaphysica* 194.28–33. See also 246.16–21.

5 Alexander, *In metaphysica* 195.13–14.

6 Alexander, *In metaphysica* 195.13–27.

7 Alexander, *In metaphysica* 245.32–246.2; 251.34–36.

8 Alexander, *In metaphysica* 1004a18–19; 1005a12: 16–18. For a more detailed discussion of this problem, see Madigan 1999, 50.

9 For a detailed discussion of Alexander's discrepant accounts of the object metaphysics, see Bonelli 2001, 199–235. For the view that the object of metaphysics is the divine substance, see Merlan 1957, 90–92; Verbeke 1981, 120–122; O'Meara 2012, 40–41. For the view that metaphysics is a universal science, see Genequand 1979.

and (3) an underlying genus (75a39–b1). Following Aristotle's claim that "being" is not an univocal term, but has many senses related to one central sense (1003a33–34), Alexander holds that metaphysics lacks the third component. In his commentary on *Metaphysics* IV.2, he explicitly says that being is not a genus strictly speaking,[10] but a common nature whose instances do not have it in a like manner and to the same degree, as the instances of genera do.[11] In keeping with this account, he describes metaphysics as both primary and universal, saying that, in things that have a common nature to a different degree, the primary instance is also universal because it is the cause of the others.[12] While the description of metaphysics as primary and universal allows metaphysics, as a science that studies one class of objects, i.e., the primary substances, to be demonstrative, it does not warrant the conclusion that it is a universal science that demonstratively studies the attributes that all beings have in common because its object is not a universal genus, as Aristotle's theory of demonstration requires, but a common cause. Alexander is aware of this consequence. In his commentary on *Metaphysics* III.2, he stresses that the subject matter of any science should be a genus, strictly speaking, and not the highest and most common genus from which all things are derived.[13]

The difficulty in understanding the grounds upon which Alexander bases his view that metaphysics is a demonstrative science is indicative of his motivation. Specifically, his choice to present this view precisely in the problematic contexts that imply that metaphysics as a universal science is demonstrative suggests that he attempts not only to secure its status as a science, but also to distinguish its subject matter from the subject matter of other sciences and to subsume them under it. The following examination of scientific texts from the second and third centuries AD offers a plausible explanation for this motivation and prepares the ground for understanding Alexander's account of metaphysics as a universal science.

3. Scientists on philosophy and philosophers

At the end of his monumental work entitled *On the Usefulness of the Parts*, Galen describes the results of his anatomical study as follows:

The work on the usefulness of the parts will truly become the principle of accurate theology, which is a far greater and a far nobler matter than all of medicine. Thus, the work on the usefulness of the parts is serviceable not only to the physician but still more

---

10 Alexander, *In metaphysica* 242.6–8.
11 Alexander, *In metaphysica* 243.33–244.3.
12 Alexander, *In metaphysica* 246.10–12; 266.6–12.
13 Alexander, *In metaphysica* 193.16–20.

to the philosopher who is eager to acquire knowledge of the whole of nature [...]. This is one of the greatest advantages that we gain from this work not as physicians but much better as men who need to know something about the useful power of which some philosophers say that it does not exist at all, let alone providing (προνοεῖσθαι) for animals.[14]

Here, Galen describes his painstaking anatomical study of bodily parts as contributing first and foremost not to his own discipline – medicine – but to philosophy's most important branch, i.e., theology. In his view, this study lays down the foundation for accurate (ἀκριβής) theology and addresses the philosophical questions of whether natural phenomena are governed by a certain power and whether this power is providential. This description places medicine on an equal footing with philosophy, and, at same time, challenges philosophers. It implies that the task of studying the supreme being does not exclusively belong to philosophers, and also that the method that Galen employs in *On the Usefulness of the Parts* leads to accurate knowledge that settles the very problems that philosophers debate.

The greatest and most necessary part of philosophical discourse is that which concerns tranquillity, about which a great many investigations were made and still are made by those pursuing wisdom; and I believe that the investigation of this [subject] by means of arguments will never come to an end. But mechanics, surpassing the teaching of this [subject] through arguments, taught all human-beings to know how to live tranquilly by means of a single and very small part thereof; I mean, of course, the one dealing with so-called artillery construction, through which [human beings] will never be disturbed during a state of peace by the assaults of adversaries and enemies, nor when war is upon them will they ever be disturbed, thanks to the philosophy that artillery construction hands down by means of instruments.[15]

Similarly to Galen, Hero describes his scientific discipline, mechanics, and, more specifically, artillery construction, as a philosophical discipline, and identifies its subject matter with philosophy's ultimate goal, as it was perceived by the Hellenistic philosophical schools, i.e., tranquillity. In so doing, he does not merely state that artillery construction and philosophy share their subject matter, but argues that the former is superior to the latter. He distinguishes "investigation by means of arguments" from "philosophy by means of instruments", saying that the former will never come to an end, whereas the latter is conclusive.[16] This contention calls to mind the argument from disagreement used by sceptics who argued against dogmatic philosophers that their disputes will persist, as Sextus Empiricus

---

14 Galen, *de usu partium*, II.447.22–449.19 Helmreich.

15 Hero, *Belopoiika*, I.1–20 Diels and Schramm.

16 Hero draws a similar distinction in his *Pneumatica*, in which he says that philosophers study pneumatics through arguments, whereas scientists study it through the activity of perceptible things (*Pneumatica*, 2.4–7 Schmidt) and deems the former method plausible and the latter certain (*Pneumatica*, 16.16–26 Schmidt).

says, "as long as water flows and tall trees grow",[17] but Hero's argument differs from the sceptical argument in one crucial respect.[18] Whereas the sceptics regard disagreement as an indication of an epistemological problem that entails a suspension of judgement, Hero regards it as a methodological problem. He holds that philosophical matters can be known with certainty and that philosophical disagreement results merely from the failure of philosophers to study their subject matter by the right method. By this argument, then, Hero challenges philosophers, and not philosophy. He argues that, owing to its method, mechanics leads to conclusive and certain results not only in its own domain, but also in the philosophers' domain, i.e., tranquillity and the happy life.

A similar criticism that turns on metaphysics rather than on ethics, and which specifically appeals to an Aristotelian conception of the sciences appears in the introduction to Ptolemy's *Almagest*. Here, Ptolemy divides theoretical philosophy into three parts: (1) theology that studies the first, invisible, and unmoved cause; (2) physics that studies material and moving objects as well as qualities such as white, hot, sweet, and soft; and (3) mathematics that studies locomotion, shape, number, size, place, and time. This division goes back to Aristotle's *Metaphysics* VI.1 (1026a18–19) but, through his characterisation of the objects of the theoretical parts of philosophy, Ptolemy departs from Aristotle and places mathematics, rather than metaphysics, at the top of this classification:

> From all this, we concluded that the two other genera of the theoretical [part of philosophy] should be called conjecture rather than knowledge – the theological due to its complete invisibility and incomprehensibility, and the physical because of the instability and unclearness of matter. As a result, [we resolved], on account of this, never to hope that philosophers will agree about these [subjects] and that only mathematics, if one approaches it rigorously, can give to its practitioners sure and indisputable [knowledge] because its demonstration is carried out by means of the most indisputable method of arithmetic and geometry [...] Further, [mathematics] contributes to the other [two parts of theoretical philosophy] no less than these [parts] themselves. For this is the most [suitable science] to pave the way to theology, because only [this science] can guess well at the unmoved and separate activity from the nearest activity [manifested in] the attributes, locomotion and order of motions, that belong to substances that are, on the one hand, perceptible and move and are moved, and on the other hand, eternal and unaffected.[19]

Ptolemy's view is closer to the sceptical stance than Hero's in excluding the possibility of attaining indisputable knowledge in theology and physics, but, like Hero, he holds that mathematicians fare better than philosophers in studying philosophy's subject matter. In Ptolemy's view, only astronomy that studies the

---

17 For example, *PH* II.37.
18 It is unclear whether the argument from disagreement implies that dogmatic philosophers' debates are unresolvable. For this question and the relevant secondary literature, see Machuca 2011.
19 Ptolemy, *Alamagest*. I.1.6–7 Heiberg.

heavenly bodies and their motions by means of the indisputable demonstrative method used in arithmetic and geometry can lead to better conjectures about the object of metaphysics, i.e., the invisible, unmoved and divine substance.[20]

These different accounts of the relationship between the sciences and philosophy have one feature in common. They seek to appropriate the subject matter of philosophy on the grounds that the scientific method leads to more secure knowledge in the domains that philosophers study, but fail to attain indisputable and conclusive results. Thus, the challenge that they pose to philosophers is not whether a scientific or demonstrative method is applicable to philosophical inquiries, but whether philosophy is the discipline that should study ethical or metaphysical matters. Alexander's interpretation of the fourth aporia cannot adequately counter this challenge. It shows that metaphysics as the science that studies primary substances is demonstrative, but it does not imply that it is a philosophical science. After all, Galen and Ptolemy conclude from a similar claim that medicine and astronomy are the sciences that lead to more accurate knowledge of divine substances.[21] The view that metaphysics, as a universal science, is demonstrative addresses this challenge better. It assigns to philosophy a subject matter that none of the sciences study, thereby re-drawing the boundary between philosophy and the other sciences that the above accounts threaten to cross. It also secures the autonomy and superiority of metaphysics, which Ptolemy questions. It implies not only that metaphysics is on a par with the other sciences because it employs the same indisputable method used in the sciences, but also that the other sciences depend on metaphysics because being a universal science of all beings it studies their subject matter and examines questions that they do not address. Admittedly, these considerations do not ascertain beyond doubt that the above accounts directly motivated Alexander's interpretation, but the following examination of his commentary on *Metaphysics* IV shows that he addresses the questions that they raise. It also prepares the ground for understanding why the view that metaphysics is a demonstrative science has consequences for later thinkers' accounts of the principles of demonstration.

---

20 For these and other similar passages as representing a single tradition, see Feke 2014.
21 Alexander is aware of this challenge. In the introduction to his commentary on the *Prior Analytics*, he stresses that geometry is not the first and principal part of philosophy, although one of its branches, i.e., astronomy, deals with divine objects. Alexander, *In analytica priora* 3.30–31.

4. Alexander and Themistius on metaphysics and the principles of demonstration

In his commentary on *Metaphysics* IV.3, Alexander describes the relationship between philosophy and the sciences as follows:

He says that the first philosopher enquires about the axioms not as demonstrating one of them (for, as he says, the principles of demonstrations are indemonstrable) but [the first philosopher asks] what their nature is, how they come to be in us, how one should use them and all the other [questions] about them discussed in the *Posterior Analytics*. For just as the account of the axioms belongs to the philosopher, so does the account of demonstration; it is not about this or that demonstration, but about what demonstration generally is and how it is carried out. For demonstration is not [a subject] that belongs to one particular genus of [the genera] that falls under the sciences, but demonstration in each science is in respect of the proper [genera] of the science and each [science] uses [it] hypothetically, taking from the philosopher [the answer to the question] of how one should demonstrate.[22]

The characterisation of metaphysics as a universal science whose subject matter is distinct from that of the other sciences serves Alexander in securing its methodological superiority to the other sciences. He views metaphysics as a regulative discipline that determines the methodological rules that the other sciences should follow: it instructs them how to use the axioms, how to demonstrate, and, as he says later, how to find the suitable demonstrative premises, and how to combine them properly.[23] By this argument, Alexander addresses the contention that the sciences can contribute to, as Galen and Ptolemy claims, or even replace, as Hero claims, metaphysics or ethics, because the scientific method leads to more accurate or certain knowledge. He shares with the scientist their view of the worth of their method, but stresses that they receive it from the philosophers, and not the other way round as Hero and Ptolemy hold. At the end of this passage, he takes this claim one step further and characterises the sciences as hypothetical, but leaves the exact significance of this characterisation unclear. The term "hypothetical" suggests that the dependence of the sciences on philosophy qualifies their epistemic worth, but here, Alexander does not explain why the use of a method that another science studies and develops has consequences for the knowledge attained through this method. In another passage found in his commentary on *Metaphysics* IV.2, Alexander offers a more promising argument for his characterisation of the sciences as hypothetical:

When he [sc. Aristotle] says that the study of these [sc. the attributes of being as being] does not belong to the geometer, he adds 'except hypothetically' (1005a12–13); this is because the geometer, too, uses them. Surely, he does not prove what each of them is, but

---

22 Alexander, *In metaphysica* 266.19–28.
23 Alexander, *In metaphysica* 268.2–6.

assumes and takes [them] from the philosopher. For example, when he assumes that similar magnitudes are those whose sides are proportional, he uses this [definition] not as proven but as posited by him, and similarly he uses [the terms] 'equal', 'identical', and the others. And the arithmetician, too, assumes that a perfect number is equal to all its constituents and examines which numbers have this [attribute], but generally about the perfect he knows nothing. For knowledge of these [attributes], i.e., what each of them is, belongs to the philosopher alone.[24]

Through this account of the relationship between philosophy and the other sciences, Alexander comes closer to qualifying the latter's epistemic worth. He holds that only the philosopher knows the definitions of the attributes that the other sciences study, whereas scientists merely use and assume them. On closer examination, however, this account is strained. Alexander's distinction between using and assuming, on the one hand, and proving and knowing, on the other hand, suggests that the philosopher has proven knowledge of the definitions that scientists merely use and assume, but this suggestion is incompatible with Alexander's interpretation of the fourth aporia. The above geometrical example implies that the philosopher proves that similar magnitudes are those whose sides are proportional, whereas the geometer assumes this definition, but in Alexander's view, the study of definitions belongs to the theoretical and not to the demonstrative branch of each science because definitions cannot be proved.[25] The arithmetical example avoids this difficulty. It implies that the philosopher knows the general definitions of *terms* that arithmeticians use and not that he proves the *definitions* used in arithmetic, but this example is also problematical. It gives rise to the question of why the mathematician's ignorance of the general definition of the term "perfect" qualifies his knowledge of the definition of perfect numbers where this term is used metaphorically.[26] These difficulties notwithstanding, Alexander's attempt to secure the epistemic superiority of metaphysics through the distinction between proving and using the principles which shaped the interpretation of Aristotle's theory of demonstration.

In the *Posterior Analytics* I.9, Aristotle says that demonstrations should proceed from the proper principles of a given science, stressing that true, indemonstrable, and immediate premises that do not meet this requirement do not yield knowledge. Themistius, the author of the earliest extant interpretation of Aristotle's *Posterior Analytics* dated to the fourth century AD, understands this claim as qualifying the epistemic worth of the sciences. He concludes from it that no science demonstrates its own principles, adding that principles that are posited as evident (ἐναργεῖς) are not principles, and that a person who knows (ὁ εἰδώς) these principles knows their consequences better than a person who merely uses (ὁ χρώμενος)

---

24 Alexander, *In metaphysica* 264.8–17.
25 Alexander, *In metaphysica* 194.26–27.
26 Indeed, in *Metaphysics* V.16, in which Aristotle discusses the different meanings of the term "perfect" the mathematical sense is not mentioned.

them.[27] In view of these conclusions, he raises the question of whether the principles of the sciences are demonstrable:

> Is it in no way possible to demonstrate the geometrical principles, the arithmetical principles, the musical principles, and the principles of the other sciences? Or it is possible, but not by the very science that uses them as principles (for this, science cannot assume other principles of the principles) but [they can be demonstrated] by a certain other [science] higher than all the others, under which all the sciences [are subsumed]. For, in this way, it will be possible to use these consequent [principles]; that is, if all of them will be subsumed under this [science], just as optics is subsumed under geometry. For it is inconceivable [to do so] in another way, if indeed demonstration proceeds from proper and cognate [principles]. And this [science] is the much-famed wisdom, and is worthy of the name of science strictly speaking and the best science, which studies the first causes of everything and the highest causes, for the highest causes are those of which there is no cause.[28]

Here, Themistius develops Alexander's account of the relationship between metaphysics and the other sciences, and clearly states that metaphysics is the supreme science that demonstrates the principles of the other sciences. In so doing, he revises Aristotle's claim, found in this chapter, that the theorems of a subordinate science (e.g., harmonics) can be proved by a higher science (e.g., arithmetic) because the latter provides the explanation (τὸ διότι) of the fact (τὸ ὅτι) that the former studies (76a11–12). He understands this claim as implying that the higher science proves the principles of its subordinate science, he applies this interpretation to all sciences, and consequently subordinates them to metaphysics.[29] Through this interpretation, Themistius deprives the sciences of the autonomy that Aristotle's theory of demonstration grants them. Having argued that scientists use, but do not know, their proper principles, he stresses that they can use these principles because the sciences are subordinate to metaphysics.

The immediate consequence of this account is that the principles of demonstration are not indemonstrable, as Aristotle holds, but evident premises that scientists can use because metaphysics demonstrates them. In his paraphrase of Aristotle's discussion of the principles of demonstration in the *Posterior Analytics* I.2, Themistius comes close to drawing this conclusion. He introduces cognitive considerations absent from Aristotle's account of the principles, characterising the axioms as known to everyone by nature, the hypotheses as given by an expert (τίθεσθαι παρὰ τοῦ τεχνίτου) but familiar (γνώριμοι) to the learner, and postulates as neither clear (σαφεῖς) nor familiar to the learner.[30] In propounding this view, The-

---

27 Themistius, *In analytica posteriora*. 22.10–16.

28 Themistius, *In analytica posteriora*. 22.16–26.

29 Aristotle's distinction between demonstration of the reason why and demonstration of the fact is a distinction between explanatory and non-explanatory proofs of the same proposition; it does not imply that the former proves the principles of the latter.

30 Themistius, In *analytica posteriora*. 7.1–28. In the *Posterior Analytics* I.2 Aristotle distinguishes three types of principles: (1) axioms that anyone who intends to learn something should know; (2)

mistius borrows elements from the *Posterior Analytics* I.10 where Aristotle discusses provable premises called hypotheses in relation to the learner, and postulates (76b27–34). Following this discussion, he lists the postulates among the principles of demonstration and classifies the principles according to the knower's cognitive attitude to them.[31] Yet, at the end of his account, he carefully distinguishes the demonstrable premises discussed in the *Posterior Analytics* I.10 from the principles discussed above:

> Now, certain hypotheses and certain postulates are presently [sc. in the *Posterior Analytics* I.10] said to be neither immediate nor indemonstrable, but require demonstration and are taken without demonstration in the arguments. And these are not hypotheses and postulates, strictly speaking, but only in relation to the person who presents and grants them. However, demonstrations are certainly not from these but from those that were defined above.[32]

Like Alexander, Themistius holds the rope at both ends. He considers the possibility that metaphysics demonstrates the principles of the other sciences, and, at the same time, adheres to Aristotle's view that the principles of demonstration are indemonstrable. In propounding this view, however, he goes beyond Alexander. He weakens the epistemic worth of the principles of demonstration, by denying evident premises the status of principles and qualifying the knowledge attained through them. This view paves the way to Proclus' construal of the sciences as hypothetical.

5. Proclus on the sciences as hypothetical

In the second prologue to his commentary on the first book of Euclid's *Elements*, Proclus presents the following classification of the principles of demonstration:

> Next he [sc. Euclid] divides the common principles themselves into hypotheses, postulates, and axioms, for these differ by all means from each other, and axiom, postulate, and

---

hypotheses that state that something is or is not the case; and (3) definitions that state what the thing is (72a16–24).

31 A similar classification of the principles features in Philoponus' commentary on the *Posterior Analytics* (especially 34.5–36.17 Wallies). Richard McKirahan traces Philoponus' account to Proclus and understands it as a confused attempt to reconcile Aristotle's account of the principles with Euclid's *Elements*. See McKirahan 2009, 230–233. This interpretation is problematic for two reasons. First, as we saw, Philoponus' account of the principles predates Proclus and second, it may explain the addition of the postulates to the list of principles but not the introduction of epistemic considerations. The present study shows that confused or not, this account reflects a deliberate attempt to weaken the principles of demonstration that aims to secure the superiority of metaphysics to the other sciences.

32 Themistius, *In analytica posteriora* 7.29–33.

hypothesis are not the same, as the angelic Aristotle somewhere says. But when the proposition admitted into the rank of a principle is familiar (γνώριμον) to the learner and credible in itself (καθ' αὐτὸ πιστόν), such a proposition is an axiom [...] But when the listener does not have a self-credible notion of the thing said, but he nevertheless posits (τίθεται) and concedes (συγχωρεῖ) the assumed [proposition], such a proposition is a hypothesis [...] And when again the said thing is unknown and, although one does not concede it, one nevertheless posits it, then, he says, we call it a postulate.[33]

Like Themistius, Proclus understands Aristotle's account of the principles of demonstration in the light of the *Posterior Analytics* I.10. He adds the postulates to the list of principles, appeals to the learner's cognitive attitude to the principles, and regards the axioms as known and the postulates as unknown to the learner. His account of the hypotheses differs from that of Themistius. Whereas in Themistius' view, the hypotheses, although received from an expert, are familiar to the learner, in Proclus' view, they are assumed and conceded. This view does not imply that the hypotheses are mere assumptions; they are not merely posited, as the postulates are, but also conceded, i.e., accepted as true.[34] While it is far from clear whether and how conceded principles differ from Themistius' familiar principles, the absence of the terms "evident" or "familiar" from Proclus' account is informative.[35] It reflects his attempt to weaken the principles of the other sciences, thereby avoiding the questions that Themistius leaves open: how evident principles differ from known principles, and why knowledge based upon the former falls short of knowledge based upon the latter. The following passage from the second prologue to Proclus' commentary on the *Elements* brings to light the consequences of this view:

Since we say that this science of geometry is hypothetical and proves, from definite principles, the consequent propositions – for there is one un-hypothetical science and the other sciences receive the principles from it – he who arranges the elements in geometry should present separately the principles of the science and separately the conclusions that follow from them, and give no account of the principles but of the [propositions] that follow from the principles. For no science proves (ἀποδείκνυσιν) its own principles or pre-

---

33 Proclus, *In Euclidis*: 76.4–20.

34 Gregory MacIsaac understands this passage as implying the seemingly contradictory view that the principles of demonstrations are both hypothetical and self-evident and therefore argues that in the above passage Proclus does not express his own view (MacIsaac 2014, 50–52). However, in this passage Proclus expresses the same view that MacIsaac ascribes to him, i.e., that hypotheses are not merely assumed (MacIsaac 2014, 69 and 74). Further, the assumption that the principles are both hypothetical and evident is not even seemingly contradictory. As we saw above, in the commentary tradition on the *Posterior Analytics* evident premises are not indemonstrable principles but assumptions posited without demonstration.

35 In the first prologue to his commentary on the *Elements*, Proclus stresses that the mathematician is not ignorant of the proper principles of his science and characterises mathematics as γνωριστική (Proclus, *In Euclidis*: 32.5, 16).

sents an argument about them, but regards them as self-credible, and within this science they are more evident than their consequences.[36]

Here, Proclus justifies Themistius' view that the other sciences are subordinate to metaphysics on different grounds. Whereas Themistius focuses on the onto-logical dependence of the principles of the other sciences on higher principles, but retains their epistemological priority, by viewing them as evident or familiar, Proclus weakens their epistemic worth. He adds to his characterisation of the principles as self-credible the reservation that they are more evident than their consequences, thereby suggesting that they are not evident strictly speaking, but only in comparison to other propositions. Through this account, Proclus avoids the ambiguity that prevented Themistius from drawing the conclusion that the principles of the other sciences are demonstrable. He does not weaken the other sciences by arguing, as Themistius does, that evident principles are not principles strictly speaking. Rather, he weakens the principles themselves, arguing that they are not evident strictly speaking, but relatively to other propositions.

Proclus' account of the relationship between metaphysics and the other sci-ences differs from Themistius' account in another respect. In subordinating the other sciences to metaphysics, he does not appeal to Aristotle's account of sub-ordinate sciences but to Plato's claim in the *Republic* VI that the starting-points of the sciences are not truly first principles but hypotheses (511b5). In so doing, he modifies Plato's view. First, he does not regard the hypotheses upon which the sciences are based as stepping-stones (ἐπιβάσεις) that lead to the un-hypothetical principle, as Plato does, but holds that the highest science gives the other sciences their principles, and, second, he describes as un-hypothetical not the principle of the highest science but the highest science itself. The significance of this inter-pretation becomes clear from the passage above. There, Proclus appeals to the distinction between the hypothetical sciences and the un-hypothetical science in explaining the *Elements'* axiomatic-deductive structure. He says that, since geom-etry is a hypothetical science, the geometer should clearly distinguish the princi-ples of his science from the conclusions that follow from them. This view also finds expression in the difference between Proclus' two elementary works: the *Elements of Theology* and the *Elements of Physics*. The former is not an axiomatic-deductive work. It does not proceed from a list of principles to the propositions proven from them, but immediately opens with a demonstration of the proposi-tion "Every manifold participates in unity in some way". By contrast, the *Elements of Physics* has, in a way, an axiomatic-deductive structure; it opens with a list of definitions and then turns to the proofs. This structural difference reflects Pro-clus' view of the difference between metaphysics and the other sciences. The former, being a metaphysical work, is un-hypothetical, and, hence, does not posit

---

36 Proclus, *In Euclidis*: 75.6–18.

first principles, whereas the latter, dedicated to a subordinate science, i.e., physics, is hypothetical, and, hence, assumes, but does not prove, a set of first principles. Thus, in distinguishing metaphysics from the other sciences in terms of the distinction between un-hypothetical and hypothetical science, Proclus offers a fundamentally different conception of metaphysics; in his view, it is a superior science, not because it is based upon the highest principle, but because it is independent from any principle.

Although Proclus' conception of metaphysics is different from his predecessors' conceptions, it takes its cue from Themistius' account of the principles of demonstration. Following Hellenistic philosophers, Themistius introduced into Aristotle's theory of demonstration epistemological considerations and classified the principles of demonstration according to the knower's attitude, viewing certain principles as known by nature, others as evident, and yet others as mere assumptions. However, unlike Hellenistic philosophers, he does not use these epistemological considerations for guaranteeing strong knowledge, but for weakening the other sciences on the grounds that the knowledge that they produce is relative to what appears to the knower as evident or worthy of consent. The conception of knowledge on which this view rests is different from the conception on which the scientists' criticism of philosophers and Hellenistic epistemology rests. Whereas the latter distinguishes strong knowledge from weak knowledge in terms of the distinction between indisputable and disputable knowledge, Themistius takes the first step towards distinguishing these grades of knowledge in terms of the distinction between absolute and relative knowledge. He regards knowledge based upon evident principles as weaker than knowledge based upon demonstrated principles, but fails to secure the epistemic superiority of metaphysics. He holds that it is based upon the highest principle but does not explain how it yields stronger knowledge, given that both this principle and the evident principles of science are assumed without demonstration. In regarding metaphysics as an un-hypothetical science, Proclus avoids this question. He holds that metaphysics is epistemologically superior to the other sciences, in yielding absolute knowledge that does not depend at all on the knower's cognitive attitude or consent to principles.[37]

Apparently, this account gives the ultimate reply to the scientists' criticism of philosophers. Whereas Alexander argues that the sciences depend on metaphysics for their method and definitions. but does not explain how this dependence weakens scientific knowledge, and Themistius considers the possibility that metaphysics demonstrates the principles of the other sciences, but adheres to Aris-

---

37 Proclus' teacher Syrianus offers a clearer formulation of this view: "And those who specialise in nature, the mathematician, and the first philosopher ought to use [the essential attributes]; the former on the basis of faith (πιστευτικῶς), whereas only the first philosopher [uses them] scientifically (ἐπιστατικῶς) and intellectually (νοερῶς)." (Syrianus, *In metaphysica* 6.4–6)

totle's view that the principles of the other sciences are immediate and indemonstrable, Proclus unambiguously holds that metaphysics is epistemologically superior to the other sciences. By viewing the other sciences as hypothetical, he regards their principles as demonstrable, and weakens their epistemic worth on the ground that they depend on what appears to the knower as evident or worthy of consent.

However, like his predecessors, Proclus fails, in effect, to establish the epistemic superiority of metaphysics. The structural distinction between hypothetical or axiomatic-deductive sciences and the un-hypothetical deductive science does not amount to an epistemic difference. In as much as Proclus adheres to the idea that metaphysics is a demonstrative science, he is bound to base his proofs upon assumptions, even though he does not present them separately from their consequences. Accordingly, his notion of un-hypothetical science does not free metaphysical knowledge from the knower's consent to assumptions, but if anything, casts doubt on the idea that metaphysics can be a demonstrative science because it sets an ideal that no discursive method can attain. Damascius, the last head of the Platonic school of Athens, draws this conclusion. In his metaphysical treatise *Puzzles and Solutions Concerning the First Principles*, he says that the most venerable principle must be incomprehensible (ἀληπτός) and likens our soul's attempt to grasp it to walking in void (κενεμβατεῖν).[38] In keeping with this view, he no longer pursues the idea that metaphysics is a demonstrative science but adopts an aporetic approach and presents arguments for conflicting views; for example, if the principle is absolute, it cannot serve as a principle or a cause of something; and if it is a principle or cause of something, it is not absolute.[39] Thus, rather than establishing the epistemic superiority of metaphysics to the other sciences, Proclus' too strong conception of knowledge exposes philosophers once again to the argument from disagreement.[40]

References

Primary sources

Alexander of Aphrodisias:

Alexandri Aphrodisiensis in Aristotelis metaphysica commentaria, edidit M. Hayduck (Commentaria in Aristotelem Graeca 1). Berlin: Reimer, 1891.

---

38 Damascius, *Traité des premiers principes*: 7.18–8.5.

39 Damascius, *Traité des premiers principes*: 2.9–20.

40 Damascius is not a sceptic. Although, in his view, discursive methods do not lead to absolute knowledge, they can lead us through indications (δι' ἐνδείξεις) to what lies beyond their limits (i 8.12–20 Westerink and Combès). See O'Meara 2012, 52.

Alexandri Aphrodisiensis in Aristotelis analyticorum priorum librum i commentarium, edidit M. Wallies (Commentaria in Aristotelem Graeca 2.1). Berlin: Reimer, 1883.

Aspasius:

Aspasii in ethica Nicomachea quae supersunt commentaria, edidit G. Heylbut (Commentaria in Aristotelem Graeca 19.1). Berlin: Reimer, 1889.

Damascius:

Damascius, Traité des premiers principes. Texte établi par L.G. Westerink, traduit par J. Combès. Vol. 1. Paris: Les Belles Lettres. 1986.

Galen:

Galeni de usu partium libri XVII, edidit G. Helmreich. Vol. 2. Amsterdam: Hakkert, 1968.

Hero of Alexandria:

Herons Belopoiika (Schrift vom Geschützbau). Griechisch und Deutsch von H. Diels und E. Schramm (Abhandlungen der Königlich Preussischen Akademie der Wissenschaften, Jahrgang 1918, Philosophisch-Historische Klasse Nr. 2). Berlin: Verlag der Königlichen Preussischen Akademie der Wissenschaften, 1918.
Heronis Alexandrini opera quae supersunt omnia, edidit W. Schmidt. Vol. 1. Leipzig: Teubner, 1899.

Philoponus:

Ioannis Philoponi in Aristoteles analytica posteriora commentaria cum anonymo in librum ii, edidit M. Wallies (Commentaria in Aristotelem Graeca 13.3). Berlin: Reimer, 1909.

Proclus:

Proclus: Elements of Theology. A Revised text with Translation, Introduction and Commentary by E.R. Dodds. Oxford: Clarendon Press, 1963.
Procli Diadochi in primum Euclidis elementorum librum commentarii, edidit G. Friedlein. Leipzig: Teubner 1873.

Ptolemy:

Claudii Ptolemaei opera quae extant omnia, edidit J.L. Heiberg. Vol. 1.1. Leipzig: Teubner, 1898.

Sextus Empiricus:

Sexti Empirici opera, edidit H. Mutschmann. Vol. 1. Leipzig: Teubner, 1912.

Syrianus:

Syriani in metaphysica commentaria, edidit W. Kroll (Commentaria in Aristotelem Graeca 6.1). Berlin: Reimer, 1902.

Themistius:

Themistii analyticorum posteriorum paraphrasis, edidit M. Wallies (Commentaria in Aristotelem Graeca 5.1). Berlin: Reimer, 1900.

Secondary literature

Bonelli, Maddalena (2014): *Alessandro di Afrodisia e la metafisica come scienza dimostrativa*. Napoli: Bibliopolis.

Feke, Jacqueline (2014): "Meta-mathematical Rhetoric: Hero and Ptolemy against the Philosophers." *Historia Mathematica*, 41: 261–276.

Genequand, Charles (1979): "L'object de la métaphysique selon Alexandre d'Aphrodisias." *Museum Helveticum*, 36: 48–57.

Machuca, Diego E. (2011): "The Pyrrhonian Argument from Possible Disagreement." *Archiv für Geschichte der Philosophie*, 93: 148–161.

MacIsaac, D. Gregory (2014): "Geometrical First Principles in Proclus' Commentary on the First Book of Euclid's Elements." *Phronesis*, 59: 44–98.

Madigan, Arthur (Translation & commentary) (1999): *Aristotle: Metaphysics Books B and K 1–2*, Oxford: Oxford University Press.

McKirahan, Richard (2009): "Philoponus' Account of Scientific Principles in his Commentary on Aristotle's Posterior Analytics." *Documenti e studi sulla tradizione filosofica medievale*, 10: 211–263.

Merlan, Philip (1957): "Metaphysik: Name und Gegenstand." *Journal of Hellenic Studies*, 77: 87–92.

O'Meara, Dominic J. (2012): "The Transformation of Metaphysics in Late Antiquity." In: G.T. Doolan (Ed.): *The Science of Being as Being: Metaphysical Investigations*, 36–52. Washington DC: The Catholic University of America Press.

Verbeke, Gérard (1981): "Aristotle's Metaphysics Viewed by the Ancient Commentators." In: Dominic J. O'Meara (Ed.): *Studies in Aristotle*, 107–127. Washington DC: Catholic University of America Press.

Comment: Weak Knowledge in the History and Philosophy of Ancient Science: Trajectories of Further Studies

Annette Imhausen

Abstract

The analysis of "weak knowledge" which was undertaken in several projects of the CRC 1095 has proven an interesting line of enquiry for the history of science in all periods. However, it is especially profitable for the history of ancient science, as it can, on the one hand, and like in its modern counterparts, be applied to developments in specific scientific disciplines. Here, the analysis, according to the model of a variety of ways in which knowledge can be called weak (epistemic, social, practical) that was developed in the History of Science project A06 of the CRC, can be shown to be equally fruitful for the analysis of ancient knowledge. On the other hand, however, the concept of weakness with regard to knowledge can also be used for a critical reflection of the historiographical development that the history of ancient science has undergone since its beginnings and thus reveal its Eurocentric and Orientalist weaknesses, which – although first criticised decades ago – have proven to be surprisingly persistent. This analysis ultimately leads to another old, but not yet satisfactorily answered, question, namely, "What are the specific characteristics of *scientific* knowledge?". The attempt to answer this question (which, historically, can only be raised for specific periods and cultures), from an ancient point of view may provide new ideas for addressing the demarcation problem in later periods.

1. Introduction

The aspect of weak knowledge is of special concern to those historians of science who work on ancient texts. Compared to studies of later bodies of knowledge (weak or strong), the situation that a researcher finds himself or herself in, is weakened from the outset by at least two issues in which research conditions are different from those of researchers focusing on more recent periods. First, the available source material is usually very restricted, and the numbers of extant sources easy to overview. What sources are still extant is often dependant on the vagaries of preservation rather than importance or relevance in ancient times.[1] In addition, the available sources are usually not distributed equally over the period in which an ancient culture existed, but tend to be concentrated in specific periods (and places) leaving the researcher practically without any evidence for other times (or places). Second, the historiographical treatment that ancient science, and, in particular, some pre-Greek science, has suffered at the hands of modern researchers points to a methodological weakness that was (and, in part, still is) a problem in the history of science that should be addressed.

It is often stressed how much ancient science differs from its modern successor.[2] The contributions on weak knowledge pertaining to the ancient periods in this volume touch upon several of these aspects, for example, the question of authorship (Laurence Totelin) or what counts as scientific knowledge (Daryn Lehoux), and how it is argued (Orna Harari). In addition, this commentary hopes to indicate some further directions for research about ancient knowledge which can be illuminated using the framework of weak knowledge. In exploring these possibilities, and the contributions on more recent weaknesses of knowledge in this volume, it is to be hoped that a picture emerges that diverges from the traditional simplistic view, i.e., that strength of knowledge simply grows with time. In fact, as is presented by Moritz Epple in the introduction to this volume, several types of weaknesses can be differentiated and discerned in individual periods and circumstances. The study of these weaknesses may even bring to light not only *differences between*, but also *similarities bridging* both times and cultures, and thereby help to overcome the usual anachronistic prejudice of modern scientists as well as some historians of modern science against earlier scientific knowledge, which has long since been recognised (for example, Sommer et al. 2017, 8–10), but is still not extinct (thus, the contributions for

---

1 This is not supposed to argue that relevance in ancient times had no bearing at all on what is extant – the *Tale of Sinuhe*, for example, was obviously a much read and copied literary text in ancient Egypt for at least 750 years (Parkinson 1997, 21), as is suggested by the comparatively large number of extant copies (four papyrus copies from the Middle Kingdom and some twenty-eight later copies; see Parkinson 1997, 26). However, the fact that we have less extant copies of other literary texts (e.g., only four Middle Kingdom papyri for the *Tale of the Eloquent Peasant*) does not necessarily imply that it was less popular (there is evidence that the *Tale of the Eloquent Peasant* was still quoted in the Ramesside Period, see Parkinson 1997, 57). For the vagaries of preservation, see also the medical text Louvre E32847 mentioned later in this contribution).

2 While the basic statement is clearly valid, the way that this was used in the history of science often implied a depreciation of ancient science. In the history of mathematics, Karine Chemla has exemplified this with "mathematical proofs" (Chemla 2012). Francesca Rochberg has taken up this "prejudice" and used it in her latest book as a point of departure: "The aim of this book is to raise and explore questions about observing and interpreting, theorizing and calculating what we think of as natural phenomena in a world in which there was no articulated sense of nature in our terms, no reference or word for it." (Rochberg 2016, 1).

ancient science in Sommer et al. 2017, still adhere to the "traditional" disciplines based upon modern science for the ancient periods).[3]

2. Weakness of ancient scientific texts

The research programme of the CRC 1095 investigates the weaknesses of collections of knowledge and how these weaknesses affected their further development. Project A06 has developed a finer structure for this research question, differentiating weakness into epistemological, practical, and social categories. As research in project A03 has confirmed, all of these are relevant, even where ancient scientific knowledge is concerned. This differentiation into the aforementioned categories also reflects the results that were obtained during the past fifty years in the history of science, namely, that the development of knowledge is usually complex, involving theoretical developments as well as practical and social elements.[4] With regard to ancient scientific texts, the analysis of the individual areas of weaknesses can also be used fruitfully, as the contributions of Harari, Lehoux, and Totelin in this volume exemplify. In addition, the analysis of the past historiography also reveals weaknesses that should be addressed in future research.

2.1. The source situation

Written sources constitute the foundations of the history of science of all periods. The situation concerning the availability of written sources is very different for

---

3 This criticism is valid for my own contribution in that volume as well as for the section on antiquity, in which astrology and alchemy are referred to as border areas (*"Grenzbereiche"*), see Sommer et al. 2017, 125. The awareness that ancient science has not (yet) received an appropriate treatment has been criticised several times in the past (examples from the area of mathematics included Unguru 1975; Robson 1999, 3; Cuomo 2001, 1–2; Høyrup 2002, 8; Imhausen 2003a, 11–12), which has prompted a series of publications (for mathematics, see, for example, the source book by Katz 2007, and the following individual studies by Robson 2008, Plofker 2009, and Imhausen 2016) and has since found recognition in overviews such as Sommer et al. 2017. However, this awareness has so far not led to changes in the treatment of ancient science; thus, Sommer et al. 2017, still confines the areas of ancient sciences covered to those that were once prompted by respective modern successors. The historiography of ancient science has undergone and still is undergoing a development to recognise what is part of the field (for an early attempt in this direction for ancient Mesopotamia, see Ritter 1989a).

4 While this general statement is, at this point, probably uncontroversial in the academic field of the history of science, what is still not agreed (and possibly not homogeneous) are the roles and the significance of the individual aspects. For an overview of individual lines of enquiry and references to further literature, see Chalmers 2013, and Sommer et al. 2017, 20–106.

ancient cultures compared to more recent periods, but it also differs significantly between ancient Egypt, Mesopotamia and ancient Greece (Imhausen and Pommerening 2010, 1–10). Many classical ancient scientific texts were translated from Greek into Syriac during the sixth century AD, and into Arabic during the eighth and nineth centuries, and from Arabic and Greek into Latin especially from the eleventh until the fourteenth century, thereby providing an unbroken line of tradition.[5] In contrast, the knowledge transmitted by Egyptian and Mesopotamian sources was not available to us until the re-discovery of their script and grammar in the early nineteenth century.[6] Then, the first scholars working on the newly discovered scientific texts of Egypt or Mesopotamia were faced with a technical vocabulary of an unknown scientific culture, which was initially treated from an anachronistic modern point of view, until, at least in some aspects, an emic perspective could be gained. However, even after over 100 years of work on Egyptian and Mesopotamian science, their status and concepts remain not fully understood (Imhausen and Pommerening 2016, 1–13).

As a consequence of the choice of writing material (clay tablets in Mesopotamia and papyrus in ancient Egypt), the source situation is often weaker for Egypt than for its contemporary fellow culture Mesopotamia. This fragmentation of available texts for ancient Egypt is evident, on the one hand, from the number of texts of a certain kind, for example, the earliest Egyptian mathematical texts (written in hieratic) originate from the Middle Kingdom, and only half a dozen hieratic texts are extant. They hold approximately 100 problems and some tables from which to re-construct Egyptian mathematics (for a list of these and their description, see Imhausen 2016, 63–69). The consequences of these limitations for assessing ancient scientific disciplines cannot be under-estimated, as the recent publication of a new medical text (Louvre E32847) has demonstrated with its section on the mummification of high ranking officials of the royal court (Bardinet 2018, 211–226). Before the publication of this papyrus, indigenous information about Egyptian embalming methods was obtained using their products, mummies, as well as ritual texts from the context of the embalming process (Bardinet 2018, 211), although the most informative texts were those by the Greek authors who wrote about Egyptian mummification, namely, Herodotus (*Histories* II, 85–88) and Diodorus Siculus (*The Library of History* I, 91). Papyrus Louvre E32847 not only contains information about the substances and practices used in embalming, but also indicates the medical context in which the knowledge of embalming a person was set in ancient Egypt, since it is part of a larger composition, which, from its other content (for example, texts about problems with the vagina, skin problems, and bloody diarrhoea, as

---

5 See, for example, Gutas 1998; Ragep 2013; Burnett 2013; Burnett and Juste 2016.

6 Transmission of knowledge between ancient cultures is still an area in which much more research should be done; see, most recently, Steele 2016.

well as recipes for medications to treat pain in the abdomen), belongs to the medical texts. On the other hand, the fragmentation is also an issue in each extant document from which smaller or larger parts may be missing, with serious consequences for those attempting to read it. Thus, the re-construction of mathematical procedures from administrative texts is mostly impossible because of their fragmentary state.[7]

At the same time, the source situation even for Egypt may be considered strong in comparison to the classical scientific texts, such as Euclid's *Elements*, for example, because the sources are "original texts", copied in the time when they were still used and presumably contemporary or almost contemporary to the time in which they were written, while the manuscripts of the Greek scientific texts are often medieval copies, and only very few, if any, contemporary sources exist (for the transmission of Euclid's *Elements*, see Cuomo 2001, 126–135).[8]

Finally, the question of a strong or weak source situation for Mesopotamia, is not as straightforward as it may seem at first glance. While there are periods with abundant sources (for example, the Ur III period for administrative texts), and others in which Mesopotamia is at least clearly much richer than Egypt (compare, for example, the roughly 100 mathematical problems found in a dozen mathematical texts from Middle Kingdom Egypt with the approximately 150 published (by 1999) problem texts (some containing large numbers of problems) from contemporary Old Babylonian Mesopotamia),[9] the situation is still far from evenly spread for times and places (see the overview of mathematical tablets from post Old Babylonian periods given in Robson 2008, 327–342). Indicating the source situation is a common feature of many historiographical works on ancient science, since it allows us to estimate what kind of questions can be asked with the chance of obtaining reliable answers. This awareness of a certain "weakness" of the available sources that can be studied has forced historians working on ancient material to reflect carefully regarding what can be done with their texts.

---

7 Examples of administrative texts that are sufficiently well preserved to be used for mathematical analyses include Papyrus Reisner I (Rossi and Imhausen, 2009) and Papyrus Berlin 10005 (Imhausen 2003b; Vymazalová 2016).

8 It should be noted that what counts as a scientific text is also less straightforward (even for classical antiquity) than is often presented; see Taub 2017, on the range and variety of formats used in writing scientific texts.

9 Robson 1999, 7. Nemet-Nejat (1993) provides an overview of tablets with their respective problem numbers; for corrections to this list, see Robson 1999, 7, note 30. For a list of tablets with mathematical problems since 1999, see Robson 2008, 324. Additional tablets are published in Friberg 2007 (tablets of the controversial Schøyen collection); Proust 2008; Friberg and George 2010; and Friberg and Al-Rawi 2016.

2.2. Historiographical weaknesses: Anachronism, eurocentrism and orientalism

The historiography of pre-Greek ancient science has undergone a complex history from its early stages in the nineteenth century. In its beginnings, after the cuneiform, hieratic and hieroglyphic scripts were deciphered, and their respective languages became accessible again to modern researchers, the idea of the earliest science had already been shaped by what had, until then, been the earliest scientific texts attributed to Greek writers from the seventh century BC onwards. Individual texts, for example, Euclid's *Elements*, the *Enquiry into Plants* (*Historia Plantarum*) by Theophrastus, or even fragments of texts (for optics, see the second chapter of Smith 2015) were accepted as the origins of the respective disciplines by representatives of their modern counterparts.[10] In addition, some of the methodological features of these texts still have hallmark status within the discipline (for example, the axiomatic-deductive structure of Euclid's *Elements*).[11]

The evidence provided by the Egyptian and Mesopotamian texts after they became accessible again proved, however, that those cultures had assembled the first written collections of knowledge for a variety of areas, some of which have successors up to modern times, while others do not. It also became clear that the idea of science being born out of nothing in ancient Greece had to be reconsidered. A key figure in the early historiography of Egyptian and Mesopotamian mathematics and astronomy was Otto Neugebauer,[12] whose legacy is key publications in the history of Egyptian and Mesopotamian mathematics as well as Mesopotamian astronomy.[13]

Nonetheless, what was not immediately apparent even after the publication of a number of Egyptian and Mesopotamian sources (and, even today, is far from being exhaustively researched) was the exact relation between Egyptian and Mesopotamian and Greek sciences. While the Greek authors themselves indicate that the origin of at least some of their sciences is to be located in Egypt or Mesopotamia, some aspects of their texts are strikingly different.

Whichever area of ancient bodies of knowledge a researcher wants to explore, there are certain practical difficulties that he or she will have to face, especially

---

10 For the problem of homonymy exemplified for the case of physics, see Pellegrin 2000. The problematic source situation for optics is sketched in Smith 2015, 23–25.

11 As Charette 2012, points out, this is used as a characteristic feature to distinguish (the superior) Greek (and modern European) mathematics from non-Western mathematical traditions. "Systematic" and "axiomatic-deductive" is contrasted with "intuitive" (at best inductive), "illustrative" and "unreflected" (Charette 2012, 291).

12 For a collection of various aspects of Neugebauer's works, see Jones et al. 2016; for his motivation, see the contribution of Jens Høyrup in Jones et al. 2016: especially 184–187; for the early historiography of Mesopotamian mathematics, see, also, Høyrup 1996; Robson 1999, 1–3, and Robson 2008, 4–8.

13 For example, Neugebauer, 1926, 1934, 1935–1937, 1955, and 1975, to name just some monographs.

when dealing with ancient bodies of knowledge, and, even more so, with sources from pre-Greek cultures. This is not meant to underplay the difficulties of dealing with ancient classical texts (Imhausen and Pommerening 2016, 405–570), but rather to underline that working on ancient materials differs with regard to the available sources and how they are typically accessed. Historiographical issues arise on two levels. First, the researcher can safely assume that some, or even most, of the conceptual framework will be fundamentally different from those that are taught in current counterparts of that area of knowledge (if there is a current counterpart). As has been demonstrated by Jens Høyrup in the case of pre-Greek mathematics, not even arithmetical operations as basic as addition or subtraction can be taken to have been understood as we understand them today (Høyrup 2002, 19–21). The extent of such conceptual differences should never be under-estimated, not even in studies of more recent materials, as the classic study of Ludwik Fleck illustrates (Fleck 1935, Chapter 1). These issues (and others that arise in the context of working with ancient scientific texts) are exemplified in a recently published volume (Imhausen and Pommerening 2016).

Second, despite all the historiographical insights that were gained in the past fifty years, the history of ancient science still holds a special place within the discipline. In the historiography of science, the naïve assumption that "later" knowledge is supposedly *per se* "superior" – as it is the result of an improvement of earlier bodies of knowledge, methodologies, etc., – can still be found, especially in the encounter with ancient sources. A certain frustration with this situation was explicitly voiced[14] some years ago by representatives of the field as being some sort of strange specimen of a discipline whose respectability seems to grow in inverse proportion with the age of the sources that are studied (supposedly indicating that the quality of knowledge, and hence its value to be studied, increases with time) can still be encountered today. The line of reasoning can rather bluntly be summarised as follows: more recent knowledge is superior in quality to earlier knowledge.[15] Those who study earlier bodies of knowledge therefore choose to work on inferior, or "easier" content. This choice reflects the abilities of the researcher, and therefore the judgement of the quality of the knowledge of the respective sources is transferred to the regard of the historian working with these sources. However, the credit of the historian working on ancient sources is enhanced by acknowledging his or her ability to read dead languages. Thus, a significant part of the appreciation that historians studying ancient materials receive is due to their philological knowledge, while their work of exploring former (foreign) concepts is – at least in contexts that include a

---

14 See, for example, Ritter 1989b, 39, or Cuomo 2001, 1.

15 While this statement hopefully seems absurd to any historian (of science) – it expresses an underlying prejudice that is often encountered implicitly or explicitly in conferences and publications that encompass larger time spans, e.g., from pre-modern to modern periods.

variety of periods – depreciated. This anachronistic attitude towards earlier science resulted in the evaluation of ancient scientific texts as weak. In mathematics, this is exemplified by the lack of algebraic formulae and proofs in these texts, which are common elements of "our" mathematics. The anachronistic depreciation of previous scientific cultures in comparison to their modern western counterparts can be pigeon-holed in the larger concept of Eurocentrism,[16] and, although a number of studies have appeared in the history of ancient mathematics in the past 20 years which mark the recognition of this problem and the change of the conceptual framework upon which the study of ancient mathematics is based,[17] the former attitude is still encountered not only in certain academic contexts, but also in public perception. The difficulties that are encountered when trying to overcome the Eurocentric approach are also related to the Orientalism issue that was raised in 1978 by Edward Said.[18] Thus, although Egypt and Mesopotamia are recognised as the earliest civilisations in which scientific concepts may be found, their depiction is usually that of cultures which have since perished, were superseeded by modern (stronger and better) successors, and whose characteristic is that of being different, (of "otherness") from modern (western) cultures.[19]

---

16 For Eurocentrism in (the history of) mathematics, see Ritter et al. 1996.

17 See Selin 2000, Høyrup 2002, Robson 2008, to name just three examples.

18 Said 1978, for a recent introduction to the concept that also discusses the various criticisms that Said met in response, see Dhawan and Castro Varela 2015, 91–150; for Said's relevance to the historiography of Mesopotamian mathematics, see Robson 2008, 273–274.
Similar to the criticism that can be voiced against Orientalism, exceptions from a "general" depreciation of ancient sciences in modern historiography can (easily) be found. However, as with Orientalism, this is not enough to invalidate the recognition of a situation that deserves to be addressed. Pinarello (2015, 16) applies the criticism of Orientalism to the treatment of scribes in Egyptology, criticising the "scribe" category as something invented by Europeans in order to "confirm the supposed deep social division between the educated elite and the vast ignorant majority". While I agree that the spectrum of literacy in Egypt was probably wider than is traditionally acknowledged in literature (and a comparison with Mesopotamia seems to confirm this as was presented by Eleanor Robson during the conference on weak knowledge), it seems not in line with the evidence of scribal work and self-depictions to deny the category as a whole.

19 Another interesting development that can be traced with past historiography is the comparison between Egypt and Mesopotamia in regard to the assessment of their sciences. Since Mesopotamia has not only more extant sources to offer than Egypt, but also in terms of what can be translated into our modern mathematics has the more advanced texts ("second degree equations"), and, it developed the first mathematical astronomy, Egypt has become its poor cousin. Thus, Otto Neugebauer began his historical work on Egyptian fraction reckoning, but then switched to Mesopotamian mathematics and astronomy ("But the paucity of the Egyptian material compared to the Mesopotamian, and its more elementary nature meant that the early 'desire to investigate the logico-conceptual foundations of mathematics of one of the most interesting people in Antiquity" ["die logisch-begrifflichen Grundlagen der Mathematik eines der interessantesten Völker des Altertums", Neugebauer 1926, Vorwort], gave way to the sheer intellectual challenge of the sophisticated application of arithmetic methods and their

Despite this persistence of outdated perceptions on the earliest sciences, as recent careful historical studies have uncovered,[20] the history of scientific evolution is neither straightforward nor simple. Thus, it can be demonstrated even in the area of mathematics that it is not always a better "quality" of science that drives or determines changes. The procedure to calculate the area of a circle that was used in Middle Kingdom Egypt yielded a more accurate result than that used in Demotic Egypt, which had been adopted from Mesopotamia (which has a better reputation in the history of mathematics than Egypt (Imhausen 2009).[21] Knowledge, including scientific knowledge, never exists in isolation, but is always an essential part of the society and culture in which it is produced.[22] The relations of (scientific) knowledge, methods, actors (scientists and patrons), institutions and instruments are often complex and have proven to be an immensely fruitful area of studies in all periods.

Because of its otherness and its temporal distance from modern science, the history of ancient science offers the history of science the possibility to explore significant questions more independently from the current conceptions of science, such as the key question of "What qualifies as science?", for example.[23]

2.3. Weak or strong? The epistemological status of ancient knowledge

Historiographically, the question of the epistempological status of ancient knowledge is probably the most complicated one to be answered, because, on the one hand, scientific knowledge supposedly evolves (we know more today than we did, say, 2000 years ago), while, on the other, an analysis of the epistemological status of this knowledge requires a careful and sophisticated approach in order to avoid the traps of anachronism. Judging from the variety of examples on the

---

application to physical phenomena in Mesopotamian mathematical astronomy. And to this Neugebauer, Egypt had nothing more to offer." Ritter 2016, 159–160).

20 For example, Robson 2008.

21 For a recent article that raises the same question (using, however, an outdated historiographic paradigm), see Warburton 2016.

22 This is illustrated for the example of Mesopotamian mathematics in Robson 2008. Chemla and Keller 2017 provide further examples from a variety of fields and periods. The most prominent claim of the close relation between societies and their scientific knowledge was put forward as the *strong programme* of the sociology of scientific knowledge by Bloor 1976; see also Bloor 2004. For a modern example, see Pickering 1984.

23 The problems that arise when attempting to answer this question are detailed in Chalmers 2013. A related question is "How can 'scientific' knowledge be distinguished from 'other' knowledge?", the so-called demarcation problem, for which Laudan 1983 has become the classical study. For research that attempts to isolate a corpus of texts that belonged to the "domain of rational practice" in Mesopotamia, see Ritter 2010. For ancient science and humanities, Jens Høyrup has proposed a definition that considers various issues raised in the historiography of science; see Høyrup 1995, x.

evolution of scientific knowledge, the question of its epistemological status in those periods that witnessed evident progress is far from simple (see the examples given in Chalmers 2013, 84–94). One feature that seems to be characteristic for assessing scientific knowledge at various (if not all) times is the ability to solve problems that may arise in the future and predict their solution(s) – an ability that could be taken as one exemplary measurement for epistemological strength. Pre-Greek, as well as Greek, scientific texts explicitly indicate concern with this aspect, as will be briefly sketched in the following section with examples mostly from the area of mathematics.

Among the prominent collections of scientific knowledge that are extant from ancient Egypt are mathematical and medical texts.[24] Both, mathematical and medical, texts include procedure texts that indicate how specific mathematical or medical problems are to be tackled and solved.[25] In the Egyptian (and Mesopotamian) mathematical texts, the individual problems are always indicated with concrete numerical examples.[26] However, the *opinio communis* is that what was taught with those texts were the procedures (or algorithms) to solve a specific type of problem, so that the scribe would also be able to solve a problem of the same type with different numerical values.[27] At least two problems of the Rhind Mathematical Papyrus indicate this explicitly. In problem 61b (the calculation of 2/3 of a fraction) the final sentence states: "Behold, calculating is likewise for any simple fraction that will occur."[28] Problem 66, the calculation of a daily portion from the given amount for the year, ends: "You should calculate likewise about anything that is said to you as in this method."

---

24 This perception of mathematical and medical texts constituting "Egyptian science" is in part due to the former high status of the types of knowledge that have a counterpart in modern science. There are several other domains which would per emic view be categorised in the group of privileged knowledges, such as the knowledge about the topography of the netherworld, the knowledge of the quality of certain days in the calendar, ritual knowledge and others. These have mostly been ignored by modern historians of science (see most recently my own contribution in Sommer et al. 2017), but should have a place in this category. For a collection of characteristic features of Egyptian and Mesopotamian scientific texts from a wider area of disciplines, see Bawanypeck and Imhausen 2014.

25 Procedure texts for various disciplines are also extant from many other early cultures (e.g., Mesopotamia and China) as a means to organise and transmit bodies of knowledge.

26 The format of Egyptian and Mesopotamian mathematics has been characterised as numeric, rhetoric and algorithmic, which names the three most striking features of the problem texts; see Ritter 1989b.

27 The sequence of the aHa-problems of the Rhind Mathematical Papyrus illustrates this idea of arranging knowledge according to the structural type of the problem; see Imhausen 2003a. A more detailed analysis of the structure of this problem group is currently being prepared by Jim Ritter. On the analysis of algorithms in mathematical cultures, see Bullynck 2015. Research has shown the usefulness of the concept for Greek mathematics as well, see Ritter and Vitrac 1998, and Bernard and Christianidis 2011.

28 For the unusual way in which problem 61b is phrased, see Ritter 1989b, 58–59.

However, nowhere in the Egyptian mathematical texts is the issue of the reliability of the procedure itself raised – an issue that becomes central in later mathematical writing. Then, the value of a mathematical procedure – or a mathematical statement – is measured by the extent and proof of its validity. In later mathematics, proofs are an integral element of collections of mathematical statements. One prominent difference between pre-Greek and Greek texts from a modern point of view, is this lack of proof. The correctness of the result that a procedure from a mathematical text yielded (for the specific numerical values that were indicated at the beginning of the text) is sometimes confirmed by a verification, which is added to the text after the solution has been indicated. The lack of a general proof in the earliest mathematical texts has, in past historiographical descriptions, been used to denigrate them.[29] This standard narrative fits well with the perception of "Eastern" cultures as it was explicitly voiced in 1841 by Jean-Baptiste Biot:

> One finds renewed evidence for this peculiar habit of mind, following which the Arabs, like the Chinese and Hindus, limited their scientific writings to the statement of a series of rules, which, once given, ought only to be verified by their applications, without requiring any logical demonstration or connections between them: this gives those oriental nations a remarkable character of dissimilarity, I would even add of intellectual inferiority, comparatively to the Greeks, with whom any proposition is established by reasoning, and generates logically deduced consequences. (Translation cited after Charette 2012, 274)

The general devaluation of non-western cultures found in the statement above is characteristic for of the attitude of the historiography of a certain time.[30] How then should a "missing" general proof be treated historiographically without resulting in the stating of the inferiority of a given culture *versus* another? While comparisons between mathematical cultures are apt to indicate their differences, it seems, at this point in our knowledge about the development of sciences, historiographically doubtful to place too much emphasis on the absence of specific so-called characteristic features, thereby granting them a primary status with supposed general validity for various times and cultures. Thus, each scientific culture, and its concepts, deserves to be treated based upon its own emic concepts and formal features. The task for the historian is to understand these concepts and features.[31] For an assessment of the epistemological status of Egyptian

---

29 For a detailed assessment and revision of this view, see Chemla 2012.

30 One might argue that this attitude can also be detected – if not as bluntly – in the other example (the German Siegmund Günther on the difference between Indian and Greek mathematics) cited in Charette 2012, 275–276, which Charette (2012, 276) describes as "more respectful and nuanced". This, too, has a parallel in the general Orientalism debate; see Dhawan and Castro Varela 2015, 107. For this issue with regard to the history of science, see Chemla and Keller 2017.

31 For examples of how this might be done, see Imhausen and Pommerening 2016, or Pommerening and Bisang 2017.

written knowledge, the cultural connotations of writing in ancient Egypt have to be taken into account. The invention of writing and numeracy was attributed to the god *Thoth*, who is also closely connected to *maat*, the Egyptian concept of the way things should be, including truth, balance and order, morality and justice.[32] For the scientific texts, the idea that written words are non-negotiably true has found its reflection in the usage of a specific verb form, the *sḏm.ḥr.f* that is used to express the necessity of the action described by the verb, and is used in the instructions of the mathematical (and medical) procedures. Thus, in ancient Egypt, the status of being written down implied epistemological strength, and further discussion of validity was not part of the formal framework.

In the cultural comparison of concepts and features, if it is to be done in a historically sophisticated way (i.e., not simply by granting the later culture the victory), the individual points of departure must also be taken into account. Thus, Egypt and Mesopotamia are both examples of cultures that built collections of knowledge from scratch. In Greece (and all later cultures), we find a fundamentally different situation, because forms of knowledge of these cultures used (sometimes indicating this explicitly) the results of earlier scientific cultures. While initial historiography has focused on key features of each culture in their development towards modern science, later studies have begun to explore the individual cultures in more detail.

Another difference between pre-Greek and later written collections of knowledge that is linked to their epistemological status – as well as to the social status of the ancient experts – is that of explicit authorship. Laurence Totelin indicates a further implication of this at the beginning of her contribution to this volume – the existence of anecdotes, that is to say, stories told about famous authors. The indication of "prominent" authorship, which can even become problematical when a text is falsely ascribed to a prominent author, in order to grant it strength, becomes popular in Greek science. From what we know so far about the context of sciences in Greece, a competitive culture which is first tangible in the letters of experts to their king within the Mesopotamian culture, has now become the standard mode of developing, testing and transmitting scientific ideas. This feature of competition in Greek science is also dealt with in the contribution of Orna Harari on Proclus' *Elements of Theology* in this volume.

---

32 On *Thoth*, the most detailed accounts can still be found in the article of the Lexikon der Ägyptologie (Kurth 1986) and in the even older monograph by Boylan 1922. For more recent monographs, see Bleeker 1973, and Stadler 2009 (the latter also includes a short historiography).

2.4. Social strength and weaknesses of ancient experts

Knowledge has always been linked with power.[33] This becomes traceable with the first writing – invented in Egypt and Mesopotamia likewise to record knowledge of ownership (see the respective contributions in Houston 2004, also Robson 2007). The available sources from Egypt and Mesopotamia complement each other in various respects, and can also be used to indicate differences between those two cultures. In both cultures, the invention of writing can be shown to have been stimulated, if not prompted, by economic needs of some sort. Both cultures include numerical values among their first extant sources. In Mesopotamia, the available source material to trace the evolution of the writing system is much richer than that of Egypt, thus allowing us to trace several stages in the development of the eventually emerging cuneiform script.[34] In Egypt, the first available evidence already presents us with the duality of the later writing system, namely, hieroglyphic writing and hieratic.[35] In addition, even the early evidence of Egyptian writing indicates that it was not only used to represent economic data, but also to convey power.[36]

Throughout all periods of ancient Egyptian history, writing remained the monopoly of the élite (the king and his entourage either located in administration or in temples). Those who were entrusted with collecting, organising and transmitting knowledge, designated as "scribes" by the basic requisite to fulfil these tasks, the ability to read and write, were supposedly socially-strong representatives of their respective cultures. However, as so often is the case, a more detailed analysis of these scribes indicates that the combination of knowledge and power did not always lead to a predictably strong social position, and even if this had been obtained, it was not guaranteed to remain that way in the future.[37] For the group of Mesopotamian scholars around the Neo Assyrian

---

33 This can be exemplified by tracing the means by which scientists were supported by the rulers (or in later times governments) of their times. In most (if not all) periods and cultures, a relation between scientists and rulers can be determined. For ancient periods, the scribes at the court of Ashurbanipal during the Neo-Assyrian Empire, Aristoteles as the teacher of Alexander the Great, the Library of Alexandria (a royal project of the Ptolemaic kings) are prominent examples of the relation between knowledge and political power.

34 On the invention and early uses of writing and number system in Mesopotamia, see Robson 2007. For a detailed study of cuneiform writing and early philology, see Glassner 2003, and Cancik-Kirschbaum and Kahl 2018.

35 In Egypt, as in Mesopotamia, the invention of writing was probably stimulated by the invention of numbers; see Imhausen 2016, 15–17. The evidence of first writing and number signs is published in Dreyer 1998. For discussions of the early evidence of writing in Egypt, see Breyer 2002, Kahl 2003, and Cancik-Kirschbaum and Kahl 2018.

36 A prominent example is the decoration of the mace-head of king Narmer that includes the depiction of a tribute given to this king; see Imhausen 2016, 24–25.

37 In this context, it must be taken into account that there were supposedly various degrees of literacy among those scribes (see Veldhuis 2011). Not much attention has, as yet, been devoted

king, a fierce rivalry to curry favour can be detected in the letters, and the ever present fear of falling from grace with the king, which was the same as losing one's livelihood.[38] A different aspect of the relation between knowledge and power can be traced within the Egyptian material, namely, the autobiographies of scribes.[39] The comparison between the autobiographies of high officials from the Old Kingdom and the First Intermediate Period indicates that, while, during the former period, the proximity to the king and what the official achieved for him were essential for his social position, during the latter, the status of officials was dependant on the ability to care for the people in his immediate village or region.[40]

3. Conclusion

The topic of weak knowledge as studied in the context of the CRC 1095 provides the possibility for diachronic research without the (habitual but outdated) bias that earlier knowledge (and, by implication, those cultures that produced it) were necessarily inferior. The individual projects and their case studies, ranging from studying forms of knowledge and their weaknesses in a variety of cultures and periods, can help to overcome traditional prejudices against ancient sciences in the history of science and open the way for a historiography that both acknowledges its strong past and focuses on the different aspects of its seemingly ever recurring weaknesses.

In addition, the concept can also be used for a critical assessment of past (and present) historiography in the history of science. While the focus of this contribution has been on ancient science, it should be clear that the claims are also likely to affect the work of historians working on more recent periods. There, too, the present scientific concepts should not be taken for granted. The historiography of ancient science can help to alert a historian working on more recent periods to the possible pitfalls that he or she may face, because these may be easier to discern and to analyse in material which is farther removed.

---

to the bottom end of the spectrum, namely, persons that one would consider socially weak and whose abilities and output of writing have not yet been recognised, as was presented during the conference by Eleanor Robson.

38 The example *par excellence* of this is probably the scribe Urad-Gula (see Parpola 1987).

39 This text corpus is used by Nadine Eikelschulte in her dissertation to compare experts that lived and worked during the Old Kingdom with those living and working during the First Intermediate Period.

40 The comprehensive analysis will be given by Nadine Eikelschulte in her dissertation. A more restricted analysis focusing on mathematical knowledge can be found in Imhausen 2013.

References

Classical Sources

Diodorus of Sicily (1933). *The Library of History* (Loeb Classical Library 279). Cambridge MA: Harvard University Press, available at: https://www.loebclassics.com/view/LCL279/1933/pb_LCL279.i.xml, last accessed 10 July 2018.

Herodotus (1920). *Histories* (Loeb Classical Library 117), Vol. 1: Books I and II. Cambridge MA: Harvard University Press.

Secondary Literature

Bardinet, Thierry (2018): *Médecins et magiciens à la cour du pharaon. Une étude du papyrus médical Louvre E32847*. Paris: Édition Khéops.

Bawanypeck, Daliah, and Annette Imhausen (Eds.) (2014): *Traditions of Written Knowledge in Ancient Egypt and Mesopotamia (Alter Orient und Altes Testament 403)*. Münster: Ugarit.

Bernard, Alain, and Jean Christianidis (2012): "A New Analytical Framework for the Understanding of Diophantus's *Arithmetica* I–III." *Archive for History of Exact Sciences*, 66 (1): 1–69.

Bleeker, C.J. (1973): *Hathor and Thoth: Two key Figures in Ancient Egyptian Religion (Studies in the History of Religions XXVI)*. Leiden: Brill.

Bloor, David [1976] (1991): *Knowledge and Social Imagery*. 2nd edn. Chicago IL: University of Chicago Press.

Bloor, David (2004): "Sociology of Scientific Knowledge." In: Ilkka Niiniluoto et al. (Eds): *Handbook of Epistemology*, 919–962. Dordrecht: Springer.

Boylan, Patrick (1922): *Thoth the Hermes of Egypt: A Study of some Aspects of Theological Thought*. Oxford: Oxford University Press.

Breyer, Francis Amadeus (2002): "Die Schriftzeugnisse des prädynastischen Königsgrabes U-j in Umm el-Qaab." *Journal of Egyptian Archaeology*, 88 (1): 53–65.

Bullynck, Maarten (2015): "Histories of Algorithms: Past, Present and Future." *Historia Mathematica*, 43 (3): 332–341.

Burnett, Charles (2013): "Translation and Transmission of Greek and Islamic Science to Latin Christendom." In: David C. Lindberg and Michael H. Shank (Eds.): *The Cambridge History of Science. Volume 2: Medieval Science*, 341–364. Cambridge: Cambridge University Press.

Burnett, Charles, and David Juste (2016): "A New Catalogue of Medieval Translations into Latin of Texts on Astronomy and Astrology." In: Faith Wallis and Robert Wisnovsky (Eds.): *Medieval Textual Cultures: Agents of Transmission, Translation and Transformation*, 63-76. Berlin: de Gruyter.

Cancik-Kirschbaum, Eva, and Jochem Kahl (2018): *Erste Philologien. Archäologie einer Disziplin vom Tigris bis zum Nil*. Tübingen: Mohr Siebeck.

Chalmers, Alan (2013): *What is this Thing called Science?*. 4th edn. New York: Open University Press.

Charette, François (2012): "The Logical Greek versus the Imaginative Oriental: On the Historiography of 'non-Western' Mathematics during the period 1820–1920." In: Karine Chemla (Ed.): *The History of Mathematical Proof in Ancient Traditions*, 274–293. Cambridge: Cambridge University Press.

Chemla, Karine (Ed.) (2012): *The History of Mathematical Proof in Ancient Traditions*. Cambridge: Cambridge University Press.

Chemla, Karine, and Evelyn Fox Keller (Eds.) (2017): *Cultures without Culturalism: The Making of Scientific Knowledge*. Durham NC-London: Duke University Press.

Cuomo, Serafina (2001): *Ancient Mathematics*. London-New York: Routledge.

Dhawan, Nikita, and María do Mar Castro Varela (2015): *Postkoloniale Theorie. Eine kritische Einführung*. 2. Auflage. Bielefeld: Transcript.

Dreyer, Günter (1998): *Das prädynastische Königsgrab U-j und seine frühen Schriftzeugnisse*. Mainz: von Zabern.

Fleck, Ludwik (1935): *Entstehung und Entwicklung einer wissenschaftlichen Tatsache. Einführung in die Lehre vom Denkstil und Denkkollektiv*. Basel: Bruno Schwabe & Co.

Friberg, Jöran (2007): *A Remarkable Collection of Babylonian Mathematical Texts. Manuscripts in the Schøyen Collection – Cuneiform Texts I*. New York: Springer.

Friberg, Jöran, and Andrew George (2010): "Six more Mathematical Cuneiform Texts in the Schøyen Collection." In: Dileeto Minuto and Rossario Pintaudi (Eds.): *Papyri Graecae Schøyen. Essays and Texts in Honour of Martin Schøyen (Papyrologica Florentina 40)* , 123–195. Florence: Edizioni Gonnelli.

Friberg, Jöran, and Farouk N.H. Al-Rawi (2016): *New Mathematical Cuneiform Texts*. Basel: Springer International Publishing.

Glassner, Jean-Jacques (2003): *The Invention of Cuneiform. Writing in Sumer*. Baltimore MD-London: Johns Hopkins University Press.

Gutas, Dimitri (1998): *Greek Thought, Arabic Culture: The Graeco-Arabic Translation Movement in Baghdad and Early 'Abbāsid Society (2nd–4th/8th–10th Centuries)*. London: Routledge.

Houston, Stephen (2004): *The First Writing: Script Invention as History and Process*. Cambridge: Cambridge University Press.

Høyrup, Jens (1995): *As Regards the Humanities. An Approach to their Theory through History and Philosophy*. Roskilde: Roskilde Universitet.

Høyrup, Jens (1996): "Changing Trends in the Historiography of Mesopotamian Mathematics: An Insider's View." *History of Science*, 34 (1): 1–32.

Høyrup, Jens (2002): *Lengths, Widths, Surfaces: A Portrait of Old Babylonian Algebra and its Kin*. New York: Springer.

Jones, Alexander, Christine Proust and John M. Steele (Eds.) (2016): *A Mathematician's Journeys. Otto Neugebauer and Modern Transformations of Ancient Science*. New York: Springer.

Imhausen, Annette (2003a): *Ägyptische Algorithmen. Eine Untersuchung zu den mittelägyptischen mathematischen Aufgabentexten (Ägyptologische Abhandlungen 65)*. Wiesbaden: Harrassowitz.

Imhausen, Annette (2003b): "Calculating the Daily Bread: Rations in Theory and Practice." *Historia Mathematica*, 30 (1): 3–16.

Imhausen, Annette (2009): "Traditions and Myths in the Historiography of Egyptian Mathematics." In: Eleanor Robson and Jacqueline Stedall (Eds.): *The Oxford Handbook of the History of Mathematics*. Oxford: Oxford University Press.

Imhausen, Annette (2013): "Mathematik und Mathematiker im pharaonischen Ägypten." *Mitteilungen der Mathematischen Gesellschaft Hamburg*, 33 (1): 75–97.

Imhausen, Annette (2016): *Mathematics in Ancient Egypt: A Contextual History*. Princeton NJ: Princeton University Press.

Imhausen, Annette, and Tanja Pommerening (Eds.) (2010): *Writings of Early Scholars in the Ancient Near East, Egypt, Rome, and Greece. Translating Ancient Scientific Texts.* (Beiträge zur Altertumskunde 286). Berlin-New York: Walter de Gruyter.

Imhausen, Annette, and Tanja Pommerening (Eds.) (2016): *Translating Writings of Early Scholars in the Ancient Near East, Egypt, Greece, and Rome. Methodological Aspects with Examples.* (Beiträge zur Altertumskunde 344). Berlin-New York: Walter de Gruyter.

Kahl, Jochem (2003): "Die frühen Schriftzeugnisse aus dem Grab U-j in Umm el-Qaab." *Chronique d'Egypte*, 78 (1): 112–135.

Katz, Victor J. (Ed.) (2007): *The Mathematics of Egypt, Mesopotamia, China, India, and Islam: A Sourcebook.* Princeton NJ: Princeton University Press.

Kurth, Dieter (1986): "Thot." In: Wolfgang Helck and Wolfhart Westendorf (Eds.): *Lexikon der Ägyptologie*, 497–523. Vol. VI. Wiesbaden: Otto Harrassowitz.

Laudan, Larry (1983): "The Demise of the Demarcation Problem." In: R.S. Cohen and Larry Laudan (Eds.): *Physics, Philosophy and Psychoanalysis: Essays in Honor of Adolf Grünbaum*, 111–127. Boston Studies in the Philosophy of Science, 76. Dordrecht: D. Reidel.

Nemet-Nejat, Karen Rhea (1993): *Cuneiform Mathematical Texts as a Reflection of Everyday Life in Mesopotamia (American Oriental Series 75)*. New Haven CT: American Oriental Society.

Neugebauer, Otto (1926): *Die Grundlagen der ägyptischen Bruchrechnung*. Berlin: Springer.

Neugebauer, Otto (1934): *Vorlesungen über Geschichte der antiken mathematischen Wissenschaften. Erster Band: Vorgriechische Mathematik.* Berlin: Springer.

Neugebauer, Otto (1935–1937): *Mathematische Keilschrift-Texte (Quellen und Studien zur Geschichte der Mathematik, Astronomie und Physik A3).* 3 vols. Berlin: Springer.

Neugebauer, Otto (1955): *Astronomical Cuneiform Texts*. London: Lund Humphries.

Neugebauer, Otto (1975): *A History of Ancient Mathematical Astronomy*. Berlin: Springer.

Parkinson, Richard B. (1997): *The Tale of Sinuhe and other Ancient Egyptian Poems 1940–1640 BC*. Oxford: Oxford University Press.

Parpola, Simo (1987): "The Forlorn Scholar." In: Francesca Rochberg-Halton (Ed): *Language, Literature, and History. Philological and Historical Studies Presented to Erica Reiner*, 257–278. American Oriental Series 67. New Haven CT: American Oriental Society.

Pellegrin, Pierre (2000): "Physik." In: Jacques Brunschwig and Geoffrey Lloyd, *Das Wissen der Griechen*, 388–403. Munich: Wilhelm Fink Verlag.

Pickering, Andrew (1984): *Constructing Quarks: A Sociological History of Particle Physics*. Chicago IL: The University of Chicago Press.

Pinarello, Massimiliano Samuele (2015): *An Archaeological Discussion of Writing Practice. Deconstruction of the Ancient Egyptian Scribe.* London: GHP Publications.

Plofker, Kim (2009): *Mathematics in India*. Princeton NJ: Princeton University Press.

Pommerening, Tanja, and Walter Bisang (Eds.) (2017): *Classification from Antiquity to Modern Times. Sources, Methods, and Theories from an Interdisciplinary Perspective.* Berlin-Boston MA: Walter de Gruyter.

Proust, Christine (2008): *Tablettes mathématiques de la collection Hilprecht*. Wiesbaden: Harrassowitz.

Ragep, F. Jamil (2013): "Islamic Culture and the Natural Sciences." In: David C. Lindberg and Michael H. Shank (Eds.): *The Cambridge History of Science. Volume 2: Medieval Science*, 27–61. Cambridge: Cambridge University Press.

Ritter, Jim (1989a): "Babylone – 1800." In: Michel Serres (Ed.): *Éléments d'Histoire des Sciences*, 16–37. Paris: Bordas. (English translation: (1995): "Babylon – 1800." In: Michel

Serres (Ed.): *A History of Scientific Thought: Elements of a History of Science*, 44–72. Oxford: Blackwell.

Ritter, Jim (1989b): "Chacun sa vérité: les mathématiques en Égypte et en Mésopotamie." In: Michel Serres (Ed.): *Éléments d'Histoire des Sciences*, 38–61. Paris: Bordas. (English translation: (1995): "Measure for Measure: Mathematics in Egypt and Mesopotamia." In: Michel Serres (Ed): *A History of Scientific Thought: Elements of a History of Science*, 44–72. Oxford: Blackwell.

Ritter, Jim, and Bernard Vitrac (1998): "Pensée grecque et Pensée "orientale"." In: Jean-François Mattéi (Ed.): *Encyclopédie Philosophique. Vol. IV: Le discours philosophique*, 1233–1250. Paris: Presses universitaires de France.

Ritter, Jim (2010): "Translating Rational-practice Texts." In: Annette Imhausen and Tanja Pommerening (Eds.): *Writings of Early Scholars in the Ancient Near East, Egypt, Rome, and Greece. Translating Ancient Scientific Texts*, 349–383. Beiträge zur Altertumskunde 286. Berlin-New York: Walter de Gruyter.

Ritter, Jim (2016): "Otto Neugebauer and Ancient Egypt." In: Alexander Jones, Christine Proust and John M. Steele (Eds.): *A Mathematician's Journeys: Otto Neugebauer and Modern Transformations of Ancient Science*, 127–163. New York: Springer.

Ritter, Jim, Catherine Goldstein and Jeremy Gray (1996): *L'Europe mathématique: Mathematical Europe*. Paris: Maison des Sciences de l'Homme.

Robson, Eleanor (1999): *Mesopotamian Mathematics, 2100–1600 BC. Technical Constants in Bureaucracy and Education*. Oxford: Clarendon Press.

Robson, Eleanor (2007): "Literacy, Numeracy and the State in Early Mesopotamia." In: K. Lomas, R.D. Whitehouse and J.B. Wilkins (Eds.): *Literacy and the State in the Ancient Mediterranean*, 37–50. London: Accordia Research Institute.

Robson, Eleanor (2008): *Mathematics in Ancient Iraq: A Social History*. Princeton NJ: Princeton University Press.

Rochberg, Francesca (2016): *Before Nature. Cuneiform Knowledge and the History of Science*. Chicago IL-London: University of Chicago Press.

Rossi, Corinna, and Annette Imhausen (2009): "Architecture and Mathematics in the Time of Senusret I: Sections G, H, and I of Papyrus Reisner I." In: Salima Ikram and Aidan Dodson (Eds.): *Beyond the Horizon: Studies in Egyptian Art, Archaeology and History in Honour of Barry J. Kemp*, 440–455. Cairo: Supreme Council of Antiquities Press.

Said, Edward (1978): *Orientalism*. New York: Pantheon.

Selin, Helaine (Ed.) (2000): *Mathematics Across Cultures: The History of Non-Western Mathematics*. Dordrecht-Boston MA-London: Kluwer.

Smith, A. Mark (2015): *From Sight to Light: The Passage from Ancient to Modern Optics*. Chicago IL-London: University of Chicago Press.

Sommer, Marianne, et al. (Eds.) (2017): *Handbuch Wissenschaftsgeschichte*. Stuttgart: J.B. Metzler.

Stadler, Martin Andreas (2009): *Weiser und Wesir. Studien zu Vorkommen, Rolle und Wesen des Gottes Thot im ägyptischen Totenbuch*. Tübingen: Mohr Siebeck.

Steele, John M. (2016): *The Circulation of Astronomical Knowledge in the Ancient World*. Leiden: Brill.

Taub, Liba (2017): *Science Writing in Greco-Roman Antiquity*. Cambridge: Cambridge University Press.

Unguru, Sabetai (1975): "On the Need to Rewrite the History of Greek Mathematics." *Archive for History of Exact Sciences*, 15 (1): 67–114.

Veldhuis, Niek (2011): "Levels of Literacy." In: Karen Radner and Eleanor Robson (Eds.): *The Oxford Handbook of Cuneiform Culture*, 68–89. Oxford: Oxford University Press.

Vymazalová, Hana (2016): "Ration System." In: Willeke Wendrich et al. (Eds.): *UCLA Encyclopedia of Egyptology*. Available at: https:// escholarship.org/content/ qt8g74r617/qt8g74r617.pdf, last accessed 10 July 2018.

Warburton, David (2016): "Egypt's Role in the Origins of Science: An Essay in Aligning Conditions, Evidence, and Interpretations." *Journal of Ancient Egyptian Interconnections*, 9 (1): 72–94.

Failure and the Imperfections of Artisanal Knowledge in the Early Modern Period

Sven Dupré

Abstract

Artisanal textual practices are strategies to deal with the uncertainty of artisanal processes and the whims of materials. Confronted with the precarious nature of artisanal knowledge, variation had always been the most important strategy of error management. Following the dissatisfaction with ways of writing down knowledge, hiding the imperfection of the process of knowledge production and in response to the limits of language in articulating skills, the codification of error emerged as a new strategy in the seventeenth century, pointing to a new conception of the epistemic value of failure and error in the early modern arts and sciences.[1]

1. Introduction

"Ever tried. Ever failed. No matter. Try again. Fail again. Fail better."[2] Samuel Beckett's words expressed his belief that failure is an essential part of the artist's work. Nevertheless, for Beckett, this did not mean that failure relieves the artist from the task of trying to succeed, however impossible the mission might be. Beckett's embracing of a culture of fallibility is in stark contrast with the historiography of technology. Graeme Gooday has aptly observed that in the history of technology, failure has been typically used to categorise pathological technologies that clearly demarcate them from successes (Gooday 1998). Another historiography, that of craft theory, treats failure as a mundane occurrence in technological design, in line with Beckett's thinking on failure. In his theory on the nature of design and craft, woodworker and professor at the Royal College

---

1 This research has received funding from the European Research Council (ERC) under the European Union's Horizon 2020 research and innovation programme (grant agreement No 648718).
2 Burton 2005; Kinnucan 2011.

of Art, David Pye argues that design cannot be failure-free (Pye 1978, 70). A craft object or technology cannot meet all requirements, especially not those imposed by economy, and is always based upon a compromise between design requirements to be fulfilled in order to create an ideal object. According to Pye, such a compromise is always a sort of failure. Failure is then unavoidably ubiquitous in all design and technology. Even if it were possible for a technology to succeed at any moment, later users would come with different requirements, again making failure inevitable.

Different from Pye, Michael Polanyi sees failure as an inevitable step towards success. In connection to "rules of skill and connoisseurship which comprise important technical processes", Polanyi speaks of "the usual process of unconscious trial and error by which we feel our way to success and may continue to improve on our success without specifiably [sic] knowing how we do it." (Polanyi 2005, 65) For Polanyi, this error is "good error". There is also "bad error", which follows from our limited powers of articulation:

> Although the gains made by casting our thoughts into articulate terms eventually outweigh by far these initial disadvantages," Polanyi admits, "there will always remain certain chances of error … which arise from our very adoption of an articulate interpretative framework. (Polanyi 2005, 98)

Language is the source of error and of the imperfection of artisanal knowledge. Another way of formulating this is that artisanal knowledge is strong for skilled masters, as it depends upon performance, and its transmission does not occur exclusively, or mainly, via language. However, for those lacking skill, the limits of language make artisanal knowledge weak. This chapter deals with both types of error, good and bad. It argues that the recognition of the limits of language – giving rise to bad error – led to new ways of writing down artisanal knowledge in the seventeenth century. However, at the same time, the recognition of good error – that one can learn from mistakes – in the arts was also adopted in the sciences, which came to recognise the epistemic value of failure.

In this chapter, I do not make a clear distinction between errors and mistakes, nor do I offer a word history of the terms used for errors and mistakes in different languages. While it has been recently attempted to demarcate errors from mistakes, for example, along lines of distinction between thought and action, or between the absence or presence of rules or norms, it turns out that, historically, the distinction between error and mistake is fluid and that different word categories are used in various ways.[3] In this chapter, I explore artisanal textual practices as strategies to deal with the uncertainty of artisanal processes and the whims of materials. As we will see, confronted with the precarious nature of artisanal knowledge, variation has always been the most important strategy for error manage-

---

3 Bondio and Bagliani 2012, vii-xiii; Neumaier 2010.

ment. However, I will argue that, following the dissatisfaction with ways of writing down knowledge, thus hiding the imperfection of the process of knowledge production, and in response to the limits of language in articulating skills, the codification of error emerged as a new strategy in the seventeenth century. This points to a new conception of the epistemic value of failure and error in the early modern arts and sciences. I will show that the early modern sciences adopted, what I will call, a poetics of failure. This rhetorical move made imperfect knowledge stronger.

2. Recipes as error management

Famously, the French potter Bernard Palissy made "Practice" reluctant to tell "Theory" the secret of white enamel. Palissy had "Practice" say that this was not a refusal for economic reasons, but simply because words were an ineffective way to learn a craft. "Even if I used a thousand reams of paper to write down all the accidents that have happened to me in learning this art," Practice says, "you must be assured that, however good a brain you may have, you will still make a thousand mistakes, which cannot be learned from writings, and even if you had them in writing you wouldn't believe them until practice has given you a thousand afflictions."[4] Only long and sustained experience, including the making of mistakes inherent to the apprenticeship, leads to the acquisition of knowledge. The insufficiency of discursive language to teach the arts was recognised even by enlightenment projects, such as the *Encyclopédie*, which were deeply invested in the description of the arts.[5] "It is handicraft which makes the artist, and it is not in books that one can learn to manipulate [...] there are many things that one learns only in the shops," Denis Diderot warned (Roberts 2012, 49). In his descriptions, Diderot's emphasis was on physical objects and fairly basic processes; fitting his idea of science as a system of rules, Diderot had no place for skills, gestural knowledge, experimentation, failures or errors.

Since Antiquity, one of the most common formats used to reproduce artisanal experience was the "recipe" telling the reader "how-to".[6] Typically consisting of a description of the ingredients and the instructions on how to process them, the format of the recipe remained remarkably stable. Their format also made recipes an excellent vehicle of transmission. Recipes in sixteenth-century books of secrets often had their origin in manuscript collections moving along chains of transmission going back centuries, sometimes even to Antiquity. For example, the optical

---

4 Palissy 1957, 192; Shell 2004.
5 Stalnaker 2010, 99-123; Pannabecker 1994; Roberts 2012.
6 Clarke et al. 2012; Leong and Rankin 2011; Smith 2010.

secret of how to make an image float in the air in Giovanni Battista Della Porta's "Natural Magick", one of the best-selling books of secrets of the sixteenth century, is a variation on a secret already found in the *Secretum Philosophorum*.[7] This manuscript, circulating in numerous copies, was originally composed in England around the year 1400. Devoted to the seven liberal arts (grammar, rhetoric, dialectic, arithmetic, music, geometry, astronomy), it was nevertheless more than just another university textbook. The first section on grammar consisted of recipes explaining how to construct a pen and how to make inks, and the third section, on dialectic, listed secrets about how to deceive the senses, including some about how to deceive the sense of sight; among others, the secret of the image in the air, which was later adopted by Della Porta.[8]

Recipes in books of secrets were considered always to give the desired result, that is, to be tried out and verified by experiment. As William Eamon has shown, professors of secrets operated in a competitive social environment in which they needed to fight for their place in the marketplace (Eamon 1994). Books of secrets served their authors to establish their authority as experts. Readers of the books of secrets were thus not supposed to deviate from the instructions in the recipe; they were to follow the rules. For authors who primarily aimed to establish their authority, there was no space for failure or to acknowledge that things could go wrong. It is not that, during processes of transmission, which could connect a sixteenth-century book of secrets to an ancient recipe, the authors did not change recipes. They did, but the changes were silent and invisible to the readers; authors made changes without explicit notification, adapting recipes to new local and material conditions, because, tried in new contexts, recipes seemed no longer to work, or the results were considered to be unsuccessful. By inclusion in a book of secrets, a recipe verified its efficacy, as Eamon noted.

As much is true of artisanal recipes, collected in books of secrets circulating in manuscripts. A very similar picture emerges from the treatise entitled *The Three Books of the Art of the Potter*, written and illustrated between the years 1558 and 1575 by Cipriano Piccolpasso. Today, the book is known because of one manuscript copy at the Victoria and Albert Museum in London. Though it has long been acknowledged as the first contemporary account of the manufacture of pottery produced in Europe, it was not intended as an instruction manual upon the basis of which the reader could make pottery. The treatise was packaged as a book of secrets. So much is clear from its full title:

The three books of the art of the potter in which is discussed not only the practice but briefly all the secrets of this thing that even to this day have always been kept concealed.

---

7 Goulding 2006; Clarke 2009.
8 Dupré 2019.

Far from being the revelation of instructions to apprentice potters, the treatise is a literary and visual celebration of their art, convincingly selling the skill and knowledge of the potter to its intended audience of élite patrons. It is a celebration of the tin-glazed earthenware produced by the potters of Castel Durante and Urbino during the late-fifteenth and early-sixteenth centuries. Secrets were included, especially if the recipes were ingenious, difficult or beautiful, according to Piccolpasso, but there was no mention of failures, nor any indication of errors.

Of course, if tried, artisanal recipes often failed to deliver the desired result. The most common strategy to deal with the uncertainty of artisanal processes and the whims of materials was variation. Authors of "how-to" books listed several ways of making or preparing of a material with slight variations so the reader could try the next variation if he failed in his attempts to follow the first recipe. One of the more extreme examples is found in a sixteenth-century Venetian manuscript which lists no less than seventeen different ways to make chalcedony glass – just one after the other, without distinction (Moretti and Toninato 2001, 43). Confronted with the precarious nature of artisanal knowledge, variation in practice and writing was the most important strategy for error management.[9]

3. Codification of error

Failure and error were typically not noted in books of secrets. Writing about doing things wrong, in fact, only seems to emerge in the seventeenth century, and in another genre of artisanal writings than books of secrets. This is not to say that, occasionally, the readers of secrets, who tried out the recipes, did not jot down that a procedure did not work in the margin of a recipe book. Here is just one example that this was indeed the case: Wolfgang Seidel wrote three *Kunstbücher* between 1540 and 1550, collecting recipes from the libraries of Tegernsee and from the libraries of neighbouring cloisters during his stay in Augsburg (Neven 2014, 30–36). Seidel's margin annotations record his comments on the recipes. For example, Seidel noted down in the margin of a recipe for the melting of crystal that the recipe was of no use to him and that a better way to melt crystal was found in another folio of the same manuscript.

In the seventeenth century, such evaluative notes moved from the margin of the text to the body of the text. What emerges is the process of writing "how-to" texts, as found in earlier named or anonymous sources, followed by the explicit signal that a recipe does not work and suggestions for ways to change it in order to make it work. This is (what I have called elsewhere) "the codification of error" (Dupré 2017). Here, I will show that the emergence of the codification of error

---

9 For precarious knowledge, see Mulsow 2012.

reflects a new conception of knowledge, upon the basis of an analysis of the works of Francis Bacon and Johannes Kepler. Bacon and Kepler are seemingly different characters, but they were nevertheless both avid readers of books of secrets, who used Della Porta's book of secrets as a source.

Peter Harrison has argued that Francis Bacon was one of the most prominent spokesmen for the understanding of the enterprise of natural philosophy as the undoing of the errors consequent of the Fall of Man (Harrison 2007, 172–185). Since sin was equated with error, the Fall was considered the source of ignorance and epistemic error. It was also the moment when sensory knowledge, which, until the Fall, had only been a distraction from the direct perception of knowledge with the eye of the soul, attained a certain value. It was only through externally imposed methodological constraints that "fallen" human minds could avoid error and be rightfully guided. Experimental natural philosophy, as it emerged in the seventeenth century, then aimed at the restoration of Adamic knowledge, a state which could be reached by developing methods such as experimental testing to avoid and erase error. Bacon described the sources of error – the "idols of the mind" – which included sensory errors as well as errors of the internal senses and the intellect. He also believed that errors could be rectified by natural means, and he suggested the use of optical instruments to circumvent the failures of the human senses and the practice of note-taking to combat the errors of memory.

For Bacon, to obtain the right material for experimental histories, on which natural philosophy was built, it was necessary for experience to become "literate". Experience could only obtain this literate stage – that is, transform into *"experientia literata"* – if it were written down in reports:

When all the experiments of all the arts have been collected and arranged, and come with one man's knowledge and judgement, many new things, useful to our life and condition, can be discovered by means of that very translation of experiments from one art to others, i.e., by that experience which I have called literate. (Bacon [1604] 2004, 161)

For Bacon, the recording of experience had to follow strict rules so that the resulting experimental history was not *any* collection of experiments, but a collection of relevant experiments generated in a controlled manner, according to the true order of experience and digested according to the rules of *experientia literata* (Jalobeanu 2014). The codification of error had an important place in Bacon's literate experience. He advised that the errors that the researcher committed during his enquiries and discoveries be included in experimental histories (Pastorino 2011, 545). Cesare Pastorino has shown that an embryonic version is already to be found in Bacon's conception of mechanical history. For Bacon, to be included in such a history are:

first the materialls, and their quantities and proportions; Next the Instrumts and Engins requesite; then the use and adoperation of every Instrumt; then the woork it self and all the processe thereof wth the tymes and seasons of doing every part thereof., whereby he listed the typical elements of recipes, and then he concluded by adding a new element to the traditional recipe format, that is, error codification:

Then the Errors wch may be comytted, and agayn those things wch conduce to make the woorke in more perfection.[10]

Bacon stressed the necessity of keeping both experimentation and its reporting open-ended, an attitude which implied a change in the epistemic value of failure and error. In contrast to books of secrets, Bacon's experimental histories were considered as open to improvement. As Cesare Pastorino has recently observed,

the acknowledgment of the provisional, historical character of knowledge was a tenet of what Bacon called an 'initiative' method of knowledge transmission, or a method of 'probation.' According to this approach, Bacon stated, knowledge 'ought to be delivered and intimated, if it were possible, in the same method wherein it was invented' and discovered. Only the display of its tentative features would encourage and stimulate others to improve and advance it. The format of the new genre of natural and experimental histories grew out of Bacon's dissatisfaction with the way in which recipes hid the imperfection of the process of knowledge production. (Pastorino 2011, 545)

I do not want to suggest that the emergence of the codification of error is a consequence of Bacon's conception of the project of experimental natural philosophy. Not only was the development of the Baconian style of experimental reporting left to other natural philosophers after Bacon, in particular Robert Boyle, as Steven Shapin (1984, 516) has famously argued, the dissatisfaction with the ways of writing down knowledge hiding the imperfection of the process of knowledge production, in conjunction with a belief in the open-endedness of processes of knowledge-making, was also much more widely shared at the beginning of the seventeenth century. It is, for example, equally present in the work of Johannes Kepler, whose poetics of science (Hallyn 1990) is, in fact, a poetics of failure. In several of his books in the broader field of mathematics, Kepler presented his knowledge as a narrative of the historical development of his own paths of inquiry. Here, I take as an example his presentation in the "Paralipomena" of his investigation of the measure of refraction (or what came to be known as Snell's law) – an example thus from his *Optics*. I think that this is appropriate given that, in this same book, he re-worked the secrets of Della Porta, which Bacon also transformed to make his experimental histories.[11] Kepler clearly indicated the reasons for, and benefits of, his poetics of failure:

The means and measure of refractions, even by itself, is established at a high price, and thus, reader, you may not be admitted without adverse consequences: not without first being led through the same briar patch of enquiry that I myself have crept through, on the grounds that since you are going to partake of the common fruit, you should pour out

---

10 Pastorino, forthcoming 2019.
11 Garber 2014; Dupré 2012.

labor as a first libation. This, however, turns out to be for your benefit, that, since there is not yet nothing left over that you might desire in the cause of refractions, you might nevertheless that no other measure remains, since all crannies have been thoroughly gone over; and also, that you might have the method of seeking before your eyes, cognizance of which alone serves as the greatest argument that this way of measuring has not been assumed arbitrarily. (Kepler [1604] 2000)

Kepler's narrative of his research into refraction consists of three approaches which he tried out and which, in the end, all failed to different degrees. Kepler started with the data which he had received from the measurements of atmospheric refraction by Tycho Brahe and Christoph Rothmann and the tables of refraction which he gathered from medieval optics such as Witelo's. This approach failed, he tells his reader, and characterising his first strategy of discovery of the measure of refraction as "an almost blind plan of enquiry", he switched gear and moved on to a second method. His second path of investigation was fuelled by analogies between refraction and reflection, which, however productive, also failed in delivering the measure of refraction, as Kepler had hoped. Addressing his reader with the words, "I have kept you and myself hanging long enough now", he moved on to his third path of investigation, in which he thought through his considerations of the causes of refraction. This third way allowed Kepler to discover a constant relation between angles of incidence and angles of refraction, which nevertheless only held for angles smaller than 30 degrees, and thus fell short of his objective of the discovery of the measure of refraction.

In sum, Kepler's historical account of his paths of investigation, characterising them as failures, was a strategy to cope with the imperfections of knowledge-making, opening it up for correction and improvement. In the terms of Polanyi's typology of error, Kepler recognised "good" error and the significance of learning from failure. For Kepler, the codification of error was not a response to the limits of language; instead, it was a rhetorical strategy to cope with the imperfections of knowledge-making. His poetics of failure served the goal of making weak knowledge stronger.

4. Poetics of failure

The imperfection of knowledge was also embedded in practices of book production and the culture of correction which emerged in the early modern print shop. The printing of a book was a social practice involving the collaboration of authors, publishers, and correctors. Printing a text did not entail the erasure of all typographical errors, as even Elizabeth Eisenstein in clarification of her claims for the fixity of print already pointed out. In fact, print was the kingdom of errors, because "in the hands of ignorant craftsmen, the printing of texts led to the multiplying of error" (Eisenstein 2002, 92). While many aspects of this culture of correction have ancient roots, Anthony Grafton has argued that a shift occurred in the late sixteenth century. This shift entailed a new sense of responsibility towards the transmitted text, reflected in the Antwerp publisher Christoph Plantin's comments that:

> we never make it our practice to change anything in an author's manuscript deliberately. This is so much our policy that I would sometimes rather print what we do not understand, even if it seems to be an error, as it is in the copy given to us, than to replace it with something on the basis of conjecture or some other source.[12]

In the printing shop, correctors seem to have understood their work as always provisional and open for further improvement. Their idea that perfection was impossible to attain shines through in their puzzled comments on the imposition of censorship and the Index:

> If all the troubling errors in our writers are corrected, will we not be asserting, against the truth, that they surpassed all the powers of weak humanity and gained perfect knowledge and understanding?[13]

Printers evolved their own new ways of reporting and correcting errors. In the sixteenth century, they invented the *errata*, listing the mistakes in the text, which could range from typographical errors to substantive changes. Not only did the codification of error underscore the imperfection of knowledge which Bacon and Kepler embraced, it is important to realise that it also emerged and was embedded in the context of early modern print culture through inventions such as *errata*.

The recognition of the epistemic value of error and failure is reflected in new ways of organising artisanal knowledge, which significantly differed from the format of the books of secrets. One format was the commentary, consisting of an edition and sometimes translation of a collection of artisanal recipes, including annotations pointing out the errors, a format which emerged in the seventeenth century. An excellent example of such a text is Johannes Kunckel's *Ars vitraria experimentalis oder Vollkommene Glasmacher-Kunst* (1679). I have discussed Kunckel's book elsewhere in relation to the codification of error, primarily considered in response to the limits of language, and so here I summarise only the most important points (Dupré 2017).

First of all, it is important to point out that elements of the magisterial account, as embodied in books of secrets, are still present in Kunckel's text. Kunckel does not just pride himself on first-hand experimentation, he also warns his reader that the recipes found in the book might not work upon the reader's first trial. This does not mean that the recipes are wrong; it is more likely that the reader made a mistake. If the reader finds himself in such a situation, Kunckel's

---

12 Quoted in Grafton 2011, 161.
13 Quoted in Grafton 2011, 137.

advice is to try again, and again, and again. After all, he reminds his reader, it requires practice to be a master. Here Kunckel's text supports Pamela Smith's argument that artisanal recipes and "how-to" books were not always, or not only, about telling readers how to get something done, but about how to do things right (Smith 2012). They are not – or not only – about the transmission of knowledge, but about the transmission of epistemic values which were very important in artisanal workshops. One example of such a value is continuous attention, and indeed, the repetition of practices on which Kunckel also places so much emphasis.

Kunckel was very conscious of the limits of language in expressing artisanal knowledge. It was a matter of practice. The glassmaker needed to be equipped with a good eye, as Kunckel called it, *Augenmaß*.[14] *Augenmaß* was called for when judging the quantities of ingredients crucial to obtaining colours; small differences of quantities could result in big differences of colour. "None of this can be taught on paper," Kunckel[15] concluded, proclaiming the limits of language. It was to characterise this unspeakable property of artisanal knowledge that Albrecht Dürer had already evoked the term which Kunckel used for the same reason, *Augenmaß*. Dürer's *Augenmaß* was *Wissen* (knowledge) partly acquired through practice (Doorly 2004, 272). *Augenmaß* guided the hand of the skilled artisan and allowed him to avoid *yrthumb* (error) and *falscheit* (falseness).

Kunckel's *Ars vitraria experimentalis* was a multi-layered book, consisting of several layers of texts, translations, annotations and comments. The book contains: firstly, Kunckel's translation and comments on Antonio Neri's *L'arte vetraria*, the first printed book on glass-making, published in 1612; secondly, Kunckel's German translation of Christopher Merrett's *The Art of Glass*, published in 1662. Merrett was a practising physician in London, a fellow of the Royal College of Physicians and a founding member of the Royal Society in London (Allen 2004). As part of the Royal Society's history of trades programme, he translated Neri's *L'arte vetraria* into English as *The Art of Glass* in 1662. This was a considerably expanded translation, not just a rendering in English, but with the addition of Merrett's "Observations". In this separate section of *The Art of Glass*, Merrett discussed his views on the nature, antiquity and use of glass, followed by notes on the different recipes of Neri. Thus, the second part of Kunckel's book is a translation of Merrett's book, which is itself already a translation of Neri's book. Moreover, in the third part of his book, Kunckel includes his *Observationen und curieusen Erinnerungen* on Merrett's notes on Neri's book. Kunckel's book thus consists of layers of annotation and comment on Neri.

Experimentation led Kunckel to evaluate Neri's recipes. Kunckel used his translation of Neri as a vehicle not just for making changes, adapting to local

---

14 Kunckel 1689, Vorrede.
15 Kunckel 1689, Vorrede.

circumstances and procedures whenever those differed from those found in Neri, but also to note whenever Neri went wrong. A recipe could be wrong in different ways. A first type of error, perhaps the least interesting one, was a typographical error. A second kind of error concerned the materials, especially the quantities of ingredients, or the material conditions of the processes, such as furnaces and temperatures. A third important error was a violation of the idea that a good recipe should not be too complex without good reason. The procedures followed by Neri were wrong, according to Kunckel, not because they led to the wrong result, but because they contained operations conducted in vain, which were not necessary to reach the goal or were simply too cumbersome. For example, on one of Neri's recipes, Kunckel noted that, "The author makes this recipe difficult and expensive, while it can be done with much less effort and expense" (1689, 75).

The full impact of Kunckel's codification of error becomes clear when compared with books of secrets. Authors of recipes corrected a recipe, but they did not note that they had corrected their source recipe, or how exactly the source recipe was lacking; and they certainly did not maintain the source recipe as Kunckel did. Kunckel's magisterial account in his preface is borrowed from books of secrets, and as much might be expected from a book which also served to establish Kunckel as an expert on glassmaking upon his move to the court of Brandenburg. Nevertheless, Kunckel's layering of recipes, annotating the errors he finds in them, also sets him significantly apart from books of secrets, which destroyed the previous layer by replacing the source recipe. Kunckel's book reveals the traces of his testing of recipes, and by adding translation upon translation, and comment upon annotation, it also suggests the open-ended character of the process, as if Kunckel expected another author to add another layer of comment and annotation to the layer which he had added to the text.

Even if the process of knowledge-making was open-ended, as Kunckel expected to be corrected and emended, the errors which he himself codified and corrected were not his own, but those of Neri and Merrett. In the process of testing recipes, Kunckel experienced the errors whenever Neri's recipes failed to deliver the desired results. The format of comment and annotation which Kunckel used allowed readers to experience the errors for themselves if they were so inclined, while attributing these errors to his predecessors rather than to his own failures. This use of codification of error to establish authority and expertise is not unusual in the artisanal world. A famous example comes from a narrative of making by the sixteenth-century sculptor Benvenuto Cellini. His account of the casting of a monumental bronze in his *Treatises on Goldsmithing and Sculpture* emphasised the difficulty of this process, placing it on a par with Michelangelo's carving of marble statues from one single block of marble, and the ingenuity of accomplishing the casting of the statue in one pour. Cellini underscores that he had to rescue the metal when the professional bronze casters failed. He narrates that, when he had to retreat to bed because of sickness, the craftsmen to which he entrusted the project negligently allowed a cake to form on the metal. Leaping from his sick-bed, Cellini reproached them:

Oh you good-for-nothings! Who not only know nought, but have brought to nought all my splendid labours, at least keep your heads on your shoulders now and obey me; for from my knowledge of the craft I can bring to life what you have given up for dead, if only the sickness that is upon me shall not crush out my body's vigour. (Cellini 1967, 123)

Instructing his craftsmen on how to proceed with handling the materials, Cellini then succeeded in liquefying the metal and thus in "bringing it back to life" (Cole 1999). This narrative strategy of attribution of errors to others, either predecessors or workers of perceived lower epistemic status, was much more widely used than was commonly thought, and was not limited to the artisanal world. It has been shown to have been already quite common in ancient, medieval and early modern medicine (or "*téchne iatriké*") and alchemy. Paracelsus made ample use of it.[16]

While Kunckel acknowledged the epistemic value of error, other artisanal writings more fully embraced (what I have called in connection to Kepler) a poetics of failure. In fact, I would like to suggest that a poetics of failure characterises those artisanal writings which we might call "manuals", in the sense that they claim to serve the learning of a craft, whether it be surgery or goldsmithing, in opposition to the *Encyclopédie*, in which Diderot followed a logic of representation in his description of the arts, and which was not intended to be used in the context of instruction. I illustrate this with one example of such a manual: the eighteenth-century *Guidebook for Upcoming Gold- and Silversmiths* (1721) by the Dutch silversmith Willem van Laer (1674–1722). Rather than a book of secrets, van Laer's guide presents itself as a sort of structured *curriculum* for the apprentice, although it is in no way intended to replace, but rather to complement, hands-on education on the workshop floor (Hagendijk 2018). Van Laer wrote down his instructions and description of techniques in ways suggesting alternative histories of his own failures. A typical pattern is that van Laer suggests that one way of proceeding would fail and the result could be potentially disastrous. One example is his suggestion that, without the preparation of the Brussels sand to make the mould, the cast will be undesirably "rough". But this is just one example; in his book, failures are ubiquitous, and he regularly, for example, in his discussion of soldering, includes extensive trouble-shooting sections. As a master silversmith, van Laer describes failures only to suggest how to correct them, but it is clear that the failures are his own. The failures that he describes are based upon his own workshop experience.

---

16 Bondio 2011; Pereira 2012.

5. Conclusion

Artisans knew that one could only learn by doing, and that this meant making mistakes. It is this epistemic value of error and failure which Palissy and so many others voiced when expressing scepticism about the didactic value of their own writings. In contemporary art theory, the cause of the occurrence of error in the arts was considered to be deficiency in judgement, which meant that artists failed to adhere to the rules (Ostrow 2006, 278–279). These rules could sometimes be formulated mathematically, such as in the sixteenth-century work of Paolo Pino and Giovanni Paolo Lomazzo, in which errors were associated with the ignorance of perspective and the absence of good proportions. For example, Prospero Bresciano's statue of *Moses* was criticised for not using the proper working methods of the sculptor, and precisely in terms of "*Moses*" being ill-proportioned. Other artists, such as the painter Pieter Aertsen, were even thought to play wilfully with such proportional and compositional "*errata*" (Falkenburg 2006). However, these are errors with regard to the finished art work, while Palissy and other authors of recipes, secrets and instructions, such as Kunckel and van Laer, whom we have discussed in this chapter, wrote about error and failure in relation to the process of making.

At the beginning of the seventeenth century, the epistemic value of error and failure became recognised in the world of scholarship, from the mathematical sciences to natural history. This can be seen as a recognition that humans, including mathematicians and natural and experimental philosophers, are all weak actors who need to develop strategies of error management. More than knowledge of materials and techniques or the value of attention and repetition, one could argue that it was the value of error and failure which the likes of Kepler and Bacon, developing new ways of knowing in the sciences at the beginning of the seventeenth century, adopted from the world of artisans. It is telling that recent work on medical ethics – on how to deal with errors in medical practice – explicitly harks back to the work of Albrecht Dürer as a source of inspiration and a model of the recognition of the imperfections of knowledge and the ideal of openness encouraging the publication of knowledge, expecting others to detect and correct errors and thereby perfecting knowledge (Bondio 2012, 295–296). It thus seems that artisanal knowledge remains a source for the recognition of the epistemic value of error and failure to this day, in the same way that it was around the year 1600.

The adoption of the apprentice model in the world of scholarship coincided with new ways of writing down and organising artisanal knowledge, including the invention of the manual. There are two issues at play here, I have suggested, which relate to Polanyi's distinction between good and bad error, as I introduced them at the beginning of this essay. For Polanyi, bad error was the consequence of the impossibilities of fixing skills in words, and I have suggested that the codification of error emerged in response to the limits of language. However, the recognition of good error, in Polanyi's conception, and of failure and the imperfection of knowledge, also sits in uneasy tension with the establishment of authority. Therefore, I have argued, authors turned to formats, such as van Laer's manual, adopting a poetics of failure, which replaced the book of secrets. This allowed them to recognise the value of failure, while, at the same time, establishing themselves as experts. Confronted with the imperfections of knowledge, they adopted a rhetorical strategy to make weak knowledge stronger, that is, to package failure as being essential to success.

References

Allen, D.E. (2004): "Merret, Christopher (1614–1695)". In: Oxford Dictionary of National Biography. Oxford: University Press; Online Edition. May 2013, available at: http://www.oxforddnb.com/view/article/18599, last accessed 1 June 2015.

Bacon, Francis [1604] (2004): *The Instauratio magna Part II: Novum organum and Associated Texts*. Edited by Graham Rees and Maria Wakely. *The Oxford Francis Bacon*, Vol. 11. Oxford: Oxford University Press.

Bondio, Mariacarla Gadebusch (2011): "Die Fehler und Irrtümer der Ärtze – Paracelsus' Kritik und ihr medizinethisches Potenzial." In: Albrecht Classen, *Religion und Gesundheit: Der heilkundliche Diskurs im 16. Jahrhundert*, 215–230. Berlin: Walter de Gruyter.

Bondio, Mariacarla Gadbusch (2012): "Vom Ringen der Medizin um eine Fehlbahrkeitskultur. Epistemologische und ethische Reflexionen." In: Mariacarla Gadebusch Bondio and Agostino Paravicini Bagliani (Eds.): *Errors and Mistakes: A Cultural of Fallibility*, 291–311. Firenze: Sismel – Edizione del Galluzzo.

Bondio, Mariacarla Gadebusch, and Agostino Paravicini Bagliani (2012): "Fallibility and its Cultures – Introduction." In: Mariacarla Gadebusch Bondio and Agostino Paravicini Bagliani (Eds.): *Errors and Mistakes: A Cultural of Fallibility*, vii–xiii. Firenze: Sismel – Edizione del Galluzzo.

Burton, Brian (2005): "The Art of Failure: Samuel Beckett and Derek Mahon." *Irish Studies Review*, 13 (1): 55–64.

Cellini, Benvenuto (1967): *The Treatises of Benvenuto Cellini on Goldsmithing and Sculpture*. New York: Dover Publications Inc.

Cole, Michael (1999): "Cellini's Blood." *The Art Bulletin*, 81 (2): 215–235.

Clarke, Mark (2009): "Writing Recipes for Non-specialists c.1300: The Anglo-Latin Secretum Philosophorum, Glasgow MS Hunterian 110." In: Erma Hermens and Joyce H Townsend (Eds.): *Sources and Serendipity: Testimonies of Artists' Practice*, 50–64. London: Archetype Publications.

Clarke, Mark, et al. (Eds.) (2012): *Transmission of Artists' Knowledge*. Brussels: Koninklijke Vlaamse Academie van België.

Doorly, Patrick (2004): "Dürer's *Melencolia I*: Plato's Abandoned Search for the Beautiful." *The Art Bulletin*, 86: 255–276.

Dupré, Sven (2012): "Kepler's Optics without Hypotheses." *Synthese*, 185 (3): 501–525.

Dupré, Sven (2017): "Doing it Wrong: The Translation of Artisanal Knowledge and the Codification of Error." In: Matteo Valleriani (Ed.): *The Structures of Practical Knowledge*,167–188. Cham et al: Springer International Publishing.

Dupré, Sven (2019): "How-To Optics." In: Sven Dupré (Ed.): *Perspective as Practice: Renaissance Cultures of Optics*, 279-300. Turnhout: Brepols.

Eamon, William (1994): *Science and the Secrets of Nature. Books of Secrets in Medieval and Early Modern Culture*. Princeton NJ: Princeton University Press.

Eisenstein, Elizabeth (2002): "An Unacknowledged Revolution Revisited." *The American Historical Review*, 107 (1): 87–105.

Falkenburg, Reindert L. (2006): "On Compositional 'Errata' in Pieter Aertsen's Peasant Scenes." In: Jeffrey F. Hamburger and Anne S. Kortweg (Eds.): *Tributes in Honor of James H. Marrow: Studies in Painting and Manuscript Illumination of the Late Middle Ages and Northern Renaissance*, 197–205. Turnhout: Harvey Miller Publishers.

Garber, Daniel (2014): "Merchants of Light and Mystery Men: Bacon's Last Projects in Natural History." *Journal of Early Modern Studies*, 3: 91–106.

Gooday, Graeme (1998): "Re-writing the 'book of blots': Critical Reflections on Histories of Technological 'Failure'." *History and Technology*, 14 (4): 265–291.

Goulding, Robert (2006): "Deceiving the Senses in the Thirteenth Century: Trickey and Illusion in the Secretum philosophorum." In: Charles Burnett and W.F. Ryan (Eds.): *Magic and the Classical Tradition*, 135–162. London: Warburg Institute and Nina Aragno Editore.

Grafton, Anthony (2011): *The Culture of Correction in Renaissance Europe*. London: The British Library.

Hagendijk, Thijs (2018): "Learning a Craft from Books: Historical Re-enactment of Functional Reading in Gold- and Silversmithing." *Nuncius*, 33 (2): 198–235.

Hallyn, Fernand (1990): *The Poetic Structure of the World: Copernicus and Kepler*. Cambridge MA: The MIT Press.

Harrison, Peter (2007): *The Fall of Man and the Foundations of Science*. New York: Cambridge University Press.

Jalobeanu, Dana (2014): "Constructing Natural Historical Facts: Baconian Natural History in Newton's First Paper on Light and Colors." In: Zvi Biener and Eric Schliesser (Eds.): *Newton and Empiricism*, 39–65. Oxford: Oxford University Press.

Kepler, Johannes [1604] (2000): *Paralipomena ad Vitellionem & Optical Part of Astronomy*. Santa Fe NM: Green Lion Press.

Kinnucan, Michael (2011): "Beckett and Failure." *Hypocrite Reader, Issue 5: Realism*, available at: http://hypocritereader.com/5/beckett-and-failure, last accessed June 2018.

Kunckel, Johannes (1689): *Ars vitraria experimentalis oder vollkommene Glasmacher-Kunst*. Frankfurt-Leipzig: Kunckel.

Leong, Elaine, and Alisha Rankin (Eds.) (2011): *Secrets and Knowledge in Medicine and Science, 1500–1800*. Farnham: Ashgate Publishing.

Moretti, Cesare, and Tullio Toninato (2001): *Ricettario vetrario del Rinascimento. Trascrizione da un manoscritto anonimo veneziano*. Venice: Marsilio Editori.

Mulsow, Martin (2012): *Prekäres Wissen. Eine andere Ideengeschichte der Frühen Neuzeit*. Berlin: Suhrkamp Verlag.

Neumaier, Otto (2010): "Wer oder was fehlt bei einem Fehler?" In: Otto Neumaier (Ed.): *Was aus Fehlern zu lernen ist in Alltag, Wissenschaft und Kunst*. Vienna-Berlin: LIT Verlag.

Neven, Sylvie (2014): "Transmission of Alchemical and Artistic Knowledge in German Mediaeval and Premodern Recipe Books." In: Sven Dupré (Ed.): *Laboratories of Art: Alchemy and Art Technology from Antiquity to the 18th Century*, 23–52. Cham et al: Springer.

Ostrow, Steven F. (2006): "The Discourse of Failure in Seventeenth-Century Rome: Prospero's Bresciano's *Moses*." *The Art Bulletin*, 88 (2): 267–291.

Palissy, Bernard (1957): *The Admirable Discourses of Bernard Palissy*. Urbana IL: University of Illinois Press.

Pannabecker, John R. (1994): "Diderot, the Mechanical Arts, and the *Encyclopédie*. In Search of the Heritage of Technology Education." *Journal of Technology Education*, 6 (1): 45–57.

Pastorino, Cesare (2011): "Weighing Experience: Experimental Histories and Francis Bacon's Quantitative Program." *Early Science and Medicine*, 16 (6): 542–570.

Pastorino, Cesare (forthcoming 2019): "The Baconian Natural and Experimental Histories as an Epistemic Genre". *Centaurus*, 61.

Pereira, Michela (2012): "Il primo errore: Problematiche epistemologiche dell' alchimia." In: Mariacarla Gadebusch Bondio and Agostino Paravicini Bagliani (Eds.): *Errors and Mistakes: A Cultural of Fallibility*, 97–128. Firenze: Sismel – Edizione del Galluzzo.

Polanyi, Michael (2005): *Personal Knowledge: Towards a Post-Critical Philosophy*. London: Routledge.

Pye, David (1978): *The Nature and Aesthetics of Design*. London: Barrie & Jenkins.

Roberts, Lissa (2012): "The Circulation of Knowledge in Early Modern Europe: Embodiment, Mobility, Learning and Knowing." *History of Technology*, 31(1): 47–68.

Shapin, Steven (1984): "Pump and Circumstance: Robert Boyle's Literary Technology." *Social Studies of Science*, 14 (4): 481–520.

Shell, Hanna Rose (2004): "Casting Life, Recasting Experience: Bernard Palissy's Occupation between Maker and Nature." *Configurations*, 12 (1): 1–40.

Smith, Pamela H. (2010) "Why Write a Book? From Lived Experience to the Written Word in Early Modern Europe. *Bulletin of the German Historical Institute*, 47: 25–50.

Smith, Pamela H. (2012): "Craft Techniques and How-to Books." In: Mark Clarke et al. (Eds.): *Transmission of Artists' Knowledge*, 75–84. Brussels: KVAB.

Stalnaker, Joanna (2010): *The Unfinished Enlightenment: Description in the Age of the Encyclopedia*. Ithaca NY: Cornell University Press.

On Literary Knowledge:
The Conceptual, the Figurative and the Performative

Rivka Feldhay

Abstract

This essay is an attempt to analyse the knowledge of possible worlds that is deposited in literary texts. Its main arguments concern the conditions under which the creation of meaning in literary form constitutes systematisable knowledge. My point of departure is Aristotle's *Poetics*, where he articulates the claim that literature is closer to philosophy than to history. Aristotle's method of analysis offers three categories – the "elements" of "poetic works": the medium of literary works that is language; the object of analysis which are the actions, character and thoughts of the protagonists; and the "manner" of presentation. Relying on the work of modern theoreticians of literature, among them George Lukács, Mikhail Bakhtin, Hans Blumenberg, Tzvetan Todorov, Robert Louis Jackson, and Barbara Cassin – I adapt Aristotle's "elements" to the analysis of the modern literary form that is the novel, suggesting a modification of Aristotle's "elements": the emergence of modern subjectivities as the main "object" of the novel, which I exemplify through Dostoevesky's novel *Demons*. I deem this element to constitute the conceptual backbone of *Demons*. In analysing the "medium" of this novel, I focus on the "figurative" dimension of its language, in particular the figure of a "wrecked ship" linked to the life experience of the protagonists in the chaotic Russia of the time. Finally, I analyse Dostoevsky's narratorial devices to account for the "perfomative" (the "manner" in Aristotle's terms) aspect of the novel. The analysis of *Demons* on the three levels of the conceptual, the figurative and the performative purports to show how in novels universal aspects of human experience assume particular meaning in specific time and space. Such coincidence of the particular and the universal, I think, is rather unique for literary knowledge.

1. Some introductory analytical remarks

This essay brings to the table the topic of "literary knowledge" in order to throw light on traditional distinctions between theoretical knowledge, on the one hand, and poetics – the art of producing literary meaning in the most general sense, including literary fiction and novels, on the other.[1] These distinctions, assuming socio-institutional and cultural meanings, tend to create hierarchies that translate into concepts of "strong" (scientific) and "weak" (humanistic) knowledge.

I offer, therefore, an attempt to undermine the dichotomous nature of the epistemic/non-epistemic distinction, thereby questioning the hierarchical connotations associated with it. Here, in fact, I have two different claims. The first concerns the kind of knowledge offered by literary texts, and my point of departure is taken from Hilary Putnam in his essay entitled "Literature, Science, and Reflection" (1976), where he insists that literature gives us plausible accounts of how it feels to live through experiences such as being a communist in the 1940s, for example (Putnam 1976, 489). "Being aware of a new interpretation of the facts," he writes, "is knowledge of a possibility. It is conceptual knowledge." (1976, 488) In addition, on what relates to "theoretical knowledge", I am joining many historians of science who have questioned the view of scientific knowledge as merely embodying "pure cognition" given to logical proof. Indeed, a turn towards the historisation of scientific epistemology can be traced back to the late nineteenth century,[2] stressing the practical and contingent aspects of scientific knowledge later on (Valleriani 2017). My attempt to analyse what I call "literary knowledge" – knowledge of the possible human worlds that is deposited in literary texts – indeed, continues a contemporary trend within the field of science studies (Meyer 2018), pushing us to elaborate our thinking in new ways about the boundaries between "science" and "literature".

In what sense, and under which conditions, does the creation of meaning in literary form constitute systematisable knowledge within a differentiated field, with its own objects, boundaries and institutionalised spaces, and embedded in a socio-cultural environment of specific time and place (Brooks 1981, VIII–IX; XIX)? And, furthermore, what is the status of such "knowledge" on the spectrum stretching between "weak" and "strong"?

From the dawn of the Western philosophical tradition, discussion of such questions was guided by two seemingly contradictory intuitions, articulated, how-

---

1 In the Greek classical tradition, *poesis* refers to all forms of verbal composition and also to the production of "imitations" or representations in other fields, such as painting and sculpture. See Else 1957. Poetics in the modern sense, however, refers to literary production of meaning within a well bounded cultural field – "literature" – where the consensus about "what is literary" changes according to the context of time and place. See Eagleton 1996, especially "Introduction: What is Literature?", and Chapter 1, "The Rise of English".

2 Rheinberger 2010; Daston 1994.

ever, within a common understanding of the nature of literary activity. Both Plato[3] (*Republic* X) and Aristotle (*Poetics*)[4] presupposed that the art of verbal and musical composition was an act of imitation/representation, closer to the art/*techne* of painters or sculptors than to intellectual reflection and deliberation, the domain of philosophers. Plato, however, believed that poetry was three times removed from Truth, being but an imitation of things that are imitations of "ideas", and hence a "corruption of the mind of all listeners who do not possess as antidote a knowledge of its real nature",[5] while Aristotle speaks of poetic imitation of "men in action", whose cause is a natural instinct common to all people who "enjoy seeing likeness", because, as we look, we learn and infer what each is, for instance, "that is so and so".[6]

While Plato and Aristotle differed substantially in their explicit judgement of the nature of different kinds of verbal meaning production, their positions are complex, and do not simply contradict each other, for Plato's philosophical dialogues are far more distinguished by their literary flavour than Aristotle's treatises, including his treatise on *Poetics*. Furthermore, both denied poetics the highest epistemic status equal to that of theoretical knowledge. And yet, while Plato states that "it is phantoms, not realities that they [the poets – R.F.] produce",[7] Aristotle, dedicating a whole treatise to the art of poetry, seems to be guiding a systematic "inquiry" into its very "nature" as well as the various "parts" – aspects or "specific differences" – that distinguish it from other practices of *poiesis* (such as painting or sculpture). By comparing poetry later on in his text to philosophy, on the one hand, and to history, on the other, he endorses poetry as a unique source of learning about men's actions, their characters, values and emotions, their experiences and thoughts – in short, their *Lebenswelt* or life world. In the introduction to his treatise, Aristotle writes:

Let us here deal with Poetry, its essence and its several species, with the characteristic function of each species and the way in which plots must be constructed if the poem is to be a success; and also with the number and character of the constituent parts of a poem, and similarly with all other matters proper to this same inquiry (μέθοδος); and let us, as nature directs, begin first with first principles.[8]

Choosing the word *methodos* to describe his endeavour, Aristotle invokes his ambition to find a "way" to organise and systematise the practices of "poetic imitation" analogous to the "scientific procedures" used in Physics and Metaphysics, the most prestigious *scientiae* in his system of knowledge. Aristotle's systematic

---

3 Plato, *Republic*, 595a–608b.
4 Aristotle 1932, *Poetics*, 1447a.
5 Plato, *Republic*, 595b.
6 Aristotle 1932, *Poetics*, 1448b.
7 Plato, *Republic*, 599a.
8 Aristotle 1932, *Poetics*, 1447a.

inquiry into poetics is thus considered by Tzvetan Todorov (1939–2017), one of the most prominent theoreticians of modern poetics, as the first point of reference in the quest of modern scholars for a "theory of literature" (Brooks 1981, VIII). This kind of theory, it is claimed, provides us with an understanding of literary production that transcends the series of interpretations or commentaries on specific literary texts while anchored in a well bounded, differentiated literary field. Following Todorov's judgement about Aristotle, I shall use Aristotle's text as a point of departure for my argument that literary texts must not necessarily be read as works of art *tout court* – that is to say, judged merely by aesthetic criteria. Rather, they should be conceived as suggesting knowledge about possible forms of living in particular historical and cultural contexts. Such knowledge, however, is given to us in a different "way" than the way knowledge is offered by history or philosophy. Furthermore, Aristotle's *Poetics* will also be my inspiration for deriving a series of parameters for analysing literary/"poetic" texts which, after having read Aristotle's *Poetics*, I shall accommodate for reading and systematically analysing one specific literary text, the novel *Demons* by Fyodor Dostoevsky (1821–1881), and the knowledge which it has offered to his readers ever since.[9]

While Aristotle provides my point of departure for studying the literary production of meaning through a series of specific "elements",[10] an account of the genre of the novel – Dostoevsky's novels in particular – and the adaptation of the contents of Aristotelian parameters to this genre, will constitute the third section of my theoretical introduction.[11]

In his *Theory of the Novel* (1920), George Lukács (1885–1971) posited the novel as a new literary form born out of a "complete change in our [modern – R.F.] concept of life and its relationship to essential being" (Lukács 1971, 41–42). Immanence, he argues, "is banished from the cosmos as though by the gradual working of a spell", while "the longing for its return remains alive and unsatisfied" (1971, 42). Lukács further develops his argument by discussing the historico-philosophical background to the transition from classical and medieval literary forms to the novel, a trajectory I shall not elaborate upon here. Suffice it to accept his conclusion concerning the "objective imperfection" of the novel's world and the "interiority" of its subjective one (Lukács 1971, 70). This allows him to claim that "the novel appears as something in the process of becoming" (Lukács 1971, 46), and that "its nature as a process excludes completeness only so far as content is concerned" (1971, 72). "As a formal constituent of the novel form", he continues, "this signifies an interior diversion of the normatively crea-

---

9 Here is a quotation from a letter written by Dostoevsky in Florence to his niece: "I must return to Russia; here I will end by losing any possibility of writing for lack of my indispensable and habitual material – Russian reality (which feeds my thoughts) and the Russians." In: Frank 2010, 592, note 3.

10 Aristotle 1932, *Poetics*, I.2.

11 Aristotle 1932, *Poetics*, I.3.

tive subject into subjectivity as interiority", a diversion that "strives to imprint the contents of its longing upon the alien world" (1971, 74).

The emergence of the novel as a new literary form, expressing a deep change in the modern view of life and a new understanding of the modern subject, does not necessarily undermine Aristotle's view of the status of poetic production of meaning in the order of knowledge and art. Rather, I will suggest that, while literature maintains its status as a special kind of knowledge/praxis (*poiesis*), Aristotle's parameters for analysing poetic works need to be accommodated[12] in the spirit of George Lukács, and with the help of other modern critics and theoreticians, in particular, Mikhail Bakhtin (1895–1975),[13] Hans Blumenberg (1920–1996)[14] R.L. Jackson (1923–)[15] and David Stromberg.[16] Such accommodation will lead into my reading of Dostoevsky's novel *Demons* ([1873] 1995) as a source of knowledge about "plausible" actions, feelings and ideas of particular, (fictional) individuals living in Russia between the 1840s and 1860, whose forms of life were the possible products of a specific time, physical, social and ideological space and personal circumstances. In Part 2, I shall also draw on Aristotle's and some of the modern critics, in order to argue that this novel simultaneously carries universal significance and relevance for understanding human beings in very diverse historical contexts.

2. Poetry as a source of knowledge about possible human worlds

Aristotle opens his discussion of poetics by specifying its different kinds: "Epic poetry and tragedy, comedy and Dithyrambic poetry and music of the flute and the lyre", all of them are "modes of imitation".[17] He differentiates among them, however, in three respects: according to "the medium, the objects, the manner or mode of imitation".[18] Taking "medium" as the first "specific difference" that characterises poetic works, he turns to the language of tragedy and epic poetry, which "imitate by means of language alone",[19] a language that is "embellished

---

12 Aristotle 1932, *Poetics*, I.3.

13 Bakhtin 1984.

14 Blumenberg 1996.

15 Jackson 2013.

16 Stromberg 2012.

17 Aristotle, Poetics, I.I.2. All quotations from Aristotle's *Poetics* in this section are taken from S.H. Butcher's translations in the *The Internet Classic Archive*, available at: http://classics.mit.edu/ Aristotle/poetics.1.1.html, last accessed 8 August 2017. The reference numbers give the section and part in Roman numerals, followed by paragraph numbers in Arabic numerals.

18 Aristotle, *Poetics*, I.I.3.

19 Aristotle, *Poetics*, I.I.5.

with each kind of artistic ornament".[20] Poetic language thus appears not merely as the product of a system of symbols representing beings in the world and used in accordance with a set of conventional rules in the creation of meaning. Rather, language also signifies on a plurality of levels – among them metaphors, intonation and rhyme – that are the poet's tools for creating a world common to himself or herself, the agents represented in his or her work, and the audience of the poetic work.

Referring, then, to the second specific difference of poetic imitation – namely, its objects – Aristotle says:

Tragedy is the imitation of an action; and an action implies personal agents, who necessarily possess certain distinctive qualities both of character and of thought.[21]

By Character I mean that in virtue of which we ascribe certain qualities to the agents. Thought is required wherever a statement is proved, or it may be, a general truth enunciated.[22]

By plot I here mean the arrangement of the incidents [...] most important of all is the structure of the incidents. For tragedy is an imitation not of men, but of an action and of life, and life consists of action, and its end is a mode of action.[23]

Hence the incidents and the plot are the end of a tragedy; and the end is the chief thing of all.[24]

The plot [...] is the first principle, and as it were, the soul of a tragedy.[25]

In the category of the "objects" of poetic imitation, then, Aristotle includes the plot, built upon the agents' actions, their character and thoughts in so far as these provide the necessary background for understanding their actions and the plot. Plot is the most important, for it is an imitation of a series of incidents that constitute "an action" that is "serious, complete and of a certain magnitude".[26] Action or plot, however, imply personal agents – hence, characters – made, in Silvia Carli's apt phrasing, of "that which determines the quality of the agents", namely, their moral values and emotions (Carli 2010), as well as their thought or intellect, a power of judgement which is "required wherever a statement is proved, or it may be, a general truth enunciated".[27]

Turning now to the third element of poetic/literary works, Aristotle uses the term "manner", or "mode" of imitation. *Manner*, however, hardly receives any

---

20 Aristotle, *Poetics*, I.VI.2.
21 Aristotle, *Poetics*, I.VI.6.
22 Aristotle, *Poetics*, I.VI.4.
23 Aristotle, *Poetics*, I.VI.4–5.
24 Aristotle, *Poetics*, I.VI.5.
25 Aristotle, *Poetics*, I.VI.6.
26 Aristotle, *Poetics*, I.VI.2.
27 Aristotle, *Poetics*, I.VI.4.

further comment, apart from appearing in a list of "elements" distinguishing the poetic work, under the term *opsis*, or "spectacle".[28] Commentators tend to interpret *opsis* as *mise-en-scene*, which I understand to be the performative aspect of the drama, following Aristotle, who emphasised its spectacular effects on the audience,[29] or, in other words, the effective power of the drama in the real world.

The three distinguishing features or elements of poetry are therefore its medium (language), its objects (plot, character and thought/ideas), and its manner (performative quality). With these features in place, Aristotle is now ready to state the epistemic status of the art of poetry in Chapter 9 of his text. Convinced of the existence of a structure that must emerge by interweaving the three elements of poetry mentioned above, Aristotle declares that poetry "is a more philosophical and a higher thing than history: for poetry tends to express the universal, history the particular".[30]

Where, according to Aristotle, does the universality of poetry – tragic and epic drama – lie, and what is its relation to particulars? Apparently, there is a tension between Aristotle's claims that poetry is an imitation of men's action and life – a realm where chance and fortune prevail – and his insistence that poetry speaks of universals, to wit, human actions subjected to the universal laws of probability and necessity. But Aristotle seems to succeed in bridging over such tensions by further explaining the nature of the objects of poetic art: dramatic plots and "*dramatis personae*".

"Tragedy is an imitation of an action that is complete, and whole... which has a beginning, a middle, and an end."[31] While the beginning "does not itself follow anything by causal necessity", it is "naturally" followed by something that "comes to be", and an end "is that which itself naturally follows some other thing, either by necessity, or as a rule, but has nothing following it".[32] Aristotle never tires of stressing that the plot of a drama means a series of events "artistically constructed",[33] that is, it "must neither begin nor end at haphazard".[34] The worst, he continues, are episodic plots, "in which the episodes or acts succeed one another without probable or necessary sequence".[35] The plot, then, consists of a series of events linked by relations of probability and necessity. So are also the thoughts and opinions of the actors – the "*dramatis personae*", endowed with "the faculty of

28 Aristotle, *Poetics*, I.VI.4.
29 Aristotle, *Poetics*, I.XIV.1.
30 Aristotle, *Poetics*, I.IX.1.
31 Aristotle, *Poetics*, I.VII.2.
32 Aristotle, *Poetics*, I.VII.2.
33 Aristotle, *Poetics*, I.VI.5.
34 Aristotle, *Poetics*, I.VII.2.
35 Aristotle, *Poetics*, I.IX.2.

saying what is possible and pertinent in given circumstances",[36] and their actions which must conform with what is possible in terms of their values and emotions.

The quotations above – and many others that might have been given – confirm Carli's claim that the art of poetics, engaged in imitation/representation, shows the form of a chain of events enacted by the characters – "types" rather than individuals – events that are never severed from the experiential (Carli 2010, 305). In this sense, poetics "moves from what is better known to us to what is better known in itself", and thus moves in between *empeiria* and *philosophia*, between the particular and the universal. Malcolm Heath remarks that the well-constructed plot must show to the viewer or reader that the events are causally connected, and this is the source of their universality.[37] Finally, Stephen Halliwell, in his *Aesthetics of Mimesis*, claims that poetic universals are "embodied and discernible only through [...] the causally and intelligibly unified structure of the plot", hence they are found "on the level between abstract-ion and common sense experience and are present in poems as implicit embodied properties".[38]

To conclude my reading of Aristotle, let me add one final remark. By positing poetry between the historical and the philosophical, I see Aristotle pointing out the irreducibility of poetics to either *scientia* (theoretical knowledge) or art/*techne* (poetic practice). On the one hand, good "poetry" (including fiction) is anchored in a specific time and place, and, in this sense, it is historical. Nevertheless, there is another sense in which poetry lives "outside time", as its "objects" – in Aristotle's vocabulary are the actions of "types", not individuals capable of connecting the moment of experiencing the impact of a poem/novel or drama and the moment of its making. This is the space necessary for the universal "pleasure" and "learning" that occur "naturally" while "contemplating" poetry.[39] In this space, author and reader/spectator belong to one world that contains them both. And it is this common world, "our world" – a specific, non-abstract world – which is the domain of poetry that mediates, if you like, between the contingency of historical experience and the abstraction of philosophical truth. Thus, according to Aristotle, history is the domain of contingency; philosophy is the domain of necessity, and poetry finds itself between them, namely, in the domain of the possible which is not actual (as opposed to the real world, which is both actual and possible). While philosophy is true in all possible worlds, and history is true in a particular world, poetry is true in the world created by an author, and common to the people of his or her time, but relevant also for the present experiences and thoughts of the reader/spectator. In this sense, poetry lives within the tension

---

36 Aristotle, *Poetics*, I.VI.7.
37 Quoted in Carli 2010, 304, footnote 4.
38 Quoted in Carli 2010, 304, footnote 6.
39 Aristotle, *Poetics*, I.IV.1.

between history and philosophy, but is not *weakened* by it. Rather, it undermines the dichotomy between them. Here lies its *strength*.

3. After Aristotle: "The Elements" of the novel

3.1. The "objects": Subjectivity, inter-subjectivity and the polyphonic form of Dostoevsky's novels

Following Aristotle's remarks on poetry,[40] I believe that reading novels provides one with knowledge and pleasure. I also follow Aristotle in his claim that acquiring knowledge through poetic works entails a systematic analysis of three basic aspects/elements interwoven in the work: the medium, the objects, and the manner. For *mimêsis* (imitation; representation), in Aristotle's understanding is a construction in accordance with a plan, namely, the idea in the mind of the artist. Hence, the reader will acquire knowledge by recognising the way in which structure emerges from the arrangement of the basic components of a mimetic construction. Yet, the three "aspects" or "elements" suggested by Aristotle assume different or additional meanings in a nineteenth century novel, in contradistinction to the tragic and epic drama and poetry of the fourth century B.C. of which Aristotle was thinking.

Let me change the order of Aristotle's analysis and start with the "objects" which, according to him, consist mainly in the plot evolving from the characters' actions. Unlike Aristotle, Dostoevsky does not speak in terms of "actions" while trying to point out the essence of being human. In his *Notes from Underground* (1864), the narrator deliberately undermines the credibility of men of action, whom he presents as inferior human beings, limiting their aspirations to utilitarian needs and rational calculations of the ways to fulfil them. To be truly human, in terms of the narrator's beliefs – the underground man, whose diary is admitted by the author, Dostoevsky, to be fictive – means to have the freedom to become whatever one desires, sometimes against reason and at one's own expense:

[…] man, whoever he might be, has always and everywhere liked to act as he wants, and not at all as reason and profit dictate; and one can want even against one's own profit […]. One's own free and voluntary wanting, one's own caprice, however wild, one's own fancy, though chafed sometimes to the point of madness – all this is that same most profitable profit, the omitted one, which does not fit into any classification, and because of which all systems and theories are constantly blown to the devil.[41]

---

40 Aristotle, *Poetics*, I.IV.1.
41 Dostoevsky [1864] 1994, 16.

The will, then, not the actions, is the key to Dostoevsky's understanding of man and of human life. Human interior self, as depicted in the *Notes*, is a stage where men's irrational desires are dramatised as working against their rational calculation of interests, thus creating endemic inner conflict. Speaking in his own voice, Dostoevsky actually writes that "in discordance, in struggle, that is when he [man – R.F.] lives most fully" (Frank 2010, 308). Robert Louis Jackson comments on this by saying that:

Man's being is [...] crucified by the opposite strivings of his divided nature: his corporeal self, with its destructive, carnal drives, and his spiritual self, with its higher strivings [...] the pleasure man finds [...] in the ideal of Sodom, coexists in lacerating contact with his higher ideal (Jackson 1978, 60).

Some critics tend to interpret Dostoevsky's view of man living in constant inner struggle in terms of a reaction to the contradictions of modern life. Gary Morson, for example, following Mikhail Bakhtin, describes the life world which Dostoevsky and his generation experienced as an "unfinalised world without plan" that fits Lukács' view of the novel as a "process [that – R.F.] excludes completeness".[42] Bakhtin himself expresses the same idea by saying that "the ultimate word of the world and about the world has not yet been spoken, the world is open and free, everything is in the future and will always be in the future" (Bakhtin 1984, 166).

In such a world, actions do not capture human subjectivity, as articulated in Dostoevsky's novels. Rather, the open-endedness of the human subject, as expressed both in speech and in actions, underlies the representation of the characters who populate the novels. The polyphonic form, brilliantly analysed by Bakhtin in his *Problems of Dostoevsky's Poetics*, is built upon an understanding of human subjectivity that emerges out of the author's literary craft. And it is through the polyphonic form that we learn about Dostoevsky's intuitive understanding of modern human subjectivity. Hence, the first element of Aristotle's poetic work – the "objects", recognised by their actions, turns out, in Dostoevsky's novels, to be characters individualised by their subjectivity which motivates their actions and interactions, thereby constituting the plot.

Moreover, Bakhtin understood Dostoevsky's view of the subject not merely as an intuitive reaction to the modern world, but also as a fruit of philosophical conceptualisation:

To such an artist and observer of images as Dostoevsky, there must have occurred in a moment of profound contemplation on the meaning of phenomena and the secret of the world, this particular form of philosophical *conceptualization*, in which every opinion becomes a living creature and is expounded by an impassioned human voice.[43]

---

42 Morson 1986; Morson 1996, 72.
43 Bakhtin 1984, 16. My emphasis– R.F.

The human subject who is fragmented, not stable, always "in motion", oscillating between intentions, actions and their justifications, "not one" with himself or herself, appears in the polyphonic form crafted by Dostoevsky. This form expresses Dostoevsky's views of human subjectivity as an embodied voice heard through the character's partial discourse about itself or with itself, reflected and complimented by the speech of its interlocutors and *vice versa*, and heard in their dialogues and quarrels with each other.

Dostoevsky's protagonists are nihilists and believers, liberals and socialists, Slavophiles and Westernizers, exemplifying both satanic and martyr like qualities. And, as a collective, they appear to be a kind of heterogeneity irreducible to any objectifying concept such as "society". For there is no synthetic point of view relative to which these characters can be perceived as objects, there is no "one who knows". Even for the author, there is no privileged point of view from which he can judge them. In an earlier text by Dostoevsky, *Notes from the House of the Dead*, the narrator comments that "reality strives toward fragmentation",[44] and yet the author insists that "art imposes order upon reality…", and artistic form, for Dostoevsky, "is inseparable from idea" (Jackson 1978, 76). I believe that he found the idea – or the form – of the chaotic world which he strove to represent in the polyphonic novel. Or, in Bakhtin's words:

[…] the utterly incompatible elements comprising Dostoevsky's material are distributed among several worlds and reveal autonomous consciousnesses, they are presented not in a single field of vision but within several fields of vision, each full and of equal worth; and it is not the material directly but these worlds, their consciousness with their individual fields of vision that combine in a higher unity […] of the second order, the unity of a polyphonic novel. (Bakhtin 1984, 16)

Demons, the novel which I analyse, manifests an implicit conceptualisation of split or fragmented subjectivities as well as an idea of perspectivism, both embedded in the polyphonic form. I shall thus speak about "the conceptual" as the first element required for systemizing the knowledge embodied in this novel. At this level, it is the subjects and their voices in this nineteenth century novel of Dostoevsky that replace Aristotle's objects, understood as men's actions, which express values, emotions and ideas.

3.2. The medium: The "figurative" in poetic language

Now back to Aristotle's second element of poetic works: the medium, namely, language. Here too, Bakhtin's is a good point of departure, as he was one of the early theoreticians who emphasised the socio-biological nature of language: language is an act of sound-production (given to physiological analysis), and simul-

---

44 Quoted in Jackson 1978, 76.

taneously intersubjective or social in its meaning production aspect: it always addresses someone who does not assume a passive role – an interlocutor who participates in the formation of meaning, and a social context of reception. As he puts it,

No utterance […] can be attributed to the speaker exclusively; it is the product of the interaction of the interlocutors and, broadly speaking, the product of the whole complex social situation in which it has occurred. (Todorov 1984, 30, 18)

While Bakhtin draws our attention to the inter-subjectivity that precedes subjectivity and constitutes the communicative action represented by the polyphonic form of Dostoevsky's novels, it was Julia Kristeva who endowed us with theoretical tools for analysing the intra-psychic dynamics of the subject and of inter-subjectivity. According to Kristeva, currents of psychic energy traverse the subject's speech and are recognisable in his or her idiosyncratic intonation, accents and break in the flow of his or her speech, without interrupting, however, the continuous articulation of ego-images, ideals and judgements expressed in normal, symbolic language.[45]

Finally, Hans Blumenberg's discussion of images and their textual function, in his *Shipwreck with Spectator. Paradigm of a Metaphor for Existence*, will guide my analysis of the medium of poetic works. Metaphor, Blumenberg argues is "an authentic way of grasping connections", directed not mainly "toward the constitution of conceptuality, but back toward the connections with the life-world as the constant motivating support […] of all theory" (Blumenberg 1996, 81). In this connection, Robert Louis Jackson invokes Dostoevsky quoting (in his *Diary of a Writer*, 1877) Belinsky's praise of his *Poor Folk*:

[…] it had conveyed in one stroke, 'in an image', Belinsky exclaimed, the very essence of what the publicists and critics try to explain 'in words'. This is the secret of artistry, 'here is truth in art'![46]

According to Jackson, Dostoevsky's poetic language, blown up as it is with images, complements his understanding of man as "incomplete, at variance with himself and therefore always seeking completion, unity, wholeness, and harmony" (Jackson 2013, 158).

All this means, in my understanding, that intonations, speech interruptions, and metaphors all point to the inner split that characterises people's *psyche* and signify the connection of ideas, thoughts and emotions to the life-world represented in the novel exactly where concepts fail to do so. This will thus be the centre and point of my analysis of "the figurative" in the novel *Demons*.

---

45 Kristeva 1984, Chapter 2.
46 Jackson 2013, 162 and note 19.

3.3. The manner: Performativity in Dostoevsky's novels

In her essay entitled "Sophistics, Rhetorics and Performance; or How to Really Do Things with Words", Barbara Cassin defines the performative dimension of a text as that which transforms or creates a world; "what has [...] a 'world effect'" (Cassin 2009, 349). She examines the term "performance", and connects the word to the old French *parfournir*, related to the medieval Latin *perfournir* or *parformer*. She then concludes that the performance of the text refers to the manner in which a theme is developed within it, which depends on the techniques available to the writer and chosen by him or her, but also on the aims that he or she sets himself or herself in writing.

As I limit my analysis to one novel, I shall focus my gaze on two levels of performativity: the way – or manner – by which the author claims to represent reality; and the role of the narrator in performing such reality. *Demons*, first published in the *Russian Messenger* in 1871 and 1872,[47] purports to give access to the experiences of individual fictive characters, invented by an author who claimed that:

Altogether when I describe conversations, even tête-a-tête conversations between two people – don't worry: either I have hard facts, or perhaps I am inventing (*sochiniaiu*) them myself – but in any case rest assured that everything is true (*verno*).[48]

As an author, Dostoevsky thus committed himself to the painting of a realistic picture of individual and communal life in the Russia of his time. However, in his view, such a realistic picture is not exhausted by the compilation of more and more details and facts. Jackson succinctly defines the difference between "mirroring" and "telling":

The artist does not mirror reality (the ordinary observer performs this essentially unperceptive act a hundred times); rather he acts upon reality, 'explains' it through the shaping he gives to it, through form; he gives us a unique 'impression' of it. (Jackson 2013, 72)

My exploration of the performativity of the text thus aims to expose some of the techniques by means of which readers were supposed to acquire insights into the complex psychological, social and ideological realities of their time, the dangers that they presented, but also the hope and ideal of beauty that they offered. Dostoevsky expected that his text would deliver a moral vision about the role of art and the artist as the keepers and guardians of lofty humane and religious ideals, images and icons, not in the form of preaching, of course, but through literary effects capable of illuminating, signifying and emotionally activating readers imaginations.

---

47 See Translator's Note in Dostoevsky's *Demons*, 2006 edition, XXVI.
48 Quoted in Stromberg 2012, 463.

3.3.a Prologue to the text

What does it mean to create a world that is shared by the author, his or her characters, and the reader, a world that is not organised around one hero or one life, and the plot of which dissolves into many subplots?

Demons revolves around a series of "strange", enigmatic events that happen in a small, provincial town in Tsarist Russia of the 1860s. Against the background of a detailed account of gentry life-routines, old landed aristocrats, liberal intellectuals, the petty *bourgeoisie*, sympathisers of Westernizers and Slavophiles, socialists, radicals, professionals, servants, employees and reckless drunkards – the re-appearance of a second generation, the sons of the protagonists, is marked by acts of violence that undermine conventional manners, private relations and basic trust among neighbours, events that finally culminate in a series of provocations, strikes, fires and social chaos.

At the centre of the "main plot" is an abominable political murder committed within a small, secret society of radical opponents of the regime. Group leader Peter Verkhovensky, the neglected son of the liberal, respected historian Stepan Trofimovitch, ruthlessly shoots his comrade Shatov, demanding secrecy from the small group of his confidants in an attempt to test both the loyalty of the partners to his vision and the cohesion of the group. Behind Verkhovensky stands the aristocratic Nicholas Stavrogin – son of General Stavrogin and his wife Varvara, owner of a large estate on the outskirts of town, who had chosen Verkhovensy for his companion but whose relation to the crime remains obscure until the very end of the story.

The political murder echoes an extreme form of crime, universal and yet fully embedded in the concrete Russian context of the day. Dostoevsky's *Diary of a Writer* testifies to the life-materials that he drew upon while planning his books. An avid newspaper reader, some of his plots appear to be based upon cases published in the press. It turns out that the story of *Demons* is based upon a well-known historical event: the murder of a member of Sergey Nechayev's conspiratorial group that took place in 1869 and has agitated and divided Russian public opinion ever since (Frank 2010, 602–16).

To exemplify the thematic core of the novel, introduce some of the characters, as well as a few literary techniques used in the production of this text, I chose to focus first on one episode that functions as a synecdoche of the life world represented throughout the whole. It is a one-day event – "a *fête*" – conceived and organised by the district governor's wife, Yulia Mihailovna. The event is expected to become the highlight of social life in town – thus rewarding its initiator – Yulia – with the social prestige that she badly covets. The narrator actually presents the event as the climax of her desire: the *fête* is "the goal and crown of her diplomacy".[49]

The *fête* invites a detailed account of the physical space where the event takes place as well as of the participants: their physical looks; their clothes; shoes; hats and gloves; and even their hair arrangements, all serving as "attributes" – signifying their social status, mood and self-expression:

> Silks, velvets, diamonds shone and sparkled on all sides; fragrance permeated the air. The men were wearing all their decorations, and the old men were even wearing their uniforms.[50]

In addition, the narrator also accounts for the idea behind the event, which reveals that, in the eyes of the hostess, Yulia Mihailovna, it was intended to reconstitute the local bond of a community consisting of high and low, periphery and centre and reflecting her (fake) image of the generous, humble and united, Russian people. Hence, according to her, the event should not focus on bodily pleasures, but rather on a spiritual experience:

> The public must understand [...] that the attainment of an object of universal human interest is infinitely loftier than the corporeal enjoyments of the passing moment, that the *fête* in its essence is only the proclamation of a great idea.[51]

Under her leadership, it is decided to divide the day into two parts: public reciting of literary texts in the morning, and a ball in the evening.

Two speakers are invited to the literary recital: A canonic author – Karmazinov, whose representation is readily identified, by both readers and critics, with the most popular Russian author of the time, Ivan Turgenev (1818–1883). He is expected to recite his farewell message to his Russian public before leaving Russia to spend his old age in Europe. The second speaker, Stepan Trofimovitch Verkhovensky, is a local literary *savant* and private tutor, much respected in his own local community, but also known to the wider educated Russian public. No less meaningful, the evening ball is also planned around a cultural highlight, namely, an allegorical dance, "a literary quadrille". Planned to demonstrate social cohesion, the chaotic violence that develops during the *fête* and underlies the plot as a whole soon reveals the evening ball as a *façade*. Moreover, the "symbolic" *façade* assumes the form of literary practices, which purports to carry a spiritual message that thematizes the role and function of literature in the novel's represented life world.

Finally, the real disintegration of the provincial community behind the symbolic cover is exemplified in the narrative techniques behind the account of the event: long, detailed, exhausting descriptions of the external "attributes" of phys-

---

49 Dostoevsky [1873] 1995, 483.
50 Dostoevsky [1873] 1995, 468–69.
51 Dostoevsky [1873] 1995, 478.

ical space, such as a magnificent, "big White Hall, despite its already decrepit structure", or marble statues ("such as they were, still they were statues" (Dosto-evsky [1873] 1995, 468), all carrying ambivalent (ironic) messages. In fact, the narrator is here using allegorical techniques – a non-organic, artificial manner of connecting signifiers and signified – to signal the loss of coherence of traditional ways of life – the mark of modernity everywhere. It is not by chance, then, that the "allegorical quadrille" intended as the climax of the evening ball expresses no meaning other than the frustration of the messianic hope attributed to literature by the *fête*'s organiser, Yulia Mihailovna.

3.3.b Conceptualising subjectivity in dialogue

Here is a passage from the narrator's description of the essay read by Karmazinov on the morning of the fête:

An oration commenced! God, what wasn't in it! I will say positively that even a metropol-itan public would have been reduced to stupor, not only ours. Imagine some thirty printed pages of the most mincing and useless babble; what's more, the gentleman was reading somehow superciliously, ruefully, as if for a favour, so that it even came out offensive to our public [...]. But, who could make out the theme? It was some sort of account of some sort of impressions, some sort of recollections. But what about? [...] True, much was said about love, about the genius's love for some person, but I confess it came out rather awkwardly. The short, fattish little figure of the writer of genius somehow did not go very well, in my opinion, with the story of his first kiss [...] and, which again was offensive, these kisses occurred somehow not as with the rest of mankind [...] In short, I may not be telling it right and perhaps cannot, but the sense of the blather was precisely of that sort.[52]

The fantastic-realist literary genre, in Hoffmann's style, chosen by Karmazinov, is mixed in his impossibly long oration, with some romantic memories articulated in the confessional manner that tends to combine aesthetic with moral ideals – and both ridiculed by the narrator echoing Karmazinov with his own critical voice:

There are lines [...] which sing themselves from a man's heart as cannot be told, and such a sacred thing simply cannot be laid before the public (why was he laying it, then?).[53]

Though he praises the author for his earlier stories, there is hardly any trick that the narrator misses while trying to undermine Karmazinov's present status, either by mockingly pointing to his treatment of his own speech as a "sacred thing", or by showing that he is actually recycling Nikolai Gogol's words quoted by the drunkard Lebyadkin from Gogol's *Last Story*:

---

52 Dostoevsky [1873] 1995, 477–78.
53 Dostoevsky [1873] 1995, 476.

[…] remember, how he announced to Russia then that it 'sang itself' out of his breast.[54]

Parodying some of Turgenev's popular pieces such as *Phantoms* and *Enough*,[55] the narrator highlights Karmazinov's romantic cliché's such as the yellow, purple, orange hues providing a coloured background to the author and his lover sitting in the midst of some rare kind of greenery; or framing some mythico-historical scene dealing with Ancius Marcius, one of Rome's ancient kings, with a mermaid whistling Chopin. Then comes the vision of the great author, crossing the frozen Volga while boasting his brilliant talent: his ability to observe, in the last minute of his life, a tiny, but pure and crystal piece of ice, sparkling with memories of his beloved Germany and reminding him of his lover's tear over human inability to distinguish bad ("crime") from good ("the righteous").

Karmazinov's arrogant, condescending and self-centred personality clearly emerges from this wicked caricature, his narcissistic nature being underlined by the dramatisation of his tendency to feel rejected, by his complaints, and by his craving for praise: "But praise me anyway, praise me, I do love it terribly."[56] No less ridiculous are the organisers' attempts to flatter him by handing to him "a wreath of laurel, on a white velvet cushion, inside another wreath of live roses".[57] The accumulating effect is to arouse boredom and anger among his listeners and intensify their protests. For the *fête*, which was meant to entertain them and stir their communal emotions, turns out to be utterly alien to their needs and desires:

'Lord, what rubbish' […]. 'Precisely', another voice picked up at once, 'there are no ghosts nowadays, only natural science. Look it up in natural science.'[58]

Gentlemen, it's sheer deception.[59]

The last word, though, belongs to the narrator:

However, it must be admitted that all these unbridled gentlemen were still very afraid of our dignitaries, and also of the police officer who was there in the hall […].[60]

No less accurately does Stepan Trofimovich's speech, communicated by the voice of the narrator, delineate the contours of his personality and beliefs:

'Ladies and gentlemen! Only this morning there lay before me one of those lawless papers recently distributed here, and for the hundredth time I was asking myself the question: What is its mystery? The entire hall instantly became hushed, all eyes turned to him, some in fear. Yes, indeed, he knew how to get their interest from the first word […]. I have solved the whole mystery. The whole mystery of their effect lies – in their stupidity […].

---

54 Dostoevsky [1873] 1995, 265.
55 Dostoevsky [1873] 1995, 729, note 6.
56 Dostoevsky [1873] 1995, 479.
57 Dostoevsky [1873] 1995, 482.
58 Dostoevsky [1873] 1995, 479–80.
59 Dostoevsky [1873] 1995, 482.
60 Dostoevsky [1873] 1995, 482.

This is the shortest, the barest, the most simple hearted stupidity – *c'est la bêtise dans son essence la plus pure, quelque chose comme un simple chimique* […]. For *en parenthese* stupidity, like the loftiest genius is equally useful in the destinies of mankind […].'

'Puns from the forties!' came someone's […] voice […].

'Away' shouted some.

'Quiet, let him speak […].' another part yelled. […]

'*Messieurs*, the last word in this matter is all-forgiveness. I, an obsolete old man, I solemnly declare that the spirit of life blows as ever and the life force is not exhausted in the younger generation. The enthusiasm of modern youth is as pure and bright as in our time. Only one thing has happened: the displacing of purposes, the replacing of one beauty by another! The whole perplexity lies in just what is more beautiful: Shakespeare or boots, Raphael or petroleum?'

'Is he an informer?' grumbled some. […]

'*Agent provocateur!*'

'And I proclaim […] that Shakespeare and Raphael are higher than the emancipation of the serfs, higher than nationality, higher than socialism, higher than the younger generation, higher than chemistry, higher than almost all mankind, for they are already the fruit, the real fruit of all mankind, and maybe the highest fruit there ever may be! A form of beauty already achieved without the achievement of which I might not even consent to live.'[61]

Here is a vivid sketch of a middle-aged gentleman, speaking a mixture of languages, local and French, a tribute to his inclination towards liberal, enlightenment, cosmopolitan ideas, popular in Russia during the 1840s, but rejected by many, especially among the next generation in the 1860s. He is excited to the depth of his soul, but still charismatic enough to attract his audience's interests. Deeply involved in current events, he opens by reference to the wave of "illegal leaflets" – spreading anti-regime propaganda – that shook Russian society around 1860s to its core. Leaflets were the main weapon in the hands of groups of anarchists who aimed at undermining the existing power, using terroristic methods and leaning on a Western rational, utilitarian discourse to justify their quest for the destruction of the old in the name of a utopian future of liberty and equality. Their effect in spreading fear and suspicion was enormous.

Unfortunately, Stepan Trofimovich's message of "forgiveness" and recognition of the other, a figure of the "beautiful soul", steeped in Hegelian ideas about the "spirit of life", is not well received among the young generation of nihilists, who try to silence him: "'Is he an informer?' grumbled some.[…] '*Agent provocateur!*'"[62] For him, the secret of the mythical leaflets is nothing but pure stupidity

---

61 Dostoevsky [1873] 1995, 484–485.
62 Dostoevsky [1873] 1995, 485.

(*"C'est la bêtise dans son essence la plus pure"*), which he attempts to meet while compromising the young people engaged in writing and distributing those leaflets. The rising generation, he states, are as pure, and enthusiastic, and bright, as we were in our own days.

But his counter-vision – that Shakespeare and Raphael are more important than the liberation of the serfs, that culture and literature are superior to science and philosophy, and are the most precious fruit of humanity – only serves to raise his listeners' rage at the hypocrisy of an older generation that knew how to speak about poetry but did nothing to improve the living conditions of the people. Thus, he has to confront a young seminary student shouting from the audience:

Here in town [...] we've now got Fedka the Convict, an escaped convict, wandering around. He robs people, and just recently committed a new murder. Allow me to say: if you had not sent him to the army fifteen years ago to pay off a debt at cards [...] tell me, would he [...] go around putting a knife in people, as he does now, in his struggle for existence? What have you got to say, mister aesthete?[63]

It seems, then, that Trofimovich is, after all, and in spite of the tears and sobs he breaks into during his performance, as incapable as Karmazinov of opening his eyes and mind to his fellows, who, for their part, treat them both as hypocrites, strong in words and ideas, but lacking in action and involvement in the real world. Worst of all, while Karmazinov is convinced that there is no future for people like him in Russia, Stepan Trofimovich is incapable of grasping what the leaflets really mean. Instead, he continues to defend his old message, blind to the tectonic changes that stir Russian society below the surface.

The muddy atmosphere, the scandals and violent episodes culminating with the fire and a series of murders at the end of the evening, constitute the main plot of the chapters on the *fête*. All these are instigated by Peter Verkhovensy, Trofimovich's neglected son, who represents the next generation in his father's speech. I shall refer to just one quotation from his discourse which exposes both the naïveté and self-deception of the father's generation of educated liberals – the élite of the 1840s – as well as the destruction brought about by the new generation of "nihilists", negating in response to the naïve, humanistic élite, any value in the name of an instrumental rationality, science, utility and practicality that leaves them devoid of all traditional values of love and compassion, and prone to evil:

'To my mind' – here is Verkhovensky's voice – 'all these books, Fourier, Cabet, all this talk about the "right to work" [...] all are like novels of which one can write a hundred thousand – an aesthetic entertainment [...].'

'[...] one or two generations of vice are essential now [...] monstrous, abject vice by which a man is transformed into a loathsome, cruel, egoistic reptile.' (Frank 2010, 634)

---

63 Dostoevsky [1873] 1995, 486–87.

Peter Verkhovensy – an intelligent charmer and a newcomer to the town – quickly gains for himself the respect of the aristocratic élite, exploiting Karmazinov's "fake", inauthentic personality. Thus, Verkhovensky succeeds in gaining the trust and friendship of Yulia Mihailovna, who relied on his friendship to turn the *fête* into a great social success that she believes will secure her a position of power in the region. However, under the guise of his nihilist, destructive ideology, Verkhovensky uses his great acumen for flattery and deceit to enthral Yulia Mihailovna into blind commitment to his personality. Thus, she is unable to recognise the danger which he actually represented both for her and for society at large. His plot finally ruins the *fête* and turns it into a nightmare of chaos, dissatisfaction, hate and violent reactions against the organisers, and especially against Yulia Mihailovna herself. Her blindness to Verkhovensky's real intentions and motivations then transpires in the narrator's voice:

The poor woman was deceived right to her face, and I could do nothing. Indeed, what could I tell her? I had had time to come to my senses somewhat and to realise that all I had were just certain feelings, suspicious presentiments, and nothing more […] Alas the poor woman still wanted so much to be deceived! […] She looked upon him [Verkhovensky – R.F.] as an oracle.[64]

My close reading of the "literary speeches" of Karmazinov and Trofimovich, interrupted by the audience's responses, and commented upon by the narrator, is intended to provide a window to the author's laboratory. This laboratory is where the author develops his experiences and insights into human nature in general, and Russian men and women in particular, thus exposing their self-images, interactions, emotions, opinions, and ideological conflicts. In a word, it is the laboratory where literary knowledge is produced.

Karmazinov, Trofimovitch, Verkhovensky and Yulia Mihailovna – each is an individual whose split-subjectivity emerges through inner speech and reflection, through their conversations, at times in public discourse interrupted by the voices of friends and foes, at times accompanied by the narrator's interactions with them or by his reflections about them.

I shall give just one example. While Karmazinov boasts of his lofty aesthetic ideals – Hoffman, Gluck and Chopin – his voice, "rather shrill, even somewhat feminine",[65] according to the narrator, betrays his alienation from the public, all those voices who interrupt his speech, protecting themselves against his arrogance. While reading "superciliously",[66] he is immediately confronted by "the others": "someone permitted himself to laugh loudly."[67] His reputation as a genius notwithstanding, he cannot hide his physical appearance (his "short, fattish

64 Dostoevsky [1873] 1995, 493.
65 Dostoevsky [1873] 1995, 476.
66 Dostoevsky [1873] 1995, 477.
67 Dostoevsky [1873] 1995, 476.

little figure"[68]) nor his vain and petty pursuit of recognition and honour. No less is he torn between his status of "national author" and his preference for living in Europe.

Furthermore, he seems to exist in an ambiguous cloud, unable to decide whether "there is crime, there is no crime; there is no right, there are no righteous men; atheism; Darwinism; Moscow bells".[69] Actually, he is judged by the narrator to be a hypocrite, demonstrating a terrible gap between his aristocratic, enlightened, liberal beliefs and claims to truth and realism, on the one hand, and his dependence on flattery, on the other. Similarly, Trofimovich is split between his need for political action and his engagement in literature and art; Verkhovensky between his endless strategies of deceit and betrayal and his attraction to Stavrogin, whom he admires and loves; and Yulia between her drive for domination and her internal subordination to Verkhovensky.

Simultaneously, each individual also represents a fully-fledged "social type", to use Dostoevsky's words, carrying ideas with which they sometimes seem to merge, and ideologies that lay deep in the socio-political conflicts of Russia in the 1860s. Thus, the main socio-political conflict that animates the *fête* is between generations: liberals of all types, from Karmazinov to Trofimovitch, and nihilists of the young generation, educated and semi-educated newcomers to the intellectual élite like Verkhovensky, brainwashed by Western, rationalist – instrumental scientific – ideologies (Frank 2010). And yet, following the complex picture delineated in this text, the reader is never allowed to forget the precarious status of knowledge about the represented world, and, more generally, about any world. A healthy dose of scepticism, necessary for taking a position in any field of knowledge, is injected into the performance of the narrator, who is always alert to the limitations of his knowledge and to the credibility of his analyses, while still developing himself as a character with an ethical commitment to truth:

All I had were just certain feelings, suspicious presentiments, and nothing more.[70]

At this stage, the conceptual dimension of Dostoevsky's discourse starts to break through and may be articulated in two points. First, in the practice of producing split/fragmented subjectivities mainly by means of the dialogical form of the novel. Second, in a merging of personalities with their opinions that reveals the power of literature to demonstrate the entanglement of ideas with emotions, with pain, and interests, to show, in short, that ideas are never purely abstract, since, ultimately, in real life, they are inseparable from bodies. In addition, on the thematic level, the embodiment of ideas has a paradoxical effect: for, once ideas are embodied – charged with emotions and interests – it is no longer possible to see

---

68 Dostoevsky [1873] 1995, 477.
69 Dostoevsky [1873] 1995, 479.
70 Dostoevsky [1873] 1995, 493.

them as merely healing forces – as Trofimovich or Yulia like to believe. Rather, while embodied, they sometime transform into very destructive forces.

And yet, the fully-fledged meaning of the conceptual dimension of literature is inseparable from the two other levels of Dostoevsky's discourse, the figurative and the performative. These three interwoven aspects of the novel culminate in the story of Nicholas Stavrogin, on which I shall now comment in more detail.

3.4. Performing subjectivity in medium: Language and figure

Stavrogin, the son of a prestigious general, whose aristocratic status is also backed by his mother's (Varvara Petrovna) estate, is tutored from his childhood by Stepan Trofimovich and endowed with extraordinary physical beauty. Unlike the elaborated voices of the other protagonists, which allow the reader gradually to grasp their personality through their discourse on themselves and their conversations with others, Stavrogin's conversation is sparse. The details of his life are mysterious and amount to no more than unclear rumours. His character emerges instead in gestures – often violent, and mostly uncanny, like his secret marriage to the crippled sister of the drunkard Lebyadkin. Here is the narrator, telling the story of Stavrogin as a young student and then as an officer in St. Petersburg:

When he was taken to the lycée in his sixteenth year he was puny and pale, strangely quiet and pensive (Later on he was distinguished by his extraordinary physical strength.). Stepan Trofimovitch managed to touch the deepest strings in his friend's heart and to call forth in him the first, still uncertain sensation of that age-old, sacred anguish which the chosen soul, having once tasted and known it, will never exchange for any cheap satisfaction.[71]

Later on, in St. Petersburg:

He was received everywhere with pleasure. But very soon rather strange rumours began to reach Varvara Petrovna [the mother – R.F.]: The young man, somehow madly and suddenly, started leading a wild life [...] there was [...] talk of some savage unbridledness, of some people being run over by horses, of some beastly behaviour towards a lady of good society with whom he had had a liaison and he afterwards publicly insulted. There was something even too frankly dirty about this affair. It was added, furthermore, that he was some sort of swashbuckler, that he picked on people and insulted them for the pleasure of it.[72]

Stavrogin's personality seems to be constructed on an enigma – an empty core, an unknowable void, or split: the dreamy, sacred yearning youngster is completely disjointed from the reckless bully. Likewise, his social being is marked by abstention: never clearly articulating his ideological stance between fathers and sons, between liberals and socialists, between atheists and believers, between Slavophi-

---

71 Dostoevsky [1873] 1995, 41.
72 Dostoevsky [1873] 1995, 41–42.

les and Westernizers. Moreover, the void is also signalled by his absence from the city's prominent social events, such as the *fête*. Around this void, Dostoevsky constructs the final episode of the book.

On the last day of his life, Stavrogin pays a visit to the "holy fool",[73] the monk Tychon, who lives in a monastery by the river on the outskirts of the city. Their conversation is marked by sharp turns and twists in Stavrogin's mood: between absent-minded reflection and sudden fits of anxiety and rage; between truthful frankness, sincerity, even warmth, and a mocking tone directed at himself, occasionally at Tychon, and mostly against all others for whom he only feels contempt:

I don't invite anyone into my soul, I don't need anyone. I'm able to manage myself [...] you think I'm afraid of you? I shall reveal nothing to you, no secret, because I don't need you at all.[74]

The encounter of Stavrogin with Tychon, which lasts a few hours, is framed by the narrator's testimony and comments which assume various functions throughout the novel. First, the narrator serves as a mediator and amplifier of endless rumours that constitute the background to social and personal life in a nineteenth century provincial town. Thus, directly upon his arrival, Stavrogin questions his interlocutor about the rumours of his own scandalous behaviour, "[...] have you heard about the slap? And about the duel?",[75] to which Tychon answers positively, admitting that rumours about Stavrogin have indeed reached him. Stavrogin's response is not slow to come: "You've heard quite a lot here. No need for newspapers in this place."[76] Similarly, it is the narrator who informs the reader that Tychon is judged by people to be both crazy and blessed with a divine spark; that he is visited by poor folk and rich aristocrats alike; and that the father superior "even nursed a certain hostility towards him, as it were, and denounced him (not to his face, but indirectly) for careless living and almost for heresy".[77]

The narrator, however, fulfils many other roles besides being a medium to rumours that are often abused by those interested in creating an atmosphere of suspicion and fear, thus undermining the existing socio-political order. It is through the narrator that the text represents the physical environment – like a space full of heavy clumsy furniture, interspersed with a few refined objects that Tychon inhabits, the protagonists' physical appearance, as well as their conversations, through which their personality, thoughts, ideas and opinions gradually emerge.

---

73 Dostoevsky [1873] 1995, 682, 689.
74 Dostoevsky [1873] 1995, 689.
75 Dostoevsky [1873] 1995, 685.
76 Dostoevsky [1873] 1995, 685.
77 Dostoevsky [1873] 1995, 685.

Moreover, it is through the narrator that the text also "performs" the voices of the speaking subjects, their changing intonations, their gestures, their facial expressions, their moods. Thus, for example, Stavrogin "was somewhat pale, his hands were trembling slightly".[78] He "[…] sat all the while silent and motionless. Strangely, the shade of impatience, distraction, and as if delirium that had been on his face all that morning almost disappeared, giving way to calm as if a sort of serenity which lent him an air almost of dignity".[79]

Finally, by no means does the narrator simply perform a static textual function. Rather, from an anonymous person with no name at the beginning of the text, presenting himself as a town dweller burning with ambition to become the chronicler of the strange events he witnessed, he gradually transforms into a character, not only known by his full name, but also taking moral responsibility for the truth of the events, for their reality, which he is trying to communicate as faithfully as he can. Hence, by the last chapter of the book, the narrator is outraged at the information spread by a "dignified little old club gentleman", claiming that "this Tychon is all but mad, a totally giftless being in any case, and unquestionably a tippler", to which he, G.V., reacts: "I will add […] that this […] is decidedly nonsense, that he simply had a chronic rheumatic condition in his legs and now and then some nervous spasms."[80]

Stavrogin's meeting with Tychon is thus portrayed as a micro-cosmos of Stavrogin's life world in general, of his own personality and that of his interlocutor, marked as they are by contradictions, ambiguities and enigma, and by the multi-level discourse of Dostoevsky's literary art. It is written in a style that encapsulates the dialogical spirit of the novel as a whole, questioning every possible factual statement, truth or moral value, and is effective on all three levels of poetics: the conceptual, the figurative and the performative.

A wide range of materials underlies Stavrogin's discourse about himself. These materials include not only his exchanges with Tychon on the principles of life, on faith, trust and belief, but also his hallucinations and visions, his written confession and his dream. The confession mainly contains the tale of a series of cold-blooded experiments on women, child abuse, duels and murder, which reveal the pathological nature of the speaker, which he himself attempts to analyse and explain to Tychon. He also announces his decision to publish and distribute his confessed life story, which culminates in the rape of Matryosha – a poor, thin, little girl who, soon after the traumatic event is driven by her unbearable pain to commit suicide. I shall not dwell on this confession, beyond quoting the essence of Stavrogin's self-judgement and Tychon's reaction to it:

---

78 Dostoevsky [1873] 1995, 690.
79 Dostoevsky [1873] 1995, 705.
80 Dostoevsky [1873] 1995, 683.

Every extremely shameful, immeasurably humiliating, mean, and above all, ridiculous position I have happened to get into in my life has always aroused in me, along with boundless wrath, an unbelievable pleasure [...] It was not meanness that I loved [...] but I liked the intoxication from the tormenting awareness of my baseness.[81]

While Stavrogin perceives himself as a soulless human being, an image which he summarises with the statement: "I neither know nor feel good and evil." (Frank 2010, 646), Tychon is extremely impressed by his confession. In spite of Stavrogin's coarseness, and occasional violent reactions, Tychon is convinced of Stavtogin's sincerity. Confessing was a great deed, he thinks, but he is not yet sure of Stavrogin's ability to repent. Therefore, he responds in the following words:

This document comes straight from the need of a mortally wounded heart [...] Yes, it is repentance and the natural need for it that have overcome you, and you have struck upon a great path [...] But it is as if you already hate beforehand all those who will read what is described here and are challenging them to battle [...].[82]

Stavrogin presents the dynamics within himself as a continuous movement between outrage at his nastiness and great enjoyment in recognising his baseness. In response, Tychon insists on his own experiences with evil and sin: "I am a great sinner, perhaps more than you are."[83] Both are aware of a kind of "internal other" within their own selves with whom they maintain an ongoing inner dialogue. This may be the structure of subjectivity which allows for their openness towards each other and to the logic behind Stavrogin's spontaneous, unexpected words to Tychon: "You know, I love you very much", to which Tychon responds: "And I too."[84] Such openness leads Tychon to account for the process that Stavrogin is undergoing in terms of a deep wound at the heart of his being, to which he reacts by committing crimes. At the same time, Tychon also recognises Stavrogin's quest for repentance, which he diagnoses, however, as being blocked by the kind of "*jouissance*" that Stavrogin experiences at his own depravity. It seems as if "the internal other", with both Stavrogin and Tychon opens a crack that enables the flow of dialogue. It may have even prevented the tragic end of Stavrogin.

And yet, the surprising development of Stavrogin's discourse on himself and the network of his relationships – no one is alone, we are all products of our speech to an Other, as Bakhtin reminds us, brings it to the limit of conceptualisation as a practice of making meaning. One cannot further conceptualise Stavrogin's relationship to the others, to the world and to himself, for it is a relationship steeped in contradictions, ambiguity and enigma. It simply does not appear in the form of a concept, or an idea. To capture the character Stavrogin in his

---

81 Dostoevsky [1873] 1995, 692–93.
82 Dostoevsky [1873] 1995, 706.
83 Dostoevsky [1873] 1995, 708.
84 Dostoevsky [1873] 1995, 689.

right context, one must turn to the other dimensions of Dostoevsky's literary discourse: to the figurative and the performative dimensions that support his concept of inter-subjectivity and dialogue, but cannot be reduced to it.

Actually, Stavrogin's conversation opens with a hallucination told to Tychon and transmitted to us by the narrator:

And suddenly, though in the most brief and curt expressions, so that some things were even hard to understand, he told how he was subject, especially at night, to hallucinations of a sort; how he sometimes saw or felt near him some malicious being, scoffing and 'reasonable', in various faces and characters, but one and the same, and I always get angry [...]. [...] But it's all rubbish [...] It's I myself in various aspects and nothing more [...] you must be thinking I'm still doubtful and am not certain that it's I and not actually a demon?[85]

In response to this question, Tychon keeps asking him: "Do you see him really [...] do you actually see some sort of image?"[86]

It turns out that Stavrogin's fragmented subjectivity is also expressed in the figure of a double, a "malicious being", which Tychon insists on treating as a real, sensible and concrete image of a demon. No less symptomatic, the existence of such a "creature" within himself materialises on an extraordinary level of speech, "brief and curt expressions [...] hard to understand".

But there is more to come. The last episode told by Stavrogin in his written confession is a dream he had, which he associates with Claude Lorrain's (1600–1682) painting of Ovid's scene of *Acis and Galatea*, a painting he named to himself as "the golden age". Here is Stavrogin's account of the "action" that he saw in his dream, inspired by Lorrain's painting:

In Dresden, in the gallery, there exists a painting by Claude Lorrain [...] It was this painting that I saw in my dream, though not as a painting, but as if it were some kind of verity. A corner of the Greek archipelago; blue, caressing waves, islands and rocks, a luxuriant coastline, a magic panorama in the distance, an inviting sunset – *words cannot express it* [my emphasis – R. F.]. Here European mankind remembered its cradle, here were the first scenes from mythology, its earthly paradise [...] Here beautiful people lived! They rose and lay down to sleep happy and innocent; the groves were filled with their merry songs, the great abundance of their untapped forces went into love, into simple-hearted joy. The sun poured down its rays upon these islands and this sea, rejoicing over its beautiful children. A wondrous dream, a lofty delusion! The most incredible vision of all that have ever been, to which mankind throughout its life has given all its forces, for which it has sacrificed everything, for which prophets have died on crosses and been killed, without which people do not want to live and cannot even die.[87]

---

85 Dostoevsky [1873] 1995, 686.
86 Dostoevsky [1873] 1995, 686.
87 Dostoevsky [1873] 1995, 702–703.

This dream, however, does not erase the image of the "demon" reported by Stavrogin above. The dream, it turns out, is followed by another vision of a red spot that seems like a tiny spider that Stavrogin associates with Matryosha's death. He then has a vision of the girl, threatening him with her little fists. That vision is unbearable to him. After a few more exchanges with Tychon, he angrily leaves Tychon's rooms and commits suicide that very night.

Demons, water and land, divided by seashore, a red spot embodied in a spider – this string of metaphorical figures coming from the mouth of Stavrogin encapsulates much of what the novel is about, and delineates the role of the main character in it. It is thus through images that the particular, the individual, is tied up with a life world. No wonder that Dostoevsky, communicating with his editor, said that he was engaged in writing a "tragic poem". Let me elaborate a little on the metaphorics as well as on the effects of this last scene on potential and actual readers.

In the grip of his hallucinations, Stavrogin sees a demon, which he identifies as an embodiment of himself, a cruel, mocking, yet smart, villain hiding behind a beautiful face that often looks like an artificial mask. It is the demon in himself who enjoys violence and humiliation, who sustains his egotistic will and impedes his ability to devote himself to anything, even when he is on the brink of self-destruction.

But demons play a much broader role in the novel. Dostoevsky believed that the Russian cultured élites of the 1840s, torn by ideological struggles such as Westernizers against Slavophiles, liberals versus socialists, brought about the demonic rage of their sons' generation, which took the form of nihilism and a drive for destruction. He thus imagined Russian society as possessed by demons in analogy to the way demons penetrated the bodies of the swine in the Gospel of Luke. His epitaphs to his book – a Pushkin poem and a chapter from Luke – constitute a meaningful link in this string of demonic metaphors.

Pushkin's poem alludes to some individuals bewitched by demons into losing their way – a universal theme from Dante to Chernishevsky and many others between them. Pursuing this theme further, Dostoevsky subtly sends the reader back to Luke's story of Jesus exorcising the demons from the body of a man to the body of a herd of swine who, as a result, start running madly down the slope to a lake, where they are drowned, while the man who had been possessed now sits at the feet of Jesus.

The recurring figure of demons in Dostoevsky's novel invokes a picture of a society threatened by demons, that has lost its power to exorcise them, just as it has lost its faith in Jesus. There is nowhere to exorcise the demons in the midst of the crisis of modernity and secularisation. Stavrogin epitomises this picture. He is a man who has lost his roots in the orthodox religion, the heart of Russian national culture, as Dostoevsky was seeing it. He first looks to Europe in the

hope of liberating himself from a petrified class society and corrupt political regime, only to become a nihilist, turning away from any ideology or value in the
private and the public sphere alike. But, somehow, he is incapable of giving up
completely his higher, spiritual yearnings. "In my opinion he is Russian, and a
typical character" (Frank 2010, 606), Dostoevsky writes to his editor Katkov, a
Russian portrayed by the author as a man on a slope who is slipping into water
in which he shall drown, a human being described by Tychon as suffering from
a "deeply wounded heart". He thus becomes the embodiment of a split, modern
subject who is simultaneously particularly Russian.

This picture is intensified by the tale of Stavrogin's dream, inspired by the
painting of *Acis and Galatea* on the seashore (See Figure 1), on a corner of the
Greek archipelago. By telling this dream to Tychon, Stavrogin interprets it as expressing a wish for original purity and beauty. All he can see is the blue colour of
the water and the sky, caressing waves, spellbinding sunsets with innocent, loving,
happy people living in their paradise on earth, which he associates with the origins
of European/Universal myths, vision and ideals of peace and justice and expia-
tion of all human sins. And so, for a short while, he is flooded by happiness,
wiping the tears away from his eyes and momentarily erasing the ominous signs
inscribed in the painting, which he claims inspired the dream. What he does not
see, however, provides access to the literary strategies and meaning-making practices of the author.

Claude Lorrain's painting offers an idyllic representation – in the pastoral tradition – of the two lovers, Acis and sea-nymph Galatea, finding happiness in each
other's arms for a brief, transitory moment. It may also represent Dostoevsky's
belief in the power of art to store and deliver aesthetic and moral ideals whose
reproduction and dissemination he saw as the quintessential mission of art, never
capable of materialising in real life, and yet the spirit of human civilisation (Jackson 1978).

However, the image is framed by a threatening storm inscribed in darkish
clouds just appearing in the blue sky, by the sea, traditionally symbolising dangers
of the unknown and the uncivilised, and by the fragile ships seen on the horizon.
Most ominous, however, is the dark rock – perhaps alluding to Mount Etna – on
top of which Polyphemus, the Cyclops, son of Neptune, God of the sea, who is
in love with Galatea, is hiding, in wait – according to Ovid's *Metamorphoses* – to
kill Acis, whose blood Galatea then transforms into a clear river.

It is well known that, during his time in Dresden, Dostoevsky fell in love with
Lorrain's paintings, especially *Landscape with Acis and Galatea* – the same Lorrain
who kept painting wrecked ships (see Figure 2). In *Acis and Galatea*, he sends us
to Ovid's tragic story, a story that ends with murder and blood, two elements also
appearing in Stavrogin's vision of a red spot transforming into a spider, and finally
to Matryosha's fists threatening him. Would it be too far-fetched to associate

Figure 1: Claude Lorrain, Paysage côtier avec Acis et Galatée *(1657), Oil on canvas, 102,3 x 136 cm, Gemäldegalerie Alte Meister (Dresden).*

Figure 2: Claude Lorrain, La Tempête *(1630), Etching on ivory laid paper, 12.6 x 17.4 cm, Musée du Louvre, Paris.*

Stavrogin's dream, not only with his own individual tragedy, but more generally
with the imagery of shipwrecks throughout the novel? The narrator tells us, the
readers, about Karmazinov's text on a shipwreck which he had witnessed in the
following words:

> He described the wreck of a steamer somewhere on the English coast, of which he himself
> had been a witness, and had seen how the perishing were being saved and the drowned
> dragged out. The whole article, quite a long and verbose one, was written with the sole
> purpose of self-display. [...] Why look at this drowned woman with the dead baby in her
> dead arms? Better look at me, at how I could not bear the sight and turned away.[88]

Karmazinov, whose very name invokes the "crimson" of blood, here embodies
a spectator standing on safe land and yet unable to observe, to look at the horrific
views in front of him, really to see a drowned woman with a dead baby in her
arms. In the eyes of the narrator – now a character with moral responsibility –
such a position implies self-centredness verging on indifference to the other,
which is then covered over by exaggerated verbosity. But while Karmazinov fails
to play the classical role of a spectator, fails to use his privileged point of view in
the face of the disaster of another, he does not avoid using the figure of a shipwreck to account for the situation of Russia when he himself is on board:

> I understand only too well why the moneyed have all been pouring abroad, more and
> more of them every year. It's simple instinct, if a ship is about to sink, the rats are the first
> to leave it.[89]

He thus embodies a more general human inability to see, the lack of a perspective
that may allow one to know what should be done in times of turbulence.

4. Conclusion

In conclusion, I would like to return to my main argument about literary
knowledge, deposited in Dostoevsky's novel, the robustness of which I am trying
to "demonstrate" – in the sense of showing, not proving. It is knowledge of possible human worlds which I am trying to analyse by pointing to the art of interweaving three levels of discourse in poetic works in general, and in Dostoevsky's
novel *Demons* in particular. The first level is conceptual; it is concerned with human subjectivity and expressed in a new literary form: the polyphonic novel. The
second level, of metaphorics, directs the reader's intuition towards making connections between the text and the life world in which it is embedded. In this
world, danger hovers over the wrecking ship of Russian society, while the author

---

88 Dostoevsky [1873] 1995, 85.
89 Dostoevsky [1873] 1995, 370.

– himself imprisoned in his own perspective – cannot directly conceptualise the danger. Finally, the third level is the level of the performativity of the text, which produces a narrator separated from the author, on the one hand, and from the characters, on the other, and playing the role of a spectator who is not endowed with a privileged, synthetic perspective on the world represented in the text.

In addition, I point out the narratorial techniques of commenting and allegorising that de-stabilise the narration and already signal "social disintegration" connected to modernisation and secularisation. In interweaving these three levels, the author has created a world shared not only by the characters, himself and his contemporary readers, but also by some of us, readers of today, who share the historical memory of past atrocities of revolutions and wars, who are sensitive enough to identify in this text some of our chaotic experiences of the present, and find it intellectually relevant, instructive and emotionally touching.

References

Primary Sources

Aristotle, *Poetics:* Aristotle in 23 Volumes, Vol. 23 (1923). Translated by William H. Fyfe, Cambridge, MA: Harvard University Press; London: William Heinemann Ltd., Perseus Digital Library, available at: http://www.perseus.tufts.edu/hopper/text?doc=Perseus%3Atext%3A1999.01.0056%3Asection%3D1448b, last accessed 7 August 2018.

Aristotle, *Poetics*: Translated by Samuel H. Butcher. *The Internet Classic Archive*, http://classics.mit.edu/Aristotle/poetics.1.1.html, last accessed 8 August 2017.

Plato, *Republic*: Book 10, *Plato in Twelve Volumes*, Vols. 5 & 6 (1969). Translated by Paul Shorey, Cambridge MA: Harvard University Press. Perseus Digital Library, available at: http://www.perseus.tufts.edu/hopper/text?Doc=Perseus%3Atext%3A1999.01.0168%3Abook%3D10%3Asection%3D595a, last accessed 7 August 2018.

Secondary Literature

Bakhtin, Mikhail (1984): *Problems of Dostoevsky's Poetics*. Edited and translated by Caryl Emerson, introduction by Wayne C. Boot, Minneapolis MN-London: Minnesota University Press.

Blumenberg, Hans (1996): *Shipwreck with Spectator: Paradigm of a Metaphor for Existence.* Translated by Steven Randall. Cambridge: The MIT Press.

Brooks, Peter (1981): "Introduction." In: Tzvetan Todorov, *Introduction to Poetics*, Minneapolis MN: University of Minnesota Press: VIII–IX.

Carli, Silvia (2010): "Poetry is more Philosophical than History: Aristotle on Mimêsis and Form." *The Review of Metaphysics*, 64 (2): 303–336.

Cassin, Barbara (2009): "Sophistics, Rhetorics and Performance; or How to Really Do Things with Words." *Philosophy and Rhetoric*, 42 (4): 349–372.

Daston, Lorraine (1994): "Historical Epistemology." In: James K. Chandler et al. (Eds.): *Questions of Evidence: Proof, Practice, and Persuasion Across the Disciplines*, 282–289. Chicago IL: University of Chicago Press.

Dostoevsky, Fyodor [1864] (1994): *Notes from the Underground*. Translated by Richard Pevear and Larissa Volokhonsly. New York: Vintage Books.

Dostoevsky, Fyodor [1873] (1995): *Demons*. Translated by Richard Pevear and Larissa Volokhonsky, New York: Vintage Books 1995.

Eagleton, Terry (1996): *Literary Theory: An Introduction*. Minneapolis MN: University of Minnesota Press.

Else, Gerald F. (1957): *Aristotle's Poetics: The Argument*. Leiden: Brill.

Frank, Joseph (2010): *Dostoevsky: A Writer in his Time*. Princeton NJ-Oxford: Princeton University Press.

Jackson, Robert Louis (1978): *Dostoevsky's Quest for Form: A Study Of his Philosophy Of Art*. Bloomington IN: Bloomington Distribution Group.

Jackson, Robert Louis (2013): *Close Encounters: Essays on Russian Literature*. Boston MA: Academic Studies Press.

Kristeva, Julia (1984): *Revolution in Poetic Language*. Translated by Margaret Waller. New York: Columbia University Press.

Lukács, Georg (1971): *The Theory of the Novel: A Historico-Philosophical Essay on the Form of Great Epic Literature*. Translated by Anna Bostock, Cambridge MA: The MIT Press.

Meyer, Steven (Ed.) (2018): *The Cambridge Companion to Literature and Science*. Cambridge: Cambridge University Press.

Morson, Gary S. (1986): "The Baxtin Industry." *The Slavic and East European Journal*, 30 (1): 81–90.

Morson, Gary S. (1996): *Narrative and Freedom: The Shadows of Time*. New Haven: Yael University Press.

Putnam, Hilary (1976): "Literature, Science, and Reflection." *New Literary History*, 7 (3): 483–491.

Rheinberger, Hans-Jörg (2010): *On Historicizing Epistemology: An Essay*. Stanford CA: Stanford University Press.

Stromberg, David (2012): "The Enigmatic G-V: A Defense of the Narrator Chronicler in Dostoevsky's *Demons*." *The Russian Review*, 71 (3): 460–481.

Todorov, Tzvetan (1984): *Mikhail Bakhtin: The Dialogical Principle*. Translated by Wlad Godzich, Manchester: Manchester University Press.

Todorov, Tzvetan (1981): *Introduction to Poetics*. Minneapolis MN: University of Minnesota Press.

Valleriani, Matteo (2017): "The Epistemology of Practical Knowledge." In: Matteo Valleriani (Ed.): *The Structures of Practical Knowledge*, 1–19. Cham et al.: Springer.

Economy *as if*: On the Role of Fictions in Economics in the 1920s

Monika Wulz

Abstract

Since the 1990s, philosophers, historians, and sociologists of economics have examined the use of fictions in economics and highlighted its epistemic productivity. This essay focuses on an earlier version of fictionalism in economics, namely, the reception of Hans Vaihinger's Philosophy of "As if" in economics during the 1920s, a period of hyper-inflation and economic turbulences after the First World War. Rather than proposing fictionalism as a fruitful methodological tool, the essay argues for re-historicising and re-contextualising arguments for fictionalism in economics, and for analysing their strategies of relevance within constellations of economic transitions, crises, and debates.

Introduction

Since the 1980s, the use of fictions as epistemic tools has been raised as an issue both by historians and by philosophers of science. The emerging realism/anti-realism debate and Bas von Fraassen's intensely discussed "constructive empiricism" created the need for a closer understanding of the imaginary and fictional aspects in the generation of knowledge.[1] While the debate first concentrated on the question of how fictitious reasoning was related to the "real world", the discussion since the 1990s has shifted towards understanding the specific ways in which fictional methods are implemented within different scientific disciplines, and, specifically, in economics. Historians and philosophers have done much work in examining the specific practices and technologies of modelling in the sciences and of fictional reasoning as its integrated aspect.[2] These studies mainly focused on understanding the productivity and importance of fictions, identifying them as an indispensable part of scientific practice. Not so much work has been

---

1 Fine 1993; Cat 2012.
2 Morgan and Morrison 1999, and Morgan 2012; Suárez 2009.

done, however, on understanding why specific disciplines themselves advocated a fictionalist methodology. What is the relevance of fictionalist discourses to scientists themselves? And why were fictions, as a form of empirically weak knowledge, advocated so self-confidently in certain disciplines, above all, in economics? What could an examination of the social, political, and economic contexts add to an understanding of the importance of fictionalist epistemology within scientific discourses themselves?

In this chapter, I will focus on the discourse of fictionalism in the first decades of the twentieth century. It prominently emerged when Hans Vaihinger published his influential *Die Philosophie des Als Ob: System der theorischen, praktischen und religiösen Fiktionen der Menschheit auf Grund eines idealistischen Positivismus* (*The Philosophy of "As if": A System of the Theoretical, Practical and Religious Fictions of Mankind*) (1911) in which he advocated fictions as the most important foundation for generating knowledge. His approach was adopted in economic theory during the 1920s – a period in which the methodological foundations of modern economics were debated and the German economy was shattered due to the after-effects of the First World War. I will discuss the relation between fictionalism and economic thought in Vaihinger's philosophy, as well as in the economic reception of his *Philosophy of "As if"* in the 1920s. Considering the historical constellation of the crises of the economy as well as of economics in the 1920s in Germany, I argue that the advocacy of a fictionalist epistemology can only be understood within the framework of historical controversies of the time. In the 1920s, economic fictions thus appear to provide a way of consolidating the idea of the market economy at a time when the foundations of economic knowledge were in question. Although fictions are a form of empirically weakly-grounded knowledge, in the 1920s, they were meant to provide robust knowledge about the economy when empirical details for understanding the dynamics of economic processes were lacking or when the interpretation of the empirical data was called into question.

1. Economical fictions (Vaihinger's *Philosophy of "As if"*)

In 1911, Hans Vaihinger published his important work entitled *Die Philosophie des "Als Ob"* (*Philosophy of "As if"*), in which he sketched a theory of reasoning based upon a fictionalist epistemology. Vaihinger's *The Philosophy of "As if"* was a big success: it was published in ten revised editions during the following 15 years and translated into twelve different languages, among which the English translation was published in 1924 (Neuber 2014). The book is today classified as the first comprehensive treatise on the epistemological theory of fictionalism, a theoretical trend that has been debated prominently in the field of philosophy and history of science since the 1990s, both in the realism/antirealism debate and in the discussions on modelling.[3] In this highly successful book, Vaihinger argued for the role of fiction in knowledge production on the grounds of an economisation of thought based upon a combination of Neo-Kantian, Nietzschean and pragmatist thought. Addressing the nineteenth century methodological controversy in the philosophy of science between idealist positions on the one hand, and materialist and positivist ones on the other, he aimed at an epistemological reconciliation of empiricist and idealist aspects of knowledge by emphasising the primary relevance of fiction in the process of cognition. In line with Kant's characterisation of "ideas of reason" as "heuristic fictions", he argued that fiction is to be understood as a heuristic tool: fictions do not represent reality "as it is". On the contrary, they are constructs of ideas that indirectly and in a mediated way are useful for facilitating empirical observation. Propositions about reality are possible only upon the basis of assumptions that may be even unreal or "consciously false", as Vaihinger emphasised. Fictions thus present a kind of knowledge that is empirically weakly grounded and that can even be unrealistic.

Embracing a pragmatist understanding of knowledge in relation to the contemporary functional psychology (the reflex arc concept), Vaihinger nevertheless also emphasised the biological importance of fictions for orientation in real life situations as well as in science to explore heretofore unknown regions of knowledge.[4] He argued that the value of fictions is not to be assessed with regard to their realisticness but with regard to their usefulness in acquiring knowledge and experience in life as well as in science. He pointed out that they enable a practical and pragmatic relation towards our environment. He described the role of fictions in the basic forms of causal reasoning and analogies, in grammatical constructions, as well as in ethics, jurisprudence, and economics, in mathematics, physics, logics, geometry, etc. For all of these disciplines, Vaihinger tried to show that fictions no longer represented a threat to knowledge; instead, he argued for the indispensable importance of the methodology of fiction in epistemic processes.

The publication history of *The Philosophy of "As if"* dates way back to the nineteenth century, as in the years 1876–77, Vaihinger had already prepared the first manuscript of the volume, which served as his habilitation thesis. The publication of his theory of fictions, however, was deferred for economic and health reasons. Due to the need for paid work in the academic field, Vaihinger had to postpone the publication of his book for many years. Instead, he wrote a commentary on Kant's *Critique of Pure Reason* for the 100th anniversary of its publication and – after a period of bad health – he founded the *Kant-Studien* (1895) both of which kept him from publishing his fictionalist theory. In the history of philosophy,

---

3 Fine 1993; Suárez 2009; Frigg 2010.
4 Spariosu 1989, 246-258; Ceynowa 1993.

Vaihinger is therefore mostly known as a Kant researcher and organiser who was the first to institutionalise the research on Kant in Germany at the end of the nineteenth century. Only at the beginning of the twentieth century and after his attention had been drawn to Friedrich Nietzsche's fictionalist philosophy was he ready to prepare the publication of *The Philosophy of "As if"*, which was finally published in 1911. Vaihinger's *The Philosophy of "As if"* can thus be described as a theory of the nineteenth century, which embraces biological and energetic thought as well as an economic rationale, which only became influential in the twentieth century – after taking a long, uneconomic "detour", waiting, as he mentioned in the preface to the second edition, until the time was ripe to develop its effectiveness.[5]

For Vaihinger, the method of fictional reasoning was linked to economic perspectives in two ways: on the one hand, he understood fictions as an economical form of reasoning; he emphasised that every kind of mental activity, and thus also scientific reasoning, was an organic process showing functional behaviour. By repeatedly applying similar lines of thought and epistemic tools, he suggested reasoning would adapt to practical situations. In line with pragmatist and evolutionary thought, he argued that reasoning could become more and more organically functional and thus economically valuable. For Vaihinger, fictions were the most important instruments for this economic way of reasoning. He understood them as a "technology of reasoning", enabling us to act in view of the confusing and contradictory sensations of the outside world (Vaihinger [1911] 1922, 178–180). In his view, fictions are an imaginary form of reasoning without empirical basis. He argued that fictions usually proved to be false with regard to our empirical sensations, although he did emphasise the eminently practical value of these consciously mistaken assumptions because they enabled man to find orientation in the outside world, and, in so doing, preserve the living organism. Thus, in Vaihinger's account, fictions do not generate representational knowledge of reality, but, instead, a kind of knowledge that pursues its own logical operations. He described fictions as a skilful, inventive, and tacit kind of knowledge which created indirect methods of reasoning for those epistemic situations in which an empirical approach did not prove to be fruitful (Vaihinger [1911] 1922, 17–19). Proceeding in an experimental and abstract, and thus economical, way, fictions can help the organism conserve energy. Vaihinger emphasised that fictions served as a useful epistemic tool even within scientific practice. Whereas Kant's concept of "heuristic fiction" provided an important background for his *The Philosophy of "As if"*, at the same time, Richard Avenarius' "principle of the least expenditure of energy" was a valuable reference. Moreover, he mentioned that his thoughts developed along similar premises as Ernst Mach's "economy of thought" as well as Ferdinand C.S. Schiller's and Charles S. Peirce's pragmatism. With his philosophy

---

5 Vaihinger [1911] 1922, i-vii and Vaihinger 1921.

of "as if", Vaihinger wanted to reconcile the prevailing methodological debate between positivism and (Neo-Kantian) idealism. Pointing out the relevance of fictions for the production of knowledge, Vaihinger ([1911] 1922, 193) criticised the reductionist approach of positivism and, instead, emphasised the pragmatic and constructive role of ideas. He was convinced that reasoning correlated with the real world only in as far it proved to be useful.

In Vaihinger's approach, fictions can be understood as a form of empirically weakly-grounded knowledge that will turn into a robust knowledge, in as much as they prove to be useful in the outside world, thereby facilitating observations and practical interventions. For Vaihinger, fictions – although weak knowledge in an empirical sense – represented the most economic and thus the most rational form of reasoning for achieving orientation in our environment.

There is yet another economic aspect of Vaihinger's fictionalist epistemology: fictions were not just economical with regard to their functional and practical role for reasoning as part of the living organism. Vaihinger also argued that fictions could be found as heuristic tools within the discipline of economics. In his *The Philosophy of "As if"*, fiction turned out to be the most economic form not only of reasoning in general, but also, more specifically, of reasoning about the economy. He argued for fictions in economics against the background of a kind of methodological "two cultures" debate *"avant la lettre"*. In the field of economics, this debate goes back to the 1880s *"Methodenstreit"* between the German Historical School of Economics (Gustav von Schmoller) and the so-called Austrian School (Carl Menger) and was still prevailing during the first decades of the twentieth century (Köster 2011, 121–128): in contrast to the Historical School, Vaihinger argued that it was only the natural sciences that could rely on inductive reasoning based upon empirical observation and denied that induction was possible in the social sciences and humanities since the phenomena of social and individual behaviour were too manifold to be observed under controlled conditions. Social and individual phenomena are too variable and too heterogeneous with regard to their causal relations and effects. Based upon these methodological considerations, Vaihinger ([1911] 1922, 343) suggested that fiction was the most fruitful instrument for the study of economic phenomena. It relies on abstraction and selective neglect, economically "as if" the too heterogeneous details simply did not exist (Vaihinger [1911] 1922, 343). In contrast to the Historical School of Economics which invoked empirical and inductive reasoning for the discipline of economics, Vaihinger thus argued for the role of theoretical assumptions in economic reasoning. However, within the range of theoretical reasoning, he explicitly ruled out hypotheses since he argued that the method of hypothesis aimed at empirical testing and verification.[6] Instead, fictions were for him the most useful method in so far as they were non-empirical epistemic instruments that neither could nor should be verified. Instead, as Vaihinger argued, they were useful epistemic instruments, especially for scientific disciplines without a clearly-defined empirical basis, such as the discipline of economics, precisely because they were "consciously false" assumptions.

For Vaihinger, economic reasoning was based upon fictional assumptions right from the foundation of classical economics in the late eighteenth century: Adam Smith's economic thought, famous for its theory of self-interest as the basis for economic prosperity, figured as his most prominent example for the role of fictions in economics (Vaihinger [1911] 1922, 341–354). In his reading of Smith's economic theory, Vaihinger was influenced by the nineteenth century philosopher Friedrich A. Lange and the economist August Oncken, who had both worked on a rehabilitation of Smith's theory of economic self-interest in the light of a Kantian interpretation (Wolff 1923/24). In contrast to representatives of the Historical School of Economics, who had argued that the concept of pure economic self-interest was an unrealistic assumption that had no empirical reference and thus could not be a useful instrument for general economic analysis (Plumpe 2016, 57–60), Vaihinger argued that the abstract assumption of self-interest was a useful "fiction" for understanding the laws of the economic market. Although it did not allow economic forecasting, it proved fruitful for economic practice in everyday life. Vaihinger emphasised that it was precisely because Smith's economic theory was based upon fictional assumptions that Smith was the first to establish economics as a scientific discipline.

That fictions are organically the most rational and thus the most economic form of reasoning thus even holds true for the discipline of economics in Vaihinger's approach: based upon his epistemology of fictions, Vaihinger rejected the idea that economics could be a purely empirical science; instead, he argued that fictions enable economic reasoning as well as economic practice. Taking Smith's classical economics and its theory of self-interest as the most important example of fictionalist epistemology in economics, Vaihinger presented Smith's version of economics as the epistemologically most convincing understanding of the economy. Emphasising the organic functionality of the fiction of self-interest in classical economics, Vaihinger, in contrast to the Historical School of Economics, dehistoricised Smith's version of economics and instead interpreted it as the biologically most appropriate way of understanding the economy. But why would this organicist version of a fictionalist epistemology of economics seem to be fruitful in the first decades of the twentieth century and, more specifically,

---

6 Vaihinger was aware that the role of hypotheses had been prominently discussed by Henri Poincaré only some years before Vaihinger himself published his *The Philosophy of "As if"* ([1911] 1922, xvii).

after the First World War? A look at the reception and development of Vaihinger's *The Philosophy of "As if"* in the field of economics during the 1920s will give us some clues.

2. Fictional economics (1920s)

After the long incubation period from the manuscript (1876–77) to its first publication in 1911, the time seemed to be ripe for Vaihinger's fictionalism during, and especially after, the First World War.[7] In 1920, *The Philosophy of "As if"* received the literary award of the Nietzsche Archive in Weimar and was sometimes described as being as influential for contemporaries as Oswald Spengler's *The Decline of the West* (Vol. I, 1918; Vol. II, 1922) since it was read not only among experts but also by a wide audience (Vaihinger [1911] 1922, XIa).[8] In 1917–1918, Vaihinger, together with Raymund Schmidt, at that time a member of the staff of the Meiner publishing house and later to become known as the editor of the 1926 Meiner edition of Kant's *Critique of Pure Reason*, had founded the journal *Annalen der Philosophie* and devoted it especially to the concerns of "as if" observations.[9] The journal provided a platform for discussing issues of fictionalist epistemology in diverse disciplines such as physics, in particular the theory of relativity, the life sciences, mathematics, geometry, linguistics, law, and economics, all of which were also represented by members of the advisory board of the journal. Scholars such as Ludwig Bertalanffy, Wilhelm Roux, Julius Schaxel, Oswald Külpe, Hans Kelsen, Karl Jaspers, Otto Weininger, and Ludwig Klages contributed articles. Moreover, *The Philosophy of "As if"* was received in medicine, architecture (Mies van der Rohe), sociology (Wilhelm Jerusalem), and psychology (Alfred Adler).[10]

---

7 The third edition of the book was printed during World War I which Vaihinger attributed to an enormous interest in the *Philosophy of "as if"* even during war times: "Die Daheimgebliebenen haben sich mit erhöhtem Interesse mit seinen Problemen beschäftigt, aber auch in den Lazaretten, Gefangenenlagern, ja selbst bis in die Schützengräben hinein hat es aufmerksame Leser gefunden." (Vaihinger [1911] 1922, viii)

8 The third edition of the book was printed in 1918 when World War I was still in course. Vaihinger attributed this success to an enormous interest in *The Philosophy of "as if"* even during wartime (Vaihinger [1911] 1922, viii).

9 Hegselmann and Siegwart 1991. From 1930 onwards, Rudolf Carnap and Hans Reichenbach became editors of the journal and transformed it into the philosophy of science journal *Erkenntnis*, which was the major scientific journal for the philosophical discussions that emanated from the context of the Vienna Circle until 1939. It is interesting, however, that the Vienna Circle philosophers had no scholarly exchange with Vaihinger, and predominantly even rejected Vaihinger's *Philosophy of "as if"* (Fine 1993).

10 Jerusalem 1925; Seidel 1932; Rieken 2004; Weber 2013.

Hereafter, I will focus on the economic concerns of Vaihinger's *The Philosophy of "As if"* and its reception and further development in the discipline of economics in the 1920s. What could a fictionalist approach towards economics offer to the situation of the economy and to the debates in economics during the 1920s in Germany? German economists such as Hellmuth Wolff, Erich Gutenberg, and Edmund Herzfelder referred to Vaihinger in order to argue for the epistemic value of non-empirical knowledge in economics. They discussed such diverse topics as the conceptual role of the state for economics (Gutenberg 1922), monetary theory,[11] and the concept of the "*homo economicus*" (Wolff 1926). All of these authors adopted the epistemology of fictions within economics and discussed the methodological status of theoretical assumptions for economic thought. For these authors, the epistemology of fictions seemed to be helpful for finding solutions for the urgent economic challenges after the war. Germany was in a period of various transformations. Not only was the constitutional monarchy replaced by a democratic republic that came to be known as the Weimar Republic, but the reformation of economic life was also in question: after the war, economic life in Germany was confronted with an extended period of strikes and revolutionary situations. Different forms of economic policy were discussed, not only the conditions of free market, but also conceptions of basic income and planned economies; a form of planned economy was, at least for a short period, even realised in the Bavarian Soviet Republic (Sandner 2014, 109–155). The socialist calculation debate and the critique of planned economies by marginalist economists such as Ludwig von Mises in Vienna must be understood as only one arena of controversies (Lavoie, 1985). Moreover, the "gold standard" that had been the leading monetary policy in the decades around the turn of the century (1870–1914) had failed during the First World War, and conceptions of a new functional monetary theory were subject of much debate (Eichengreen 1992). Above all, and most noticeable in everyday life, in industry, and in the national economies, the Weimar Republic and many other of the newly-established European states faced a severe period of hyperinflation between 1918 and 1924. Attempts at governmental price regulations failed to provide relief. Due to the inflation, the breakdown of the national currency, and the resulting decline of consumption, the German economy was crisis-shaken. Economists, such as the "As if" supporter Ludwig Pohle, warned of economic chaos and the decay of the societal order in Europe (Pohle [1908] 1923, 140, 144). Due to this economic and political turbulence, the fear of a breakdown of the existing societal and economic order was enormous. In view of all of this turbulence, statistics failed: as Adam Tooze has shown in his book entitled *Statistics and the German State*, in the early Weimar Republic, there was a complete lack of information on the state of the economy since surveys on the dynamics of the economy, on earnings and prices were too slow with regard to

---

11 Herzfelder 1919, 1928, and 1932.

the very high and erratic inflation. The need for information was great, and the exigency to revive commerce urgent. The economy was in flux and too unstable to be efficiently recorded in terms of statistical data. It was not only as period of "Great Transformation", but also a period of "Great Disorder", as Tooze emphasises:

[...] the vacuum of knowledge was almost complete. There was no working indicator of inflation, the national trade statistics were in disarray, the unemployment figures were regarded with suspicion even by the Labour administration, the level of employment, production and earnings were unknown. The Weimar Republic was attempting to make economic policy for the first time, without knowledge of the basic parameters. (Tooze 2001, 84)

The first "*As if*" conference, that Vaihinger and Schmidt organised in May 1920, was held exactly within these politically, socially, and economically turbulent times. It aimed at promoting autonomous thought ("*eigengesetzliches Denken*") precisely within this situation, "amidst famine and dearth, in between election battles, numerous *putsch* attempts, and threats of strikes" (Schmidt 1921, 504).

The lack of empirical data constituted a specific situation in the shattered post-war economy that seemed to call for theoretical concepts in order to stabilise if not the economic performance in general, at least the epistemic framework of what was meant to become the economy of the Weimar Republic. Already on the eve of the First World War, and even more strongly in its aftermath, not only were the practical measures for political, social, and economic changes being debated, but, as Roman Köster has shown in his book on the discipline of national economics in the Weimar Republic, the methodological foundations of economics in Germany were also prominently being discussed. In opposition to the Historical School of Economics that had argued for economic analysis upon the basis of empirical historical research and, upon this basis, rejected the general assumptions of classical economics in the tradition of Adam Smith, younger economists opted for more theoretically-based approaches in economics. In critique of the political and moral perspectives that the older Historical School (such as the "*Kathedersozialisten*") had incorporated into their economic analysis, economists such as Pohle, who was a member of the advisory board of Vaihinger's *Annalen der Philosophie* and the editor of the journal *Zeitschrift für Sozialwissenschaft* from 1911, promoted a liberal economic approach oriented towards classical economics, which explicitly criticised the anti-business attitudes of the previous generation of economists (Köster 2011, 43–45). In this way, these economists critical of the Historical School wanted to promote what they understood to be a more "scientific" conception of economics; methodological discussions about the role of theory and of the assumptions of classical economics provided the basis of their allegedly unpolitical approach towards the discipline of economics. Referring to Vaihinger, economists such as the above-mentioned Wolff, Gutenberg

and Herzfelder understood an economic theory based upon fictionalist epistemology as an important way of approaching the economic and the methodological problems of national economics during times of unstable economic situations
such as those in the early 1920s and especially in cases when empirical data on
the economic developments was lacking. And it was, presumably, precisely due
to his methodologically framed critique of the political direction of the Older
Historical School and due to his advocacy of a both entrepreneurial and theory-
based version of economics that Pohle joined the advisory board of Vaihinger's
journal *Annalen der Philosophie*, which was devoted to the promotion of the fictionalist epistemology of "as if".[12]

Hereinafter, I will focus on Hellmuth Wolff's studies on "*homo economicus*" as
a fictionalist instrument in economics. In his study on the fictional character of
"*homo economicus*", Wolff described this concept as a useful methodological tool
that was essential for economic reasoning (Wolff 1926). While the Historical
School had, upon the basis of historical analysis, argued that there was no empirical evidence for the concept of the "*homo economicus*", Wolff suggested that Adam
Smith's proposition of self-interest and egoism as the basis for economic
prosperity was a useful fiction of heuristic value in the discipline of economics:
only by assuming that self-interest was the basic behaviour of economic practice
of all the individuals involved in free trade, was knowledge about the economy
of the market feasible. Although he conceded that there was no empirical evidence that self-interest was equally distributed among all the participants in real
economic life, he was convinced that the fictional concept of "*homo economicus*"
would prove helpful for formulating doctrines for understanding economic reality. The empirically weakly-grounded epistemic instrument of fiction was, for
Wolff, the most appropriate method for generating robust knowledge about the
economy, for establishing economics as a scientific discipline, and even for establishing practical guidelines for economic activities (Wolff 1926, 52–54). In this
way, he argued that economics should not be a historical, but only a theoretical
discipline that logically builds the economic principles of free trade and competition upon the fictional assumption of the self-interest of "economic man". He
explicitly warned against attempting to take "economic man" as a hypothesis,
trying to verify it. Neither did the epistemic value of fictions consist in forecasting
economic developments. Instead, the fiction of "*homo economicus*" – the average
economic man trading within the free market of the modern state – seemed to
be the most appropriate epistemic tool for understanding economic reality – "as

---

12 Another "As if" economist, Edmund Herzfelder, who had formulated a fictionalist critique of
the gold standard as the basis for monetary theory, worked, for example, in the 1920s at Bernhard Harms' *Institut für Seeverkehr und Weltwirtschaft* in Kiel. Also, Harms was one of the most
prominent critics of the Historical School and promoted the study of global economy (Köster
2011, 45-47).

long as the present economic system holds", as Wolff suggested in his study.[13] Although, for him, "*homo economicus*" did not exist as a real person, he emphasised that it was heuristically valuable as a fictional average person who shaped economic life.

Ever since he had finished his dissertation in political economics at the university of Freiburg, Wolff (1876–1961) spent most of his career in statistics agencies, first in Munich, then in Zürich, and finally, from 1908 to 1933, as the director of the Bureau of Statistics at Halle/Saale.[14] Working in the allegedly empirical field of statistics, it is remarkable that Wolff started to work on the methodological role of fictions in economics precisely in the period of hyperinflation and economic turbulence after the First World War, when statistics completely failed to provide any useful guideline for understanding the contemporary state and dynamics of the economy. Bringing together Vaihinger's "as if" with Max Weber's concept of "ideal types", he emphasised that economic ideal types were fictions and that they served as the most appropriate methodology for economics as a scientific discipline (Wolff 1923, 543–547). Wolff even related the fictionalist approach to his studies in economic statistics which he published from 1927 onwards. Although he agreed with the economist and statistician Ernst Wagemann, President of the Reich's Statistical Office and the founder of the German "*Institut für Konjunkturforschung*" (Institute for Business Cycle Research), that statistics was the most appropriate way to study business cycles,[15] he explicitly argued that statistics was based upon the method of fictionalism (Wolff 1932). Average figures, frequency rates, index figures and percentages could be only ascertained upon the basis of fictional assumptions (such as the concept of the average population per year which, in point of fact, does not exist in reality). He emphasised that economic statistics did not study the economy as it really is; instead, statistics examined economic principles beyond the individual occurrences. "Economic rationality", which formed the basis of the "fictional" character of the economic individual, was, for him, the object of statistical research in economics (Wolff 1927, X–XI). Even the allegedly "empirical" discipline of statistics was, for Wolff, thus part of a fictionalist approach to economics.

---

13 Wolff 1923, 550, and 1926, 79.

14 In 1933, Wolff was retired as a state official at the Bureau of Statistics due to an institutional reorganisation and was, instead, appointed as the director of the newly-founded institute of traffic at the university of Halle. During national socialism, he became the responsible for bicycle routes, and later he was commissioner for land use planning as well as for space research. After a process of de-nazification, Wolff became the curator of the library collection of the economics department at the university of Halle; in 1949, he was appointed professor for statistics and the Soviet economy in Halle and remained in this position until his retirement in 1952 (see http://www.catalogus-professorum-halensis.de/wolffhellmuth.html, last accessed 19 June 2018). Wolff's life and scientific activities from 1933 onwards still provide opportunities for further research.

15 Wolff 1928, 285; Tooze 2001, 103–122; Köster 2011, 242.

Wolff distinguished his approach both from the historical perspective on economics purported by the Historical School and from the emerging mathematical versions of economics (Morgan 2003). In this way, he provided a both non-historical and non-calculatory understanding of fictions. On the one hand, he explicitly argued for de-historicising the assumptions of classical economics and for re-using them for contemporary economic analysis (Wolff 1923, 550). He related his approach to Eduard Spranger's humanistic understanding of the "economic man" as a "life-form" ("*Lebensform*"), and, in this way, understood the conservatively-oriented version of German humanities as a background to the discipline of economics and of economic statistics in particular.[16] Spranger's humanistic concept of the "economic man" as an essentialist ideal form of life, acting in a non-hierarchical competitive realm free of domination, helped Wolff to de-historicise and de-contextualise Smith's historically-situated assumptions of classical economics (Wolff 1927, X–XI). Moreover, in his statistical study of business cycles, he rejected the idea that statistics would subordinate the individual to a merely calculatory rationale; nor would it be able to forecast economic developments; with the help of statistics, Wolff, emphasising the need for orientation in practical economic life, wanted, instead, to contribute to create economic actors that were mature to understand and react in the face of unfavourable economic situations (Wolff 1928, 301). In the approach of both Wolff and Vaihinger, it was thus the fictionalist distance to individual empirical reality that was meant to facilitate both theoretical and practical knowledge about "the economy". The epistemic tool of fiction related economics to the perspective of an essentialist version of the humanities, which focused on ideal types of the human mind. Based upon fiction, economic analysis seemed to be able to prescind from the manifold observations, and, instead, focus on a specific kind of economic activity, namely, the free trade of the economic individuals. The fiction of *homo economicus* was meant to secure autonomy of research on the market economy precisely because it declared individual motives to be insignificant, refrained from the historical specificity of economic occurrences, and, instead, focused on fictional ideal types (Plumpe 2016, 60). Both Wolff and Vaihinger argued that the organically useful and de-historicising epistemic instrument of fiction constituted economics as a science; thus, abstraction promised to be a scientific strategy for understanding economies of free trade (Morgan 2006, 22).

---

16 Spranger [1914] 1925, 145-164; Schlüter 2001.

3. Re-historicising fictionalism in economics

Philosophers, historians, and sociologists of economics have examined the methodological use of fiction in economics and highlighted its epistemic productivity;[17] they have criticised the mistaken self-conception of economics which failed to acknowledge its own uses of fiction (McCloskey 1990). As we have seen, however, in the "as if" discourse in the 1920s, it was not only science studies of economics, but even economists themselves who emphasised that theoretical constructs and, even more, fictions were the most important foundation of economic knowledge. Even more, the relevance of fiction for economics' methodology can be found in a series of neoclassical positions of economists from the 1950s onwards, including, among others, the neoclassical economists, Milton Friedman and Fritz Machlup, and the behavioural economist, Robert Sugden – to name just a few of them.[18] Pointing to the use of fiction in economics is, thus, not only an analysis and critique of economics' epistemology, it is, in fact, as Philip Mirowski pointed out, a "harmonious shared narrative" of the philosophy and history of economics and the discipline of economics itself (2016, 4). Emphasising the productive role of fiction in economics, has thus, as Mirowski criticises, suppressed the key question of "who is doing the thinking in the economy" (2016, 19). When, in the discipline of economics itself, the role of thought, of theory, fictions, and abstractions, is emphasised, a historical epistemology of fictions in economics is needed – not only an analysis of its epistemic productivity and creativity, but also a re-historicised understanding of the how, where, and when of the fictionalist discourse of economics: Against the background of which contexts do economists themselves long for fictions? What are the controversies in economics and in the economy itself due to which economists call for a fictional epistemology? What is at stake when economists defend fictions as the appropriate methodology for economic knowledge?

Vaihinger's and Wolff's fiction of "*homo economicus*" as the crucial concept of economics is tied to a specific historical and institutional framework: the historical index of modern capitalism.[19] The concept historically refers to the times when the liberal and bourgeois economy developed after a period of mercantilist economy. Instead of corporations and guilds, the nation was henceforth the basic economic entity in which the personal freedom of the individual, private property, free trade, and economic competition were the pre-conditions for all economic activities (Plumpe 2016). Based upon these conditions, Adam Smith developed the principle of self-interest as the guiding principle of economic life – hence, the principle of minimising costs and maximising utility when producing

---

17 Mäki 2002; Morgan 2006; Knuuttila 2009; Frigg 2010; Beckert 2016.
18 Mäki 2002; Knuuttila 2009.
19 Wolff 1926, 55; Köster 2011, 130f.

market goods. Instead of the accumulated wealth of the rich, the industrious "*homo economicus*" was, from then on, regarded as the main character of the nation's wealth in eighteenth century classical economics and, since the end of the nineteenth century, neoclassical economics. In contrast to the historical analysis of economic "ideal types" in the Historical School of Economics, Wolff advocated for de-historicising the historical figure of the "economic man" and for re-using it to understand the contemporary economic situation. The method of economic fiction, for him, was the appropriate epistemological tool to deal with historical economic concepts in an unhistorical way. Wolff went even further and affirmed that the more economics developed into the discipline of the present, the more the method of fiction would become useful in economics (Wolff 1923, 550). In contrast to the Historical School of Economics, pure historical analysis for understanding the present no longer seemed promising for Wolff, and empirical economic analysis did not provide sufficient evidence for understanding the turbulent national economy of the time.

As Roman Köster has shown, in view of the hyperinflation and economic turbulence that raged in the years after the First World War, the discipline of economics in Germany, facing the urgent challenge of understanding the economy and giving guidelines to economic decisions, found itself under immense pressure. Perplexed by the instability of the economic situation, it underwent a crisis and lost itself in methodological debates; a heterogeneity of concepts and methods characterised the discussion on economic issues. Theoretical approaches proved to be a way of stabilising economic knowledge as well as economic action in view of the shattered economy and of the lack of an empirical basis for understanding its dynamics. Only those theories that managed to describe the economy as an autonomous realm were understood as being successful in providing an interpretation of economic developments, despite the heterogeneous and empirically under-determined economic events (Köster 2011, 311–318). Fictionalism was presented as a theoretical tool to consolidate economic knowledge in this period. Taking up Smith's economic theory, Wolff's emphasis on the fictional concept of the "*homo economicus*" could be understood as an argument for market economy and free trade against the contemporarily competing approaches in economics, such as planned economy or as the historical plurality of economies that the proponents of the Historical School, such as Gustav Schmoller or Karl Bücher, for example, had worked out (Wolff 1923, 538–542). In this way, Wolff argued that the fiction of the "*homo economicus*", the rationality of economic self-interest, and the economy of the market were still the most appropriate principles for economic life even though at the same time, the markets after the First World War were out of order (1923, 550). Although the fiction of "*homo economicus*" bears the historical index of eighteenth-century economic transformation, Wolff was convinced that it was still valuable for his period, especially, for the shattered

German economy of the interwar years. To him, the fiction of the *"homo economi-cus"* seemed to be the only stable heuristic value for economic reasoning and for economic practice in view of the crisis of the economy as well as of economics.

Neither Vaihinger's nor Wolff's fictionalist epistemology promoted a "neutral" method of economic science. Their epistemological debates about the role of fiction in economics and the topics of classical economics were intimately tied up. Considering the historical index of classical economics implied in the method of economic fictionalism pursued by Vaihinger and the other "as if" economists in the 1920s, I suggest that fictionalism in economics did not develop as a method for analysing the diversity of different economic systems in general, but only for substantialising the use of specific arguments of classical economics, such as the assumptions of free competition and profit maximisation, needed for maintaining free market economies.[20] The epistemological tool of fiction helped economists at that time to de-historicise the eighteenth century classical economics and to claim its relevance for the present by naturalising fictions as a biological necessity of the living organism and, moreover, the fiction of the *"homo economicus"* as an ideal form of life. The epistemological debate about fiction was, at the same time, a debate about the relevance of the assumptions of classical economics. The empirically weakly-grounded epistemic instrument of fiction thus appeared (and in neoclassical economics still appears) to be the most rational form of reasoning about the economy in the period of modern capitalism (Beckert 2016, 285). Fictions seemed to be the appropriate epistemology for free market economies, although – or rather because – empirical evidence for competition and free market behaviour was unattainable.

Since the 1980s, economic methodologists have discussed fictionalism with regard to the realism/antirealism debate, by asking in which way the fictionalist method in economics was related to reality (Mäki 2002 and 2004). Moreover, historians of economic thought have looked at fictionalist approaches in economics.[21] Both have emphasised the productive role of fictions for economic reasoning and within economic modelling. In so far as Vaihinger's "as if" epistemology is mentioned, it is by referring to him as a forerunner and founding father of fictionalism in support of a constructivist and creative, but nonetheless realistic, version of science (Mäki 1998). However, we are missing a more thorough understanding of why, under which conditions, and in which contexts, fictionalism seemed and still seems to promise to be such an attractive and self-confidently chosen methodology for economists throughout the twentieth century and beyond.

---

20 On an interpretation and critique of the concept of "homo economicus" according to systems theory, see Hutter and Teubner 1994.

21 Knuuttila 2009; Morgan 2006 and 2012.

Looking back at the 1920s can teach us to draw more attention to constellations of crises, debates, controversies, and economic transitions when investigating the occurrence of fictionalist epistemologies in economics. For the relevance of fictionalist arguments in the rise of neoclassical economics since the 1930s, Michel Zouboulakis has similarly shown that neoclassical free market economics had come under attack during the Great Depression and Keynesian interventionist politics (Zouboulakis 2014, 57–68). Maurice Lagueux, moreover, pointed to the realist challenges of neoclassical theoretical assumptions during the 1940s. Against these anti-marginalist attacks, the proponents of the liberal market economy once more promoted fictionalist methodologies. Lagueux has shown that Chicago school economist Milton Friedman had formulated his famous "as if" epistemology in his influential essay entitled "The Methodology of Positive Economics", in response to these.[22] Drawing parallels to examples of physics and biology, Friedman had naturalised the historical fictional assumptions of (neo-) classical economics into law-like propositions of economic activity. In this way, he fortified the importance of unrealistic assumptions in economics and even understood assumptions that proved to be inconsistent with factual observations as an epistemic virtue of economics as a scientific discipline. Friedman's colleague, Fritz Machlup, had emphasised that the concept of the "*homo economicus*" was a "ideal type", referring to Max Weber's and Vaihinger's philosophy of "as if", and thus understood the concept as a necessary heuristic fiction for economics.[23] Both Friedman and Machlup played a decisive role in overcoming the anti-marginalist attacks and resolving the "marginalist controversy" of the 1940s; both took part in the re-consolidation of liberal market ideas and the formation of neoliberal economics after the Second World War.[24] Taking these controversies into account, Lagueux suggests shifting the focus of fictionalism in economics from questions of realism to questions of relevance (Lagueux 1994, 163). Instead of arguing about the realism or anti-realism of the fictional assumptions and about their usefulness in neoclassical economics, historical studies of economics should thus analyse how and in which contexts the relevance of specific assumptions and of specific methodological considerations is generated at a specific point in time.

In order to understand and critically evaluate the strategies of fictionalist accounts in economics, further work still needs to be done: Only recently, the behavioral economist Robert Sugden has decidedly emphasised fictionalist methodology in economic modelling (Sugden 2002). Taking examples from the behavioural economics which emerged in the 1970s (George Akerlof's 1970 "market for lemons", famous for introducing the concept of asymmetric information, and

---

22 Friedman 1953; Lagueux 1994.
23 Machlup 1978; Knuuttila 2009.
24 Backhouse 2009; Zouboulakis 2014.

Thomas Schelling's 1978 "checkerboard model" of "racial sorting"), he argued for the continued relevance of fictional reasoning for economics and for understanding economic behaviour, in particular. Why were these fictionalist methods becoming relevant in the emerging behavioural economics in the 1970s – in a period of de-regulation when behavioural economics seemed promising to provide answers to market failure? And why has Sugden's fictionalist methodology been important in behavioural economics during the last two decades?

Only recently, Philip Mirowski added a further chapter to the history of fictionalist economics by providing a fictionalist interpretation of "information" in computational economics and in recent trends of "market design". He argued that computational modelling used computer technology for generating fictional markets and in this way promised to consolidate markets as the "final arbiter of Truth". He criticised that "the overt fictional stance towards models" in contemporary economics rendered economic knowledge impervious both to critique, to empirical disproof, as well as to the role of philosophy for questions of knowledge in the economy (Mirowski 2016).

These are just very few and brief examples of more recent fictionalist accounts in economics. While questions of fictionalism are mostly treated as a purely methodological and thus as a de-historicised discourse, it is time to re-historicise and re-contextualise the promise of the epistemic productivity of fictional knowledge. Neoclassical economics provides a broad realm of fictionalist endeavours. What are the strategies of their specific fictionalist discourses? Within which historical, economic, and disciplinary discourses are they situated? In which ways do they react to historical or contemporary constellations of economic transitions, crises, and debates? As the reception of Vaihinger's work in economics during the 1920s shows, the advocacy of fictions in economics at that time appeared as a response to controversies on the role of empiricism, both historical and statistical, for economics. Fiction in economics, as a form of empirically weak knowledge that comes, however, with specific strategies of claiming its relevance, was advocated as an epistemic tool in a time when neither empirical data nor historical analysis seemed to provide a basis for understanding the contemporary dynamics of the economy, when the consolidation and institutionalisation of liberal economy seemed to be at stake, and when the idea of the market as the guiding principle of economics seemed to be under threat.

References

Backhouse, Roger (2009): "Friedman's 1953 Essay and the Marginalist Controversy." In: Uskali Mäki (Ed.): *The Methodology of Positive Economics: Reflections on the Milton Friedman Legacy*, 217–240. Cambridge: Cambridge University Press.

Beckert, Jens (2016): *Imagined Futures: Fictional Expectations and Capitalist Dynamics*. Cambridge MA: Harvard University Press.

Cat, Jordi (2012): "Review: Mauricio Suárez (Ed.): Fictions in Science. Philosophical Essays on Modeling and Idealization." *Journal for General Philosophy of Science*, 43 (1): 187–194.

Ceynowa, Klaus (1993): *Zwischen Pragmatismus und Fiktionalismus: Hans Vaihingers "Philosophie des Als Ob"*. Würzburg: Königshausen & Neumann.

Eichengreen, Barry (1992): *Golden Fetters: The Gold Standard and the Great Depression, 1919–1939*. New York: Oxford University Press.

Fine, Arthur (1993): "Fictionalism." *Midwest Studies in Philosophy*, 18 (1): 1–18.

Friedman, Milton (1953): "The Methodology of Positive Economics." In: Milton Friedman: *Essays in Positive Economics*, 3–43. Chicago IL: University of Chicago Press.

Frigg, Roman (2010): "Models and Fiction." *Synthese*, 172 (2): 251–268.

Gutenberg, Erich (1922): *Thünens isolierter Staat als Fiktion*. (Bausteine zu einer Philosophie des "Als-ob" 4). Munich: Rösl & Cie.

Hegselmann, Rainer, and Geo Siegwart (1991): "Zur Geschichte der 'Erkenntnis'" *Erkenntnis*, 35 (1–3): 461–471.

Herzfelder, Edmund (1919): *Die volkswirtschaftliche Bilanz und eine neue Theorie der Wechselkurse. Die Theorie der reinen Papierwährung*. Berlin: Springer.

Herzfelder, Edmund (1928): *Die Goldwährung als eine Fiktion der Nationalökonomie* (Bausteine zu einer Philosophie des "Als-ob" 14). Berlin: Paetel.

Herzfelder, Edmund (1932): "Fiktionen der Nationalökonomie, der Wertlehre und des Geldwesens." In: August Seidel (Ed.): *Die Philosophie des Als Ob und das Leben. Festschrift zu Hans Vaihingers 80. Geburtstag*, 22–41. Berlin: Reuther & Reichard.

Hutter, Michael, and Gunther Teubner (1994): "Der Gesellschaft fette Beute. Homo juridicus und homo oeconomicus als kommunikationserhaltende Fiktionen." In: Peter Fuchs and Andreas Göbel (Eds.): *Der Mensch – das Medium der Gesellschaft?* 110–145. Frankfurt a. M.: Suhrkamp Verlag.

Jerusalem, Wilhelm (1925): "Die Logik des Unlogischen." In: Wilhelm Jerusalem: *Gedanken und Denker: Gesammelte Aufsätze*, 173–186. Vienna-Leipzig: Braumüller.

Knuuttila, Tarja (2009): "Representation, Idealization, and Fiction in Economics: From the Assumptions Issue to the Epistemology of Modeling." In: Mauricio Suárez: *Fictions in Science: Philosophical Essays on Modelling and Idealization*, 205–231. New York-London: Routledge.

Köster, Roman (2011): *Die Wissenschaft der Außenseiter. Die Krise der Nationalökonomie in der Weimarer Republik*, (Kritische Studien zur Geschichtswissenschaft 198). Göttingen: Vandenhoeck & Ruprecht.

Lagueux, Maurice (1994): "Friedman's 'Instrumentalism' and Constructive Empiricism in Economics." *Theory and Decision*, 37 (2): 147–174.

Lavoie, Don (1985): *Rivalry and Central Planning: The Socialist Calculation Debate Reconsidered*, (Historical Perspectives on Modern Economics). Cambridge: Cambridge University Press.

Machlup, Fritz (1978): *Methodology of Economics and Other Social Sciences*. New York: Academic Press.

Mäki, Uskali (1998): "As if." In: John B. Davis et al. (Eds.): *The Handbook of Economic Methodology*, 25–27. Cheltenham-Northampton MA: Edward Elgar Publishing.

Mäki, Uskali (Ed.) (2002): *Fact and Fiction in Economics: Models, Realism, and Social Construction.* Cambridge: Cambridge University Press.

Mäki, Uskali (2004): "Realism and the Nature of a Theory: A Lesson from J.H. von Thünen for Economists and Geographers." *Environment and Planning A: Economy and Space*, 36 (10): 1719–1736.

McCloskey, Deirdre N. (1990): "Storytelling in Economics." In: Christopher Nash (Ed.): *Narrative in Culture: The Uses of Storytelling in the Sciences, Philosophy, and Literature*, 5–22. London: Routledge.

Mirowski, Philip (2016): "Information in Economics: A Fictionalist Account." *Journal of Contextual Economics – Schmollers Jahrbuch*, 136 (1): 109–130.

Morgan, Mary S., and Margaret Morrison (Eds.) (1999): *Models as Mediators: Perspectives on Natural and Social Science.* Cambridge: Cambridge University Press.

Morgan, Mary S. (2003): "Economics." In: Theodore Porter and Dorothy Ross (Eds.): *The Cambridge History of Science*, 275–305. (Vol. 7: The Modern Social Sciences). Cambridge: Cambridge University Press.

Morgan, Mary S. (2006): "Economic Man as Model Man: Ideal Types, Idealization and Caricatures." *Journal of the History of Economic Thought*, 28 (1): 1–27.

Morgan, Mary S. (2012): *The World in the Model: How Economists Work and Think.* Cambridge: Cambridge University Press.

Neuber, Matthias (Ed.) (2014): *Fiktion und Fiktionalismus. Beiträge zu Hans Vaihingers "Philosophie des Als Ob"*. Würzburg: Könighausen & Neumann.

Plumpe, Werner (2016): "The Birth of the Homo economicus: Historical Thoughts on the Origins and Significance of this Model of Human Behavior for the Modern Economy." In: Werner Plumpe: *German Economic and Business History in the 19th and 20th Centuries*, 51–79. London: Palgrave Macmillan.

Pohle, Ludwig ([1908] (1923): *Die Entwicklung des deutschen Wirtschaftslebens im letzten Jahrhundert.* 5th edition, Leipzig-Berlin: Teubner.

Rieken, Bernd (2004): "Die Individualpsychologie Alfred Adlers und ihre Bedeutung für die Erzählforschung." *Fabula: Journal of Folktale Studies*, 45 (1–2): 1–32.

Sandner, Günther (2014): *Otto Neurath: Eine politische Biographie.* Vienna: Zsolnay.

Schlüter, Marnie (2001): "Die Aufhebung des humanistischen Bildungsideals. Eduard Spranger im Spektrum des Weimarer Konservatismus." In: Hans Jürgen Apel et al. (Eds.): *Das öffentliche Bildungswesen. Historische Entwicklung, gesellschaftliche Funktionen, pädagogischer Streit*, 309–321. Bad Heilbrunn: Klinkhardt.

Schmidt, Raymund (1921): "Die 'Als Ob'-Konferenz in Halle 29. Mai 1920." *Annalen der Philosophie. Mit besonderer Rücksicht auf die Probleme der Als-Ob-Betrachtung*, 2 (4): 503–514.

Seidel, August (Ed.) (1932): *Die Philosophie des Als Ob und das Leben. Festschrift zu Hans Vaihingers 80. Geburtstag.* Berlin: Reuther & Reichard.

Spariosu, Mihai (1989): *Dionysus Reborn: Play and the Aesthetic Dimension in Modern Philosophical and Scientific Discourse.* Ithaca NY-London: Cornell University Press.

Spranger, Eduard [1914] (1925): "Der ökonomische Mensch." In: Eduard Spranger: *Lebensformen. Geisteswissenschaftliche Psychologie und Ethik der Persönlichkeit*, 145–164. 5. Auflage. Halle (Saale): Niemeyer.

Suárez, Mauricio (2009): "Fictions in Scientific Practice." In: Mauricio Suárez (Ed.): *Fictions in Science: Philosophical Essays on Modeling and Idealization*, 3–15. New York: Routledge.

Sugden, Robert (2002): "Credible Worlds: The Status of Theoretical Models in Economics." In: Uskali Mäki (Ed.): *Fact and Fiction in Economics: Models, Realism, and Social Construction*, 107–136. Cambridge: Cambridge University Press.

Tooze, J. Adam (2001): *Statistics and the German State, 1900–1945: The Making of Modern Economic Knowledge*. (Cambridge Studies in Modern Economic History 9). Cambridge: Cambridge University Press.

Vaihinger, Hans [1911] (1922): *Die Philosophie des Als Ob. System der theoretischen, praktischen und religiösen Fiktionen der Menschheit auf Grund des idealistischen Positivismus*. 7th and 8th edition. Leipzig: Meiner.

Vaihinger, Hans (1921): "Wie die Philosophie des Als Ob entstand." In: Raymund Schmidt (Ed.): *Die deutsche Philosophie der Gegenwart in Selbstdarstellungen*. Leipzig: Meiner.

Weber, Paul (2013): "Ludwig Mies van der Rohes moderne Architekturentwürfe und Hans Vaihingers Philosophie des Als Ob". In: Kerstin Plüm (Ed.) (2013): *Mies van der Rohe im Diskurs: Innovationen – Haltungen – Werke. Aktuelle Positionen*, 13–62. Bielefeld: Transcript.

Wolff, Hellmuth (1923): "Volkswirtschaftliche Idealtypen als Fiktionen." *Annalen der Philosophie*, 3 (3): 527–550.

Wolff, Hellmuth (1923/24): "Das Selbstinteresse bei Adam Smith und Kants kategorischer Imperativ." *Archiv für Rechts- und Wirtschaftsphilosophie*, 17 (3): 313–336.

Wolff, Hellmuth (1926): *Der homo economicus. Eine nationalökonomische Fiktion* (Bausteine zu einer Philosophie des "Als-ob" 11). Berlin-Leipzig: Gebrüder Paetel.

Wolff, Hellmuth (1927): *Wirtschaftsstatistik*. Jena: Fischer.

Wolff, Hellmuth (1928): *Lehrbuch der Konjunkturforschung. Zugleich eine kritisch-theoretische Untersuchung von Struktur und Konjunktur*. Berlin: Spaeth & Linde.

Wolff, Hellmuth (1932): "Die Fiktion in der Statistik." In: August Seidel (Ed.): *Die Philosophie des Als Ob und das Leben. Festschrift zu Hans Vaihingers 80. Geburtstag*, 123–139. Berlin: Reuther & Reichard.

Zouboulakis, Michel (2014): *The Varieties of Economic Rationality: From Adam Smith to Contemporary Behavioural and Evolutionary Economics*. New York: Routledge.

Weak and Strong Knowledge in Industrial Research: The Rise of the "Third" Physicist

Falk Müller

Abstract

Although physicists are generally seen as reliable contributors of (epistemically, culturally, socially and practically) "strong" scientific knowledge, they often fail to meet these expectations. This is not only due to the dynamics of a scientific field that tries to integrate new domains of research that initially lack the appropriate epistemic tools and strategies of legitimation, but also to the adaptation of physics to external influences and requirements – be they scientific, social or cultural. The focus of this essay will be on conflicts over the place of physics and physical knowledge in industrial research in the interwar period. Using the institutionalisation of industrial physics and the foundation of the German Society for Technical Physics as examples, I wish to discuss how industrial physicists used the weaknesses and strengths of their position to gain more recognition and eventually manage to transform the disciplinary self-understanding of physics.

1. The rise of the "third" physicist

At the end of the nineteenth century, new career prospects emerged for university-trained physicists in the optical and chemical industries in Germany. Since the early twentieth century, they had increasingly found employment in the electrical engineering industry as well. Reluctantly, the educational system responded to these developments with the establishment of professorships for applied physics at the technical colleges and universities. These physicists were part of a growing group of scientific professionals who, in the broader sense, were involved in building up a physical-technical infrastructure for the rapidly developing industrial society in Germany, for example, physicists who developed new measuring devices or standardisation procedures at the *Physikalisch-Technische Reichsanstalt* in Berlin.[1] After World War I, in which physicists amply demonstrated the value of

---

1 The foundation of the *Zeitschrift für Instrumentenkunde. Organ für Mittheilungen auf dem gesammten Gebiete der wissenschaftlichen Technik* in 1881 and of the *Physikalisch-Technische Reichsanstalt* in 1887 are generally seen as indications for the growing institutionalisation and acceptance of a new

their knowledge for war purposes, the group of applied physicists no longer saw their interests adequately represented by the *Deutsche Physikalische Gesellschaft* (German Physical Society or DPG). In 1919, they gathered in the newly-founded *Deutsche Gesellschaft für technische Physik* (German Society for Technical Physics or DGtP) to complement the "orientation of the German Physical Society towards pure science" (Gehlhoff 1920, 4).[2]

With "pure" science, Georg Gehlhoff, the society's first chairman, mainly referred to recent developments in theoretical physics such as quantum theory and relativity theory, but he also included the work of experimental physicists who held professorships at the universities.[3] In his understanding, the agenda of the DPG was no longer compatible with the interests and daily challenges of physicists working in industrial companies. There was a growing gap between physicists aiming at the theoretical and experimental exploration of natural laws and the generation of new experimental methodologies, on the one hand, and "technical" physicists aiming at the production and optimising of technological systems, devices and procedures, on the other. Comparable to the rise of theoretical physics as a new sub-field of physics with its own agenda and its own chairs at the universities – following Jungnickel and McCormmach: the rise of the "second physicists" – the applied physicists tried to demarcate their activities and practices from those of "pure" physicists by establishing themselves as yet another sub-field, which I propose to call the "third" physicists.[4] The "disunity of science"

---

group of professionals in Germany, which Terry Shinn and others have called "research technologists" – researchers "whose principle objective was the design, construction and diffusion of high performance devices for the purposes of detection, measurement and control" (Shinn 2001, 29). In my understanding, many but not all technical physicists can be described as "research technologists".

2 See Swinne (1994, 42–44) for the founding process and Hoffmann (1994) for a general discussion of the early years of the DGtP. Unless indicated otherwise, the German texts have been translated into English by the author.

3 "Pure" science was (and today still is) a problematical term in as much as it was used in a very inconsistent way equipped with various meanings. In many discussions in the history of science and technology, "pure" science or research is mainly referred to as devoid of "contaminations" coming from "outside" of science (political or commercial). In these accounts, "pure" science or physics is negatively defined as excluding "applied" or "technical" objectives. In this text, "pure" physics is an actor's category that particularly in the 1920s indicated a difference between "pure" as "abstract" and "idealised" physics and physical research dealing with the complexity of technical objects, which demanded new forms of physical knowledge.

4 "The Second Physicist" is the title of Christa Jungnickel's and Russel McCormmach's recently re-edited standard work on the development of theoretical physics in Germany (Jungnickel and McCormmach 2017), which was originally published under a different title in 1986. Until the late nineteenth century, physics was taught at most German universities by a single professor. Because the teaching load and the establishment of research laboratories increasingly overburdened the "first" generation of university physicists, in many cases the "second physicist" was a more theoretically minded colleague. As a result, the physics discipline split up into subfields with their own "comprehensive course of study, advanced training in research, and research by

has been introduced as a counter-model to an understanding of science, by emphasising the unified, the homogeneous, or the pure. For many scholars, these concepts still characterise central aims of scientific endeavour in general, and of scientific practices leading to "strong" forms of knowledge (for example, epistemically, socially, or practically strong knowledge) in particular.

In Peter Galison's understanding, disunity in science must not be seen as a sign of weakness, but ought to be seen as an important factor for the strength of a scientific discipline. For example, Galison sees the partition of physics into experimental, theoretical and instrumental sub-cultures as a prerequisite for an understanding of the dynamics and stability of twentieth century physics (Galison 1997). The technical physicists would have consented to such a statement because it would have supported their claim for greater recognition and their effort to gain greater independence of what they perceived as the realm of "pure" physics.

Historically, the disciplinary emancipation of the "third" physicist turned out to be a short-termed episode in the history of German physics. It started after World War I and ended with World War II. The society had its heydays in the mid-1920s with 1,700 members. In 1929, it counted 1,450 members; in 1939, at the beginning of World War II, the number had already declined to 1,275 (Hoffmann 1994, 16). In this chapter, I wish to discuss some of the reasons why the Society for Technical Physics must be seen as a phenomenon of the interwar period and a temporary effect of the professional conflicts and opportunities that accompanied the rise of industrial physics.

In the first issue of the society's journal, the *Zeitschrift für technische Physik*, the editors claimed that technical physics was an "independent domain of intellectual activity", which, compared to experimental and theoretical physics, demanded a distinct way of thinking, dealt with different problems, applied different problem-solving strategies, and developed a different relationship to the role of innovation in scientific research. According to the editors, there was "probably no greater opposition between the general foundations of two sciences than the opposition between technical and pure physics" (Gehlhoff et al. 1920, 2). Because the technical physicists did not want to be understood as mere users of "pure" physical knowledge or a mere appendage of the DPG, they claimed that their work generated and demanded idiosyncratic forms of physical knowledge and therefore contributed not only to the development of technology, but also to the development of general physics.

---

established scientists who are the mentors" (Jungnickel and McCormmach 2017, xi). For the authors, Max Planck serves as an early example of a German professor of physics who did no experiments on his own. The rise of the "third" physicist differs from the rise of the "second" in as much as most chairs of technical physics were established at the technical colleges and not at universities where the guardians of a humanistic educational ideal opposed applied research (Hoffmann 1994, 13–15).

In order to stress its independent status, the initially proposed name, *German Society for Applied Physics*, was changed in the course of 1919 to *German Society for Technical Physics* (DGtP).[5] The number of members of the new society increased rapidly and soon surpassed that of the DPG.[6] There were good reasons for this development. The technical physicists were not a small group of dissatisfied employees, but represented the increasingly self-confident majority of working physicists. As Gehlhoff proudly claimed in 1920, two thirds of German physicists worked "in technology", and only one third "in science" (Gehlhoff 1920, 4).[7]

In the initial phase, the DGtP pursued several main objectives. One aim was to develop further "the intellectual foundation of the technical domains of culture" (Gehlhoff et al. 1920, 4). This included the publication of the *Zeitschrift für technische Physik* (from 1920), which aimed at the swift publishing of research results in the rapidly expanding field of applied physics, and was financed by donations from industrial companies.[8] Its main goals were to improve and demonstrate the utility of physical methodologies and physical knowledge to industrial research and production, to promote (physics-based) technology as a new cultural force as well as to make clear that the physicists would not entrust technical research and the further development of technology to engineers.

A second aim was to contribute to the resurgence of German science and industry after World War I under the conditions of economic crises, the aftermath of the Versailles Treaty as well as additional threats, such as the occupation of the Ruhr valley with its coalmines and steelworks by the French and Belgian military. Gehlhoff responded directly to the occupation when he wrote in 1924 that the "scientific spirit", the general level of education and "the leading intel-

5 On 17 June 1919, Gehlhoff addressed Felix Klein still on behalf of the Society for Applied Physics (NSUB Göttingen, Cod. Ms Felix Klein 5B). Thanks to Birgit Bergmann for pointing me to this correspondence.

6 At that time, the DPG counted about 1,300 members (Hoffmann 1994, 16–17). Helga Schultrich emphasised that the DGtP primarily served the mutual interests of industrial scientists and companies. It mostly attracted higher ranked industrial physicists such as directors of factories or industrial laboratories while lower ranked employees rather joined the *Bund angestellter Akademiker* that operated more like a labor union (Schultrich 1985, 91). The applied physicists gathering in the DGtP were seeking to enhance their status by utilizing the "institutional strength" of a scientific discipline.

7 Around 1930, of approximately 1,600 professional physicists (without physics teachers) in Germany, 500 were employed as professors or *Assistenten* at the universities and technical colleges, 100 at governmental institutions, 100 in the patent system and about 800 in industrial companies. In total, about two thirds of professional physicists worked in "technology", because, in many governmental institutions, physicists were involved in applied research as well (Schultrich 1985, 90).

8 Another journal largely financed by the DGtP was *Physikalische Berichte*. The journal was founded in 1920 by merging three review journals into one (the *Fortschritte der Physik, Halbmonatliche Literaturverzeichnis der Fortschritte der Physik* and *Beiblätter* to the *Annalen der Physik*). The DGtP contributed 65,000 Reichsmark to its publication, the DPG 5,000 Reichsmark and the Prussian Academy of Science 10,000 Reichsmark. See Anonymus 1920, 235; Swinne 1994, 37–39.

lectuals" were "some of the very few raw materials that we do not have to import and we cannot be forced to hand over" (Gehlhoff 1924, 204). The physicists would ensure industry and technology a competitive advantage by providing Germany as a country with poor natural resources with the necessary intellectual resources:

The way our technology is instructed by scientific knowledge is still ahead of other countries. [...] Only intellectual forces, the maximum possible rationalisation of work processes and the highest standards of our technical design can help us to leave misery behind and work our way up to better times. (Gehlhoff 1924, 204)

Accordingly, a third aim was to emphasise the value of physical knowledge and methodology for the technical education system because the obvious "lack of intellectuality" made its reform inevitable (Gehlhoff et al. 1920, 3).[9] Thus, it was particularly important for the society to step into the lion's den and demand a reform of physics education at the technical colleges. Previously, most technical colleges had allowed physics only the status of an auxiliary science.[10] The goal was to establish physics as a "full science" and obtain permission to grant diplomas, and doctoral as well as post-doctoral degrees in physics. If not guided by the capacities of physical knowledge, the representatives of the society argued, technology could not take a healthy route with its strong "accentuation on form to the disadvantage of content", since "this content dominates technical construction while the latter is only secondary. The knowledge of physical processes and their effects is primary." (Gehlhoff et al. 1920, 3)

Technical physicists presented themselves as two-faced, Janus-type researchers. Nobody else was able to survey and connect the primary and the secondary realms of science and technology production at the same time – in particular, in times of radical change of the theoretical foundations of physics, which was undermining traditional understandings of the material, the elemental and the factual. Nobody else was able to look beyond the daily needs of technological development and link specialised domains of technology with general scientific developments. Thus, the technical physicists demanded the hierarchical sub-ordination of engineers and technicians:

---

9 One reason for the engagement of the DGtP can be sought in the development of the engineering education. The first professorships for electrical engineering were established at the technical colleges in the early 1880s. These were mostly filled with experienced industrial engineers and not with physicist – against their own perception of electrical engineering as applied physics. This was mostly due to the rise of heavy-current electrical engineering, the generation and utilisation of electric energy by means of powerful electrodynamic machines, which was above all a mechanical engineering challenge. See König 1996.

10 Exceptions were the technical colleges in Dresden and Munich, see Swinne 1994, 40; Hashagen 2003.

The science represented by [technical physicists] is not only appointed to answer day-to-day technological questions but also, since no one else has the ability to survey the technical and scientific potentials at one and the same time, to instruct technical progress. Eventually, technical physics is not only a consultant of technology but its leader.[11]

Such statements were expressions of a feeling of cultural superiority over engineers. At the same time, they were a reaction to the sometimes bigger, sometimes smaller, professional competition with the engineers, and therefore an expression of social fears.[12]

2. The creation and control of complex things

For some contemporary observers, the distinction between technical physicists and engineers made little sense. Richard von Mises, the director of the Institute for Applied Mathematics at the Friedrich-Wilhelms-University in Berlin, asked whether the activities of technical physics should be referred to as scientific at all, or rather as engineering in more advanced and modern fields. For him, the "so-called 'technical physics'" was "partly a mere aggregation of the instructions and methods of physical technology that are relevant for experimental investigations, partly it performs tasks that normally belong to the domain of mechanical engineering for special fields of technology such as the construction of apparatuses, thermionic tubes, etc." (Mises 1921, 13)[13]

As they had to establish and position themselves not only in relation to the community of academic physicists but also in relation to the engineering sciences and engineers, the technical physicists were caught in a double-bind, which demanded boundary-work – collaboration as well as demarcation – in two directions. If technical physicists wanted to impress their colleagues and demonstrate the independence of both "pure" physics and engineering, one central question remained unanswered: If the "pure" physicists provided primary "content" to

---

11 Schack 1926, 378.

12 I am not arguing here for or against the "primacy" of science over technology or vice versa (for a detailed discussion, see for example, Forman 2007). I am interested in the attempts of the historical actors to explore the constraints and challenges, and to exploit the opportunities that they encountered in the intermediate space between physics and technology in the interwar period.

13 Richard von Mises's remarks were published in the first issue of the *Journal of Applied Mathematics and Mechanics* (ZAMM). The Society of Applied Mathematics and Mechanics (GAMM), which was founded in 1922 by von Mises, Ludwig Prandtl and Hans Reissner, can be seen as the mathematical counterpart to (and partly in competition with) the DGtP in its effort to foster and advance the exploration of mechanics, mathematics and physics as knowledge bases of the engineering sciences and technology (Mehrtens 1990, 377–401). Thus, von Mises was not a disinterested observer.

secondary technological developments, what was the contribution of the technical physicists?

The attempt to answer this question was an important reason why technical physicists sought to demarcate their activities not only from those of engineers, but also from those of "pure" physics. This was partly due to the still felt condescension that the applied or technical physicists experienced from their academic colleagues, for example, if they were reviled as mere "paid labourers" or clerks (Hoffmann 1994, 11). In part, the technical physicists felt that many of the successes of "pure" physics were built on their experience and technological expertise – contributions to the progress of physics for which they did not, in their view, receive adequate attention and acknowledgement. In part, they felt that the exploration and construction of technical devices and appliances followed different rules, because these devices had to function under conditions that for the most part diverged from the idealised requirements of theoretical abstractions or laboratory physics.

"Pure physics", the introductory programmatic text of the *Zeitschrift für technische Physik* claimed, was a cultural achievement. It had taken several centuries and demanded the "intellectual collaboration of all cultural nations" to develop into an autonomous science (Gehlhoff et al. 1920, 2). Two essential principles had been at the centre of this development: first, to purify and isolate "every phenomenon in a pure state" ("*Reindarstellung*") and second, to process further and record the facts collected in this way ("*Tatsachenstoff*"), "by means of laws that are comparatively easy to formulate" (Gehlhoff et al. 1920, 2). Neither of these principles was normally applicable in technical research and development.

Technical physics differed from a conventional understanding of physics by the fact that, in the design of technical devices, individual physical processes could rarely be singled out and dealt with independently. The processes in a modern high-performance incandescent lamp were, for example, "electrical, thermodynamic, optical and mechanical at the same time" (Gehlhoff et al. 1920, 2). While "pure" physicist sought to treat each aspect of a phenomenon in isolation, technical physicists had to "start from the impossibility of isolating the individual physical processes in technical processes" (Gehlhoff et al. 1920, 2). They always had "to face a plurality of components of a phenomenon, the mutual conditionality of which and their unification into a specified effect must first and foremost be the subject of the investigation" (Gehlhoff et al. 1920, 2). In most cases, a comprehensive theoretical representation of the underlying processes was not possible; the enhancement of a light bulb, for example, demanded a complicated trade-off among various interdependent, occasionally conflicting, requirements.[14]

---

14 The incomplete representation and the "trade-off" between various conflicting processes and representation was a central dilemma in the engineering sciences as well. See, for example, Vincenti 1990, 20 on the design of airplane wings.

The terms *"Reindarstellung"* and *"Tatsachenstoff"* were deliberately adopted from chemistry. Chemical substances had to be isolated, transmuted and purified from a miscellany of various components by a sequence of procedures; using comparable procedures, physical facts had to be treated accordingly.[15] Historically, the equipment or materials necessary for physical experiments and the preparation of physical facts had mainly been provided by the experimenters themselves or by their laboratory assistants.[16] They were complemented by professional instrument makers who provided not only standardised laboratory devices but also conducted original research on the utilisation of specific methodologies or materials and the construction of sophisticated apparatuses.[17] These tasks increasingly fell within the scope of technical physicists who saw the constant supply of new instruments and methodologies as a central contribution to knowledge production.[18] Without the expertise of technical physics, Gehlhoff argued, "pure" physics would soon reach its limits; thus, the progress of "pure" physics would become almost inconceivable (Gehlhoff 1929, 194).

However, this was not the end of the complexity of the task. In contrast to "scientific" researchers, the primary goal of "technical" researchers was to contribute to the generation of technical devices and industrial products. Much more than scientific researchers, technical researchers had to submit the products of their research to the "principle of economic development in human culture" (Gehlhoff et al. 1920, 2).[19] Eventually, the devices had to be transformed into mass-producible items, they had to comply with legal boundary conditions – for example, national patent laws and possible conflicts with already existing patents – meet the taste, the demands and habits of customers and users, and thereby

---

15 The goal, though, was not to amplify and isolate apparent properties, but to attain a deeper understanding of the underlying processes. Referring to chemical practices as well, Gaston Bachelard called the experimental ensembles with which scientists prepare scientific objects and "realise" their properties "phenomeno-techniques": "Its purpose is to amplify what is revealed beyond appearance. It takes its instruction from construction" (Bachelard 1986, 13).

16 Steven Shapin and Simon Schaffer have shown how "matters of fact" emerged in the early Royal Society through the effort of Robert Hooke and other (more or less "invisible") technicians (Shapin and Schaffer 1985). In their account, the process of fact making was even more complex because it included the legitimation of the experimental observations by presenting the results in front of the exclusive "public" of gentlemen of the Royal Society – a strengthening of knowledge claims by their institutional embedment.

17 Two examples for the close collaboration of experimentalists with instrument makers (and theoretical scientists) in the field of gas discharge physics in the late nineteenth century are discussed in Müller 2004 and 2011.

18 The impact of this new group of researchers was not restricted to physics. Carsten Reinhardt has shown how the massive application of new physical technologies, methodologies and instruments radically transformed the practices and the disciplinary self-understanding of chemistry during and after World War II. Reinhardt 2006.

19 I do not think that Gehlhoff and his colleagues refer here to Ernst Mach, who claimed in his philosophy and epistemology that scientific thinking and the generation of scientific knowledge has to comply with economic principles, but to their daily experiences as industrial physicists.

compete with the products of other companies. In addition, these devices could not be dealt with individually, but had to be seen as integral components of complex systems. Did the processing of all these challenges and tasks still belong to physics?[20]

In 1929, the physicist and philosopher Hans Reichenbach published an article on "The Aims and Methods of Physical Knowledge" in the fourth volume of the *Handbuch der Physik*, in which he briefly referred to technical physics as well. In his understanding, technical physics helped to utilise "new discoveries of theoretical science" in technical applications and to adapt technological methods to new theoretical developments. Technical physics thus combined the ability to "prepare" theoretical knowledge for technology and to equip technology with a "theoretical instinct" that could help to anticipate technological developments (Reichenbach 1978, 132). Apart from these advantages and positive prospects, Reichenbach rejected the emancipatory claims of the technical physicists:

Important, then, as technical physics is, and develop as it may from sociological necessity – for it requires a new form of union between scientific knowledge and technological goals – it is, after all, by nature technological and not scientific. (Reichenbach 1978, 132–133)

He was able to recognise a "completely different way of thinking and a different kind of use of the scientific tools", Reichenbach admitted, "yet the clarity of conceptual definition demands a strict separation" of science and technology (Reichenbach 1978, 133). In other word, "technical physics" was not and could not be an "exact" science. Accordingly, technical physics found no further mention in Reichenbach's remarks. In his understanding, science could not be "anything more than a resource" for technology – "a powerful resource, to be sure, yet never an end. Technology can be forced to undertake scientific investigation in order to solve its problems of application, but it will always rest content once practical utilisation has succeeded, and will abandon theoretical research to the scientists." (Reichenbach 1978, 130)

If higher mathematics were an indispensable requirement, and abstract or theoretical representations the central aim and result of proper physical research, most technical physicists would have consented to Reichenbach's assessment. Often, the development of a technical device resembled more an erratic or evolutionary process than a theory driven or rationalised scientific process – as in the

---

20 Another challenge was the inclusion of the "individual" into the equations and methodologies of physics: "How can one measure the comfort of a floor? In years gone by this would not have been a proper question to ask a physicist, but in the past decade those physicists concerned with the measurement of color or with the measurement of acoustical properties have discovered, somewhat to their amazement, that these border-line problems in which an individual is part of the measuring system can sometimes be solved. Thus, the broadening of physics to include physiological manifestations is now well established" (Robinson 1948, 5).

case of the modern high-performance light bulb that developed only after "its predecessors, starting with the Edison-lamp, managed to climb the subjacent steps of luminous efficiency" (Gehlhoff et al. 1920, 2). However, the aim of the technical physicists was not only to achieve the functionality of a process or device under specific conditions, but also – a trait which, in their view, distinguished them from engineers – to generalise problems and develop methodologies that allowed for the theoretical-mathematical treatment and presentation of a whole class of problems. Even if they did not come up with theoretical solutions to specific problems themselves, they helped to formulate and pre-configure problems that otherwise would never have occurred to theoretical or experimental physicists as being particularly relevant or even solvable.

Following Hans-Jörg Rheinberger, experimental investigations pursue two distinct, but mutually interdependent, objectives: the generation, functional design and utilisation of "technical objects" or ensembles of "technical objects", on the one hand, which, on the other, were used to frame the properties of the often blurry and vaguely defined research objects or "epistemic things" and make them thereby scientifically intelligible (Rheinberger 1997). While scientific researchers were more interested in the refinement of the epistemic dimension of things and processes, technical physicists focused on the further development and utilisation of technical objects – or what Terry Shinn has called "things of function" (Shinn 2017) – and of the technical and scientific ensembles that Rheinberger has called "experimental systems". The physical researchers learned that often what they perceived as means – ways to prepare complex things, problem-solving strategies, a better understanding of systemic contexts, methodologies and research tools (including theoretical or mathematical tools) – became valuable ends of scientific research in their own right and turned out to be more important than what they had previously understood as the ends of physical research.[21]

---

21 In his account of the early history of quantum theory, Suman Seth distinguished between a "physics of principles" and a "physics of problems" (Seth 2010). According to Seth, Max Planck was an adherent of the first approach, Arnold Sommerfeld, who had been professor of applied mathematics at technical colleges before he turned into one of the most influential mathematical physicists of the early twentieth century, was an adherent of the second approach. Sommerfeld did not restrict his theoretical and mathematical problem solving strategies to physical problems but also included technological problems; vice versa, adopting technical problem-solving strategies to theoretical physics, Sommerfeld can be seen as a theoretical toolmaker who sought to bridge gaps between mathematics, physics and technology, and thus was "crafting the quantum".

3. Boundary work with the engineers

The boundary work between "pure" and "technical" physicists did not obstruct the collaboration of the DPG and the DGtP. Apart from many double memberships, both societies jointly organised the *Physicists' and Mathematicians' Days* together with the German Mathematical Society from 1921 (which took place annually from 1929). Instead, one should speak of a division of labour in which both societies took on complementary tasks, with the technical physicists commissioned to improve the contact between physics and industry and to allocate additional resources and financial support to the formerly mostly government-funded German physics community.[22] In its first year, the society received, for example, donations of 274,000 *Reichmarks* (RM) including 100,000 RM from *Siemens*, 50,000 RM from *AEG*, 30,000 RM from *Osram* and 25,000 RM from *Carl Zeiss* in Jena (Anonymus 1920, 234).

With their attempt to supply the university-educated élites with new capacities to act in a society increasingly shaped by industry and technology, the DGtP followed the example of institutions and organisations such as the *Physikalisch-Technische Reichsanstalt*, the *Göttinger Vereinigung zur Förderung der angewandten Physik und Mathematik* (the Göttingen Association for the Promotion of Applied Physics and Mathematics, which was founded in 1898) or the *Kaiser-Wilhelm-Society* each of which aimed at a better collaboration of science and industry as well as a better utilisation of industrial resources to the benefit of science and *vice versa*. Each helped to facilitate and consolidate what Mitchell Ash described as a relationship in which the partners served as "resources for one another" and mutually exchanged services and resources to achieve objectives which they would not have achieved otherwise (Ash 2002).[23] In our case, the academic scientists tried to mobilise resources that had formerly been utilised by engineers and engineering schools. This status enhancement at the expense of others shows, on the one hand, the growing interest of industry in the utilisation of resources offered by science, while, on the other, it inevitably led to interdisciplinary conflicts.

The relationship between the representatives of the German universities, who wanted to establish applied or technical sciences at their institutions, and the re-

---

22 On funding schemes and funding institutions supporting physics research, which emerged after World War I in Germany, see Forman (1974).While Forman emphasized the important role of the *Notgemeinschaft der deutschen Wissenschaft* (the predecessor of the German Research Foundation) and the *Helmholtz-Gesellschaft zur Förderung der physikalisch-technischen Forschung* (which continued the work of the Göttingen Association for the Promotion of Applied Physics and Mathematics after its liquidation), both organisations that were founded in 1920, he does not refer to the activities of the DGtP.

23 Ash introduced the concept for the investigation of scientific "resource ensembles" under the influence of varying political conditions. In his article, Ash's focuses on the relationship of science and the National Socialist state, but he has (in previous and subsequent articles) explored other constellations as well.

presentatives of the technical colleges, who rejected any attempts by the universities to interfere in the interests of their institutions, deteriorated into open conflict for the first time in the 1890s. The leading combatants were the Göttingen mathematician Felix Klein and Alois Riedler, professor of mechanical engineering at the *Technische Hochschule Berlin-Charlottenburg*. Klein promoted the establishment of institutes for applied research at the German universities as well as a stronger mathematical-scientific orientation of engineering education at the technical colleges (Manegold 1970). In 1898, he initiated, together with the industrialist Heinrich Böttinger, the foundation of the Göttingen Association for the Promotion of Applied Physics and Mathematics in order to collect funds from industry for the establishment of institutes of applied science at the universities (Mehrtens 1990, 377–401).

Riedler was concerned with the autonomy of the technical colleges as well as with the right to award doctorates (which was granted by the German Kaiser Wilhelm II to all Prussian technical colleges in 1899). While the latter was an important step forward in the attempt to enhance the cultural and social status of the academically educated engineers, their professional status was, according to Riedler, under permanent pressure from "non-academic" engineers who were educated outside the technical colleges and often had better opportunities on the job market because they earned lower wages (Gispen 2002, 194–196). In his view, there was no need for additional competition coming from the universities.

Riedler expressed his disgust for his more theoretical or more abstract-minded colleagues (such as his intimate enemy, the professor of technical mechanics at the Berlin *Technische Hochschule*, Franz Reuleaux) in pithy rhetoric.[24] Possibly in response to the foundation of the Society for Technical Physics, he took the physicists to task as well. He accused "inexperienced theorists" of re-building the "theoretical ruins" under the new names of "technical mechanics" and "technical physics", and predicted that they would suffer shipwreck just like their predecessors.[25] Only recently, in a polemical pamphlet directed against those "blind to reality" in science and technology, had Riedler renewed his role as a defender of a practical education at technical colleges against claims for a stronger theoretical and scientific education:

'Abstraction' is not an independent scientific means but an auxiliary means, a makeshift that is being used for the time being to gain a simplified and partial view. (Riedler 1919, 9)

Only researchers who were captive to this partial perspective on the world could prefer "exact" over "technical" knowledge:

---

24 On the relationship between Reuleaux and Riedler, see König 2017.
25 Riedler, quoted in Hort 1924, 317.

Usually, scientific and technical tasks can only be solved approximately. Only some of the many given connections of reality can be determined. In technology, as a rule, only individual conditions can be fulfilled, usually at the expense of the others. Frequently mistakes have to be made consciously, important conditions have to be neglected and inappropriate pre-conditions have to be assumed. The challenge of reality can be solved in different ways, but not 'exactly'.[26]

In Riedler's understanding, "exact" knowledge corresponded to a practically unattainable ideal of knowledge. It was an illusion that had little to do with reality – not only in technology, but also in science – and should not be taken and taught as a scientific standard at universities and technical colleges:

Instead of pretending to young people the delusions of 'exact' knowledge and procedures, they should rather be systematically informed (by means of 'error science') about the most essential, recurring errors in one-sided comprehension, observation and judgement. (Riedler 1919, 8)

The technical physicists would have approved of much of what Riedler wrote. However, with his last comments, Riedler overstretched the physicists' goodwill because he under-estimated the value of (theoretical or abstract) scientific knowledge as a basis for the development of new fields of technology.

Until after World War I, the physicists had largely avoided direct conflict with the engineers, as the technical physicist Wilhelm Hort, one of the co-founders of the society and co-editor of the *Zeitschrift für technische Physik*, had to admit in 1921: "Even in the technical-scientific avant-garde battles of the [eighteen] nineties [...] the physicists at the universities left it to the mathematicians alone to fight 'practice' on the side of 'theory'" (Hort 1921, 133). It was time now for the physicists to assume responsibility as well, and counter the attacks of the aged, but still combative, Riedler.[27]

In a harsh review of several of Riedler's publications, Hort lamented Riedler's apparent "deep hatred" of scientific research and of intellectuals, including physicists. Furthermore, he derided his claim that several nineteenth century scientists, such as William Herschel, Michael Faraday, John Tyndall, and Heinrich Hertz, were actually "men of practice" – trained musicians, bookbinders and laboratory technicians or engineers (Hort 1924, 316). In Hort's understanding, Riedler's emphasis of "*Sachwollen*" – his over-emphasis of empirical knowledge and experience – and his campaign against the teaching of advanced scientific theory at the technical colleges had reached a dangerous condition because these

---

26 Riedler 1919, 8. In techno-scientific research, scientists and engineers largely attempted to approximate the "exact" by achieving higher "precision" – mostly as a result of the interaction between theory, experiment and instrument development, see Epple 2002.

27 Hort, who worked as chief engineer at the turbine plant of AEG and at the Heinrich-Hertz-Institute of Oscillation Research in Berlin, was a specialist in the theory of (mechanical) oscillations and the application of differential equations to the solution of technical problems.

ideas no longer suited the requirements of current technology. In particular, he criticised Riedler's intuitive approach and questioned his claim that, at the present stage of technological development, even experienced engineers could "behold" or "visually anticipate" the design of a complex technical device: "Technological 'anticipation' unfortunately belongs in the realm of the impossible, as Riedler himself proved with his own designs. Twenty years ago, Riedler 'visually antici-pated' the Riedler-Stumpf-Turbine, which was a complete failure." (Hort 1924, 316)[28]

According to Hort, the realisation of modern technology had to depend on scientific-mathematical abstractions and tools; in addition, it demanded the par-ticipation of a large group of specialists (among them theoretically-educated en-gineers and physicists), not, as Riedler suggested, as mere auxiliaries, but as fully-fledged or even guiding collaborators.

The history of the development of all the technical ideas that eventually led to success proves how much time and effort is needed to give an initial anticipatory vision a shape that possesses viability. Thanks to the collaboration of numerous 'computers and draughtsmen', the final work oftentimes looks quite different from what the 'experienced anticipator' originally wanted. Sometimes the anticipations lead to nothing, as the Riedler-Stumpf-Turbine proves.[29]

Beyond these expressions of mutual dislike, both opponents knew that they were operating in an interstice between physics and technology that was still insuffi-ciently developed and institutionalised.[30] Both opponents saw deficits in their own methodology and knowledge. Both sought for solutions that would benefit their own community and prevent them from surrendering the interstice to other groups. However, at the same time, the groups involved over-estimated the cap-abilities of their means and under-estimated the complexity of the tasks. Further-more, they under-estimated the benefits of utilising as resources the means offe-red by other groups and the challenge of educating researchers who were able to shape and occupy the intermediate space.

For example, Riedler remarked that the "theoreticians of technology" were not able to mediate between the rapid transmutations of the physical sciences – "new, strange, partly completely visionary assumptions: ions, electrons, etc." – and technology (Riedler 1919, 49–50). In 1919, the concepts of the electron and ion still held many surprises, but, in physical research, they were no longer "visi-onary assumptions"; the better understanding of these scientific objects, on the

---

28 Despite his alleged "incompetence" (according to Hort), Riedler was successfully marketing his inventions and became a millionaire (König 2017).

29 Hort 1924, 316–17.

30 On the complexity of the task to estimate and understand the challenges of interstitial commu-nities, landscapes or arenas between science, industry and technology, see Shinn and Joerges 2001.

contrary, had an immense impact on the further development of incandescent lamps and electron tubes. In the research laboratories of American electrotechnical companies, university-educated physical chemists with an extensive knowledge on the properties of electrons and ions contributed immensely to the advances of electrical engineering and to the rise of electronics as a new branch of technology (Wise 1983). Although Riedler urged engineers to engage with developments in contemporary physics as well, he himself seems not to have realised how much the understanding and experimental exploration of these new scientific objects owed to theory and an understanding of theoretical concepts.

As became increasingly apparent, the technological and industrial creation of value was based upon the differentiation of specialised groups of researchers with their particular forms of knowledge as well as upon the collaboration and symbiosis among these groups. A common task of the involved groups was to establish, shape and institutionalise intermediate or interstitial spaces or "trading zones" where the exchange of resources and the establishment of mutually assessable resource ensembles, the development of hybrid languages or "interlanguages" (Galison 1997), the utilisation of boundary objects and different constellations of "means" and "ends" could be explored and possible solutions tested.[31] In Germany, the *Physikalisch Technische Reichsanstalt* was one institution in which the requirements of technology and science could interfere; others developed at the universities and technical colleges. The most dynamic experimental space in which the division of labour and new forms of collaboration could be tested and trained, in which new forms of organising research and new types of researchers emerged, was the industrial research laboratory.

Research laboratories served as boundary spaces in which several interest groups tried to implement their own systems of rules and constraints, to establish their own operational rationale and adjust research and development to their own goals and practices. The practical work in these laboratories meant a reality check and reality shock for many claims and expectations of the members of each group involved in joint research and development.

---

31 Sungook Hong has suggested a threefold differentiation of the concept of "boundary objects" – an analytical tool for investigating the complex interactions and relationships in heterogeneous groups – for analysing the relationship of science and technology: "Instruments as a material boundary object; new institutions and laboratories as a spatial boundary object; and new group of people who mediate between science and technology as a boundary person or a human hybrid" (Hong 1999, 296).

4. The technical physicist as mediator

A central problem for the further profiling of technical physics was that the engineers and engineering schools were not idle, but continually improved their own programmes and agendas – which included a growing awareness that some modern physical and mathematical methodologies proved to be beneficial for the further development of technology and production processes.[32] The early development of electrical engineering at the technical colleges as an "industry-based science" was gradually transformed by the requirements of a "science-based industry" (König 1996).

In economically difficult times, the industrial physicists became painfully aware of the growing competition. In 1932, in the middle of the Great Depression, the estimated annual number of physicists graduating in Germany was 250, with additional 400 unemployed physicists seeking work; the estimated demand was for between 90 to 100 physicists (Anonymus 1932, 83).[33] The blame for this misery was also sought among the engineers. In a professional advice brochure published in 1932, physicists were thus urged to defend existing jobs against engineers, who were generally working for lower wages. One way to deal with the resulting pressure was continuous innovation:

The physicist is a pioneer. If he forgets this and does not continue to create something new, the company's operations will inevitably be determined by fixed procedures. Instead of pushing forward on new paths, the technical development of existing methods will dominate. The factory will be 'mechanised', and the physicist will not be replaced by a physicist but by a specialist engineer when the position becomes vacant. [...] The jobs for physicists, at least in industry, are not permanent; they must be conquered again and again.[34]

Clearly, the disciplinary self-confidence did not correspond to the professional status and the reality of the job-market. Picking up contemporary discussions on the "mechanisation" of society and subsequent decay of culture – particularly expressed in the dichotomy of negatively connoted (technical) "civilisation" and positively connoted (primarily, German) "culture" – the physicists tried to strengthen their status by placing themselves on the side of culture.[35] They styl-

---

32 A good example of this is the education and later performance of Ernst Ruska who studied electrical engineering at the technical colleges in Munich and Berlin in the late 1920s, early 1930s. In 1986 he was awarded the Nobel Prize in Physics for his contributions to the development of electron optics and the construction of electron microscopes (Müller 2009).

33 The numbers show that physics was still a profession of a manageable size in the interwar period. In 1920, *Carl-Zeiss* in Jena employed 25, *Siemens* 55 physicists; around 1930, *Osram* employed 60 and *I.G.-Farben* 70 physicists (Schultrich 1985, 90).

34 Anonymus 1932, 72.

35 In his bestseller "The Decline of the West", Oswald Spengler makes frequent use of this distinction. Fritz Ringer cites a definition from the German encyclopedia *Der große Brockhaus*, which

ised themselves as creative spirits and as the engines of industrial innovation and progress – not only for the advantage of the company or their own benefit, but also for the renewal and re-generation of culture as a whole. Some physicists even mobilised the *motif* of bodily de-generation. According to them, the current mismatch between technology and culture showed "signs of a not yet sufficiently advanced technology", and they diagnosed a "transitional diseases of an incomplete development" (Schack 1926, 377) – which only the physicists were able to heal. In most of these statements, though, the authors left open why the practices of the technical physicists legitimised such a superior status.

A second way to deal with the pressure grew out of the gradual acceptance of the usefulness of recent developments in "pure" physics. Technical physicists increasingly accepted the role as translators between the realms of "new" and "old" physics. "Oftentimes it is said," George Gehlhoff remarked in 1929, "pure physics consists (today) of atomic physics, the physics of space structure, of radiation, the axiomatic foundation; and technical physics consists of so called 'old physics' such as mechanics, thermodynamics, optics, electricity, or the physics of oscillations and vibrations" (Gehlhoff 1929, 195). With the growing ability to transform the "new", which was often perceived as something merely intellectual, into something functional and manageable, the physicists proved that these effects were more than illusions or mere auxiliary concepts. While some physicists formed the *avant-garde* of theoretical and experimental development, the technical physicists served not as rearguard, but as an essential group of general physics that helped to transform the new into something familiar: "Anything that today belongs to the realm of pure physics; tomorrow it will belong to technical physics." (Gehlhoff 1929, 195)[36] This not only helped to develop new perspectives on technol-

---

beautifully captures the positioning of the physicists in relation to engineers: "[C]ivilisation is to culture as the external is to the internal, the artificially constructed to the naturally developed, the mechanical to the organic, 'means' to 'ends' (Spengler)" (Ringer 1969, 89); one could add: the "secondary" to the "primary". The engineers reacted to their alleged lack of cultural responsibility with attempts to develop and establish their own understanding of a modern, technologybased culture (Voskuhl 2016; Hård and Jamison 1998). Jeffrey Herf has pointed out that many attempts in Germany to appropriate technology culturally or to appropriate culture technologically showed a high affinity to reactionary and national socialist ideas (Herf 1984).

36 According to Dieter Hoffmann, this translation process was an important reason why the interest in disciplinary autonomy abated and technical physics was reintegrated into "traditional physics" in the 1930s and 1940s (Hoffmann 1994, 18). With their conviction that the new or not-yet-applied could somehow be appropriated by, or integrated into, the old technical physicists were not alone. Theoretical physicists, such as Max Planck and Albert Einstein, were critical of many implications of quantum mechanics as well and they were seeking for ways to reintegrate the world of quantum mechanical objects into what was increasingly perceived as "classical physics" (Staley 2005).

ogy, but also to compensate for the damage of modernisation experienced by some of the "older" physicists.[37]

In some areas, these hopes were justified. In most cases, the utilisation of "pure" or "abstract" knowledge for the improvement of existing products or for the generation of new classes of technological devices turned out to be too optimistic – for example, the technical utilisation of the "physics of space structure", namely, the equations of Einstein's general theory of relativity. Many results of academic research were not – or only in the distant future became – suitable for technical exploitation or could be technically exploited only in contexts that no one had previously foreseen. For those interested in the constructive exchange of science and technology, one central objective was to create an environment in which the probability for such an exchange was significantly enhanced.

In the course of the 1920s, industrial companies offered a growing number of physicists jobs and the opportunity to prove their worth. Several companies built up physical laboratories where not only specialists found well-paid and well-appointed jobs in a growing number of fields, but also physicists with a broad and general education. In industrial laboratories, the search for challenging research topics and the call for a stronger focus on original and "pure" research became more and more intense, especially in the electrical engineering industry, which demanded a high input from scientific research to foster the development of new fields of technology such as electronics. The larger companies soon introduced a division of labour between several laboratories. Some of them converged their efforts on single purposes; others covered multiple purposes and various fields of research. The latter were the laboratories where most physicists were employed.

In some cases, companies managed to employ high-profile physicists as directors of research laboratories or as amply funded associated scientists.[38] To be

---

37 To some extent, the DGtP served as one of several retreats for physicists who felt repelled and overwhelmed by the recent developments in theoretical physics. Anti-modern sentiments, the revulsion of the Weimar Republic, and a growing antisemitism led to the formation and strengthening of nationalistic and ultra-conservative networks (Wolff 2008) and eventually to the rise of the national socialist "Aryan" physicists (Eckert 2012). Philipp Lenard, a protagonist of "Aryan" physics, left the DPG in 1923 but remained a member of the DGtP. In contrast to other organisations, many members of the DGtP adopted a pragmatic attitude towards modern theoretical physics. They were experts for the "mediation" between different positions – network-builders – and not for polarisation and "purification"; following Bruno Latour, they could be referred to as amodern (Latour 1993).

38 On the development of research in the electrotechnical industry until 1914 (and preceding developments in the chemical industry), see Fox and Guagnini 1999. The establishment of central research laboratories at the electrotechnical companies in the USA was inspired by the successful promotion of industrial research in the German chemical industry in the second half of the nineteenth century (Homburg 1992; Wise 1985; Reich 1985). The German electrotechnical companies established central (physical) research laboratories mostly after the example of their US-American competitors and collaborators (Schubert 1987; Erker 1995).

able to compete with other companies and attract high-profile scientists, these scientists were granted the liberty to choose their own research topics and publish their results in competitive scientific journals. While the "technical" physicists had initially emphasised the differences from their academic colleagues, a new generation of industrial physicists sought close contact with, and competed with, university physicists – for fame and increasingly for Nobel Prizes as well.[39]

One prominent example can be found in Irving Langmuir, a physical chemist working at the General Electric Research Laboratory (Reich 1983). For several German industrial physicists, Langmuir was exemplary as a scientist who managed to conduct path-breaking research in an industrial environment, and successfully generated new methodologies and products because (and not despite the fact that) he was given the freedom and the capacities to choose his research projects mostly independent of the company's immediate needs (Ramsauer 1929, 224). In a lecture given in 1928, Langmuir emphasised the purely scientific character of his research on atomic hydrogen, which proceeded "without thoughts of practical application" and led to several most valuable discoveries and innovative technologies, including the invention of the gas-filled incandescent lamp (Langmuir 1928, 201).[40]

Langmuir differentiated between two types of industrial research. It was "logical and often extremely profitable to organise research laboratories to solve specific problems. Efficiency requires that the director shall assign to each worker a carefully planned programme. Experiments which do not logically fit in with this programme are to be discouraged" (Langmuir 1928, 202).[41] However, "organised industrial research" and the "programming" of researchers had "serious limitations".[42] First, because organised research often resembled engineering work more than research and usually went "along lines that were already foreseen"; second,

---

39 One can argue, though, that only high-profile physicists such as Ernst Abbe at Carl Zeiss opened up opportunities for other types of physical researchers in industrial companies. In the 1930s, the first Nobel Prizes were awarded to researchers working at electrotechnical companies (for example, Irving Langmuir at GE and Clinton J. Davisson at Bell-Laboratories).

40 The lecture was translated into German immediately after its publication and appeared in the widely-read journal *Die Naturwissenschaften*.

41 The idea (or rather the ideal) that scientific research can be organised and planned in a rational way, was supported by contemporary philosophers of science as well, who referred to similar attempts to "organise" research in "pure" science – only that the constraints imposed on the researchers were of a different nature: "The theoretician puts certain definite questions to the experimenter, and the latter, by his experiments, tries to elicit a decisive answer to these questions, and to no others. All other questions he tries hard to exclude. [...] Theory dominates the experimental work from its initial planning up to the finishing touches in the laboratory." (Popper [1935] 2002, 89–90).

42 This applies to the relation of theory and experiment as well. As Ian Hacking put it, partly in response to Popper: "Experimentation has a life of its own" (Hacking 1983, 159). Following Peter Galison and others, the same is true for the role of instrumentation and technology in scientific research (Galison 1997).

because very few directors were capable of foreseeing "the solution sufficiently well to plan a good campaign of attack in advance"; and third, because "the best type of research man does not like to be told too definitely what must be the objective of his experiments. To him scientific curiosity is usually a greater incentive than the hope of commercially useful results" (Langmuir 1928, 202). For Langmuir, curiosity served as a valuable guide leading the second type of industrial researcher to fundamental discoveries and helping him solve specific problems "in still better ways than could have been reached by a direct attack" – a style of research that furthermore often resulted in "valuable by-products in the form of new lines of activity for the industrial organization" (Langmuir 1928, 202).

Langmuir himself belonged to the "best type of research man"; he would not have entered industrial research without the freedoms granted to him by Willis Whitney, the head of General Electric's research laboratory. The majority of scientists, though, had to submit to the regime of collective and organised research. Adopting a phrase of General Electric's *spiritus rector*, Charles Proteus Steinmetz, Whitney celebrated a "socialism of the laboratory" and put it against individual claims to fame and for the recognition of some researchers working in his laboratory – "imbued with the German idea of individualistic, secretive research" (Miller 2011, 34, 36; Wise 1985, 101). Only outstanding researchers were allowed a high degree of personal freedom and security of employment – and this was true for German industrial laboratories as well; the rest had to work under highly-regulated laboratory procedures and continued to be replaceable (Schultrich 1985, 89).

Industrial companies increasingly upheld the ethos of free and pure research because they not only profited from their researchers as a scientific workforce generating surplus value in the form of discoveries, new methodologies, and the utilisation of scientific knowledge as a productive force. With the help of successful scientists such as Langmuir, the companies hoped to oppose the negative image of profit-oriented monopolists and to stress their contribution not only to technological, but also to general scientific progress and thereby to cultural and social progress. Langmuir's public lectures and the public presentation of his research were an integral part of what David Miller has called "the political economy of discovery stories" (Miller 2011, 57). This was all the more so after Langmuir received the Nobel Prize for Chemistry in 1932.

Hans Gerdien, the director of the central Research Laboratory at Siemens and one of the German authors who referred to Langmuir's lecture, described Langmuir's approach as "general research work taking place in a technologically inclined environment"; in his experience, it was characteristic for the "industrial *milieu*" that "most research projects that began without any specific application in mind will very soon bring forth useful appliances" (Gerdien 1929, 221). In order to channel "pure" or independent research into new products, research in the "industrial *milieu*" had to be organised and institutionalised in specific ways – including a functional division of labour and the training and specialisation of various types of researchers who, for example, did much of the groundwork and post-treatment for researchers such as Langmuir. If these conditions were fulfilled, there was no danger that industrial researchers would become too alienated from the company's goals even if their research was as close to academic research as was the case with Langmuir. The question was whether an autonomous and self-confident group of technical physicists was still needed.

5. The organisation of research in an industrialised society

For Carl Ramsauer, the director of the Research Institute at the German electro-technical company AEG, a central physical research laboratory that was founded in 1928, professional changes such as the growing professional differentiation or the prospect for young as well as established physicists to pursue a career as industrial physicist were accompanied by disciplinary changes, or at least by a growing awareness that the old disciplinary self-understanding was no longer sufficient.

He could well imagine, Ramsauer wrote in 1929, "pure" research taking place in research projects which not only aimed at "purely scientific" results, but also targeted technological objectives. In his understanding, the shifting meaning of "pure" research would affect the field of physics without harming its general constitution. Rather, it would help to adapt research as a cultural activity to the needs of an industrialised society. The application of an idealised conception of "pure" science in an ethical sense of a "disinterested quest for knowledge" would rarely be heard of anyway "in times in which the sciences have become much sought after professions" (Ramsauer 1929, 223).[43] To accept things technical or functional as legitimate objects of "pure" physics research was integral to his *realpolitik* of physics and his attempt to provide space for manoeuvring to a physics community under changing social, economic, and political conditions.[44] In his under-

---

43 Following in the footsteps of Max Weber's famous lecture on "Science as Vocation", which resonates in Ramsauer's statement as well, and Robert K. Merton's sociological analysis of the influences of political and economic objectives on the development of science, Steven Shapin discusses the rise of industrial physics, the shifting focus of scientific research from "truth" to "profit" and its impact on the professional "ethos" and the general system of values in physics in Shapin 2008.

44 Ramsauer's preference for *realpolitik* was a driving force behind the engagement of the Research Institute during World War II. Already in the mid-1930s, the AEG Research Institute started to be committed to armament research in collaboration with the *Reichswehr*. During the war, the

standing, though, the formation of an autonomous discipline of technical physics was nonsense.

As already mentioned, the popularity of the Society for Technical Physics declined in the late 1920s and technical physics was gradually re-integrated into the disciplinary context of general physics. One sign for the re-integration was the enhanced status of industrial physicists in the DPG and their growing importance as players in the political arena. The industrial physicist Karl Mey was president of the DPG from 1933 to 1935. His successor was Jonathan Zenneck, who headed the Physical Laboratory at the chemical company BASF from 1907 to 1911. From 1941 until 1945, Ramsauer took over the responsibility for the concerns of the German Physical Society. Although he was not a member of the National Socialist party and did not hold a political office, Ramsauer was a political figure in as much as he maintained regular contact with the highest-ranking representatives of the military and the political field, and tried to mediate (as far as this was possible and necessary) between politics and physics (Hoffmann 2012). One result of these negotiations was the almost complete mobilisation of the activities of the community of physicists to armament research and development.

After the end of the war, Ramsauer, who had also served for several years as a member of the directorate of the DGtP and as co-editor of the *Journal for Technical Physics*, tried to draw a line under the sub-disciplinary discourse of "technical physics" – and thus also under that of the "third" physicist. He rejected Georg Gehlhoff's earlier attempt to give physics education at technical colleges a practical and more technology-oriented form, for example, by offering courses on materials or machine science, economics or legal doctrine (Gehlhoff 1921). Like Gerdien and Langmuir, he was convinced that industrial physicists needed a general education, and that they would specialise automatically under the influence of the *milieu* of industrial laboratories or factories. Regarding the three-volume textbook of technical physics published by Gehlhoff in the mid-1920s, he wrote, after the war, that it was "a clear failure, simply because nobody can write a textbook for a discipline that does not exist" (Ramsauer 1949, 30). Based upon his initiative and those of others, the DGtP was not founded again after its dissolution in 1945.[45]

Research Institute became one of the largest industrial facilities for armament research in Germany (Weiss 2002).

45 The DPG was dissolved in 1945 as well. The work was continued in a loose association of regional physical societies until the DPG was founded again in 1963. The preamble to the statute states that the DPG considers itself as the successor organisation of the German Society for Technical Physics as well. Hoffmann assumes that the legislation of the Allied Control Council, which suppressed applied research, prevented the re-establishment of the DGtP (Hoffmann 1994, 19). With its 61,000 members, the DPG is currently the largest national physical society in the world. Today, the biggest member groups are students and early career academics; 11.7% of the members regard themselves as industrial physicists (available at: http://www.dpg-physik.de/dpg/profil/struktur.html, last accessed 28 January 2019).

On several occasions in the 1940s, Ramsauer presented his ideas in a diagram which aimed at a better understanding of the role of physics in an industrialised society (in a state of war):[46]

If physics research and education is to be encouraged to the degree that meets the actual importance of physics as a whole or if German physics is to be assessed accurately as a factor of military strength, we must first of all understand the precise nature of physics.[47]

This demanded a fresh perception on the social and cultural embedding of physics – "physics should not only be considered as an isolated science, but should be seen simultaneously in the light of its general importance that extends well beyond the bounds of an individual scientific field" (Ramsauer 1996, 315).

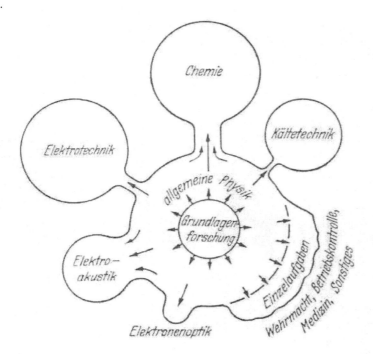

Figure 1: Carl Ramsauer's 'amoeba' model of the "nature" of physics, first published in 1943.

A central objective of presenting the diagram was to convince the political and military leaders that physical research needed a greater governmental support. In addition, Ramsauer offered a model for disciplinary unity, which tried to integrate

---

46 The diagram was first shown during a talk given by Ramsauer at the *Lilienthal Gesellschaft für Luftfahrtforschung* in 1942 but it expanded on ideas that Ramsauer developed in the 1930s. I will refer to the translation of Ramsauer (1943) in Ramsauer (1996).

47 Ramsauer 1996, 315.

the work of technical physics as well. Eventually, the diagram was a propaganda tool that sought to convey a unified image of physics to a wider public as well as to the physicists themselves.

The physicists' remits expressed in the diagram are fourfold. First, they had to conduct *Grundlagenforschung* – foundational or basic research – that encompassed primarily the investigation of "the fundamental laws of all existing things and all events". It was to serve as a foundation for the development of all other domains of science and technology, "since obviously every natural science and every technology is ultimately built upon these fundamental laws" (Ramsauer 1996, 315). This happened in the inner core. Second, the physicists had to adapt new questions, ideas, things, and methodologies coming from the inner core; they had to evaluate and enhance these *stimuli* and integrate them into the broader conceptual and pragmatic context of "general physics" and its separate branches mechanics, acoustics, thermodynamics, optics, electrical science, magnetism, and atomic physics (Ramsauer 1996, 317). The classification, ordering and legitimation of practices and knowledge claims happened in the zone surrounding the core.

Third, physicists had to guide and supervise the technological implementation of physical principles as well as the further development of new technical devices. New domains of science and technology – in Ramsauer's understanding fields of "specialised" physics – such as electrical engineering, electroacoustics, or heat technology would only emerge, mature and eventually separate from the realm of general physics if they sufficiently (and exhaustively) adapted and implemented the impulses coming from physics. "From the nucleus of this amoeba," Ernst Brüche, the head of the laboratory for "General Physics" in the AEG-Research Institute (since 1940, it was called laboratory for "Fundamental Research in Physics"), later wrote, "the domains of applied physics emanate like pseudopodia. In an advanced stage of development, they make themselves independent as autonomous (and self-confident) technological domains" (Brüche 1956, 229).[48] To gain independence, any such field had to develop a methodology of its own that no longer could be subsumed under "general physics", and it had to be taught in an autonomous and specialised system of education (Ramsauer 1996, 318). Even then, these fields had to maintain contact with physics.

As a fourth aspect, Ramsauer mentioned "special fields of application closely associated with physics" with three groups standing out in particular: military physics, the physico-medical field, and manufacturing control in the chemical in-

---

48 Since the early 1930s, Brüche himself was involved in the development of electron optics – a new branch of physics and technology that is shown at the bottom of the diagram in a nascent state – and of electron microscopes. Brüche's biggest rival was the electrical engineer Ernst Ruska. Thus, Brüche was well aware of the growing competition of physicists with engineers even in advanced fields such as electron physics and electron optics (Müller 2009).

dustry (Ramsauer 1996, 317). At the time of the first publication of the diagram, the military aspect reigned supreme.

The organic form of the diagram and Brüche's comparison with an amoeba was not accidental, but resulted from Ramsauer's understanding of physics as an organism in permanent interaction with a supportive, demanding, and partly hostile environment. As we have seen, the organism had an internal structuring that came along with a functional (professional as well as inner disciplinary) differentiation that was particularly visible in the separate domain of *Grundlagenforschung*. The core or nucleus served as the creative centre where the organism generated the knowledge and intellectual energy – be it "difference" (in systems theory), "information" or "negentropy" (in information theory) – for its own reproduction and renewal, and for the creation of impulses whose impact reached beyond the disciplinary borders of physics. The direction of the arrows can be interpreted as a kind of osmotic pressure caused by a flow of knowledge or energy that counterbalanced the pressure exerted by the environment and gave the organisms its specific shape.

The diagram could be read as an expression of strength. It appears as an illustration of a (organic) machine that counteracts the entropic decay and cultural decline (a machine constructed to work against a Spenglerian type of cultural pessimism) by generating an offspring of scientific activity, new fields of technology and thereby new forms of physical order.[49] However, the common use of the term *Grundlagenforschung*, with which Ramsauer tried to capture the operations at the core of this machine, was rather novel; it reached a wider distribution in Germany only in the late 1930s (Schauz 2014, 288). One reason for its emergence was the increasing occupation of physicists in armament research and the need to introduce a term that was able to close the gap between the actual professional practices of the majority of physicists and a disciplinary self-understanding and vocational self-esteem that was still oriented towards the ethos of "pure" science. The use of the term *Grundlagenforschung* allowed them to signal to politicians, the military, and the majority of physicists, that a central task of physics research was to provide a foundation not only to general physics and other fields of science but also to technology. In this way, the introduction and use of the concept of *Grundlagenforschung* helped to re-integrate those physicists who felt excluded in older models of physics.[50]

---

49 These new forms of physical order were partly developed and tested inside of the Research Institute, for example, electron optics as a new branch of physics and technology. In many ways, the structure and dynamics of the Research Institute resembled the understanding of the structure and dynamics of the whole field of physics as depicted by Ramsauer in his diagram – with Ernst Brüche's Laboratory for Fundamental Research in Physics at the core.

50 The diagram could also be interpreted as a mere variety of the "linear model of innovation" which shaped the post-World War II debates on the relation of science and technology. However, Ramsauer was aware that he presented a narrow and politically-motivated view of the

5.1. Discussion

Right after World War I, the technical physicists felt that their contribution to general physics was not sufficiently appreciated and that they did not obtain the support they demanded or wished for from their colleagues at the DPG and sought to strengthen their position institutionally by founding a new physical society. The knowledge of the technical physicists was epistemically and culturally weak, because their claim to contribute original "physical" knowledge was not taken seriously by many of their colleagues. Occasionally, the "pure" physicists even put themselves forward as the defenders of "culture" against the takeover of (technological) "civilisation" – which included not only the work of engineers but of industrial and other applied physicists as well. While they had to defend themselves in inner-disciplinary conflicts against attacks from their academic colleagues, the technical physicists were competing with the engineers on a professional level. Despite their claim to be producers of utilisable knowledge, this knowledge could be seen as weak even from a practical point of view because the technical physicists first had to build up an educational infrastructure and develop a cognitive framework that was able to contribute to promising fields of technology which demanded the expertise of a physicist and were not easily accessible to engineers.

After the foundation of the DGtP, many things changed – some due to the activities of the society, such as the establishment of chairs for (technical) physics at the technical colleges and universities, others due to general social developments, such as the growing demand of physicists in war-related research. If the aim of the technical physicists was to make new forms of collaboration with institutions and organisations outside or at the margins of the physics community possible, to make physics more compatible with the demands and challenges of industrialised societies, to mobilise new resources in economically difficult times, and gain additional freedoms of action for the community of physicists, the loosening of disciplinary integrity and the temporary rise of the "third" physicists must be seen as a success-story. But there were disadvantages as well.

For Ernst Brüche, the dangers of the concept of *Grundlagenforschung* outweighed the benefits. For him, the creative engine of progress in physics remained

---

relation of physics and technology. After the war, he referred positively to a definition given by the German philosopher Bernhard Bavink, which suggests that Ramsauer did not reduce technology to the role of a mere recipient or user of scientific knowledge: "Technology is not, as is currently still generally believed, only 'applied science' (physics or chemistry); it is a cultural domain sui generis, which exists on an equal footing with art, science, and the ethical and moral realm as the forth realm of values" (cited in Ramsauer 1949, 19). For him, the central question was in which system of values one wanted to participate, and how the physicists manage to position themselves and enforce their claims in the interstice with other sciences and with technology.

"free" or "undirected" research – to use Irving Langmuir's metaphor: driven by curiosity – and not *Grundlagenforschung*, which was somehow a bluff package.[51] In his understanding, the introduction of this concept was a compromise and an attempt to satisfy the growing demand for applied science and the gradual adoption of technology as the main and foremost aim of physical research – no longer "nature" and its general laws, no longer the promotion and enhancement of physical methodology, no longer knowledge of a higher order. *Grundlagenforschung* was – similar to applied research – already goal-oriented and not free to adapt its investigative pathway to new findings or even adopt new goals if they seemed more interesting. For Brüche, "free" research as an activity was "physical art" practised by individuals. In contrast, *Grundlagenforschung* was "physical craft" conducted by groups of people. Its effectiveness was based upon the division of labour.

> Those who work on the solution of goal-oriented tasks, often operating in a larger community, will work to a great extent according to the clear rules of the 'physical craft', which one can learn, and they strive to solve usually clearly-defined tasks. (Brüche 1944)

Grundlagenforschung was already an expression of a utilitarian or industrial research regime. In Brüche's understanding, it still preferred short-termed research goals over research with a long-time perspective. In times of war, most physical researchers were engaged in war-related and technological research; eventually, the majority of physicists had become "technical" physicists contributing, in one way or another, to the war machine.

The attempt by some physicists to incorporate technology into their discipline and to benefit from the allocation of resources associated with the development of technology can be regarded as a dubious success in the light of the contributions of physicists to the development of new war technology (including nuclear bombs) in World War II. The community of physicists has bought itself many advantages from this commitment, especially the greatly improved professional perspectives and the resources available to researchers. However, there were also disadvantages, such as the immensely increased dependence on governmental or industrial resources, and the associated loss of autonomy. An entry in his diary from early 1945 summarising a late night talk of Ernst Brüche with his colleague Hans Mahl makes this position quite clear:

> We soon agreed: Change the profession. Become a farmer. Write books (but not about physics). The best would be not to hear anything about physics anymore – because physics is no longer a science. It is a whore of technology, belongs to foreign power groups. The calm and peacefulness of science in earlier decades – gone! Thus, become a biologist or botanist or join an expedition! Only leave physics, which is no more but a mere battle of

---

51 Brüche refers to a preceding article by Jonathan Zenneck, the wireless pioneer and, at that time, director of the *Deutsches Museum* in Munich, in which Zenneck proposed *Grundlagenforschung* to be a suitable term primarily for research aiming at technological objectives.

interests on the ground of physics. Withdraw from a science that is valued today only because its children make useful slaves.[52]

References

Anonymus (1920): "Bericht über die Jahresversammlung." *Zeitschrift für technische Physik*, 1: 232–236.

Anonymus (1932): "Bedarf und Nachwuchs an Physikern." In: *Volkswirtschaftliche Zentralstelle für Hochschulstudium und akademisches Berufswesen* (Ed.): Untersuchung zur Lage der Akademischen Berufe, 5, 68–84. Berlin: Struppe und Winckler.

Ash, Mitchel (2002): "Wissenschaft und Politik als Ressourcen für einander." In: Rüdiger vom Bruch and Brigitte Kaderas (Eds.): *Wissenschaften und Wissenschaftspolitik. Bestandsaufnahme zu Formationen, Brüchen und Kontinuitäten im Deutschland des 20. Jahrhunderts*, 32–51. Stuttgart: Franz Steiner Verlag.

Bachelard, Gaston (1986): *The New Scientific Spirit*. Boston MA: The Beacon Press.

Brüche, Ernst (1944): "Anmerkungen des Herausgebers für den Nichtphysiker." *Physikalische Blätter*, 1: 12.

Brüche, Ernst (1956): "Gedanken über Physik und Technik, Ingenieure und Physiker." *Physikalische Blätter*, 12: 229–232.

Eckert, Michael (2012): "The German Physical Society and Aryan Physics." In: Dieter Hoffmann and Mark Walker (Eds.): *The German Physical Society in the Third Reich: Physicists between Autonomy and Accommodation*, 96–125. Cambridge: Cambridge University Press.

Epple, Moritz (2002): "Präzision versus Exaktheit: Konfligierende Ideale der angewandten mathematischen Forschung. Das Beispiel der Tragflügeltheorie." *Berichte zur Wissenschaftsgeschichte*, 25: 171–193.

Erker, Paul (1995): *The Choice between Competition and Cooperation: Research and Development in the Electrical Industry in Germany and the Netherlands, 1920–1936*. In: François Caron, Paul Erker and Wolfram Fischer (Eds.): *Innovations in the European Economy between the Wars*, 231–253. Berlin-New York: Walter de Gruyter.

Forman, Paul (1974): "The Financial Support and Political Alignment of Physicists in Weimar Germany." *Minerva*, 12: 39–66.

Forman, Paul (2007): "*The Primacy of Science in Modernity, of Technology in Postmodernity, and of Ideology in the History of Technology*." *History and Technology*, 23: 1–152.

Fox, Robert, and Anna Guagnini (1999): *Laboratories, Workshops and Sites. Concepts and Practices of Applied Research in Industrial Europe, 1800–1914*. Berkeley CA: Office for the History of Science and Technology, University of California.

Galison, Peter (1997): *Image and Logic: A Material Culture of Microphysics*. Chicago IL: University of Chicago Press.

Gehlhoff, Georg (1920): "Zur Gründung der Deutschen Gesellschaft für technische Physik." *Zeitschrift für technische Physik*, 1: 4–5.

---

52 Ernst Brüche, entry in his diary, 12 February 1945 (Technoseum-Mannheim, Nachlass Ernst Brüche II/66).

Gehlhoff, Georg (1921): "Die Ausbildung der technischen Physiker." *Zeitschrift für technische Physik*, 2: 121–127.

Gehlhoff, Georg (1924): "Fünf Jahre Deutsche Gesellschaft für technische Physik." *Zeitschrift für technische Physik*, 5: 201–204.

Gehlhoff, Georg (1929): "Zehn Jahre Gesellschaft für technische Physik." *Zeitschrift für technische Physik*, 10: 193–198.

Gehlhoff, Georg, Hans Rukop and Wilhelm Hort (1920): "Zur Einführung." *Zeitschrift für technische Physik*, 1: 1–4.

Gerdien, Hans (1929): "Ziele und Aufgaben technisch-physikalischer Forschungsinstitute in der Industrie." *Zeitschrift für technische Physik* 6: 218–222.

Gispen, Kees (2002): *New Profession, Old Order: Engineers and German Society, 1815–1914*. Cambridge: Cambridge University Press.

Hacking, Ian (1983): *Representing and Intervening. Introductory Topics in the Philosophy of Natural Science*. Cambridge: Cambridge University Press.

Hård, Mikael, and Andrew Jamison (Eds.) (1998): *The Intellectual Appropriation of Technology. Discourses on Modernity, 1900–1939*. Cambridge MA: The MIT Press.

Hashagen, Ulf (2003): *Walther von Dyck (1856–1934): Mathematik, Technik und Wissenschaftsorganisation an der TH München*. Stuttgart: Steiner.

Herf, Jeffrey (1984): *Reactionary Modernism. Technology, Culture, and Politics in Weimar and the Third Reich*. Cambridge: Cambridge University Press.

Hoffmann, Dieter (1994): "Zur Etablierung der 'technischen Physik' in Deutschland." In: Dieter Hoffmann and Edgar Swinne (Eds.): *Über die Geschichte der "technischen Physik" in Deutschland und den Begründer ihrer wissenschaftlichen Gesellschaft Georg Gehlhoff*, 7–22. Berlin: ERS-Verlag.

Hoffmann, Dieter (2012): "The Ramsauer Era and Self-mobilization of the German Physical Society." In: Dieter Hoffmann and Mark Walker (Eds.): *The German Physical Society in the Third Reich: Physicists between Autonomy and Accommodation*, 126–168. Cambridge: Cambridge University Press.

Homburg, Ernst (1992): "The Emergence of Research Laboratories in the Dyestuffs Industry, 1870–1900." *British Journal for the History of Science*, 25: 91–111.

Hong, Sungook (1999): "Historiographical Layers in the Relationship between Science and Technology." *History of Technology*, 15: 289–311.

Hort, Wilhelm (1921): "Die Technische Physik als Grundlage für Studium und Wissenschaft der Ingenieure." *Zeitschrift für technische Physik*, 5: 132–140.

Hort, Wilhelm (1924): "Besprechung (Review of Alois Riedler (1919): *Wirklichkeitsblinde*; idem (1921): *Akademische Pneuma und die Drehkranken*; idem and St. Löffler (1921): *Reibungstriebwerke und ihre Missdeutung durch Theoretiker*)." *Zeitschrift für technische Physik*, 5: 316–17.

Joerges, Bernward, and Terry Shinn (Eds.) (2001): *Instrumentation between Science, State and Industry*. Dordrecht et al.: Kluwer.

Jungnickel, Christa, and Russell McCormmach (2017): *The Second Physicist. On the History of Theoretical Physics in Germany*. Cham: Springer.

König, Wolfgang (1996): "Science-Based Industry or Industry-Based Science? Electrical Engineering in Germany before World War I." *Technology and Culture*, 37: 70–101.

König, Wolfgang (2017): "Engineering Professors as Entrepreneurs: The Case of Franz Reuleaux (1829–1905) and Alois Riedler (1850–1936)." *History and Technology*, 33: 53–69.

Langmuir, Irving (1928): "Atomic Hydrogen as an Aid to Industrial Research." *Science*, 67: 201–208.

Latour, Bruno (1993): *We have Never been Modern*. Cambridge MA: Harvard University Press.

Manegold, Karl-Heinz (1970): *Universität, Technische Hochschule und Industrie. Ein Beitrag zur Emanzipation der Technik im 19. Jahrhundert unter besonderer Berücksichtigung der Bestrebungen Felix Kleins*. Berlin: Duncker und Humblot.

Mehrtens, Herbert (1990): *Moderne – Sprache – Mathematik. Eine Geschichte des Streits um die Grundlagen der Disziplin und des Subjekts formaler Systeme*. Frankfurt a. M.: Suhrkamp.

Miller, David Philip (2011): "The Political Economy of Discovery Stories: The Case of Dr Irving Langmuir and General Electric." *Annals of Science*, 68: 27–60.

Mises, Richard von (1921): "Zur Einführung: Über die Aufgaben und Zielen der angewandten Mathematik." *Zeitschrift für Angewandte Mathematik und Mechanik*, 1: 1–15.

Müller, Falk (2004): *Gasentladungsforschung im 19. Jahrhundert*. Berlin-Diepholz: GNT-Verlag.

Müller, Falk (2009): "The Birth of a Modern Instrument and its Development during World War II: Electron Microscopy in Germany from the 1930s to 1945." In: Ad Maas and Hans Hooijmaijers (Eds.): *Scientific Research in World War II. What scientists did in the war*, 121–146. New York-London: Routledge.

Müller, Falk (2011): "Johann Wilhelm Hittorf and the Material Culture of 19th Century Gas Discharge Research." *British Journal for the History of Science*, 44: 211–244.

Popper, Karl (2002) [1935 (German edition); 1959 (English edition)]: *Logic of Scientific Discovery*. London: Routledge.

Ramsauer, Carl (1929): "Sollen die technisch-physikalischen Forschungslaboratorien der Industrie rein wissenschaftliche Forschung betreiben? *Zeitschrift für technische Physik*, 10: 223–226.

Ramsauer, Carl (1943): "Die Schlüsselstellung der Physik für Naturwissenschaft, Technik und Rüstung." *Die Naturwissenschaften*, 31: 285–288.

Ramsauer, Carl (1949): *Physik, Technik, Pädagogik. Erfahrungen und Erinnerungen*. Karlsruhe: Braun.

Ramsauer, Carl (1996): "The Key Position of Physics in Science, Technology and Armament." In: Klaus Hentschel (Ed.): *Physics and National Socialism: An Anthology of Primary Sources*, 315–321. Transl. Ann M. Hentschel. Basel: Birkhäuser.

Reich, Leonard S. (1983): "Irving Langmuir and the Pursuit of Science and Technology in the Corporate Environment." *Technology and Culture*, 24: 199–221.

Reich, Leonard S. (1985*): The Making of American Industrial Research: Science and Business at GE and Bell, 1876–1926*. Cambridge: Cambridge University Press.

Reichenbach, Hans (1978): "The Aims and Methods of Physical Knowledge (1929)." In: M. Reichenbach et al. (Eds.): *Hans Reichenbach Selected Writings 1909–1953*, 120–225. Dordrecht: D. Reidel Publishing Company (originally in: Hans Geiger and Karl Scheel (Eds.) (1929): *Handbuch der Physik, Band IV, Allgemeine Grundlagen der Physik*, 1–80. Berlin: Springer).

Reinhardt, Carsten (2006): *Shifting and Re-arranging – Physical Methods and the Transformation of Modern Chemistry*. Sagamore Beach MA: Science History Publications.

Rheinberger, Hans-Jörg (1997): *Toward a History of Epistemic Things. Synthesizing Proteins in the Test Tube*. Stanford CA: Stanford University Press.

Riedler, Alois (1919): *Wirklichkeitsblinde in Wissenschaft und Technik*. Berlin: Springer.

Ringer, Fritz (1969): *The Decline of the German Mandarins: The German Academic Community*, 1890–1933. Cambridge MA: Harvard University Press.

Robinson, Howard A. (1948): "The Challenge of Industrial Physics." *Physics Today*, 1 (2): 4–7.

Schack, Alfred (1926): "Technik und Physik." *Die Naturwissenschaften*, 14: 377–383.

Schubert, Helmut (1987): "Industrielaboratorien für Wissenschaftstransfer. Aufbau und Entwicklung der Siemensforschung bis zum Ende des Zweiten Weltkrieges anhand von Beispielen aus der Halbleiterforschung." *Centaurus*, 39: 245–292.

Schultrich, Helga (1985): "Industriephysiker in der deutschen Elektroindustrie von den Anfängen bis zur Weltwirtschaftskrise." *Zeitschrift für Geschichte der Wissenschaften, Technik und Medizin*, 22: 85–92.

Seth, Suman (2010): *Crafting the Quantum: Arnold Sommerfeld and the Practice of Theory, 1890–1926*. Cambridge MA: The MIT Press.

Shapin, Steven (2008): *The Scientific Life: A Moral History of a Late Modern Vocation*. Chicago IL: University of Chicago Press.

Shapin, Steven, and Simon Schaffer (1985): *Leviathan and the Air-Pump: Hobbes, Boyle, and the Experimental Life*. Princeton NJ: Princeton University Press.

Shinn, Terry (2001): "The Research-Technology Matrix: German Origins, 1860–1900." In: Bernward Joerges and Terry Shinn (Eds.): *Instrumentation between Science, State and Industry*, 29–48. Dordrecht et al.: Kluwer.

Shinn, Terry (2017): "The Silicon Tide: Relations between Things Epistemic and Things of Function in the Semiconductor World." In: Jed Z. Buchwald and Robert Fox (Eds.): *The Oxford Handbook of the History of Physics*, 860–891. Oxford: Oxford University Press.

Staley, Richard (2005): "On the Co-Creation of Classical and Modern Physics." *Isis*, 96: 530–558.

Swinne, Edgar (1994): "Georg Gehlhoff. Gründer der Deutschen Gesellschaft für technische Physik." In: Dieter Hoffmann and Edgar Swinne (Eds.): *Über die Geschichte der "technischen Physik" in Deutschland und den Begründer ihrer wissenschaftlichen Gesellschaft Georg Gehlhoff*, 24–50. Berlin: ERS-Verlag.

Vincenti, Walter G. (1990): *What Engineers Know and How they Know it. Analytical Studies from Aeronautical History*. Baltimore MD-London: The Johns Hopkins University Press.

Voskuhl, Adelheid (2016): "Engineering Philosophy. Theories of Technology, German Idealism, and Social Order in High-Industrial Germany." *Technology and Culture*, 57: 721–752.

Weiss, Burghard (2002): "Rüstungsforschung am Forschungsinstitut der AEG bis 1945." In Helmut Maier (Ed.): *Rüstungsforschung im Nationalsozialismus. Organisation, Mobilisierung und Entgrenzung der Technikwissenschaften*, 109–141. Göttingen: Wallstein.

Wise, George (1983): "Ionists in Industry: Physical Chemistry at General Electric, 1900–1915." *Isis*, 74: 6–21.

Wise, George (1985): *Willis R. Whitney, General Electric, and the Origins of U. S. Industrial Research*. New York: Columbia University Press.

Wolff, Stefan L. (2008): "Die Konstituierung eines Netzwerkes reaktionärer Physiker in der Weimarer Republik." *Berichte zur Wissenschaftsgeschichte*, 31: 372–392.

Weak Knowledge and the Epic Theatre of Science: Papers of the Pre-Conference Workshop

Nitzana Ben David, Corinna Dziudzia, Martin Herrnstadt, Lukas Jäger Natalie Levy, Linda Richter, and Sebastian Riebold

Abstract

The following joint chapter brings together the case studies and reflections of the participants of a Pre-Conference Workshop on the historiography of weak knowledge held in Frankfurt am Main on 1 July 2017. The empirical cases discussed include the marginalisation of female writers in the German enlightenment, the critical sociology of mixed schools in Israel, early modern knowledge of the weather, and hierarchies between lay knowledge and professional knowledge in the Juvenile Court of Palestine. Reflections include another look at the debate on Chinese "science" and a comparison of the historiography of weak knowledge and the "weak science paradigm" in Latour's writings.

Introduction

Martin Herrnstadt and Lukas Jäger

> To estrange means [...] to historicise, to represent processes and persons as historical, that is to say frail. [...] What is won with this? It is won that the spectator no longer sees the people on stage represented as completely unchangeable, uninfluenceable, helplessly delivered to their destiny.
> *Bertolt Brecht, 1933*[1]

Producing works of research in the history of science or producing a theatre play are clearly two very different occupations. Yet both practices share an initial question: What is the story that needs to be told, and how and with which means do we need to tell it in order to achieve the desired effect? In other words, and more related to our sphere of action, what kind of history of science do we want to tell,

---

1 Brecht [1933] 1967, 301–302. Translation by Martin Herrnstadt.

what kind of image of science do we want to draw, and what are the tools and instruments at our disposal? The strangeness effected by the title of the conference "Weak Knowledge", one that inverts the commonplace that usually equates knowledge with power, needs to be understood as a call to reflect upon the question of how the history of science and science studies should be performed today. It invites us to look at science not only with a capital letter, a heroic "Science" that shines its light upon the world, but also on the construction of the stage and its very "apparatus of illumination" (Brecht 1967, 454). In its estranged form as weak knowledge, science makes an appearance on the stage of the epic theatre. In this light, the point of convergence of epic theatre and the historiography of weak forms of knowledge can be seen precisely in the way that their objects are staged or situated. In the case of Bertolt Brecht, "Art" is staged and stripped of its sublime status in order to make its illusions accessible; in the case of a history of weak forms of knowledge, "Science" is placed in a specific situation in order to show how the claim to scientificity is actively produced. It is thus revealed to be a struggle for intellectual, social and material resources, not as a set of fixed abstract rules.

In both cases, this critique of the production, circulation and consumption of scientific knowledge does not reject the concept of science (or of art, as in the case of Brecht); it is no attempt to revive Schmittian truth politics that seeks to undermine any possible distinction between science and politics.[2] Contrary to some contemporary models and methodologies of Science and Technology Studies, a history of weak forms of knowledge holds on to the concepts of "knowledge" and "science" as legitimate units of investigation and as a horizon of the work of researchers in the humanities and the social sciences. Yet the adherence to these concepts is a strange one. If taken seriously, it comes with a commitment to change the way in which work in the humanities is done, to climb outside the ivory tower and to make one's own production(s) relatable to colleagues from other disciplines and fields as well as accessible and relatable to the eyes of a wider audience. To borrow another phrase from Brecht, its purpose is to "show the world [of science] in a way that makes it manageable" (Brecht 1967, 260), and that allows the researcher as well as the audience to change from passive spectator to active observer. The history of weak forms of knowledge thus demands not only the production of an "epic" perspective on diverse historical materials and sciences following the thesis that the way things have happened never precludes the possibility that they could have happened any other way (Elkana 1981, 67). It is, moreover, to reflect upon and change the way in which we do or

---

2 One of the more fashionable examples for the use of Carl Schmitt's political philosophy as a reference-point to understand the politics of scientific knowledge is the work of Bruno Latour. See Harman 2014, 133.

perform science, who we talk to, what kind of languages, formats and technologies we use, etc., – in short, to switch our work into an "epic" mode.

To start the initial dialogue on the presumed potentials of a concept of weak knowledge and/or a history of weak forms of knowledge, a pre-conference workshop was planned and organised. The event was put together by graduate and post-graduate students of the Collaborative Research Centre *Discourses of Weakness and Resource Regimes*, and the Study Group *Historical Epistemology* at the Goethe University, Frankfurt am Main, in cooperation with the Cohn Institute for the *History and Philosophy of Science and Ideas* at Tel Aviv University, Israel. The workshop thus organised was held on the 1 July 2017 in Frankfurt am Main ahead of the international conference entitled "Weak Knowledge: Forms, Functions, Dynamics". The workshop allowed us to assess the heuristic potentials and limits of this approach in preparation of the conference. Our approach was twofold. First, we presented our specific methodological framework developed in the Frankfurt Working Group on the History of Science and discussed it with young researchers from different fields of the humanities and the social sciences. In addition, we encouraged our guests to introduce the concept of weak knowledge into their respective fields of research and apply it to their materials, in order to evaluate its methodological potential. As we did not determine definitive outlines of the concept of weak knowledge in advance, we left space for the participants to come up with their own interpretation and understanding of the research terminology.

The ensuing text is the initial outcome of our meeting and discussions. The short reflections, mostly case studies, reflect the different research interests of the participants and their interest in a variety of topics, all of which use the workshop theme as their point of departure. The contributions presented here address a great variety of issues. They reflect both the heterogeneity of the disciplinary backgrounds and the heuristic potential of a historiography of weak knowledge. Each contribution explores, in its own way, both the potential and the challenge to investigate a history of weak forms of knowledge. The order of the essays in this chapter reflects both the epistemological as well as the institutional dimension of a history of weak forms of knowledge. Whereas the first section, *Strengthening and Weakening Knowledge* turns to the question of the socio-historical foundations of weak and strong forms of knowledge, the second section, *Hierarchies of Knowledge*, deals with problems of institutional, technological and cultural strength and weaknesses of knowledge.

1. Strengthening and weakening knowledge

Mechanisms of canonisation – or: Why female writers of the Enlightenment are not part of the German literary canon today

Corinna Dziudzia

After a long-lasting focus on memory and remembrance in cultural studies, a recent shift to the aspect of what is forgotten can be recognised (especially with regard to the works of Aleida Assmann). The literary canon as the practice of what is read in schools or universities and considered worth passing down to the next generation can be seen as an embodiment of what is remembered and "dominant" or "strong" knowledge. Likewise, non-canonical authors can be seen as an embodiment of "weak" knowledge. In its absolute extreme, non-canonical authors have to be regarded as forgotten. But why are certain authors part of the "dominant" cultural memory while others are not? What are the mechanisms behind these processes?

Overall, especially the canon of German literature seems strikingly homogeneous (Braam and Hagstedt 2017, 83) and is criticised as being too male.[3] Taking a look at the current reading lists of the German Departments at Universities,[4] as well as the introductions to literature for both students and pupils, confirms this.[5] Rarely do they list any female writer before 1800. If they do, Catharina Regina von Greiffenberg is mentioned, a writer of pious poems in the seventeenth century. Seldom, and mostly because of the current efforts of Women's Studies, are Luise Gottsched or Anna Luise Karsch listed, two re-discovered female writers of the eighteenth century. However, not every reading list or introduction currently names female writers at all, let alone before 1800. Often, this is attributed to a missing constant or continuous female writing tradition, especially before 1800: if, apparently, there had been no female writers, no texts would exist that could be remembered (Sylvester-Habenicht 2009). Moreover, it is assumed that the male scholarly dominance prevented the canonisation of female authors (Sylvester-Habenicht 2009).

Actually, there is more to this observation than meets the eye: what the canon does not include points to almost systematic voids. Not only are female writers a small minority in general, but, moreover, they are also restricted to specific literary forms in the representation of the canon, i.e., small forms such as poetry. In addition, there is a peculiar time gap in the representation: what is not included in

---

3 See, for example, Winko 1996.

4 This is based upon a sample of 24 online available reading lists of German Literary Departments of Universities.

5 This finding is based upon Willems 2015; Brenner 2011; Boyle 2009; Bremer 2008; Fischetti 2009; Kaiser 2007; Schlosser 2006; Wellbery 2004.

the literary canon are female authors of the early Enlightenment period, as their names cannot be found on the reading lists or in the introductions to literature,[6] such as, for example, Christiana Mariana von Ziegler. Indeed, the majority of the names of female writers before 1800 seem to be forgotten as a standard work of the nineteenth century discloses: Karl Goedeke's multi-volume *Grundriss* (first edition in 1859), basically lists German authors, male and female, with short biographical information and the titles of their work. For roughly 150 years (from the beginning of the Thirty Years' War to the end of the Seven Years' War) and only in a sub-genre, the *Holy Lyric*, Goedeke lists an impressive number of 75 female poets in the second edition of the *Grundriss* (Goedeke 1887, 317–331). Only one of them is part of the literary canon today: Greiffenberg.

Remarkably, today a writer of pious Baroque sonnets *is* remembered, but female writers of the subsequent epoch of the Enlightenment are not. What could be the reasons why a writer such as Ziegler is not remembered in the canon even though she was honoured by contemporaries with a doctorate by the University of Wittenberg for her writing, was a member of the German Society in Lipsia, winner of the society's prize, and an acquaintance of Johann Sebastian Bach, who used her texts for his cantatas?[7] Only recently, and mostly because of the extended musicological research on Bach, is Ziegler, as well as her work, slowly being re-discovered.[8] But why was she forgotten in the first place? Goedeke (1887, 330) still knew about her, 120 years after she was proclaimed a *poeta laureata* in 1733. But at the end of the nineteenth century, a process of forgetting, i.e., a weakening of former dominant knowledge, seemed to have set in. Several aspects have to be considered regarding this shift during which fewer female writers were remembered, and most were, slowly but surely, forgotten. In the scope of a general scientification and a standardisation of terms regarding epochs and genres, art history terms were transposed into literary history. In addition, Wilhelm Scherer popularised the notion that there were special heydays in the German literature, with phases of decay between them. Subsequently, the research focus had been more on the epochs of the heydays, their characteristics and especially the works of authors who were considered to be representative for that epoch.[9] Their work served as a benchmark for a literary history that was increasingly structured in these epochs and alongside the respective masterpieces. This implied a selection and a focus on single examples. In addition, in the nineteenth

---

6 Conspicuous by their absence are also Jewish female authors before 1900, female authors of plays, especially tragedies, writers of pacifist texts, writers with politically non-conservative convictions, etc.

7 See Dziudzia 2017.

8 See Peters 2008.

9 In the Ngram Viewer based upon Google Books, it becomes apparent that certain terms are not used before 1880, for example, "Barock", "Klassik" and "Vormärz", which are terms for literary epochs.

century, this was coined by the conviction of male geniuses. Furthermore, in this period of fervent nationalism, epochs that seemed to represent a more unique period of German literature gained more attention. The Baroque period, with its German societies and the emphasis on using the German language, was favoured over the subsequent epoch, the Enlightenment, which was seen as being dominated by French language and culture. During the nineteenth century, there was an increasingly stronger focus on the particular "Germanness", the assumption of a specific national essence that should be found especially in literature.[10] Around 1900, a very specific, normative image of how German literature should be, became dominant and finally all-encompassing. While, in the middle of the nineteenth century, both Jewish and female writers contributed to the literary field, different political convictions as well as different methodological approaches could be seen in the writing, alternative, diverse voices seemed to become quieter as the notion of the nation became the dominant narrative, especially after 1871, and were silenced after 1933. This entanglement of different aspects yielded consequences that can be conceptualised as a homogenisation of the literary field which eventually led to today's homogenous canon.

The answer to the question of why only Greiffenberg, out of Goedeke's list, was not forgotten is probably that she was the most compatible female author with the normative conviction of German literature which explicitly formed around 1900, or rather, could be made compatible, whereas many others could not. But, whereas forgetting might be a passive process, remembrance is not: over the span of roughly a hundred years, beginning at the end of the nineteenth century, Greiffenberg was promoted from a local writer to an increasingly more important poet, first for the Baroque era, later for the whole German-speaking area, and finally for the whole seventeenth century.[11] Even the spelling of her surname follows suit, changing from the French *Catherina* to the German *Katherina*. Part of the reason why Greiffenberg became a canonical author might be that she was a Baroque writer and did not, like Ziegler, translate from French literature. Another reason might be that her pious poems fitted far better to the propagandised subordinated female role than a self-conscious writer of satirical songs about men that can be found among Ziegler's texts.[12] Overall, the canonisation of some authors, accompanied by a concomitant strengthening of the knowledge about

---

10 Whittle 2013, 38–40. This notion of an increasing, male-dominated nationalism also sees a rise in anti-Semitism. Whittle points to this analogy of an exclusion of both female and Jewish writing, especially after 1871.

11 Paradoxically, as she is seen as more typical and significant for her time, the actual information about her and her works is getting shorter; today, one almost never finds an example of one of the poems for which she is so much praised, which is weakening her status as a canonical author among her male counterparts.

12 Ultimately, it had been Professors of German literature who still in the 1920s refused to admit women to their courses: Hermand 1994, 83.

them, seems to have led to a marginalisation of texts and authors who did not fulfil these specific norms, not only with respect to female writing but, furthermore, also regarding Jewish authors.

The struggle for weakness: Perspectives and problems in critical sociology – The case of mixed schools in Israel

Natalie Levy

This essay aims to offer an empirical analysis of student social-identification in Jewish-Arab mixed schools in Israel. My research focuses on the discourse and institutionalisation of critical sociology and its objective to empower weak social actors in the Israeli school system. Building upon sociological fieldwork, I criticise what I perceive to be the epistemological shortcomings of critical sociology and the ways in which it affects the research and activist field in Israel.

In Israel, the Arab minority and Jewish majority are sharply segregated. This is especially true in graded schooling, since primary school enrolment is based upon residential area and more than 90 per cent of the Arabs and Jews in Israel live in separate communities (Smooha 2013). This has led to two distinct systems: Arab and Jewish, compounded by two different languages.[13] Having said that, in the last two decades, a small, but rising, number of Arabs who live in mixed Jewish-Arab cities and neighbourhoods have entered predominantly Jewish schools. This trend is attributed to the flourishing Arab middle-class, whose members seek quality education for their children, and acknowledge the importance of acquiring high-level Hebrew to improve educational and occupational attainment in Israel. We term these schools as "circumstantially mixed".

The Hebrew-language mixed schools promote a homogeneous Hebrew-Jewish-Zionist culture and expect their Arab (as well as their immigrant Jewish) students to adapt. Arab students are expected to be proficient and interact in Hebrew, to join in the celebration of Jewish and national holidays, and to internalise the Jewish-Zionist narrative. These schools teach neither Arab culture, nor Muslim/Christian curricula. This is generally consistent with the aspirations of Arab parents that, by attending Hebrew schools, their children will gain fluency and familiarity with Hebrew and Jewish culture (Levy and Shavit 2015).

In addition to the circumstantially mixed Hebrew schools, since 1997 several NGOs committed to promoting Arab-Jewish co-existence have founded a few (currently eight) bi-lingual schools, motivated by a declared multi-cultural educational policy.[14] These schools aspire to a numerical balance between Jews and Arabs at all levels – students, staff, and management. Both the *curricula* and the

---

13 Al-Haj 1996; Gavison 1999.
14 Bekerman and Horenczyk 2004; Bekerman and Maoz 2005.

school calendar are adapted to both national groups and to the three main religions to which the students belong. Zvi Bekerman suggests that the emphasis of bi-lingual schools on "weak" and "strong" identities highlights the centrality of national identification and might encourage distinctions between Jews and Arabs in comparison to other schools – to wit, Hebrew mixed or segregated (Bekerman 2009). My research leans on Bekerman's claim, and aims to examine it empirically in comparable, different school contexts.

One of the main focuses of critical sociology is the research of inequality between groups, in terms of distribution and recognition. In the Israeli context, the strengthening of a weak Arab-Palestinian identity is one of its key topics, as well as an arena of intervention into the social conflicts of Israeli society. Research on Arab-Palestinian identity in Israel focuses for the most part on the collective identity of Palestinians,[15] almost leaving no conceptual or intellectual space for other sets of explanation(s) or meanings, and relying upon a multicultural conception of identity politics (Rabinowitz 1993) that offers Palestinians their oppressed national identity as the only source of self.

According to Luc Boltanski, such a sociological vision, which assumes the struggle for identity exclusively through existing power relations, does not grant enough space to understand the full experience of people *beyond* the constraints of structural inequality (Boltanski 2011). Following this line of critique, I claim that concentrating on collective identity and on the liberation of a "weak" Palestinian identity in Israeli society as one of the main projects of critical sociology leads us to grasp "the Palestinian" as an essentialised identity, thus neglecting other experiences and interpretations of reality. The research which I am about to present adopts a relational approach which perceives identity not as a fixed attribute, but as negotiable, dynamic and dialectic.[16]

The survey that I conducted is composed of three parts, combining questions on culture and social identification. In the following, I describe the social identification section, in which I attempt neither to force national affiliations, nor to ignore their importance. The research is aimed at challenging critical sociology's assumptions in several ways. First, by comparing the effects of schools on the students' perception of self, I postpone the use of reified social "weak" and "strong" identification, and treat it as an acquired feature, related to the ideology of the school in question. Methodologically speaking, allowing subjects in the field, in surveys, to decide how to describe their own "self" without reinforcing the importance of collective categories, can allow new phenomena to be discovered.

The results reveal that, in general, the majority of students, when asked to describe themselves freely, do not use collective affiliations at all. 7.4 per cent of

---

15 Bishara 1993; Rouhana and Ghanem 1998; Rekhess 2007; Ghanem 2000.
16 Monterescu 2001; Bernstein 1995; Dar 2008.

the Jews mention their national or religious affiliation, compared to 28 per cent of the Arabs. Most of the Jews who mentioned it are studying in Hebrew mixed schools, while the majority of the Arabs are from segregated schools. The Jewish students generally neglect collective attributes, which can be explained by their dominant position in Israel, and therefore the transparency of that domination. Arab students, on the other hand, emphasise it mainly when they study in segregated schools, where social encounter does not exist. Generally, students preferred to describe themselves in terms of personal attributes, tastes or social ties. However unexpectedly, the results enabled the recognition of different cultural ideal types which require further analysis. Postponing critical logic as the base line of the study can therefore reveal new cultural meanings in the lives of children, challenging the automatic distinctions based upon national logic.

To conclude, the study and the partial results presented above offer an integration between the relational sociological approach and the survey methodology, in order to avoid the conceptual pitfalls of critical sociology, when dealing with "weak" and "strong" social actors. The study attempts not to reify the collective identification of group members, or presume the importance of their social position in advance, but allow other aspects to be examined in order to discover new and maybe surprising phenomena. Applying this epistemic approach in the case of mixed and segregated schools in Israel sheds light on the outcomes of different ideological encounters or the lack of them.

The weak-science paradigm and its challenges for a relational history of weak forms of knowledge

Martin Herrnstadt

In this short reflection, I want to raise the following rather heretical questions that came up during the workshop discussions: Has the programme of weakening "strong science" and the concept of "weak knowledge" not already been part of a well-established and influential paradigm in Science and Technology Studies, Sociology of Scientific Knowledge, and among the proponents of the more general cultural turn in the study of science since the 1980s (Zittel 2014)? In which way has this mode of doing or performing the history of science reformulated the very concept of knowledge? And how does the programme of "a history of weak forms of knowledge" formulated in the framework of the conference relate or respond to the challenges posed by this paradigm? To do this, I will give a short account of what I call the weak-science paradigm, as it is most famously outlined in the work of Bruno Latour. In a second step, I will highlight some essential limitations and shortcomings of this paradigm, and I will close with the challenge that Latour's system poses for the formulation of a "history of weak forms of knowledge", as outlined in the frame of the conference.

In order to present Latour's programme of "weak knowledge", it is useful to start from his basic anti-epistemologic intuitions, which were formulated in his early philosophical work *Irréductions*. Written in the form of aphorisms and ironically mimicking the style of Wittgenstein's *Tractatus*, Latour presents the outlines of his system:

1.1.1 Nothing is, by itself, either reducible or irreducible to anything else.
1.1.2 There are only trials of strength, of weakness [...].[17]

As Latour states, his attack is directed against the basic presupposition on which "all theories of knowledge" are built, namely, that "force (or weakness) is different in kind to reason", and that "right can never be reduced to might" (Latour [1984] 1993, 153). In Latour's system, "thought" is not a valid category for historical descriptions. "We neither think nor reason," he states, "we work on fragile materials – texts, inscriptions, traces, or paints – with other people." (Latour [1984] 1993, 186) In order to leave the narrow perspective offered by epistemology, the historian of science needs to replace the category of "thought" with "work". Consequentially, the focus from scientific objects, and their strong and exclusive claim to reality needs to be shifted to the "so-called weak objects".[18] To put it more simply, Latour is not interested in the question of *how we know things*, but in a description at the level of existence itself. What *is* are merely more or less weak and strong associations, i.e., networks, between objects done and undone by "trials of forces, of weaknesses" that are not decided by corresponding more or less to reality, but by the sheer solidity (financial, institutional, technical, etc.) of the reality which they are able to produce and maintain. Knowledge then needs to be understood as a specific *mode of existence* (Latour 2004) among others, not as representation. To put it into Latour's bellicose language, "science is not politics. It's politics by other means" (Latour [1984] 1993, 229). Accordingly, what we call *Truth*, then, is nothing but the outcome of a struggle to mobilise and maintain a system of references, the flow of materials, actors, gods, etc. Latour's project to re-tell the story of science starts with the assumption of the *weakness* of knowledge.[19] It is the basic assumption of an ontology of things and the fundamental operation of a strong programme to empower and liberate the agency of objects from the "prison of the subject/object division" (Latour 2014, xxvi). In Latour's account, *weakening* a strong concept of science does not only allow us to give a realistic account of how science is actually done, but, moreover, also con-

---

17 Latour [1984] 1993, 158.
18 Latour [1984] 1993, 170; Latour 2004, 243.
19 "If the word 'force' appears too mechanical or too bellicose, then we can talk of weakness. We all play with different fields of force and weakness, we do not know the state of force, and this ignorance maybe the only thing we have in common." (Latour [1984] 1993, 155)

nects to a specific *ethos* and the attempt to open a horizon of empowerment for *weak actors*. "If the weak had in front of them only the array of weaknesses that I have described, they would dirty their hands and transform it as they pleased." (Latour [1984] 1993, 234–235)

One of the main groups of weak actors that Latour seeks to empower is the scientists themselves. In the case of contested climate science, for example, the only way to challenge the crisis of objectivity of the disciplinary field in the face of systematic production of doubt, is, according to Latour, to create a self-under-standing of the scientists that is not dependent on objective truths, but rather on a description of scientific practices "that will make it possible to regain trust at last in a profoundly redefined scientific institution" (Latour 2014, 11). According to Latour, this emancipation of the *weak actors*, this re-definition of the scientific project depends essentially on a renunciation and radical break with the tradition of *critical theory*, i.e., any attempt to give a social explanation of knowledge or science (Latour 2004 and 2014). *Critique*, as Latour understands it, depends on the pre-supposition of an "objective" reality of the world and the assumption of the mind, the subject of the critic as privileged access to its *truth*. In Latour's eyes, this conception fails to account for reality, as it relies on a twin operation that simultaneously over-emphasises and devalues the power of objects. While the first operation aims to devalue the idea of the agency of objects as a false belief which refers to the cognitive power of projection and ideology, the second operation, in turn, mobilises "matters of fact" in order to demonstrate how ideas and forms of behaviour are determined by "objective reality" (Latour 2014, 237–242). This contradictory critical reductionism of *fetish* and *fact*, so Latour argues, is part and parcel of every attempt to give a social explanation of scientific objects.

In order to give a realistic description of how science is carried out, Latour proposes to stop talking about *facts*, *matters of fact*, or *scientific objects*, and to start understanding all these entities as *matters of concern*. Referring to the Heideggerian etymology of *Thing* as a gathering, the object of science, the *fact*, can no longer be seen as determined by categories of understanding, but as an assembly of a variety of different materials and practices, of "gods, passions, controls, institutions, techniques, diplomacies" (Latour 2004, 236). *Matters of concern* are thus understood as arenas of contestation where the reality of, and knowledge about, a *thing* is produced by means of ongoing negotiations. Consequentially, *critique* and its privileged subject of knowledge need to be replaced by *diplomacy*, which negotiates the matters of concern for a "new *civilisation* to come" (Latour 2014, 481, 485).

But at what price does this turn to the ontology of things and their negotiations come? It performs itself as a reduction of the critical concept and the object of fetishism. For Marx, commodity-fetishism refers to a historically-specific social practice independent of the division of mind and matter. Commodity form is an abstraction that has no roots in human thought, but springs from a social relation, i.e., an exchange relationship. As abstraction, it is embodied in the physical object but is independent of its material qualities. As Marx put it, commodities are "sensuous things which are at the same time supra-sensible or social".[20]

Thus, the critique of fetish does not primarily refer to a misconception, or misrepresentation of the world,[21] but to a historically specific order of things. By ignoring the analysis of the social form as "real abstraction" (Sohn-Rethel 1978, 57) and its relation to the way in which objects are produced, circulated, and consumed as commodities, Latour withdraws from the need to situate his own concept of things and their associations historically. The detrimental effect of this is not just the loss of historical depth, but also the closure of any alternative way of associating and distributing things beyond Latour's own timeless cosmology of actor-networks. Furthermore, under these conditions, the empowering aspect of liberating weak actors, human and non-human, becomes questionable. If there is no way beyond the ontology of networks and their streams of actants, goods and values, the emancipation of weak actors is tantamount to the voluntary adoption and submission to Latourian cosmology. But does this radically anti-utopian cosmology not nullify one of the main sources of strength of weak actors, which is the force or weakness to claim and reclaim the relative autonomy and historical specificity of forms of thought and being?

In his *Theaitetos Problem,* Moritz Epple opposes traditional forms of the history of science guided by strong normative conceptions of knowledge in the tradition of Plato's *Theaitetos,* and his famous distinction between science, *logos,* and mere opinion, *doxa.* In accordance with the larger paradigm of weak science described above, the *history of weak forms of knowledge* opposes any possibility of creating a fixed hierarchy between forms of knowledge, whether they refer to the correspondence with a higher reality of ideas (Platonic tradition), or to "collective recognition" as criteria for truth (social explanation of science). Both variations of normative definitions of scientific knowledge are detrimental to the *practice* in the history of science, as they jeopardise and misrepresent, so Epple argues, the largest parts of its historical archives. Instead of presupposing a strong concept of scientific knowledge, the historian of science should reconstruct the dynamic between "guiding definitions of knowledge" and forms of knowledge which, upon the basis of any of these definitions (e.g., a definition A), were diagnosed as "weak" (A-weak). These (historical) diagnoses of weakness of knowledge (or traces thereof) are the starting-point for historical analysis. They are supposed to serve as vantage points for a history of science that studies complex dynamics of knowledge production situated at the level of the historical actors in their socio-cultural environment.

---

20 Marx 1990, 165; for a discussion of the Chapter "Fetishism and the Commodity Form", see also Harvey 2010, 39.
21 See also White 2013.

Thus, a relational history of weak forms of knowledge connects its critique of a normative concept of scientific knowledge with an analysis of diverse and historically-specific forms of knowledge, and is therefore not bound to the limitations encountered in the Latourian frame. But while it holds on to a concept of knowledge, it avoids thematising the "guiding concept of knowledge" that informs and grounds its own historiographic operation of diagnosing weaknesses.

2. Hierarchies of knowing

How to know about the weather?

Linda Richter

The point of departure for this reflection was a thought, or rather a series of questions, that developed during the concluding discussion of the workshop: Can we think of so-called common knowledge, i.e., knowledge that is believed to be true across societal layers, as *strong* knowledge? If the relational nature of what historical actors term "weak knowledge" rings true, a benchmark of either a knowledge ideal or a strong body of knowledge is needed. But what, then, could this be? Does the dimension of socio-cultural strength specifically imply that a body of knowledge is perceived to be strong once it permeates from learned contexts into the wider public? Is common knowledge necessarily epistemically and practically strong? Are both features, indeed, a prerequisite for knowledge to spread and be used? Or is it possible for epistemically weak knowledge to become widely accepted? These questions grapple with the socio-cultural dimension of weak or strong knowledge in particular, its meaning, its relations to the epistemic and practical dimension, and its possible dynamics.

But some of these questions are, perhaps, not posed correctly. Diffusionist models of popularisation of knowledge with their imagery of knowledge slowly trickling down from the laboratories at the top of the ivory tower have received extensive criticism in the historiography of science.[22] Suggestions to think about the social dynamics of natural knowledge in a more differentiated way include focusing on locations of knowledge production and the forms of its transmission (Fissell and Cooter 2003, 131). Famous examples, which unite the spatial as well as the media aspect, include Simon Schaffer and Steven Shapin's "three technologies" (material, literary, social) employed by Robert Boyle to render his air-pump experiments credible to a wider public (Shapin and Schaffer 1985, 25–26). The concept of weak knowledge, I argue, provides an additional layer to this approach because it helps us to zoom in on the question of how historical actors perceived,

---

22 For example, Brecht and Orland 1999; Fissell and Cooter 2003.

negotiated and evaluated different ways of knowing relative to one another. Such processes were particularly pronounced within a body of knowledge that was of high day-to-day relevance for many people in the eighteenth and nineteenth centuries: knowledge about the weather. At the same time, this case study reveals knowledge about the weather, which, according to contemporary sources, was very widely diffused, although it was thought to be epistemically weak.

During the Enlightenment era, several scholars of diverse backgrounds set out to reform a practice that they perceived to be very widespread in rural communities, but deeply rooted in superstition and an imminent threat to agricultural yields: predicting the weather with farmers' rules. To them, the kind of weather knowledge codified in calendars and almanacs was epistemically weak because it was often based upon astrology or attributed prognostic powers to certain holidays.[23] For this reason, one of the means to achieve this was by reforming these calendars and rationalising the content according to Enlightenment standards (Böning 2002). As has been shown in similar instances, such reform efforts were often neither asked for nor necessarily well-received on the part of farmers (Rásonyi 2000, 116–124). Calendar reforms intended to abolish astrological elections for bloodletting and other purposes were met with harsh protests and boycotts. The Berlin Academy of Sciences, for example, saw no other way than to reinstate astrological weather predictions in 1780 after they had been left out the year before (Böning 2002, 96–98), signalling a remarkable persistence of this variety of common knowledge.

Historians of meteorology have stressed that it was always a "democratic" science, in the sense that the atmosphere was literally out in the open, an object of inquiry accessible to anyone, and of practical and economic relevance for many in agrarian communities.[24] Not all learned actors, however, welcomed this. To some, indeed, it posed a threat: If everyone could have a say, who was to distinguish between true and false? An anonymous author lamented in 1787 that no "right vantage point" from which the weather could be "surveyed" had yet been established, and nobody could clearly distinguish false from correct weather signs (T. 1787, 2). The fact that the weather was of such relevance to daily activities and accessible to everyone created the problem that everyone could claim expertise regardless of their education and scholarly ambitions (T. 1787, 11).

The farmer's rules thus proved to be a remarkably recalcitrant method of forecasting, although its scope was decidedly local. It is hard to say, from the historian's point-of-view, why or how successfully they were actually used. While most of the reform-minded authors acknowledged a true core in some of them, it was a core that, as far as they were concerned, was to be unearthed empirically through repeated observations. Until then, the farmer's rules would remain epis-

---

23 For example, T. 1787, 49–52; Adelbulner 1768, 8–20.
24 Coen 2010, 125; Golinski 2007, 53–54; Janković 2002, 142.

temically weak.[25] The learned authors who commented on these matters oscillated between admiring the perseverance of superstition and the firm conviction that they knew better. Horace Bénédict de Saussure (1740–1799), for example, conceded in 1784 that it was "very humiliating" that a "seaman or farmer who has neither instruments nor theory can predict changes in the weather many days ahead with admirable success, that the naturalist with all his scholarship and art would not have surmised" (Saussure 1784, 403). The problem with the seaman's and farmer's knowledge was, Saussure was certain, that it was restricted to a certain location. As opposed to the potentially universal knowledge of a naturalist like himself, a farmer would be completely helpless if he were to be moved only a few miles from his home (Saussure 1784, 404).

One could assume that this kind of weather lore had the advantage of old age – that most farmers had a conservative tendency, especially when their livelihood depended on the outcome of a forecast (Brakensiek 2016, 101–102). However, the widespread use of barometers as weather glasses shows how an invention that was relatively recent in the eighteenth century[26] could become common in many households even though nobody was quite sure how the changes in the quicksilver column were related to impending weather changes or why. The traditional body of weather lore was thus able to integrate new technical objects such as the barometer. As Jan Golinski has shown for Great Britain, the material consumer culture of the Enlightenment era entailed sales of these instruments to a surprisingly diverse group of customers (Golinski 2007, 108–136). The barometers' key selling factor was its supposed ability to predict weather changes. Thus, they often came (and occasionally do today) with engraved indicators ranging from "dry" to "stormy" to underline this claim (Golinski 2007, 130). In his overview of several weather instruments, Michael Adelbulner (1702–1779), professor of mathematics at the University of Altdorf, sensibly cautioned his readers in 1768 that barometers merely indicated changes in the "weight of the air" (Adelbulner 1768, 45). How those, in turn, were related to changes in the weather remained to be determined. Therefore, wrote Adelbulner, it was one thing to consult the barometer with such questions, but an entirely different matter to understand its answers correctly (Adelbulner 1768, 45–46). He was not opposed to installing indicators on the instrument, but proposed that each observer create a made-to-measure paper scale to plaster on to the instrument to account for differences in the height and climate of the respective locale (Adelbulner 1768, 55–58).

The "blackboxing" of barometers as commodities of weather prediction thus had its limits and required substantial interaction with the instrument, as well as maintenance. In addition, the way an instrument was used depended on the educational background of its owner. Those who lacked the mechanical skill, warned

---

25 For example, Adelbulner 1768, 16.
26 For a detailed account, see Middleton 1964.

Adelbulner, had better not buy a barometer for "loss of time and quicksilver" (Adelbulner 1768, 48). Barometers in the eighteenth century were popular household items, which could, if they were of proper quality, measure a certain physical parameter of the air – that much seemed certain. Little was known, on the other hand, about the correlation of that parameter with weather changes. The promise of prediction was, however, a key element of their marketing strategy that was bound to be disappointed time and time again. Consequently, Johann Georg Krünitz insisted in his *Oekonomische Encyklopädie*, "that many people know full well that the calendar often lies, but this does not cause them to lose trust in it. The barometer, they object, lies almost as frequently" (Krünitz 1784, 542).

In this brief section, we have encountered two popular methods of weather prognostication. One of them was based upon folklore and printed calendars, the other upon a commercialised version of an instrument adopted from a laboratory context into salons and private homes – and both were thought to be epistemically weak. In practical terms, Enlightenment scholars could offer no rational forecasting method that would have been more reliable than weather lore. Notably, weather rules and signs codified in calendars were apparently valuable enough for the farmers to protest once the rules were removed. Their practical value is, among others, a possible reason for this. Weather knowledge as well as the authority to prescribe how to apply it were contested. It was by no means obvious in the late eighteenth century that the instrument-based claim invested in natural laws would eventually triumph (albeit continuing to struggle with epistemic and practical weaknesses). However, in a somewhat ironic twist of history, the barometer together with other measuring instruments would later become part of the standard equipment for any meteorological observatory, thereby shedding its dubious reputation as the "weather glass".

Regarding the questions posed at the beginning, this case study has provided empirical material for three tentative conclusions. Firstly, we have seen that epistemic strength was not a prerequisite for barometers or weather lore to appear as socio-culturally strong. Secondly, socio-cultural strength is a vague term that can be applied rather arbitrarily to a wide variety of phenomena: a great number of followers, the high social standing of followers, old age and tradition, accordance with rational Enlightenment ideals, and the benefit of a marketable commodity for people to purchase. A typology of such weaknesses, as articulated in the sources, might offer interesting points of comparison between case studies. As some of the above-mentioned strengths overlap with epistemic or practical dimensions, finally, we also need to think further about the interdependencies between epistemic, social and practical ascriptions of weakness.

On the hierarchies between lay knowledge and professional knowledge in the Juvenile Court of Palestine

Nitzana Ben David

In this essay, I shall examine the dynamics between actors with weak knowledge and actors with stronger knowledge, in the field of the juvenile justice system in Palestine, from the 1920s to the 1930s. I will attempt to diagnose types of knowledge – both lay and professional, legal and therapeutic – in colonial, social, and gender contexts. An important diagnosis in this respect pertains to the hierarchy between various actors in this field, be it against the background of the authority vested in them or against the background of the epistemic status of the knowledge possessed by them.

In many Western countries, the function of a juvenile court was founded during the early years of the twentieth century. The reformers in Britain (and other Western countries) led the legislator to distinguish the justice system of juvenile offenders from the justice system of adult criminals through the Children Act of 1908, adopting the penal-welfare model, while extending legal protection to adolescents (Bradley et al. 2009, 4). In the examination of juvenile delinquency in biological, psychological or psycho-social terms, this model shifted the focus from the crime to the criminal, concentrating on factors that led the juvenile delinquent to violate the law, together with re-habilitation possibilities (Clarke 1975, 231). Legal knowledge alone failed to furnish the judge with tools to adjust between the developmental stage of the child and the methods of treatment or punishment which would secure the well-being of both the delinquent and society. The starting-point of legal knowledge is the normative system of society. The jurist takes an interpretative position – interpreting the reality that prevailed in the past, and determining whether the norm had been violated, what the severity of the transgression was and what the social price imposed upon the offender was to be. Legal knowledge lacks the means to understand the causes and motivations of delinquent behaviour and the measures that would prevent such behaviour in the future.

Given this inherent epistemic weakness of legal knowledge, a different kind of knowledge is required. The court was authorised to appoint probation officers, whose function it was to provide the judge with information concerning the condition of the juvenile delinquent within his or her family and community, and to assist by locating a studying framework or work place for the child, verifying that he or she would not return to criminal activity. The probation officers were usually middle-class women volunteers. The foundation of the juvenile court was a middle-class initiative, emerging from the concept of judges and probation officers, whereby the court and probation procedures ought to educate working-class parents, usually poor mothers, about how to raise their children. In this fashion, class divisions were established and consolidated upon the basis of a hierarchy between different kinds of lay knowledge: between the parental knowledge of lower-class mothers and the lay knowledge of judges and volunteers who belonged to the middle class.

In the early days of the twentieth century, the British Mandate's legislator introduced the probation method and the Penal-Welfare Model in Palestine and other colonies through the Juvenile Delinquent Order of 1922.[27] This change had an immense effect on the development of juvenile judgment in Palestine. The president of the district court appointed volunteers from the community as probation officers. However, with time, the court found it difficult to locate appropriate candidates,[28] and therefore only a few probation officers were appointed.

In the early 1930s, the Colonial Office, in accordance with the instructions of the League of Nations, sought to promote the notion, concerning the need to separate the juvenile judgment court from the general judgment court while applying the probation model. It made it clear, however, that the model should be adapted to local circumstances and resources.[29] Until the mid-1930s, judging juvenile delinquents in Palestine remained in the hands of British judges, who were thought to be familiar with the special legal model. The judge possessed the legal knowledge, and the trial was held according to legal practices, preserving the status of the judge above the status of all other actors in this field. However, the judge was now urged to find a solution for the problem of the juvenile accused, applying the probation model in the local Jewish and Arab communities. For this purpose, the judge could restrict the freedom of movement of the accused through judgment, determining where he or she would stay, study or work.[30] The legal knowledge of judges was of no avail for this task, as British judges were strangers to local Jewish and Arab communities, and therefore were denied the possibility of properly assessing the prevailing social circumstances and norms. Two supervisors were appointed beside the judges, as non-expert governmental officers,[31] whose function it was to supervise the accused either by themselves or by means of others. However, even such appointed governmental probationary

27 In reference to juvenile delinquency – policy and actions of the Colonial Office, October 1942. London National Archive, CO 859/73/11.

28 A letter from the Chief Justice, Michael McDougal, to the presidents of the district courts, 11/4/1932, Haifa Municipal Archive, 00077/10.

29 Lord Passfield memorandum 1929/10/05, London National Archive, CO 323/1026/6.

30 See the terms of the probationary order, specified in the order's form, Haifa Municipal Archive, 00077/10.

31 M. Nixon MBE, a missionary between 1919 and 1939, who supervised "neglected" girls as a governmental welfare supervisor, appointed by the Juvenile Delinquency Sub Committee, Meeting No. 6, dated 20–21 April, London National Archive, CO859/73/13. Kenneth H. Reynolds, a missionary, who, from 1905, treated "neglected" boys in Palestine. In May 1931, he was appointed as the juvenile probation officer. See the letter of Reynolds, dated 18 June 1935, Israel State Archives, M 272/1.

officers found it difficult to fulfil the supervisory function, both due to the scope of this requirement and because they were unfamiliar with the minors, especially of the Jewish community, as they even did not speak, let alone have a command of, their language.[32]

The Jewish communal institutes were quick to solve this problem through the Social Department of the National Committee of the Jewish community. The Social Department proposed an arrangement, which laid specific foundations to a centralised supervisory system, under the mutual management of the British Mandate and the Social Department. The establishment of a communal system was consistent with the policy of transferring the responsibility for care to the community. During these years, both in Palestine as in other western countries, the field of treating juvenile delinquency underwent a process of rejection of lay knowledge and its substitution by scientific and professional knowledge. The authority to diagnose juvenile delinquents and to treat them was redistributed again: it was shifted from volunteers to experts of psychiatry, psychology, medicine and social work, arguing that they held the therapeutic knowledge necessary for examining and curing the delinquent. The cooperation between British judges and the Social Department of the National Committee was founded on a joint cultural colonialist stand, whereby modern western therapeutic knowledge was to govern the methods of raising and educating children, and was, therefore, to be favoured over primitive eastern lay knowledge.

In October 1932, a managerial system was established whereby two volunteer supervisors were appointed to assist the juvenile court – a Jewish and an Arab probation officer. Arab children were referred to male volunteers in the community, while Jewish children were treated by the Social Department of the National Committee. The probation officers, most of whom were female social workers in the community, had mixed knowledge, professional and lay, and the judges adopted their recommendations so that most of the Jewish boys were given a probation order in the community. In the Arab community, the previous practice was still upheld – judges continued to appoint esteemed men from among the communal school headmasters or merchants, while determining the legal solution based upon the lay knowledge provided to the judges. The Arab probation officers were perceived by the judges to be lacking professional knowledge, and unable to provide a suitable solution in the community, with the result that most of the Arab boys were sent to corrective facilities outside the community.

Now, there were distinct practices for each community, which led to distinct structures of hierarchy between the judges and the probation officers. In the Arab

---

32 Children from the Arab community, Christians and Muslims, studied in the educational institutions of the Christian mission institutions in Palestine. Children from the Jewish community studied in the educational institutions of the Jewish community, and therefore the experience of Christian missionaries with the children of the community was limited.

community, the previous hierarchy of knowledge and functions was preserved. The probation officer, a native male, who had lay knowledge, sat opposite a male judge, who held the legal knowledge. In the Jewish community, the hierarchy between the actors was completely turned upside down in the context of knowledge, function and gender. A female probation officer, a social worker with a strong therapeutic knowledge, sat opposite a male, colonialist judge with weak legal knowledge. In this fashion, the epistemic strength of the therapeutic knowledge was translated into an institutional and political strength.

In the report of the probation officer for 1934,[33] the chief judge was exposed to the difference between punishing Jewish and Arab children, which led to a move to restore control of the probation services to the government. In 1935, the colonialist government appointed Mr. Wilfred H. Chin, a British probation officer and a social worker, as the supervisor of the probation services, and presented a statement that the appointment was intended to assure that the work of the probation service in Palestine would be broadened and subsequently founded upon scientific methods.[34] As professional knowledge took priority over the female professional volunteers of the Jewish community, governmental agents, professional judges and probation officers won back their traditional dominance in the field.

Lay knowledge is frequently looked upon as weak knowledge, and legal knowledge is frequently looked upon as strong knowledge. This essay provides a different angle on this notion. The situation of a foreign judge, ruling in the matter of local juvenile offenders, demonstrates the limits of legal knowledge. As such, judges were oblivious to the local social circumstances and processes, i.e., to lay knowledge, and to the interpretation of the circumstances towards ways of treatment, i.e., therapeutic knowledge. This essay has sought to present an example of how – in a single time space, under the influence of political, social and professional conditions – distinct structures of hierarchy were formed between lay knowledge and professional knowledge and between their holders. Perpetual negotiations took place between various holders of knowledge over the status of their knowledge, creating coalitions between different areas of knowledge, aspiring to fend off undesirable actors from the field. At times, an agreement is achieved, whereby another field of knowledge is required – be it professional or lay. Such an agreement upset the hierarchy between knowledge holders in that field, undermining the control of the dominating holder. As the threat persisted and as there was a growing fear that the dominating holder would lose his ranking in the hierarchy, he might choose to strengthen his position by introducing a knowledge

---

33 Report of the probation officer for 1934, Israel State Archive, M 272/19.
34 The letter of Wauchope to the Colony State Secretary, January 1935, Israel State Archive, M 272/1.

holder on his behalf. This actor provided him with the missing knowledge, but did not threaten his ranking in the hierarchy.

The existence of "Chinese" science: Variations on a theme

Sebastian Riebold

Any account of the history of technology and natural thought in China sooner or later must confront the fact that certain key developments responsible for the genesis of science in the West simply did not occur in the Chinese tradition. For example, there is scant evidence for sustained efforts to formalise and mathematise natural laws and, in a broader sociological context, the crucial convergence of artisanal expertise and natural philosophy, which has been argued to have been formative for the scientific "habitus" in Europe (Zilsel 2000, 3–21), did apparently not take place. Finally, "science" in China never developed a concept that would distinguish it from other fields of scholarly activity (Sivin [1982] 2005, 3–6). In mid-nineteenth century China,[35] "science" (understood in the sense outlined above) was thus socially and institutionally *weak*. The proponents of scientific knowledge – as it had developed in the West – were convinced of its *practical strength* but first had to secure a place for it next to traditional Chinese learning (Huters 2005, 1–73).

The observation that there was no scientific revolution in the Chinese context is widely known as the basis for the "Needham Question", asking for an *explanation* of this observation (Needham [1969] 2005, 16). As a matter of fact, its namesake was hardly the first to formulate it. Around the year 1900, approximately forty years prior to Needham, the first wave of newly returned, Western-trained Chinese scientists had already bemoaned and attempted to explain the absence of science in their homeland (Amelung 2014, 197–201). At least since the Second Opium War (1856–60), reform-minded officials and intellectuals in all echelons of society had been convinced that "science" (broadly understood) was indispensable for safeguarding the sovereignty of the Qing Empire. Accordingly, the state commenced a broad "Self-Strengthening" (*ziqiang*) programme and enabled a huge influx of Western technology, learning, and institutions (Elman 2005, 355–395).

It must thus be noted that science in post-1860 China was lauded less for its *epistemic*, but rather for its *practical*, strength, i.e., its potential to foster industrial and military development. We find this pronouncement as early as 1857 in an article by Scottish missionary Alexander Williamson (1829–1890), but it was re-

---

35 I will not discuss the "first phase" of transmission of scientific knowledge to China, which occurred via Jesuit missionaries in the seventeenth and eighteenth century (Mungello 2000, 17–51; Elman 2005, 61–221).

iterated by Chinese reformers as well: "A country's strength derives from the people. The people's strength derives from the mind. The mind's strength derives from science." (Elman 2005, 301–302) The discourse of weakness concerning China's disadvantaged situation on the international stage arguably privileged those branches of learning that could be most readily capitalised on politically and militarily. Williamson and others may have labelled these as "science" (*gezhi*), but the Chinese who had been trained abroad brought with them a new concept of science (*kexue*), which they distinguished from mere technical learning. They essentially asserted that forty years of "Self-Strengthening" had utterly failed to institutionalise "genuine" science based upon experimentation and theorising (Elman 2005, 396–419).

But does this mean that China *never had* science? After Qing-China's defeat in the First Sino-Japanese War (1894–95), the prolific translator and political activist Yan Fu (1853–1921) decried questions of this kind as untimely and esoteric (Amelung 2014, 196–197). However, they were of central concern for a host of thinkers between roughly 1860 and 1900, who were (naïvely, perhaps) unwilling to break completely with China's past even in the face of the growing foreign and domestic threats.

One prominent idea in this context was that "Western" learning had originated in Chinese antiquity and been brought to Europe by certain "cultural brokers". The West, allegedly utterly inept in original thinking, was nonetheless able to comprehend this knowledge and even *improve* upon it, and was now returning to China in more sophisticated form what had always belonged to it. This "theory" has often been treated as an instance of a "discourse of self-assertion" (Lackner 2008, 200). It was a rhetorical tool that could be wielded to integrate a vast body of "barbarian" knowledge into the Chinese canon without calling into question the axiomatic superiority of Chinese learning and civilisation. At court, the trope was an important rhetorical asset in countering allegations of attempted "Westernisation" from the conservative camp (Jenco 2015, 67–82). By the 1890s, the idea had seeped deeply into the public consciousness.

I argue that the "Chinese Origins" discourse between 1860 and 1895 betrays a marked unease concerning the relative strengths of the European and Chinese traditions, an unease shared by those who have posed the "Needham Question". I shall illustrate this by way of example. Zhang Zimu's (1833–1886) treatise entitled "Lice zhiyan" of 1877 (a widely-circulated text at that time, albeit by an obscure author), is particularly densely filled with "Chinese Origins" stories. In one section, we find the typical assertion that "Western" learning was institutionally strong in Chinese antiquity.

In the Three Dynasties and earlier [i.e., prior to the eighth century BCE], there were experts in every generation of Heavenly Officers (*tianguan*) [a high official rank] and the 'Nine Arithmetical Arts' were listed among the Six Arts [i.e., rites, music, archery, charioteering, writing, and mathematics]. The scholars (*ru*), as a matter of course, learned them all from childhood. Therefore it is said: 'Those who thoroughly comprehend heaven and earth are called scholars (*ru*)'. (Zhang [1891] 1985, 500)

The "Nine Arithmetical Arts" serve here as a *pars pro toto* for science in general. The sage rulers of antiquity had realised its virtue in governing a state and created the appropriate institutions. However, as mentioned above, there is little evidence, in the eyes of Zhang, that these sages valued science as a means of producing a superior form of knowledge. Zhang's "scholars (*ru*)" had social rivals, whom he refers to as "*literati (shidafu)*". Whereas the former were well-disposed towards non-literary, practical pursuits, and the sciences, the latter despised these as base and undignified activities, "delightedly engaged in metaphysical speculations and did not study solid principles" (Zhang [1891] 1985, 500).

The *literati* had their hearts and thoughts [fixed on] talent and ability. Without exception, they patterned themselves after the 'Great and Far' [like small-minded men]. Therefore, it became a widespread [attitude] not to have the leisure to [practice] any art or technique and the specialists along with their apprentices 'grabbed their arts and travelled to the western territories'.[36] The bright and intelligent men among (the Westerners) had never heard of the Great Way of the sages, so they had nothing in which to exercise their wisdom. [Therefore] they spent a lifetime to devote their mental and physical efforts to arts and techniques, developing unique skills that were surely [not equalled] in thousands of years. When it comes to arts and techniques specifically, [the Westerners] of course overshadow the Song and Ming, there is absolutely no use in concealing this fact. [Works on] astronomy after the Wanli period (1572–1620) and mathematics after the Kangxi reign (1661–1722), attest to this most clearly; but when all is said and done, [even] the best [works] on any particular art are still nothing but the 'skimmings and residues' (*xuyu*) of China. (Zhang [1891] 1985, 500)

Here, all tendencies of the "Chinese Origins" trope come together. In the end, it is asserted that the "true" knowledge ("the Great Way of the sages", which can be roughly understood as "good governance") remained confined to China proper, and that it was an ultimately lesser form of knowledge ("arts and techniques") that travelled West. However, it is also pointed out that 1) the technical knowledge ("science") subsequently developed in the West is far superior to anything accomplished in the field in China, and 2) that the Chinese scientific tradition all but died out.

Culturally, Chinese superiority remained unassailable for Zhang: no matter how impressive the accomplishments of the West in the realm of science and technology might be, these remained inferior pursuits when compared to the wisdom of the sages of Chinese antiquity. "Science" thus emerged as a *culturally weak* form of knowledge. In contemporary politics, however, it became ever harder to

---

36 This is a quotation from a canonical historiographical text that identifies the "cultural brokers" alluded to above.

deny that China was lacking something vital, as the country repeatedly showed itself to be unable to compete on the world stage. "Science", owing to its practical merits, would conceivably be able to redeem China's weakness in the international arena, provided one was to strengthen it sufficiently institutionally – which undoubtedly *did* happen in a number of reform measures during the last decades of the Qing dynasty (Zarrow 2015, 15–26). However, this did not prevent Ren Hongjun (H.C. Zen, 1886–1961), co-founder of the Science Society of China (*Zhongguo kexueshe*) from asking yet again in 1915 why science *(kexue)* did not develop in China (Amelung 2014, 200). Ren also correlated national strength and scientific development, although, for him, science was not a body of exploitable practical knowledge; it was a *method of knowledge production*. It is strongly implied in his article that science education in China in the late nineteenth and early twentieth century had taken a completely wrong path: "[T]he essence of science lies not in materiality (*wuzhi*), it lies in method (*fangfa*)." (Ren 1915, 13) In other words, only science understood as a method to produce *epistemically strong knowledge* can create a strong nation, and the like was not to be found in all of Chinese intellectual history.

Conclusion

Martin Herrnstadt and Lukas Jäger

Our first section entitled *Strengthening and Weakening Knowledge* calls for a switch in the historians' perspective, and grapples with its consequences and challenges. All the case studies mark a shift towards what we have called an epic mode of writing the history of science: from monolithic results of monumental history of knowledge (such as the contemporary German literature canon) towards a history of the practices of "purifying" knowledge; from the (paradoxical) theoretical presupposition of a weak collective identity intended to strengthen (but actually weakening) social actors, to the intersubjective experiences and interpretations of the actors themselves; and, finally, from the epistemology of knowledge to the ontology of networks and the question of whether we can get rid of epistemology as easily as contemporary approaches in science studies would have us believe. This shift towards an epic mode of historicising science does not bid farewell to the investigation of debates on the value of bodies of knowledge in general, far from it. Rather, it takes seriously the struggles for, and evaluations of, those bodies undertaken by the historical actors themselves. This shift to an epic mode should prevent us, as historians of "weak" forms of knowledge, from imposing upon ourselves an ideal of knowledge so utterly strict that, in consequence, the majority of historically traceable bodies of knowledge would have to appear as "weak", "deficient" or "precursory" forms of it, if they were to come into view at all. Contrary to such a view, studying "weak" forms of knowledge aims to illuminate these as under-estimated or disregarded, but integral all the same, because they are crucial parts of knowledge production. To be sure, neither the historical actors' vantage-points nor the forms of knowledge identified by them as "weak" (or "strong") are to be taken as ends in themselves or to be reified as alleged ideals of knowledge, but as empirical traits of the epic plays that we call science and society demanding further investigation.

Hence, in addition to our focus on epistemology, the three case studies of the second section, entitled *Hierarchies of Knowing* locate the work of science inside diverse social and cultural struggles. Here, the difference between social and epistemic strengths and weaknesses emerges as an illuminating distinction. As the cases show, social or institutional strength did not necessarily entail epistemic strength or *vice versa*. Institutionally strong actors, such as juvenile judges, lacked the social knowledge of the local actors. At the same time, providing social knowledge and negotiating its legal implications created opportunities to strengthen the social and institutional position of female social workers inside Mandatory Palestine. In another case, the history of meteorological knowledge shows how epistemic weaknesses of traditional knowledge, such as weather lore did not necessarily entail the success of scientific knowledge and research technology. On the contrary, the epistemic weakness of weather lore was an integrated part of its cultural and practical strength. These and other examples point to the dynamic and complex – institutional as well as social – constellation in which knowledge is produced and put to work.

Yet, the emphasis on *Hierarchies of Knowing* leads us to another problem raised in the framework of our research programme. The historian of weak knowledge or of any other such programme is inevitably situated in the contemporary power relations on a global scale, profiting from, as well as critically participating in, the institutional endeavours called "Science". It is a reminder for us historians that we need to make ourselves accountable not only for our relation to, responsibility for, and statements about, the past (Benjamin 2007, 253–264), but also for our own engagement in shaping the image of contemporary knowledge production and its socio-political role.

References

Adelbulner, Michael (1768): *Kurze Beschreibung der Barometer und Thermometer auch andern zur Meteorologie gehörigen Instrumenten nebst einer Anweisung wie dieselben zum Vergnügen der Liebhaber, und zum Vortheil des Publici gebraucht warden sollen.* Nürnberg: Fleischmann.

Al-Haj, Majid (1996): *Education of Arabs in Israel: Control and Social Change.* Jerusalem: Magness Press.

Amelung, Iwo (2014): "Lokalität und Lokalisierung – zur Entwicklung der Wissenschaften im China des späten 19. und frühen 20. Jahrhunderts." *Jahrbuch für Europäische Überseegeschichte*, 14: 193–214.

Bekerman, Zvi (2009): "Identity versus Peace: Identity Wins." *Harvard Educational Review*, 79: 74–83.

Bekerman, Zvi, and Gabriel Horenczyk (2004): "Arab-Jewish Bilingual Coeducation in Israel: A Long-Term Approach to Intergroup Conflict Resolution." *Journal of Social Issues*, 60 (2): 389–404.

Bekerman, Zvi, and Ifat Maoz (2005): "Troubles with Identity: Obstacles to Coexistence Education in Conflict Ridden Societies." *Identity*, 5 (4): 341–357.

Benjamin, Walter (2007): "Theses on the Philosophy of History." In: Walter Benjamin: *Illuminations*, 253–264. New York: Schocken Books.

Bernstein, Deborah (1995): "Jews and Arabs in the 'Nesher' Cement Works." *Cathedra: For the History of Eretz Israel and its Yishuv*, 78: 82–107.

Bishara, Azmi (1993): "On the Question of the Palestinian Minority in Israel." *Theory and Criticism*, 3 (1): 7–20.

Boltanski, Luc (2011): *On Critique: A Sociology of Emancipation.* Cambridge: Polity Press.

Böning, Holger (2002): "Volksaufklärung und Kalender: Zu den Anfängen der Diskussion über die Nutzung traditioneller Volkslesestoffe zur Aufklärung und zu ersten praktischen Versuchen bis 1780." *Archiv für Geschichte des Buchwesens*, 56: 79–107.

Boyle, Nicholas (2009): *Kleine deutsche Literaturgeschichte.* München: C.H. Beck.

Braam, Hans, and Lutz Hagstedt (2017): "Lyrische Wunderkammern der 'Sattelzeit': Gedichtsammlungen als Instrument bürgerlicher Kanonstiftung." *German Life and Letters*, 70 (1): 79–99.

Bradley, Kate, Anne Logan and Simon Shaw (2009): "Youth and Crime: Centennial Reflections on the Children Act 1908." *Crimes and Misdemeanours: Deviance and the Law in Historical Perspective*, 3 (2): 1–17.

Brakensiek, Stefan (2016): *Grundzüge der Agrargeschichte, 2: Vom Dreißigjährigen Krieg bis zum Beginn der Moderne (1650–1880).* Cologne, Weimar, Vienna: Böhlau.

Brecht, Bertolt (1967): "Über eine nicht-aristotelische Dramatik (1933–1941)." Bertolt Brecht: *Schriften zum Theater I*, 228–338. Gesammelte Schriften, 15. Frankfurt a. M.: Suhrkamp Verlag.

Brecht, Christine, and Barbara Orland (1999): "Populäres Wissen." *Werkstatt Geschichte*, 23 (1): 4–12.

Bremer, Kai (2008): *Literatur der Frühen Neuzeit: Reformation – Späthumanismus – Barock.* Paderborn: Fink.

Brenner, Peter J. (2011): *Neue Deutsche Literaturgeschichte.* 3rd ed. Berlin: Walter de Gruyter.

Clarke, John (1975): *The Three Rs: Repression, Rescue and Rehabilitation: Ideologies of Control for Working Class Youth.* Birmingham: Centre for Contemporary Cultural Studies, University of Birmingham.

Coen, Deborah (2010): "Weatherwiser?" *Historical Studies in the Natural Sciences*, 40 (1): 125–135.

Dar, A. (2008): "Palestinians and Jews at Work: The Sociology of Labor Practices in Israel and its Contribution to Understanding the Conflict." *Soziologia Yisraelit (Hebrew)*, 2: 287–306.

Dziudzia, Corinna (2017): "Eine apokryphe Geschichte der deutschen Literatur: Deutschsprachige Frauenliteratur der Frühen Neuzeit und ihre Abwesenheit in der neueren Literaturgeschichtsschreibung." *Comparatio*, 9: 169–180.

Elkana, Yehuda (1981): "A Programmatic Attempt at an Anthropology of Knowledge." In: Yehuda Elkana and Everett Mendelsohn (Eds.): *Sciences and Cultures. Anthropological and Historical Studies of the Sciences*, 1–76. Dordrecht-London: Reidel Publishing.

Elman, Benjamin A. (2005): *On their own Terms: Science in China, 1550–1900*. Cambridge MA: Harvard University Press.

Fischetti, Renate (Ed.) (2009): *Barock*. Stuttgart: Reclam

Fissell, Mary, and Roger Cooter (2003): "Exploring Natural Knowledge: Science and the Popular." In: Roy Porter (Ed.): *The Cambridge History of Science, 4: Eighteenth-Century Science*, 129–158. Cambridge: Cambridge University Press.

Gavison, Ruth (1999): *Does Equality Require Integration? The Case of the Public Schools System in Jaffa*. Jerusalem: The Van Leer Jerusalem Institute.

Ghanem, As'Ad. (2000): "The Palestinian Minority in Israel: The 'Challenge' of the Jewish State and its Implications." *Third World Quarterly*, 21 (1): 87–104.

Goedeke, Karl (1887): *Grundriss zur Geschichte der deutschen Dichtung aus den Quellen*. Vol. 3, 2nd ed. Dresden: Verlag von L. S. Ehlermann.

Golinski, Jan (2007): *British Weather and the Climate of Enlightenment*. Chicago, IL: University of Chicago Press.

Harman, Graham (2014): *Bruno Latour: Reassembling the Political*. London: Pluto Press.

Harvey, David (2010): *A Companion to Marx's Capital*. London-New York: Verso.

Hermand, Jost (1994): *Geschichte der Germanistik*. Reinbek: Rowohlt.

Huters, Theodore (2005): *Bringing the World Home. Appropriating the West in Late Qing and Early Republican China*. Honolulu, HI: University of Hawai'i Press.

Janković, Vladimir (2000): *Reading the Skies: A Cultural History of English Weather, 1650–1820*. Chicago IL: Chicago University Press.

Jenco, Leigh (2015): *Changing Referents. Learning Across Space and Time in China and the West*. Oxford: Oxford University Press.

Kaiser, Gerhard (2007): *Aufklärung, Empfindsamkeit, Sturm und Drang*. Tübingen et al.: Francke.

Krünitz, Johann Georg (1784): "Kalender". In: *Oekonomische Encyklopädie oder allgemeines System der Staats- Stadt- Haus- und Landwirthschaft*, Vol. 32, 443–603. Berlin: Joachim Pauli.

Lackner, Michael (2008): "Ex Oriente Scientia? Reconsidering the Ideology of a Chinese Origin of Western Knowledge." *Asia Major*, 21 (2): 183–200.

Latour, Bruno [1984] (1993): *The Pasteurization of France*. Cambridge MA-London: Harvard University Press.

Latour, Bruno (2004): "Why has Critique Run out of Steam? From Matters of Fact to Matters of Concern." *Critical Inquiry*, 30 (2): 225–248.

Latour, Bruno (2014): *An Inquiry into Modes of Existence: An Anthropology of the Moderns*. Cambridge, MA: Harvard University Press.

Levy, Natalie, and Yossi Shavit (2015): "A Chronicle of Disappointment: Integration between Arabs and Jews in a Jewish-Israeli Elementary School." *Soziologia Yisraelit*, 16 (2): 7–30.

Marx, Karl (1990): *Capital: A Critique of Political Economy, Volume I*. London: Penguin Classics.

Middleton, William Edgar Knowles (1964): *The History of the Barometer*. Baltimore, MD: Johns Hopkins University Press.

Monterescu, Daniel (2001): "A City of 'Strangers': The Socio-cultural Construction of Manhood in Jaffa." *Journal of Mediterranean Studies*, 11: 159–188.

Mungello, David E. (2009): *The Great Encounter of China and the West, 1500–1800*. 3rd ed., Lanham, MD et al.: Rowman & Littlefield Publishers.

Needham, Joseph [1969] (2005): *The Grand Titration*. London-New York: Routledge.

Peters, Mark (2008): *A Woman's Voice in Baroque Music: Mariane von Ziegler and J. S. Bach*. Aldershot-Burlington VT: Ashgate Publishing.

Rabinowitz, Dan (1993): "Oriental Nostalgia: How the Palestinians Became 'Israel's Arabs'". *Teorya Uvikoret (Hebrew)*, 4: 141–52.

Rabinowitz, Dan (2002): "Oriental Othering and National Identity: A Review of Early Israeli Anthropological Studies of Palestinians." *Identities: Global Studies in Culture and Power*, 9 (3): 305–325.

Rabinowitz, Dan, and Khawla Abu-Baker (2002): *The Stand Tall Generation: The Palestinian Citizens of Israel Today*. Jerusalem: Keter.

Rásonyi, Peter (2000): *Promotoren und Prozesse institutionellen Wandels: Agrarreformen im Kanton Zürich im 18. Jahrhundert*. Berlin: Duncker & Humblot.

Rekhess, Elie (2007): "The Evolvement of an Arab-Palestinian National Minority in Israel." *Israel Studies*, 12 (3): 1–28.

Ren, Hongjun (1915): "Shuo Zhongguo wu kexue zhi yuanyin" [The Reason behind the Absence of Science in China]. *Kexue*: 8–13.

Rouhana, Nadim, and As'Ad Ghanem (1998): "The Crisis of Minorities in Ethnic States: The Case of Palestinian Citizens in Israel." *International Journal of Middle East Studies*, 30 (3): 321–346.

Saussure, Horace Bénédict de (1784): *Versuch über die Hygrometrie*. Leipzig: Junius.

Schlosser, Horst Dieter (2006): *dtv-Atlas Deutsche Literatur*. 10th ed. München: dtv.

Shapin, Steven, and Simon Schaffer (1985): *Leviathan and the Air-Pump. Hobbes, Boyle, and the Experimental Life*. Princeton, NJ: Princeton University Press.

Sivin, Nathan [1985] (2005): "Why the Scientific Revolution did not Take Place in China – or did it?" *Environment Systems and Decisions (formerly Enviromentalist)*, 5 (1): 39–50.

Smooha, Sammy (2013): *Still Playing by the Rules: Index of Arab-Jewish Relations in Israel 2012: Findings and Conclusions*. Haifa: University of Haifa.

Sohn-Rethel, Alfred (1978): *Intellectual and Manual Labour. A Critique of Epistemology*. London: Macmillan.

Sylvester-Habenicht, Erdmute (2009): *Kanon und Geschlecht: eine Re-Inspektion aktueller Literaturgeschichtsschreibung aus feministisch-genderorientierter Sicht*. Sulzbach: Helmer.

T., P. (1787): *Die Witterungsprophezeyungen unpartheyisch beurtheilet: Nebst Winken zu einer neuen sichrern Theorie*. Berlin: [no publisher].

Wellbery, David E. (Ed.) (2004): *New History of German Literature*. Cambridge, MA.: Harvard University Press.

White, Hylton (2013): "Materiality, Form, and Context. Marx contra Latour." *Victorian Studies*, 55 (4): 667–682.

Whittle, Ruth (2013): *Gender, Canon and Literary History: The Changing Place of Nineteenth-Century German Women Writers (1835–1918)*. Berlin: Walter de Gruyter.

Willems, Gottfried (2015): *Geschichte der deutschen Literatur*, Band 1–5: *Humanismus und Barock; Aufklärung; Goethezeit; Vormärz und Realismus; Moderne*. Köln: UTB.

Winko, Simone (1996): "Literarische Wertung und Kanonbildung." In: Heinz Ludwig Arnold and Heinrich Detering (Eds.): *Grundzüge der Literaturwissenschaft*, 585–600. Munich: Deutscher Taschenbuch Verlag.

Zarrow, Peter (2015): *Educating China: Knowledge, Society, and Textbooks in a Modernizing World, 1902–1937*. Cambridge: Cambridge University Press.

Zhang Zimu (1985 [1891]): "*Lice zhiyan*" [*Humble Considerations and Scattered Notes*]. In: Wang Xiqi (Ed.): *Xiaofang huzhai yudi congchao*, 496–509. Reprint. Hangzhou: Hangzhou gujishudian.

Zilsel, Edgar (2000): *The Social Origins of Modern Science*. Dordrecht: Kluwer Academic Publishers.

Zittel, Claus (2014): "Wissenskulturen, Wissensgeschichte und historische Epistemologie." *Rivista internazionale di filosofia e psicologia*, 5: 29–42.

Climate and Environment

A Weaker Form of Knowledge?
The Case of Environmental Knowledge and Regulation

Dominique Pestre

Abstract

Environmental knowledge has every reason to be weak because there is not one problem, one preoccupation, but a myriad of troubles tackled by a myriad of disciplines, because the problems are political through and through, and only "technical" in a minor part, and because environmental troubles are the reverse side of production and consumption. The solutions are thus heavily sensitive to economic and political interests. Temporarily, environmental questions could rise to pre-eminence: when major accidents happen, when public opinion ignites about particularly unfair matters – when business and politicians cannot but *do something* about the negative effects of progress. In what follows, I come back to these claims, show the extreme variety of solutions that have been proposed since the late 1960s, and analyse in detail two particular moments: around 1970 when the "environmental question" took the form we are still familiar with and when economists and states were the central actors; and around 1990, when global business and managers advanced new frames and tools, and progressively imposed their solutions – notably in the Global South. In both cases, however, the results were poor and this paradox is remarked on: thousands and thousands of actions and projects have been proposed over the last 50 years to cope with environmental deterioration – but without significant results.

Introduction

There is no intrinsically strong or weak knowledge, as Moritz Epple shows in his contribution to this anthology – it is always in context that knowledge claims are defined as stronger or weaker. At any given time, they could be judged to be quite convincing or most dubious by different people, for varying reasons, without ways to arbitrate easily between them. This is true with scientific claims when they mobilise alternative visions – i.e., different kinds of disciplinary lenses. During the nineteenth century debate over the age of the Earth, for example, geologists tended to give far longer time-spans that physicists (who gave extraordinary short ones) and they were under constant pressure to reduce their evaluations by Lord Kelvin and others – because there were always hierarchies of disciplines, of certified knowledge.[1]

Strong knowledge is often the sign of a socially recognised set of claims, while weak knowledge is that of claims that are, for the most part, contested. Stakes are often high between competing forms of knowledge – and this implies not only disciplinary and epistemic differences, but also political and social values. Sociologically speaking, some people are more at the margins than other, and their knowledge tends, more often than not, to be seen by professionals as the knowledge of amateurs, and thus is weaker. Hierarchies and hegemonic forms exist at any given time, that is clear, but hegemonies are never total, and they regularly show limits, weaknesses. Dynamics are thus necessarily complex as what has once been socially rejected could re-emerge in another guise, and what has been judged strong could be forgotten, or could later be said to be an error.

In other words, it is most pertinent, in these matters, to be radically historicist – but sociological and political, too; and never to forget what Bruno Latour showed us about Louis Pasteur at *Pouilly-le-Fort* – his theory of microbes became strong because of this well-managed public experiment; or what Steven Shapin and Simon Schaffer taught us – that solutions to the problem of knowledge are solutions to the problem of social order. Knowledge claims and know-how are rarely the only province of official sciences: they are produced, scrutinised and evaluated by military engineers and business leaders; they are proposed by ordinary people, displayed in public spaces and mobilised or criticised by "civil society" actors; they are food for the media and for the ideological mill – and all these people, institutions and spaces contribute to the strength or the weakness of knowledge proposals.

1. Environmental knowledge and weakness: An organic relationship?

Environmental knowledge has good reason to be and to remain particularly weak: diagnosis and solutions are rarely consensual, conflicts are recurrent between disciplinary fields, and environmental claims are easily dismissed or ignored. The reasons are many. The "environment" is quite complex and large as an object of investigation, it implies studies ranging from physical and biological phenomena to human and animal forms of behaviour, and studies are performed on various

---

1 Burchfield 1975 and 1990; Pestre 2000.

spatial and temporal scales. They mobilise a large variety of tools and techniques and combine different angles and points of view. Observation and measurements might imply satellites and sensors of all kinds, but also direct visual identifications by amateurs, and epidemiology, toxicology, economic calculus, as well as political and moral judgements. Finally, models, simulations and the devising of scenarios are often decisive, and each of these tools implies decisions on what counts and matters, what is central and what is not.

In a way, environmental knowledge is a set of studies and techniques that are not hierarchised, and which could be criticised – in the data that they provide (varied in nature and difficult to assemble and ascertain), in the tools that they deploy (they lack, for example, the instrumental efficiency of laboratory knowledge that could be sanctioned by technological development) and in "the negative flavour" that environmental knowledge has *vis-à-vis* "progress" – in a sense, it has some of the weaknesses of the social and critical sciences. Of course, we know from social studies of science that any scientific practice cannot but be selective and partial, since simplifications and hypotheses are part of the game, but, in the case of environmental knowledge, the problems are one or two orders of magnitude more complicated. And the nature of its results could not be compared to those of physics, material sciences, or biology. And it should come as no surprise that the latter alone, and not environmental knowledge, are used to define "scientificity" both in the specialised literature and in the popular imagination.

Environmental knowledge also tends to be weak because of its uneven relationships with power. On the one hand, to talk like Jürgen Habermas, there are *systems* that organise innovation, production, regulation and safety – in short, (laboratory) science, business and the state, the backbones of our material lives (Habermas 1985). On the other, there are the *life worlds*, the many forms of social life and experience – which could mobilise people who put pollution and environmental degradation on the public agenda. They might be scientists or medical doctors but they also might be ordinary people. Whistleblowing and environmental knowledge, two things that are closely-linked, are often "cooked on the spot" by people trying to connect the troubles that they have identified with local industrial or agricultural activity. In short, environmental knowledge is easily looked upon by experts as weak – just think of the *Amoco Cadiz* trial in the United States (Fourcade 2011) – and it tends to weigh only on the margins of "serious knowledge".

Temporarily, and in certain contexts, environmental knowledge could rise to pre-eminence and appear on the front pages of newspapers. This occurs when major accidents reach the media (Seveso or Chernobyl, for example), when public opinion ignites about a particularly unfair and dramatic affair – when *systems* are suddenly at fault. But this rarely means that environmental knowledge becomes strong enough to ground a sustained, coherent and lasting action. One reason for this is that *systems*, if one of their major interests is at stake (and this is often the case), have the resources to counteract; and they can act quickly and in a strategic way – just think of the tobacco industry or the oil companies, now well studied by social sciences.[2] Another reason is that even professional knowledge in these highly political matters is easily dismissed by fellow scientists who are not experts – suffice to think of the radical critiques often made against climate change by chemists or solid state physicists. Finally, conflicts of interests are very common (think of pesticides and endocrine disruptors at EU level, for example) and social, political and economic capital seems to be too potent a parameter for the environmentalists to assert themselves autonomously.

Scientifically speaking, the relation between the disciplines involved in environmental knowledge is also a major weakness since their differences in the framing and definition of environmental problems are difficult to overcome. Economists, for example, tend to start from what economic theory says (the inclusion of negative environmental externalities into prices via fees or markets of pollution rights offers the most efficient solution for both growth and environmental protection),[3] whereas ecologists might be more interested in the materiality of relations and be centred on *milieus* and local evaluations. The former might consider economic *growth* (sustainable, of course) to be the most important target, while the latter might put the emphasis on ecological conservation and local functionalities – and epidemiologists on the protection of the health of the population. So what matters, at the end, is which discipline has the upper hand for decision-making – which comes down to who, in social and political terms, has the power to impose it. It might just be political power, as in 1970, when the OECD, under pressure from some of its key member states, transferred its environmental unit from the scientific to the economic directorate; or, as occurred in the late 1980s, when international business led by the International Chamber of Commerce succeeded in marginalising both state and Keynesian approaches and replacing them with private law-making, contracts and voluntary commitments, which meant, this time, that industrial managers partly replaced economists as the most important figures for designing proper environmental action.

Differences between political cultures might also be decisive. In the United States, the de-regulation of the 1980s and 1990s was motivated by two main considerations: arguments in favour of the universal superior efficiency of "the market", and a belief in the intrinsically corrosive and harmful nature of the state –

---

2 Oreskes and Conway 2010; Kaiser and Wasserman 2016.

3 Conceptually speaking, this idea of optimisation (proposed by economics) when applied to heterogeneous entities as "growth" and "environmental protection" raises major questions. Barde and Gerelli wrote in 1977, for example, that the fee "allows us to get at the optimal level of pollution", a statement worth discussing.

which had a long history there, one which was largely absent on the European continent, which was often more "social democratic" and inclined to social negotiation through states.[4] Differences in approaches to the environment could also refer to differences in legal cultures, to what forms the basis of law. In the United States, what is degraded is often the object of assessments by comparison with reference sites with a view to compensation. On the European continent, on the other hand, action more often aims at maintaining functional situations, which more often means the protection of ecosystems and makes the state or the local authorities the central actors (Bouleau 2011).

2. Posing the problem, listing questions and solutions

The structural weakness of environmental knowledge is well illustrated by a paradox, namely, the gap between the time, work, intelligence and quantity of money invested to save the environment – and the quite low level of end results. For half a century, the environmental question has been central in the public space and thousands of commitments have been taken annually by governments, business, NGOs and international organisations. For nearly 50 years, agencies and ministries dedicated to environmental protection have existed in the United States, Japan, and Europe, and by now are nearly everywhere; dozens and dozens of intergovernmental agreements have been signed and ratified internationally; and, since the 1990s, thousands of companies have annually produced voluntary commitments which have been audited by professional experts. The United Nations Environmental Programme (UNEP) was established in 1973, following the Stockholm Conference on the Human Environment, and the one which deals with Climate Change today is most powerful. The OECD has published more than 500 reports on the topics since 1972, as well as hundreds and hundreds of declarations, recommendations, decisions, guidelines, procedural rules, principles, and technical notes – most of them accepted by its member states. A large number of consultant firms and financial institutions evaluate "ecosystems services" and climatic impacts today; the World Bank has declared the environmental quality of the projects that it finances since the 1970s; and it now plays a central role in the global political economy of environmental questions.

---

4 Short 2012 provides an excellent study on this point. It analyses the discussion on deregulation that is deployed in law journals between 1980 and 2005. Through a quantitative study, it shows the growing importance of the argument of the coercive state (towards that of the market) and adds: "framing regulation as a problem of coercive state power" tends to favour "a logic of governance uniquely suited to self-regulatory solutions that promised noncoercive ways of governing".

The extent and variety of the solutions put into place to limit the damage that is inflicted on the environment are thus most noticeable. The results, however, seem to remain unequal and give no cause for strong optimism. At local levels in the Global North (I mean in richer countries), some results are noteworthy. The quality of the waters of the main European rivers has partly been under control since the 1990s or 2000s, and that of air in most cities has improved since the London smog of 1952. This improvement is not general, however: fine particle pollution often remains worrying, that of agricultural soils is rarely reduced, and long-term reduction of pollution due to chemical molecules remains weak and is marked by recurrent conflicts of interest.[5] In the Global South, the situation is worse in almost all registers. I do not intend to give an inventory here – that would be impossible in so few pages. But there is no great risk in claiming that the environmental situation is still deteriorating, a fact often repeated in UNEP reports – even if certain countries, India and China, for example, have recently put determined actions into place for the more serious damage (Huchet 2016). The situation in regions where extractive activities are essential – as in the Gulf of Guinea in Africa, for example – often show how pollution – in this case oil pollution – is profoundly devastating, without serious studies being carried out, without recognition, nor compensation being paid (Ferguson 2005). Two last indexes of the weakness of results could be the alerts on climate warming, which are more and more pressing, and the curves that define the anthropocene, that moment of terrestrial life geologically marked by human enterprise: these curves have globally remained, since the 1940s, on their historical trajectory of deterioration, without notable inflexion or progress – as if the thousands and thousands of projects and financing set up over the last 50 years had not had any impact proportionate to the situation (Bonneuil and Fressoz 2016).[6]

How are we to understand this extraordinary paradox? How are we to account for it?

The first and most important parameter to take into account is that environmental destruction essentially *derives from* production, from economic growth and our modes of life – that it is the other side of the same coin; and that seriously reducing the former will affect the latter. For this reason, environmental damage has rarely been taken in itself and for itself; instead, it has been common practice, over the last two centuries, to devise forms of protection of the environment that do not affect economic activity too much. What is behind the solutions that try not to affect industrial progress unduly is the importance of economic develop-

---

5 Högselius et al. 2016, notably Chapters 7 and 8. Valo 2016 and 2017.

6 For a study on the (weak) regulation of chemical product in environment, see Jas 2014. A last example: according to World Scientists' Warning to Humanity: A Second Notice, BioScience, published online, 13 November, 2017, 9 Gt of CO_2 were emitted at global level in 1960, they were 22 in 1992, and 36 in 2016.

ment, the seduction of the affluent society, and the necessity not to weaken, in global contexts of war and economic competition, the economic strength of one's own nation. So any response to pollution over the last two centuries has tended to consider what the other countries were doing, and weigh the benefits (for health, nature and the environment) against the costs (for employment, national strength and industrial competitiveness). Notably, in times of crisis, the means deployed for environmental protection tend to remain strictly subservient to the needs of the economy. And the recent election of Donald Trump, or the complex negotiations with industry after each scandal, show this with the utmost clarity.

The second parameter that might explain this paradox is that there is not *one* problem, *one* environment, *one* preoccupation; there is, instead, an infinite myriad of problems, some very local, other quite global. "The environment" is a large set of concerns, and environmental protection is not an entity to which a coherent field of research could be dedicated. For Orville L. Freemann, the US Secretary of Agriculture at the end of the 1960s, for example, the environmental question refers to quality of life and rurality (Roslansky 1967). For Roger Revelle, the ocea- nographer and the director of the *Centre of Population Studies* at Harvard – and for the experts from the Global South present at the preparatory meeting to the Stockholm Conference hold in Founex in Switzerland in June 1971 – poverty is the primary cause of environmental disasters: in poor countries, surviving is the priority and socio-environmental solidarity is central in guaranteeing the co-exis- tence of all in a given *milieu* (UN Geneva and EPHE 1971). At the same time, the economist Kenneth E. Boulding claims that the living standards in the Global North are responsible for the progressive destruction of the Spaceship Earth; anticipating the Club of Rome report of 1972, he says that the question of the Earth's *limits* has to be put central stage (Boulding 1966). For the OECD in the 1970s, the questions that mattered were the quality of the air and the waters, noise near airports, the place of motor cars in towns, the quality of energy production, the impact of chemicals and pesticides, industrial releases, cross border pollution – all of which call for technological policies, recycling, and collaboration with industry. The numerous conferences organised by the United Nations in the 1970s indicate another range of preoccupations: overpopulation (in Bucharest in 1973), food production (in Rome), sea protection (Caracas, Geneva, New York), human settlements (Vancouver), access to water (Mar del Plata), desertification (in Nairobi in 1977). For the UNEP, the urgency is in the writing of international law, planning at country level, the evaluation and control of terrestrial ecosystems, the scientific monitoring of the global environment – and it is UNEP that puts the Global Environmental Monitoring System into place.

I will not go on with as detailed an enumeration for the following decades – that would become fastidious. I just would like to draw attention to the extreme variety of stakes and add a short Borgesian list. For some people, what matters is to save whales, pandas and elephants, to recover and restore nature to its original state, to create sanctuaries and parks – from which local populations could be excluded, as was not uncommon in Africa in the colonial tradition of hunting preserves (Blanc 2015). The protection of the environment could imply the choice for other agricultural practices, certified wood production, measures to protect resources in the long run. It could suppose industrial ecology, the sorting of waste at home, the mastering of environmental damage via its inclusion in prices, via fees, or Total Quality Industrial Management. It could aim at protecting regional biodiversity, rescuing wetlands, attenuating climate change (Janković and Bowman 2014).

Chronologically, the 1970s and 1980s generally use the term "environment" whereas the 1990s and 2000s more often talk about "global climate change" and "sustainable development". The change is most significant but nothing should lead us to accept the evidence that the global scale is the only or most important parameter (Taylor and Buttel 1992). And the words "environment" and "sustainable" could be absent altogether (as in the Marpol Convention for the Protection of the Sea), only to appear recently (in tension with other words such as "nature" and "*milieus*"), and then be replaced or marginalised (by "biosphere" and "ecosystems" here, "climate change" there).

The last parameter to consider is that there cannot be one type of solution to this complex set of problems, and, in particular, *no scientific or technological fix*. The range of solutions varies in nature and reflects the variety of values, objectives and knowledge that could be mobilised.

Two solutions are old, but still quite topical. They date from the turn of the nineteenth century, are part and parcel of any liberal economic order, and are still essential today. The first one consists in *financially compensating* for damage. The compensation could derive from an arrangement between polluters and victims or an administrative obligation; it could be taken over by insurance companies or imposed by a legal decision of justice. Today, this is quite popular around ecosystems, since their destruction now has to be legally compensated in most countries in the Global North. The second consists in *permitting* – in administratively authorising the opening of a new plant. This refers to the geographical conditions of production and allows zoning, a political management of space (a business which pollutes must be outside city centres or residential areas, for example). Compensating, which amounts to including damages in the production costs, is an easy solution for polluters, since it is a way to absolve oneself, to maintain social peace with neighbours – and to continue producing (Fressoz and Pestre 2013).

The second main group of instruments consists in promulgating norms and standards, to establish material limits for pollution; to which one could add, for new projects, the Environmental Impact Assessments, designed in the 1970s by administrations working with scientists and professional organisations. These instruments largely rely on toxicicology and epidemiology, but also depend on production imperatives and social values: the level of a norm (the legal threshold for the presence of a carcinogenic in a product, for example) has derived, since the nineteenth century, from arbitration between the negative effects of the pollution (on the immediate environment or health, for example) and the requirements of the production process. Up to the 1950s, this was often done empirically, by negotiations between professional experts and medical doctors; since the 1960s, cost-benefit analysis (CBA) has officially been required. CBA is a solution that looks scientific, but that is particularly prone to biases and approximations (the number of parameters and choices to be made implies a limited form of objectivity), and this tool, de facto, was massively used by regulators to limit the demands of environmental activists that wanted to "impose" too heavy costs on production. And, in reality, a product or process considered vital for production is rarely forbidden or banned before a replacement has been provided.[7]

The third group, that of "economic instruments", was initiated in the 1970s and 1980s by economists when they were put at the centre of the decision process. Economic instruments were also part of the battle fought by the new liberal and conservative think tanks (i.e., Heritage and Enterprise) against the social role of states and Keynesianism to show the superiority of markets over political regulations, over norms and standards.[8] The first ones were the Polluter Pays Principle (PPP) and the fee which aimed at including the negative environmental externalities of the production process in prices. According to economic theory, the fee would lead to an optimum for economic growth and the environment. In the 1980s, markets of rights – which later became known as cap and trade – were said to be more efficient than fees. In this schema, a global ceiling of pollution is allowed by someone, generally political powers (i.e., a certain quantity of SO_2 or CO_2 emissions), and a market allows the exchange of "rights to pollute" between producers. In practice, apart from CO_2 markets, these tools were not used very often. And cap and trade markets, when they existed, demonstrated varied trajectories with uneven effects – suffice to think of the failure of the CO_2 market established in Europe in the last two decades.[9]

Taking care of the environmental damage induced by our modes of development, however, was not only the province of legal or public authorities – it was also done at the level of production by industrial managers. Knowledge about recycling was already being mobilised in the late 1970s and governments helped companies develop technical standards for "clean production" – what was known

---

7 For convincing remarks by an expert on these calculations, Kelman 1981 (in 1981, Steven Kelman was associate director for management planning at the United States Federal Trade Commission). See, also, Boudia 2014; Boudia and Henry 2015; Boudia 2016; Hays 2000.

8 OECD 1972 and 1985; Cook 1988.

9 For studies on the efficiency of these tools, Ercmann 1996; Schreurs 2002; Driesen 2003; Vig and Faure 2004; DG Environment 2004; Toke and Lauber 2007.

in the 1980s as the Best Available Technologies. One must be cautious, however: since nobody is ready to save the environment if the price to pay is too high, the complete formulation was that of the Best Available Technologies *not entailing excessive costs* – which left many ways to escape from too drastic solutions.[10] Around 1990, industrialists extended Total Quality Management to include environmental interests; and they tried to formalise lifecycle analysis, albeit with little success because of the sheer complexity of the work.

In connexion with NGOs, they also promoted labels – the *Forest Stewardship Council* label, for example – that were ways of developing socially responsible products and sustainable practices.[11] Initially, labels were often interesting for environmental protection, even if they had only limited impact in terms of market shares because they were generally created by companies occupying market niches. But their success among consumers and citizens led to their submersion and the dilution of their impact: competitors, who were much bigger on the markets, started, in turn, to create their own labels with rules as glowing as they were vague. In this way, they were able to trump the force of initial labels and dissolve what made them worthwhile in the first place (Abbott and Snidal 2009).

More recently, auto-organisation, codes of good conduct, guidelines, sustainable finance and charters of Environmental and Social Responsibility – in short, moral and voluntary commitments on the part of companies – have become most common. This move in the 1990s reveals a new attitude on the part of global corporations that thought they were now strong enough, globally speaking, to take the leadership in environmental protection. Their solutions did not initially replace the previous ones, notably, formal, state-based regulations, but they became more and more popular in the 2000s. They notably gained in importance on global issues and it was "voluntary commitments" that have prevailed in international conferences since the failure of the Copenhagen COP meeting in 2009 – for example, during the Paris COP 21 in 2015.

Similarly, private contracting and soft law-making became new tools. Around some key tropical agricultural products such as palm oil in the mid-2000s, for example, "multi-actor round tables" were set up to define what would count in international trade as a *sustainable* product. These round tables gathered the major global companies of agro-business such as *Unilever* and *Nestlé*, representatives of local populations and conservation NGOs such as the WWF. "Collectively", they set the norms of "sustainable products" – even though the latest developments in Indonesia and Malaysia (the key producers of palm oil) show how the palm oil

---

10 EEC, Directive du Conseil 84/360, 28 juin 1984. Baya-Laffite 2015.
11 On labels, Bartley 2007, and Marx 2010.

plantations remain destructive of the primary forest and why they are now contested on all fronts.[12]

Finally, this arsenal of tools – this cabinet of curiosities, one might say – should not mask a major fact – that many practices at world level *ignore any rule*. I have mentioned some of the cases in the Global South (the Gulf of Guinea, for example), but one should not forget the non-respect of laws or sheer deception in the Global North itself – suffice to think this time of the recent *VW* diesel motors scandal or *Syngenta* practices.[13]

Numerous means for integrating environmental degradation and economic realities were thus deployed in parallel over time. And the result is not systemic, since the new tools rarely replaced the old ones – they just tended to pile one onto the other. The "advantage" of this piling of knowledge, tools and spaces of regulation was that it allowed the people who had sufficient power to choose how they intended to tackle the problems, and where to do it.

3. History, Part 1: An economic revolution, 1968–1972

To understand better how power and knowledge are intertwined around environmental knowledge, I will consider two historical moments. These moments were chosen because they were essential in the solutions that were finally accepted, in the kinds of knowledge that were considered to be the best. One deals (this section) with the new role given, from the late 1960s to the mid-1970s, to economists and economic knowledge in environmental protection, and the solution that was agreed on by experts and governments, notably at the OECD. The second analysis (Section 4) considers the late 1980s and early 1990s, the role played by business leaders and managers at that time, and the break it represented in terms of what should count as good knowledge.

3.1. How were economists made the ultimate experts on environmental protection?

Putting environmental questions in political settings took a new shape in the late 1960s and early 1970s. The United States Environmental Protection Agency was created in 1969, the European and Japanese equivalent institutions in the following years. The American government was aware of the implied costs for its own

---

12 On multi-actors round tables, Glasbergen and Schouten 2011; Cheyns 2011; Ruysschaert and Salles 2014.
13 About Syngenta: see Foucart 2015. See, also, Green and Berry 1985, and Park and Vetterlein 2010, who indicate, around the World Bank, that rules are far from being systematically applied.

industry, and it tried to internationalise its policy. It did so through the OECD and the international conference prepared by the United Nations and held in Stockholm in 1972 on "human environments".

The OECD was the most decisive and its economists proposed the principles that were to form the backbone of most of the regulations (its solutions were accepted by the European Commission, see, for example Meyer 2017). The central role of the OECD in developing rules to manage environmental destruction depended on its nature: a space in which economists were to help Western countries on their road to "economic growth", the OECD's *raison d'être* since WWII; and a place where the long-term international challenges faced by the Western countries could be openly discussed: the OECD was the place where their experts could meet and define common solutions. The OECD did this in the mid-1970s for the global trade rules that were to be put in place for the investments of multi-national corporations in developing countries[14] – it did it in 1970 for the environment.

In the 1960s at the OECD, it was the directorate for scientific affairs that first took responsibility for the emerging environmental "challenge". It considered it as a practical set of problems and looked at noise in urban areas, the pollution of the water and the air, and toxic products such as lead or asbestos. For the automobile industry, it proposed creating technical norms for engines, showed the advantage of public transport and suggested limiting the circulation of cars in towns (Schmelzer 2012). In 1970, the OECD Council of Ministers radically reversed this logic, this way of framing questions: it withdrew the environmental question from the scientific directorate and put it under economists' leadership. In 1972, the new directorate said how things should be taken and stated that there was a universal principles of action, the Polluter Pays Principle, and one concrete solution, the integration of environmental negative externalities into prices *via* fees. According to economic theory, markets would thus lead to optimal solutions, at the lowest global cost for society. For the first time, a unique and universal solution was said to exist and be the only rational, science-based way of acting.[15]

The reasons for this "economic revolution" were explicit. In October 1970, the Secretary-General wrote that the ministerial-level council "recognized that governmental interest in maintaining or promoting an acceptable human environment *must now be developed in the framework of economic growth*".[16] In February 1971, he added that the OECD had "a special responsibility to see that stable economic growth continues within the market economy and that institutional arrangements are made so that pollution control works towards a stronger and more effective

14 Petrini 2011; Hadjuk 2013.
15 Bohm and Kneese 1971, 1–2. OECD 1972.
16 *1971 Programme of Work for the OECD*, presented by the Secretary General to the Council on October 1970 (C(70)125), as quoted by Long 2000, quotation on 36 (my emphasis).

market economy" (Schmelzer 2013, 311). And his deputy, Gérard Eldin, backed him by adding: "we, in the OECD, do not believe there to be any fundamental conflict between economic growth and environmental protection."[17]

In short, the OECD tried to domesticate the spectre of the "limits to growth" that the Earth could inflict on our ways of living and producing. The choice was made to re-assert the centrality of growth, give priority to GATT rules (i.e., not promulgating protective measures against countries that were without environmental standards), and give the central role to economists. The solution was to go through the tool decided upon by theory, and rely on cost-benefit analysis to help fix the priorities.

A last word on this turning-point. The preparation of the Stockholm Conference was seen with fear in developing countries. The dominant feeling there was that "environmental concerns were a neat excuse for the industrialized nations to pull the ladder up behind them." (Rowland 1973, 47) To defuse criticism and prevent the Stockholm Conference from turning into a public failure, Maurice Strong, in charge of its preparation, brought together in Founex, Switzerland, twenty-seven scientists and economists, half of whom were from developing countries. What was striking here was the way the environmental problem was defined:

Environmental problems [first] reflect [in Southern countries] the poverty and very lack of development [...]; life itself is endangered by poor water, housing, sanitation and nutrition [and] these are problems, *no less than those of industrial pollution*, that clamour for attention. (UN Geneva and EPHE 1971, 6-7)

On the other hand, the solution that was advocated was not surprising: environmental problems would eventually be solved "by the process of development itself".[18]

The prevailing tone – and this is essential – was thus congruent with that of the OECD. Despite another definition of what was to be put behind the word "environment", the solution was of the same kind: there is no contradiction between economic development (or growth) and the protection of the environment, and detailed analyses and "trade-offs" need to be negotiated between economic and environmental interests (Handl 2013).

3.2. Environmental economics and the Spaceship Earth

Let me now consider a very small sub-group among economists, the economists specialised in environmental management. To show what they were doing, I will start with a seminar held at the *Resource for the Future Foundation* in 1966. It was

17 Gérard Eldin as quoted by Schmelzer 2013, 298.
18 UN Geneva and EPHE 1971, 6–7 (my emphasis).

organised around a question: Wasn't the destruction of our environment the price to pay for unlimited growth? To what extent could we have a growth policy before we found ourselves up against the impenetrable wall of damage? The framing of the answer was that of Spaceship Earth. An article by Kenneth E. Boulding, entitled "The Economics of the Coming Spaceship Earth", was very influential; often cited, it was radical in its critique of the blindness of mainstream economics (Boulding 1966).

Boulding started from the premise that we must learn how to live in a terrestrial economy without reservoirs of anything, neither for resources nor for discharges. He stated that this system, closed in upon itself, "requires economic principles which are somewhat different from those of the open earth of the past". He noted that this idea was not popular among economists who, for the majority, preferred to continue thinking in terms of "income-flow concepts to the exclusion, almost, of capital-stock concepts". Refusing to draw conclusions from a situation about to occur, they continued to act, says Boulding, as if "production, consumption, throughput, and the GNP were the sufficient and adequate measure of economic success". In brief, he claimed that mainstream economics was epistemologically weak (even if politically strong), and that the economists of the environment were in a position to propose a better form of knowledge.

A Quaker and great moralist before God, Boulding may not have been representative of economists; however, his voice was heard. In 1969, Kneese and Ayres, two other experts in environmental economics, took up the issue again. They insisted on the fact that negative environmental externalities (in particular, pollution) were not local "*freakeries*", as economic theory tended to assume – they were indeed central, since they were the reverse side of the same production and consumption processes; they grew very rapidly in developed countries, in a non-linear manner; the fees that needed to be implemented in order to integrate them in prices would never be sufficient; anyway, theory cannot calculate them, and massive investment (in energy savings, transport systems, waste treatment, etc.) would be necessary, independently of fees. Experts in the flow of materials, they used this knowledge to propose alternative models for economic issues; they noted that the Earth's absorption capacity was real but not infinite, and that it varied depending on pollutants and environments. While concluding about "the impossible difficulty [of planning], both from the standpoint of data collection and computation", they nevertheless thought that this kind of work was necessary. In short, they gave attention to the immensity of concrete questions, to new forms of modelling, to theoretical problems – and they had a clear objective: to take seriously what was then emerging as inevitable on the horizon (Ayres and Kneese 1969).

For Boulding, Kneese and Ayres, the issue of pollution and resources was thus part of what could be described as a "thermodynamic" understanding of economic processes, a vision of an economy also made of flows of materials. This idea was, at first, well received by mainstream economists: Ayres and Kneese published their article in the *American Economic Review*, and Solow himself, who was then one of the most recognised economists (and a Nobel Prize laureate in 1987) stressed its importance; this work, he wrote in 1971, included "an important message that economists have to transmit to others".[19] In the same way, these material-based approaches, which also took into account the differentiated social effects of environment policies, occupied a notable part of debates between economists during OECD seminars. For example, during the 1971 seminar, New York University professor William Baumol stressed the potentially adverse social effects of environmental policies. For his part, Alan Coddington from Queen Mary College in London disputed the fact that norms were less economically efficient than fees, notably in information costs. Along with Pearce and Opschoor, he insisted on the limitations of cost-benefit analyses and the unconvincing nature of the techniques used to evaluate the "benefits" of environmental policies (notably, the "consent to pay" technique). They also insisted on the need for physical analyses through input-output matrixes and material balances through biological and ecological statistical data. "Our fear," they wrote, "is that by adopting [only] cost/benefit analyses, decision makers (...) do not recognize that we are dealing with a closed system." In fact, the most surprising thing about the OECD seminars of 1971 and 1972 is that doubts were strongly present and economic orthodoxy was supported by only a limited number of people.[20]

The trend, however, came to a definitive halt around 1973/74. The discipline of economics no longer worked based upon these approaches – which is clear when comparing the articles published by Solow on this issue in 1971 and in 1973.[21] Another example dates from 1974 with Yale economics professor and vocal opponent to the Club of Rome William D. Nordhaus; he indeed spoke of the shift from "a cowboy economy, where space is unlimited, both in terms of resources to draw from and capacity to store waste, to a spaceship economy, where waste takes away available space and needs to be recycled"; but he did not refer to Kneese or Boulding, whose works were about to be forgotten by the profession; nor did he draw substantial conclusions from these observations. Similarly, the OECD leadership (and the economists who made it) quickly returned to orthodoxy, only focused on fees, forgot the question of limits and did

19 Robert Solow is quoted by Pottier 2014. There is a certain arrogance in Solows sentence since economists are among *the last* to consider the question.
20 The 1971 seminar is published in 1972 under the title *Problèmes d'économie de l'environnement*.
21 Details and references are given in Pottier 2014.

not consider as interesting the variety of positions that emerged during the seminars that they *themselves* had organised.

This clear setback, which was never intellectually justified, seems to be correlated to three events that occurred in quick succession between 1972 and 1974. The first was the intellectual debate launched by the Club of Rome's *Limits to Growth* report, after which economists, industry and politicians mainly repeated that growth was *not* to be limited: nothing was insurmountable and theory showed how to reconcile environmental protection and growth (Thurow 1977). The second event was the oil crisis, which was considered a geopolitical issue. This was not false but such a characterisation helped to erase the central idea of a possible *intrinsic crisis* over resources, of physical limits at Earth level (Hourcade and Combet 2017). The third event was the economic recession that followed, which brought the necessity of growth back to the front of politicians and economists' minds. If we add the inertia of theoretical thinking, in economics as in other fields, we could understand why the Spaceship Earth disappeared from an economic science that could have followed another trajectory.[22]

4. History, Part 2: A business revolution, 1988–1992

The first transformation, around 1970, rested on the claim that economic theory knew how to deal with environmental damage, and the fact that the political authorities (notably the OECD secretary-general and the EU Commissioners) put economists in the leadership position. A second transformation, as important and as massive as the first, occurred around 1988–92. It was essentially different, and amounted, for global business, to putting itself at the centre of the game and declared the ecological modernisation of production. The idea was to act from inside by greening industrial processes and products, and by properly managing resources and waste. In discursive terms, "sustainable development" was the oxymoron that sealed the contract that they proposed – which relied on "responsibility" and the "participation" of all to the "governance" of the world. In other words, a move of global corporations defined by two novelties: on the one hand, they offered to improve environmental action thanks to internal management, audits, labels and certifications – by transforming their core business. This was where environmental problems could best be identified and solved. But this solution also targeted state roles and Keynesian policies and promoted the auton-

---

22 For tensions between environmental and trade economists *inside* the OECD, see Dohlman 1990.

omy of partners engaging freely in contracts. And this solution was built on their new power, which had dramatically increased during the previous decade.[23]

They took their inspiration from the autonomy and firepower that they had accumulated throughout the 1980s, with the multiplication of regional free trade agreements, thanks to the rules which they had been able to impose on countries concerning investment policies, through the privatisation of dispute settlements with states via private arbitration tribunals, through the promotion of good practices against hard law in terms of labour rights, etc.[24] Global corporations, which had become quite powerful entities in a world that they shaped in their own image, undertook, at the turn of the 1990s, to make the business world the nerve centre of a renewed architecture of social relations, the core of a new social contract (Mattli and Woods 2009). In this process, the environmental issue was used as a lever: corporations, witnessing the emergence of a "civil society" concerned with environmental issues, decided to take leadership in the area and advocate sustainable and contractually designed growth.[25]

This "revolution" started at the turn of the 1980s and 1990s, when management gurus such as Luntz and Harrison suggested that companies and political leaders should become *green* and *participative*[26] – since people were becoming so. Between 1988 and 1991, industrial companies, through their professional associations, published hundreds of reports and declarations, and organised dozens and dozens of events. In 1990, for example, the *Coalition for Environmentally Responsible Economics* was established, the *Prince of Wales Business Leaders Forum* considered the question of environmental protection, and the *Global Environmental Management Initiative* was created to transform TQM into Total Quality *Environmental* Management. Along with many other newly created *fora*, they advised companies on the transformations needed to promote sustainable growth.[27]

The preparation of the Rio conference speeded up things. In 1991, the *World Industry Conference on Environmental Management*, organised by the International Chamber of Commerce and UNEP published the *Business Charter for Sustainable Development*; the same year, the *Business Council for Sustainable Development* ("a CEO-led organization of forward-thinking companies that galvanizes the global business community to create a sustainable future") was launched by Stephan Schmidheiny, a Swiss businessman close to Maurice Strong;[28] the International

---

23 The term "governance" appeared for the first time in the World Bank lexicon in 1990. Moretti and Pestre 2015.

24 Mallard and Sgard 2016; Flores-Zendejas 2016; Van Harten and Loughlin 2006; Dezalay and Garth 1996; Dezalay and Garth 2012; Boyer 1996.

25 Chatterjee and Finger 1994; Falkner 2008.

26 Harrison 1992 and 1993; Pestre 2008; Rowell 1996, notably Chapter 4.

27 For details, Pestre (forthcoming): *Environment: The Business Revolution, 1988–1992. Voluntary Commitments, Green Management and Labels*.

28 Schmidheiny (with the BCSD) 1992.

Organization for Standardization set up a working group, which led to the ISO 14000 (environmental) standards (IISD 1996); business environmental audits spread;[29] and state and private funds started to circulate massively *via* NGOs.[30] As a sign of the speed of the transformation, the first *Environmental Strategies Handbook*, prefaced by Schmidheiny himself and more than 1,000 page long, was published in 1994. And the following year *Green, Inc*, appeared, the best-seller by Frances Cairncross, editorialist at the *Economist*.[31]

What we should remember here is that the main global industrial actors changed course in an organised and strategically conceived manner, that they triggered a fast-developing dynamic, that the core of the proposals was made of charters, codes, guidelines and voluntary commitments, that green management was to become "a corporate priority" enabling the implementation of the *Pollution Prevention Pays* principle (they tended not speak anymore of the *Polluter Pays Principle*), and that the right path was joint work with NGOs and governments, for pragmatic and realistic reasons.

In other words, a displacement from a system centred on states and intellectually dominated by economic thinking, to a universe made of voluntary commitments, in which business managers were central; from economic instruments to management, recycling and labels; from "national economies" to the "global market place"; from the political as the legitimate space for regulation to "distributed" arrangements built according to opportunities, favouring free contracting and private law-making.

One should finally realise that the environmental policies set up in the 1970s and 1980s appeared, at the turn of 1990s, to be quite inefficient before the exponential growth of production and consumption caused by globalisation – and of the pollution that mechanically derived from them. The OECD expressed itself in this manner in 1990 and suggested abandoning the idea of controlling industrial waste at the "end of pipe"; it instead promoted radical changes in producing processes – which might explain why business proposals were welcomed by many at the time. Nothing proves that what they did reversed the trend, on the contrary, but it did open another discursive and practical world made of sustainable growth, responsibility commitments and shared governance.

---

29 ICC 1991; Smart 1992; UNEP IE 1992; UNEP IE 1994.
30 Goldman 2005; Park and Vetterlein 2010.
31 Kolluru 1994; Cairncross 1995. For international trade, Anderson and Blackhurst 1992.

5. As a way of conclusion: What sort of arrangement for which sort of hegemony?

In order to capture the implications of the business move of the late 1980s, and to come to broader conclusions, I suggest beginning from an observation: the victory of business around 1990. It had managed to become autonomous at global level, and, from then on, was in a position to define the rules and knowledge that counted at that level. Environmental protests, particularly vivid around 1988-1992, showed that the victory of this form of globalisation was not complete, however: industrial practices encountered opposition among educated élites for whom the defence of Gaïa and the climate were essential.[32] The "social question" was no longer threatening the hegemony of the business world, as in previous decades, but environmental damage was doing it; and it seemed preferable to those speaking on behalf of industry to propose solutions and tame environmental protest.

In keeping with what they had advocated for the previous fifteen years, global corporations proposed to create, on environmental issues, a world of *private solutions and lawmaking* – a world without mandatory norms. And the starting-point consisted of promoting agreements with organised NGOs about "sustainable" products and processes – to define the future jointly.[33]

Many people have interpreted this move as the creation of a *sustainable development historical bloc*.[34] If we understand hegemony (or historical *bloc*) as a strategically designed alignment of social and interest groups; if we understand hegemony as values and knowledge shared by members of these "coalitions"; and if we also understand here the creation of a new conception of the social and political order – then we can reasonably see, between 1988 and 1992, the emergence of a new form of hegemony which was trying to take over, different from the post-World War Two one. Things are, however, more complex, since companies are not a homogenous *bloc*. The business world has no head or hierarchy, it is divided by antagonistic interests and is not as consistent as the world of politics, which is based upon the legitimacy of elections and the verticality of the state apparatus. This led to strategies that varied from company to company and depended on their technological advantages, the activity sectors in which they operate, the political options of their leaders, and on the historical differences between Europe and the United States.[35]

---

32 On the role and action of environmental NGOs (and, in particular, the *Big Ten*) in the United States, Gottlieb 1993.

33 Abbott and Snydal 2009 provide a detailed analysis of the intellectual/political games in those negotiations.

34 Levy and Newell 2002; Sklair 2001.

35 Schreurs 2002; Wurzel et al. 2003; Vig and Faure 2004; Toke and Lauber 2007; Kelemen and Vogel 2010.

Environmental pressure was, for example, highest on the energy, motor car, cement, aluminium, steel, chemistry, and paper sectors. Here, there was a permanent temptation to weigh on the public and political space and launch disinformation campaigns – in parallel to publicly accepting the charters of the International Chamber of Commerce. And Exxon, Texaco, General Motors and Ford, among others, played a key role in the creation of the *Global Climate Coalition* in 1989, whose goal was to create doubt about climate science. Such strategies of denying or minimising the existence of problems were brought into prominence when Republicans endorsed climate denial in the mid-1990s; and it has remained central in American politics since then – Donald Trump today being the latest proof of it.[36]

This development brings about two possibilities. On a global level, as the United States is obviously not the whole world, nothing enables us to say that denegation will generalise and become the norm. The worsening climate crisis and its impact (on floods, for example), the increased attention given to the environment in China and India, the persistence of the preoccupation with the state of the environment among major companies (including in the United States; in California, for example) – like the continuation of strong protests – may lead to the sustainable growth paradigm advocated by companies at the turn of 1990s becoming hegemonic again. In that case, the developments in the United States today may have only been a contained deviation, possibly linked to stakeholders in decline (such as coal industries) (Levy and Egan 2003).[37]

But one should certainly avoid over-hastiness. The persistent economic difficulties and challenges of unemployment, the extreme development of social inequalities, and the sense of abandonment felt by many populations are as cruel today on one side of the Atlantic as on the other. The most pauperised populations and regions, both in the United States and in Europe, are also the most sceptical about the reality of climate change and the urgency of action.[38] And if the currently emerging political expressions of the Trump type (or Austrian or Italian types) were to become electorally successful at world level, environmental protection could be seriously weakened – and, with it, the proposal of hegemony that most industry representatives tried to put in place in the late 1980s.

---

36 Dunlap 2008; Hoffman and Forbes 2011.
37 They, for example, comment "that the change in the US fossil fuel industry's position is attributable to endogenous dynamics, including a series of strategic miscalculations, interactions with events in Europe, and shifts in the discursive, organizational, and economic spheres".
38 Scruggs and Benegal 2012; Hennes et al. 2016.

References

Abbott, Kenneth W., and Duncan Snidal (2009): "The Governance Triangle: Regulatory Standards Institutions and the Shadow of the State." In: Walter Mattli and Ngaire Woods: *The Politics of Global Regulation*, 44–88. Princeton NJ: Princeton University Press.

Anderson, Kym, and Richard Blackhurst (1992): *The Greening of World Trade Issues*. New York: Harvester Wheatsheaf.

Ayres, Robert U., and Allen V. Kneese (1969): "Production, Consumption, and Externalities." *The American Economic Review*, 59 (3): 282–297.

Barde, Jean-Philippe, and Emilio Gerelli (1977): *Economie et politique de l'environnement*. Paris: PUF.

Bartley, Tim (2007): "Institutional Emergence in an Era of Globalization. The Rise of Transnational Private Regulation of Labor and Environmental Conditions." *American Journal of Sociology*, 113 (2): 297–351.

Baya-Laffite, Nicolas (2015): "Gouverner par la promesse du développement durable. Évaluation d'impact environnemental et Meilleures Techniques Disponibles dans le conflit des usines de pâte à papier sur le fleuve Uruguay." Doctoral Dissertation, Paris: École des hautes études en sciences sociales.

Blanc, Guillaume (2015): *Une histoire environnementale de la nation. Regards croisés sur les parcs nationaux du Canada, d'Ethiopie et de France*. Paris: Publications de la Sorbonne.

Bohm, Peter, and Allen. V. Kneese (1971): *The Economics of Environment*. New York: St Martin Press.

Bonneuil, Christophe, and Jean-Baptiste Fressoz (2016): *The Shock of the Anthropocene. The Earth, History and Us*. London-New York: Verso Books.

Boudia, Soraya (2014): "Gouverner par les instruments économiques. La trajectoire de l'analyse coût-bénéfice dans l'action publique." In: Dominique Pestre (Ed.): *Le gouvernement des technosciences. Gouverner le progrès et ses dégâts depuis 1945*, 231–260. Paris: La Découverte.

Boudia, Soraya (2016): "Des instruments pour mettre en économie l'environnement. L'économicisation par approximation et occultation." *Ecologie & politique*, 52: 45–61.

Boudia, Soraya, and Emmanuel Henry (Eds.) (2015): *La mondialisation des risques*. Rennes: Presses Universitaires de Rennes.

Boulding, Kenneth E. (1966): "The Economics of the Coming Spaceship Earth." In: Henry Jarrett (Ed.): *Environmental Quality in a Growing Economy*, 3–14. Baltimore MD: Resources for the Future, Johns Hopkins University Press.

Bouleau, Gabrielle (2011): *Ambiguïtés du leadership européen sur l'environnement. Ecological Modernisation: Construction and Biases of a European Environmental Ideology*. Available at: https://hal.archives-ouvertes.fr/hal-00750172, last accessed January 2019.

Boyer, Robert (1996): "State and Market: A New Engagement for the Twenty-First Century?" In: Robert Boyer and Daniel Drache (Eds.): *States against Markets: The Limits of Globalization*, 62–85. London and New York: Routledge.

Burchfield, Joe D. (1975, 1990): *Lord Kelvin and the Age of the Earth*. Chicago IL: Chicago UniversityPress.

Cairncross, Frances (1995): *Green, Inc. A Guide to Business and the Environment*. London: Earthscan Publications.

Chatterjee, Pratap, and Matthias Finger (1994): *The Earth Brokers*. London: Routledge.

Cheyns, Emmanuelle (2011): "Multi-stakeholder Initiatives for Sustainable Agriculture: Limits of the 'Inclusiveness' Paradigm." In: Stefano Ponte et al. (Eds.): *Governing through Standards: Origins, Drivers and Limitations*, 210–235. Basingstoke: Palgrave Macmillan.

Cook, Brian J. (1988): *Bureaucratic Politics and Regulatory Reform: The EPA and Emission Trading*. New York: Greenwood.

Dezalay, Yves, and Bryant Garth (1996): *Dealing in Virtue: International Commercial Arbitration and the Construction of a Transnational Legal Order*. Chicago IL: Chicago University Press.

Dezalay, Yves, and Bryant Garth (2012): "Corporate Law Firms, NGOs, and Issues of Legitimacy for a Global Legal Order." *Fordham Law Review*, 80 (6): 2309–2345.

DG Environment (2004): *Comparison of the EU and US Approaches towards Acidification, Euthrophication and Ground Level Ozone*, 4 October 2004, available at: http://ec.europa.eu/environment/archives/cafe/activities/pdf/case_study1.pdf, last accessed January 2019.

Dohlman, Ebba (1990): "The Trade Effects of Environmental Regulation." *The OECD Observer*, February-March: 28–32.

Driesen, David M. (2003): *Does Emissions Trading Encourage Innovation?* Washington DC, DC: Environmental Law Institute. Available at: http://www.eli.org, last accessed January 2019.

Dunlap, Riley E. (2008): *Climate-Change Views: Republican-Democratic Gaps Expand*, 29 May, available at: http://www.gallup.com/poll/107569/climatechange-views-republican democratic-gaps-expand.aspx, last accessed January 2019.

Ercmann, Sevine (1996): "Enforcement of Environmental Law in United States and European Law: Realities and Expectations." *Environmental Law*, 26 (4): 1213–1239.

Falkner, Robert (2008): *Business Power and Conflict in International Environmental Politics*. London: Palgrave.

Ferguson, James (2005): "Seeing like an Oil Company: Space, Security, and Global Capital in Neoliberal Africa." *American Anthropologist*, 107 (3): 377–382.

Flores-Zendejas, Juan (2016): "Financial Markets, International Organizations and Conditional Lending: A Long-term Perspective. In: Grégoire Mallard and Jérôme Sgard (Eds.): *Contractual Knowledge: One Hundred Years of Legal Experimentation in Global Markets*, 61–91. New York: Cambridge University Press.

Foucart, Stéphane (2015): "Failles dans l'homologation de six OGM en Europe." *Le Monde*, 15 Octobre 2015.

Fourcade, Marion (2011): "Cents and Sensibility: Economic Valuation and the Nature of 'Nature'." *American Journal of Sociology*, 116 (6): 1721–1777.

Fressoz, Jean-Baptiste, and Dominique Pestre (2013): "Critique historique du satisfecit-postmoderne. Risque et 'société du risque' depuis deux siècles." In: Dominique Bourg et al. (Eds.): *Du risque à la menace. Penser la catastrophe*, 19–56. Paris: PUF.

Glasbergen, Pieter, and Greetje Schouten (2011): "Creating legitimacy in global private governance. The case of the Roundtable on Sustainable Palm Oil." *Ecological Economics*, 70 (11): 1891–1899.

Goldman, Michael (2005): *Imperial Nature: The World Bank and Struggles for Social Justice in the Age of Globalization*. New Haven CT: Yale University Press.

Gottlieb, Robert (1993): *Forcing the Spring: The Transformation of the American Environmental Movement*. Washington DC: Island Press.

Green, Mark, and John F. Berry (1985): "White-collar Crime is Big Business." *The Nation 240*, 8 June 1985: 689.

Grevsmühl, Sebastian (2014): *La Terre vue d'enhaut*. Paris: Seuil.

Habermas, Jürgen (1985): *The Theory of Communicative Action*. Vol. 2, *Lifeword and System: A Critique of Functionalist Reason*. Boston MA: The Beacon Press.

Hajduk, Thomas (2013): "A Code to Bind them all. The Multinational Dilemma and the Endeavour for an International Code of Conduct." In: Sandra Brändli et al. (Eds.): *Multinationale Unternehmen und Institutionen im Wandel – Herausforderungen für Wirtschaft, Recht und Gesellschaft*, 311–339. Berlin: Stämpfli.

Handl, Günther (2013): *Environment: Les déclarations de Stockholm (1972) et Rio (1992)* available at: http://legal.un.org/avl/pdf/ha/dunche/dunche_f.pdf, last accessed January 2019.

Van Harten, Gus, and Martin Loughlin (2006): "Investment Treaty Arbitration as a Species of Global Administrative Law." *The European Journal of International Law*, 17 (1): 121–150.

Harrison, E. Bruce (1992): *Environmental Communication and Public Relations Handbook*. Government Institute, 2nd edition.

Harrison, E. Bruce (1993): *Going Green: How to Communicate Your Company's Environmental Commitment*. Burr Ridge IL: Irwin Professional Publishing.

Hays, Samuel P. (2000): *A History of Environmental Politics Since 1945*. Pittsburgh PA: University of Pittsburgh Press.

Hennes, Erin P. et al. (2016): "Motivated Recall in the Service of the Economic System: The Case of Anthropogenic Climate Change." *Journal of Experimental Psychology*, 145 (6): 755–771.

Hoffman, Andrew J., and Melissa Forbes (2011): "The Culture and Discourse of Climate Skepticism", *Strategic Organization*, 9 (1): 77–84, available at: http://www.eenews.net/assets/2010/11/12/document_cw_01.pdf, last accessed January 2019.

Högselius, Per, et al. (2016): *Europe's Infrastructure Transition. Economy, War, Nature*. Basingstoke: Palgrave Macmillan.

Hourcade, Jean-Charles, and Emmanuel Combet (2017): *Fiscalité carbone et finance climat. Un contrat social pour notre temps*. Paris: Les petits matins/Institut Veblen.

Huchet, Jean-François (2016): *La crise environnementale en Chine: Evolutions et limites des politiques publiques*. Paris: Presses de Sciences Po.

ICC (1991): *ICC Guide to Effective Environmental Auditing*, Paris: ICC Publishing.

IISD (1996): *Global Green Standards: ISO 14000*. Winnipeg, Manitoba: IISD.

Janković, Vladimir, and Andrew Bowman (2014): "After the Green Gold Rush: The Construction of Climate Change as a Market Transition." *Economy and Society*, 43 (2): 233–259.

Jas, Nathalie (2014): "Gouverner les substances chimiques dangereuses dans les espaces internationaux." In: Dominique Pestre (Ed.): *Le gouvernement des technosciences. Gouverner le progrès et ses dégâts depuis 1945*, 31–63. Paris: La Découverte.

Kaiser, David, and Lee Wasserman (2016): "The Rockefeller Family Fund vs. Exxon." *The New York Review of Books*. 8 December 2016: 22.

Kelemen, R. Daniel, and David Vogel (2010): "Trading Places: The Role of the United States and the European Union in International Environmental Politics." *Comparative Political Studies*, 43 (4): 427–456.

Kelman, Steven (1981): "Cost-Benefit Analysis. An Ethical Critique." *Regulation, AEI Journal on Government and Society*, January-February: 33–40.

Kolluru, Rao V. (Ed.) (1994): *Environmental Strategies Handbook*. New York: McGraw-Hill.

Levy, David L., and Peter J. Newell (2002): "Business Strategy and International Environmental Governance: Toward a Neo-Gramscian Synthesis." *Global Environmental Politics*, 2 (4): 84–101.

Levy, David L., and Daniel Egan (2003): "A Neo-Gramscian Approach to Corporate Political Strategy: Conflict and Accommodation in the Climate Change Negotiations." *Journal of Management Studies*, 40 (4): 803–829.

Long, Bill L. (2000): *International Environmental Issues and the OECD, 1950–2000. An Historical Perspective*. Paris: OECD.

Mallard, Grégoire, and Jérôme Sgard (Eds.) (2016): *Contractual Knowledge: One Hundred Years of Legal Experimentation in Global Markets*. New York: Cambridge University Press.

Manulak, M.W. (2017): "Developing World Environmental Cooperation. The Founex Seminar and the Stockholm Conference." In: Wolfram Kaiser and Jan-Henrik Meyer (Eds.): *International Organizations and Environmental Protection. Conservation and Globalization in the Twentieth Century*, 103–127. New York: Berghahn.

Marx, Axel (2010): "Global Governance and the Certification Revolution." Leuven Center for Global Governance Studies, Working Paper 53, available at: http://papers.ssrn.com/sol3/papers.cfm?abstract_id=1764563, last accessed January 2019.

Mattli, Walter, and Ngaire Woods (2009): *The Politics of Global Regulation*. Princeton NJ: Princeton University Press.

Meyer, Jan-Henrik (2017): "Making the Polluter Pay. How the European Communities Established Environmental Protection." In: Wolfram Kaiser and Jan-Henrik Meyer (Eds.): *International Organizations and Environmental Protection. Conservation and Globalization in the Twentieth Century*, 183–210. New York: Berghahn.

Moretti, Franco, and Dominique Pestre (2015): "Bankspeak: The Language of World Bank Reports." *New Left Review*, 92: 75–99.

OECD (1972): *Problèmes d'économie de l'environnement*, Paris.

OECD (1985): *Environments and Economics*, Paris.

Oreskes, Naomi, and Erik M. Conway (2010): *Merchants of Doubt: How a Handful of Scientists Obscured the Truth on Issues from Tobacco Smoke to Global Warming*, London: Bloomsbury.

Park, Susan, and Antje Vetterlein (2010): *Owning Development: Creating Policy Norms in the IMF and the World Bank*. Cambridge: Cambridge University Press.

Pestre, Dominique (2000): "The Art of Science or How to constantly (Re)invent Nature and Mask Humain Ingenuity. In: Helga Nowotny and Martina Weiss (Eds.): *Shifting Boundaries of the Real: Making the Invisible Visible*, 97–110. Zurich: Collegium Helveticum in der Semper-Sternwarte.

Pestre, Dominique (2008): "Challenges for the Democratic Management of Technoscience: Governance, Participation and the Political Today." *Science as Culture*, 17 (2): 101–119.

Pestre, Dominique (forthcoming): "Environment: The Business Revolution, 1988–1992. Voluntary Commitments, Green Management and Labels." *Economy and Society*.

Petrini, Francesco (2011): "Who'll Stop the Runaway Shop? The Battle to Regulate the Multinational's Activities in the EEC at the Dawn of Globalization." EUSA 12th Biennial International Conference, Boston, 3–5 March 2011.

Pottier, Antonin (2014): *L'économie dans l'impasse climatique: développement matériel, théorie immatérielle et utopie auto-stabilisatrice*, Ph.D, Paris: EHESS.

Roslansky, John D. (Ed.) (1967): *The Control of Environment. A Discussion at the Nobel Conference*. Amsterdam: North Holland.

Rowell, Andrew (1996): *Green Backlash: The Global Subversion of Environmental Movement*. London: Routledge.

Rowland, Wade (1973): *The Plot to Save the World: The Life and Times of the Stockholm Conference on the Human Environment*. Toronto: Clarke, Irwin & Co.

Ruysschaert, Denis, and Denis Salles (2014): "Towards Global Voluntary Standards: Questioning the Effectiveness in Attaining Conservation Goals. The Case of the Roundtable on Sustainable Palm Oil (RSPO)." *Ecological Economics*, 107: 438–446.

Schmelzer, Matthias (2012): "The Crisis before the Crisis: The 'Problems of Modern Society' and the OECD, 1968–74." *European Review of History/Revue européenne d'histoire*, 19 (6): 999–1020.

Schmelzer, Matthias (2013): *The Hegemony of Growth. The Making and Remaking of the Growth Paradigm and the OEEC/OECD, 1948–1974*. Ph.D. Frankfurt a.d. Oder: Europa-Universität Viadrina.

Schmidheiny, Stephan (with the BCSD) (1992): *Changing Course. A Global Business Perspective on Development and the Environment*. Cambridge MA: The MIT Press.

Schreurs, Miranda (2002): *Environmental Politics in Japan, Germany, and the United States*. Cambridge: Cambridge University Press.

Scruggs, Lyle, and Salil Benegal (2012): "Declining Public Concern about Climate Change: Can we Blame the Great Recession?" *Global Environmental Change*, 22 (2): 505–515.

Short, Jodi (2012): *The Paranoid Style in Regulatory Reform*. Washington DC: Georgetown University.

Sklair, Leslie (2001): *The Transnational Capitalist Class*. Oxford: Blackwell.

Smart, Bruce (1992): *Beyond Compliance: A New Industry View of the Environment*. Washington DC: World Resources Institute.

Taylor, Peter J., and Frederick H. Buttel (1992): "How do we Know we have Global Environmental Problems? Science and the Globalization of Environmental Discourse." *Geoforum*, 23 (3): 401–416.

Thurow, Lester C. (1977): "The Implications of Zero Economic Growth." *Challenge*, 20 (1): 36–43.

Toke, David, and Volkmar Lauber (2007): "Anglo-Saxon and German Approaches to Neoliberalism and Environmental Policy: The Case of Financing Renewable Energy." *Geoforum*, 38: 677–687.

UNEP IE (1992): *From Regulations to Industry Compliance*. Technical Report no. 11.

UNEP IE (1994): *Company Environmental Reporting*, Technical Report no. 24.

UN Geneva, and EPHE (VIe section) (1971): *Development and Environment. Report and Working Paper of a Panel of Experts (…)*. Founex: Switzerland: 4–12 June 1971.

Valo, Martine (2016): "Pesticides en hausse dans les campagnes françaises." *Le Monde*, 10 March 2016.

Valo, Martine (2017): "La qualité de l'eau se dégrade encore en France." *Le Monde*, 18 October 2017.

Vig, Norman J., and Michael G. Faure (2004): *Green Giants? Environmental Policies of the United States and the European Union*. Cambridge MA: The MIT Press.

Wurzel, Rüdiger K.W. et al. (2003): "From High Regulatory State to Social and Ecological Market Economy? New Environmental Policy Instruments in Germany." *Environmental Politics*, 12 (1): 115–136.

Knowledge Production with Climate Models: On the Power of a "Weak" Type of Knowledge

Matthias Heymann

Abstract

From the early 1950s, computer simulation was quickly adopted in the atmospheric sciences. Successes in weather and climate simulation increased the attraction and authority of this approach. From the 1970s, the prediction of climate change based upon model simulations became an important goal. The way to climate modelling and prediction, however, was neither straightforward nor linear, but involved competition, disagreement, conflict and negotiation. The inherent uncertainties in simulation approaches to predict future climate changed raised controversy about the validity of simulation models and results. Was knowledge production with climate models a weak type of knowledge? Was it appropriate to simulate future projections of climate change, in spite of the uncertainties and limits of climate models, and make use of that knowledge in the public and for political purposes? This chapter discusses how the competition between different research interests and directions and different scientific norms played out in the development of climate modelling and climate prediction. It focuses on the formative period of climate prediction in the 1970s and shows that scientists in the USA and in the UK disagreed deeply about the power of climate simulation and its use for the prediction of climate change.

1. Introduction

Climate modelling has become a powerful and influential research direction. It serves to model and simulate atmospheric and climate processes and provide an understanding of changes of climate over time. Currently, it is best-known for simulating projections of climate change for many decades and even centuries into the future (Figure 1).

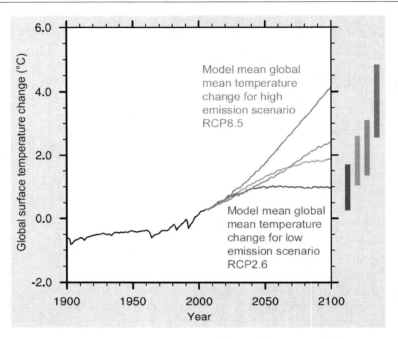

Figure 1: Climate projections to the year 2100 by the IPCC (2013, 1037).

Such projections serve to analyse the possible development of future climate and to inform policy-makers and the public about future climate change. Graphical depictions of such projections have become iconic images of the representation of global climate change. In our current project, entitled "Shaping Cultures of Prediction: Knowledge, Authority and the Construction of Climate Change", we propose to investigate the production of climate projections as a historical phenomenon.[1] Why did scientists take an interest in quantifying future climate for decades and centuries ahead, for periods of time which most of those alive today will not experience, and which cannot take account of many unforeseeable events that have an impact on climatic development and human culture? Why did scientists trust that this was reliable and useful information? Why did such information and the practices behind it gain scientific and social authority?

The way to climate modelling and prediction was neither straightforward nor linear, but involved competition, disagreement, conflict and negotiation. In this chapter, I will re-visit the well-established narrative about the emergence of meteorology and climatology as sciences based upon the laws of physics from Vilhelm Bjerknes to numerical weather prediction and climate modelling and offer a more complicated one. The established narrative has emphasised the *struggles of*

---

1 This contribution draws on the work of the whole project team Janet Martin Nielsen, Gabriel D. Henderson and Dania Achermann.

scientists with the complexities of the atmosphere and described how scientists – in the context of the Cold War and ample research funding – managed to tackle the enormous scientific challenges of realising computer-based weather and climate modelling and prediction.[2] I would like to shift this narrative to include the *struggles of scientists with each other, and their dissenting scientific convictions, values and identities,* and include the junctions and decisions taken, and the debates and controversies about the directions taken and the practices which they involved.

If we portray the professional trajectories of climate researchers in the post-WWII era, they all take their departure in scientific interests in climate, but lead in very different directions. Figure 2 represents a rough sketch of selected research trajectories and serves as a starting-point in our project.

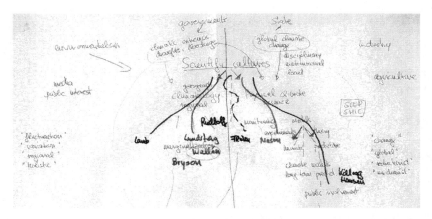

Figure 2: Hand drawn sketch of different professional trajectories of climatologists and climate scientists in the Post-WWII era (drawn during a project meeting and discussion by the author in autumn 2013).

It shows that some scientists pursued the strong geography-oriented research directions that had dominated in traditional climatology (the trajectories to the left, for example, show Hubert Horace Lamb in the UK and Helmut Landsberg in the USA). Others took an interest in the mathematical modelling of physical processes in the atmosphere (the trajectories to the right, for example, Syukuro Manabe and Norman Phillips in the USA, and Basil John Mason in the UK). Some scientists, such as William Welch Kellogg, Stephen H. Schneider and James E. Hansen, even sought to use climate modelling for the prediction of future climate. The figure is not comprehensive. It only represents notable examples and aims to highlight the diversity of directions and research interests, but it is nevertheless revealing. These trajectories not only represent different research interests, but also deep disagreement about epistemic values and standards. They sig-

---

2 Harper 2008; Edwards 2010; Fleming 2016; Weart 2008 and 2010; Heymann 2010b.

nify more than scientific ideas and directions, but represent different, partly inconsistent, scientific *cultures*.[3]

Climate modelling has played a major role in forging a scientific consensus about climatic change, and, according to a range of authors, plays a hegemonic role in climate science.[4] On the other hand, this scientific consensus and hegemonic character tends to hide the social relations, complex negotiations, and tangible interests underlying the consensus itself. It flattens the diversity of scientific perceptions and the complexities of historical processes that have shaped it. Historical investigation of research into problems of climate reveals that a large *variety* of interests in climate and *directions* in climate research existed. Scientists pursued radically different directions investigating climate and subscribed to very different epistemic values and standards.[5] Assessments about the epistemic strength of research directions and types of knowledge were dependent on the relative perspective of specific scientific cultures. Such assessments depend on fundamental decisions about which types of knowledge are important, which epistemic standards are used to judge this knowledge, and which applications of this knowledge are regarded as useful and socially relevant.

In addition, disagreement about the epistemic strength of climate models raises the question of whether knowledge based upon climate modelling represents a strong or weak type of knowledge and what the labels "strong" and "weak" may possibly mean. One the one hand, this type of climate knowledge appears to be a strong type of knowledge in several ways. It carries the authority of almost universal acceptance in the relevant scientific communities, as is powerfully documented in the influential reports by the Intergovernmental Panel on Climate Change (IPCC). While dissenting voices still exist today, they mostly belong to scientists not directly involved in climate research or originate from political, rather than scientific, motivations.[6] Furthermore, climate knowledge based upon climate modelling has a very strong social and political impact, has given rise to numerous conferences at the highest political level, has spurred extraordinary media coverage and has supported the establishment and institutionalisation of an extended political negotiation regime.[7] On the other hand, climate knowledge based upon climate modelling may, arguably, be considered to be a weak type of knowledge. It is subject to irreducible, even unquantifiable, uncertainties.[8] Climate models are inherently complex, opaque and, only to a limited degree, accessible to empirical validation. Results in climate simulation – and atmospheric simulation in general – depend on a very large number of computations and ap-

---

3 Heymann et al. 2017, particularly Chapter 2; Fine 2007.
4 Shackley et al. 1998; Hulme 2008.
5 Heymann 2009 and 2010a.
6 Oreskes et al. 2004; Oreskes and Conway 2010.
7 Luterbacher and Sprinz 2001; especially Bodansky 2001.
8 van der Sluijs 1997; Shackley et al. 1998; Lahsen 2005; Petersen 2006.

proximations. If model results compare well with data based upon empirical observation, it is not easily possible to decide whether they do so for the right or the wrong reasons.[9]

I will describe the scientific cultures of climate modelling and prediction by the emergence and stabilisation of specific codes, which characterise these cultures. I use the concept of "code" broadly, as comprising cultural elements with strong symbolic meaning, such as foundational interests, concepts, language, practices, approaches, values, standards and rules.[10] Codes in science comprise all kinds of representations which carry meaning, inform behaviour, align practice and contribute to create coherence. The narrative which I suggest highlights the contested character of these codes, and shows that these codes and their authority were in competition with others. The investigation of different codes and cultures in the history of climate research shows that there was usually no agreement on the epistemic strength of different types of climate knowledge. Scientists disagreed on the epistemic status of scientific approaches and claims. Their assessments were dependent on the scientific cultures in which they were raised and of which they felt to be a part.

2. Taking off: The formation of a heuristic research programme (1945–1970)

In 1904, the Norwegian physicist Vilhelm Bjerknes formulated the basic, so-called primitive equations: non-linear, partial differential equations, which, in principle, described the state of the atmosphere in every point in space and time. Bjerknes wanted to elevate meteorology to a quantitative science based upon the laws of physics and thereby open the perspective of weather prediction. These equations proved a foundational step for the further development of dynamic meteorology.[11] They represented a powerful code for the development of a new culture in weather and climate science. First, the primitive equations bore the promise of a comprehensive physical understanding of the atmosphere and represented a boost for dynamic meteorology. Second, with this promise, the primitive equations carried the revolutionary power to reverse priorities in meteorology and climatology. Both disciplines were characterised by a strong empirical tradition of data collection and a bottom-up research strategy which aimed at accumulating an archive of data as a basis for the understanding of atmospheric

---

9 Oreskes et al. 1994; Lenhard and Winsberg 2010.

10 One of the definitions of code offered by the *Oxford English Dictionary* is "a system or collection of rules or regulations on any subject" (1933, vol. II, 582).

11 Bjerknes 1904/2009; Gramelsberger 2009; Friedman 1989.

phenomena. Theorists such as Bjerknes attempted to overcome the limitations of this bottom-up approach with the help of physical theory. Third, climatology was a discipline strongly interested in the interactions of human beings and climate: in questions related not only to climate and agriculture, climate and human health, but also to the impact of human action on local climates. The primitive equations effectively cancelled human affairs out of the equation – another far-reaching example of physical reductionism.[12]

While the primitive equations represented a powerful code, just as important were their limitations. The fact that the primitive equations had no analytical solutions strongly reduced their effectiveness and required the means of approximation, which was usually an accepted circumvention of an *impasse*, of a blocking impediment in scientific practice. Scientists prefer to be exact, however, and usually take exactitude as a norm of their profession. Approximation forces compromise with exactitude. In atmospheric modelling and simulation, approximation became a necessity, an unavoidable need, another code, we might say, of post-WWII modelling practice. The first to attempt to make the primitive equations operational with the help of approximation was the British scientist Lewis Fry Richardson.[13]

During World War I, Richardson applied a numerical approximation scheme for solving the primitive equations in order to calculate a weather prediction. In practice, this meant the introduction of a geographical grid and solving the equations numerically for grid elements instead of individual points (Figure 3). Such a grid represented a move from local precision to averaged information. Grid-based numerical approximation was to become another foundational code in atmospheric modelling and simulation. All weather and climate modelling requires numerical approximation over a pre-defined geographical grid. Richardson's attempt failed (his calculations turned out to be wrong and were so laborious that numerical approximation of the primitive equations proved ineffective when computed by humans). But he paved the way for the theory-based top-down approaches and numerical approximation by future generations with the help of non-human computers.

---

12 Bjerknes was certainly not the only scientists contributing to the physicalization of the atmosphere. Gunnar Ellingsen has recently argued that the unusual historiographic recognition that he and his famous Bergen School of Meteorology received strongly overrates his role. Ellingsen 2016; see, also, Friedman 1989.

13 Richardson 1922, iii; Lynch 2006.

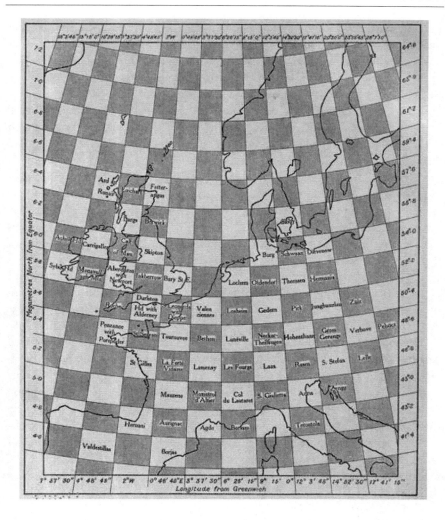

Figure 3: A representation of the grid on which Lewis Fry Richardson performed his numerical approximation of a weather prediction for 20 May 1910 (1922, ii).

The primacy of reductionism and approximation, which today is so plausible to atmospheric scientists, represented a significant revolution. It was deeply suspect to empirical-minded scientists, who based their scientific wisdom primarily upon careful and detailed observation. The well-known story of young British engineer Guy Stewart Callendar's climate theory is an instructive example.[14] During the 1930s, Callendar developed a theory of global warming to explain the significant warming phenomena that had been observed in the Northern Hemisphere. Buil-

---

14 For a biographical account of Callendar, see Fleming 2007.

ding on work about the greenhouse effect by Joseph Fourier, John Tyndall and Svante Arrhenius, he re-worked the theory of infrared radiative transfer and calculated a warming that roughly fit with observational temperature data. The majority of climatologists, however, questioned the explanatory power of Callendar's theory and his conclusions, and remained very reluctant to accept his far-reaching claims. When Callendar presented his calculations at the Royal Meteorological Society in London in 1938, the objections were manifold. Callendar only focused on infrared radiative transfer, and failed to consider any other meteorological and climatological processes and all geographical detail. George Simpson, director of the Meteorological Office in London, concluded that the increase in carbon dioxide and temperature "must be taken as rather a coincidence". The observed rise in temperature "was probably only [...] one of the peculiar variations which all meteorological elements experienced" (Callendar 1938, 237). This episode shows that it was not an easy task for theoreticians to establish epistemic authority of their codes of scientific practice, even if some features and patterns matched observations. Climatologists, immersed in a tradition of studying a great wealth of detailed data, placed great emphasis on local difference and diversity and – even decades later – were highly suspicious of generalised "big" explanations, such as global climate change, as suggested by Callendar.[15]

Immediately after WWII, decisive efforts for the development of improved weather prediction with the help of computers were made. Scientists such as Vladimir Zworykin, John von Neumann and Carl Gustav Rossby grasped the unique combination of technical chance (the development of computers) and funding opportunity (by military agencies). They boldly sold the perspective of developing the ability to manipulate weather and climate (Rosol 2017). The objective of weather prediction was only a means to achieve more: the manipulation of weather and climate – a goal that certainly was of interest to military agencies. Climate and weather modification became a deeply entrenched code for the framing of issues of and interests in climate during the early years of the Cold War. This was to dominate research on weather and climate in the USA for the next 20 years (Fleming 2010). Von Neumann's and Rossby's approach to weather prediction focused on solving simplified versions of the primitive equations. Even though computers promised to offer enormous computational power, the mastering of the primitive equations for numerical weather prediction was so demanding in terms of computing power that it still required radical simplifications. It was not clear from the outset, however, which approach would be effective and epistemically justified. Rossby took a radically pragmatic approach. He pondered that a short-term prediction over a few days did not require the inclusion of processes which had relevance only on timescales that were of longer duration. This was the

---

15 von Rudloff [1670] 1982; Lamb 1982.

starting-point for the barotropic model, which neglected vertical movements of the air.

British meteorologist Reginald Sutcliffe, in contrast, Assistant Director and Head of Forecasting Research at the UK Meteorological Office from 1948, demanded a baroclinic approach which did include vertical motion. Sutcliffe considered precipitation, which depended on vertical motion, as the essence of weather forecasting. Both Rossby and Sutcliffe pursued different philosophies and disagreed deeply. In practice, the more realistic ambition of UK meteorologists turned out to be a great disadvantage and threw British attempts to realise numerical weather prediction many years back. While Sutcliffe had no confidence in Rossby's radical simplification, it was Rossby's approach that paved the way for success. The baroclinic approach was still proving much too demanding for what computer-based numerical modelling approaches could master at this point in time.[16] Rossby's radical pragmatism became another foundational code in computer-based atmospheric modelling. Limits of data, knowledge and computing power forced the modellers to accept drastic simplifications and approximations, even if they were knowingly – and to the dismay of many theoretical physicists and meteorologists – not realistic.

The ideal operator in order to pursue and realise Rossby's ideas and develop them further proved to be the young meteorologist Jule Charney, a close associate and friend of Rossby, who led the Princeton Meteorology Project to develop numerical weather prediction. As has often been narrated, Charney and his team determinedly pursued Rossby's barotropic approach and famously finished their first successful simulations in 1950.[17] The historian of science Amy Dahan Dalmedico has shown that Charney was instrumental in establishing a heuristic approach to computer-based numerical simulation. Following Rossby, he did not shy away from radical simplification of meteorological models for experimental reasons. As Charney explained later (in 1972):

The computer is used heuristically to build highly simplified models as a means to discover new relationships in the atmosphere.[18]

He developed the idea of experimenting with models, and of a hierarchy of models with different complexity, which served to provide an understanding of specific processes or to solve specific questions, even though these models were knowingly not realistic.

Two brilliant Norwegian meteorologists, Arnt Eliassen and Ragnar Fjørtoft, helped in the Meteorology Project and supported Charney's weather-prediction work during research stays at Princeton. Even though they dutifully accepted

16 For the conflicting approaches of Rossby and Sutcliffe, see Persson 2005.
17 Harper 2008; Nebeker 1995.
18 Quoted in: Dalmedico 2001, 420.

Rossby's and Charney's research programme, they felt rather suspicious and uncomfortable with the engineering-like pragmatism that it entailed. Both originated from the excellent Oslo school of hydrodynamic theory and were much less inclined and less optimistic about bending and abusing theory all too drastically. The surprising success of Charney's approach represented a first type of proof of a concept that raised a lot of attention and enthusiasm, and paved the way for the development of operational numerical weather prediction. Eliassen and Fjørtoft, however, back in Europe, did not focus on this direction of research in the following years, though both had served many years in practical weather forecasting, and Fjørtoft, in 1955, had become director of the Norwegian Meteorological Institute.[19]

The power of Charney's approach was impressively confirmed by Norman Phillips, who was often called the inventor of the first General Circulation Model (GCM). Phillips, a member of von Neumann and Charney's team, simulated a much longer forecast period of 30 days with a further simplified version of the weather model. While this was only an experiment and not a simulation based upon a realistic situation, it turned out to be surprisingly successful. Phillips' model experiment reproduced patterns of the atmospheric circulation. He concluded that "the verisimilitude of the forecast flow patterns suggests quite strongly that it [the model] contains a fair element of truth" (Phillips 1956, 154). The experiment was path-breaking in two ways and raised a lot of enthusiasm: first, it showed that computer-based simulation could serve to simulate atmospheric phenomena; second, it proved that "[n]umerical integration of this kind [...] give[s] us [the] unique opportunity to study large scale meteorology as an experimental science", as British meteorologist Eric Eady concluded in 1956.[20] Model experimentation with a hierarchy of models of different degrees of complexity and realism proved another decisive code in atmospheric modelling and simulation. Its epistemic justification was not rooted in the realism and mathematical rigour of the treatment of physical equations (which had to be compromised with simplification and approximation), but in the encouraging results that modelling and simulation efforts generated. Simulations were compared to observational data, which partly could be reproduced. This comparison procedure, albeit not without its pitfalls,[21] became another foundational code in atmospheric modelling. Scientists called it "verification" or "validation" (Oreskes et al. 1994).

---

19 Eliassen, who became lecturer and professor in geophysics at the University of Oslo in the 1950s, made very significant theoretical contributions to dynamic meteorology. Fjørtoft, as professor of meteorology at the University of Copenhagen, developed a sophisticated graphical method to approximate solutions of the primitive equations in the early 1950s. Kristiansen 2016.

20 Quoted in Lewis 1998, 52.

21 These pitfalls included the lack of observational data (especially in higher layers of the atmosphere), the differences between statistical model results on a grid element and observational data

Phillip's work paved the way for heuristic climate modelling, the investigation of atmospheric and climatic processes with computer models with the aim of understanding and quantitatively describing these processes. Climate modelling was significantly different from numerical weather prediction, even though it was partly built on the same equations. Weather prediction models served the deterministic calculation of the short-term changes of atmospheric variables, which was limited to a few days due to the chaotic character of the atmosphere. Climate models, in contrast, provided statistical information of large-scale, long-term calculations with a focus on energy exchange processes, which were crucial for the developments of climate.

The first generation of climate modellers, Joseph Smagorinski and Syukuro Manabe in Princeton, Yale Mintz and Akio Arakawa in Los Angeles, Warren Washington at the NCAR in Boulder, and Cecil Leith at the Livermoore Laboratory, all started modelling work in the late 1950s and early 1960s. They all belonged to the type of heuristic modellers, dedicated to improving their understanding of the atmosphere. The research strategy consisted of an expansion of GCMs by including and improving sub-models, which described atmospheric processes that had not been considered in the models to date, such as radiative transfer, convection and thermal equilibrium, and the role of the oceans (Manabe) and the representation of the planetary boundary layer and cloud processes (Arakawa) (Edwards 2010, 154–171). These additional sub-models often concerned so-called sub-scale processes, processes which took place on scales smaller than the grid resolution (which was in the order of a magnitude of 500 km) and, hence, caused significant additional challenges. Processes such as cloud dynamics and radiation transport (among many others) could not be modelled explicitly, because their size was smaller than the model grid. The model, so-to-speak, could not see realistic clouds. These, instead, had to be approximated with so-called parameterisations, artificial auxiliary constructions, which professedly were not (and could not be) a realistic representation.[22]

By the 1960s, climate modelling had become a small, but well-established research culture, which was characterised by codes such as theory-based mathematical modelling (Bjerknes), grid-based numerical approximation (Richardson), radical reductionism (Rossby), heuristic modelling, model experimentation and validation (Charney, Phillips), parameterisation and model expansion (Manabe, Arakawa, and many others). These codes were generally accepted in the small climate modelling community, but remained controversial in the broader climatological discipline.

---

representing one point in space and time, and the opacity of models which made it hard to decide whether a fit of simulated and observation-based data was appropriate for the right or the wrong reasons. See, for example, Guillemot 2010.

22 Gramelsberger 2010; Guillemot 2017.

A notable example of the tensions surrounding these novel codes was the deep conflict between Hubert H. Lamb and John Mason at the UK Meteorological Office (hereinafter referred to as MetOffice) during the late 1960s. Lamb was one of the pioneers of historical climatology. After the war, he joined the MetOffice's climatology section. There, he discovered an archive with a rich collection of past weather data, and he specialised in using and analysing this weather archive to investigate climatic changes in the past. Lamb was convinced that understanding the climate and its changes required a detailed analysis of climates of the past. He was raised in the empirical climatological tradition and placed great emphasis on the collection of empirical information. When the British cloud physicist, John Mason, was appointed director of the MetOffice in 1965, Lamb's situation changed drastically. Mason transformed the culture at the MetOffice deeply, and focused operations systematically on numerical simulation, while other fields of activity were drastically reduced or closed. Lamb lost his scientific staff and all financial support.[23]

Lamb was not only frustrated by the massively deteriorating conditions for his work, he was also opposed to the way in which climate was being investigated by numerical simulation. Numerical modelling, Lamb believed, reduced climate to a purely physical phenomenon with no associations to culture, geography, or human history – a reductionist approach that he found to be misguided at best, and harmful at worst. In 1971, this clash came to a head. Lamb left the MetOffice after 36 years of service to found the Climatic Research Unit at the University of East Anglia, where he continued historically-based investigations of climate. Lamb explained the reluctance with which he had perceived numerical simulation on several occasions. In a paper in the journal *Nature* in 1969, he wrote:

The computer models of atmospheric behavior and other climatic areas may be unrealistic, and may therefore proceed too far and too fast on faulty basic assumptions. Such developments should be preceded by acquiring fuller and firmer factual knowledge.[24]

In a later article, he explained:

Without a record of climate's past behavior extending back […], the subject would be in the situation of a branch of physics in which the basic laboratory observations of the phenomena to be explained had not been made. There can be no sound theory without such an observation record. (Lamb 1986, 17)

Lamb stood as a representative of those who did not easily accept the epistemic strength and scientific priority of numerical simulation and had little trust in numerical models and the codes of the atmospheric and climate modelling culture.

---

23 Martin-Nielsen 2015 and 2017.
24 Lamb 1969.

3. Making politics: The shaping of climate prediction science (1970–1990)

Historians have described the 1970s as a time of deep social, political and cultural transformation.[25] This time of transformation proved to be of foundational importance to changes in the perception of climate and climatic problems. Developments in climate modelling were strongly influenced by the rise of the environmental movement and the perceptions and cultural values that it brought. According to political scientist Lynton Keith Caldwell, the environmental movement represented "an expression of a changing view of mankind's relationship to the earth". He called this mindset the "new environmental paradigm". This paradigm marked a general change of perspective from "an earth unlimited in abundance and created for man's exclusive use to a concept of the earth as a domain of life or biosphere for which mankind is temporary resident custodian." (Caldwell 1996, 48)

This change of perspective also slowly took root in the atmospheric sciences around 1970. Robert M. White, director of the U.S. Weather Bureau, explained in 1969: "Since time immemorial, we have been trying to protect man against his environment. Now we must try equally hard to protect the environment against man" – a neat summary of the environmental paradigm (White 1969, 343). Moreover, the influential Committee on Atmospheric Sciences of the U.S. National Academy of Sciences adopted the perspectives of the environmental paradigm in its report entitled "The Atmospheric Science and Man's Needs", which was published in 1971. This report defined priority areas for research funding during the 1970s. It focused on challenges in "weather prediction" and "air quality". The problem of rising carbon dioxide levels in the atmosphere, the so-called "carbon dioxide problem", had still not received high priority. It was rather hidden in a minor chapter on "weather and climate modification" under the name "inadvertent modification". Inadvertent climate modification was perceived as being not very important. The report explained that, according to preliminary simulations by Manabe, "the expected increase of perhaps 18 percent in atmospheric CO_2 by the year 2000 might result in a surface temperature increase of 0.5°C. This is comparable to the natural variability of climate over 30 years; consequently, the CO_2 problem is not likely to be critical in the next few decades".[26] A few scientists, such as the oceanographer Roger Revelle, had been raising attention about the carbon dioxide problem since the 1950s. This group only represented a very small minority of the larger atmospheric science communities. Around 1970, most atmospheric scientists, including climate modellers, perceived the so-called carbon-dioxide problem, and future climate change, not as an important issue.

---

25 Ferguson et al. 2010; Döring-Manteuffel and Raphael 2008; Jarausch 2008.
26 Committee on Atmospheric Sciences of the National Research Council 1971, 46.

From about 1970, however, the new environmental paradigm set the stage for significant long-term changes in the culture of climate science. Charles Keeling, who became famous for taking the first representative measurements of CO_2 concentrations in the atmosphere and establishing the later so-called Keeling curve which showed rising CO_2 levels, was an early example of a scientist who offered a much stronger interpretation of the carbon-dioxide problem. In April 1969, Keeling was invited to give a lecture at a Symposium on "Atmospheric Pollution: Its Long-Term Implications", at the meeting of the American Philosophical Society. Keeling summarised the recent findings derived from his measurements. A significant fraction of about 40 per cent of carbon dioxide emissions due to fossil fuel combustion remained in the atmosphere and could lead – as Manabe's preliminary simulations had already suggested – to climate warming. Keeling used this lecture to express his personal concerns strongly. He revealed himself to be a reader of the *Sierra Club Bulletin*, from which he took the following quotation to characterise the situation:

The image which comes to my mind as applicable today is that of a Kafka-like toboggan, running down a slope at ever-increasing speed. Most of the passengers are completely unaware that the slope is becoming steeper; in the front, the official drivers are too busy quarreling over possession of the steering-bar to notice anything at all. Here and there among the passengers are a few individuals who recognize the danger. Some of these, convinced that a precipice lies ahead, shrilly exhort the others to 'Turn! Turn!'" (Keeling 1970, 16–17)

In Keeling's perception, human society, emitting rising amounts of atmospheric pollutants, was such a toboggan running down the slope. He continued at the end of his lecture:

If the human race survives into the twenty-first century with the vast population increase that now seems inevitable, the people living then, along with their other troubles, may also face the threat of climatic change brought about by an uncontrolled increase in atmospheric CO_2 from fossil fuels. (Keeling 1970, 17)

Keeling was one of the first climate scientists to express the question of climate in strong language and give it a new meaning. He offered, we may say, a re-coding of the CO_2 question by linking it to terms such as "danger", "threat", and to normative conclusions such as "Turn! Turn!" with capital letters and exclamation marks. For the time being, however, Keeling was only an exception. His "code" had not yet travelled very far in the climate science community.

Two unusual conferences in 1970 and 1971 were to help make Keeling's concern gain much further ground. An outstanding and unusual personality, Carroll Louis Wilson, professor of management at the Massachusetts Institute of Technology (MIT), organised the *Study of Critical Environmental Problems* (SCEP) in 1970. Wilson had had a remarkable career as an administrator, businessman and university professor with excellent contacts and ties to the worlds of politics and business. He had no environmental expertise, but he was nonetheless a kind of élite activist of high-level projects with outstanding political relevance (Lomask 1987/2016). In 1969, he recognised the environment as a profitable topic for a new project and planned a study conference of experts, the *Study of Critical Environmental Problems* (SCEP), which was to last a full month in July 1970 at Williams College in Williamstown, Massachusetts. Work at this conference had the goal of establishing and synthesizing the state of knowledge about environmental problems. It was organised in four work groups dealing with 1) Climatic Effects, 2) Ecological Effects, 3) Monitoring, and 4) Implications of Change. All the participants at the conference, including many leading scientists, "acted as individuals, not as representatives of the agencies or organizations with which they were affiliated".[27] The SCEP report, published only three months after the end of the conference, provided a comprehensive assessment of environmental problems. A language of concern prevailed. The potentially dire climatic impact of human activity was outlined in the first few lines of the introduction.

The Work Group on Climatic Effects was chaired by meteorologist William Welch Kellogg, director of the Laboratory of Atmospheric Sciences at the National Center for Atmospheric Research (NCAR) at Boulder, Colorado. It included 19 experts, which included noted and heavy-weight climate and atmospheric scientists such as Robert G. Fleagle, John Murray Mitchell, Joseph Smagorinsky, and Charles Keeling. The SCEP Report included, among others, the following assessment of this work group:

Although we conclude that the probability of direct climate change in this century resulting from CO_2 is small, we stress that the long-term potential consequences of CO_2 effects on the climate or of social reaction to such threats are so serious that much more must be learned about future trends of climate change. Only through these measures can societies hope to have time to adjust to changes that may ultimately be necessary. (SCEP 1970, 12)

A few pages later, the authors asked: "What is our best guess about the future?" And answered: "The picture is far from clear, but we do have a fairly good idea of what is happening – even if we sometimes have difficulty assigning the right numbers" (SCEP 1970, 49). This last sentence offered a striking contradiction within only 18 words between "far from clear" and "fairly good idea". The report summarised that a "projected 18 percent" increase of carbon dioxide would cause a warming of 0.5° C by the year 2000 (as Manabe's simulations had suggested). It added that "a doubling of the CO_2 might increase mean annual surface temperatures by 2° C", even though the uncertainty of such an estimate was emphasised.

William Kellogg's preparations for the work at the SCEP Conference included a background paper which he wrote and circulated among the participants (1971). In this paper, he set the tone right from the outset by emphasising that:

---

27 SCEP (Study of Critical Environmental Problems) 1970, xiv.

there is the haunting realization that man may be able to change the climate of the planet Earth. This, I believe, is one of the most important questions of our time, and it must certainly rank near the top of the priority list in atmospheric science. (1971, 123)

Kellogg not only employed strong language and re-ordered priorities in the atmospheric sciences, his chapter also drew a decisive conclusion, which he put most visibly in the title of the paper: "Predicting the Climate". Climate models, he argued, had to be developed further and improved to gain not only scientific understanding, but also to serve and furnish politics with knowledge about future climate change.

The SCEP Conference was followed by a similar one focusing on climate a-lone, the Study of Man's Impact on Climate (SMIC) in July 1971 in Stockholm, which came to similar interpretations and conclusions, and further increased their visibility.[28] The immediate impact of SCEP and SMIC on political institutions and processes was, however, limited. The scientific and technical information it represented was not novel. Nonetheless, SCEP and SMIC made a significant difference and must be regarded ground-breaking, albeit in less visible and more indirect ways. First, SCEP and SMIC established a new framing of climate issues within the environmental paradigm, which replaced the traditional Cold War framing of climate modification. Climate was – so to speak – re-coded from an atmospheric state that offered the option of deliberate change by human forces, to an atmospheric state that was in danger of being changed by, and, at the same time, become a threat to, human society. Second, the SCEP and SMIC conferences and reports placed the problem of climate change as their highest priority, which was not the case in most other environmental assessments of the time.[29] Third, with the re-framing of the issue of climate change in terms of a significant potential future risk, the prediction of climate for many decades emerged as an important scope of climate modelling. While the problem of predicting weather and climate, days or even seasons ahead, had occupied practical meteorologists and climatologists since the nineteenth century, science-based predictions for many decades into the future was a unique and novel ambition in the meteorological profession.

In the following years, Kellogg remained one of the most active scientists endeavouring to make these messages heard. He was supported by a new generation of climate modellers who put a strong focus on predictive modelling, notably, Stephen H. Schneider and James E. Hansen. Schneider was an engineering student at Columbia University when he started a first atmospheric modelling experiment in 1970 and was immediately drawn to the power of simulation. Kel-

---

28 SMIC (Study of Man's Impact on the Climate) 1971.
29 The Committee on Atmospheric Sciences of the U.S. National Academy of Sciences defined weather prediction, air quality, weather and climate modification and weather danger and disasters as priorities. Committee on Atmospheric Sciences 1971.

logg invited Schneider in 1971 to serve as a *rapporteur* at the SMIC conference. In 1973, Schneider joined NCAR and, in many regards, professional forces with Kellogg.[30] He was concerned about a range of climate-related problems from drought and food shortages to long-term climate change. He became a dedicated science activist, sympathising with the environmental left and not shying away from going public with his scientific and moral convictions. Schneider not only engaged regularly in the media with his concerns and warnings, in 1976, he also published a popular book with the title *The Genesis Strategy: Climate and Global Survival.* In this book, Schneider emphasised the importance of climate models for climate prediction. Although he admitted the significant limitations and uncertainties of these models, he argued in favour of using them all the same:

Unfortunately, for the task of estimating the potential impact of human activities on climate the models are just about the only tools we have. Should we ignore the predictions of uncertain models? [...] I think not – a political judgment, of course [...] The real problem is: If we choose to wait for more certainty before actions are initiated, then can our models be improved in time to prevent an irreversible drift toward a future calamity? [...] This dilemma rests, metaphorically, in our need to gaze into a very dirty crystal ball; but the tough judgment to be made here is precisely how long we should clean the glass before acting on what we believe we see inside. (Schneider 1976, 147–149)

This book found a big audience and made Schneider a well-known public figure. He was invited to Congress hearings and, among others, appeared on the Johnny Carson TV show. While he could not definitely say, one way or the other, how hazardous climate would be in the near future, he took every opportunity to go public about his concerns about the future. Schneider's scientific convictions and style also brought him considerable criticism and, notably, a deep controversy with the much older, world-renowned climatologist Helmut Erich Landsberg. Landsberg, who was born and educated in Germany and had emigrated to the USA in 1934, was one of the leading experts in fields such as bioclimatology, urban climatology, and microclimatology, and was strongly dedicated to maximising the usefulness of climatology to human society. He served as director of the U.S. Weather Bureau's Office of Climatology between 1955 and 1966, and established the National State Climatologist Program, which placed a trained climatologist in each state in the USA to conduct climate research and impact analysis for the benefit of local businesses, industries, and federal states.[31]

Landsberg perceived the emergence of Schneider on the political scene as being inconsistent with the established norms, and he reacted particularly strongly to this transgression. He criticised Schneider, first, for the lack of credible science and, second, for the fact that, with his book and his public appearances, a "my-

---

30 Henderson 2014, 61–63; Heymann and Hundebøl 2017, 111.
31 Henderson 2017 and 2016, 216.

thology of climate has been spilled on the public".[32] Schneider's science was, in Landsberg's opinion, far from convincing. In one article, he wrote that:

Cause and effect relationships of climate are known in only a rudimentary way; hence predictions for either short or long intervals are afflicted with great uncertainties. Shouldn't this be persuasive enough to send at least the scientists back from the television cameras to their laboratories and studies in order to perfect their knowledge?[33]

In Landsberg's eyes, going public with such highly uncertain claims was a serious breach of the well-established norm of reticence. Appearing on television shows, in magazine articles, and publishing popular works suggested that Schneider was sacrificing the credibility of the scientific profession for the purpose of raising his own political profile. Landsberg vehemently challenged the usefulness of the current climate models to both science and to the development of policy. While he appreciated their potential usefulness over the long-term, he believed that Schneider's use of model-based estimates to guide policy development overlooked the fact that models did not adequately represent the real atmosphere and their uncertainties were not quantified. In his hostile review of Schneider's book, Landsberg emphasised:

Crude or premature estimates can be very misleading in providing guidance for such far-reaching decisions and may be far more damaging than no estimate at all [...] we should be wary of basing broad national or international decisions on hand-waving arguments or back-of-the-envelope calculations.[34]

According to Landsberg, Schneider represented a new kind of climate scientist, who appeared to circumvent established traditions for the purpose of unifying politics, the public, and science. Schneider, however, continued his own mission unabated.

The "prediction of climate" goal was far from easy to accomplish. Mathematician Edward Lorenz provided strong arguments which supported Landsberg's critique of numerical modelling. Lorenz' theoretical work questioned the possibility of climate prediction altogether. He had investigated the chaotic structure of the atmosphere, which, in his view, caused indeterminacy and limited its predictability. This was the deeper reason for the fact that numerical weather prediction was not able to attain useful predictions beyond a few days ahead. According to Lorenz, climate models did not reflect the chaotic behaviour of the atmosphere and treated the impact of CO_2 as being deterministic. In his eyes, climate models potentially behaved in too stable a manner, although it was not possible to decide on this point.[35] Both Schneider and Kellogg were well aware of the primitive state

---

32 Quoted in Henderson 2014, 73.
33 Landsberg 1976, quoted in Henderson 2014, 74.
34 Landsberg 1977, 122, quoted in Henderson 2014, 75.
35 Lorenz' arguments are discussed in more detail in Heymann and Hundebøl 2017, 106–108.

of climate models and the uncertainty inherent in the representation of atmospheric processes, and, hence, in simulation results. In their eyes, nothing much could be done other than to accept uncertainty, and nevertheless prepare ourselves for worsening times. The attempt to establish certainty from uncertain models is typically shown in a report entitled "Effects of Human Activities on Global Climate", which Kellogg was commissioned to prepare for the World Meteorological Organization (WMO) in 1977. In this report, Kellogg discussed Lorenz' critique in some detail and proposed to assume "a more pragmatic view" (1977, 4). He argued:

It can be seen, then, that there is an entire hierarchy of models of the climate system [...] It is reassuring to see that, when we compare the results of experiments with the same perturbations [...] but using different models, the response is generally found to be either about the same or differs by an amount that can be rationalized in terms of recognized model differences or assumptions. (Kellogg 1977, 4)

Immediately following this sentence, Kellogg added a qualification, which, in his eyes, however, did not invalidate the argument:

Of course, it is possible that all our models could be utterly wrong in the same way, giving a false sense of confidence, but it seems highly unlikely that we would still be so completely ignorant about any dominant set of processes [...].[36]

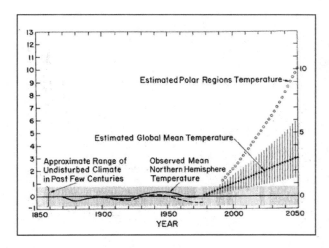

Figure 4: Kellogg's prediction of future climate based upon simulation results of climate models (1977, 24).

---

36 Kellogg 1977, 9. This combination of argument and qualification was a typical element in the writings of Kellogg, Schneider and others. It served to consider uncertainty, but effectively made it secondary to the argument. Heymann 2012.

In the WMO report, Kellogg went a significant step further. He suggested a powerful symbol by showing probable future warming in a graph (Figure 4). His graph was one of the first long-term predictions of climate warming, which was based upon computer simulations, and was the first in an actual scientific report. This type of graph established a visual code, which soon found emulators, and later made its way into IPCC reports and thus became an iconic emblem of climate change. It transmitted the message much more effectively than the vague estimates of temperature change in the case of doubled CO_2 concentrations, which served as a benchmark in most assessments at that time.

Whereas Kellogg and Schneider advocated for pragmatism in the use of climate models in order to provide predictive knowledge about future climate, another young scientist, climate modeller James E. Hansen of the Goddard Institute of Space Studies (GISS) in New York, adopted this pragmatism and developed a simple model dedicated to calculate future projections of climate. In 1981, Hansen and co-workers published a landmark paper in the journal *Science* based upon simulations with a one-dimensional climate model. In this paper, the authors accurately discussed a large range of problems and uncertainties, which covered more than half the article. At the end of the article, they published the first simulated climate projections for a range of different carbon dioxide emission scenarios (Figure 5).

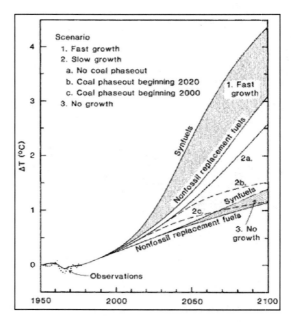

Figure 5: Hansen's climate projection with a 1-dimensional climate model to the year 2100 (1981, 963).

Hansen's ambitions, however, reached beyond the publication of a bold article in one of the most prestigious journals. A week before the article appeared in print, he sent it to the science journalist of the *New York Times*, Walter Sullivan. Sullivan recognised the importance of the work and prepared a title page article entitled "Study Finds Warming Trend that could Raise Sea Levels" (Sullivan 1981). Hansen's article and its sensational public marketing in the *New York Times* brought him a wave of very hostile responses. His projections were based upon a very simple model, and were subject to enormous uncertainties. While the authors admitted the limits of knowledge and discussed the uncertainties extensively, they nevertheless proposed the strong conclusion of an "improved confidence in the ability of models to predict future CO_2 climate effects". Their projections, however, were nothing but a bold bet on the future, which most scientists considered to be premature.[37] Marketing such work in a newspaper ran contrary to scientific etiquette. In spite of the furious outcry, however, this work and, more importantly, many of the codes and practices that it entailed, not only were to stay, but also to inform future work.

Predictive use of climate models, as proposed by Kellogg, Schneider and Hansen, was controversial. Many scientists interested in climate modelling and prediction did not easily accept it. An instructive case of significant reservations about pursuing predictive modelling can be found in the climate modelling effort at the UK Meteorological Office.[38] In the UK, the MetOffice pursued small-scale climate modelling work from 1963. In 1968, a first climate model was finished, and, in the early 1970s, the first publications based upon simulation experiments appeared. These publications – as well as internal discussion – were characterised by a strong cautiousness with regard to the model and its simulation results. Roger L. Newson, one of the scientists in the team, wrote in 1972:

It is not appropriate to attach much weight to the results of such a coarse predictor of the Earth's climatology as the present Met O[ffice] [...] general circulation model.[39]

This was also the opinion of MetOffice director John Mason. Mason, in spite of his enthusiasm about numerical simulation and weather prediction, regarded climate simulation only a slowly developing research domain, in which an adequate understanding of atmospheric processes had to be gained first. An application of the model for practical purposes was out of the question. As Mason wrote in 1976:

Our understanding of the mechanisms and causes of climatic trends and fluctuations is inadequate to allow their prediction.[40]

---

37 Heymann and Hundebøl 2017, 114–115.
38 This part of the story is described more detailed in Martin-Nielsen (forthcoming).
39 Quoted in Martin-Nielsen (forthcoming), 8.
40 B. John Mason 1976, 51. Quoted in Martin-Nielsen (forthcoming), 8.

Mason was clearly in favour of developing numerical approaches, as his conflict with Lamb illuminated. At the same time, he remained very cautious about its limitations to protect the scientific authority of the MetOffice.

In the UK, in contrast to the USA, it was the government that requested politically relevant information about future climate. From 1974, the carbon dioxide problem and potential future warming – as well as predictions of cooling and future ice ages – were discussed in the Cabinet Office of the British government. As one government official noted:

in my view, the UK should consider the extent and priority given to long-term forecasting of climatic change to see whether it would be wise to increase the amount of research undertaken.[41]

In 1975, the government asked the MetOffice for a statement about potential climate change. The interest of the government had less to do with concern about climate change than concern about British industry in case demands for emission reduction resulted. The head of the MetOffice research department, John Stanley Sawyer, wrote in his conclusion that a "fundamental understanding has not reached a stage which permits a reliable computation of future climate".[42] Such statements by MetOffice officials were not perceived as an encouragement to shed light on this question. As Mason continued undeterred in his cautious philosophy, Cabinet Secretary John Hunt visited Mason personally in September 1977, again to no effect. Hunt tried to insist on an intensification of the MetOffice's climate modelling and prediction efforts. In early 1978, the Cabinet Office had characterised the CO_2 question as "the most serious potential man-made threat to the global climate".[43] The government's chief scientist concluded:

Clearly, therefore, there must be a global modelling capacity outside the US.[44]

Mason, concerned about MetOffice funding, eventually responded to the government's calls, and asked his staff for detailed climate projections. These efforts, however, quickly lost their importance when Margaret Thatcher became Prime Minister in 1979. Thatcher did not see a political priority in the CO_2 problem and, for the time being, put a stop to the MetOffice's reluctant efforts.[45]

---

41 British National Archive, TNA CAB 164/1379. Warren to Press, 14 October 1974, quoted in Agar 2015, 608–609.
42 British National Archive, TNA CAB 184/567. "The Weather", Ashworth to Berrill, 23 February 1977, quoted in Agar 2015, 611.
43 Proposals for a National Climatology Research Programme, Annex 1, British National Archive, CAB 164/1423, KEW, 4–6, quoted in Martin-Nielsen (forthcoming), 17.
44 British National Archive, TNA CAB 184/567. Ashworth to Berrill, 4 April 1978, quoted in Agar 2015, 619.
45 Only in 1988, Thatcher radically changed her mind, accepted the risks of climate change and took the decision to establish the Hadley Centre for Climate Prediction and Research. Mahony and Hulme 2016; Folland et al. 2004.

4. Conclusions

The post-war period was a formative period for the negotiation and establishment of atmospheric simulation and the specific codes that it entailed. Practices such as radical reductionism, approximation, computer experimentation and parametrisation had been invented, travelled throughout the world, and quickly came to be generally accepted codes in the specialised sub-communities of atmospheric and climate modellers and numerical weather-prediction experts, although they still remained controversial nonetheless. While some scientists immersed in traditional practices and values rejected them and continued to see numerical simulation with significant reluctance, others were drawn to the power of simulation by its successes, its versatility, and the promises that it entailed. Meteorologists and climatologists, such as George Simpson, Hubert H. Lamb and Helmut Landsberg, viewed the reductionist approach and the generalised and simplified theoretical treatments and big claims derived from atmospheric modelling with great caution, or even reluctance. Computer models seemed able to show anything, whereas the empirical validation and corroboration of such claims appeared limited and piecemeal. Theoretically versed meteorologists such as Reginald Sutcliffe, Arnt Eliassen and Ragnar Fjørtoft, on the other hand, felt uncomfortable with the immense engineering-like pragmatism involved in the treatment of the physical equations.

The 1970s, in contrast, was a formative period for the emergence of foundational codes of a culture of climate prediction. The decision for predictive modelling was a significant one, because it involved new priorities and research tasks, as well as adjusted practices and strategies. It channelled scientific and institutional resources from the development and testing of models to their application. Predictive modelling and its specific codes were motivated by a wave of environmental concerns. The possibility of changes of climate was re-interpreted from an optimistic framing of controllable weather and climate modification to a pessimistic framing of a significant future threat to human society and the biosphere, often even addressed with apocalyptic undertones. Some scientists, such as William Kellogg, Stephen Schneider and James Hansen, pushed climate prediction many decades into the future, even though they were aware of the limitations of the models and the uncertainties involved in such predictions.

In the eyes of these scientists, the perception of political urgency justified a shift of established scientific norms. First, while the problem of uncertainty could not be solved, proponents of climate prediction proposed to take a pragmatic stance and argued that, even from uncertain models, useful knowledge could be derived. Established modelling successes, and the fact that all climate models largely agreed in the modelling experiments, appeared re-assuring enough, Kellogg claimed. A "dirty crystal ball" was not good enough, Schneider admitted, but better than no crystal ball at all, given the need to investigate the threat of climate warming. Second, the urgency assigned to the problem of climate change was taken, by concerned scientists, as not only a justification but also a responsibility to go public and make political statements. Deliberately, they compromised or deliberately overcame the norm of reticence. Both these transgressions were deep and lasting. In the long-term, they effectively caused a change or adjustment of established epistemic standards, a re-coding of what represented good or bad science. Again, these new codes fuelled a lot of controversy and conflict. Lorenz' cautious warning about a potentially under-estimated indeterminacy of the climate, Mason's careful appreciation of the premature state of climate modelling, and Landsberg's furious critique of going public and spilling "mythologies of climate change" on laymen and politicians was only representative for the majority of scientists, who placed high esteem on the established values and norms of scientific cautiousness, scepticism and reticence.

The acceptance or rejection of the codes which characterised atmospheric modelling and prediction related to diverse scientific and political cultures. Lamb and Landsberg, who had been raised in an observation-focused climatological tradition, valued detailed empirical knowledge higher than simulation-based knowledge. Theoreticians such as Sutcliffe, Eliassen, Fjørtoft and Lorenz had certain reservations with the pragmatism of scientists such as Rossby, Charney, Kellogg, Schneider and Hansen. Conservative scientists such as Mason and Landsberg, defending scientific diligence and rigor and feeling a responsibility for protecting the authority of science, clashed with a (mostly) younger generation's environmental concerns, ideas of political responsibility and public ambitions, as well as with governmental demands of "politically convenient" knowledge. These cultural affinities and subscriptions to a diversity of scientific codes also determined perceptions of knowledge as being "strong" or "weak". Lamb and Landsberg considered numerical approaches, with their inherent approximations and uncertainty, as limited, and, in the case of climate modelling, premature and "weak". Rossby, Mason and many others, in contrast, rather saw the immense strength and opportunities of computer-based numerical approaches, whereas they perceived Lamb's historical empiricism as an irrelevant and "weak" research strategy. Mason decidedly embraced numerical weather forecasting and endorsed heuristic climate modelling. At the same time, he recognised the limitations of climate models. In contrast to Kellogg, Schneider and Hansen, he perceived the results of climate simulation as being epistemically too "weak" to allow for useful climate prediction.

The competition of research directions, scientific standards and cultural codes depended significantly on political and cultural contexts. In the early Cold War era, military tensions and geopolitical interests provided an ideal breeding ground for the high-flying ambitions of technology-based atmospheric sciences, which held the promise of not only numerical weather prediction and satellite surveillance, but also of weather and climate control. A strong scientific and technological optimism characterised this era and rewarded the bold and ambitious, rather than the conscientious and scrupulous minds. Computer-based numerical approaches neatly fit this ambitious mindset and early accomplishments quickly silenced its critics. In the 1970s, the enthusiasm for environmental control had largely faded and given way to the opposite perceptions of environmental concern, whereas the confidence in numerical approaches persisted and, among many (often younger) scientists, even increased. This context fuelled the demands for long-term climate prediction among those, who shared strong concerns about future global warming and its impact on human society. While this ambition remained contested, it took increasingly root – and, with it, the codes it resulted. The establishment of the Intergovernmental Panel on Climate Change (IPCC) in 1988 provides evidence both for the contested character of climate prediction – called climate "projections" in scientific terminology – and, at the same time, for the spread and acceptability of its codes, which, by then, had travelled far enough and were, more or less, firmly established. A scientific culture and identity had emerged and consolidated, which included climate prediction, public communication and the deliberate connection of science and politics. Kellogg's call for prediction was finally heard and Hansen had won his bet on the future.

References

Agar, Jonathan (2015): "'Future Forecast – Changeable and Probably Getting Worse': The UK Government's Early Response to Anthropogenic Climate Change." *Twentieth Century British History*, 26 (4): 602–628.

Bjerknes, Vilhelm (1904/2009): "Das Problem der Wettervorhersage, betrachtet vom Standpunkte der Mechanik und der Physik." (The problem of weather prediction, considered from the viewpoints of mechanics and physics) *Meteorologische Zeitschrift*, 21: 1–7 (translated and edited by Volken E. and S. Brönnimann. *Meteorologische Zeitschrift*, 18 (6): 663–667).

Bodansky, Daniel (2001): "The History of the Global Climate Change Regime." In: Urs Luterbacher and Detlef F. Sprinz (Eds.): *International Relations and Global Climate Change*, 23–40. Cambridge MA: The MIT Press.

Caldwell, Lynton Keith (1996): *International Environmental Policy: From the Twentieth to the Twenty-first Century*. 3rd edn. Durham NC: Duke University Press.

Callendar, Guy S. (1938): "The Artificial Production of Carbon Dioxide and its Influence on Climate." *Quarterly Journal of the Royal Meteorological Society*, 64 (3): 223–40.

Committee on Atmospheric Sciences of the National Research Council (1971): *The Atmospheric Sciences and Man's Needs: Priorities for the Future*. Washington DC: National Academy of Science.

Dalmedico, Amy Dahan (2001): "History and Epistemology of Models: Meteorology as a Case Study (1946–1963)." *Archive for the History of the Exact Sciences*, 55 (5): 395–422.

Döring-Manteuffel, Anselm, and Lutz Raphael (2008): *Nach dem Boom: Perspektiven auf die Zeitgeschichte seit 1970*. Göttingen: Vandenhoeck & Ruprecht.

Edwards, Paul N. (2010): *A Vast Machine: Computer Models, Climate Data, and the Politics of Global Warming*. Cambridge MA: The MIT Press.

Ellingsen, Gunnar (2016): *The Bergen School: Rethinking how Scientific Meteorology Began*. Unpublished manuscript, University of Bergen.

Ferguson, Nigel, et al. (Eds.) (2010): *The Shock of the Global: The 1970s in Perspective*. Cambridge MA: Harvard University Press.

Fine, Gary A. (2007): *Authors of the Storm: Meteorologists and the Culture of Prediction*. Chicago IL-London: University of Chicago Press.

Fleming, James R. (2007): *The Callendar Effect: The Life and Work of Guy Stewart Callendar (1898–1964)*. Boston MA: American Meteorological Society.

Fleming, James R. (2010): *Fixing the Sky: The Checkered History of Weather and Climate Control*. New York: Columbia University Press.

Fleming, James R. (2016): *Inventing Atmospheric Science*. Cambridge MA: The MIT Press.

Folland, Chris K., et al. (2004): "History of the Hadley Centre for Climate Prediction and Research." *Weather*, 59 (11): 317–323.

Friedman, Robert Marc (1989): *Appropriating the Weather, Vilhelm Bjerknes and the Construction of a Modern Meteorology*. Ithaca NY-London: Cornell University Press.

Gramelsberger, Gabriele (2009): "Conceiving Meteorology as the Exact Science of the Atmosphere: Vilhelm Bjerknes's Paper of 1904 as a Milestone." *Meteorologische Zeitschrift*, 18 (6): 669–673.

Gramelsberger, Gabriele (2010): "Conceiving Processes in Atmospheric Models – General Equations, Subscale Parameterizations, and 'Superparameterizations'." *Studies in History and Philosophy of Modern Physics*, 41 (3): 233–241.

Guillemot, Hélène (2010): "Connections between Simulations and Observation in Climate Computer Modelling. Scientists' Practices and 'Bottom-up Epistemology' Lessons." *Studies in History and Philosophy of Modern Physics*, 41 (3): 242–52.

Guillemot, Hélène (2017): "How to Develop Climate Models? The "Gamble" of Improving Climate Model Parameterizations." In: Matthias Heymann et al. (Eds.): *Cultures of Prediction in Atmospheric and Climate Science: Epistemic and Cultural Shifts in Computer-based Modelling and Simulation*, 120–136. New York: Routledge, Series Environmental Humanities.

Hansen, James E., et al. (1981): "Climate Impact of Increasing Atmospheric Carbon Dioxide." *Science*, 213 (4511): 957–966.

Harper, Kristine C. (2008): *Weather by the Numbers: The Genesis of Modern Meteorology*. Cambridge MA: The MIT Press.

Henderson, Gabriel D. (2014): "The Dilemma of Reticence: Helmut Landsberg, Stephen Schneider, and Public Communication of Climate Risk, 1971–1976." *History of Meteorology*, 6: 53–78.

Henderson, Gabriel D. (2016): "Governing the Hazards of Climate: The Development of the National Climate Program Act, 1977–1981." *Historical Studies in the Natural Sciences*, 46 (2): 207–242.

Henderson, Gabriel D. (2017): "Helmut Landsberg and the Evolution of 20th Century American Climatology: Envisioning a Climatological Renaissance." *WIREs Climate Change*, 8 (2): 1–14.

Heymann, Matthias (2009): "Klimakonstruktionen. Von der klassischen Klimatologie zur Klimaforschung." *NTM. Journal of the History of Science, Technology and Medicine*, 17 (2): 171–197.

Heymann, Matthias (2010a): "The Evolution of Climate Ideas and Knowledge." *Wiley Interdisciplinary Reviews Climate Change*, 1 (3): 581–597.

Heymann, Matthias (2010b): "Understanding and Misunderstanding Computer Simulation: The Case of Atmospheric and Climate Science — An Introduction." In: Matthias Heymann and Helge Kragh (Eds): "Modeling and Simulation in Atmospheric and Climate Sciences." Special issue, *Studies in History and Philosophy of Modern Physics*, 41 (6): 193–200.

Heymann, Matthias (2012): "Constructing Evidence and Trust: How did Climate Scientists' Confidence in their Models and Simulations Emerge?" In: Kirsten Hastrup and Martin Skrydstrup (Eds.): *The Social Life of Climate Change Models: Anticipating Nature*, 203–224. New York: Routledge.

Heymann, Matthias, and Randlev Hundebøl (2017): "From Heuristic to Predictive: Making Climate Models Political Instruments." In: Matthias Heymann et al. (Eds.): *Cultures of Prediction in Atmospheric and Climate Science: Epistemic and Cultural Shifts in Computer-based Modelling and Simulation*, 100–119. New York: Routledge, Series Environmental Humanities.

Heymann, Matthias, et al. (Eds.) (2017): *Cultures of Prediction in Atmospheric and Climate Science: Epistemic and Cultural Shifts in Computer-based Modelling and Simulation*. New York: Routledge, Series Environmental Humanities.

Hulme, Mike (2008): "Geographical Work at the Boundaries of Climate Change." *Transactions of the Institute of British Geographers*, NS 35: 5–11.

Jarausch, Konrad H. (Ed.) (2008): *Das Ende der Zuversicht? Die siebziger Jahre als Geschichte*. Göttingen: Vandenhoeck & Ruprecht.

Keeling, Charles D. (1970): "Is Carbon Dioxide from Fossil Fuel Changing Man's Environment?" *Proceedings of the American Philosophical Society*, 114 (1): 10–17.

Kellogg, William W. (1971): "Predicting the Climate." In: W.H. Matthews et al. (Eds.): *Man's Impact on the Climate*, 123–132. Cambridge MA: The MIT Press.

Kellogg, William W. (1977): *Effects of Human Activities on Global Climate*. Geneva: WMO (Technical Note).

Kristiansen, Thorleif Aass (2016): *Meteorologi på reise: Veivalg og impulser i Arnt Eliassen og Ragnar Fjørtofts forskerkarrierer*. Dissertation, University of Bergen.

Lahsen, Myanna (2005): "Seductive Simulations? Uncertainty Distribution around Climate Models." *Social Studies of Science*, 35 (6): 895–922.

Lamb, Hubert H. (1969): "The New Look of Climatology." *Nature*, 223 (5212): 1209–1215.

Lamb, Hubert H. (1982): *Climate, History and the Modern World*. London: Methuen.

Lamb, Hubert H. (1986): "The History of Climatology and the Effects of Climatic Variations on Human History." *Weather*, 41 (1): 16–20.

Landsberg, Helmut (1976): "Whence Global Climate: Hot or Cold?" *Bulletin of the American Meteorological Society*, 57 (4): 441–43.

Landsberg, Helmut (1977): "Comment on Review of 'The Genesis Strategy'." *EOS*, 58 (3): 122.

Lenhard, Johannes, and Eric Winsberg (2010): "Holism, Entrenchment, and the Future of Climate Model Pluralism." *Studies in History and Philosophy of Modern Physics*, 41 (6): 253–262.

Lewis, John M. (1998): "Clarifying the Dynamics of the General Circulation, Phillips' 1956 Experiment." *Bulletin of the American Meteorological Society*, 79 (1): 39–60.

Lomask, Milton (2016/1987): "One of a Kind: Carroll L. Wilson." In: Carroll L. Wilson 1910–1983, Report of The Carroll L. Wilson Awards Committee January 1987, The MIT Libraries, Institute Archives and Special Collections. available at: https://gecd.mit.edu/sites/default/files/abroad/files/carroll-wilson-report.pdf, last accessed 30 October 2016.

Luterbacher, Urs, and Detlef F. Sprinz (Eds.) (2001): *International Relations and Global Climate Change*. Cambridge MA: The MIT Press.

Lynch, Peter (2006): *The Emergence of Numerical Weather Prediction, Richardson's Dream*. Cambridge: Cambridge University Press.

Mahony, Martin, and Mike Hulme (2016): "Modelling and the Nation: Institutionalising Climate Prediction in the UK, 1988–92." *Minerva*, 54 (4): 445–470.

Martin-Nielsen, Janet (2015): "Ways of Knowing Climate: Hubert H. Lamb and Climate Research in the UK." *WIREs Climate Change*, 6 (5): 465–477.

Martin-Nielsen, Janet (2017): "A New Climate: Hubert H. Lamb and Boundary Work at the UK Meteorological Office." In: Matthias Heymann et al. (Eds.): *Cultures of Prediction in Atmospheric and Climate Science: Epistemic and Cultural Shifts in Computer-based Modelling and Simulation*, 85–99. New York: Routledge, Series Environmental Humanities.

Martin-Nielsen, Janet (forthcoming): "Computing the Climate: When Models Became Political." *Historical Studies of the Natural Sciences*.

Mason, B. John (1976): "The Nature and Prediction of Climatic Changes." *Endeavour*, 35: 51.

Nebeker, Frederik (1995): *Calculating the Weather: Meteorology in the 20th Century*. San Diego CA: Academic Press.

Oreskes, Naomi, et al. (1994): "Verification, Validation and Confirmation of Numerical Models in the Earth Sciences." *Science*, 263 (5147): 641–646.

Oreskes, Naomi, et al. (2004): "The Scientific Consensus on Climate Change." *Science*, 306 (5702): 1686.

Oreskes, Naomi, and Erik M. Conway (2010): *Merchants of Doubt. How a Handful of Scientists Obscured the Truth on Issues from Tobacco Smoke to Global Warming*, 169–215. New York: Bloomsbury Press.

Persson, Anders (2005): "Early operational Numerical Weather Prediction outside the USA: An Historical Introduction, Part III: Endurance and Mathematics – British NWP, 1948–1965." *Meteorological Applications*, 12 (4): 381–413.

Petersen, Artur (2006): *Simulating Nature: A Philosophical Study of Computer Simulation Uncertainties and their Role in Climate Science and Policy Advice*. Apeldoorn: Het Spinhuis.

Phillips, Norman (1956): "The General Circulation of the Atmosphere: A Numerical Experiment." *Quarterly Journal of the Royal Meteorological Society*, 82 (352): 123–164.

Richardson, Lewis Fry [1922] (2007): *Weather Prediction by Numerical Process*. Cambridge: Cambridge University Press, available at: https://archive.org/detailsweatherpredictio00richrich, last accessed 30 October 2016.

Rosol, Christoph (2017): "Which Design for a Weather Predictor? Speculating on the Future of Electronic Forecasting in Post-war America." In: Matthias Heymann et al. (Eds.): *Cultures of Prediction in Atmospheric and Climate Science: Epistemic and Cultural Shifts in Computer-based Modelling and Simulation*, 68–84. New York: Routledge, Series Environmental Humanities.

Rudloff, Hans von [1670] (1967): *Die Schwankungen und Pendelungen des Klimas in Europa seit dem Beginn der regelmässigen Instrumenten-Beobachtungen*. Braunschweig: Vieweg.

SCEP (Study of Critical Environmental Problems) (1970): *Man's Impact on the Global Environment. Assessment and Recommendation for Action*. Cambridge MA: The MIT Press.

Schneider, Stephen H. (1976): *The Genesis Strategy: Climate and Global Survival*. New York: Plenum Press.

Shackley, Simon et al. (1998): "Uncertainty, Complexity and Concepts of Good Science in Climate Change Modelling: Are GCMs the Best Tools?" *Climatic Change*, 38 (2): 159–205.

Sluijs, Jeroen, van der P. (1997): *Anchoring amid Uncertainty. On the Management of Uncertainties in Risk Assessment of Anthropogenic Climate Change*. Ph.D. thesis, University of Utrecht.

SMIC (Study of Man's Impact on the Climate) (1971): *Man's Impact on the Climate*. Cambridge MA: The MIT Press.

Sullivan, Walter (1981): "Study Finds Warming Trend that could Raise Sea Levels." *New York Times*, 22 August 1981.

Weart, Spencer R. (2008): *The Discovery of Global Warming*. Revised and expanded edition, Cambridge MA: Harvard University Press, updated available at: https://www.aip.org/history/climate/ index.htm, last accessed 30 October 2016.

Weart, Spencer R (2010): "The Development of General Circulation Models of Climate." *Studies in History and Philosophy of Modern Physics*, 41: 208–217.

White, Robert M. (1969): "Remarks at the Dedication of the ESSA Geophysical Fluid Dynamics Laboratory, Princeton, New Jersey." *Bulletin of the American Meteorological Society*, 50 (5): 341–343.

Partisanal Knowledge:
On Hayek and Heretics in Climate Science and Discourse

Richard Staley

Abstract

This essay examines the legacy of Friedrich von Hayek and the positions developed by climate-change sceptics, who currently cast themselves as heretics arguing against the corrupted and politicised science of the Intergovernmental Panel on Climate Change (IPCC), in order to characterise the features of what I will describe as "partisanal knowledge". Oreskes and Conway have analysed how such sceptics worked to produce doubt on a series of issues, and Joshua Howe has argued that most critique of climate change science has been reactive, shaped in response to the research and advocacy of scientists who had already made carbon and climate a policy concern. I aim to complement these studies of sceptical strategies with an analysis of the forms of knowledge that avowed partisans assert – both of the subject at issue, and of their opponents – when arguing from a position of weakness. Given the centrality of Hayek's 1944 *The Road to Serfdom* to the political and economic stances advocated by many climate sceptics, I will link a study of Hayek's work to an analysis of two recent sceptical accounts of the climate consensus, Singer and Avery's *Unstoppable Global Warming* (2007) and Idso, Carter and Singer's, *Why Scientists Disagree About Global Warming* (2015). Historians and sociologists of science have often studied the development of knowledge through scientific controversies. I hope that articulating the characteristics of "partisanal knowledge" will help us to better understand controversies across scientific, political and economic stances.

1. A classroom visit

In the Spring semesters of 2011 and 2012, I taught an undergraduate honours seminar on "Global Warming: History, Science, Politics" in the History of Science Department at the University of Wisconsin-Madison. I offered students the opportunity to invite four researchers to class, asking them to select university researchers who worked on different aspects of climate change, who would each send one research article and one article on the public dimensions of their work, and then join the class for an open discussion of their work. The second time I ran the course, students asked me to invite a climate sceptic, so I contacted the Heartland Institute in suburban Chicago to ask whether they could suggest someone.[1] They put me onto Steven J. Welcenbach of Menomonee Falls (WI), a trained chemist and long-time member of the American Chemical Society, who owns a chemical waste and recycling firm and runs a subscription news service that he calls Reality News. Steven did not refer us to his own publications but brought a bag full of books into the classroom and unpacked them onto the seminar table. One pile featured a host of colourful covers, and he told us that these were his authorities, the literature he relied on in developing his understanding of climate change; prominent amongst them was the 2008 edition of S. Fred Singer and Dennis T. Avery's *New York Times* bestselling book, *Unstoppable Global Warming*.[2] There was another pile of thin books in grey-green covers which Steven handed out, giving us each a copy of the condensed, *Reader's Digest* version of Friedrich von Hayek's *The Road to Serfdom* that was first published in 1945, a year after the original book came out (our copies bore a sticker noting that they had

---

1 The Heartland Institute is a leading free-market think tank that has been in operation since 1988. The four primary foci of its advocacy work are reflected in a set of policy newspapers sent monthly to "every national and state elected official in the United States and thousands of civic and business leaders", dealing with *Budget & Tax News, Environment & Climate News, Health Care News,* and *School Reform News*. Their website is at: https://www.heartland.org, and their index page on climate change notes that, on 26 May 2012, they were described in the *Economist* as "the world's most prominent think tank promoting scepticism about man-made climate change", available at: https://www.heartland.org/Center-Climate-Environment/index.html, last accessed 17 June 2017.

2 Welcenbach is President of the waste disposal and recycling firm Alchemical Ventures Inc. and proprietor of the subscription based newspaper and website Reality News, available at: http://www.realitynewsmedia.com/news. In June 2017, the front page of the website listed a set of "featured books from Amazon", whose titles will indicate the character of the books that Steven brought to the classroom five years earlier: *Merchants of Despair* by Robert Zubrin, *Carbon Gauntlet* by Donn Dears, *Unstoppable Global Warming* by S. Fred Singer and Dennis T. Avery, *The Solar Fraud* by Howard C. Hayden, *The Climate Caper* by Garth W. Paltridge and Christopher Monckton, *Energy Keepers Energy Killers* by Roy Innis, *Ecoimperialism: Green Power, Black Death* by Paul Driessen, *The Deep Hot Biosphere* by Thomas Gold and Freeman Dyson, *Climate: The Counter Consensus* by Professor Robert M. Carter, *A Primer on CO2 and Climate* by Howard C. Hayden. Friedrich von Hayek's *The Road to Serfdom* was also listed (in The Definitive Edition edited by Bruce Caldwell), together with six other books which I will list for the sake of completeness: *Islam: An Overview* by Richard Ghyselinck, *Psalms of Promise* by E. Calvin Beisner, *The Gospel under Fire* by William Thomas Bray and Nora Lam, *Common Sense on Mass Immigration* by Ed John Tanbon, *Rewards* by Herbert J. Wahlbert and Joseph L. Bast, and *Ever Wonder Why and other Controversial Essays* by Thomas Sowell.

been provided courtesy of the Wisconsin Chapter of Americans for Prosperity).[3] Steven said that this book would show us the world view underlying his approach. This experience of pairing a forthright critique of the scientific consensus on climate change with a background in neoliberal political and economic thought forms the kernel for the present essay, and I have set out the nature of this classroom visit at some length because it reflects many significant features of the complex of problems that I wish to discuss.

I will argue here that to understand better the on-going disputes that chase climate change across scientific, political and economic spheres, historians of science should go beyond the analyses of controversy that have been our staple, and extend still further the rich studies of strategies of denial that have been developed by Oreskes and Conway in their well known book *Merchants of Doubt* (2010). Oreskes and Conway have shown conclusively that adherence to free market liberalism underlay the stances developed by such early critics of climate change as Fred Singer, William Nierenberg and Frederick Seitz, whose consistent critiques of scientific consensus on tobacco and cancer, acid rain, and ozone also furthered their arguments against the regulatory power of the state. But, in common with the excellent work of Joshua Howe, and Eric Pooley's study *The Climate War: True Believers, Power Brokers, and the Fight to Save the Earth*, Oreskes and Conway have focused most closely on instances in which Singer and others attacked specific findings from the IPCC. Thus, to date, climate sceptics have usually been considered as being principally engaged in manufacturing doubt and creating ignorance, although this only describes part of their work.[4] I will endeavour to re-construct broader features of the intellectual framework underlying these climate sceptics' stances.

My analytic aim will be to complement earlier studies of sceptical strategies by articulating a number of revealing characteristics of what I will call "partisanal knowledge". We have recognised the practical, sometimes tacit and unwritten knowledge of craft workers and others with the concept of "artisanal knowledge".[5] I think it may be similarly helpful to explicitly consider the particular features of approaches to knowledge that have been developed in situations of contest, when slogans are at issue as well as theorems, and mottos and motives may be more important than models. Scientific controversies have proven highly valuable sites for sociological and historical analysis in large part because they reveal assumptions otherwise taken for granted amongst research communities. The circumstances that we are concerned with here are related, but are somewhat

---

3 An electronic copy of the *Reader's Digest* version is available from the website of the Institute of Economic Affairs: https://iea.org.uk/publications/research/the-road-to-serfdom, last accessed 17 June 2017.

4 Howe 2014; Pooley 2010; Proctor and Schiebinger 2008; Biddle and Leuschner 2015.

5 See, for example, Secord 1994; Ingold 2000.

different in character, because they typically involve rather different, in some senses more distributed stakes, being engaged amongst a still broader community than that of research scientists and involving not only scientific, but also economic, political and ideological issues. I will analyse here the forms of knowledge asserted by avowed partisans, considering the distinctive nature of their perspective on both the subject at issue (in this case, climate science), and their opponents (who they often describe as climate "alarmists"), when arguing from a position of weakness, without the support of the majority of the scientific community. I have used the term "partisanal *knowledge*", rather than "partisanal *science*" because I am concerned with cases involving commitments that are distinctly broader than the subject matter of scientific debates narrowly construed, but I do not want to tie this concept too closely to the specific politically- or ideologically-partisan stances evident in climate change (such as those exhibited by Republicans and supporters of the free market). Rather, outlining characteristics of partisanal knowledge may prove helpful in considering other cases in which agendas bridge distinctively different intellectual commitments (or this is argued by those asserting or denying particular knowledge claims). Many of the elements I will be concerned with were represented in my classroom that day, but empirically my account will primarily be based upon the study of a small group of books. I have already mentioned the first, in which Singer and Avery set out their positive case for an understanding of global warming based largely on solar cycles and the contention that recent warming fits within the bounds of natural variability: *Unstoppable Global Warming: Every 1,500 Years*, with its first edition of 2006 followed by an updated and expanded version in 2008.[6] The second is the 2015 book in which Singer together with Craig D. Idso and Robert M. Carter set out their negative case, arguing that there is no scientific consensus for anthropogenic global warming in *Why Scientists Disagree About Global Warming*, probably their most direct intellectual response to the challenges represented by the work of Oreskes, Conway and others who have helped characterise the distinctions between climate science consensus and its critics (Idso et al. 2015; 2017).

I have a further historical aim that will emerge from following the cue provided by Steven Welcenbach's gift to our class. Hayek's extraordinary *The Road to Serfdom* also emerged from contest.[7] Analysing the circumstances of its publication in several distinct and influential forms, as well as its central arguments, will show that, in addition to its advocacy of individual economic freedom, Hayek's book provides a potential source for several other features of the complex set of views advocated by climate sceptics now. In particular, as well as articulating some of the key values that sceptics support, it may have helped to shape assumptions about the scientific community and intellectuals that are still influential

---

6 Singer and Avery 2006; 2008. Later references will be to the 2008 edition.
7 Hayek [1944] 2007; Hayek [1945] 2005.

amongst the conservative movement in the U.S. today – as well as stimulating the neoliberal think tanks now utilised by climate sceptics.

2. Roads to and beyond *Serfdom*

Anyone leafing through the pages of the economist Friedrich A. von Hayek's most well known book will recognise that a very strong account of its origins in the middle of World War II is etched into its central argument. Having completed a highly technical book on economic theory in *The Pure Theory of Capital* in 1941, Hayek wrote *The Road to Serfdom* in response to his alarm at the extent to which the economic planning being pursued in the course of the war had come to be taken for granted in Britain and America. Dedicating it ironically to all socialists, Hayek included a telling epigraph from David Hume, "It is seldom that liberty of any kind is lost all at once". One of his most significant and oft-repeated arguments was that few people – be they socialist or not – recognised clearly the danger that they faced of losing their freedom to the seductive certainties of economic planning. Hayek thought that the central problem with the rise of the Nazis in Germany stemmed from their national socialism. Re-interpreting early socialist attacks on the Nazi party, and the Nazi suppression of communist thought, Hayek offered an alternative history in arguing forthrightly that the inevitable corollary of socialism was totalitarianism.[8]

Hayek cast himself as a lonely prophet representing views that were far from dominant, describing "democratic socialism" as a utopian ideal that most expressed without recognising that its two terms were incompatible, and "conservative socialism" as having prepared the ground for Nazism and representing the dominant trend in England and the U.S (Hayek [1945] 2005, 44). This rhetorical setting – depicting neoliberal thought as marginal at the time – has survived in many accounts of the book, without reflecting on its extraordinary commercial success, except to describe this as surprising. The first two British print runs of *The Road to Serfdom* were quickly sold out, and the Conservative Party dedicated a substantial portion of its allocation of paper under post-War rationing to printing further copies of the book in order to aid its chances in the 1945 election – but lost to an unprecedented swing to Clement Attlee's Labour Party. Although U.S. publishers were initially reluctant to take it on, and the University of Chicago Press set

---

8 He argued that "the rise of fascism and Marxism was not a reaction against the socialist trends of the preceding period but a necessary outcome of those tendencies"; Hayek [1945] 2005, 39–40. For a detailed account of the origins of the book, see Caldwell 2007, "Introduction", in Hayek [1944] 2007. An understanding of the importance of quite specific historical perspectives in framing such understandings of political economy is underlined in both the draft and final statement of aims accepted by the Mont Pèlerin Society in April 1947. See Plehwe 2015.

its first print run at 2,000 copies, it had sold 30,000 copies within six months, and, by February 1945, had also spawned a condensed version for *Reader's Digest*, with approaching 10 million copies in circulation and on newspaper stands, and customers taking the opportunity offered to order more than one million reprints of the article.[9] Thus, perhaps Hayek's original depiction of his views as unpopular, and certainly later repetitions of this framing, should be recognised as – at least in part – a rhetorical strategy, even if the scale of the book's success surely did surprise all involved; and we should also note that the ideological contest between planning and liberal thought that was integral to Hayek's argument played a significant role in political contests in both Britain and the United States, although Hayek himself was somewhat taken aback that his work should be so thoroughly appreciated by the members of one party and excoriated by those of another (some American reviews were particularly savage). Hayek's own commitment was more strongly to a long-term political agenda rather than to any particular party – he was ideologically committed to neoliberalism, rather than politically partisan.

But focusing on the immediate circumstances of its publication would risk neglecting some of the most important grounds for the success of *The Road to Serfdom*. Hayek had first encountered debates on planning in post World War I Vienna as he finished doctorates in law and political science, when Ludwig von Mises' 1922 book *Die Gemeinwirtschaft: Untersuchungen über den Sozialismus* shifted Hayek from his early sympathy with socialism, and he followed Mises in attacking Otto Neurath's proposals for a moneyless economy. In 1931, Hayek was brought to the London School of Economics by Lionel Robbins, in good part to provide an intellectual counterweight to the success of John Maynard Keynes' work in Cambridge, and Hayek published forerunners to aspects of his argument in *The Road to Serfdom* in academic papers and magazine articles in the 1930s (Caldwell 2004). Yet historians such as Johanna Brockman and Ben Jackson have emphasised that from the late nineteenth century through to the interwar period, neoliberal and socialist thought emerged in dialogue, with models of socialism and markets often used side by side methodologically, sometimes combined, as in the work of Walras, Pareto and Barrone, and sometimes even regarded as equivalent under specific assumptions. Jackson emphasises that, like other neoliberal thinkers in the 1930s, Hayek expressed suspicion about the moral values of *laissez faire*, shared value commitments with socialists and also endorsed significant state re-gulation and re-distribution (in Chapter 3, for example).[10] If such common ground was important in the 1930s, we have already seen enough to know that many elements of it were re-interpreted or discarded in *The Road to Serfdom*. This

---

9 Caldwell 2007, 19; Blundell 2005.
10 Bockman 2011; Jackson 2010. His biographer recommends that those on the left read Chapter 3, and those on the right consider the foreword to the 1956 paperback edition in order to challenge their preconceptions about Hayek's views; Caldwell 2007, 2.

is particularly true of both the highly streamlined, condensed version that the *Reader's Digest* editors produced to fit into 20 pages (which Hayek praised), and the 18-panel cartoon that was published in *Look* magazine and then reproduced by General Motors as the 118th volume in their "Thought Starter" series.[11]

Hayek's intellectual and physical migrations surely helped him to develop a message that engaged with political thought across different national contexts, and Hayek followed American enthusiasm for his work to take up a position at the University of Chicago in 1950, where his first faculty seminar was in the philosophy of science (it was attended by the physicists Enrico Fermi and Leo Szilard, and the geneticist Sewall Wright). Although the forced diasporas of the twentieth century necessitated many personal and intellectual migrations that were to have significant consequences for disciplines such as physics, economics and the philosophy of science, Hayek's relevance in diverse political cultures is striking and unusual, matching the role of Marx, Engels and Lenin in international socialism and similarly built, in part, upon having experienced different political systems. It is surely also important to note how ready Hayek was to adapt his message for different media, and critically, his interest in addressing political cultures in and beyond academia.

This was an important aim that reflected his analysis of the strongholds of socialism, and he pursued it both strategically and broadly, carefully targeting specific audiences. When the British businessman Antony Fisher approached Hayek to say that, having read *The Road to Serfdom*, he now wished to go into politics to implement it, Hayek told him that he shouldn't. Rather, as Fisher recalls, Hayek argued that:

Society's course will be changed only by a change in ideas. First you must reach the intellectuals, the teachers and writers, with reasoned argument. It will be their influence on society which will prevail, and the politicians will follow. (Blundell 2005, 28)

In 1955, Fisher founded the free market think tank called the Institute for Economic Affairs with this very much in mind. Thus, intellectuals were an important audience for Hayek, but he also regarded them as more likely than not to be inclined towards socialism. In his 1949 article on "Intellectuals and Socialism", he offered an account of what he described as the "professional second-hand dealers in ideas", arguing that socialism had never been primarily a working-class movement, but had always depended centrally upon those he called intellectuals (Hayek [1949] 2005, 105). This was a wide class of people – not scholars and experts in a given field, but journalists, teachers, ministers, cartoonists, writers, and radio commentators – amateurs with respect to the subject matter that they conveyed, including many scientists and doctors who could command respect.

---

11 This is included in the Institute of Economic Affairs edition of the *Reader's Digest* version, Hayek, [1945] 2005.

Hayek thought them constitutionally inclined towards socialism, and regarded this as partly due to the rise of engineering and the natural sciences in the last hundred years, leading to the thought that similar forms of organisation could be applied to the social realm (Hayek [1949] 2005, 18–19). These were the people who had to be won away from socialism, and he gave an account of why one found so many of them amongst the faculties of universities (who, he thought in this respect, had largely to be classed as intellectuals rather than as experts) (Hayek [1949] 2005, 119–22). With his website, discussion in my classroom and other activities, Steven Welcenbach fills very well the role of the intellectual that Hayek thought was critical to the success of his message.

Taking Hayek's political advocacy as a guide, we can already point to several important features that might be regarded as characteristic of partisanal knowledge. Critically, it includes a contextually based and highly detailed account of the opponent, one that is capable of explaining the grounds for the opponents' views – of knowing the opponent, perhaps, better than they do themselves. Often depicting the opponent as being at present more powerful than oneself, partisanal knowledge is thus likely to be subtle in its framework, and blunt in its labelling; and adherents recognise that they may well need to craft messages strategically for diverse audiences – in this case, the intellectual class. (These are all features that may well be shared by knowledge practitioners in general, but they are surely given less emphasis in most research fields.)

If reasoned arguments might be the central need for intellectuals, Hayek also showed a sharp brilliance in simplifications. He wrote a set of jacket notes for the first edition of *The Road to Serfdom* that provide a kind of summary in what we might call bullet points, setting out his contentions about Nazis, totalitarianism, socialism, the need to provide economic freedom (and, critically, not the freedom from economic care that socialists promised), and the role of the system of private property in safeguarding the freedoms even of those who do not own (Hayek [1945] 2005, "Summary"). The cartoon version in *Look* and General Motors dispensed with the language of socialism in favour of featuring "Planners" as its central character. It finished with an actual bullet point, depicting an execution in totalitarian hands when disciplining is planned:

'If you're fired from your job, its apt to be by a firing squad. What used to be an *error* has become a *crime* against the state. **Thus ends the road to serfdom!**' [emphasis in the original]

In this grim account – which might be called alarmist – the planning of thought was the third last step in planning finality. After planned professions and wages, and before planned recreation and disciplining,

Your thinking is "planned" . . . .

In the dictatorship, unintentionally created by the planners, there is no room for difference of opinion. Posters, radio, press—all tell you the same lies!

Figure 1: from Hayek 1945.

In the *Reader's Digest* version, a similar point was made with the example of relativity, opposed both as a Jewish attack on Christian and Nordic physics, and for being in conflict with dialectical materialism. This was because totalitarian systems such as those in Germany and the Soviet Union could not afford to cease before they controlled every act. As Hayek put it:

collectivism means the end of truth. To make a totalitarian system function efficiently it is not enough that everybody should be forced to work for the ends selected by those in control; it is essential that the people should come to regard these ends as their own. This is brought about by propaganda and by complete control of all sources of information.[12]

In the examples he gave, Hayek would uphold science in the face of totalitarian arguments against particular findings; and, despite promoting economic competition as the only means of avoiding the "coercive or arbitrary intervention of authority", he also recognised that government interference on working hours, sanitation and social services were compatible with preserving competition, and further that competition was impractical in fields dealing with pollution or deforestation, for instance, where harmful effects were not confined to property owners (Hayek [1945] 2005, 43–44). Given these views, then, Hayek might have seen grounds for a regulatory response to the science of climate change.

Hayek had a clear eye for the tactics required by totalitarian rulers, and whether he was conscious of this or not, up to a point, at least, these were tactics that he, too, followed in convincing a wide class of readers of his own stances (and it is worth noting that Hayek had volunteered to write propaganda for the British to be distributed in Europe in the course of the war). Hayek noted that the totalitarian leader's search for large-scale agreement would be unlikely to settle with the best, but would rather have to make do with the worst elements of any society, for higher education and intelligence implied differentiated views. Finding uniformity of outlook therefore required descending to regions of lower moral and intellectual standards, "where more primitive instincts prevail". This group would need to be enlarged still further, "by converting more to the same simple creed", amongst the docile and gullible. And, as a third step, he noted that, given the difficulty of uniting people through positive aims, the leader must appeal to a common weakness in finding an internal or external enemy (Hayek [1945] 2005, 52–53).

It is true that Hayek provided subtle discussions of power, authority, freedom and property in considered language written for expert readers, but he also offered condensed versions of his work for intellectuals, and even more graphic accounts that turned on simple slogans; and he, too, had found an enemy within when urgently combatting the imperfectly recognised socialism of Western societies and warning so stridently of its threats to truth and freedom. Arguably, all these factors in the pragmatics of persuasion have been as significant as the more positive vision of a new liberalism that Hayek also sought. In 1947, he organised the Mont Pèlerin Society to allow a committed group of thinkers who shared liberal concerns to develop and articulate a common perspective, free of the relentless debate of first principles that had dominated public discussions of the free market and planned society in the 1920s and 1930s.[13] Accounts of the nature

---

12 Hayek [1945] 2005, 54–56 at 54.
13 For accounts of the emergence of neoliberalism, see Mirowski and Plehwe 2015; Burgin 2012; Jones 2012.

of economic and social knowledge – and freedom – were both central to this endeavour, and these were shaped by Hayek's emerging understanding of the market. A decade earlier, Hayek had described the division of knowledge as the central problem of economics as a social science – every bit as important as the division of labour. In 1945, he gave his first confident account of the price system as a kind of machinery (writing "it is more than a metaphor") that enabled the transfer of information between myriad individual and corporate agents and allowed the entire economic system to function as a single market.[14] *The Road to Serfdom* represented his first major attempt to bring economic thought and political philosophy together; and the assertion that private property and the market competition that Hayek regarded as central to economic freedom are also foundational for free societies became integral to the stated aims of the Mont Pèlerin Society in its founding meeting (Plehwe 2015, 24–25). Yet, as historians of neoliberalism have shown, reaching consensus on the nature of freedom and the appropriate degree of state control (both issues taken up in *The Road to Serfdom*) proved difficult even within this group – and, although formulated in contrast to totalitarian systems, the concept of the free market that they elaborated is not necessarily congruent with the idea of liberal democracy; neoliberals have been able to reconcile liberal economics with authoritarian regimes such as Pinochet's Chile. Historians have also emphasised how hard neoliberals worked to win a distributed footing for their views in the face of their initial marginality in academia. What Plehwe and Mirowski call the neoliberal "thought collective" was steered by the regular meetings of the Mont Pèlerin Society but engaged several layers of activity, with the relations between them often invisible to outsiders. With some representation in academic departments in the LSE, the University of Chicago, Geneva and Freiburg (often unrecognised by outsiders), they were also able to use foundations such as the Volker Fund and the Relm Foundation to promote and help fund their activities, and provide neoliberal education, as well as entrepreneurial think tanks providing two further layers of still more politically direct advocacy. Early think tanks such as the Foundation for Economic Freedom that Leonard Read, Henry Hazlitt and others founded in Manhattan in 1946, and Fisher's Institute of Economic Affairs provided general position statements and advice on principle; and, from the 1970s, satellite think tanks were founded that offered timely position papers on current policy (as the Heritage Foundation sought to do under Edwin Feulner's leadership in Washington, D.C., from 1973).[15]

This account of the avowedly partisan work of Friedrich von Hayek has picked out some features that we might identify more generally with the distinctive kind of knowledge that partisans profess, my primary analytic aim. But, in addi-

---

14 Hayek [1937] 2014; Hayek 1945, 521.
15 See especially Mirowski 2015; Jones 2012, Chapter 4.

tion, it has provided historical grounds for our study of climate change, for, as we shall see, late twentieth and early twenty-first century critics of the scientific consensus on climate change have adopted some of the same concerns as Hayek, and have made use of the institutional achievements of Hayek's advocacy.

3. Unstoppable?

In 2008, the back pages of the second edition of *Unstoppable Global Warming: Every 1,500 Years* introduced its two authors as a climate physicist internationally known for his work on climate, energy and environmental issues, S. Fred Singer; and as a senior fellow of the Hudson Institute – a non-profit conservative think tank – who had previously worked as a senior analyst at the U.S. Department of State, Dennis T. Avery. Both were seasoned writers who had contributed to controversial topics in diverse media. Singer's brief biography mentioned his four books on aspects of climate change, from *Global Climate Change* in 1989 to *Climate Policy – From Rio to Kyoto* in 2000, but also noted his more than four hundred technical papers in scientific, economic and policy journals, and explicitly mentioned his recent co-authorship of a series of peer-reviewed papers on disparities between terrestrial and balloon- and satellite-based temperature measures. Although the book was written for a lay audience, Singer's expertise was clearly critical for its profile and scientific credentials. Avery's biographical sketch noted his work for dozens of newspapers as well as his 1995 book *Saving the Planet with Pesticides and Plastic: The Environmental Triumph of High-Yield Farming*, with a second edition in the year 2000. The stimulus for their collaboration had been Avery's argument that the Medieval Warm Period was one of the most favourable in history, expressed in a 1998 article on global warming as a boon to mankind, first published in Hudson's *American Outlook* – which had also been condensed and reprinted in the August 1999 issue of *Reader's Digest* (Singer and Avery 2008, 277–78).

The authors built on Avery's account of the potential benefits of global warming, but their principal argument was that a natural and moderate if somewhat irregular cycle of warming and cooling lasting about 1,500 years could be identified throughout the past one million years, and that what they called the Modern Warming would last a few more hundred years before giving way to cooling. They argued that this cycle, first identified in Greenland ice cores analysed by Dansgaard and Oeschger, was based in the physical evidence rather than being "an unproven theory like the model-based predictions used by advocates of the theory of man-made global warming" (Singer and Avery 2008, 28). Inevitable and unstoppable, they thought it was triggered by the sun, despite the absence of a solar cycle of that same length, being amplified by cosmic rays and ozone chemistry, and they argued that a computer model run by Holger Braun and colleagues at the Potsdam Institute for Climate Impact Research had found that superimposing the sun's well-known 87 and 210 year cycles could create such a cycle here on earth (Singer and Avery 2008, 25–27).

In the first edition, the authors' account of this climate cycle was interspersed with discussions of the Intergovernmental Panel on Climate Change and the Kyoto Protocol, and punctuated by chapters on numerous "baseless fears" – of sea level rise and species extinction, for example. This was an approach that thoroughly mixed their arguments against particular scientific views and policies with their account of a different view of climate change. Updating and revising the second edition with the assistance of the chair of the Heartland Institute, Joe Bast and his wife Diane, the authors noted that they had found a more logical organisation, now separating the first part with its discussion of the climate cycle from three different parts on the flaws of the greenhouse theory and climate models, baseless fears, and the costs and futility of the Kyoto Protocol. The effect was dramatic, pulling four related but distinct stories into focus. The first was a human history of the rise and fall of civilisations based upon climate change, which stressed the need to fear ice rather than warmth. Then followed the unfolding story of the scientific discovery of a 1,500-year climate cycle and a discussion of the different kinds of evidence upon which it was based. Punchy accounts of what the authors argued was a scientific fraud in the deliberations of the IPCC and a policy mistake in international protocols took up the bulk of the book in its final two parts.

This organisation cleverly put Singer and Avery's own interpretation of climate change before entering into detailed attacks on the IPCC and outlining their critique of the Kyoto Protocol and policy recommendations. As to the science of climate, this manifested an important subtext to some of their arguments more fully than the first edition had: the common view that the scientific findings should stand on their own, and that failures in science reflect the unwarranted intrusion of politics. It also brought into clearer relief the authors' distinction between the sceptical scientist – wary of alarmism and aiming for truth – and their vision of the consensus scientific view as one driven by an environmentalist agenda and the current ease of obtaining funding for climate research. In some respects, then, Singer and Avery shared a valorisation of science with the climate scientists that they attacked, but offered sharply different versions of what counts as good and bad science. As to the international attempt to combat climate change politically through the Kyoto Protocols, Singer and Avery offered an interpretation of their phased structure and the distinctions between the participation of first world and developing countries that treated them relentlessly in terms of the economic interests of the nations involved, thereby rendering the protocols a cynical attempt from various European nations to gain economic advantage and for the UN to become the "rationing board" planning the world's use of energy. Singer and Avery's positive policy recommendation for the U.S. was to concentrate on mitigating effects without attempting to alter what they thought were largely the result of natural variations in climate.

This brief portrait will have suggested how combative the book is, but will have shown that the authors also offered their own, engaging perspective on climate science and the human history of adaptations to climate. Both aspects of their work have evidently been persuasive for many, as the back-cover endorsements (prominently from three climatologists), the best-seller status of the book, and the continued life of some of their arguments in American political culture all indicate. Yet, despite upholding common perspectives on the purity of science, the specific images of science and politics that Singer and Avery present also reflect partisan priorities that might well make their account immediately persuasive to some readers (although they are likely to alienate others), while also being so selective as to be vulnerable to critique from more comprehensive perspectives. One way of putting this would be to say that their work often shows a brilliant engagement with momentary contests – told so as to highlight sceptical victories – without responding to the full breadth and long-term evolution of the research fields at issue. Another would be that the force of their arguments often depends upon equivocating between local and global perspectives.

Both these factors are at issue in Singer and Avery's treatment of the status of the Medieval Warm Period (MWP), first illustrated in their prologue by reprinting a graph from the 1995 edition of the IPCC report, which showed a distinctive increase in temperatures in the period from about 900 to 1300 AD (Singer and Avery 2008, xxi). Only in a later section do they refer to the way that the findings of this graph had been questioned by the argument that, rather than being global, the MWP was merely regional to Europe – but arguing, themselves, that this was untrue. On the face of it, they back their point up well by discussing a range of evidence from China, Japan and North America, but a careful reading of their footnotes would show that all the evidence considered is drawn from papers published before 1999 (Singer and Avery 2008, 46–50). Later in the book, they return to the topic in a section on "The 'Hockey Stick' Scandal" in which they discuss the work of Michael Mann and colleagues as this was incorporated in the 2001 report of the IPCC and widely publicised thereafter (Singer and Avery 2008, 127–32). Mann's studies of more globally distributed data using tree rings, corals, ice cores and historical records had shown far less evidence for a distinctively warm period (which now disappeared into the relatively uniform handle of the "hockey stick" graph), but his results and statistical analysis had been challenged by a small group of scholars. Singer and Avery discuss all their criticisms in some detail – without noting that these critiques of Mann had, in turn, been rebutted, and that, in its Fourth Assessment Report in March 2007, the IPCC had published an account of 14 further reconstructions, which upheld Mann's work.

This period is central to Singer and Avery's argument in two ways. The existence of the MWP is integral to their understanding of the natural cycle which they see as explaining the phenomena, and its relative height allows them to argue that current high temperatures fall within the limits of natural variation; yet the controversy is described as bearing solely on the credibility of the consensus view of anthropogenic global warming, and not on that of their own theory. Singer and Avery's discussion of this debated issue is thus interestingly selective – and, in at least two ways that might not have been evident to many readers.

By devoting significant attention only to critiques of Mann and the IPCC discussion, they offer what can be described as a partisanal "campaign story" of the exposure of apparent scientific errors. Failing to alert their readers to the selective nature of their account surely helped sceptical attacks on the consensus scientific position seem to be considerably more telling than they were held to be amongst scientists. Thus, their work did not provide the kind of comprehensive and longer-term treatment of this evolving field of research that would allow readers to appreciate fully the scientific stakes involved.

But it is also revealing that while Singer and Avery emphasise that Mann's hockey stick graph was picked up by the Clinton administration (as "the quick answer they wanted"), they refrained from pointing out that Republican controlled House committees had issued congressional investigations of this climate research in 2006 (Singer and Avery 2008, 128–29). Thus, they made it look as though politics was involved in support for global warming, but that attacks on it were simply scientific – thereby also obscuring the full nature of the political stakes involved, and the extent to which these had led Republicans to pursue prosecutorial tactics (which, although deployed in different ways over many years, have failed to indicate any substantial difficulty with Mann's work) (Mann 2012).

Summing this up, we can make the two distinct points that, for these proponents of partisanal knowledge, it has been strategically significant to describe their opponents as partisan, while also minimising recognition of the partisanal nature of their own work. This is because it is more important for them to count as scientists than as partisans, for this helps them open up to debate what might otherwise be regarded as settled knowledge. Conversely, they can gain an advantage or at least level the field of contest if they can convince others that their opponents are partisans. Their attempt to leverage significant asymmetries in the relations between science and partisanship has required the exercise of substantial finesse on the part of climate sceptics, and also led to some institutional innovation – for they must invert typical understandings of institutional power in the sciences to elevate the voices of a few contrarians above widespread consensus. Between the two editions of *Unstoppable Global Warming*, Fred Singer founded the

Nongovernmental International Panel on Climate Change (NIPCC), which over time has published a series of reports countering the IPCC (*Climate Change Reconsidered*, with four major instalments and an interim report from 2009 to 2017). The character and aims of the NIPCC articulate an understanding of science and the political which seeks to take advantage of their own lack of formal government or academic affiliations without drawing attention to the support of the Heartland Institute, while utilising the fact that the IPCC had been founded to provide an analysis of the state of scientific understanding of climate change relevant to policy but also neutral with respect to policy, to describe it as politically motivated. As their website puts it:

NIPCC has no formal attachment to or sponsorship from any government or governmental agency. It is wholly independent of political pressures and influences and therefore is not predisposed to produce politically motivated conclusions or policy recommendations.

NIPCC seeks to objectively analyze and interpret data and facts without conforming to any specific agenda. This organizational structure and purpose stand in contrast to those of the United Nations' Intergovernmental Panel on Climate Change (IPCC), which *is* government-sponsored, politically motivated, and predisposed to believing that climate change is a problem in need of a U.N. solution.[16]

Both the IPCC and the NIPCC must negotiate the relations between science and politics, but in contrast to the way the IPCC explicitly incorporates both peer review and government review on an international basis in order to achieve an understanding of science relevant to policy, the NIPCC has presented its stance as being independent of politics. They have had some success in propagating their perspective, especially in the U.S., partly because of their ability to address the intellectual circles that Hayek highlighted – and aided surely by aspects in which their account of the climate sciences with their footings in academia, government funded research and international organisations can mesh with current Republican distrust of these grounds. In these disputes, then, what counts as partisan and as science are potentially at issue in ways that are rare in controversies within research fields, where all share the status of scientist; and there are substantial advantages (and potential costs) to opening them up to debate.

Some of these benefits and costs are registered in the diverse images of science, its methods and institutions that are conveyed in *Unstoppable Global Warming*, which share many features with typical understandings of the climate sciences, but also feature aspects that support sceptics' arguments against the predominant view of the subject. I will consider both a point of commonality and one of difference before turning to the diverse strategies which Singer and Avery use to

---

16 Emphasis in the original. See their website: http://climatechangereconsidered.org/about-nipcc, last accessed 27 June 2017.

explain their difference from consensus views. In general, Singer and Avery support – and express eloquently – a common view of the interdisciplinary nature of the climate sciences and their dependence on a wide range of evidentiary supports, each of which, alone, would be insufficient, but which together allow comprehensive arguments to be identified. For example, their climate cycle argument is presented as a discovery of this nature that took place in the years since 1983 and across the work of hundreds of researchers. The authors emphasise this point without making the contrast that could be drawn to the chronology and scale of the argument for anthropogenic warming, built up since the early 1860s through the work of thousands; since then, Singer has sought to nullify this disadvantage by citing thousands in the reports of the NIPCC (Singer and Avery 2008, 7).

In contrast to this shared commitment to interdisciplinary empiricism, Singer and Avery largely dismiss the general circulation models and computerised forecasting programmes that the IPCC have relied on in discussing scenarios for future climates, arguing that these assume a stable climate in the absence of anthropogenic effects, also assume that climate change will be linear, do not match observed measures from satellite observations, and are based upon questionable data.[17] Yet, however just such criticisms may have been at a given point in the development of climate models, they could hardly be regarded as telling against their use in principle; and we have also noted that Singer and Avery themselves are quite ready to draw on similar resources when it suits them, yet sought to distinguish their climate cycle from the "theory" of anthropogenic climate change, relying as it did on models.[18] Indeed, their arguments against abstract theoretical approaches in favour of more empirical work might seem reminiscent of the strategy followed by the proponents of German and Nordic science who, Hayek noted, had argued against relativity.

This observation reminds us that bad science is often explained by recourse to social arguments, such as the thought control, forms of propaganda, and ultimately political power, to which Hayek referred. Singer and Avery develop several different strategies to manage the complex move of valorising science while themselves attacking widely-held views, and perhaps the most obvious is to explain how their opponents and their institutions have succumbed to bad science. Examining some of the diverse strategies that Singer and Avery deploy to explain their difference from the scientific consensus will highlight how wide-ranging and opportunistic their approach is.

The first strategy that I wish to mention involves offering an account of the diverse reasons which different groups might have for accepting anthropogenic climate change that ties them to the politicisation of the IPCC in support of an

---

17 Singer and Avery 2008, 137–48 on 47–48.

18 See also the contributions of Matthias Heymann (also in this conference) and especially Paul Edwards, e.g. Heymann 2010.

environmentalist agenda, journalists' interest in scare-mongering, politicians' support for bandwagons, and – something that Singer and Avery see to be new – climate scientists' readiness to chase funds in the direction of climate science research (Singer and Avery 2008, 104–05). These structural reasons are supported by numerous accounts of particular exchanges or controversies that show purportedly fraudulent behaviour on the part of climate scientists. One particularly revealing example involves Singer and Avery's strident critique of the ways that Ben Santer changed the language used in Chapter 8 of the Second Assessment Report as lead author in 1995, without ever acknowledging that Santer followed closely-defined protocols in acting as he did (Singer and Avery 2008, 118–22). This is an instance in which Singer and Avery's account selectively details aspects of the way in which these events were debated in the IPCC, scientific journals and the *Wall Street Journal*. As Oreskes and Conway have shown, mastery of the diverse media of the intellectual and academic sphere has been critical in attempts to manage perceptions of climate change, and climate sceptics such as Singer, Fred Seitz and Patrick Michaels have countered the lack of peer reviewed papers that are sceptical about anthropogenic climate change with publications in news media and other forums that support their own stances. Having published sceptics' attacks on Santer, for example, the editors of the *Wall Street Journal* simply did not give him or his colleagues the opportunity to publish their response, except in a heavily edited version which eventually appeared in full in the *Bulletin of the American Meteorological Society*, but this was then followed by Singer and Seitz repeating the erroneous charges that they had made in both the *Wall Street Journal* and the *Washington Times* (Oreskes and Conway 2010, 204–15).

A second strategy was simply to deny that consensus is important to science – a methodological point that Singer and Avery (2008, 7) saw exemplified in Galileo's famous resistance to the Church's argument that the Earth was stationary. This readiness to stand against common belief has been embraced by many climate sceptics or contrarians who take a certain pride in their status as heretics. But despite arguing that consensus does not necessarily define scientific truth, it is clear that Singer and Avery would prefer to claim the ground of common belief and consensus for their own views, for the third strategy which they follow has been to argue that the appearance of consensus is illusory – that most climate scientists do not support the IPCC position.

4. Scientists disagree?

In support of their contention, Singer and Avery begin by citing a list of petitions with varied numbers of signatories that are designed to show dissent in the scientific community, though as they recognise there are questions about the pertinence of different forms of expertise in evaluating such petitions for or against anthropogenic climate change (Singer and Avery 2008, 123–25). They then consider a "startling" piece that Naomi Oreskes had published in *Science* in 2004. Oreskes had sought to determine whether the consensus view stated by the IPCC was widely held by those publishing on global climate change in the peer-reviewed literature, or whether, in fact, it was subject to the kind of dispute that climate sceptics had averred. The importance of the issue to sceptics is indicated both by Singer and Avery's response to her brief but influential paper, and the fact that this has since become the kernel of a 106 page publication that Singer co-authored with Craig Idso and Robert Carter in 2015, *Why Scientists Disagree About Global Warming: The NIPCC Report on Consensus*, with a revised version appearing in 2017.

The changing ways that Singer and his co-authors describe both Oreskes and the article reveal their basic assumptions about the communities capable of judging work on climate change. Singer and Avery describe Oreskes as a "professor of history", and a page later we learn from an Internet discussion reproduced from the mathematician David Wojick that, as a student of history of science, "she really doesn't understand very well how science actually functions".[19] In the 2015 NIPCC report, Oreskes is described as a "science historian", while, two years later, she is described instead as a "socialist historian", although on both occasions the authors go on to note that she is "not a scientist" (Idso et al. 2015, 10, 11). The latter point neglects the fact that Oreskes has worked as a research assistant and teaching assistant in geology and the earth sciences, but it is emphasised because of doubts about whether historians can understand the nature and limitations of scientific abstracts (which she is described as having read "quickly") (Idso et al. 2015, 11). The former point about "socialism" indicates the continued relevance of Hayek's problematic in the present, and it is accompanied by the attempt to suggest that the authors have encapsulated the essence of Oreskes' work in addressing this single article. The authors suggest that the essay became the basis for Oreskes and Conway's 2010 book *Merchants of Doubt: How a Handful of Scientists Obscured the Truth on Issues from Tobacco Smoke to Global Warming*, and for an academic career "built on claiming that global warming 'deniers' are a tiny minority within the scientific community", as well as for a film and (perhaps especially critically), the notoriety of having been repeated in Al Gore's *An Inconvenient Truth* (Idso et al. 2015, 11).

Oreskes' article and its methods are also described in rather glib terms. In 2008, Singer and Avery describe her method as querying the Internet with the search words "global climate change" and consulting 928 abstracts between 1993 and 2003 (Singer and Avery 2008, 125). In 2015 and 2017, a fuller description

19 Singer and Avery 2008, 122–26, at 125–26.

notes the important point that Oreskes had used a search of the Institute for Scientific Information database to identify peer-reviewed articles on the topic – something that explains why her approach did not pick up the extensive non-peer-reviewed literature dissenting from the consensus view – which Idso, Singer and Carter nevertheless describe as inexplicably absent (Idso et al. 2015, 11). Many of their other critiques concern points that are good in principle, but are also clearly recognised in Oreskes' brief article itself – such as the distinction between explicitly and implicitly supporting a statement, and the potential irrelevance of attribution statements to the particular subject of the study concerned.

Oreskes' 2004 article is just one of many surveys that the NIPCC must deal with in order to maintain the absence of a meaningful consensus on the central issues concerning anthropogenic climate change, but their treatments often involve reading against the grain of the original study in order to pick out perspectives that were not central to the authors themselves. But the major concern of the NIPCC report on consensus is to summarise the elements of their argument that the IPCC is agenda driven and a political, rather than a scientific, body. In this, they return to the concerns that Singer and Avery had outlined – only a little less briefly – in *Unstoppable Global Warming*.

5. Partisanal knowledge

In my introduction, I noted that *Why Scientists Disagree About Global Warming* probably constitutes Singer's most direct response to the challenges posed by the work of historians of science such as Oreskes and Conway, and Joshua Howe, with their detailed analyses of the scientific and political environment in which both the IPCC and a community of climate sceptics have arisen. In keeping with their responses to other aspects of the climate sciences, we have seen now that Singer and other climate sceptics have responded to this kind of historical knowledge indirectly and selectively, offering strategic replies to critical claims that conduct a vigorous defence by attacking the messenger while addressing the message somewhat glancingly. As these historians have shown in earlier work, climate sceptics have learned from past engagements, built robust structures relating think tanks to select media, and they have been reactive, with their combative tactics shaped largely by the claims and institutions that they seek to counter. My account of Hayek indicates that elements of their playbook may also be due to the similarly combative origins of neoliberal economic and political thought, which featured a broad-scale analysis of the critical intellectual community that should be addressed for political gain. Climate sceptics have noted this well, and a brief study of Singer's earlier career will also suggest further concrete links that significantly complicate the image that Singer and Avery give of the asymmetric relations between politics and science when discussing the climate consensus and the stances that they take as critics.

To date, in order to give an understanding of how the public might perceive Singer, my portrait of his background has been based upon the brief biography in the back pages of *Unstoppable Global Warming*. This makes clear his longstanding work in environmental science, without detailing the extent to which Singer had also been involved in governmental work, or disclosing that Singer had aligned his scientific and political perspectives rather closely from at least the late 1970s.[20] After his 1948 Ph.D. in physics at the University of Princeton (NJ) and early work in cosmic ray physics and atmospheric sciences, Singer was the first director of the National Weather Satellite Center in the U.S. Department of Commerce from 1962–64, before becoming the founding Dean of the School of Environmental and Planetary Sciences at the University of Miami. In 1967, Singer took a position as Deputy Assistant Secretary in the U.S. Department of the Interior in the Lyndon B. Johnson administration, where he was responsible for Water Quality and Research. Under Richard Nixon in 1970–71, he served as Deputy Assistant Administrator (Policy) of the newly founded U.S. Environmental Protection Agency, chairing an Interagency Work Group on Environmental Impacts of the Supersonic Transport. Singer was building significant expertise in policy, and began publishing on environmental pollution and population levels. As Oreskes and Conway show, at this time, he also represented a typically "environmentalist" stance, arguing for the need to reduce "the environmental impact of population growth [...] above all by choosing lifestyles which permit 'growth' of a type that makes a minimum impact on the ecology of the earth's biosphere".[21] In 1971, Singer was a Federal Executive Fellow at the Brookings Institution, an independent research institute that describes itself as non-partisan, where he undertook cost-benefit analyses of environmental regulation; but he moved back into the academic sector later that year as Professor of Environmental Sciences at the University of Virginia. By 1978, Oreskes and Conway point out, his perspective had changed to express significant caution about the costs of environmental protection and to seek potential solutions to environmental problems in the technological innovations that one might expect from the free market (Oreskes and Conway 2010, 84).

Towards the end of Ronald Reagan's first year of the presidency, in November 1981, Singer sent his CV stressing that he was a long-time Republican and

---

20 Singer has offered relatively little biographical information on his career but notably disputed Scheuering's brief comment on his funding from oil companies and threatened (but not pursued) legal action against the archivally-based work of Oreskes and Conway that I will draw on here: Scheuering 2004; Oreskes and Conway 2010.

21 Singer 1971, 256, as cited in: Oreskes and Conway 2010, 84.

member of the Republican National Committee, with "the right political-econo-mic philosophy to mesh with the Reagan administration". Singer turned down the offer of second in command at the National Oceanic and Atmospheric Administration, because this would not provide him enough scope for policy initiatives, but he soon found a different form of opportunity through engagement in committee work (Oreskes and Conway 2010, 85). Proposed by the White House to be a member of a National Academy of Sciences Acid Rain Peer Review Panel that convened in early 1983 and was chaired by William Nierenberg, Singer effectively became a dissenting voice. He argued consistently throughout the deliberations that the science was not settled (as he would later do in debating climate change), and also developed a cost-benefit analysis so far at odds with the rest of the report that, rather than being published as a chapter as originally planned, it was instead included as a signed appendix. There, going beyond the committee's charge to summarise and critique the science of technical working groups on acid rain in the US and Canada, Singer concluded that the government could set a maximum level of acceptable pollution, and establish transferable emissions rights that could be used, sold or traded. This was a then-novel market-based solution that (without much analysis) Singer wrote, "would guarantee that the market will work in such a way as to achieve the lowest-cost methods of removing pollution".[22] Perhaps Singer's readiness to act in this way reflected a further element in his political experience. In 1982–83, Singer was also a Senior Fellow at the Heritage Foundation, the prominent neoliberal think tank run by the Secretary-Treasurer of the Mont Pèlerin Society, Edwin J. Feulner; and this was in the bellwether period after Reagan had enthusiastically adopted their 1981 report entitled Mandate for Leadership, proposing ways to reduce the size of the Federal Government. When Singer first cut his teeth in arguments against scientific consensus, it was within committees of experts, furthering policy aims associated with the Reagan administration and neoliberal political and economic agendas.

My analysis here has shown that when Fred Singer approached climate change two decades later, he addressed intellectual and politically partisan circles far more thoroughly and effectively than he did the scientific community, but chose to do so as a scientist, rather than as the politically-motivated partisan that he also was. But, in conclusion, I would like to draw attention to several respects in which partisanal knowledge is unlike artisanal knowledge. Rather than being characterised by tacit skills embodied in product and process, difficult to communicate as knowledge except through practice, partisanal knowledge is a child of persuasion and communication, flaunting its status as knowledge perhaps too flamboyantly. Practitioners such as Singer are highly explicit about the framework for the knowledge asserted by opponents, offering insight into their motivations, critical assumptions and the patronage network to which they are beholden, all features

---

22 Oreskes and Conway 2010, 82–102, at 93.

that help to explain why their opponent's work should not be taken as certain knowledge. Partisanal accounts of the enemy are blunt and crude, offering urgent attention to framework and strategic detail, and, in the examples we have seen, neglecting a sustained and comprehensive account of the field of research involved. It is characteristic that, for all the positive features of Singer and Avery's account, their argument for a new climate cycle has not been widely upheld, but merged with a more general sceptical argument that present climate phenomena can be explained by natural variability. Finally, proponents of partisanal knowledge offer distinctive accounts of the foundations of their own knowledge, in this case tying it to institutions formed in contrast with the international and governmental basis for some of the institutions of climate science, and rejecting or obscuring the arguments that might tie them to the partisanal foundations that support them. Critically, they aim to claim that they are not partisans.

References

Biddle, Justin B., and Anna Leuschner (2015): "Climate Skepticism and the Manufacture of Doubt: Can Dissent in Science be Epistemically Detrimental?" *European Journal for Philosophy of Science*, 5 (3): 261–78.

Blundell, John (2005): "Introduction: Hayek, Fisher and *the Road to Serfdom*." In: *The Road to Serfdom: With The Intellectuals and Socialism*, 22–33. London: The Institute of Economic Affairs.

Bockman, Johanna (2011): *Markets in the Name of Socialism: The Left-Wing Origins of Neoliberalism*. Stanford CA: Stanford University Press.

Burgin, Angus (2012): *The Great Persuasion: Reinventing Free Markets since the Depression*. Cambridge MA-London: Harvard University Press.

Caldwell, Bruce (2004): *Hayek's Challenge: An Intellectual Biography of F.A. Hayek*. Chicago IL: University of Chicago Press.

Caldwell, Bruce (2007): "Introduction." In: *Friedrich A. Hayek, the Road to Serfdom: Text and Documents*. Edited by Bruce Caldwell. Collected Works of Friedrich August Hayek, 1–33. Chicago IL: University of Chicago Press.

Edwards, Paul N. (2010): *A Vast Machine: Computer Models, Climate Data, and the Politics of Global Warming*. Cambridge MA: The MIT Press.

Hayek, Friedrich A. von [1949] (2005): "The Intellectuals and Socialism." In: *The Road to Serfdom: With The Intellectuals and Socialism*, 105–29. London: The Institute of Economic Affairs.

Hayek, Friedrich A. von [1945] (2005): "The Road to Serfdom." In: *The Road to Serfdom: With The Intellectuals and Socialism*, 39–70. London: The Institute of Economic Affairs.

Hayek, Friedrich A. von [1945] (2005): "*The Road to Serfdom in Cartoons*." In: *The Road to Serfdom: With The Intellectuals and Socialism*, 71–89. London: The Institute of Economic Affairs.

Hayek, Friedrich A. von [1944] (2005): "Summary." In: *The Road to Serfdom: With The Intellectuals and Socialism*, 35–36. London: The Institute of Economic Affairs.

Hayek, Friedrich A. von (1945): "The Use of Knowledge in Society." *The American Economic Review*, 35 (1945): 519–30.

Hayek, Friedrich A. von [1937] (2014): "Economics and Knowledge." In: *The Market and Other Orders*. Edited by Bruce Caldwell. The Collected Works of F.A. Hayek, 57–77. London/New York: Routledge.

Hayek, Friedrich A. von [1944] (2007): *The Road to Serfdom: Text and Documents*. Collected Works of Friedrich August Hayek. Edited by Bruce Caldwell. The Definitive Edition. Chicago IL: University of Chicago Press.

Heymann, Matthias (2010): "Understanding and Misunderstanding Computer Simulation: The Case of Atmospheric and Climate Science – An Introduction." *Studies in History and Philosophy of Modern Physics*, 41 (3): 193–200.

Howe, Joshua P. (2014): *Behind the Curve: Science and the Politics of Global Warming*. Weyerhaeuser Environmental Books. Seattle WA-London: Washington University Press.

Idso, Craig D. et al. (2015): *Why Scientists Disagree About Global Warming: The Nipcc Report on Scientific Consensus*. Arlington Heights IL: Nongovernmental International Panel on Climate Change.

Idso, Craig D. et al. (2017): *Why Scientists Disagree About Global Warming: The Nipcc Report on Scientific Consensus*. 2nd ed. Arlington Heights IL: Nongovernmental International Panel on Climate Change.

Ingold, Tim (2000): *The Perception of the Environment: Essays on Livelihood, Dwelling and Skill*. London-New York: Routledge.

Jackson, Ben (2010): "At the Origins of Neo-Liberalism: The Free Economy and the Strong State, 1930-1947." *The Historical Journal*, 53 (1): 129–51.

Jones, Daniel Stedman (2012): *Masters of the Universe: Hayek, Friedman, and the Birth of Neoliberal Politics*. Princeton NJ: Princeton University Press.

Mann, Michael E. (2012): *The Hockey Stick and the Climate Wars: Dispatches from the Front Lines*. New York: Columbia University Press.

Mirowski, Philip (2015): "Postface: Defining Neoliberalism." In: Philip Mirowski and Dieter Plehwe (Eds.) (2015): *The Road from Mont Pèlerin: The Making of the Neoliberal Thought Collective, with a New Preface*, 417–55. Cambridge MA-London: Harvard University Press.

Mirowski, Philip, and Dieter Plehwe (Eds.) (2015): *The Road from Mont Pèlerin: The Making of the Neoliberal Thought Collective, with a New Preface*. Cambridge MA-London: Harvard University Press.

Oreskes, Naomi (2004): "The Scientific Consensus on Climate Change." *Science*, 306 (5702): 1686.

Oreskes, Naomi, and Erik M. Conway (2010): *Merchants of Doubt: How a Handful of Scientists Obscured the Truth on Issues from Tobacco Smoke to Global Warming*. New York: Bloomsbury Press.

Plehwe, Dieter (2015): "Introduction." In: Philip Mirowski and Dieter Plehwe (Eds.): *The Road from Mont Pèlerin: The Making of the Neoliberal Thought Collective, with a New Preface*, 1–42. Cambridge MA-London: Harvard University Press.

Pooley, Eric (2010): *The Climate War: True Believers, Power Brokers, and the Fight to Save the Earth*. New York: Hyperion.

Proctor, Robert, and Londa L. Schiebinger (2008): *Agnotology: The Making and Unmaking of Ignorance*. Stanford CA: Stanford University Press.

Scheuering, Rachel White (2004): "S. Fred Singer (1924-)." In: *Shapers of the Great Debate on Conservation: A Biographical Dictionary*, 115–27. Westport CT: Greenwood Publishing Group.

Secord, Anne (1994): "Science in the Pub: Artisan Botanists in Early Nineteenth Century Lancashire." *History of Science*, 32 (3): 269–315.

Singer, S. Fred (Ed.) (1971): *Is There an Optimum Level of Population?* Population Council Book. New York: McGraw-Hill.

Singer, S. Fred, and Dennis T. Avery (2006): *Unstoppable Global Warming: Every 1,500 Years*. Lanham MD: Rowman & Littlefield Publishers.

Singer, S. Fred, and Dennis T. Avery (2008): *Unstoppable Global Warming: Every 1,500 Years*. Updated and expanded ed. Lanham MD: Rowman & Littlefield Publishers.

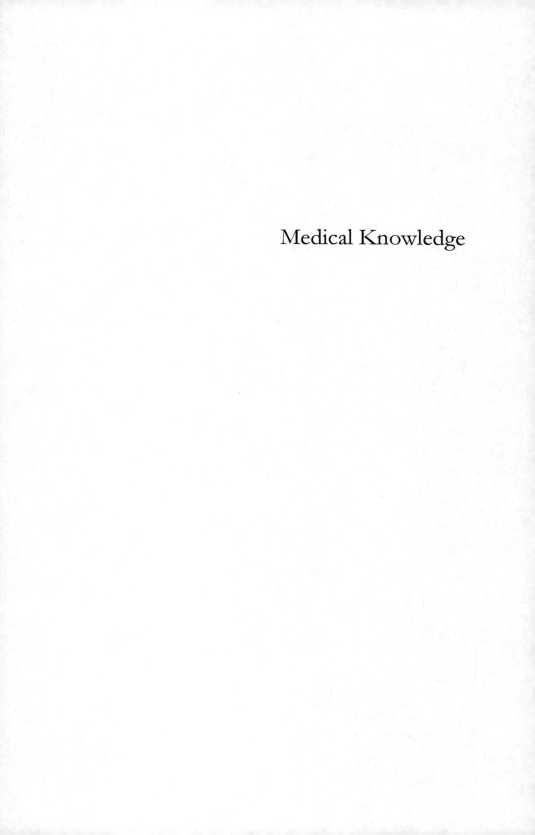

Medical Knowledge

The Weak and the Strong:
Medical Knowledge and Abolitionist Debates in the Late Eighteenth Century

Suman Seth

Abstract

In the late eighteenth century, both British abolitionists and their opponents could agree on a fact: the slave population in the West Indies was not self-sustaining. Deaths outnumbered births. Where the two sides disagreed was over the cause of this demographic decline. This essay focuses on a subsection of this wide-ranging debate, that part involving the testimony of those who claimed some expertise in, or knowledge of, medicine. Abolitionists deployed medical logics to insist that the slave trade and the brutal practices of slavery were to blame for this shocking and disturbing numerical data. Some apologists for slavery, by contrast, used their medical training to argue that the region's deadly climate was the culprit, while others pointed fingers at the behaviour and practices of slaves themselves. Thus, this chapter is concerned with both strength and weakness: the robustness of a mutually accepted fact and the weakness of any individual interpretation, none of which managed to achieve closure or compel consensus.[1]

1. Introduction

This is a story of strength and weakness. It involves what might be considered a strong fact and multiple weak interpretations. The fact was strong in the sense that it formed the basis for a sustained, polemical, and detailed argument. The fact itself was not, for the most part, contested. The interpretations were weak in that no side was able, for reasons I shall explain in some detail, to convince the

---

1 It is with pleasure that I acknowledge here my gratitude to Moritz Epple, Annette Imhausen and Falk Müller for the invitation to participate in their "Weak Knowledge" conference and for their very helpful comments. Amber Lia-Kloppel continues to make my weak work stronger. This chapter is derived from parts of my recent book, *Difference and Disease: Medicine, Race, and the Eighteenth-Century British Empire* (Cambridge: Cambridge University Press, 2018).

other. Nor, at least within the time period I consider here – the 1760s to the 1790s – was either side able to achieve closure. As is common in debates that are not easily resolved, the fundamental problem was that the sides could not really agree on what the terms of the debate were. This is another element of weakness. Strong forms of knowledge compel those with disparate interests to debate on common terrain.

The fact was this: in the eighteenth century, slave populations in the West Indies were not self-sustaining. Numbers of births were outweighed by numbers of deaths, so that slaves needed to be imported for the population even to stay steady. The fact was notorious. As Richard Sheridan has noted, both Edmund Burke and David Hume commented upon it, with Hume suggesting "that a stock of slaves grow worse five per cent, every year, unless new slaves be bought to recruit them". Exact numbers were disputed, but even an estimate by a source sympathetic to planters and intentionally aiming for "very low calculation" suggested that six slaves per two hundred (so, around 3 per cent) were needed every year to maintain the current population (Sheridan 1972, 26). For abolitionists, the fact was powerful evidence for the brutality of the slave system and a key reason that the "man-trade" should be ended. For those in support of slavery, the fact was distressing, but population decrease could not be blamed on plantation owners or the practices of enslavement. Fingers were pointed in multiple directions. It was not slavery, some argued, but the brutal West Indian climate that took the lives of hundreds of thousands. Others blamed the characters and customs of slaves themselves. Perhaps slavery should be meliorated, they acknowledged, to deal with what were portrayed as isolated excesses and poor policy, but there was no reason for its eradication.

Central to these debates was the testimony of those who claimed some expertise in, or knowledge of, medicine, and it is their arguments with which this essay is concerned. Comparatively little attention within the vast literature on abolitionism has been paid to the role played – on either side – by medical men.[2] Yet medical arguments supplemented and were entwined within arguably more familiar moral, theological, and economic positions. The relationships between medicine, climate, and disease were critical for a debate that turned upon who was to blame for the inhuman and near-unimaginable losses of human life due to the "seasoning",[3] or whether black bodies were essential for the cultivation of sugar

---

2 A recent and very welcome exception can be found in Smith 2015. See, also, Sheridan 1985.

3 Hans Sloane defined "what is call'd the seasoning" as follows: "that is to say, that every New-Comer before they be accustomed to the Climate and Constitution of the Air in Jamaica are to have an acute Disease, which is thought to be very dangerous, and that after this is over, their bodies are made more fit to live there, with less hazard than before: and this is not only thought so in that Island, but in *Guinea* and all over the remote Eastern parts of the world." (Sloane 1707 & 1725, Vol. I., xcviii) In 1740, Charles Leslie estimated that "Almost half of the new imported

under a blazing New World sun. Medical men and medical logics were marshalled in arguments over African inferiority and the very question of their humanity. And doctors, surgeons, midwives and others all participated in ongoing discussions over the question of the single or multiple origins of different "races". As abolitionist critiques invoked changes – more or less cosmetic – doctors became even more thoroughly imbricated within the slave system. From the 1760s, one begins to find medical texts written on ways to handle the initial seasoning and later care of slaves. From the 1780s, the writings of men who claimed to administer to the medical needs of thousands of slaves per year were cited, critiqued, and debated in parliamentary sessions devoted to the question of the continuation of the trade within the British Empire. Abolitionists excoriated planters for the death and suffering – from disease, neglect, and harsh treatment – of the slaves they owned, while some West-Indian doctors used their experiences to offer *apologia* and negations of precisely these charges.

The medical knowledge of both abolitionists and pro-slavery writers was strong enough to command attention, but too weak to command assent. Strength and weakness are, of course, relative categories. However weak the knowledge of British medical practitioners may have been, it was still stronger – strong enough to be heard – than that of the enslaved themselves. The voices of slaves were often silenced, not least by a legal system that forbade their bearing witness or bringing charges against their owners. The voices of the formerly enslaved certainly had profound impacts on abolitionist debates, as can be seen clearly in the role played by Olaudah Equiano in publicising the horrors of the *Zong* massacre in the 1780s. And the vast majority of those providing medical treatment for the enslaved were themselves slaves. Some British authors were happy to bolster their own claims to the possession of local knowledge by citing "native" informants whom they presented as more or less reliable, although even such mentions tend to be limited, becoming less common in botanical treatises across the eighteenth century. As Londa Schiebinger has shown, the audience also mattered: "In his Jamaican *Treatise*," she writes of the author of the *Treatise on the Diseases of Negroes* (1820), "Thomson valued 'Negro' knowledge. In his European version, this knowledge often fell from view" (Schiebinger 2017, 179). In this account of medical knowledge and abolitionism, then, my focus is on the published writings of those with enough social capital to be published at all.

Negroes die in the Seasoning" (Leslie 1740, 305). For a detailed discussion of the diverse and changing meanings of the term, see Seth 2018, Chapter 3.

2. Medicine and abolitionism

In 1789, when the Jamaica House of Assembly published two reports on the slave-trade, the abolitionist debate was coming to a head (Fuller 1789). The year before, William Wilberforce had introduced a parliamentary resolution that would have committed the British House of Commons to a discussion of the trade in its next session. Petitions were already flooding in, from both sides. An investigatory report on the matter by the Privy Council was published in April 1789, and in May, Wilberforce delivered an immediately famous speech describing the horrors of the Middle Passage, the journey from the coast of Africa to the New World, and arguing that abolition would lead to a near-certain improvement of the situation of slaves in the West Indies (Foot 1792, 75). "[H]is *speech* is circulated everywhere," wrote one pro-slavery writer with chagrin in 1792, "and the cruelties recorded in it are become as familiar to *children* as the story of *Blue Beard* or *Jack the Giant Killer*." The Committee of the Jamaican House responded in October and November, dividing the criticisms levelled in the many petitions before Parliament into those that concerned the African slave trade, and those that concerned the treatment of slaves in the West Indies. On the first matter, they (disingenuously) suggested that "the inhabitants of the West-India islands have no concern in the ships trading to Africa". The African trade was a British interest. Jamaican planters were involved in the trade only as the buyers "of what British acts of Parliament have declared to be legal objects of purchase".[4] The crucial accusations, then, were those regarding the *treatment* of the enslaved within the island, which they divided into four charges: that the laws governing negroes were harsh; that the laws were executed with inhumanity and without mercy; that negroes were grossly overworked and were not granted sufficient days of rest; and that the decline in the numbers of slaves on the island was due to their poor treatment (Fuller 1789, 3). It is this last charge, and the attempts at defence against it, with which we are most concerned here.

The Committee began by contesting not the bare fact, but rather its magnitude. Deploying deeply suspicious exculpatory calculations – which two authors have recently described as "highly improbable" – they were still forced to concede that there had been a net loss of more than 26,000 lives among slaves on the island since 1655. The report then listed the two main causes of slave mortality: "The great proportion of deaths that happen among negroes newly imported" (that is, what was known as 'the seasoning'), and "The loss which prevails among the negro infants that are born in the country." (Fuller 1789, 15) The three medical men called to provide evidence to the committee (whose interviews were then published as appendices) came to the same broad conclusions on the question of the seasoning. Deaths were not to be laid at the doors of planters. Losses among

---

4 Fuller 1789, 2–3. On medicine and the Middle Passage, see Sheridan 1981.

newly-arrived slaves were due to diseases from which they were suffering prior to landing, acquired either in Africa or on-board ship. They differed more on the causes of the deaths of infants. James Chisholme and Adam Anderson both agreed that roughly one quarter of all negro children died within two weeks of their birth. Chisholme ascribed this to the lack of cleanliness and care with which the young were treated and dressed, arguing that paying greater attention to the sanitary conditions of newborn children would thus, in principle, solve the problem quite easily. "But, simple as this may appear in theory," he argued, placing the blame on the enslaved themselves, "those who are much conversant with negroes, will be aware of the difficulty, if not impossibility, of putting it in practice, in a degree sufficient to answer the purpose. For, such is the ignorance, obstinacy, and inattention of negroes: so little regard have they for each other, and so averse are they to executing the directions of white people, when repugnant to their own prejudices [...]."[5] Anderson denied that the question of dressing could solve the problem so simply, but did not regard the issue as one that was easily solvable in practice, either.[6] John Quier reported that the affliction was not common in the area of his practice and placed the blame for the island's declining slave population on the promiscuity of negro women, which led both to frequent abortions and to a lack of care for children, who were "lost through neglect and the want of maternal affection, which the mothers seldom retain for their offspring by a former husband".[7] Rehearsing standard tropes about the wickedness, ignorance, and wantonness of slaves, then, physicians lent their expertise to the apologist cause.

We shall return to some of these claims soon, but for us the most basic point to be drawn from the report of the Jamaican Assembly is the centrality of medical arguments to the abolitionist debate.[8] Reading abolitionist tracts, the public was horrified by stories of torture and punishment, and moved by descriptions of the backbreaking labour slaves were forced to perform. Almost every island passed laws in response to such critiques, but it was hard to deny charges that such laws were unenforceable (and certainly unenforced) window-dressing when faced with the strong fact of a decline in the slave population. Abolitionist claims, which held the slave-system responsible for this prodigious loss of life, required expert responses, which blamed not planters or their laws, but ship-board conditions and the practices of slaves themselves. Among the most trenchant critics of slavery were medical men – among whom Benjamin Rush and James Ramsay were perhaps the most famous. As we can see, however, physicians and surgeons also

---

5 Fuller 1789, Chisholme, Appendix Six: 26–28.

6 Fuller 1789, Anderson, Appendix Seven: 28–30.

7 Fuller 1789, Quier, Appendix Eight: 30–33.

8 Beyond the specific elements cited below, I want to cite here my more general debts to Sheridan's coverage of the relationships between medicine and slavery in Sheridan 1985.

argued for the other side. It was not slavery *per se*, that was to blame, they argued, for matters were complex. But the situation could be improved and, practised properly, medicine could aid in melioration.

If we accept that medicine played a role in abolitionist debates, we should also acknowledge the role played by abolitionist debates in pushing certain medical issues to the fore. The Jamaican Assembly seemed to make it obvious that the profound losses due to "the seasoning" should be discussed in explicitly medical terms, but this had not always been so. Charles Leslie's *New History of Jamaica* (1740) did not shy away from describing some of the worst elements of life on the island: "trivial errors" punished with brutal whippings, slaves treated cruelly simply for the pleasure of the overseer, and "their Bodies all in a Gore of Blood, the skin torn off their Backs with the cruel Whip, beaten Pepper, and Salt, rubbed in the Wounds, and a large Stick of Sealing-wax dropped leisurely upon them" (Leslie 1740, 305). And yet, only a half-dozen pages after this horrific depiction, Leslie described the stunning number of deaths due to "the seasoning" without any of this emotion or empathy. An Owner, he noted, must replenish "his Stock [...] every Year, or he would soon want Hands for his Work. Almost half of the new imported Negroes die in the Seasoning." (1740, 312) One should compare this invocation of a numerical claim to that of Anthony Benezet, the French-born Quaker who has been called the "father of Atlantic abolitionism" (Jackson 2009). In 1762, Benezet, too, noted that roughly half of the slaves imported to Jamaica died of the seasoning, while a quarter perished in Barbados, bringing the total number of deaths, including the passage, for a single year of British trading to the West-Indies and colonies in North America to twelve thousand souls.

What a sad dreadful Affair then is this Man-Trade, whereby so many Thousands of our Fellow rational Creatures lose their lives, are, truly and properly speaking, murdered every Year; I do not think there is an Instance of so great Barbarity and Cruelty carried on in any Part of the World, as is this, Year after Year. It is enough to make one tremble, to think what a Load of Guilt lies upon this Nation, on this Account, and that the Blood of Thousands of poor innocent Creatures, murdered every Year, in carrying on this cursed Trade, cry aloud to Heaven for Vengeance. (Benezet 1762, 39–40)

This was a powerful claim, made in a Christian, moral register. It relied, for its power, in being able to connect a strong fact – death-rates on the Middle Passage were agreed to be high, even if exact numbers were contested – with intentional or near-intentional murder. This reading, of course, was precisely what pro-slavery advocates denied and where they sought to blunt abolitionist criticisms by pointing to the conditions of slaves prior to their embarkation, or to uncontrollable shipboard conditions. Yet, the debate was not necessarily a stalemate, for it involved more than two sides. Fundamentally, it was fought in the public arena and the British public was increasingly horrified by the accounts that abolitionists brought to their attention.

It is surely no coincidence that the first tract on how to "season" slaves properly to avoid the kinds of losses Benezet described appeared two years after Benezet's *Short Account of that Part of Africa, Inhabited by the Negroes*. James Grainger was born in Scotland around 1721 and graduated with a medical degree from Edinburgh in 1753, before moving to St. Kitts in 1759. In publishing his "Essay on the More Common West-India Diseases" in 1764, Grainger registered his "astonishment, that among the many valuable medical tracts which of late years have been offered to the public, none has been purposely written on the method of seasoning new negroes" (Grainger [1764] 2005a, 6). This "method" was fairly straightforward, involving gradual habituation to the work of the fields. Or, as he phrased it in his poem, *"The Sugar Cane"*: "Let gentle work, / Or rather playful exercise, amuse / The novel gang: and far be angry words; / Far ponderous chains: and far disheartening blows".[9] This was valuable counter-propaganda and signalled the beginning of medicine's involvement in a discourse about the development of a more benevolent form of slavery. The "seasoning", in Grainger's work, was not a brutal numerical fact that underscored the fundamental inhumanity of the man-trade. Rather, it was a problem to be resolved by better and more medically informed management. Urging better medical treatment for the enslaved, the planter could be economically rational and take back the moral high-ground ceded to the abolitionist:

But it is not enough to take care of Negroes when they are sick; they should also be well clothed and regularly fed. Neglecting either of these important precepts is not only inhuman, it is the worst species of prodigality. One Negroe saved in this manner more than pays the additional expences which owners of slaves by this means incur. But, supposing it did not, it ought seriously to be considered by all masters, that they must answer before the Almighty for their conduct towards their Negroes. (Grainger [1764] 2005a, 51)

As Larry Tise has noted, pro-slavery writings tended to be reactive. A number appeared in response to the criticisms levelled by Benezet and others in the 1760s. A second grouping emerged after the Somerset Case in 1772, including one written, anonymously at first, by the Pennsylvanian physician, Benjamin Rush.[10] In

---

9 Grainger [1764] 2005b, 62–63. See, also, Smith 2015.

10 In March 1749, James Somerset was purchased as a slave in Africa and transported to Virginia, where he was sold to Charles Steuart on 1 August. Twenty years later, in 1769, Steuart made a business trip to England and took Somerset with him, planning to stay for as long as necessary and then return to America. In 1771, Somerset fled Steuart's service, at which point Steuart tasked James Knowles, the Captain of a ship bound for Jamaica, to seize and imprison Somerset before taking him to the West Indies for sale. When news of Somerset's capture reached several prominent abolitionists, including the lawyer Granville Sharp, they brought a writ of *habeas corpus*, which Lord Mansfield, Chief Justice of the Court of King's Bench, granted. On 9 December, Knowles gave Somerset over to the custody of the court. Mansfield delivered his judgment, in favour of Somerset, in June the next year. See Rabin 2011, 19. For an excellent discussion of the relationship between the Somerset Case and that of Mary Hylas in *Hylas* v. *Newton*, see Paugh 2014.

1773, Rush was twenty-seven years old and three years away from adding his name to the Declaration of Independence. He had completed his MD in Edinburgh under William Cullen in 1768 and had returned to Philadelphia the following year to begin his own practice, soon thereafter taking up the professorship for chemistry at the University of Pennsylvania. A figure of no mean importance, then, in spite of his relative youth, it comes as no surprise that Rush should have been approached, according to his own account, to write something in support of a petition to the Pennsylvania Assembly arguing for a higher duty to be imposed on the importation of slaves, and thus providing an economic impetus for the eventual eradication of what abolitionists called the "man-trade".

Less than thirty pages long, Rush's *Address* offered a crisp and scathing summary of the arguments put forward to defend slavery, rejecting each as only so much self-serving or simply wicked rhetoric. Proponents of slavery had declared Negroes to be the natural inferiors of Europeans in intelligence or morality: Rush denied it outright. Were slaves idle, treacherous, or inclined to thievery, then this was a result of their enslaved condition and would end when they were free. "The vulgar notion" that the colour of their skin was a mark of the curse on Cain, their forefather, Rush rejected as "too absurd to need refutation" (Rush 1773, 3). Indeed, black skin was no curse, but rather a blessing, for it "qualifies them for that part of the Globe in which Providence has placed them. The ravages of heat, diseases, and time, appear less in their faces than in a white one." (Rush 1773, 3–4) To the common economic defence of the trade – that one could not produce sugar, indigo, or rice without slave labour – Rush offered three retorts. First, were the claim true, economic necessity could hardly justify the violation of "the Laws of justice or humanity" (Rush 1773, 4). Second, the economic premise of the claim was, in fact, false: free labour in Cochin China produced sugar at prices lower than those gained from the use of slaves in the West Indies.[11] Third, and perhaps most interesting, there was something wrong with the assumption that only those born in climates similar to those of the West Indies could labour there.

I know it has been said by some, that none but the natives of warm climates could undergo the excessive heat and labour of the West-India islands. But this argument is founded upon an error; for the reverse of this is true. I have been informed by good authority, that one European who escapes the first or second year, will do twice the work, and live twice the number of years that an ordinary Negro man will do. (Rush 1773, 8)

Rush's argument was unusual, for he was suggesting that those born in Africa, where the soil supplied all that the human frame required with minimal effort, were not used to hard labour, however accustomed they might be to warm environs. A European, by contrast, could become seasoned to the climate in a year

---

11 On the debate over the economic value of free versus enslaved labour, see Drescher 2002. On the question of how 'free' some free labour was, see Major 2012.

or so, and could then use their native capacity for labour to their advantage under a different sky.

More familiar were Rush's rejections of moralist and religious pro-slavery arguments. Claiming that the trade in men served a moral purpose by introducing pagan Africans to Christianity, for example, was "like justifying highway robbery because part of the money acquired in this manner was appropriated to some religious use." (1773, 14–15) Rush had no more time for positions which held that slavery had saved Africans from death (their lives forfeit as captives of war) or which found support for slavery in the Old Testament. There was nothing decent about slavery and much that was degrading and terrible. Taking a page from the book of his fellow Philadelphian, Anthony Benezet, Rush detailed the horrors of the torture inflicted upon slaves by brutish masters:

Behold one covered with stripes, into which melted wax is poured – another tied down to a block or a stake – a third suspended in the air by his thumbs – a fourth – I cannot relate it. (Rush 1773, 23)

Magistrates and legislators, "men of sense and virtue" and – above all – ministers, all had to speak out to end a trade that violated every sense of justice, economic logic, and Christian benevolence.

The rejoinder from the pro-slavery camp was rapid.[12] Writing as "A West-Indian", Richard Nesbit sought in his *Defence of the West-India Planters* to cast stories of horrific brutality as either outright falsifications – "I never knew a single instance of such shocking barbarities" – or else as the actions not of *all* planters, but of exceptional villains within their number (Nisbet 1773, 15). Nisbet followed what would become the general trend of pro-slavery tracts in many of his other attacks and defences. He invoked "self-interest" as a reason to deny that slave-owners regularly damaged or destroyed their valuable human property. He cited the existence of slavery in the Old Testament to defend the practice of the day, suggesting also that one could not – as Rush had – use either the absence of such approval in the Gospels or Christ's "general maxims of charity and benevolence" to condemn the trade.[13] And Nisbet pointed to the plight of others, closer to home, whom abolitionists should seek to protect before they pled the cause of negroes in other lands. If the exigencies and necessities of states required a kind of slavery for soldiers and sailors, why could the same arguments not be made for labourers in sugar-fields? Were Britain to give up on the sugar trade, the king-

---

12 Rush's pamphlet, in fact, inspired three different rejoinders, which Tise has characterised as "constitute[ing] the most acute formulations of traditional proslavery thought prior to the nineteenth century". Tise 1987, 28.

13 "If the custom had been held in abhorrence by Christ and his disciples, they would, no doubt, have preached against it in direct terms." (Nisbet 1773, 8)

dom would soon be beggared and left defenceless, easy prey for the French or other powerful adversaries.[14]

As in Rush's case, however, the most unusual of Nisbet's arguments turned on the question of African physiology. Rush had attempted to turn two pro-slavery arguments against themselves, arguing that black skin was no curse, but rather an advantage in the warm climates of Africa, and also that African slaves were not the best labourers in the similarly warm climate of the West Indies. Nisbet was having none of it:

> The writer confesses, that hard labour within the tropics shortens human life, and that the colour of the negroes qualifies them for hot countries, yet he is desirous, that our white fellow subjects should toil in these sultry climates, that the Africans might indulge their natural laziness in their own country. The former are, no doubt, much obliged to him for his kind intentions. (Nisbet 1773, 10)

And Nisbet rejected completely Rush's claims for African equality. Although he acknowledged that it was "impossible to determine, with accuracy" whether European or African intellects were superior, since Africans "have not the same opportunities of improving as we have", Nisbet determined the matter in favour of Europeans in any case. With a reference to David Hume on "national characters" as support (Hume [1777] 1987), Nisbet declared that "it seems probable, that they are a much inferior race of men to the whites, in every respect" (Nisbet 1773, 20–21). Importing slaves to the New World appeared to improve both their work ethic and intellect, but Nisbet was wary of geographic explanations for what he suggested was African inferiority to all other peoples, both past and present. "The stupidity of the native cannot be attributed to *climate*," he opined, for the nearby Moors and Egyptians were not so inferior (Nisbet 1773, 23–24). Without advocating for polygenism explicitly, Nisbet opened the door to the position, and similarly left it as merely implied, that natural inferiority should serve as justification for African enslavement.

Rush would have the last word. To the planters' invocation of self-interest as a reason to doubt stories of brutality, he replied by questioning the applicability of such economic rationalities:

> It is to no purpose to urge here that Self Interest leads the Planters to treat their Slaves well. There are many things which appear true in Speculation, which are false in Practice. The Head is apt to mistake its real Interest as the Heart its real Happiness. (Rush 1773, 13)

He ceded ground on the question of African inferiority even as he suggested that physical causes (i.e., climate) could explain the discrepancy. Yet, he questioned

---

14 By freeing Africans, Nisbet intoned, "Britons, themselves, must become abject slaves to despotick power" (Nisbet 1773, 13–14).

the import of this argument in the current debate. Let it be allowed, he suggested, that his opponent had made his case:

Would it avail a man to plead in a Court of Justice that he defrauded his neighbor, because he was inferior to him in Genius or Knowledge? (Rush 1773, 33)

Rush listed his extant allies ("Montesquieu, Franklin, Wallis, Hutchinson, Sharp, Hargrave, Warburton, and Forster") and sought to win more, by analogizing the fight for African freedom to the fight against British tyranny in America (Rush 1773, 18). "Where is the difference," Rush asked, "between the British Senator who attempts to enslave his fellow subjects in America, by imposing Taxes upon them contrary to Law and Justice; and the American Patriot, who reduces his African Brethren to Slavery, contrary to justice and Humanity?" (Rush 1773, 30) If the last comparison seems something of a stretch to modern ears, it was not so at the time. As Tise has noted, public champions of slavery were hard to find in the immediate aftermath of the American Revolution, when "liberty for all" was the byword.[15]

For our purposes, among the most interesting elements of Rush's response to Nisbet is the fact that the Philadelphian physician made use of his medical expertise in a way he had not in his earlier pamphlet. The first critique of the slave trade, once theological and economic apologies were dispatched, had tended to focus on individualised barbarisms perpetrated against the bodies of the enslaved. But Nisbet had made something of a tactical error in attempting to dispose pre-emptively of what we have seen was one of the most telling abolitionist arguments, that pointing to the net decline of the native slave population in the West Indies as proof of the specific barbarity of the slave system there.[16] Nisbet termed it a "common accusation" (albeit one which was "very unjust") which held that "the West-Indies are obliged to have supplies from Africa, to keep up their numbers". Calculations were not straightforward, Nisbet argued: in any case, however, neither the failure to flourish, nor the loss of African lives in the West-Indies, could be blamed on European owners. The slave population was "checked by the irregularities of both sexes, and their carelessness in preserving their health". And further misfortunes that slaves encountered, he added with galling insouciance, "are mostly of their own seeking" (Nisbet 1773, 27). Rush, unsurprisingly, disagreed, noting that African populations in Africa were hardly in decline and invoking both their "Colour and certain Customs" to explain their ability to withstand diseases that crippled European populations. It was conditions in the New World, not native African weakness or behavioural flaws, that led to population

---

15 "So long as Americans revered the revolution and its ideology, slavery was inseparable from evil. It was only when they thought of slavery outside the perspective of Revolutionary ideology that they ascribed good to it." (Tise 1987, 37)

16 On the natalist debate, see Sheridan 1985, Chapter Eight; Tadman 2000; Paugh 2013.

decline. It had become a trope to note that childbirth was attended with less difficulty in warmer climates. Rush cited a Dr. Bancroft, who reported that "Indian
women in Guiana seem to be exempted from the Curse inflicted upon Eve",
(Rush 1773, 41) and a Dr. George Taylor, who served as physician and man-
midwife on St Kitts, who observed that white women on the island gave birth
easily.[17] Rush noted that far more children died in the West Indies soon after
birth than elsewhere, due to the disease known locally as the Jaw-Fall (infant tetanus), and blamed the fact directly on "their peculiar circumstances as Slaves"
(Rush 1773, 41). And, like many abolitionists, Rush drew attention to the effects
of "the seasoning", which "destroys many of the Negroes" (Rush 1773, 45). But
he did specifically reject the common explanation for this massive death rate,
arguing that the climate of the West-Indies was not responsible. As before, he
argued not for African weakness, but rather for a kind of relative strength:

They are even exempted from the most fatal epidemic diseases to which the White People
are subject. (Rush 1773, 45)

It was, rather, their new diet, the hardships and suffering which they were now
forced to undergo, labour "in a Climate not intended for it", and their intemper-
ance with regard to liquor that was to blame for the "immense Waste" of their
lives (Rush 1773, 44 and 45). And all of this suffering was to be charged not to a
curse, or innate debility, or African cultural failings, but to the evils of the slave
system itself.

In the 1760s, it was possible to read Benezet's description of deaths on the
Middle Passage as "murder" as either hyperbole or metaphor. In the 1780s, however, the connection between shipboard conditions and intentional slaughter became literalised in the public mind with the story of the infamous *Zong* affair. In
1781, a slaveship named the *Zong*, travelling from Africa to the West Indies, began
to run low on potable water. One hundred and thirty-three slaves, insured as
cargo, were thrown overboard to drown, ostensibly as a means of preserving the
rest of the crew and the remaining slaves. When the ship reached Jamaica, the
owners lodged an insurance claim for their lost property, a claim which the insurance company contested. Roughly two weeks after the first trial, in which a jury
had found for the owners, Olaudah Equiano – a freed slave who would go on to
pen a memoir entitled *The Interesting Narrative of the Life of Olaudah Equiano* in 1789
– brought the facts of the case to the attention of Granville Sharp, a leading abolitionist. Through the accounts of Sharp and others, the events on the *Zong* became widely known. "The *Zong* affair," write Trevor Burnard and John Garrigus,
"played a central role in making the abolition of the slave trade a matter of intense

---

17 Taylor noted, however, that "Negro Women" had a much more difficult time, putting this down
to the distortion of their pelvis by "Kicks they get when young, and to the Hardships they
undergo during their Pregnancy" (quoted in Rush 1773, footnote 41).

public interest in Britain. It served as a supreme example of the callous financial calculations on which the slave trade was based." (Burnard and Garrigus 2016, 216)

Among those to publicise the *Zong* massacre was the former surgeon, Reverend James Ramsay. His *Essay on the Treatment and Conversion of African Slaves in the British Sugar Colonies* (1784) excoriated planters for their treatment of the enslaved and drew bitter and often *ad hominem* replies. Ramsay covered some of the same ground as abolitionists before him, building, before the reader's eye, an image of the grossly excessive labour and brutal punishments to which slaves were subjected. He also added comparatively new elements, drawing on his surgical experience. Ramsay may have been the first major abolitionist writer to detail the system for caring for sick slaves. A poorly paid surgeon, he noted, was employed to care for sick slaves, with his income set at a certain amount *per* head *per* year. Some "frugal planters" eschewed the services of medical men, dosing their slaves with commercially available powders and pills, calling in a practitioner only to "pronounce them past recovery". (Ramsay 1784, 70–71) Where the plantation manager was a steady, stable and married man, Ramsay suggested, one could count on better diets and treatment for the sick, with the manager's wife taking on a supervisory role. Yet, the practice of hiring married men was becoming less common, and when such a figure was a "gadding, gossiping reveler (a character sometimes to be met with)", the sick were very poorly served.

Often, while the manager is feasting abroad, careless and ignorant of what has happened, some hapless wretch among the slaves is taken ill, and unnoticed, unpitied, dies, without even the poor comfort of a surgeon, in his last moments, to say, 'It is now too late.'[18]

And it was not unusual for as many as one in eight (presumably seasoned) negroes to die of "fevers, fluxes, dropsies" in a year, as a result of excessive labour, and minimal food and care (Ramsay 1784, 83). Even more disturbing than this portrayal of callous neglect may have been Ramsay's description of the treatment of pregnant and nursing women.[19] Plantation owners forced all who were deemed capable to work in the field gang, so that "hardly any remonstrance from the surgeon can, in many cases, save a poor diseased wretch from the labour". To this work were assigned even pregnant women in the last months of their term: "and hence suffer many an abortion; which some managers are unfeeling enough to express joy at, because the woman, on recovery, having no child to care for, will have no pretence for indulgence" (Ramsay 1784, 75). Were she to carry the child to term, Ramsay continued, the infant would be born in a "dark, damp,

18 Ramsay 1784, Note 71–72.
19 Ramsay's interest in this topic no doubt derived from his time spent training at the British lying-in hospital. See Paugh 2013, 128.

smoky hut", which explained the loss of such infants to cramps and convulsions (Ramsay 1784, 76).

Philip Gibbes published his *Instructions for the Treatment of Negroes* two years after Ramsay's *Essay*, although he was at pains, in a later edition, to stress that his "sentiments were entertained and these instructions given, long before Ramsay wrote or Wilberforce spoke".[20] His positive recommendations were fairly basic and involved allowing sufficient time for new slaves to become "seasoned" to the climate before they were put to strenuous labour, and providing them with sufficient amounts of nutritious food, after the recommendations of Count Rumford.[21] Turning to the question of whether pregnant women should work in the fields, Gibbes agreed with Ramsay (albeit for somewhat different reasons): "A small degree of the knowledge of the human frame," he asserted, "will inform you, that laborious exercise obstructs procreation: for which reason it is extremely improper and ill-judged to make females carry canes to the mill or in uneven fields." (Gibbes 1797, 86) Robert Thomas, writing in 1790, concurred, suggesting that benevolence was already a part of the care provided by several proprietors, who did not assign women to the field gang after their first three or four months of pregnancy, demanded lighter work until the seventh or eighth month, when no further duty was required, and "annually send out baby-clothes for the use of their breeding women" (Thomas 1790, xi–xii). That position marked a difference from John Quier's, in his testimony to the Assembly. Quier had insisted that he had not known of any cases of abortions to follow – as Ramsay had claimed – from excessive labour or "ill usage", and averred instead that "moderate labour is beneficial to pregnant women, as being the best means of preserving general health".[22]

Where Gibbes, Quier, Thomas and other defenders of slavery were all in apparent agreement, however, was on the necessity to move the debate on the declining slave population away from the question of death rates and towards those concerning birth rates. For, on the latter, they could dwell on questions of the promiscuity of enslaved women and avoid many of the ugly questions about infant mortality that abolitionist authors were raising. Gibbes thus claimed that "Early prostitution is the certain obstruction to population", offering a frankly

---

20 Gibbes 1797, 132. That said, he did confess that his hope in originally publishing lay in "repelling the illiberal attacks of dangerous and mistaken zealots" (1797, 68).

21 Gibbes' Instructions are perhaps most remarkable for the execrable poetry they contain. Gibbes reproduced songs intended to be sung by slaves and written by "a very ingenious Lady". For example, this one, on labour: "How useful is labour, how healthful and good! / It keeps us from mischief, procures wholesome food; / It saves from much sickness and loathsome disease / That fall on the idle and pamper'd with ease." Or this one, on the curse of Ham: "We're children of Cham! He his father offended, / Who gave him the curse which to us is descended. / 'A servant of servants' alas! is our curse; / And bad as it is, it has sav'd us from worse." (1797, 107, 33)

22 Fuller 1789, Appendix eight, 32.

graphic farming analogy (derived from a "very sensible friend") to explain his logic:

When the earth is prepared and ploughed, and the seed, at the proper season, is cast into the furrows, if it be ploughed over and over again, would the seed thus, disturbed in its germination strike root deeply, or would it vegetate at all? If sowed with different seeds, inimical to each other, how weak and mingled would be the produce! Let the divine command be carefully observed as well in your care of the women as of the soil, *Sow not thy land with divers seeds*.[23]

More standard explanations connected Afro-Caribbean hyper-sexuality with a resultant venereal infection, leading to infertility, or else tied "prostitution" to the procuring of abortions, which then led to medical difficulties.[24] Long, for example, stated simply that "the women here are, in general, common prostitutes; and many take specifics to cause abortion" (1774, 436). The Governor, Edward Trelawney, invoked abortions as the direct cause of low populations: "what chiefly contributes to their being so few Children among the *English* Negroes," he asserted, "is the Practice of the Wenches in procuring Abortions. As they lie with both Colours, and do not know which the Child may prove of, to disoblige neither, they stifle it at birth."[25] Thomas insisted that the frequency, amongst Afro-Caribbean women, of cases of "the whites" [probably Leucorrhea] was due to "the frequent abortions they designedly bring upon themselves, in order to prevent their having the trouble of rearing their offspring, to which they are seldom bound by the same ties of maternal tenderness and affection that white women are" (1790, 279). Thomas, in fact, offered a litany of reasons for the fact that "not one estate in fifty can keep up its original number, even although the greatest humanity and lenity have been practice, and all possible pains have been taken for rearing the children that have been born", ranging from early promiscuity, prostitution, abortions, early loss of infant life, and diseases with which women in warm climates were more subject than in colder ones (1790, xix–xx, xvi). How powerful was this discourse may be gleaned from the fact that even an author profoundly critical of the Report of the Jamaican Assembly, and of Quier's testimony in particular, found himself in agreement with the doctor's claim that many abortions on the island were the result of "promiscuous intercourse" (Fuller 1789, 61). Negative judgements about black female sexuality made unlikely bedfellows.[26]

---

23 Gibbes 1797, Note, 125–126.

24 "Put simply," writes Katherine Paugh, "many British authors believed that racially characteristic sexual promiscuity led to venereal disease and infertility, while they believed that Christian monogamy encouraged fertility." (2013, 129) On hyper-sexuality, see Morgan 1997; Altink 2007 and 2005.

25 Quoted in Sheridan 1985, 224.

26 For more on this point, see Paugh 2013.

Like many, if not most, of the owners of plantations in the West Indies, Gibbes was an absentee landlord, living in Britain. Such owners were, as Sheridan noted, "highly vulnerable to antislavery propaganda", and many pushed for measures to improve, although not abolish, slavery (Gibbes 1985, 230). Where general problems with the treatment of slaves were acknowledged by this group, blame was placed largely on the backs of managers and overseers, who became the public face of the atrocities and neglect abolitionists had identified. Coupled with rising prices for slaves in the last decades of the century, the weight of public opinion pushed colonial legislatures to institute new laws and codes to protect slaves from the most brutal treatment and, eventually, to encourage an increase in their population.[27] In Jamaica, the Consolidated Slave Act of 1781, for example, introduced clauses requiring adequate clothing, the allocation of provision grounds and "sufficient time to work the same", and prescribing the punishment for a master who mutilated or dismembered slaves. The Act of 1787 added further clauses, with medical elements that seem to have been a direct response to Ramsay's criticisms, allowing towns and parishes to levy taxes to provide "food, medical care, and attendance" for slaves – too old or sick to care for themselves – who had been abandoned by their owners, and requiring that a surgeon provide, under oath, an account of the increase or decrease of numbers of slaves on every plantation, with a description of the cause of each decrease, in order to "prevent the destruction of negroes, by excessive labour and unreasonable punishments". Critics noted, however, that many such laws were essentially toothless. As one writer identifying himself as a "Jamaica Planter" put it:

I have for many years been conversant with Jamaica, and know of but one instance of the law against mutilation being inforced, and that instance occurred since the people in Britain have interested themselves in favour of the poor negroes. (Fuller 1789, 20)

The editor for that work put his finger on one of the most obvious intrinsic problems with legislation that pitted masters against slaves in the realm of the law: the testimony of slaves was not admissible against owners (1789, i–ii).

Laws that mandated that medical men, dependent upon owners for their livelihoods, testify in cases of excessive neglect or unlawful deaths also seem impossibly naïve (assuming that they were intended to have real effects in the first place).[28] Indeed, the testimony of such practitioners seems to have largely served the opposite cause. Thus, Jesse Foot, who had served as a surgeon for three years in the West Indies, with the "care of two thousand negroes annually" invoked his own experiences as part of his *Defence of the Planters in the West Indies* (Foot 1792,

---

27 Ramsay noted that "slaves be now raised to a price that few old settled plantations can afford to give" (1784, 76). On the new slave laws, see Goveia 1965, 152–202.

28 As Goveia notes, the position of a doctor "was a difficult one, since he was himself an employee of the planter on whom he would be forced to inform if he took his responsibilities for his slaves more seriously than his loyalty to an employer and fellow inhabitant." (1965, 198)

31). Foot declared that he had not seen "any other treatment than that which humanity dictates," adding that "during my practice I never was called to give *surgical relief* to any negroes who had suffered from the severity of chastisement" (1792, 75–76). Robert Thomas drew on nine years of medical care for three thousand negroes a year to make a similar point: "I never was called upon," he asserted, "to administer assistance to a negro in consequence of any violence or cruelty exercised over him, either by the master, manager, or overseer" (Thomas 1790, xv). It is possible that one outcome of the new laws – coupled with the need to be seen to be responding to anti-slavery critiques and the economic incentives introduced by the increasing value of slaves – may have been a reduction in the number of planters who relied on their own judgement alone in treating sick or injured slaves. And yet, even though the number of practitioners rose, it should be clear from the sheer number of slaves under their yearly care the minimal attention each patient could receive. Foot and Thomas were hardly alone in having thousands of slaves under their charge.[29] In their testimony before the Jamaica Assembly, Chisholme, Anderson, and Quier detailed the size of their practices – around 4,000 slaves a year – as part of their credentials. The "Jamaica Planter" placed this number in some perspective by noting that a regiment or a ship of war of five hundred men was accorded a surgeon and perhaps several surgeon's mates.

Once, twice, or thrice in a week, to gallop to a plantation, to take a peep into the hospital, or hot-house, as it is called, write in a book, 'bleed this,' 'purge that,' 'blister another,' 'here give an opiate,' 'there the bark,' is not, in my opinion, taking care of, though it may be called taking charge of, the healths of 4000 or 5000 negroes. (Fuller 1789, 60)

3. Conclusion

The abolitionist debate – spearheaded, in some cases, by those with medical training – managed to place the medical care of slaves near the forefront of public concern. We might suggest, then, that, by the 1780s at least, medical knowledge *as a whole* had achieved some measure of strength as part of claims and counter-claims concerning the morality of slavery. As a measure of this, one might note that, in 1789, the Privy Council Committee systematically asked witnesses about the care of slaves in sickness, the laws that existed to regulate such care, and the provision for slaves when they were old and infirm (Sheridan 1985, 271). Colonial legislatures acted to place such laws on the books from the 1780s onwards. Yet much of the attention in the colonies had been reactive. Tracts about such med-

---

29 For average number of slaves per practitioner on different islands, see Sheridan 1985, 302 et seq.

ical care for the enslaved tended to dissipate after Wilberforce's bill - delayed until
1791 – sputtered in the House, the country's political mood swinging against radical reform in the aftermath of the French Revolution. In 1792, all Wilberforce
was able to extract from his fellow parliamentarians was the agreement on a
"gradual abolition" of the slave trade. An Act to that effect would have to wait
until 1807.

If we look beyond legislation, however, and also look more closely at specific
claims made by participants within the debates, one finds that medical expertise
was important, but hardly conclusive. Medical logics, in other words, were a key
part of the discourse around abolitionism, with practitioners arrayed on either
side of the debate. For every Rush or Ramsay who drew attention to the tremendous losses of life due to the "seasoning" or infant tetanus, or to the appalling
treatment of pregnant and nursing women and sick or aged slaves, there was a
Quier, a Foot, or a Thomas willing to testify to the exceptionality of horrific punishments, when they were meted out, or to the culpability of slaves in their own
declining population. A profession became strong, at least in part, upon the basis
of a strong fact. Here, as elsewhere, however, we see that the real battle was over
interpretations of the *meanings* of an agreed upon fact. And facts cannot speak for
themselves.

References

Altink, Henrice (2005): "Deviant and Dangerous: Pro-Slavery Representation of Jamaican
    Slave Women's Sexuality, C. 1780–1834." *Slavery and Abolition*, 26 (2): 271–288.
Altink, Henrice (2007): *Representations of Slave Women in Discourses on Slavery and Abolition,
    1780–1838*. London: Routledge.
Benezet, Anthony (1762): *A Short Account of that Part of Africa, Inhabited by the Negroes*. Phil-
    adelphia PA: William Dunlap.
Burnard, Trevor, and John Garrigus (2016): *The Plantation Machine: Atlantic Capitalism in
    French Saint-Domingue and British Jamaica*. Philadelphia PA: University of Pennsylvania
    Press.
Drescher, Seymour (2002): *The Mighty Experiment: Free Labor Versus Slavery in British Eman-
    cipation*. New York: Oxford University Press.
Foot, Jesse (1792): *A Defence of the Planters in the West Indies; Comprised in Four Arguments*.
    London: J. Debrett.
Fuller, Stephen (1789): *Notes on the Two Reports from the Committee of the Honourable House of
    Assembly of Jamaica*. London: James Phillips.
Gibbes, Philip (1797): *Instruction for the Treatment of Negroes &C. &C. &C.*, 2nd ed. London:
    Shepperson and Reynolds.
Goveia, Elsa V. (1965): *Slave Society in the British Leeward Islands at the End of the Eighteenth
    Century*. New Haven CT-London: Yale University Press.

Grainger, James [1764] (2005a): "An Essay on the More Common West-India Diseases, James Grainger, Md (1764), with Additional Notes by William Wright, MD, FRS (1802)." In: J. Edward Hutson (Ed.) (2005): *On the Treatment and Management of the More Common West-India Diseases (1750–1802)*, 1–56. Kingston: University of the West Indies Press.

Grainger, James [1764] (2005b): "The Sugar Cane", Book IV. In: J. Edward Hutson (Ed.): *On the Treatment and Management of the More Common West-India Diseases (1750–1802)*, 57–84. Kingston: University of the West Indies.

Hume, David [1777] (1987): "Of National Characters." In: *Hume: Essays, Moral, Political, and Literary*, 153–163. Edited by E.F. Miller. Indianapolis, IN: Liberty Fund.

Hutson, J. Edward (Ed.) (2005): *On the Treatment and Management of the More Common West-India Diseases (1750–1802)*. Kingston: University of the West Indies.

Jackson, Maurice (2009): *Let This Voice Be Heard: Anthony Benezet, Father of Atlantic Abolitionism*. Philadelphia PA: University of Pennsylvania Press.

Leslie, Charles (1740): *A New History of Jamaica: From the Earliest Accounts, to the Taking of Porto Bello by Vice-Admiral Vernon. In Thirteen Letters from a Gentleman to His Friend*. London: Printed for J. Hodges.

Long, Edward (1774): *The History of Jamaica*. 3 Vols. Vol. II, London: T. Lowndes.

Major, Andrea (2012): *Slavery, Abolitionism, and Empire in India, 1772–1843*. Liverpool: University Press.

Morgan, Jennifer L. (1997): "'Some Could Suckle over Their Shoulder': Male Travelers, Female Bodies, and the Gendering of Racial Ideology, 1500–1770." *The William and Mary Quarterly*, 54 (1): 167–192.

Nisbet, Richard (1773): *Slavery Not Forbidden by Scripture. Or a Defence of the West-India Planters*. Philadelphia PA: John Sparhawk.

Paugh, Katherine (2013): "The Politics of Childbearing in the British Caribbean and the Atlantic World during the Age of Abolition, 1776–1838." *Past and Present*, 221: 119–160.

Paugh, Katherine (2014): "The Curious Case of Mary Hylas: Wives, Slaves, and the Limits of British Abolitionism." *Slavery and Abolition*, 35: 629–651.

Rabin, Dana (2011): "'In a Country of Liberty?': Slavery, Villeinage, and the Making of Whiteness in the Somerset Case (1772)." *History Workshop Journal*, 72: 5–29.

Ramsay, James (1784): *An Essay on the Treatment and Conversion of African Slaves in the British Sugar Colonies*. Dublin: T. Walker, C. Jenkin, R. Marchbank, L. White, R. Burton and P. Byrne.

Rush, Benjamin (1773): *An Address to the Inhabitants of the British Settlements in America Upon Slave-Keeping (the Second Edition). To which are Added, Observations on a Pamphlet, Entitled, 'Slavery Not Forbidden by Scripture; or, a Defence of the West-India Planters.' By a Pennsylvanian*. Philadelphia PA: John Dunlap.

Schiebinger, Londa (2017): *Secret Cures of Slaves: People, Plants, and Medicine in the Eighteenth-Century Atlantic World*. Stanford CA: University Press.

Sheridan, Richard B. (1972): "Africa and the Caribbean in the Atlantic Slave Trade." The *American Historical Review*, 77 (1): 15–35.

Sheridan, Richard B. (1981): "The Guinea Surgeons on the Middle Passage: The Provision of Medical Services in the British Slave Trade." *The International Journal of African Historical Studies*, 14 (4): 601–625.

Sheridan, Richard B. (1985): *Doctors and Slaves: A Medical and Demographic History of Slavery in the British West Indies, 1680–1834*. Cambridge: Cambridge University Press.

Smith, Sean Morey (2015): "Seasoning and Abolition: Humoural Medicine in the Eighteenth-Century British Atlantic." *Slavery and Abolition*, 36: 684–703.

Tadman, Michael (2000): "The Demographic Cost of Sugar: Debates on Slave Societies and Natural Increase in the Americas." *The American Historical Review*, 105 (5): 1534–1575.

Thomas, Robert (1790): *Medical Advice to the Inhabitants of Warm Climates, on the Domestic Treatment of All the Diseases Incidental Therein: With a Few Useful Hints to New Settlers, for the Preservation of Health, and the Prevention of Sickness*. London: J. Strahan and W. Richardson.

Tise, Larry E. (1987): *Proslavery: A History of the Defense of Slavery in America, 1701–1840*. Athens GA-London: University of Georgia Press.

Inflamed Spines and Anarchical Minds: Dynamics of Medical Testimony on Nervous Shock in Late Nineteenth Century England

José Brunner

Abstract

This chapter brings to light the discursive codes that two leading Victorian doctors, John Eric Erichsen and Herbert William Page, shared, even though they addressed the issue of "nervous shock" from different angles. Although they held contradictory views on the nature of nervous shock, a topic that achieved prominence in the context of railway accidents, both of them depicted it as resulting from a moment of excess leading to a loss. Moreover, though they drew on different metaphorical registers, they shared extensive recourse to analogical reasoning. Although this indicated that medical knowledge of nervous shock was still in the making, in their eyes, this did not mark it as epistemically weak. Instead, leading British doctors were concerned with the institutional weakness of medical knowledge on nervous shock, which was formed and articulated, principally, as expert testimony in court. Above all, they were apprehensive that dissension among doctors testifying for conflicting parties in an adversary legal setting might undermine the status of the medical profession and its claim to objective knowledge.

Introduction

This chapter is devoted to an analysis of the medical discourse on "nervous shock" in England in the last third of the nineteenth century. It seeks to reveal the institutional setting, imagery, conflicts, and codes of knowledge that governed this discourse, and to trace their development from the mid-1860s to the early 1880s.

As has been noted widely, the origins of this medical discourse lay in the rapid expansion of the railway system in Britain in the mid-nineteenth century. Trains transformed land travel not only by virtue of their speed and capacity, but also by the extension of railway-building, which involved the largest body of public works and the most dazzling engineering achievement known at that time (Hobsbawm 1985, 70). In the second half of the nineteenth century, trains constituted the space of a highly significant collective experience of technology, evoking fantasies of what machines could effect in terms of power and speed, as well as destruction and disruption. Modern technology shrunk space and radically increased mobility. The railway held out the promise of speed, efficiency and luxury, and the transformation of nature, time and space, as well as of the economy and society. At the same time, people spent more and more time cooped up in railway carriages (Freeman 1999, 86). The mechanics of travel were believed to impose a strain on the nerves and to lead to fatigue and rapid aging (Harrington 2000, 249). The railway also displaced horse-drawn coaches and ships as a main setting for accidents, injuries and accidental death (Mendelson 1998, 36). Hence, the fuming, fire-spitting juggernaut of steel cutting across the landscape and rushing great numbers of passengers around the countryside both excited and terrified people. They thought of railway travel as dangerous. Most frightening, however, were railway accidents, when the iron monsters lost control and crashed into each other or jumped the rails.[1]

The law imposed strict liability on railway companies, making them responsible for all damages, regardless of cause or agency. This meant that, legally, any accident was the fault of the railway companies (Mendelson 1998, 47). In 1864, Parliament passed an amendment to a law that required railway companies to compensate the victims of accidents. As Allan Young reports, "the following year, juries awarded over three hundred thousand pounds to people injured on the railways" (Young 1995, 17). Compensation was integral to this framework, reflecting the understanding that accidents were an unavoidable risk of modern technology, whose enormous power meant that even a minor malfunction or mistake could lead to a frightful event in which many lives were ruined.

When passengers suffered bodily injuries in an accident, the harm inflicted on them was visible and doctors could assess the damage to their health with relative ease and transparency. However, some passengers seemed to suffer of serious health impairments after an accident, without any discernable bodily injury that could explain them. British physicians used the term "nervous shock" for invisible injuries that could have detrimental consequences for those affected by them. Although nervous shock was said to be caused not just by train accidents, railways were thought to expose passengers to the risk of especially strong shocks.

Railway companies could be held liable for invisible injuries as well as visible ones; they had to compensate passengers for a loss of work ability and for the loss of income that resulted from both types of harm. Thus, medical explanations of their causality, dynamics and consequences were of paramount importance. As a rule, doctors articulated such explanations in expert testimony in court, when passengers pressed claims against railway companies. On the one hand, since ex-

---

1 Freeman 1999, 85–86; Drinka 1984, 114.

pert testimony on nervous shock referred to invisible causes and developments, such testimony may seem weaker than testimony referring to somatic injury, which usually dealt with broken limbs or damaged organs. On the other hand, since the court had to rely entirely on expert testimony when ruling on the nature, origins and long-term effects of invisible injuries, doctors testifying in such matters played a crucial role in legal proceedings. However, in order to be effective and to explain invisible causes and processes to judges and juries, doctors had to mobilise imagery that was accessible to laypersons and endowed their testimony with credibility.

Medical testimony on nervous shock involved an interplay between medical and legal actors, with the former taking part in an institutional setting whose norms and rules were set by the latter. The implications of this hierarchy bothered doctors already at the time; they feared that the participation of doctors in adversarial disputes might diminish the public status of their profession and their knowledge claims. However, both doctors and legal practitioners could claim sophisticated knowledge regimes of their own, which, although not scientific in the "hard" sense of the word, were systematic, formalised, carried far-reaching practical implications, and were considered indispensable to any well-functioning modern society. Both professions could look back on venerable traditions; they had established strong institutions that had accumulated considerable cultural capital over the centuries. Thus, in order to assess how the entanglement of law and medicine played out in the question of nervous shock, it is necessary to have a closer look at the main actors and theories that were involved.

The wine merchant who called his wife "Sir"

In a railway collision that occurred on 23 August 1864, a forty-three-year-old wine merchant "was suddenly dashed forward and then rebounded violently backwards". Apparently unhurt, the man assisted his fellow passengers for the next two hours. The evening, however, brought restlessness and chills, a tingling in his arms and legs, and insomnia. The following day, he felt ill and shaken. Nonetheless, the merchant waited eight days before consulting a surgeon for his persistent headache and back pain. Difficulties in movement followed, as did memory loss and cognitive confusion. He even called his wife "Sir". More and increasingly severe symptoms ensued: stronger back pains, spasms, neck pains, uncertainty when walking, partial deafness, irritability of the eyes, numbness in the right arm and hand, rigidity and tenderness in the spine, noises in the head, and a feeble pulse.

Finding that he was unable to run his business, the wine merchant lodged a compensation claim against the railway company; it was tried in a London court in 1865. Together with another physician, John Eric Erichsen acted as medical expert-witness on behalf of the claimant. Already at that time, Erichsen was a medical celebrity. He was Professor of Clinical Surgery at University College, London, and Fellow of the Royal College of Surgeons. In the first half of the 1850s, he had published a book on surgery that ran into 10 editions (Erichsen 1853). During the American Civil War, the American Government issued a copy of the volume to every medical officer in the Federal Army. Later, he was appointed "surgeon extraordinary to the Queen" and, in 1895, he was honoured as a Baronet. Erichsen explained that the wine merchant "was suffering from concussion of the spine which had developed irritation and chronic inflammation of the cord and of its membranes, and that recovery was very doubtful". The jury awarded the man £6,000 (Erichsen 1866, 53–58). In a later comment, Erichsen added that he was informed in 1873 that the wine merchant's condition had still not improved (1875, 90).

Imagining nervous shock

Erichsen presented this case together with fourteen others in a series of six lectures at University College Hospital. In 1866, he published them in a book entitled *On Railway and other Injuries of the Nervous System*, which was to appear in 18 editions. As Erichsen told the reader, he wrote the book both because the injuries that it addresses had become frequent in the wake of the expansion of the railway system, and because they taxed the diagnostic skill of the surgeon. As he explained, injuries of this kind had become:

[….] a most important branch of medico-legal investigation. There is no class of cases in which medical men are now so frequently called into the witness-box to give evidence in Courts of Law, as in the determination of the many intricate questions that often arise in actions for damages against Railway Companies for Injuries alleged to have been sustained by Passengers in collision on their Lines; and there is no class of cases in which more discrepancy of surgical opinion is elicited than in those under consideration. (Erichsen 1866, 3)

How, then, did Erichsen explain what happens in nervous shock? He held that what took place in the nervous system in the wake of an accident paralleled what happened on the tracks or in the carriage during a railway collision. Already in the fourth edition of his popular textbook on *The Science and Art of Surgery* of 1864, he had explained: "The *Immediate Constitutional Effects*, or *Shock*, consist in a disturbance of the functions of the circulatory, respiratory, and nervous systems, the harmony of action of the great organs of the body becoming disarranged."[2] Surprisingly enough, in this book, Erichsen also claimed that merely thinking about an injury at the moment of an accident suffices to sustain a shock. In his 1864 portrayal, a shock and its ensuing symptoms could result from an immensely frightening thought; a state of mind could severely affect the nervous system:

In persons of a very timid character or of great nervous susceptibility, more especially in females and in children, a very trivial injury may produce an extreme degree of shock to the nervous system – indeed the mere apprehension of injury may, without any physical lesion being actually induced, give rise to all the phenomena of shock in its most intense degree. People have been actually frightened to death, without any injury having been inflicted upon them. The state of mind at the time of the receipt of the injury influences materially its effects on the nervous system. If the patient be anxiously watching for the infliction of the wound, as waiting for the first incision in a surgical operation, all the attention is concentrated upon the coming pain; it is severely felt, and the consequent shock to the system is usually great (Erichsen 1864, 101–102).

However, in *On Railway and other Injuries of the Nervous System*, Erichsen modified his position when dealing with nervous shock caused by railway accidents, claiming that a concussion of the spine produced a shock to the nervous system. What, then, was a nervous shock for Erichsen in 1866? This was his answer:

How these jars, shakes, shocks, or concussions of the spinal cord directly influence its action I cannot say with certainty. We do not know how it is that when a magnet is struck a heavy blow with a hammer, the magnetic force is jarred, shaken, or concussed out of the horse-shoe. But we know that it is so, and that the iron has lost its magnetic power. So, if the spine is badly jarred, shaken, or concussed by a blow or shock of any kind communicated to the body, we find that the nervous force is to a certain extent shaken out of the man, and that he has in some way lost nerve-power. What immediate change, if any, has taken place in the nervous structure to occasion this effect, we no more know than what change happens to a magnet when struck. But we know that a change has taken place in the action of the nervous system just as we do in the action of the iron by the change that is induced in the loss of its magnetic force. (Erichsen 1866, 94–95)

As we can see, in 1866, Erichsen cast his explanation of nervous shock in an entirely material mode, alluding to another puzzle, magnetism, which raised the question of causation at a distance. Thereby, Erichsen related nervous shock and the concussion of the spine to an issue that had attracted the attention of the leading physicists of his age, among them a famous London colleague, James Clerk Maxwell. While magnetic force and its sudden depletion served Erichsen as an analogy to portray the pathogenic effects of spinal concussion as well as to legitimise his inability to provide a proper explanation, Maxwell (1855) had not only made extensive use of a fluid analogy a decade earlier, but had also explained

---

2 Erichsen 1864, 101; emphasis in the original.

that analogical reasoning is necessary to explain phenomena for which there is still no reliable theory (Maxwell 1855, 157). As Maxwell put it:

By referring everything to the purely geometrical idea of an imaginary fluid, I hope to attain generality and precision, and to avoid the dangers arising from a premature theory professing the cause of the phenomena. [...]. The substance here treated of must not be assumed to possess any of the properties of ordinary fluids except those of freedom of motion and resistance to compression. It is not even the introduction of a hypothetical fluid which is introduced to explain actual phenomena. It is merely a collection of imaginary properties. (Maxwell 1855, 159–60)

Maxwell expanded his work on electromagnetic phenomena in the beginning of the 1860s. By the time he published his famous four-part paper entitled "On Physical Lines of Force", he had been appointed Professor of Natural Philosophy at King's College, London (Maxwell 1861). This seminal publication appeared just as Erichsen set out to write on nervous shock. Of course, one cannot know whether Erichsen read Maxwell, but one can safely assume that Erichsen knew that, when he invoked the loss of magnetic power, he related the question of nervous shock to a prominent topic in the physics of his age.

Moreover, like the physicists of his age, Erichsen took recourse to the notion of "loss" to mark a sudden depletion of energy. In the accident, he tells his readers, the patient "has lost bodily energy, mental capacity, business aptitude" (1866, 97). Loss is a recurrent trope in the book: in addition to the above-mentioned instances, Erichsen refers to a "loss of motor power" (1866, 122), or, more generally, to a "loss of power" (1866, 122), as well as a "loss of bodily activity" (1866, 128).

While Erichsen projected elements of physics and imagery from an external but also invisible force into the internal and invisible world of the nerves, there is a significant difference between the dissipation of nervous energy in people and that of a horseshoe hit by a hammer. While the latter loses its magnetic qualities at the very moment at which it is hit, people do not necessarily lose their nervous energy at the time of the accident. Nervous energy may dissipate incrementally, and only some time after the actual accident has occurred. Erichsen compensated for this incongruity by introducing the notion of an insidious inflammation in the spinal cord. He postulated that the process of inflammation starts at the moment of the accident but takes time to develop, giving the victims the impression that they are getting better while they are actually getting worse. He argued, entirely without proof, that, if an examination had been conducted immediately after the accident on those who only later suffered of the effects of nervous shock, physicians would have found evidence of a spinal cord injury.

Erichsen regarded the loss of nervous force as irrecoverable, making the effects of nervous shock practically incurable. He claimed not have met a single patient who had recovered completely after having been ill for an entire year (Erichsen 1866, 138). For a number of reasons, Erichsen's notion of a nervous shock that led to a permanent loss via an insidious spinal inflammation was rather useful to claimants in court:

First, Erichsen postulated a somatic causal link between the accident and the disabling symptoms, validating the physical nature of the injury. In legal terms, this was crucial, since in 1861, only five years before the publication of Erichsen's book, the court had refused to compensate for emotional harm in *Lynch* v. *Knight*, laying the groundwork for the rule that mental disturbance alone does not qualify as a legally recognisable harm (Chamallas and Kerber 1990, 814).

Second, Erichsen conceptualised the link between the accident and the symptoms in terms of the most reputable science of the day, physics, its central category, energy, and the method of one of its prominent scientists, analogical reasoning.

Third, since the organic inflammatory changes in the spinal cord were internal, they were not detectable from the outside. This allowed claimants to overcome the problems caused by the lack of objective evidence in these cases.

Fourth, Erichsen stressed the severity of the loss of nervous energy and work power involved, which, he argued, paradoxically was far more severe than that caused by visible somatic injuries.

To sum up, Erichsen provided claimants with a medical etiology that appeared epistemically strong, as it provided a scientific explanation for a puzzling medical phenomenon. In the British legal context of the last third of the nineteenth century, this epistemic strength could gain a strong legal momentum, because strict liability pre-empted the questions that usually arose in common law disputes. Thus, although strict liability meant that the railways had to submit to a rigid legal regime, it also meant that there was not much room for legal arguments. Instead, the courtroom turned into a venue where medical testimony became pivotal. Although this constellation endowed medical knowledge with strength in the courtroom, doctors were concerned about the broader effect of the increased visibility of doctors serving as scientific experts in court, which they regarded as detrimental to their professional reputation.

The scandal of disagreement

Commenting on what they termed "one of the most extraordinary conflicts of medical testimony ever witnessed in a court of justice", the editors of the *British Medical Journal* warned that the public would soon lose its faith in medical credibility if high-profile practitioners disagreed so strongly about the question at hand (Noble 1865, 354). In the same issue, the journal published a letter from Daniel

Noble, a physician who claimed to have been "much consulted" in railway accident litigation by both sides. Noble suggested that a collegial meeting of experts from both sides before a trial, designed to reach a consensus, might help to preserve "the honour and dignity of our profession" (Noble 1865, 361). Four months later, on 5 August 1865, the editors of the *Lancet*, the other leading British medical journal, deplored the "scandal" of the display of conflicting medical witnesses appearing in hostile array.[3] On 14 December 1867, the *Lancet* advocated that the question of injury and compensation be settled by a medical tribunal, consisting of two or three appointed practitioners. These experts would assess the evidence of the medical witnesses and arrive at a fair conclusion.[4]

As we can see, the editors of the two leading medical journals in England argued that, even though doctors played a prominent role in legal proceedings, their participation in adversarial proceedings directed public attention to the disagreements among medical practitioners, weakening medicine's claim to be objective knowledge. Both journals, therefore, advocated the de-juridification of medicine and the establishment of autonomous medical forums in which doctors could come to a consensus among peers and avoid the antagonistic public performances into which the adversarial dynamic of the legal process had forced them.

In a series of articles published in the *Lancet* in 1878, Erichsen, too, reflected extensively on the way in which doctors, by becoming players in a legal process, subordinated themselves to the logic of the law and substituted a legal vantage-point for a medical one when encountering patients, whose behaviour and even symptoms were altered by litigation. In Erichsen's depiction, medicine appears as a discipline betraying its calling by subordinating itself to law. He allows ample space to the plight of the expert witness in communicating intricate medical perspectives to a judge and a jury:

> In order to make himself at all intelligible, the witness is often obliged to be very defined in his answers, and he often becomes insensibly more positive and dogmatic in his statements [...]. He cannot venture to employ those minor shades of expression by which he could more correctly have explained his meaning had he been addressing members of his own profession. The court is much in the position of a person who is being addressed in a language with which he is but imperfectly acquainted. (Erichsen 1878, 485)

Erichsen reminded his readers that a claimant seeking compensation for nervous shock is "a man broken down in body and mind, and reduced to the condition of a nervous invalid" (1878, 601). He pointed out that, as part of the legal process, this person was subjected to several prolonged examinations, brought to the town where the trial was held and examined again by medical experts from both sides, who conducted their examinations with the legal claim in mind:

---

3 *Railway Injuries and Special Jury Damages*, 1865, 156.
4 *Medical Evidence in Railway Cases*, 1867, 741.

It is an examination of one party of medical men in the presence of another. It most improperly often assumes *quasi*-legal form [...] Confronted with hostile experts, the patient feels that he has to prove to them that he is no impostor. Since he suffers of a nervous shock, he is highly irritable and will tend to behave unnaturally [...] a false impression of his condition is conveyed to the court, which looks upon him as a malingerer and guilty of wilful exaggeration, because his nervous condition has become worse than it was even at the last medical examination, making no allowance for the aggravation of the hysterical symptoms that would necessarily be produced by the fatigue and excitement to which he is exposed. (Erichsen 1878, 601)

Thus, Erichsen concluded, "the law as at present administered in compensation cases is harassing to the practitioner of medicine, is attended by serious inconvenience to the public at large, is wasteful of the time of men otherwise much occupied, and the result, so far as the attainment of justice is concerned, is at best doubtful in many cases." (1878, 637)

As we can see, even though he had attained great prestige as a medical expert in the English courtroom, Erichsen was highly critical of the legal process. He held legal measures to be responsible for exacerbating the mental problems with which claimants approach the court, and he denounced the law for turning doctors into the agents of legal procedures. On the one hand, then, the modernisation of tort law that imposed strict liability on railway companies placed medicine at centre-stage of the legal process. On the other hand, doctors perceived the agonistic nature of the legal proceedings as having a negative impact on medical practice and as tarnishing their reputation as scientifically trained, objective professionals.

Accommodating the consensus?

Though Erichsen expressed concern about the effect of the law on medicine, there is no doubt that the legal uses of his theory made it prominent not only in English courts, but also on the other side of the Atlantic. In 1884, Charles Dana, Professor of Diseases of the Mind and Nervous System at the New York Post-Graduate Hospital and later the first Professor of Diseases of the Nervous System at the newly founded Cornell University Medical College, describes the following scene:

The physician who is called into court to testify in a case of spinal injury witnesses a curious spectacle. The lawyer for the prosecution waves before the jury a volume of 'Erichsen Upon Spinal Concussion.' He reads to them, in impressive accents, the statement that every injury to the spine, however slight, is full of danger for the sufferer. He asks, with sonorous emphasis, if Mr. Erichsen is not a surgeon of world-wide fame. (Dana 1884, 617)

Erichsen's work was of legal use to claimants due to its physicalist approach and its assertion that illnesses caused by nervous shock were severe and practically incurable. However, Erichsen modified his stance to some extent in the revised and expanded publication of his studies, which he published under a more elaborate title in 1875: *On Concussion of the Spine, Nervous Shock, And Other Obscure Injuries of the Nervous System in Their Clinical and Medico-Legal Aspects*, under which it appeared in 42 editions.

It should be noted that, while the title of Erichsen's first book referred to railways and to injuries of the nervous system, the title of the expanded version omits the reference to railways, describes the injuries in question as obscure, and alludes to the entanglement of law and medicine. Erichsen seems to have come around to the complexity of the issue of nervous shock and sought to elaborate on it in a more general fashion, even though railway accidents still served him as the paradigmatic event causing nervous shock.

The puzzle that he and other late-nineteenth century English physicians sought to solve was that of a category of patients who had been in an accident and then developed symptoms that were highly disproportionate to the bodily injuries that they had sustained, if any physical harm could be established at all. In addition, it was unclear how one could explain another puzzling feature of the disorders that resulted from such accidents: the delayed onset of symptoms. The interval of days and weeks that could separate the accident from the illness raised questions as to the causality involved. This puzzle of how even a slight jolt experienced in a railway collision or a derailment could have caused the delayed onset of such severe and long-lasting consequences for one's health, preoccupied not only the English medical community in the late nineteenth century, it was also addressed in the German, American and French medical and forensic literature.

In the revised, expanded edition, Erichsen modified the strict somatic explanation of 1866. Thus, he returned – at least partially – to the fold of the consensus in British medicine, according to which shocks endured by railway accidents were the effect of fright, rather than of physical jolts, which led to an inflammation of the spinal cord. As we have seen, Erichsen had already expressed such a view in 1864, but replaced it by a somatic understanding of nervous shock in the 1866 book. Three examples of publications dealing with shock between 1866 and 1875, the date of the publication of the second edition of Erichsen's book, may illustrate the contours of the mentalist paradigm that prevailed in British medicine in this period, which regarded shock as a psychical – emotional or cognitive – event that originated in fright.

In 1867, John Furneaux Jordan, a fellow member of the Royal College of Surgeons, published a prize-winning essay in the *British Medical Journal*, entitled "On Shock after Surgical Operations and Injuries". He argued that:

The peculiar condition which, more than any other, influences the degree of intensity of shock, is the susceptibility or excitability of the nervous system. [...] Besides the degree of sensitiveness in the nervous system, it is well to consider the influence which states of mind that are present during the reception of an injury exert on the degree and nature of shock. [...] In the great majority of cases of shock, it is probable that an extreme and indefinable dread accompanies the injury and greatly aggravates the intensity of the shock. In cases where it is possible to obtain a hopeful and calm state of mind, as in certain surgical operations, a most favourable influence on the phenomena of shock is seen.[5]

With reference to shocks caused by railway accidents, Jordan argued:

[A] psychical element is always present in its most intense and violent form. The incidents of a railway accident contribute to form a combination of the most appalling circumstances which it is possible for the mind to conceive. The vastness of the destructive forces, the magnitude of the results, the imminent danger to the lives of numbers of human beings, and the hopelessness of escape from the danger, give rise to emotions which in themselves are quite sufficient to produce shock, or even death itself. (Jordan 1867, 222)

Daniel Hack Tuke, a member of the Royal College of Surgeons like Erichsen and Jordan, published his influential treatise entitled *On the Influence of the Mind upon the Body in Health and Disease Designed to Elucidate the Action of the Imagination* in 1872. In the Preface, Tuke mentioned that the trigger for the book had been a newspaper item about the curative effect of a railway collision. The writer reported that the shock of the accident had cured symptoms of rheumatism, "an effect, perhaps unparalleled in the history of railway accidents" (1872, vii). Tuke provided 430 clinical illustrations of the influence of the mind on the body. In 153 cases, he described how fear, fright, terror or anxiety could lead to physical reactions such as convulsions, paralysis, aphonia and even death. However, he also claimed that sometimes hope and faith could induce cures of chronic diseases.

A year later, the *Lancet* published a set of clinical lectures by James Paget on "Nervous Mimicry of Organic Diseases". Paget was interested in the way in which nervous disorders could produce "an imitation or mimicry of organic local disease" (1873, 511). Paget used the word "neuromimesis" for such a condition. He argued that these patients often imitate or assume symptoms of a disease that they have seen or heard of, from close relatives or from famous people. Moreover, he argued that those who tended to neurosmimesis suffered from a "weakness of will". While some of them might be intentionally fraudulent and lying, he believed that most were like children, who involuntarily imitated diseases:

And in the frauds which some of these patients' practice, I am nearly sure that the fault is rather in weakness of the will than in its perverse strength. As other people cannot resist thieving or drinking, so these cannot resist, have not will enough to resist, the inducement to fraudulently exaggerate, their symptoms, or even to invent some. It is often very hard

---

5 Jordan 1867, 219; emphasis in original.

to distinguish between the frauds of the wilful and those of the will-less; but I have seen no reason to believe that wilful fraud in disease is much more common among those with nervous mimicry or hysteria than it is among others. [...] They say 'I cannot'; it looks like 'I will not;' but it is 'I cannot will'. (Paget 1873, 511)

These examples illustrate the broad consensus concerning the power of the mind over the body, which governed British medicine in the 1860s and 1870s. In the 1875 edition of his book, Erichsen sought to make room for this mentalist perspective alongside his physicalist conception of nervous shock:

It is important to observe that a serious accident may give rise to two distinct forms of nervous shock, which may be sufficiently severe to occasion complete unconsciousness. The first is mental or moral, and the second purely physical. These forms of 'shock' may be developed separately, or they may co-exist. (1875, 194)

Erichsen explained that what he called mental or moral unconsciousness could occur without any prior physical violence to the head or the spine. He described this kind of shock as a result of fear, explaining that it led to hysteria, a mental disorder that could also affect men, although he considered it more frequent among women (Erichsen 1875, 195). Though Erichsen may have shared the gender prejudices of his age, he diverged from the understanding of hysteria that was common among doctors of his time by stressing that only the fear instilled by a railway accident was strong enough to generate this disorder. He emphasised that, in thirty years of hospital practice, he had never come across a single instance of hysteria that had been caused by a shock that did not result from a railway accident:

The crash and confusion, the uncertainty attendant on a railway collision, the shrieks of the sufferers, possibly the sight of the victims of the catastrophe, produce a mental impression of a far deeper and more vivid character than is occasioned by the more ordinary accidents of civil life. Hence, I think, the greater degree of mental shock that accompanies them, and of the hysterical state that is apt to be induced by them. (1875, 196)

People with hysteria, Erichsen went on to explain, tended to exaggerate their symptoms without being conscious of doing so. He described these symptoms as originally being a result of the "agony of fear" into which people were thrown at the moment of an accident. Later, he argued, the symptoms were maintained by "anxieties connected with the collapse of business [...] and [...] continued indefinitely by the harass of mind consequent on the litigation in which the sufferer becomes involved in prosecuting his claim for competition" (1875, 199). When Erichsen expanded his explanation of nervous shock into a dual-track etiology, allowing for both a somatic and a mental causal chain, he related hysteria to a "loss of self-control" and "a temporary suspension of the power of will" (1875, 199). However, Erichsen argued that the two types of shock led to somewhat different symptoms. He explained that, in hysteria, there was no delayed onset, no increasing severity, the pains experienced were more diffuse, and the prognosis was more favourable (1875, 200–203).

To sum up, throughout his writings, Erichsen conceptualised the shock incurred in railway accidents in terms of loss; at first, a loss of nervous energy, and later also a loss of will. Though his later work allowed for the possibility of a purely mentalist etiology of nervous shock, perhaps in order to accommodate the dominant view, it is evident that he still held on to the physicalist explanation as the more important one.

Mental anarchy

So far, Erichsen dominated this sketch of the techno-medico-legal drama of nervous shock. Now Herbert William Page enters the stage. He is the hero of the last act, the character with the memorable closing lines. Page served as surgeon to the London and North Western Railway Company, the largest railway company at the time, and, like Erichsen, he wrote a seminal book on the disabling effects of railway accidents, which he entitled *Injuries of the Spine and Spinal Cord without Apparent Mechanical Lesion and Nervous Shock in their Surgical and Medico-Legal Aspects* (1883).

Point for point, Page refuted Erichsen's 1866 arguments concerning the organic nature of nervous shock, turning it into a purely psychical phenomenon. Finding Erichsen's idea of an invisible injury to the spinal cord highly unconvincing, he pointed out that Erichsen failed to provide any post-mortem evidence for his theory of spinal inflammation and that spinal cord injury was exceedingly rare without any signs of vertebral injury (Page 1883, 49–50). Page suggested that the term "shock" signified a mental collapse of some kind, and he explained that the vague notion of a "general nervous shock" denoted "some functional disturbance of the whole nervous balance or tone rather than structural damage to any organ" (1883, 143). Though he traced shock to fright, that is, a psychic, rather than a somatic, cause, Page stressed that, like Erichsen, he was aware of its potentially severe consequences:

[M]edical literature abounds with cases where the gravest disturbances of function, and even death or the annihilation of function, have been produced by fright and by fright alone. It is this same element of fear which in railway collisions has so large a share – in many cases the only share – in inducing immediate collapse.

Finally, Page also sought to account for the delay in the onset of symptoms after an accident by purely psychical factors. He explained that the shock could be disguised by the excitement that passengers involved in railway accidents feel while still being at the scene (1883, 148).

As an illustration, Page offered the case of a forty-six-year-old patient who had been in a severe collision. This tall and strong man had sustained several bruises and a broken nose but had not lost consciousness. The patient was in a state of "great nervous depression, with feeble and rapid pulse, and inability to eat or sleep". Moreover, he was greatly distressed by the death of a friend sitting next to him and "this seemed to prey constantly upon his mind". The man recovered from his bodily injuries, but "his mental condition showed extreme emotional disturbance". He feared doom, cried easily, had sudden sensations of being short of breath, spoke with a weak voice, slept badly, was constantly troubled by distressing dreams, and his pulse was racing. He did not get better and fifteen months after the accident his claim was settled. Despite a mild improvement, he was still "wholly unfit for work". Four years after the accident, this patient's physician reported that he still suffered from depressed spirits, palpitations, loss of sleep, bad dreams, easy fatigability, occasional loss of voice, loss of energy, dread of impending evil, and was easily upset (Page 1883, 151–153).

"For want of a better and without a shadow of reproach," Page also used the term "hysteria" to describe the condition from which such patients suffered in the wake of a general nervous shock. In keeping with the definition of hysteria of his age, he characterised a hysterical condition as "one in which there is loss of self-control and enfeeblement of the power of the will [...] loss of the habitual power to suppress and keep in due subjection the sensations which are doubtless associated with the various functions of the organic life of the individual" (Page 1883, 175).

Like Erichsen, Page portrayed what happens in a nervous shock as a loss, but he did not understand this loss in the physical terms of energy and labour power. Instead, Page claimed that the control of the psyche by the will is lost due to the fear or fright evoked by a railway collision. A chain of command breaks down, allowing lower forces to assert themselves (Page 1883, 176). This leads to a mental anarchy that allows

the mind of the patient, unhinged by the shock, and directed to the pains and other abnormal sensations of his body [...] to run riot with the symptoms which he feels. Dwelling constantly on his bodily sensations, he is on the look-out for any new sensation that may arise, and is alive to and makes discovery of sensations which to the healthy have no existence at all. (Page 1883, 174)

In a healthy person with a stable mental state, Page argued, bodily sensations do not intrude into consciousness. However, "let some sudden profound psychical disturbance arise, such as may well be induced by the shock of a railway collision", and these "organic sensations declare their being, and force themselves into the conscious life of the individual" (Page 1883, 176). They "step out of their natural obscurity, and become the foci of the uncontrolled and misdirected attention of the mind" (1883, 177). Page reiterated this hierarchical and conflictual image of the mind in manifold ways, driving home the message that shock entails the breakdown of an internal structure of mental self-government, in which, to quote from another passage, "the higher intellectual processes are [...] put *hors de combat*, and in their temporary abeyance or annihilation lies the possibility of disorder" (Page 1883, 198).

Above all, Page replaced Erichsen's physicalist rhetoric of energy loss with a quasi-political metaphor. This metaphor suggests an invisible internal revolution in which fear or fright bring about the failure of "higher" mental functions that ought to control "lower" ones. Once the lower functions intrude freely into consciousness, awareness of them comes to dominate the mind to an increasing degree. As Page put it:

[...] the patient, alive to every new sensation which may arise [...] tends to exaggerate its import, to describe it in terms which to the healthy man seem well-nigh absurd [...] And out of this exaggeration itself arises another cause of prolongation of the illness. The exaggerated estimate of the symptoms themselves leads to an erroneous estimate of the present incapacity, and to an increasing belief in the impossibility of future recovery and usefulness. (Page 1883, 180)

In Page's account, the will has become feeble; inner control has been lost; the mind yields unconsciously or wilfully to bodily sensations, leading to "the abandonment of the conscious self to the thraldom of the morbid state, the enjoyment, so to speak, of the luxury, not of woe exactly, but of gloomy hopes and feelings [...]. A vicious habit is being impressed upon his nervous system, from which the sufferer will find it difficult in the future to rid himself. [...] As he sows so also he shall reap" (1883, 187).

Page's discourse reaches a turning-point when he portrays the sufferer as enjoying his suffering. From thereon, he no longer depicts the patient merely as a victim of an involuntarily experienced shock and a loss of self-control, but as a "man who voluntarily abandons himself to the morbid state" and "submits both his moral and physical nature to a long spread-out shock from which he will find it hard to rally" (1883, 203).

Ultimately, Page presents the claimant as someone who actively and voluntarily extends the effects of the nervous shock. Hence, he also describes the symptoms as "brought on by the will of the patient himself" (1883, 203). Based upon this picture of the mind as thrown into anarchy by nervous shock, Page stresses that compensation may act as a potent element in retarding convalescence. He points to the countless instances in which a speedy recovery followed financial settlement, but surprisingly, he does not interpret this pattern as malingering. For him, the ascendance of lower mental functions in the minds of claimants is a sign of their weakness of will rather than of imposture, which would demand a strong will and self-control. In his words, their mental state is one of "a strange perversion and abeyance of volitional power or will, whereby each action, word, and thought, seem to run riot, as it were, for want of due control" (Page 1883, 235). He warns that the absence of objective signs of damage to the nerves should not lead one to impugn the "integrity and trustworthiness" of patients, for in his words, they "are really suffering from the symptoms of a general nervous shock" (Page 1883, 142).

Even though he did not dismiss them as frauds, and although he proclaimed claimants innocent of conscious deception, he still held them to be guilty of pretence (Page 1883, 255–257). Page refused to clarify this ambiguity; on the contrary, he stated that:

The borderland of conscious and unconscious yielding to this influence of compensation is ill-defined; but it is not part of our duty to express an opinion as to whether the patient is on one side of the boundary or the other. (Page 1883, 258)

Drawing on the concept of nervous mimicry developed by Paget, Page argued that the tremendous fright elicited by a traumatic experience induced an auto-hypnosis, which led the brain to mimic symptoms of somatic illnesses that the patient may have experienced in the past, without there being any actual somatic disorder. In such a state, he claimed, "patients may voluntarily submit themselves to their exhibition, and the manifestations thereof become in themselves no less real. The existence of a certain amount of control is shown moreover by the disappearance of the mimicries, when all cause for their representation is removed" (Page 1883, 204). On the one hand, Page's etiology stresses the involuntary origin of the symptoms of nervous shock by pointing to the power of fright. On the other, it attributes control over the continued existence of these symptoms to the patients. Page's ambivalence comes to the fore in the appendix to his book, which contains over two hundred cases of railway injuries, about half of which are described as deception of one form or another.

To sum up, Page opposed Erichsen on a number of levels. He unmasked the symptoms of shock as the result of a phantasm that emerges in a moment of fright. Instead of drawing on the physicalist repertoire that served Erichsen, he drew on a socio-political one, which portrayed nervous shock as the collapse of stable self-government, leading to the revolutionary – and pathogenic – overthrow of reason, and the anarchic, unconstrained running wild of lower functions. It seems that, while Erichsen's imagery imparted scientific credibility to his discourse on nervous shock, the success of Page's imagery stemmed from its resonance with widespread fears of class struggle, revolution and national decline, which, in turn, were related to mental disorders, such as hysteria and neurasthenia.[6]

Like Erichsen's book, Page's work too, became a prominent fixture in legal proceedings, where it served railway companies both in England and the US.

---

6 Nye 1984; Pick 1989.

Thus, the passage from Charles Dana that was quoted above on the way Erichsen's approach served the claimant's lawyer, goes on to present the lawyer for the defence as responding by brandishing "triumphantly a larger work, by Mr. Herbert Page, on 'Injuries to the Spine'; he reads to the jury cases of malingering therein related, shows that Mr. Erichsen has for years made a business of being an expert for people with injured spines, but that he has never yet found a case that proved fatal. He quotes Mr. Page's two hundred and thirty four cases of spinal concussion, in most of which recovery resulted" (Dana 1884, 617).

Page carried the day. Erichsen's somatic theory of nervous shock, which traced it to spinal concussion and inflammation, was rejected because he could not provide any evidence for it, because it did not accord with developments in neurology, a discipline which was taking its first steps at the time, and because it contradicted the mentalist consensus. Erichsen was dismissed as dated.

Conclusion

This chapter has brought to light the discursive codes that two leading Victorian doctors, John Erich Erichsen and Herbert William Page, shared when they addressed the puzzle of nervous shock, arguing that both of them depicted shock as a moment of excess leading to a loss. For Erichsen, an excess of technological power – paradigmatically two colliding railways – brings about a loss of nervous energy, work ability and income. In contrast, according to Page, an excess of fright and imagination again results in a loss of work ability and income, but here it is accompanied by a loss of will.

We have seen that both Erichsen and Page resort to strong imagery as a discursive resource to conceptualise a moment of transformation from health into illness. One might regard the extensive use of analogies as a sign of epistemic weakness. However, as the short digression to Maxwell has shown, analogical reasoning was considered a legitimate scientific strategy even in physics at the time, a means by which to explore and depict processes and dynamics for which there was still no sound scientific theory. Thus, albeit extensive recourse to analogies indicated that the knowledge on nervous shock was still in the making, it did not mark it as epistemically weak.

Both Erichsen's and Page's work emerged in a legal context that granted doctors a prominent public role as expert witnesses, but simultaneously subordinated their testimony to the adversary dynamics of the legal process. Leading medical practitioners and scholars were concerned that, although the regime of strict liability increased the importance of doctors in court, rather than strengthening the social status of doctors, public dissension was seen as subverting their status as objective agents of knowledge. Moreover, the simplified presentation of complex medical subjects to laypersons was also regarded as weakening the scientific authority of medicine. Thus, already at the time physicians were concerned with the hierarchical and conflictual logic of the court that medicine had to enter when doctors acted as expert witnesses. In addition, Erichsen claimed that the legal context in which doctors examined claimants affected their practice negatively. Rather than encountering those suffering from symptoms as patients, and assessing their disorder objectively, they investigated them in a quasi-forensic mode, representing a party in a legal dispute.

Finally, we have seen how Erichsen's somatic theory of nervous shock, which seemed to be strong at the outset, came to be considered as weak and dated because it could not supply the empirical evidence that it should have been capable of providing in its own terms, and did not accord with the prevailing medical consensus. It seems that, when Erichsen realised the weakness of his position, he sought to subsume the consensual position on the mental dynamics of nervous shock into his approach, by distinguishing two forms of nervous shock and developing a dual-track etiology. However, this attempt to save his theory by partial accommodation failed. Page's mentalist explanation, which built on the work of other physicians and played on widespread cultural fears, gained the upper hand both in medicine and in court, thus closing this particular chapter in the medico-legal history of nervous shock.

References

Chamallas, Martha, and L.K. Kerber (1990): "Women, Mothers and the Law of Fright: A History". *Michigan Law Review*, 88 (4): 814–864.

Dana, Charles L. (1884): "Concussion of the Spine and its Relation to Neurasthenia and Hysteria". *Medical Recorder*, 26: 617–21.

Drinka, George F. (1984): *The Birth of Neurosis: Myth, Malady and the Victorians*. New York: Simon & Schuster.

Erichsen, John E. (1853): *The Science and Art of Surgery: A Treatise on Surgical Injuries, Diseases, and Operations*. London: Walton & Maberly.

Erichsen, John E. (1866): *On Railway and Other Injuries of the Nervous System*. London: Walton & Maberly.

Erichsen, John E. (1864): *The Science and Art of Surgery: A Treatise on Surgical Injuries, Diseases, and Operations*. 4th edition. London: Walton & Maberly.

Erichsen, John E. (1867): *On Railway and Other Injuries of the Nervous System*. 2nd edition. London: Walton &Maberly.

Erichsen, John E. (1875): *On Concussion of the Spine, Nervous Shock and Other Obscure Injuries to the Nervous System in their Clinical and Medico-Legal Aspects*. New York: William Wood.

Erichsen, John, E. (1878): "On Surgical Evidence in Courts of Law, with Suggestions for its Improvement." *Lancet*, 1878, I: 411–413, 450–452, 485–486, 600–602, 637–639, 709–710.

Erichsen, John E. (1882): *On Concussion of the Spine, Nervous Shock and Other Obscure Injuries to the Nervous System in their Clinical and Medico-Legal Aspects*. A new and revised edition. New York: William Wood.

Freeman, Michael (1999): *The Railway and the Victorian Imagination*. New Haven CT: Yale University Press.

Harrington, Ralph (2000): "The Railway Journey and the Neuroses of Modernity." In: Richard Wrigley and George Revill (Eds.): *Pathologies of Travel*, 229–259. Amsterdam: Rodopi (*Clio Medica*, 56).

Harrington, Ralph (2001): "The Railway Accident: Trains, Trauma, and Technological Crises in Nineteenth-century Britain." In: Mark S. Micale and Paul Lerner (Eds.): *Traumatic Pasts: History, Psychiatry, and Trauma in the Modern Age, 1870–1930*, 31–56. Cambridge: Cambridge University Press.

Hobsbawm, Eric J. (1985): *The Age of Capital, 1848–1875*. London: Sphere Books.

"Influence of Railway Travelling on Public Health: Report of the Commission" (1862). *Lancet*, 1862, I: 15–19, 48–53, 79–85, 107–110, 130–132, 155–158, 231–235, 258–261.

Jordan, Furneaux John (1867): "The Hastings Prize Essay 1866: On Shock after Surgical Operations and Injuries." *British Medical Journal*, I: 73–76, 136–137, 164–167, 192–193, 219–224, 257–261, 281–282.

Maxwell, James Clerk (1855): "On Faraday's Lines of Force." *Transactions of the Cambridge Philosophical Society*, X, 1: 155–229.

Maxwell, James Clerk (1861): "On Physical Lines of Force." *Philosophical Magazine*, 21: 161–175, 281–345; 23: 12–24, 85–95.

"Medical Evidence" (1865). *British Medical Journal* I: 364–365.

"Medical Evidence in Railway Cases" (1867). *Lancet*, II: 741.

Mendelson, Danuta (1998): *The Interfaces of Medicine and Law: The History of the Liability for Negligently Caused Psychiatric Injury (Nervous Shock)*. Aldershot: Dartmouth Publishing.

Noble, Daniel (1865): "Medical Evidence in Railway Accidents", *British Medical Journal*, I: 361–362.

Nye, Robert (1984): *Crime, Madness and Politics: The Medical Concept of National Decline*. Princeton NJ: Princeton University Press.

Page, Herbert W. (1883): *Injuries of the Spine and Spinal Cord without Apparent Mechanical Lesion and Nervous Shock in their Surgical and Medico-legal Aspects*. London: Churchill.

Paget, James (1873): "Clinical Lectures on the Nervous Mimicry of Organic Diseases." *Lancet*, 1873, II: 511–513, 547–549, 619–621, 727–729, 763–765, 833–835.

Pick, Daniel (1989): *Faces of Degeneration: A European Disorder, c. 1848 – c. 1918*. Cambridge: Cambridge University Press.

"Railway Injuries and Special Jury Damages" (1865). *Lancet*, II: 156–157.

Schivelbusch, Wolfgang (1980): *The Railway Journey: the Industrialization of Time and Space in the Nineteenth Century*. Oxford: Basil Blackwell.

Trimble, Michael (1981). *Post-Traumatic Neurosis: From Railway Spine to the Whiplash*. Chichester, UK: John Wiley & Sons.

Tuke, Daniel H. (1872): *Illustrations of the Influence of the Mind upon the Body in Health and Disease Designed to Elucidate the Action of the Imagination*. London: J. & A. Churchill.

Young, Allan (1995): *The Harmony of Illusions: Inventing Post-Traumatic Stress Disorder.* Princeton NJ: Princeton University Press.

The Power of Weak Knowledge: Modernist Dissonances in American Medicine

John Harley Warner

Abstract

The new version of reductionist, laboratory-based scientific medicine that emerged in the final third of the nineteenth century represented a programme that was "strong" epistemologically, socially, and culturally. This chapter suggests that co-emerging with it in the 1890s was a programme to retrieve and advocate for epistemologically "weaker" forms of knowledge and their social and moral correlates that efforts to promote the new scientific medicine had disparaged, dismissed as lesser, and rendered disreputable. Sounding a note of dissonance more than dissent, some clinicians began to speak up for clinical virtues being marginalised or placed at risk of being lost, such as personal judgement, individual experience, the educated senses, and a cultivated medical artistry. Tellingly, while physicians continued to point to "the personal equation" as an impediment to precision to be eliminated, others simultaneously began to use the term in a new positive sense to refer to the clinician's personal judgement and personal knowledge of the individuated patient. This was the moment when "clinical acumen" prominently came to the fore as one way of capturing what distinguished the physician-artist from the mere technician, and when the "art" of medicine more and more came to stand for what was fragile, missing, or undervalued. This discourse of deficiency was a lament and jeremiad, but also a programme to retrieve ways of knowing and acting that had been discounted. By the mid-twentieth century, the enduring attribution of weakness to personal knowledge would give organised medicine a culturally and politically powerful resource in its successful battle to block the passage of national health insurance and to shape the structure of American health care.[1]

---

1 I am deeply grateful to Rene Almeling, Cornelius Borck, Henry Cowles, Naomi Rogers, and Joanna Radin for their comments on versions of this chapter.

Introduction

Judged by the appraisal of physicians at the time and by the assessment of later historians, the new version of scientific medicine that emerged during the final third of the nineteenth century – reductionist, mechanistic, laboratory-based – represented knowledge that was "strong" epistemologically, socially, culturally, and politically. It was a form of knowledge characterised by aspirations to precision, exactness, and standardisation, and fundamentally grounded in commitments to mechanical objectivity, self-abnegation, automaticity, and the drive to eliminate the personal equation.

My focus here, taking the case of the United States, is a programme that, in the 1890s, co-emerged with the new scientific medicine to champion and retrieve epistemologically "weaker" forms of medical knowledge that proselytisers for the new order had belittled and rendered disreputable. While celebrating the gains brought by the new scientific medicine, some physicians, concerned that its epistemological house-cleaning might have been too aggressively zealous, began to speak up for clinical ways of knowing that had been marginalised, lost, or placed at risk of being lost. Mounting aspirations to a medicine of precision, they warned, were edging out personal knowledge and personalised medicine. They insisted on the value of personal judgement, individual experience, cultivated artistry, and attention to the idiosyncrasies of individual patients. This was a diffuse but unmistakably legible call to valorise anew medical knowledge and ways of knowing that were in danger of being banished.

These two programmes for medical knowledge co-existed and, in some ways, defined one another. But it is important to say plainly that, at the end of the nineteenth century, the relationship of the weaker to the stronger programme was one of dissonance more than dissent. Between the 1860s and 1880s, the ambitions of the reductionist programme had sometimes been met with resistance and outright opposition, but that began to fade. What was new around 1890 was the vocal advocacy of a distinctly weaker form of medical knowledge by physicians who, for the most part, embraced the epistemological allegiances at the core of the new scientific medicine. In proselytising for what they recognised as comparatively weak knowledge, they were championing ways of knowing, acting, and *being* modern physicians that were in addition to, not instead of, what the epistemologically and culturally strong reductionist programme alone could provide. Their programme resonates powerfully with early twenty-first century calls to reinstate knowledge about the "patient as person" in ways that go beyond the limitations of evidence-based medicine and beyond biological individuality – to move from "precision medicine" to "personalised medicine".[2]

---

2 See, for example, Ziegelstein 2017 and Borck 2019, in this volume.

I wish to do three things here. First, I will sketch the emergence of the new version of scientific medicine between the 1860s and the turn of the century, which turned upon knowledge that I am styling as epistemologically and culturally strong. In doing so, my aim is to draw attention to the other kinds of knowledge that the physicians who promoted this programme dismissed as marginal and sometimes demonised as dangerous. Second, I will turn to what coalesced in the 1890s and early 1900s as advocacy for a distinctly weak form of medical knowledge. This was part of a programme to retrieve ways of knowing that had been diminished and discredited as the new scientific medicine gained in power, often expressed as clinical acumen, ineffable artistry, and an alternative meaning of the term "personal equation" that indicated personal knowledge and personal judgement as important attributes of the individual physician. Finally, I will turn to the 1940s, when the physician's personal knowledge and autonomous individual judgement, again held to be at risk, were at the core of a campaign that tightly bound their preservation to Cold War geopolitics and the defence of "American freedom". The enduring attribution of weakness to personal knowledge that was forged in the late nineteenth century gave mid-twentieth century organised medicine a culturally and politically powerful resource in its successful battle to block the passage of national health insurance in the United States and to shape the structure of American health care.

1. Epistemological divestment

That scientific medicine in the United States emerged during the final third of the nineteenth century is a historiographic commonplace. And yet, earlier American physicians never doubted that they already had a scientific medicine of their own – for example, the sensual empiricist programme rooted in the systematic patho-anatomical correlation of signs and symptoms observed at the bedside with lesions found at autopsy championed by the American disciples of the Paris Clinical School. What gained ascendance was a new version of scientific medicine. The fact that later physicians and historians alike tend to equate that new version with "scientific medicine" *tout court* is testimony to the remarkable success of its advocates in promoting its epistemological, cultural, and moral virtues and in rendering what had come before as lesser and somehow inauthentic. Like modernity itself, defined in significant measure oppositionally by what it excluded, the programme for a new scientific medicine was characterised as much by the kinds of knowledge that it disparaged as by the ideals that it embraced. It encompassed a project of epistemological divestment, a project that discounted and sought to shed ways of knowing that had once held pride of place.

The most ardent American proselytisers for a plan to reground medicine in the experimental sciences shared French physiologist Claude Bernard's rejection of claims by "great practicing physicians" to mastery at the bedside that came from an experientially-developed "clinical sense or instinct" (Bernard [1865] 1927, 203), that is, a command of what he sneered at as an "untenable medical claim to art". "There is no such thing as a medical work of art," Bernard insisted in his 1865 polemical *Introduction to the Study of Experimental Medicine*, "and therefore there is no such thing as a medical artist; physicians calling themselves such injure medical science, because they exalt a physician's personality by lowering the importance of science." (Bernard [1865] 1927, 204) Embracing a universalism that trounced all claims to ineffable ways of knowing that inhered in the individual clinician, Bernard proclaimed that the experimental method "is impersonal; it destroys individuality" (Bernard [1865] 1927, 220).

Americans who promoted the new programme – especially the cohort that, starting in the later 1850s, travelled to German centres of medical study – tended to elide distinctions between laboratory and clinical ways of knowing. They often conflated such social and technical hallmarks as specialism, diagnostic instruments of precision, and reliance on the experimental laboratory sciences. The *exact method* that was the distinctive hallmark of the experimental laboratory, for example, corresponded to the very deliberate quest for precision, exactness, and impersonality in the clinic. The ideal of mechanical objectivity, moreover, had a clinical counterpart in the epistemological and aesthetic preference for standardisation, precision, and visual representation of knowledge elicited at the bedside.[3] Thus, the medical professor Mary Putnam Jacobi would admonish Philadelphia students to cultivate "the laboratory habit of mind" at the patient's bedside, urging that "the clinical record gains in value with every approximation to the ideal of the laboratory notebook" (Jacobi 1900, 6). It was a multifaceted epistemological programme, but, in America, it tended to be depicted in ways that emphasised its unity and thereby enhanced its strength and cultural power.

This elision is especially clear in the kinds of knowledge celebrated and disparaged in promoting new diagnostic instruments of precision. The sphygmograph was at the vanguard of a proliferation of automatic self-recording devices that embodied reductionist aspirations and a new ideal of automaticity. Modelled on the kymograph – emblematic of the experimental physiology laboratory – it automatically inscribed a line on a revolving drum recorder indicating the strength and rate of the pulse, bringing experimental physiology's graphic method to the clinic.[4] "The tracings of the pulse-form are a literal transcript of physiological facts," a New York medical professor asserted in 1867 (Clymer 1867, 279). "The

---

3 I draw here on Warner 1998, 297–305; and see Warner 1992.

4 Borell 1987; Brain 2015; Bynum and Porter 1993; Crenner 1993; Frank 1987, 34; Frank 1988; Romano 2002. And see Wise 1995.

graphical method," another physician urged the following year, "corrects the personal errors which may be laid to the charge of the observer, whether from prejudice, from inattention, or want of sensorial acuteness, and substitutes a mathematical and positive expression of facts for the ever-varying and often contradictory appreciations of the human eye." (Anonymous 1868, 73).

From the mid-1860s, the sphygmograph became a tangible, material emblem of the impulse to find instruments of precision that would establish the power of laboratory science to transform bedside knowing. It exemplified the larger, intertwined aims of cultivating mechanical objectivity and eliminating the personal equation of the clinical observer. The experienced physician's finely-honed senses and personal judgement were to yield to objective representations in which normal and pathological nature spoke for itself, free from the clinician's sagacity and interpretation. With the sphygmograph, as one physician put it, "the heart is made to write out a description of its own ailments" (Johnson 1873, 15). Feeling the pulse – exercising the learned touch or *tactus eruditus*, which had earlier been so esteemed in the Paris Clinical School's sensual empiricist programme – one physician commented, " is a method only approximately exact; too much depends upon the factor of personal equation in the observer" (Gardiner and Hoagland 1905, 80).

Like the sphygmograph, the thermometer and graphical representation of temperature also promised to help liberate clinical medicine from its dependence on the individual physician's senses and personal judgement. In their enthusiasm for the clinical thermometer, Americans followed the lead of the Leipzig clinician Carl Wunderlich, who published his first paper on thermometry in 1857 and had become the dominant figure in the field by the time he published his massive 1868 treatise *Das Verhalten der Eigenwärme in Krankenheiten*, translated into English three years later. Thermography, he asserted, had "an advantage of almost priceless value, in as much as it gives results which can be measured, signs that can be expressed in numbers, and offers materials for diagnosis which are incontestable and indubitable, which are independent of the opinion or the amount of practice or the sagacity of the observer" (Wunderlich 1871, 48). It was an instrument of precision that "substitutes the exactness of measurement and the certainty of figures for the uncertainty and indefiniteness of judgment", an American reviewer of Wunderlich's book commented when it appeared (J.C.R 1869, 426). "It is *precise*; its results can be rendered apparent to the eye; they do not depend upon judgment or estimation, but can be rendered visible, and with that exactness which always belongs to arithmetical figures" (J.C.R. 1869, 432). It also obviated attention to what the patient had to say, for unlike patients, he asserted, "the thermometer does not lie. It neither simulates, dissimulates, nor exaggerates" (J.C.R. 1869, 433).

Medical thermometry had grown from the hospital, but, in promoting the clinical thermometer and graphical depiction of information derived from it, American clinicians took pains to identify thermometry with the laboratory.[5] Indeed, the common practice in American medical journals during the 1860s of printing temperature graphs as a white line against a black background – instead of the later convention of a black line against a white background – would surely have conjured up in the minds of the viewers the image of the white line that a kymographic or sphygmographic stylus etched onto black sooted paper (Borrell 1987, 57).

Knowledge derived though the physician's practised finger on the pulse, hand on a feverish forehead, or ear at the end of a stethoscope, New York physician Édouard Seguin argued in 1876, "are the expression of individual sensory impressions rendered in the individual's own language – impressions and language which necessarily vary from man to man, and cannot be finally adjudicated by a more stable authority" (Seguin 1876, 350). In contrast, the results obtained by the sphygmograph and thermometer "*are substitutes to our senses*, and give automatic results which cannot be influenced by the personal modalities of the senses or of the mind" (Seguin 1876, 349). Diagnostic knowledge produced by clinical thermography was "given out by the instrument itself, in traces, figures or diagrams which the imagination of the observer cannot alter, nor his power of rhetoric enlarge or color. [...] [W]hat the thermometer says no man can contradict" (Seguin 1876, 350).

2. Eliminating the personal equation

From sphygmograph to x-ray, each new instrument of precision would be praised in its turn, as one physician put it, for "leaving nothing to the fallibility of the personal equation" (Barnes 1894, 678). This construct of the personal equation gave physicians a way to capture and express the danger that individual variation posed to medical aspirations to precision and exactitude. It grew from an observation in late-eighteenth-century astronomy that observers making simultaneous measurements of star transit times would record slightly different values. Such differences in the personal equation from one person to the next in astronomical observation and reaction time in experimental psychology could be measured, and, during the second half of the nineteenth century, there were vigorous programmes of personal equation research in astronomy, physiology, and psychology.[6] While mentions of the personal equation appeared in the medical literature

---

5 Hess and Mendelsohn 2010. And see Hess 2005.

6 On the "personal equation", see Canales 2009; Boring 1957, 134–153; Daston and Galison 2007; Hoffmann 2007; Kuklick 2011; Richards 1982; and Schaffer 1988.

earlier, it was in the late 1860s and 1870s – the same moment when some physicians were celebrating the epistemological power and clinical potential of the new
instruments of precision – that the personal equation assumed a prominent place
in American medical discourse.

The aim of eliminating the personal equation – what one physician described
as "that unbidden guest that sneaks into our laboratories and clinics, and confounds the senses of the keenest of mortals" (Prince 1889, 421) – was a hallmark
of the new scientific medicine. It stood for the danger of relying on the individual
doctor's unaided senses – however "educated" and experienced – and for individual variation as a source of error. An embodied obstacle to mechanical objectivity, it pushed against uniformity, standardisation, and exactness. "The use of
apparatus for counting, weighing, and measuring, which will give results independent of the personal equation of the user, is one of the characteristics of modern
medicine," the Washington, D.C. physician John Shaw Billings asserted, singling
out the "habit of precision and accuracy" (Billings 1893, 47).

In the American medical vernacular, moreover, the meanings of the personal
equation expanded far beyond its role as the nemesis of mechanical objectivity to
encompass individual variation among physicians more broadly, ranging from individual exercise of clinical judgement, to opinions derived from "education and
reading", to their personal "feelings and emotions".[7] It could refer to "personal
peculiarities", "variation in the way of looking at things", clinical skill, or even the
distorting influence of "hero-worship" on the critical assessment of medical
knowledge.[8]

Epistemology and professional identity were tightly bound together throughout the nineteenth century, and the drive to eliminate the personal equation became part and parcel of a larger transformation in the epistemological, social, and
moral constitution of the modern physician. The embrace of reductionism, the
values of the experimental laboratory, and mechanical objectivity went hand in
hand with a transformation in identity, as did new moral convictions that hinged
upon restraining epistemological autonomy and suppressing the credit accorded
to personal experience and judgement.[9] Self-denial and self-abnegation – moral
virtues that Lorraine Daston and Peter Galison have identified as characteristic
of practitioners of other natural sciences who embraced mechanical objectivity
during precisely this period – were also critically important ingredients in the physician's new sense of self, something much too little recognised in the historiog-

---

7 Woodhull 1877, 17; Blake 1900, 482.
8 Phin 1877, 71; Richardson 1891, 13; Dolan 1887, 160. Scott Podolsky and Rory Brinkmann
   generously shared their preliminary findings on the changing use of the personal equation as
   "observer bias" in Brinkmann et al. 2019; for their springboard to this important investigation,
   see Podolsky et al. 2016.
9 See Warner 1991.

raphy of medicine.[10] In this remaking of the identity of the modern American physician, long-esteemed personal judgement grew suspect as something variable, indefinite, and subjective, which was to be reined in by disciplined self-restraint, self-abnegation.

Emerging from the 1860s alongside the impulse to eliminate the personal equation of the physician was the aspiration to liberate clinical medicine from its earlier preoccupation with the myriad individuating characteristics of each and every patient. Laboratory workers, as Robert Kohler has pointed out, contrasting them with scientists in the field, secured their epistemological credit line by stripping away the particular and local, and physicians sought to harness that power for the clinic as well.[11]

Therapeutic knowledge, for example, had been governed by the premise that treatment had to be matched to the idiosyncratic characteristics of each patient and their local physical, social, and epidemiological environments.[12] As an Ohio physician had noted in 1848, "*Individualism*, not *universalism*, attaches therefore to all our therapeutic measures".[13] Treatment was to be sensitively gauged not to a disease entity, but to such attributes of the patient as ethnicity, age, gender, occupation, socioeconomic position, and habits, and of place as climate, topography, population density, and social structure. But a new therapeutic imaginary, distinguished by an allegiance to knowledge produced and validated by experimental science, signalled a shift *from* individualism *to* universalism (Warner 1990, 207–209). This shift in clinical cognition was reflected by a telling transformation in medical vocabulary. The normal began to supplant the natural as the paradigm of bodily disorder and disease, moving clinical medicine away from its preoccupation with individuating characteristics towards a more reductionist perspective that weighed specific indicators in the patient against criteria of health expressed as objectively measurable universalised norms (Warner 1997, 85–91).

The final third of the century with its ardent celebration of new epistemological and moral commitments was a singular moment at which exactness, automaticity, and even clinical certainty seemed tantalisingly within reach. Individual judgement, the educated senses, and personal experience were devalued, albeit never discarded. Their rank in the hierarchy of ways of medical knowing had been decisively weakened.

---

10 Daston and Galison 2007; Galison 1998; Daston and Galison 1992.
11 Robert Kohler explicates this point in Kohler 2002a and 2002b.
12 Rosenberg 1979, and Warner 1997.
13 H[arrison] 1848, 122, my emphasis.

3. The discourse of deficiency

By the 1890s, programmatic calls for a new version of scientific medicine had begun to yield to self-congratulations on its arrival. Outright opposition increasingly gave way to questions about the *sufficiency* of this approach to medical knowledge. What emerged was advocacy of a diffuse but interconnected cluster of kinds of weakened and discounted medical knowledge and ways of knowing that proponents insisted should be valued in addition to, not instead of, the strong epistemological programme at the heart of the new scientific medicine – a call for pluralism.

This multivocal lament coalesced around what I will call a "discourse of deficiency", a discourse that co-emerged with modern medicine and became a lasting part of it. It included warnings about what was missing from the emerging medical order – most often epistemological and human values that had been marginalised, forgotten, or sacrificed as the new version of scientific medicine gained in power. But it was more than simply a complaint. Drawing attention to what was absent, marginalised, or at risk of vanishing was a springboard to making the case for preservation and retrieval, a programme of cultural salvage.

Protests against reductionist hubris of course continued. For some aging doctors caught up in a crisis of belonging, for example, engaging in this discourse was an occasion to rail against their alienation from the new order of things. "In the constant search for more exact and scientific methods," one doctor sniped in 1893, "we may be losing sight of the patient and his personal sufferings." (Anonymous 1893a, 56) Sometimes, this discourse of deficiency was an exercise in pastoral nostalgia, reflection on an imagined past and particularly the world of the old-time family doctor. And sometimes it took the shrill form of a jeremiad, a lamentation over the current state of medicine and a prophesy of its downfall if the headlong zeal for mechanistic reductionism was not checked, along with an exhortation to repentance.

What matters here, though, is the wide spectrum of physicians spanning from family doctors to a professional élite at the most fortified bastions of the new scientific medicine such as Johns Hopkins, who, by engaging in the discourse of deficiency, were calling attention to ways of knowing that were being forgotten, endangered, or sacrificed in a larger process of change which they applauded as progress.[14] Their lament and its animating anxieties often resonated with antimodernist strains that could be heard in other realms of American culture, including *fin-de-siècle* calls for wholeness, and stirrings of rebellion against mechanistic

---

14 Consider here also the engagement with medical history at the end of the nineteenth century, particularly by a medical élite at places such as Johns Hopkins. See Burnham 1998; Huisman and Warner 2004; Warner 2011 and 2014.

science and the wider fragmentation of modern life.[15] But, to the extent that what emerged in the 1890s was an American medical strain of anti-modernism, by and large, it was not an alienated reaction against modernism so much as a part of modernism itself.

Demonisation of the unaided senses in favour of diagnostic instruments of precision, for example, was tempered by the plea that young physicians should not neglect the cultivation of their own senses. "You will learn the use of many new and valuable instruments," William Keen told Philadelphia medical students in his 1890 address entitled "The New Era in Medicine". "But I want to urge you to do one thing more: to combine with all our nineteenth-century inventions eighteenth-century shrewdness of observation and acute cultivation of the unassisted senses, in order to make up the more perfect doctors of the twentieth century."[16]

4. Art, acumen, and personal knowledge

Such revivalist rhetoric was often couched in the language of "the personal equation", but valorising the term differently. The personal equation retained its meaning as a source of variability, uncertainty, and error. But, in the discourse of deficiency, it prominently assumed an alternative connotation as part of what made the interaction between doctor and patient more than a transaction between skilled technician and standardised machine. It was this additional, distinctly positive sense of the term that enabled one clinician in 1891 to equate "the personal equation of operator and patient" with "judicious individuation" (Edebohls 1891, 591). Regarded this way, the personal equation could represent an ingredient in the calculus of knowing to be prized and cultivated, not just a source of error to be eliminated.

This was a telling but unmarked variation in vernacular medical language. The personal equation was one of several terms (clinical acumen and art were others) used to capture and affirm the value of weak knowledge that turned upon personal experience, individual judgement, and knowing the idiosyncrasies of sick individuals. It may well have slipped into this new usage through misunderstanding of the original meaning by doctors drawn to the adjective "personal" as a way of grasping important dimensions of how the physician was to know and what

---

15 As a starting-point, see Lears 1981. I have not yet begun to compare the case of the United States with European impulses, including the holism in the natural sciences that would intensify during the interwar period; see, for example, Harrington 1996; Ash 1995; and Lawrence and Weisz 1998.

16 Keen 1905, 122–123. And see Evans 1993.

about the patient was worth knowing. Indeed, in this usage the emphasis shifted from the second word, personal *equation* (as the term originally had been used in astronomy) to the first: *personal* equation. If the former meaning was precise, the latter could be diffuse and often sloppy. Yet, American physicians widely deployed this term to insist on the value of the personal and individual as key components of medical knowing.

More and more, physicians spoke of the personal equation as a desirable attribute of the autonomous medical *persona*, re-affirming the value of personal judgement. Thus, a physician just returned in 1891 from Berlin, where he had observed the use of Robert Koch's tuberculin in treating pulmonary tuberculosis, could report admiringly on the "acumen" of the Berlin clinicians and the important role played by their "judgement and expertise – what is called the personal equation" (Quimby 1891, 75). Reliance on the individual clinician's personal equation was especially key in diagnostically challenging cases that presented unfamiliar symptom clusters. In such cases, a Philadelphia clinician maintained, "There are no rules which can be laid down with regard to symptoms to be looked for", and "therefore, the personal equation enters more largely into their successful management than usual, and a physician has rare opportunities to display his acumen as a diagnostician" (Meigs 1886, 413). So too, in a discussion on cardiac disease at a meeting of the Medical Association of the Greater City of New York, one speaker urged greater reliance on instruments of precision, "not, however, to the exclusion of a proper consideration of the personal equation and the older well-known methods of diagnosis" (Shearer 1909, 965). For him as for others, diagnostic knowledge did not depend on making a choice between instruments of precision (and all they stood for) and this rendering of the personal equation, but on both as important clinical tools.

Some physicians also began to re-assert the importance of knowing the individuating characteristics of patients and local environments. "The personal equation in disease seems to me, at present, to be of more real importance in practice than anything else," one New York physician asserted. "The old practitioner's powerful hold on the family was due essentially to the fact that it was believed he knew all about it – that no individual peculiarity or idiosyncrasy escaped him" (Robinson 1908, 663, 664). Drawing attention to the importance of "the personal equation of the patient" was a way of recovering discounted kinds of clinical knowledge. A call to attend to individuality could, in turn, be a vehicle for challenging the hubris of, as one physician put it, "modern scientific medicine in its desire for exactness and impatience of things that cannot be reduced to some more or less rigid formula" (Anonymous 1886, 128). The personal equation also began to be equated with a doctor-patient relationship being important to eliciting clinically relevant information. As one physician put it in 1908, "By the personality of the physician, or the personal equation, we simply mean the ability of the physician to gain the confidence of the patient" (Fisher 1908, 985).

Weak knowledge was further linked to devalued social forms of organising knowledge and practice. At the turn of the century, a growing chorus asked the question, "Is the General Practitioner Passing Away?"[17] Much of this lamentation was nostalgia for the figure variously called the general practitioner, country doctor, or family physician, socially and morally embedded in a matrix of personal relationships with patients, families, and communities. Concern about the fragmentation of medical knowledge and the putatively mechanical character of specialists was another expression of the anxiety about what modern medicine was at risk of leaving behind. Pointing to the ongoing "subdivision of labor", which, in industry, meant "mechanics or workmen become almost like machines", one physician cautioned those gathered in 1899 for a meeting of the American Academy of Medicine that "this has unfortunately been the tendency of specialism in medicine". He went on to warn that "there is a great danger, then, that the modern development of specialism will tend to produce a narrower type of medical men, who, like the mechanics, will know only their own department" (Bulkley 1899, 174–175). Specialism had proven key to medical advancement, he affirmed, but specialists ran the risk of becoming mere technicians.

Addressing matriculants at the Texas Medical College in Galveston on the opening of the 1893 session, the 32-year-old professor William Keiller concluded his remarks by showing his students "a picture of the goal for which you are striving" – namely, English artist Luke Fildes' sentimental painting *The Doctor* (Figure 1), which had been commissioned by Henry Tate and first exhibited in 1891 at the Royal Academy in London. The painting depicts a doctor in a rustic working-class cottage sitting in vigil over a young child laid out on a bed improvised on two chairs, with distraught parents posed in the background. Set in the home rather than a hospital and with no medical technology in sight, the composition made a stark contrast with the stripped-down reductionist aesthetic so widespread in visual images of medical modernism. It embodied virtues ascribed to both the family doctor and the physician-gentleman. "I hold up before you as a high ideal this picture of the country practitioner," Keiller told his students. "He is no brilliant specialist," he averred, but "the man whom our artist has chosen is a true man of science, but his science is a means to relieve suffering humanity."[18]

---

17 Anonymous 1893b. And Anonymous 1904, 778–779.
18 Keiller 1893. See Anonymous 1884; Anonymous 1901; Anonymous 1900.

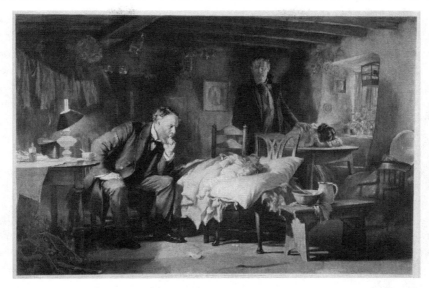

Figure 1. After English painter Luke Fildes first exhibited The Doctor *in London in 1891, more than a million engravings and prints such as this quickly appeared in American doctors' waiting rooms and parlours. Dittrick Medical History Center, Case Western Reserve University, Cleveland, Ohio.*

Keiller's admonishment was tinged with nostalgia for a world slipping away. And this nostalgia for personal relationships, a sensibility to the art of healing, and individuated attention to the whole patient was growing among doctors and patients alike. More than a million engravings of Fildes' painting appeared in doctor's offices and American parlours, it was recreated in *tableaux vivants*, and in 1911 it would appear in a Thomas Edison film – popularity that testified to longing for what the mechanistic, laboratory-based, reductionist cosmology had edged out.[19] Keiller's address to medical students took part in forging an often romantic, usually nostalgic, and remarkably durable declensionist narrative that turned upon the vanishing epistemological, moral, and social values and imagined world of the family physician.

The "art of medicine" also emerged as a central theme in the discourse of deficiency, tightly bound to positive renderings of the "personal equation" as something desirable and to calls for recognising the importance of individuality and judgement in medical knowing. Art conventionally referred to practice and science to theory, though in medical discussions the precise meaning of the terms or their relationship to grounding concepts like *techne* were seldom probed: art was, as one doctor acknowledged, "a loose form of expression" (Anonymous 1890, 64). The ideal of making medicine an exact science had set up the aim of

---

19 Lederer and Rogers 2000, 496. And see Warner 2014, especially 60–61.

supplanting the vagaries of art with an approach to automaticity and certainty – art as a foil to the new version of scientific medicine. And, in turn, the defence of art had been common in reactions against zealous programmatic depictions of a science of medicine rooted in precision, exactness, mechanical objectivity, and the power of the laboratory to direct (rather than merely to explain) practice (Warner 1991). By the 1890s, though, the championing of the healing art was voiced by some of the most eminent leaders of the profession, who welcomed, rather than resisted, the new scientific medicine.[20] "Even the foremost of diagnosticians would not claim that his special branch was a perfect science," one New York physician insisted in 1905, calling for greater attention to the "faculties which make the artist", such as unmediated touch, sight, and hearing. "He is fully aware how much depends on the personal equation." (Stern 1905, 1536, 1538)

The art of medicine retained its earlier connotations. But, starting in the 1890s, more and more "art" came to stand for knowledge and ways of knowing that were fragile, undervalued, or missing in modern medicine. Clinical artistry often figured in a contrapuntal refrain as the antithesis of that which was automatic, mechanical, and factory-like. More than this, art became a capacious umbrella category for all that was deficient and worth preserving or restoring in the face of the domination of medicine by mechanistic reductionism. This was the moment when art began to take on subtle but important new clinical and cultural meanings that were constitutive of efforts to craft a "virtuous modernity" that would be remarkably enduring.[21]

This was also the moment when the term "clinical acumen" prominently came to the fore to indicate a separate, special set of attributes that distinguished the physician-artist from the mechanic or mere technician. The term's robust deployment at the turn of the century can be understood as yet another means of trying to express and put a name to endangered kinds of medical knowing. "Our advance in scientific methods of diagnosis has led to an exaggerated estimation as to their value," a North Carolina physician asserted in his 1909 discussion of tuberculosis. "This has led to the loss of that faculty, with which our ancient colleagues were so endowed, viz: clinical acumen, the same which is so essential in the diagnosis of this disease." (Jones 1909, 425) Extolling clinical acumen re-affirmed the importance of ineffable virtues and finely-honed artistry that resided in the astute clinician. It stood for keen diagnostic discrimination, penetrating perception, cultivated judgement informed by individual experience, and wisdom – precisely those attributes of the physician-as-knower that had been discounted. It was particularly associated with élite clinicians who embraced the cognitive and material tools of the new scientific medicine while resolutely insisting that the clinical art of knowing could never by reduced to an applied science. Like "art"

---

20 I begin to pursue this in Warner 2014b.
21 See Lawrence 1998; Mayer 2000; and Rosenberg 1998.

and the positive meaning of "the personal equation", "clinical acumen" was used to identify ways of knowing to be valued in addition to, not instead of, the epistemologically stronger programme at the core of the new scientific medicine.

I have concentrated here on epistemological strength and weakness, but there were other reasons why the medical knowledge that has been my focus was weak compared with the mechanistic, reductionist, laboratory-based version of scientific medicine. One was the problem of branding. For physicians at the time, as for later historians, there was the open question of what to call this diffuse but nonetheless manifest body of weak knowledge and its signature ways of knowing. "Scientific medicine" was a powerful moniker, all the more so during the Progressive Era when scientific expertise was so prized and authoritative in all spheres of American life. But this brand was taken. "Art" was perhaps the most readily available label, but it was at once both too broad and too narrow, too bound to conventional distinctions between art and science, and lacked epistemological specificity.

A second reason was this weak knowledge's aura of pastness, its identification with older medical ways, and its increasing association with nostalgia for the social embeddedness and personal knowledge of the general practitioner. This is partly a story about the co-invention of modernity and tradition. Third, – and very much related – was its identification with weak social forms, particularly generalism in an era of intensifying specialisation. Fourth, was the problem of communication, or, rather, incommunicability. It bore a strong family resemblance to what Christopher Lawrence has termed the "incommunicable knowledge" of a turn-of-the century British clinical élite. who, in his words, "invoked an epistemology of individual experience which, by definition, defied analysis." (Lawrence 1998, 505) It was a form of knowledge that resisted articulation. Fifth, and finally was material; it did not require the bricks and mortar of laboratories, the glass and metal of instruments, and largely lacked the visible, palpable emblems of economic and institutional support that proclaimed the power of the new scientific medicine.

5. Weak knowledge and cultural power

The kinds of weak knowledge that physicians championed in the discourse of deficiency that coalesced around the turn of the century continued to temper the model that the most committed proselytisers for mechanistic reductionism had sought to establish.[22] It persisted, for example, in the élite homosocial professionalism that cultivated the cultural values of the gentleman-physician, exemplified by such figures as William Osler. It pervaded the new medical humanism that

---

22 I begin to sketch this longer trajectory in Warner 2014b.

emerged in the wake of the First World War and the calls to re-enchant the art of medicine in an age of medical science. It flourished in interwar holism and educational initiatives designed to return attention to – as medical education leader George Canby Robinson put it in the title of his 1939 book – *The Patient as a Person*. And it infused nostalgic calls during the Great Depression to retrieve the personal equation, epitomised by apprehensions about the ever-vanishing general practitioner and the enormous popular success of Kansas doctor Arthur Hertzler's bestselling book *The Horse and Buggy Doctor* (1938).

I want to close, though, by returning to Luke Fildes' *The Doctor*, the sentimental painting in Figure 1 that William Keiller had held up as a model for his Texas medical students in 1893. But here I want to turn to the 1940s and the way in which the American Medical Association (AMA) enlisted Fildes' painting as the centrepiece of its successful campaign to defeat national health insurance. In this case, it was precisely the attribution of weakness and vulnerability to the physician's personal knowledge that the painting was held to convey that accounted for its extraordinary cultural and political power. Keiller had displayed the picture as a nostalgic homage to the kind of personal knowledge about individual patients and individuated care that, in the 1890s, many feared was slipping away in the age of specialism, mechanical objectivity, and automaticity. In the 1940s, the AMA – the chief embodiment of organised medicine – placed this image at the centre of a discourse of deficiency that both celebrated the epistemological, social, and moral values which it contended that the painting expressed and warned that these values were fragile and imperiled. AMA leaders went on to make the risk of losing such personal knowledge one pivot upon which debates over the structure of American health care turned, and, in the process, tightly linked "weak" forms of medical knowledge and endangered ways of knowing to early Cold War geopolitics.[23]

Proposals for a system of national health insurance were almost implemented in 1917, and in the 1930s and 1940s support for such a move re-emerged (Numbers 1978). Beginning in 1943, the United States Congress debated a series of bills that would have established universal national health insurance of the sort that Britain adopted in 1948. "We are in an era of startling medical progress," President Harry Truman told Congress in 1949. "The technical resources available to the physician are tremendously greater than a generation ago." But "as a Nation we have not yet succeeded in making these scientific advances available to all those who need them".[24] Physicians who supported Truman's plan for national

---

23 I draw heavily in this section on Warner 2014a, 32–45; Warner 2014b; and Warner 2013, 1452–1453.

24 President Harry Truman to the Congress of the United States, draft marked "Hold for Release", The White House, 22 April 1949, White House Central Files: Official File, OF 286-A, Harry S. Truman Papers, Harry S. Truman Library, Independence, Missouri.

health insurance – a minority – went on to argue that the epistemological and technical advances of modern biomedicine had rendered some of the traditional relations between doctor and patient anachronistic. "The day of the horse and buggy doctor who, with his unaided hands and eyes and little black bag, can cure all of the ills of mankind is past," (Boas 1944, 49) insisted Ernst P. Boas, head of The Physicians Forum, a group that styled itself "the voice of the liberal doctor."[25] "It is high time that the organized profession stopped worrying about the doctor-patient relationship, and gave attention to the relationship between the profession and the people of this country."[26]

In celebrating modern biomedicine, Truman and Boas were echoing the triumphalist narrative of reductionist, mechanistic, laboratory-based medical knowledge that pervaded post-war American society. At no time before or since was the cultural authority that the medical profession derived from public faith in technoscience more robust. Expectations of medical progress stemming from laboratory research and bolstered by the development of the sulfa drugs in the 1930s intensified in the 1940s when the media lionised penicillin as a "wonder drug". Hollywood films, which often glossed over the distinction between practising doctors and medical investigators, popularised the construction of laboratory researchers as heroes, drawing on and promoting the image of the physician as biomedical scientist. And just after the war, mass crusades against specific diseases cemented in the public mind the expectation that faith in and funding for biomedical research would lead to the conquest of such feared diseases as polio. It was this adulation of reductionist scientific knowledge and its clinical and cultural power that has led historians to characterise this mid-century moment as the Golden Age of American Medicine.[27]

It is therefore remarkable that, in choosing an emblem of American medicine to rally and inspire opposition to national health insurance, the image that the AMA selected was Fildes' painting *The Doctor*. The AMA too boasted of the progress of biomedical knowledge. Yet, it eschewed a stripped-down modernist aesthetic and images that might have captured the physician's command of reductionist science – the kind of celebratory image of white-coated medical scientists surrounded by gleaming laboratory glassware and instruments of precision that were so common during the Golden Age. Instead, it chose an aesthetically dissonant, nostalgic evocation of personal knowledge and an individuated personal relationship between doctor and patient. It was the personal knowledge and per-

---

25 Boas to Milton [I. Romer] (1950) 17 July 1950, Ernst Boas Papers (MS 10), American Philosophical Society, Philadelphia, Pennsylvania. See Brinkman 1994.

26 Boas to G.M. Smith (1949), and Boas to the Editor, New York Medicine, typescript, 5 November 1948, in Boas Papers.

27 On the positive image and robust cultural authority of the American medical profession during the Golden Age, see Hansen 2009; and on the more complex realities of doctor-patient relationships during this period, see Tomes 2016.

sonalised care captured in this scene, the AMA contended, not epistemologically and culturally stronger biomedical knowledge, that the move for government control would destroy, which needed to be preserved. As one AMA spokesman tellingly put it, with the kind of "assembly line" medicine that state-controlled national health insurance would impose, "personalized medicine which now prevails would come to an end".[28]

At the same time, the opponents of national or what they named "compulsory" health insurance raised the stakes by tightly linking "personalized medicine" to Cold War fears about socialism and communism. "American medicine has become the blazing focal point in a fundamental struggle which may determine whether America remains free, or whether we are to become a Socialist State, under the yoke of a Government bureaucracy," AMA President Elmer L. Henderson told the 1949 annual meeting of its House of Delegates. Exemplifying the rhetoric typical of medical McCarthyism, he called on doctors to dedicate themselves "to the protection of our American way of life, which is the foundation of our economic health and our political freedom". The upcoming Congressional debate on what he called "socialized medicine" was to be "the Battle of Armageddon – the decisive struggle which may determine not only medicine's fate, but whether State Socialism is to engulf all America".[29]

AMA officials and their allies raised the spectre of doctors reduced to mere technicians and patients reduced to nameless automata; of the doctor-patient relationship reduced to a transaction between a skilled mechanic and a standardised machine; and of standardisation and automaticity run amuck. One widely circulated and reproduced pamphlet in the campaign quoted Lenin as saying that "Socialized Medicine is the keystone to the arch of the Socialist State" (a statement Lenin never made), and featured cartoons depicting what would happen to the American doctor in a system of national health insurance. The physician in Figure 2, a robot labelled "socialized medicine", hovers over a terrified patient – quintessentially, as the caption reads, "Mechanical Treatment". In another cartoon from the same pamphlet, the surgeon is a mindless puppet, with politicians pulling the strings.[30] In such images, Cold War fear of a communist takeover redou-

---

28 "What about Child Welfare in a Welfare State", n.d., typescript in Whitaker and Baxter Campaigns, Inc. Records, C134, Office of the Secretary of State, California State Archives, Sacramento, California (hereafter Whitaker and Baxter Papers), box 10, folder 28.

29 *News Release from the America Medical Association*, San Francisco, 27 June [1949], in: Whitaker and Baxter Papers, box 10, folder 31; Address by Elmer L. Henderson, Chairman of the Coordinating Committee, National Education Campaign, American Medical Association (prepared for delivery before the House of Delegates of A.M.A.), [1949], Whitaker and Baxter Papers, box 10, folder 28; Elmer L. Henderson, Address to the AMA House of Delegates, [1949] in Whitaker and Baxter Papers, box 10, folder 11. On the larger political battle, see Blumenthal and Morone 2009; Campion 1984; and Engel 2001.

30 *America's Vital Issue*, (Chicago IL: National Physicians Committee, pamphlet with no date n.d. but 1948 or 1949), Medical Historical Library, Harvey Cushing/John Hay Whitney Medical

bled anxieties about the loss of personalised medicine. "We do not think medicine should be regimented," a New Jersey woman wrote in a private letter to President Truman, denouncing proposals for national health insurance and asserting that "there is too much communism in this movement." Such a plan, she warned the President, was the slippery slope to doctors "who would know nothing about us".[31]

Figure 2. This widely reproduced cartoon labelled "Mechanical Treatment" captured the argument that depersonalised "socialized medicine" would reduce doctors to robots. Pamphlet titled America's Vital Issue *(Chicago, Illinois: National Physicians' Committee for the Extension of Medical Services, ca. 1948). Historical Medical Library, Harvey Cushing/John Hay Whitney Medical Library, Yale School of Medicine, New Haven, Connecticut.*

Library, Yale University, New Haven CT. The cartoon first appeared in the *Chicago Daily News* and was widely reprinted. And see Knoblauch 2014.

31 Marie Unbekamt, Teaneck, N.J., to Mr. President, 8 January 1946, White House Central Files: Official File, OF 286-A, Truman Papers.

Late in 1948, the AMA hired the Whitaker and Baxter public relations firm to sell this message to Congress, the medical profession, and the public. Since the mid-1940s, Clem Whitaker and Lenore Baxter, a husband and wife team of political consultants, had been running a campaign for the California Medical Association against what they called "compulsory" government health insurance at state level, urging in its place "voluntary" insurance free from state interference. "Your profession is in the front lines in one of the most critical struggles in the history of this Nation," Whitaker had told California doctors. "This is a cold war, right here in America."[32] In what was to be one of the great public relations campaigns of modern American politics, Whitaker and Baxter made *The Doctor* stand for everything that would be lost if the state were to impose what they denounced as "socialized medicine". They warned physicians and the public alike to "KEEP POLITICS OUT OF THIS PICTURE", as in the extensively distributed pamphlet in Figure 3 that featured the Fildes' painting.[33] Whitaker and Baxter had become "de facto, the spokesmen for organized medicine," a Lancaster, Pennsylvania physician wrote in a letter to Whitaker. "I think that you have taken on your shoulders the stupendous task of stemming the tide of degeneracy in our civilization."[34]

It would be difficult to overstate the scale of the crusade, which made the physician in Fildes' painting the most widely circulated and viewed image of a doctor in America. At the time, this was the most expensive lobbying campaign in American history. *The Doctor* appeared in pamphlets, posters, print advertisements, newspapers, roadside billboards, and gigantic banners. By 1949, as many as two-thirds of American physicians displayed a poster of the painting in their waiting rooms with the ubiquitous caption "Keep politics out of this picture". At the AMA's annual convention that year, the backdrop to the Convention Hall stage was a huge reproduction of the painting, seven meters high. From the podium, with Fildes' sentimental picture looming behind him, the incoming AMA president railed against the threat of creeping socialism and assembly-line medicine.[35]

---

32 Clem Whitaker, "Report to the House of Delegates of the California Medical Association." 11 April 1948, typescript in Whitaker and Baxter Papers, box 5, folder 6. On Whitaker and Baxter, see Lepore 2012.

33 "Your Medical Program: Compulsory? – or – Voluntary?" (Chicago IL: National Education Campaign, pamphlet with no date but 1949), American Medical Association Archives, Chicago, Illinois.

34 Edwin E. Ziegler to Clem Whitaker, Lancaster, PA, 16 May 1949, in Whitaker and Baxter Papers, box 9, folder 38.

35 National Education Campaign, American Medical Association, "Immediate Release", Atlantic City NJ, 6 June [1949]," AMA mailing #107, Whitaker and Baxter Papers, box 10, folder 25.

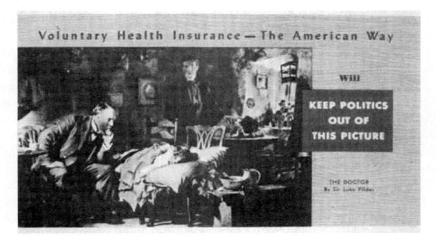

Figure 3. Whitaker and Baxter, acting for the AMA, circulated millions of posters and pamphlets featuring The Doctor *with the caption, "KEEP POLITICS OUT OF THIS PICTURE", as in this pamphlet from 1949. American Medical Association Archives, Chicago, Illinois.*

Editorials that Whitaker and Baxter drafted for newspaper editors to publish as their own charged that state medicine "destroys the doctor-patient relationship so important to diagnosis and treatment", obliterating crucial knowledge of the individual patient, and "makes automatons of patient and doctor alike".[36] To reinforce the point, Whitaker and Baxter arranged lectures and radio broadcasts by disgruntled British doctors they called "exiles" or "refugees" from socialised medicine. Asserting that British medical practice had been reduced to "three-minute assembly line consultations", Ralph Gampell – who had left Manchester for Chicago – was among those who testified on "Socialized Medicine as I Saw it in England". As a British doctor consulting a patient, "you only have time to fill in their name on the top of the official prescription form and sign your name and the date on the bottom and fill in a standard formulary and the time is up," he cautioned. "The one thing that you don't have enough of in this system is time."[37] The chairman of the AMA Board of Trustees railed against the "government herding of patients and doctors into assembly-line medical mills [that] would lower the standards of healthy America to those of sick, regimented Europe", while

---

36 "Freedom in Medicine" and "An Ounce of Prevention." Suggested Editorial for Voluntary Health Insurance Week, (n.d.) in Whitaker and Baxter Papers, box 6, folder 4.

37 Ralph J. Gampell, "Socialized Medicine as I Saw it", October 1949, typescript, in Whitaker and Baxter Papers, box 10, folder 27.

Whitaker underscored the spectre of doctors transformed into what he called "scientific robots".[38]

Some physicians, such as Boas, did object to the use of *The Doctor* to represent their profession, criticising it as a nostalgic celebration of the doctor-patient relationship that masked over the social and technological realities of modern medicine and the economic problems of health care distribution. "We agree, of course, that the picture is 'dated', if viewed literally," Whitaker retorted in a private letter to a North Carolina physician who, like Boas, had protested this choice. "But on that basis a great many things are 'dated', including the Hippocratic oath, the Bible and the works of Dickens and Shakespeare." As Whitaker went on to conclude, "'The Doctor' isn't just an out-dated painting. It is a vivid portrayal of the vitally important physician-patient relationship which has made doctors something more than medical technicians. And that relationship is out-dated only in countries which have adopted socialized medicine".[39]

By 1952, with the election of Dwight Eisenhower, the movement for national health insurance was dead. Whitaker and Baxter had succeeded brilliantly in mobilising medical and public opposition by dramatising the value and vulnerability of the personal knowledge for which they made *The Doctor* stand. In the process, however, they inadvertently incited disaffection with the medical profession by focusing the public's attention on the deficiencies in their own medical care. The AMA's campaign had encouraged American patients to expect the kind of personalised medicine that they saw displayed in the ubiquitous posters, pamphlets, and billboards depicting Fildes' painting, but as patients, by and large, this is not what they experienced.

Doctors were aware of this growing discontent and often shared it. In 1950, for example, a county medical society in California hired psychologist and marketing expert Ernest Dichter to conduct a study of "the doctor-patient relationship", and the extensive interviews that he conducted led Dichter to conclude that "the ideal doctor is gone".[40] One general practitioner, looking back nostalgically at earlier times, told Dichter that "the doctor has to treat the entire patient – the patient as a whole. That, dammit, is why I'm a general practitioner yet, and not in limited specialty, because I feel that the general practitioner is the ideal person to [...] to see the patient as a whole" (Dichter 1950, 20). Many of the respondents

---

38 Elmer L. Henderson, "American Medicine Replies to President Truman: A Doctor's Diagnosis of the President's Compulsory Health Insurance Program", Chicago, n.d., Isidore Sydney Falk Papers (MS 1039), Manuscripts and Archives, Yale University Library, New Haven CT, box 174, folder 2655; Clem Whitaker to Greer Williams, 22 March 1951, Whitaker and Baxter Papers, box 10, folder 4.

39 Clem Whitaker to Elbert L. Persons (Duke School of Medicine), 14 March 1950, Whitaker and Baxter Papers, box 11, folder 8.

40 Dichter 1950, 6. The study was initiated by the Alameda County [California] Medical Association.

reminisced about the kind of personal knowledge that earlier physicians possessed. "When I think of the ideal doctor, our old family physician comes to mine,"
commented one of them. "You had the feeling that he knew everything and that
the story of your body was safely in his hands." (1950, 9) Others bemoaned the
lack of attention to the individuated patient. A 26-year-old insurance agent com-
plained that "they turn these doctors out now on a belt system. It is mass production [...]. They are more like robots now. [...] They become automatic and lose
their humaneness. They forget that the people they are treating are human beings
and not animals." (Dichter 1950, 6–7) "When it comes to scientific know-how,"
a real estate broker observed, "the doctor doesn't have to apologize to anyone.
But in dealing with patients, he might well take a few lessons from his horse-and-
buggy ancestors."[41] The medical society that commissioned the study conceded
that the general practitioner had lost stature in American society, but asserted, as
its executive secretary put it, "it's not too late to retrieve that loss". As one way
of redressing the deficiency, the society tellingly proposed introducing a new term
– "*personal physician*" – with the aim of establishing in the public mind "the personal physician as the new ideal doctor".[42]

6. Conclusion

The weak knowledge that I have explored here played not just a complimentary,
but a compensatory, role. As it was promoted beginning around the early 1890s,
it encompassed knowledge and ways of knowing that were intended to be in addition to, not instead of, the mechanistic, reductionist impulse at the core of the
new scientific medicine. This was especially important to physicians' identity,
something that would intensify in the twentieth century. It offered something
beyond what reductionist science alone could provide – ranging from ways of
knowing illness (not just disease), to the public's estimation of the ideal doctor,
to the individual doctor's sense of authenticity. The personal, the individual, the
finely-honed senses, the ways of knowing attached to art, the values and skills
encompassed by clinical acumen – these were all attributes that affirmed medicine
to be more than *merely* an applied science and the physician more than *merely* a
highly skilled technician. This became increasingly important as physicians la-
boured to distinguish their knowledge and identity from the newly professional-
ised nurse, the Taylorised worker on Henry Ford's assembly line, and, later, the
spectre of the doctor as a robot.

---

41 Menges 1951. Menges was reporting on Dichter's study.
42 Rollen Waterson, quoted in Menges 1951, 6. Emphasis is in the original.

During the second half of the nineteenth century what counted as scientific medicine had been transformed, and the reform of medical schools and other institutions in the 1910s and 1920s consolidated the hegemony of the mechanistic-
reductionist programme. The hallmarks of the new order persisted: precision, exactness, standardisation, specialisation, automaticity, reliance on new technologies, allegiance to the laboratory and the habits of mind that it fostered, and, perhaps even more than in some other fields of natural science, to a very large extent,
mechanical objectivity and self-abnegation.

In the 1940s, the AMA was able to draw on the articulation of weakness as a
resource in enlisting both physicians and the public in a massive and successful
political campaign that fundamentally shaped the structure of American health
care. Nothing in the crusade to defeat proposals for national health insurance
questioned the epistemological, clinical, and cultural power of reductionist, high-
tech, laboratory-grounded biomedicine. It was instead its *sufficiency* that was called
to account. Yet, the authentic physician – the ideal American doctor – required
something more, a kind of knowledge about the individual patient that could be
acquired only through a personal doctor-patient relationship. The AMA's successful crusade turned upon a politically-charged discourse of deficiency that both
affirmed the importance of a form of weak medical knowledge proclaimed to be
at risk, and made a plea for its preservation.

Calls to preserve or restore the kinds of medical knowledge and ways of knowing centring on the value of the individual and the personal that began to be
articulated in 1890s would prove to be remarkably durable and enduringly dissonant. The core epistemological elements of the reductionist, mechanistic version
of scientific medicine remained unmistakably "strong", even when starting in the
1990s its hegemony came to be challenged by evidence based medicine (EBM).
At the same time, the rise of EBM invigorated lamentations over the marginalisation of the kinds of "weak" knowledge encompassed by clinical acumen and
intuition, individual experience and autonomy, clinical artistry, and attention to
the idiosyncrasies of individual patients, and helped fuel moves to retrieve them.
By the early twenty-first century, new calls for "personalised medicine" abound,
including, for example, lobbying for a new field of "personomics" – that is, "information about the individual derived from knowing the patient as a person" –
cast as "the missing link in the evolution from precision medicine to personalized
medicine".[43] The discourse of deficiency that co-emerged with the new version
of scientific medicine persists, not in opposition to, but as a constitutive part of,
modern medicine.

---

43 Ziegelstein 2015 and 2017.

References

American Medical Association (1949a): *News Release from the America Medical Association*, San Francisco, 27 June [1949], in Whittaker and Baxter Campaigns, Inc. Records, C134, Office of the Secretary of State, California State Archives, Sacramento, CA (hereafter Whittaker and Baxter Papers), box 10, folder 31.

American Medical Association (1949b): "Your Medical Program: Compulsory? - or – Voluntary?" (Chicago IL: National Education Campaign, pamphlet with no date but 1949), American Medical Association Archives, Chicago, Illinois.

American Medical Association (1949c): National Education Campaign, American Medical Association, "Immediate Release", Atlantic City NJ, 6 June [1949], AMA mailing #107, Whitaker and Baxter Papers, box 10, folder 25.

"*America's Vital Issue*" (1948/9), (Chicago IL: National Physicians Committee, pamphlet with no date n.d. but 1948 or 1949), Medical Historical Library, Harvey Cushing/John Hay Whitney Medical Library, Yale University, New Haven CT.

Anonymous (1868): "On the Principal Applications of the Graphical Method to Biology." *Medical Times and Gazette*, 1: 72–73.

Anonymous (1884): "The Family Doctor." *Massachusetts Ploughman and New England Journal of Agriculture*, 44: 4.

Anonymous (1886): "The Temperaments." *Medical Record*, 14: 128–129.

Anonymous (1890): "The Science and Art of Medicine." *British Medical Journal*, 16: 64–65.

Anonymous (1891): "Discussion. Asepsis and Antisepsis in Operative Surgery." *Transactions of the American Surgical Association*, 6: 117–131.

Anonymous (1893): "Are We on the Wrong Track?" *American Advance: A Monthly Magazine of Homoeopathic Medicine*, 30: 56–59.

Anonymous (1893): "Is the General Practitioner Passing Away?" *Medical Record*, 44: 625.

Anonymous (1900): "Nominations are Over." *Brick*, 12: 1.

Anonymous (1901): "Passing of the Family Doctor." *Christian Advocate*, 76: 829.

Anonymous (1904): "Is the General Practitioner Passing Away?" *Medical Record*, 65: 778–779.

Ash, Mitchell G. (1995): *Gestalt Psychology in German Culture, 1890–1967: Holism and the Quest for Objectivity*. Cambridge: Cambridge University Press.

Barnes, Justin L. (1894): "An Adaptation of the Maddox Cylinder for Use on the Phorometer." *Medical Record*, 15: 678.

Bernard, Claude [1865] (1927): *Introduction to the Study of Experimental Medicine*. Trans. Henry Copley Greene. New York: Macmillan.

Billings, John S. (1893): "The Effects of his Occupation upon the Physician." *International Journal of Ethics*, 4: 40–48.

Blake, Clarence John (1900): "The Sociological Status of the Physician." *Boston Medical and Surgical Journal*, 142: 482–487.

Blumenthal, David, and James A. Morone (2009): *The Heart of Power: Health and Politics in the Oval Office*. Berkeley CA: University of California Press.

Boas, Ernst P. (1944): "Medicine for All." *P.I.C.* 15: 48–49. In: Ernst Boas Papers (MS 10), American Philosophical Society, Philadelphia, Pennsylvania.

Boas, Ernst P. (1948): [Ernst Boas] G.M. Smith, 12 February 1948, in Boas Papers.

Boas, Ernst P. (1948): Ernst P. Boas to the Editor, *New York Medicine*, typescript, 5 November 1948, in Boas Papers.

Boas, Ernst P. (1950): Ernst Boas to Milton [I. Romer], 17 Jult 1950, Boas Papers.

Boring, Edwin G. (1957): *A History of Experimental Psychology*, 134–153. 2nd ed. Englewood Cliffs NJ: Prentice-Hall.

Borrell, Merriley (1987): "Instrumentation and the Rise of Modern Physiology." *Science and Technology Studies*, 5: 53–62.

Brain, Robert (2015): *The Pulse of Modernism: Physiological Aesthetics in Fin-de-Siècle Europe*. Seattle WA: University of Washington Press.

Brinkman, Jane Pacht (1994): "Medical McCarthyism: The Physicians Forum and the Cold War." *Journal of the History of Medicine and Allied Sciences*, 49: 380–418.

Brinkman, Jane Pacht, et al. (2019): "The Rise and Fall of the 'Personal Equation' in American and British Medicine, 1855-1952." *Perspectives in Biology and Medicine*, 62: 41–71.

Bulkley, Duncan L. (1899): "How Far has Specialism Benefited the Ordinary Practice of Medicine." *Bulletin of the American Academy of Medicine*, 4: 174–178.

Burnham, John C. (1998): *How the Idea of Profession Changed the Writing of Medical History*. London: Wellcome Institute for the History of Medicine.

Bynum, W.F., and Roy Porter (Eds.) (1993): *Medicine and the Five Senses*. Cambridge: Cambridge University Press.

Campion, Frank D. (1984): *The AMA and U.S. Health Policy since 1940*. Chicago IL: Chicago Review Press.

Canales, Jimena (2009): *A Tenth of a Second: A History*. Chicago IL: University of Chicago Press.

Clymer, Meredith (1867): "The Sphygmograph." *New York Medical Journal*, 4: 277–284.

Crenner, Christopher William (1993): *Professional Measurement: Quantifying Health and Disease in American Medical Practice, 1880–1920*. Ph.D. Dissertation, Harvard University.

Daston, Lorraine, and Peter Galison (1992): "The Image of Objectivity." *Representations*, 40: 81–128.

Daston, Lorraine, and Peter Galison (2007): *Objectivity*. New York: Zone Books.

Dichter, Ernest (1950): *A Psychological Study of the Doctor-Patient Relationship*. n.p.: California Medical Association.

Dolan, Th. M. (1887): "A Criticism of the Report of the English Commission on the Pasteur Method." *North Carolina Medical Journal*, 19: 159–166.

Edebohls, George M. (1891): "A Combined Laparotomy and Gynecological Operating Table." *Medical Record*, 40: 598–591.

Engel, Jonathan (2001): *Doctors and Reformers: Discussion and Debate over Health Policy, 1925–1950*. Columbia SC: University of South Carolina Press.

Evans, Hughes (1993): "Losing Touch: The Controversy over the Introduction of Blood Pressure Instruments into Medicine." *Technology and Culture*, 34 (4): 784–807.

Fisher, Edward D. (1908): Comments in "Medical Association of the Greater City of New York. Stated Meeting, Held October 19, 1908." *Medical Record*, 74: 983–985.

Frank, Robert G. Jr. (1987): "American Physiologists in German Laboratories, 1865–1914." In: Gerald L. Geison (Ed.): *Physiology in the American Context, 1850–1940*, 11–46. Bethesda MD: American Physiological Society.

Frank, Robert G. Jr. (1988): "The Telltale Heart: Physiological Instruments, Graphic Methods, and Clinical Hopes, 1854–1914." In: William Coleman and Frederic L. Holmes (Eds.): *The Investigative Enterprise: Experimental Physiology in Nineteenth-Century Medicine*, 211–294. Berkeley CA: University of California Press

"Freedom in Medicine" and "An Ounce of Prevention" (n.d.), Suggested Editorial for Voluntary Health Insurance Week, in Whitaker and Baxter Papers, box 6, folder 4.

Galison, Peter (1998): "Judgment against Objectivity." In: Caroline A. Jones and Peter Galison (Eds.): *Picturing Science, Producing Art*, 327–359. New York: Routledge.

Gampell, Ralph J. (1949): "Socialized Medicine as I Saw It", October 1949, typescript, in Whitaker and Baxter Papers, box 10, folder 27.

Gardiner, Charles Fox, and Henry W. Hoagland (1905): "Human Blood Pressure and Pulse as Affected by Altitude." *Transactions of the American Climatological Association*, 21: 80–89.

H[arrison], [John P.] (1848): "Notices of Empiricism." *Western Lancet and Hospital Reporter*, 8: 122–124.

Hansen, Bert (2009): *Picturing Medical Progress from Pasteur to Polio: A History of Mass Media Images and Popular Attitudes in America*. New Brunswick NJ: Rutgers University Press.

Harrington, Anne (1996): *Reenchanted Science: Holism in German Culture from Wilhelm II to Hitler*. Princeton NJ: Princeton University Press.

Henderson, Elmer L. (1949a): "Address to the AMA House of Delegates", Whitaker and Baxter Papers, box 10, folder 11.

Henderson, Elmer L. (1949b): "Chairman of the Coordinating Committee, National Education Campaign, American Medical Association (prepared for delivery before the House of Delegates of the A.M.A.)", Whitaker and Baxter Papers, box 10, folder 28.

Henderson, Elmer L. (1951): "American Medicine Replies to President Truman: A Doctor's Diagnosis of the President's Compulsory Health Insurance Program", Chicago, n.d., Isidore Sydney Falk Papers (MS 1039), Manuscripts and Archives, Yale University Library, New Haven CT, box 174, folder 2655.

Hertzler, Arthur (1938): *The Horse and Buggy Doctor*. New York: Harper and Brothers.

Hess, Volker (2005): "Standardizing Body Temperature: Quantification in Hospitals and Daily Life, 1850–1900." In: Gérard Jorland et al. (Eds.): *Body Counts: Medical Quantification in Historical and Sociological Perspective*, 109–126. Montreal: McGill-Queen's University Press.

Hess, Volker, and J. Andrew Mendelsohn (2010): "Case and Series: Medical Knowledge and Paper Technology, 1600–1900." *History of Science*, 48: 288–314.

Hoffmann, Christoph (2007): "Constant Differences: Friedrich Wilhelm Bessel, the Concept of the Observer in Early Nineteenth-Century Practical Astronomy and the History of the Personal Equation." *British Journal for the History of Science*, 40: 333–365.

Huisman, Frank, and John Harley Warner (2004): "Medical Histories." In: Frank Huisman and John Harley Warner (Eds.): *Locating Medical History: The Stories and Their Meanings*, 1–30. Baltimore MD and London: The Johns Hopkins University Press.

Jacobi, M.P. (1900): *Address at Semi-Centennial of Women's Medical College of Philadelphia*. Mary Putnam Jacobi Papers, Schlesinger Library, Radcliffe Institute for Advanced Study, Harvard University, Cambridge MA.

Johnson, W.O. (1873): "Modern Medicine." *North American Review*, 240: 1–37.

Jones, William M. (1909): "Fallacies Past and Present in the Treatment of Tuberculosis." *Transactions of the Medical Society of the State of North Carolina, Fifth-Sixth Annual Meeting*, 424–428. Raleigh NC: Edward and Broughton Printing Company.

Keen, William Williams (1905): *Addresses and Other Papers*. Philadelphia PA: W.B. Saunders and Company.

Keiller, William (1893): "The Country Doctor." *Medical and Surgical Reporter*, 69: 763–764; reprinted from the *Texas Medical Journal*.

Knoblauch, Heidi Katherine (2014): "'A Campaign Won as a Public Issue will Stay Won': Using Cartoons and Comics to Fight National Health Care Reform, 1940s and Beyond." *American Journal of Public Health*, 104: 227–236.

Kohler, Robert (2002a): "Place and Practice in Field Biology." *History of Science*, 40: 189–210.

Kohler, Robert (2002b): *Landscapes and Labscapes: Exploring the Lab-Field Border in Biology*. Chicago IL: University of Chicago Press.

Kuklick, Henrika (2011): "Personal Equations: Reflections on the History of Fieldwork, with Special Reference to Sociocultural Anthropology." *Isis*, 102: 1–33.

Lawrence, Christopher (1998): "Still Incommunicable: Clinical Holists and Medical Knowledge in Interwar Britain." In: Christopher Lawrence and George Weisz (Eds.): *Greater than the Parts: Holism in Biomedicine, 1920–1950*, 94–111. New York: Oxford University Press.

Lawrence, Christopher, and George Weisz (Eds.) (1998): *Greater than the Parts: Holism in Biomedicine, 1920–1950*. New York: Oxford University Press.

Lears, T. Jackson (1981): *No Place of Grace: Antimodernism and the Transformation of American Culture, 1880–1920*. New York: Pantheon Books.

Lederer, Susan E., and Naomi Rogers (2000): "Media." In: Roger Cooter and John Pickstone (Eds.): *Medicine in the Twentieth Century*, 487–502. London: Harwood.

Lepore, Jill (2012): "The Lie Factory: How Politics Became a Business." *The New Yorker*, (24 September): 50–59.

Mayer, Anna-K. (2000): "'A Combative Sense of Duty': Englishness and the Scientists." In: Christopher Lawrence and Anna-K. Mayer (Eds.): *Regenerating England: Science, Medicine, and Culture in Inter-War Britain*, 67–106. Amsterdam: Rodopi.

Meigs, Arthur V. (1886): "Constipation." *Transactions of the College of Physicians of Philadelphia*, s. 3 (8): 405–420.

Menges, Roger (1951): *Something New in Patient Relations*. Reprint from *Medical Economics* (August). In: Ernest Dichter Papers, Hagley Museum and Library, Wilmington, Delaware, box 166, folder 73.

Numbers, Ronald L. (1978): *Almost Persuaded: American Physicians and Compulsory Health Insurance, 1912–1920*. Baltimore MD: The Johns Hopkins University Press.

Phin, John (1877): *Practical Hints on the Selection and Use of the Microscope, Intended for Beginners*. New York: The Industrial Publication Company.

Podolsky, Scott H., et al. (2016): "From Trials to Trials: Blinding, Medicine, and Honest Adjudication." In: Christopher Robertson and Aaron Kesselheim (Eds.): *Blinding as a Solution to Bias: Strengthening Biomedical Science, Forensic Science, and Law*, 45–58. San Diego CA: Academic Press.

Prince, Morgan (1889): "The Occurrence and Mechanism of Physiological Heart Murmurs (Endocardial) in Healthy Individuals." *Medical Record*, 35: 421–428.

Quimby, C.E. (1891): "The Treatment of Pulmonary Tuberculosis by Koch's Method." *Medical Record*, 39: 73–76.

R., J.C. (1869): "[Review of] *Das Verhalten der Eigenwärme in Krankheiten*. Von Dr. C. A. Wunderlich. Leipzig." *American Journal of the Medical Sciences*, n.s. 64: 426–447.

Richards, Robert (1982): "The Personal Equation in Science: William James's Psychological and Moral Uses of Darwinian Theory." *Harvard Library Bulletin*, 30: 387–425.

Richardson, Maurie (1899): "Appendicitis." *Transactions of the American Surgical Association*, 17: 72–115.

Robinson, Beverley (1908): "The Personal Factor in Disease." *Medical Record*, 74: 663–664.

Robinson, G. Canby (1939): *The Patient as a Person: A Study of the Social Aspects of Illness*. New York: The Commonwealth Fund.

Romano, Terrie M. (2002): *Making Medicine Scientific: John Burdon Sanderson and the Culture of Victorian Science*. Baltimore MD: The Johns Hopkins University Press.

Rosenberg, Charles E. (1979): "The Therapeutic Revolution: Medicine, Meaning, and Social Change in Nineteenth-Century America." In: Morris J. Vogel and Charles E. Rosenberg (Eds.): *The Therapeutic Revolution: Essays in the Social History of American Medicine*, 3–25. Philadelphia PA: University of Pennsylvania Press.

Rosenberg, Charles E. (1998): "Holism in Twentieth-Century Medicine." In: Christopher Lawrence and George Weisz (Eds.): *Greater than the Parts: Holism in Biomedicine, 1920–1950*, 335–355. New York: Oxford University Press.

Schaffer, Simon (1988): "Astronomers Mark Time: Discipline and the Personal Equation." *Science in Context*, 2: 115–145.

Seguin, E. (1876): *Medical Thermometry and Human Temperature*. New York: William Wood & Co.

Shearer, Leander H. (1909): Comments in: "The Medical Association of the Greater City of New York. Stated Meeting, October 18, 1909." *Medical Record*, 76: 964–966.

Stern, Heinrich (1905): "Led Astray: Chairman's Address before the Section on Pharmacology, at the Fifty-sixth Annual Session of the American Medical Association, Portland, Ore., July 11–14, 1905." *Journal of the American Medical Association*, 45: 1535–1540.

Tomes, Nancy (2016): *Remaking the American Patient: How Madison Avenue and Modern Medicine Turned Patients into Consumers*. Chapel Hill NC: University of North Carolina Press.

Truman, Harry (1949): President Harry Truman to the Congress of the United States, draft marked "Hold for Release", The White House, 22 April 1949, White House Central Files: Official File, OF 286-A, Harry S. Truman Papers, Harry S. Truman Library, Independence, Missouri.

Unbekamt, Marie (1946): Marie Unbekamt, Teaneck, N.J., to Mr. President, 8 January 1946, White House Central Files: Official File, OF 286-A, Truman Papers.

Warner, John Harley (1990): "From Specificity to Universalism in Medical Therapeutics: Transformation in the Nineteenth-Century United States." In: Yosio Kawakita et al. (Eds.): *History of Therapy: Proceedings of the 10th International Symposium on the Comparative History of Medicine—East and West*, 193–223. Tokyo: IshiyakuEuroAmerica.

Warner, John Harley (1991): "Ideals of Science and their Discontents in Late Nineteenth-Century American Medicine." *Isis*, 82: 454–478.

Warner, John Harley (1992): "The Fall and Rise of Professional Mystery: Epistemology, Authority and the Emergence of Laboratory Medicine in Nineteenth-Century America." In: Andrew Cunningham and Perry Williams (Eds.): *The Laboratory Revolution in Medicine*, 310–141. Cambridge: Cambridge University Press.

Warner, John Harley (1997): *The Therapeutic Perspective: Medical Practice, Knowledge, and Identity in America, 1820–1885*, with a new preface. Princeton NJ: Princeton University Press.

Warner, John Harley (1998): *Against the Spirit of System: The French Impulse in Nineteenth-Century American Medicine*. Princeton NJ: Princeton University Press.

Warner, John Harley (2011): "The Humanising Power of Medical History: Responses to Biomedicine in the 20th-Century United States." *Medical Humanities*, 37: 13–24.

Warner, John Harley (2013): "*The Doctor* in Early Cold War America." *Lancet*, 381: 1452–1453.

Warner, John Harley (2014a): "The Aesthetic Grounding of Modern Medicine." *Bulletin of the History of Medicine*, 88: 1–47.

Warner, John Harley (2014b): "The Art of Medicine in an Age of Science: Reductionism, Holism, and the Doctor-Patient Relationship in the United States, 1890–1960." In: Nanami Suzuki (Ed.): *Healing Alternatives: Care and Education as a Cultural Commodity*, 55–91. Senri Ethnological Reports 120.

Whitaker, Clem, and Lenore Baxter (n.d.): "What about Child Welfare in a Welfare State", typescript in Whitaker and Baxter Papers, box 10, folder 28.

Whitaker, Clem (1948): "Report to the House of Delegates of the California Medical Association", 11 April 1948, typescript in Whitaker and Baxter Papers, box 5, folder 6.

Whitaker, Clem (1950): Clem Whitaker to Elbert L. Persons (Duke School of Medicine), 14 March 1950, Whitaker and Baxter Papers, box 11, folder 8.

Whitaker, Clem (1951): Clem Whitaker to Greer Williams, 22 March 1951, Whitaker and Baxter Papers, box 10, folder 4.

Wise, M. Norton (1995): *The Values of Precision*. Princeton NJ: Princeton University Press.

Woodhull, Alfred A. (1877): "On the Causes of the Epidemic of Yellow Fever at Savannah, Georgia, in 1876." *American Journal of the Medical Sciences*, 74: 17–53.

Wunderlich, C.A. (1871): *On the Temperature in Diseases: A Manual of Medical Thermometry*. Trans. W. Bathurst Woodman. London: The New Sydenham Society.

Ziegelstein, Roy C. (2015): "Personomics." *JAMA Internal Medicine*, 175: 888–889.

Ziegelstein, Roy C. (2017): "Personomics: The Missing Link in the Evolution from Precision Medicine to Personalized Medicine." *Journal of Personalized Medicine*, 7/11, available at: https://www.mdpi.com/2075-4426/7/4/11/htm, last accessed January 2019.

Ziegler, Edwin E. (1949): Edwin E. Ziegler to Clem Whitaker, Lancaster, PA, 16 May 1949, in Whitaker and Baxter Papers, box 9, folder 38.

Negotiating Epistemic Hierarchies in Biomedicine: The Rise of Evidence-based Medicine

Cornelius Borck

Abstract

The alliance of medicine with the laboratory revolution since the experimentalisation of the life sciences in the nineteenth century resulted in an unprecedented course of technological development, with modern biomedicine now dominating medical practice on a global scale. Towards the end of the twentieth century, however, ever more costly interventions called the established regimes of scientific expertise into question, especially in countries with a national health service. The movement for evidence-based medicine (EBM), a self-proclaimed "new paradigm" for clinical practice, challenged scientific explanations as insufficient for legitimising therapeutic interventions and called, instead, for a systematic evaluation of their clinical efficacy. The implementation of EBM re-negotiated epistemic and power relations in the health sector and resulted in a new "pyramid" of evidence with scientific explanations no longer ruling at the top but serving an explanatory role at the bottom, whereas systematic reviews of randomised clinical trials now rank at the top. Contextualising the emergence of EBM in the much longer debate on the limits of science-based medicine and in the socio-political realm of health-care services rather than the rationale for evidence levels, this chapter re-constructs EBM as the powerful product of initially weak forms of knowledge. In fact, the debate continues, as its proponents see the aims of EBM threatened by both industry and policy, whereas the advocates of science-based medicine position so-called precision medicine to their defence. In medicine, weak and strong forms of knowledge cannot be differentiated abstractly, but the strength of a particular form of knowledge depends on the epistemic framework and political context of clinical practice.

Introduction

In 1972, the British physician and epidemiologist Archibald Cochrane published *Effectiveness and Efficiency*, a critical examination of the British National Health Service (NHS), which is now recognised as a founding classic of evidence-based medicine (EBM), even though the movement of this name was announced only twenty years later. Calling for a general evaluation of medical treatments, Cochrane introduced his concerns regarding the NHS with a blatant comparison:

> I once asked a worker at a crematorium, who had a curiously contented look on his face, what he found so satisfying about his work. He replied that what fascinated him was the way in which so much went in and so little came out. I thought of advising him to get a job at the NHS, [as] it might have increased his job satisfaction, but decided against it. He probably got his kicks from a visual demonstration of the gap between input and output. A statistical demonstration might not have worked so well. (Cochrane 1972, 12)

According to Cochrane's analysis, medical progress in the form of new procedures and drugs had inflated costs without delivering at an equal pace in terms of cure(s) and saved lives. It would be a mistake, however, to regard this book as a harsh criticism of the National Health Service. On the contrary, Cochrane called for a critical evaluation of therapeutic measures in order to save money for delivering *better* care and for dealing with social inequality. He was not a neoliberal *avant la lettre* and styled himself accordingly right at the beginning of his book, referring back to his student days in London in the 1930s:

> The idea of a National Health Service was not the source of my greatest enthusiasm. Antifascist activities (and in particular Spain) headed the list, but the NHS ranked high. There was, I remembered, to be some rally about the possibility of a National Health Service in some London suburb, and I decided to go alone with my own banner. [...] After considerable thought I wrote my slogan: All effective treatment must be free. I had a deep inner feeling that this was absolutely right [...]. The slogan, I regret to say, was a flop. The only person who noticed it damned me for having 'Trotskyite' tendencies, but I still thought it had something. (Cochrane 1972, 1)

Apparently, the concern about *effective* – in contrast to scientifically justified – treatment was the driving force of his professional career from early on.

Cochrane had learned about the gap between inputs and outputs in the medical system the hard way and under severe constraints. Even before finishing his medical training in 1938, he had volunteered in the Spanish civil war, helping doctors with the triage of the wounded in makeshift hospitals, and he subsequently served in the Royal Army Medical Corps in WWII, during which he was captured by the Germans and had to work as a doctor in several prisoner of war camps:[1]

On one occasion, when I was the only doctor there, I asked the German Stabsarzt for more doctors to help me cope with these fantastic problems. He replied: 'Nein! Ärzte sind

---

[1] Apparently, Cochrane performed a clinical trial even under these circumstances; see Cochrane 1984.

überflüssig.' I was furious and even wrote a poem about it; later I wondered if he was wise or cruel; he was certainly right. (Cochrane 1972, 5)

Regardless of starvation, severe epidemics and no available treatment, surprisingly few of his patients had died, forcing him to reconsider the relevance of medical treatment.

In addition to giving a flavour of his personality, the quotations form Cochrane's book provide an outlook on his critical attitude towards medicine: the availability of new therapeutic options does not necessarily result in better outcomes, a positive effect is all too easily over-estimated, and, most importantly, the progress of medical research will not solve, but aggravate the problem if new procedures are not rigorously evaluated. Rising health costs are probably a typical feature of prosperous times through all periods; thus, it was not so much the diagnosis that made Cochrane's analysis remarkable, but the remedy that he suggested for dealing with the problem: the general implementation of an appropriate evaluation of all forms of medical treatment, "in particular by the wide use of randomized controlled trials" (Cochrane 1972, 86). Back then, these were little more than "random reflections", as Cochrane subtitled his book with British humour. He identified two main factors pushing in the wrong direction in Britain, the unquestioned esteem of basic research with its backing by the British Medical Research Council (MRC), and the unjustified eminence of individual clinical experience. When the "EBM working group" around David Sackett from McMaster University in Hamilton, Ontario, announced their "new approach" in 1992, the group argued, like Cochrane, against the eminence of clinical experience and against purely science-based, pathophysiological explanations (Evidence-Based Medicine Working Group 1992). They propagated EBM as a strategy to incorporate the latest data from clinical research into medical practice, thus replacing the existing regimes of therapeutic legitimation.

EBM marks a major transformation of Western biomedicine around the end of the twentieth century. "In the world of clinical research and practice, few will dispute that the introduction and elaboration of the concept of evidence-based medicine (EBM) has shown to be a game changer." (Knottnerus and Tugwell 2017, 1) EBM is now simply the new "gold standard" (Timmermans and Berg 2003) that changed "the art of clinical medicine" into standardised health care practice according to internationally viable guidelines. In addition to reforming clinical practice, EBM resulted in powerful new institutions in the health sector, one of the new actors being the collaboration bearing Cochrane's name that was started in Britain twenty years after his book.[2] Organised as a charity, the Cochrane Collaboration specialises in providing systematic reviews and meta-analyses of clinical studies, strongly prioritising large randomised controlled trials

---

2 For an official history of the different strands merging in EBM and diverting in the several institutions propagating it, including the Cochrane Collaboration, see Daly 2005.

(RCTs) over other forms of clinical or epidemiological data. The Cochrane Collaboration issues corroborated "evidence" which, in many countries, is funnelled directly into guidelines regulating medical practice. In addition to its many branches and local centres, the Cochrane Collaboration has opened a "consumer network", inviting patients, patient groups and other actors to engage with its now globally active network.[3] Meanwhile, the Cochrane Collaboration has also teamed up with the World Health Organization and with Wikipedia,[4] thereby demonstrating its strategic position as a clearing house and steering centre for what counts as medical evidence.

It may seem misplaced to discuss the rise of EBM as a case study for weak knowledge, if EBM must be recognised as medicine's reigning regime. The Cochrane Collaboration, for example, claims that its "work is internationally recognized as the benchmark for high-quality information about the effectiveness of health care".[5] In epistemological terms, however, medical decision-making is always of problematical status, as it faces the difficulty of applying general assumptions to the specific circumstances of single patients with highly individual problems even if they suffer from common and well-studied diseases. EBM bases its decisions on evidence from systematic reviews, whereas previously the individual experiences of a physician or scientific explanations for a case provided the rationale for an intervention. EBM can hardly be described as a result of new biomedical insights or theories, but its implementation reflects a massive re-ordering of epistemic and institutional hierarchies. It is this realm of shifting rationales that makes the rise of EBM a rich case for discussing the socio-political construction and negotiation of epistemic hierarchies in a particularly powerful sector of scientific research and practice. This chapter explores this debate in five steps in a combined chronological and thematic sequence.

The first section situates Cochrane's study of the British NHS in the larger context of the years around 1970, when individual actors, scattered more towards the margins of science-based biomedicine, started to critique medicine. The next section describes how this critique connected with concerns about the practice of medicine from within academic hospitals, focusing on Alvan Feinstein as the exemplary figure. Section 3 zooms in on the 1990s, when David Sackett and his group announced EBM as a new programme, introducing statistical data as a resource for clinical decision-making. With regard to the epistemological discussion revolving around weak knowledge, a particularly fascinating twist in the transformation of biomedicine to EBM was the concurrent rise of a new philosophy of medicine (Section 4). Real-world research and medical practice, however, hardly

---

3 See http://consumers.cochrane.org.

4 See http://www.cochrane.org/about-us/our-partners-and-funders.

5 See http://www.cochrane.org/about-us/our-vision-mission-and-principles. The Collaboration now uses the single word "Cochrane" as a brand name for this expertise.

ever follow philosophical arguments. There are many diverse actors in medicine, pushing in different directions, and the socio-political negotiation of epistemic hierarchies which took place during this period of enormous research dynamics in medicine and the life sciences offered science-based medicine new arguments for re-building its claims. The chapter finishes in Section 5 with a brief outlook on precision medicine as an attempt to re-open the debate about strong and weak forms of knowledge. Throughout these five sections, the analysis is based primarily upon publications now regarded as landmark articles. Instead of taking them as illustrating a rather well-known story, I use these sources to situate the transformations towards EBM within a larger network of socio-political changes and to contextualise how the abstract term "best available evidence" acquired more and more significance in dealing with individual cases. The debate on epistemic hierarchies is far from being closed today. The historical trajectory formats the ongoing discussions around best medical practice.

1. Incipient scepticism in a period of unlimited progress

In retrospect, the 1970s can be described as a phase which built up awareness about the problems that EBM was mobilised to solve towards the end of the century. Initially, however, there was neither a consensus about the existence of a problem, nor a shared understanding of its significance. On the contrary, Cochrane's sceptical analysis must be contrasted with the, at the time, prevailing enthusiasm about the unprecedented progress in science and technology, as most ostensibly demonstrated by the space programme and the landing on the moon in 1969. Medicine participated in such promises in many respects, its biggest triumph in terms of public recognition being the transplant of a human heart in 1967. Also, the now infamous 1962 Ciba Symposium on "Man and his Future", discussing (among other topics) the total eradication of all pathogens (Wolstenholme 1963), exemplifies this generally shared sense of unlimited technological progress. In a similar attitude, the cover story of *Life* magazine in September 1965 celebrated the new powers to the "Control of Life": with eye-catching visuals, the issue described how "audacious experiments promise decades of added life, superbabies with improved minds and bodies, and even a kind of immortality". The contemporary audience may have perceived the details of fetal surgery, ultrasound imaging, test-tube reproduction and kidney transplants with uncanny admiration, but, for citizens and experts alike, it was simply inconceivable that eradication programmes would result in the massive problems of multiple drug resistance – or the progress of medical technology in today's bioethical conundrums (Podolsky 2014).

If anything, even the Thalidomide catastrophe had demonstrated the powers of new drugs in their full ambivalence, when more than ten thousand babies were born with malformed limbs because or their mothers taking a newly released and aggressively marketed drug, before it was stopped in 1961. These events resulted in much stricter regimes for clinical testing. In the US, for example, the Food and Drug Administration (FDA) emerged during this period as a powerful actor, requiring proof of efficacy before granting approval of a new drug (Greene and Podolsky 2012). As these regulatory reforms implemented stricter test regimes, they also fostered the general appreciation of the type of evidence provided by RCTs and thus served as a blueprint for the type of evaluation later introduced by EBM. At the time, however, public funding institutions such as the National Institutes of Health (NIH) in the US and the MRC in Britain still sponsored the majority of clinical research, with the pharmaceutical industry and new private actors such as clinical research organisations (CROs) taking over only during the 1990s (Bothwell et al. 2016).

Medicine was undergoing a "therapeutic revolution" in this period, as President Gerald Ford had claimed in signing the FDA bill in 1976, expressing a widely held conviction.[6] Such an account of unprecedented medical progress conventionally refers to milestones such as organ transplants, wonder drugs or those in the story of *Life*. But the new levels of funding for basic research in the life sciences since the end of WWII did not simply deliver in forms of scientific advances, new theories or technological inventions, but also resulted in a complex reorganisation of the health sector with, for example, a sub-specialisation of hospital medicine, especially in universities. Comparing the changes in hospital practice after WWII with the introduction of the clinical examination, the post-mortem, ether narcosis and antisepsis during the nineteenth century, historical scholarship has hence re-constructed a much more convoluted process of changes, going hand-in-hand with social transformation and political reform.

A particularly important arena was to be found in the growing dominance of laboratory science in medical practice during the twentieth century.[7] The *American Medical Association*, for example, established an *Institute for Biomedical Research* in Chicago in 1963, comprising no clinic but 80 scientists for the "intensive and fundamental study of life processes particularly as related to intracellular mechanisms" (Walsh 1963, 1382). Its consequence was the appearance of the élite specialist, who was caricaturised as caring more about research findings than about his patients. Quite early on, this new trend towards basic research raised concerns about how it might push clinical care in the wrong direction and constrain efforts

---

6 "Therapeutic revolution" is primarily an actors' term, used, for example, by the pharmaceutical industry for demarcating their new status. Charles E. Rosenberg introduced it in the historiography in 1977; see Rosenberg 1977.

7 For a careful overview on recent scholarship, see Greene et al. 2016.

in "primary medical care". Kerr White, Franklin Williams and Bernard Greenberg introduced this new term in their now classic paper with the somewhat fancy title "The Ecology of Medical Care". Asking the question "Is the burgeoning harvest of new knowledge fostered by immense public investment in medical research being delivered effectively to the consumers?", and calculating the vast discrepancy between the general medical needs of the overall population and the proportion of patients seen at university hospitals and medical training centres, the authors concluded:

For many years, it was an unchallenged assumption that physicians always knew what was best for the people's health. [...] In general, this experience must be both limited and unusually biased if, in a month, only 0.0013 of the 'sick' adults (or even ten times this figure), [...] in a community are referred to university medical centers. [...] Medical, nursing and other students of the health professions cannot fail to receive unrealistic impressions of medicine's task in contemporary Western society. (White et al. 1961, 890f.)

In a graph illustrating their main argument, they showed the minute selection of patients seen in a university clinic as a small square nested in a series of much larger boxes (see Figure 1).[8] Even during the 1960s, statistics were already being employed as a technology for critiquing epistemological hierarchies in medicine – a process that resulted in the arrival of EBM in a new "evidence ecosystem" (Heneghan et al. 2017a, j2873), in which the different actors of the health sector compete over the significance of their data. White's title-giving metaphor hence invites us to reflect upon evidence as something with an epistemic life of its own, rivalling other forms of knowledge and information (see Section 5 below).

A similar, more complex history applies to the RCT, the main tool for generating reliable evidence today: so decisively introduced by Bradford Hill for testing the efficacy of streptomycin in Britain in 1948 when the drug was so scarce that a placebo control was of no ethical concern, this test strategy had emerged from multiple attempts in rigorous clinical testing, going on for at least half a century.[9] Hill's testing became possible with the funding schemes which the MRC made available for basic and clinical research in Britain, but it took a long time before academic physicians recognised the RCT as a technology offering new opportunities against excessive prescribing by their colleagues.[10]

---

8 A 3D-version of the central figure in the 1961-paper, showing nested boxes of relevance, is still used for the University of Virginia's Kerr White Health Care Collection; see http://historical.hsl.virginia.edu/kerr/home.cfm.html, last accessed 1 January 2019.

9 Medical Research Council 1948. The British Medical Journal devoted an issue to its 50th anniversary in 1998; see Chalmers 1998; Bothwell and Podolsky 2016.

10 Marks 1967; Edwards 2007.

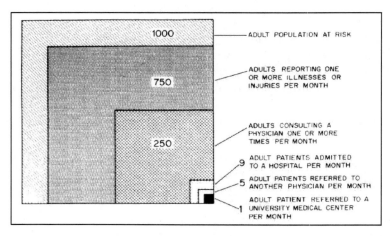

Figure 1: Graph illustrating the relative relevance of patient contacts in the medical training site (university medical centre = black box in the right-hand corner) to the proportions of the population reporting illnesses and consulting medical help (White et al. 1961, 888).

Even Hill himself expressed strong reservations against the RCT as a universal tool, stating in his Heberden Oration in 1965: "Any belief that the controlled trial is the only way would mean not that the pendulum had swung too far but that it had come right off its hook." (Hill 1965, 108) This was a single, but eminent voice; his statement can be taken as sign of how contested the RCT still was in the 1960s – and it can also encourage us to reconsider its current dominance. According to the epistemology of EBM, an RCT may accurately and sufficiently be characterised as a rational test technology delivering objective data, in historical terms, however, the construction of the RCT as such a technology transpires as a complex social process full of multi-faceted debates and involving actors pulling in different directions. The pharmaceutical industry, for example, which today is clearly the powerhouse of this knowledge technology, remained sceptical for a long time, fearing too much regulation. The RCT rose to the status of "gold standard" for sorting the "therapeutic wheat from the chaff" only during the 1980s – ironically, at a time when this standard was to be abolished in the economy (Jones and Podolsky 2015).

Focusing on the British context, Helen Valier and Carsten Timmermann have re-constructed how the relationship between experimental medicine and clinical service was changed by the new role of the state as a scientific entrepreneur and the increasing centralisation of policy and planning after the war, so that the clinical trial eventually emerged as privileged form of therapeutic evaluation (Valier and Timmermann 2008). Cochrane had already identified a shift towards pure science and basic research as one of the main factors contributing to what he had described as an inflation of medical expenditure:

[The Medical Research Council's] foundation was on the principle that it should have 'the widest possible freedom to make new discoveries unhampered by pressures to give precedence to those problems which appeared at the moment to be of the most pressing practical importance'. The idea was excellent but there have been unexpected side-effects. The MRC inevitably was biased towards the pure and opposed to applied research. (Cochrane 1972, 10)

The changing relations between laboratories, clinical settings and public health authorities have been a continuing topic in the scholarship on the emergence of biomedicine as the typical form of the post-WWII Western medical framework, but there is probably no satisfying way to summarise the history of Western medicine after 1945, as Anne Hardy and Tilly Tansey have pointed out (Hardy and Tansey 2006), because of the complexities of medicine and the political and economic forces that shape the production and circulation of medical knowledge – and it is precisely this which calls for situating the arrival of EBM in a political epistemology.

With regard to these large forces and tendencies, it is important to remember how the socio-political climate changed from the 1960s to the 1970s: besides being a period of unbroken trust in progress, the 1960s have also become synonymous with the emergence of the counterculture, the civil rights movement, the activism against the war in Vietnam and many more social changes. These tendencies may not have affected the medical sector directly, but the swing towards the political left certainly inspired a new wave of criticism and a generally more critical attitude towards medicine and its institutions. The sociologist Nicholas Jewson, for example, published his famous paper "The Disappearance of the Sick Man from Medical Cosmology" in 1976, describing the historical shift of medicine away from the patient as a whole person to organs and cells (Jewson 1976). The most radical voice was probably Ivan Illich with his *Medical Nemesis* from 1975, in which he accused medicine of "colonising" human beings by expropriating health and making people sick (Illich 1975). In a manoeuvre typical of the ideologised climate of the time, he turned the correlation between better conditions of health and larger numbers of doctors into the argument that physicians simply go where they can expect more money for their services. "Medicalisation" became a buzzword, which reflected Illich's claim that medicine had been expanded into new domains and had conquered aspects of human life and behaviour not self-evidently medical – with harmful consequences for those affected and deleterious effects on society.[11]

Illich had based his critique upon the highly influential studies by Thomas McKeown, chair of social medicine in Birmingham since 1945, who had collected demographic data from historical records for questioning the causal role of medical advances in increasing survival rates and general life expectancy during the

---

11 Conrad and Schneider 1980. For a current view on medicalisation, see Correia 2017.

last 200 years, which he instead attributed to better nutrition and economic growth. McKeown summarised his studies in *The Role of Medicine: Dream, Mirage or Nemesis?*, written with the help of a Rock Carling Fellowship by the Nuffield Provincial Hospitals Trust in 1976, the same fellowship that had enabled Cochrane to write his *Effectiveness and Efficiency* four years earlier (McKeown 1976). The discussion about the role of medicine in improving health continues (Deaton 2013); for the focus on epistemic hierarchies here, it suffices to note how these early studies mobilised statistical data as powerful arguments about medical services and the role of medicine in society.

2. Kindling awareness for a problem not yet clear

Cochrane's recommendation of RTCs did not change the field, but his book did not pass by unnoticed. It was reviewed by international medical journals, and the national press jumped on the harsh criticisms of wasted money (Thomas 1997). When a symposium in 1978 at the Royal College of Physicians in London debated "Medicines for the Year 2000", Cochrane was invited to open the first session with a critical review on the development of medicine from 1930 to 1970, but neither the representatives from medicine nor from the pharmaceutical industry recognised how his strict recommendation of RCTs could also be understood as a strategic opportunity. On the contrary, the scientist John Butterfield described Cochrane's views as an "assault on modern medicine's reputation" and Brian Cromie, director of the pharmaceutical company Hoechst UK, accused the regulatory authorities of being "mass murderers" because they delayed the availability of life-saving drugs (Butterfield 1979, 75).

Apparently, it took more steps to change the prevailing attitude towards medicine and to transform medical practice. One of these steps was a study by John Wennberg and Alan Gittelsohn, published a year after Cochrane's book in *Science*, reporting surprising treatment variations among hospitals around Boston which could not be explained by medical or social differences. Instead, they had to be attributed to individual and unjustified preferences of the physicians in charge (Wennberg and Gittelsohn 1973). Wennberg had studied with Kerr White, who had pointed him to the unique research opportunities in newly available hospital data which he then evaluated for treatment variations.[12] In the *Science* paper, he argued that variation in medical treatment amounted to a much more serious problem than a mere local curiosity or a matter of wasted money, because such idiosyncratic preferences were coupled with significantly poorer outcomes, some of which occurred at the prestigious university hospitals of Ivy League institu-

---

12 See White 1997, 18.

tions. Again, little changed immediately, and the problems lingered on: "The amount and cost of hospital treatment in a community have more to do with the number of physicians there, their medical specialties and the procedures they prefer than with the health of the residents." (Wennberg and Gittelsohn 1982, 120) *Scientific American* popularised their findings nine years later as a direct confirmation of Illich's stark thesis. Wennberg and Gittelsohn, however, did not accuse medicine in general or its scientific basis, but questioned individual expertise as a sufficient resource – a critique which would eventually result in efforts to standardise health care on an international level and scale.

These early epidemiological studies did not change medicine at once, but the public learnt about the relevance of statistics. In a political climate that viewed the reigning ideology of techno-scientific progress more and more critically, epidemiological data showed that advances in basic medical research did not pay off for patients automatically, and a growing number of experts recognised the important differences between the rationale for individual treatment decisions and the effects on the collective level. The newly established departments of epidemiology demonstrated their relevance for health policy and health care planning. Gradually, this were also to affect the hierarchy in medical schools. When EBM was started about two decades later, its actors could build on this momentum and turned to medical education with their new approach on the level of the individual decision-making for (and with) the patient. In this way, the EBM group gained strength as a reform movement from the clinic for the clinic, in contrast to earlier epidemiological perspectives on health care planning, research policy or social medicine.

This is not to say that practice – on the level of the individual patient – had been entirely absent in earlier debates, but problems of decision-making had been addressed rather differently. This is demonstrated in fascinatingly nuanced ways by Alvan Feinstein from Yale University's prestigious faculty of medicine: when David Sackett was still a young professor at a relatively unknown university, Feinstein published – together with him and Walter Spitzer – a paper criticising the state of clinical research as a "chaotic variety of activities, ranging from polemic debates about medical ethics to quantitative accounts of hospital finances to biostatistical experiments with randomized therapy" (Spitzer et al. 1975). But Feinstein pursued a slightly different agenda compared to clinical epidemiology. He was not concerned about outcomes or costs, but about medicine losing its own proper grounding as a clinical science of diagnosis and decision-making. For Feinstein, the diagnostic differences among well-trained physicians were no question of skill or quality, but a core epistemic issue of medicine as a practical science, pointing to a scientific problem. According to his analysis, such differences mirrored the various ways to group the signs and symptoms to a diagnosis and to translate the "dis-ease" of a patient into a disease in accord with a medical classification system.[13]

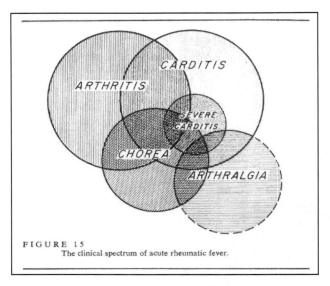

FIGURE 15
The clinical spectrum of acute rheumatic fever.

Figure 2: Alvan Feinstein's illustration of the relative overlap in clinical symptoms between a selected set of diagnoses, using a Venn diagram he knew from his studies of statistics and Boolean algebra (Feinstein 1976, 184).

Because he had studied mathematics before entering medical school, he was used to sketching such conceptual problems diagrammatically and employed sophisticated branches of statistics to address the theoretical problems of medical decision-making (Feinstein 1963). In his *Clinical Judgment* from 1967, another publication that is now often quoted as a source and starting-point for EBM, Feinstein described, for example, the usefulness of Venn diagrams for the problems in disease classification:

I began using such multi-circle diagrams in illustrations presented both in print and in lectures. Many physicians are accustomed to seeing drawings in which a single circle is 'sliced', like a pie, into radial segments that show the proportional distribution or percentages of some total entity. The circles I drew were used in a quite different way: they contained no quantitative distinctions and the 'partitions' were performed not by the radial lines of a 'pie', but the overlap of several other circles. [...] They were the type of Venn diagram devised to illustrate 'sets' studied in symbolic logic and in Boolean algebra. (Feinstein1967, 8f.)

Feinstein's esteemed colleagues in clinical medicine, however, did not share his enthusiasm; they did not even recognise the problems he intended to discuss:

---

13 The distinction between "dis-ease" and "disease" is borrowed from Feinstein 1996.

I realized that there were probably two reasons for the difficulty. The first was that my academic colleagues [...] dealt mainly with mechanisms of disease [...] and most of their research data came either from animals or from the results of patients' laboratory tests. Without the need to classify clinical symptoms and signs for specific analysis, these colleagues had seldom encountered such classifications as a challenge. [...] Another probable reason for the difficulty was that these particular colleagues, [...] were superb clinicians with excellent clinical judgment. [...] Although each colleague might have used a different system that was non-reproducible or even indescribable, he had been using the system for years and had found that it worked reasonably well for his clinical judgment. (Feinstein 1967, 12)

Clinical judgement continued to rely on tacit knowledge and the individual skills of the examiner, regardless of Feinstein's call for a "scientific methodology in clinical medicine" (Feinstein 1964).

Feinstein did not give up, but intensified his efforts, most famously by his course on *Clinical Biostatistics* in LVII parts in the 1970s.[14] A little later, while Spitzer and he served as editors of the *Journal of Chronic Diseases*, they renamed it the *Journal of Clinical Epidemiology*, thereby establishing in 1988 what can now be regarded a flagship journal of EBM (Feinstein and Spitzer 1988). These alliances notwithstanding, Feinstein conserved his scientific emphasis with distinctive nuances. In 1985, both Feinstein and Sackett published volumes entitled *Clinical Epidemiology*. But the difference shines up in their subtitles: while Sackett propagated it boldly as *A Basic Science for Clinical Medicine*, Feinstein designed it as an *Architecture of Clinical Research*.[15] Focusing on clinical practice as a science of its own, he developed strategies to embrace "indices, rating scales and other expressions that are used to describe and measure symptoms, physical signs, and other distinctly clinical phenomena", such as pain, distress and disability (Feinstein 1987, 5). Feinstein searched for abstract scientific methodology to transform as much of the art of clinical medicine into a proper science. His agenda was to clarify and elevate the epistemic status of clinical practice itself – rather than letting it be guided by its averaged effects. He hence accused EBM early on as being "cookbook medicine",[16] and his name re-surfaces frequently in the still ongoing discussions on EBM.

Neither Feinstein's *Clinical Judgment* nor Cochrane's *Efficiency and Effectiveness* transformed medicine. In retrospect, both approaches had only limited impact in their time. Cochrane and Feinstein failed to open a debate on epistemic hierarchies as they did not address the very barrier between basic research with its intrinsic epistemic ideals of scientific explanation, on the one hand, and clinical practice, on the other, relying on skills and tacit knowledge, often not even recognised as being epistemically relevant by the actors, as the responses to Fein-

---

14 Feinstein 1970–1981, the series was the basis for his monograph of this title: Feinstein 1977.
15 Sackett et al. 1985; Feinstein 1985.
16 To my knowledge, Feinstein introduced the term; see Feinstein and Horwitz 1997.

stein's book show. Perhaps it was also the economic environment that kept the established routines in their place in the US, where private health insurance paid for treatments based upon diagnoses, leaving smaller leverage to the epidemiologists. This was to change, when the discussion was taken up from inside the university in another country with a National Health Service, because this initiative approached the debate from a different angle, enrolling different actors under the new slogan of "evidence-based medicine". This new approach emerged from the activities of David Sackett's group at McMaster University in Hamilton, Ontario, Canada.

3. Building up momentum locally

The beginnings of Sackett's Department for Clinical Epidemiology date back to the same period that we have been discussing so far. Specific to the approach at McMaster University, however, was the local context of a newly established medical school that was opened around the new teaching method of problem-based learning, instead of the traditional courses in the underlying sciences and specialties of medicine. Sackett arrived at McMaster University in 1967 to start, at the young age of 32, a new Department for Clinical Epidemiology, which was at the time still an oxymoron, as it was designed to connect epidemiological, i.e., collective and statistical, data with the clinical problems of individual cases. John Evans, the new medical school's founding dean, had basically given Sackett *carte blanche* to design the department as he saw fit. For about a decade, Sackett and his team established themselves by conducting clinical trials on issues ranging from hypertension to the prevention of strokes by aspirin, thereby demonstrating the relevance of statistical evidence for common clinical problems.

Around the year 1980, however, Sackett formed a group in Hamilton for "critical thinking" based upon clinical epidemiology, and they designed a course on "critical appraisal of the medical literature", which was aimed at medical students early in their training.[17] This was the starting-point of the dynamics of EBM at micro-level: whereas Cochrane had looked at outcomes in the abstract in terms of aggregated numbers for therapeutic procedures in relation to saved lives, and Feinstein had aimed at his colleagues with the outlook on *clinimetrics* as new science, Sackett's group focused on training in the ordinary clinic and on skills in dealing with the growing literature – what was to resonate so well not only in the context of problem-based-learning at McMaster's. At the moment of its inception, however, this subtle difference was probably not clear even to the protago-

---

17 Haynes 1991; the group published a series of articles in the Canadian Medical Association Journal; see Department of Clinical Epidemiology and Biostatistics, McMaster University 1981.

nists; in 1985, the McMaster group published their textbook still under the title of *Clinical Epidemiology*. Now in its third edition, it has in the meantime evolved into the "the bible of evidence based medicine" (Smith 2015).

The term "evidence-based medicine" first appeared in the autumn of 1990 in an information document, and in 1991, Gordon Guyatt from Sackett's group used it as an editorial opening in the newly established *ACP Journal Club*, describing it as a means to extract "new, sound clinical evidence from the morass of the biomedical literature so that practitioners can get at it" (Guyatt 1991). Later, Guyatt remembered:

Meanwhile, our group of enthusiastic evidence-based medical educators at McMaster [...] were refining our practice and teaching of EBM. Believing that we were on to something big, the McMaster folks linked up with a larger group of academic physicians, largely from the United States, to form the first Evidence-Based Medicine Working Group and published an article that expanded greatly on the description of EBM, labeling it as a 'paradigm shift'. (Guyatt 2008, xxif.)

"Evidence-Based Medicine: A New Approach to Teaching the Practice of Medicine", the article of November 1992 mentioned by Guyatt here, was the first product of an alliance between the group in Hamilton and Drummond Rennie, editor of the *Journal of the American Medical Association* (*JAMA*). Rennie traded the "iconoclastic" McMaster team for a series in 32 articles in *JAMA*, as follows: "Like their leader, Sackett, they tended to be expert at working together and forming alliances with new and talented workers, and intellectually exacting." In the following year, they began together the "Users' Guides to the Medical Literature", starting in 1993 and now also available as an interactive website (Rennie 2008).

Introducing EBM as "a new approach to teaching the practice of medicine", the group positioned itself at explicit distance to the prevailing approaches to medicine, as the "EBM Working Group" explained straight away with the first lines of their seminal paper:

A NEW paradigm for medical practice is emerging. Evidence-based medicine de-emphasizes intuition, unsystematic clinical experience, and pathophysiologic rationale as sufficient grounds for clinical decision making and stresses the examination of evidence from clinical research. Evidence-based medicine requires new skills of the physician, including efficient literature searching and the application of formal rules of evidence evaluating the clinical literature. (EBM Working Group 1992, 2420)

In fact, the group discarded the three historically most important ways of legitimising medicine in just a single sentence: medicine as an art ("intuition"), as an expertise ("un-systematic clinical experience"), and as a science ("pathophysiologic rationale"). Taken together, EBM thus proclaimed to change the legitimisation of medical interventions within biomedicine: neither scientific explanations, nor clinical expertise sufficed any longer for legitimising the diagnostic and therapeutic process; what were required instead were data from clinical studies – or, even better, their consolidation in systematic reviews.

With this allegedly "new approach", theoretical knowledge and scientific explanations were downgraded epistemologically, from previously ranking as the highest form of knowledge in biomedicine to now functioning as a mere heuristic or useful strategy for identifying possible targets for new interventions (then to be evaluated by RCTs). This epistemic inversion is most explicitly demonstrated by the famous "pyramid of evidence" in EBM (see Figure 3) (Glover et al. 2006). This figure has meanwhile acquired an almost iconic status within EBM and circulates widely (sometimes with slight alterations). Showing three layers of aggregate forms of evidence at the top and three further layers of evidence from different types of clinical trials at the middle, it leaves one single bottom layer for "background information" and "expert opinion", those forms of knowledge arrived at in basic research (including their theoretical frameworks) and by the clinical examination of the patient. The illustration had been developed by Jan Glover from Yale's Cushing/Whitney Medical Library for a poster presented at a Medical Library Association meeting – in itself, a telling detail of both the central role of information management and the co-operative, anti-authoritarian spirit of the EBM movement.

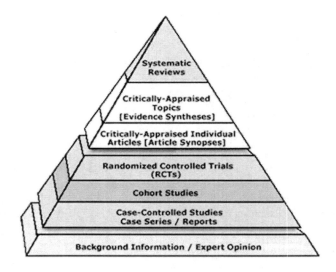

Figure 3: The "Pyramid of Evidence" in evidence-based medicine, pushing pathophysiological explanations, the individual circum-stances of patients and clinical expertise – the cornerstones of clinical practice before EBM – to the bottom (Glover et al. 2006).

Looking back on the emergence of EBM, Guyatt stated in his preface to the Users' Guide: "In fewer than 20 years, evidence-based medicine (EBM) has gone from a tentative name of a fledgling concept to the fundamental basis for clinical practice that is used worldwide." (Guyatt 2008, xxi) Compared with this new consensus on clinical evidence that was to emerge with the global implementation of EBM, the previous periods since the "laboratory revolution", which started at some time during the nineteenth century, appear to have been united under the search for pathophysiological explanations, albeit with violent and frequent debates about such explanations (Cunningham and Perry 1992). Today's regime of EBM with its emphasis on aggregate statistical data does certainly not rule uncontested, but empirical "evidence" remains unobjectionable. Evidence can be criticised as biased or incomplete but cannot be contested as such; it is rhetorically immunised. Wherever the name came from, switching from clinical epidemiology to EBM proved to be decisive.

The ensuing transformation of the medical realm went beyond mere rhetoric. There may be many different reasons why the antagonistic approaches by clinical, biological, genetic, psychological, or social explanations of medical problems have waned, but EBM certainly helped to nurture a more syncretistic attitude within medicine. This more ecumenical spirit contrasts sharply with the aspirations of the pioneers of physiology to base medicine on the natural laws of living organisms. "Absolute determinism must become the real foundation of the science of living bodies", had been Claude Bernard's famous *credo* (Bernard 1957, 80), who had hence railed against the use of averages declaring, "in physiology, we must never make average descriptions of experiments, because the true relations of phenomena disappear in the average" (Bernard 1957, 135). With EBM, however, averages reign; and this was sensed early on by science-minded clinicians such as Feinstein, who criticised it – in remarkably similar ways to Bernard – as gearing towards the "'average' randomized patient" (Feinstein and Horwitz 1997).

Not every branch of scientific medicine and biomedical research subscribed to determinism in similar ways, and statistics, in particular, had already started to play an important role in Bernard's time (Jorland et al. 2005), but, from the distant vantage-point of today's EBM, the different branches of scientific medicine had shared the trust in scientific explanations for legitimising therapeutic interventions. Compared with EBM as new and different epistemic regime, one could even argue that some of the most adversarial specialties, such as psychosomatics and surgery, had engaged in a similar thought style as they had shared the agenda of seeking causal explanations, although their therapeutic conclusions were radically divergent. From the stomach's acid imbalance as an explanation for peptic ulcers that legitimised vagotomy as a surgical procedure to restore its balance to Franz Alexander's psychodynamic explanation of the same disease as a suppressed conflict requiring psychoanalysis: during the heydays of pathophysiological reasoning, theories and explanations formed the core of the epistemology of medicine.[18] Or, to turn the same argument around, causal explanation as an overarching thought style had enabled actors from medicine's vastly different branches to engage in fierce debates on the plausibility of a theory. Evidence was brought forward *pro* or *contra* a theory and debated with regard to the strength of the underlying epistemology, whereas most discussions today seem to focus around the strength of evidence, and revolve around hidden biases. The so-called replication crisis is a timely symptom of this shift, as such a "crisis" is only conceivable on the assumption of a universal standard for hypothesis testing – something totally ignorant of historical epistemology (Atmanspacher and Maasen 2016). Empirical data had certainly been of crucial relevance also in earlier regimes, for example, for demonstrating the value of a theory and for corroborating scientific knowledge, but without a scientific theory for their explanation, data were not accepted as proper knowledge in themselves.

According to the principles of EBM, by contrast, evidence suffices even in the absence of explanations, something which is absolutely unsatisfactory for science-based medicine. The Christmas issues of the *British Medical Journal* regularly comment with wit and irony on recent trends in medicine. The issue for the year 2011 indulged in this curiosity of "evidence without explanation" by reporting the alleged effectiveness of remote, retroactive prayer in a randomised clinical trial (Leibovici 2001). The paper was not to be taken at face value – and illustrated the new spirit of EBM all the more faithfully. EBM's creed is not the religious *credo quia absurdum*, but its agnostic echo that "evidence" applies even if or when it is absurd.

Searching for factors contributing to such a radical historical and epistemological shift, many different aspects have to be factored in; and of special weight and importance was the forging of alliances. EBM participated at, and contributed to, larger socio-political transformations at the turn of the millennium, including the neoliberal agenda and new measures of efficiency and control. Already before the announcement of EBM, for example, the American Congress had initiated an Agency for Health Care Policy and Research (AHCPR) in response to "accumulated public and private frustrations about the perceived health and economic consequences of inappropriate medical care." (Field and Lohr 1990, 2) Building on the NIH Consensus Development Program, which had been limited to the research community in its activities (Solomon 2007), the agency established a Committee on Clinical Practice Guidelines for rationalising and standardising health care. The committee stressed, as its first addressees, the "patients and practitioners", but the driving force behind the new agenda were clearly the - in the

---

18 The examples chosen here are mine, but Feinstein sketched a similar perspective upon medicine's reigning paradigms in: Feinstein 1996.

public perception - escalating costs, as became clear with the committee's following publication on *Cost Analysis Methodology* (Grady and Weis 1995). Compared to the emphasis on social critiques of medicine during the 1970s, the debate on rising health costs of the 1990s took place in a neoliberal political climate, when "efficiency", "choice", and "value for money" became economic catchphrases.

This political turn applied even more radically to Britain, where Margaret Thatcher proclaimed free-market ideology and in which "economic concepts [were] no longer treated as the terminology of an alien social science, but as part of a plausible language of action" (Ashmore et al. 1989, 200). A reform of the NHS in 1989 under the slogan "Working for Patients" introduced an internal market for health care as a new "business-like" approach (Greengross et al. 1999, 11), and, in 1991, a Research and Development Programme was introduced, which focused exclusively on the evaluation of clinical trials as the appropriate measure against diversity and "unacceptable variation in the quality of treatment" (Peckham 1991, 367). In the following year, the same year that saw the announcement of EBM, British initiatives to collect available RCTs and to review their results for the different specialties were merged to a new centre, named after Archibald Cochrane (who had died in 1988). In the British context, the new thought style exposed its normative stances particularly early. Iain Chalmers, the founding director of the Cochrane Centre, appealed to the scientific audience even in his inaugural address to make a prospective registration of all clinical trials mandatory and to ban the under-reporting of results as "scientific misconduct" (Chalmers et al. 1992, 387).

Systematic reviews, as delivered by the Cochrane Centre, were "the next phase in the application of science to the art of medicine", an editorial in *The Lancet* assured its readers, thereby inadvertently pointing to the disciplining effects of the new knowledge regime.[19] In an epistemological perspective from the inside, the move from single RCTs to their compulsory introduction and collective evaluation in systematic reviews may simply be described as a rational consequence of the methods already implemented. In the light of the complexities of clinical practice and the heterogeneity of epistemologies employed for the construction of medical knowledge, however, this next step transpires as a vast exercise in homogenisation. The implementation of EBM radically changed the way in which medical problems were tackled, as they were now perceived in a standardised and universally formatted way.

It took the concerted efforts of many actors with different agendas in the political realm to make EBM pervasive. A major enabling factor was the perceived costliness and preciousness of health care that turned it into a central (and expensive) policy issue in many Western societies (Lambert 2006). Specialised institutions for the collection, digestion and management of knowledge in aggre-

---

19 *The Lancet*, Editorial 1992, 1131.

gate forms such as the guideline committees or the Cochrane Centre, hence moved to the top of the "pyramid of evidence". And this new, single pyramid replaced previously existing hierarchies of competing forms of medical knowledge, pushing clinical expertise, the hallmark of the "art of medicine" since antiquity, towards the bottom, together with theoretical explanations and pathophysiological considerations, so central to medicine as the biomedical research programme. The introduction of EBM must be appreciated in terms of a socio-political epistemology of medical knowledge, where hitherto more marginal voices gained attention, new institutions emerged, and new alliances in a changed political environment contested the established balance of powers in the health sector until "evidence" was raised to the top.

Such a larger picture of the political epistemology of EBM must also include the technical and material circumstances, such as, for example, the prevailing information infrastructure. When Wennberg and Gittelsohn reported treatment variations in the 1970s, this had required access to unique health care records, and the results were granted a publication in *Science*. Twenty years later, the Medical Literature Analysis and Retrieval System (MEDLARS) of the National Library of Medicine (NLM) made computerised literature searches possible in the US, but this still required access to a locally-stored copy of the database (Dee 2007). The *Oxford Database of Perinatal Trials*, for example, was published, in the pre-Internet age, on diskettes and distributed upon a subscription basis (Starr et al. 2009). Today, more than 350,000 searches are performed daily worldwide through its online version MEDLINE, containing more than 24 million references since 1966 from about 5,200 journals. "Critical appraisal of the literature", when introduced at McMaster's in 1980, was a laborious procedure requiring hard work in the library. If this has now turned into a relatively easy exercise, this overshadows the transformative powers of the new medium. In addition to providing a new thought style, EBM offered a "new approach" in dealing with the wealth of knowledge; it has become a necessity against an information overload.

Beyond the intellectual appeal of epistemological considerations and the hard factors of technological constraints, softer aspects also paved the way for EBM. Perhaps the most important was the rhetoric of empirical evidence: Who would or could argue *against* empirical evidence? Cochrane had railed against the ill-founded dominance of the specialists and never ceased to call for epidemiological data, Feinstein had aspired to train his fellow clinicians in esoteric statistics. The EBM group, by contrast, appealed to the young physician to stand up against authoritarianism by advertising the obvious, namely, evidence. Thus, a movement had been started, which was also an alliance against old and new authorities in medicine. There is a certain irony to the fact that EBM also offered other players in the ever more costly health sector new leverage for increasing their powers in the name of rational procedures for containing costs. With the framework of

EBM, the pharmaceutical and medical industry, for example, quickly learned the rules of the new game for demonstrating the superiority of costly pharmaceutical or technological innovations – enforcing even stricter regimes of control of medical practice by regulatory authorities.

4. EBM as thought style and the renewal of philosophy of medicine

The introduction of EBM marks the rare event that a new approach was propagated as an intervention from philosophy of science. The "EBM-Working Group" advertised its programme as nothing less than a paradigm shift, explicitly referencing Thomas Kuhn. In addition to starting their paper with the sentence "A new paradigm for medical practice is emerging", the group emphasised this by separating a paragraph under the line "A PARADIGM SHIFT" in capital letters, starting with the following lines:

Thomas Kuhn has described scientific paradigms as ways of looking at the world that define both the problems that can legitimately be addressed and the range of admissible evidence that may bear on their solution. When defects in an existing paradigm accumulate to the extent that the paradigm is no longer tenable, the paradigm is challenged and replaced by a new way of looking at the world. Medical practice is changing, and the change, which involves using the medical literature more effectively in guiding medical practice, is profound enough that it can appropriately be called a paradigm shift. (EBM Working Group 1992, 2420)

According to Kuhn's definition, however, the introduction of EBM hardly matches the criteria for a paradigm shift (Kuhn 1962). There is simply no incommensurability in the Kuhnian sense between the old pathophysiologic rationale and the new evidence from randomised clinical trials (Couto 1998). Any discrepancy between a well-defined hypothesis from laboratory research and the outcome of a clinical trial would still force biomedical research to explore and explain this discrepancy along its own terms and conditions – and not under a new theoretical framework. The BMJ's Christmas paper quoted above was not a regular publication but highlighted precisely this tension, thereby pointing to the continuance of the underlying biomedical framework. EBM pervaded medicine without any revolutionary breakthroughs in scientific theory; it offered a new algorithm for clinical decision-making without new therapeutic insights.

There can be little doubt that the introduction of EBM fails the criteria of a paradigm shift, according to Kuhn, and its explicit declaration as such a paradigm shift thus testifies to the popularity of Kuhn's philosophy of science and to the rhetorical skills of the EBM working group. However, if EBM was no paradigm change in the Kuhnian sense, its introduction nonetheless signifies a thorough transformation of medical practice. The massive re-negotiation of epistemic hierarchies described here represents an epistemic rupture, which can be related to a different thought style – to use Ludwik Fleck's term from his socio-political epistemology (1979). For a proper assessment of the swing from biomedicine to EBM, it does not suffice to mobilise the concept of paradigm from philosophy of science for comparing and contrasting science-based biomedicine with statistics-based EBM, but one has to trace how the new formats of knowledge transformed clinical practices and how new routines intervened in the power relations among the institutions in the health sector, shaping together the construction of medical reality by the various actors.

Historians and sociologists of medicine were quick to point to a much more convoluted path towards the recent debates about the best practice of scientific medicine.[20] Some located forerunners, in an attempt to create a *longue-durée* history of a form of practice that had been discredited by allegedly more science-based approaches only temporarily (Tröhler 2000). Others pointed to the ongoing debates within medicine, warning against their over-interpretation as radical shifts (Sturdy 2011). EBM resonated with earlier criticisms of medical practice and responded by a range of malleable techniques ("critical appraisal") for transforming clinical practice. Instead of declaring EBM to be the introduction of a new paradigm, it should better be characterised as an approach situated within the contemporaneous political and economic climate of declining trust and growing accountability. The implementation of EBM was, for example, part and parcel of a much larger trend towards standardisation, and its rapid implementation in many different countries fostered evaluation as governance technology far beyond medicine. Evidence-based practice has henceforth become a model that permeated from medicine to health care, education and the university sector as a "guide to doing it better" (Cartwright and Hardie 2012). "Evaluation", "evidence" and "transparency" have become the buzzwords for a new form of rigour in dealing with complex problems of control and regulation in Western societies.

This much larger trend towards a general appreciation of evaluation and accountability is aptly illustrated by the shift in the public responses to Iain Chalmers and the activities of the Cochrane Collaboration. Their pilot project on obstetrics was scandalised by "some senior obstetricians" as the effort of an "obstetric Baader-Meinhof gang" (Chalmers et al. 1989), but, just ten years later, Chalmers was invited to open an issue on "evidence-led policy" of the *Annals of the American Academy of Political and Social Science*, in which he plainly stated:

---

20 Timmermans and Berg 2003; Lambert 2006.

Because professionals sometimes do more harm than good when they intervene in the lives of other people, their policies and practices should be informed by rigorous, transparent, up-to-date evaluations. (Chalmers 2003, 22)

Regardless of the debate within medicine as to whether meta-analysis and systematic reviews of RCTs do arrive at proper representations of the reality of medical practice, evaluation has gained a status of fundamental technology of governance, and it did so probably because of its second promise, namely, transparency.

Another facet of EBM pointing to its predominant functioning as a rhetorical means rather than as a new paradigm was the missionary verve with which its advocates propagated it. Critics noted parallels to "Protestant exegesis" or went as far as to compare it with fascism.[21] It is no coincidence that these criticisms come from a later phase, when EBM had already started to control medical practice. Initially, critique came from among the proponents of clinical epidemiology. Feinstein, for example, regarded the algorithms for corroborating the results from different RCTs in systematic overviews simply as naïve (compared to his sophisticated Boolean algebra), ridiculing meta-analysis as "statistical alchemy for the 21st century" (Feinstein 1995). A year later, his co-editor Spitzer echoed this attitude, citing meta-analysis "theology", while at the same time celebrating clinical epidemiology "as one of the main basic sciences for clinical practice", that has, in the meantime, displaced pathology (Spitzer 1996). Perhaps even more telling, however, was the fact that neither of these articles mentioned EBM – so few years after its announcement, it was probably not yet what it soon turned into, a new thought style.

Jeremy Howick expressed this new status of EBM as an epistemic regime most radically in his opening sentence of the first monograph on the philosophy of EBM: "What on earth was medicine based on before evidence-based medicine?" (Howick 2011, 3) The implementation of EBM coincided, indeed, with a remarkable interest in philosophy of medicine. Within a couple of years, a rather esoteric sub-specialty of the philosophy of science turned into a substantial branch of disciplinary activity; in the meantime, about half a dozen handbooks were published on the topic (Borck 2016). The announcement of EBM as a paradigm shift may have been a rhetorical strategy for advertising the "new approach", but it was followed by a new line of work, concentrating on elucidating methodological principles, discussing the problems and rationale for different designs of clinical tests or debating the implications of the statistical approach for the classification of diseases.[22] Besides a revived debate on disease as a scientific or value-laden concept, this wave of scholarship initially concentrated on epistemological analyses of the different test methodologies and strategies for meta-

---

21 Gerber et al. 2005; Holmes et al. 2006.
22 Gifford 2011; Sadegh-Zadeh 2012; Solomon et al. 2017.

analysis, producing highly relevant arguments against over-stating the powers of RCTs, for example.[23]

Philosophers working in this arena may seem to accept, at least implicitly, EBM as a guiding paradigm of medical practice and thereby foster it. A closer look, however, reveals how this field of scholarship contributed in its own ways to the re-negotiation of epistemic hierarchies. By following EBM in its critique of science-based medicine and of the exclusiveness of pathophysiological explanations for medical decision-making, the philosophical debate opened up towards other approaches to medicine, health, and illness. Once the dominance of the sciences in biomedicine's epistemology was questioned, other voices and traditions of critical thinking called for attention: the patient perspective was brought in; nursing as a form of care, rather than the healing imperative of medicine. Pain, suffering and disability – core topics of healing practices in most cultures, but relegated to the subjective side in biomedicine – re-surfaced as heavily unrecognised and under-theorised topics of medical thinking.[24] *Medical humanities* may still be the name for a rather loose field (of mainly frustrating activities) mediating between the factual necessities of hospital medicine and the needs of the patient, but there was a remarkable renaissance of continental philosophy in thinking about medicine.[25]

The plea for efficacy and for a critical evaluation of medical treatment that was once started at the margins of medicine's institutional hierarchy has reached the centre stage of medicine. By taking EBM as the guiding framework of medical practice, however, this philosophy of medicine ignores the negotiations about epistemic hierarchies that accompanied its implementation and the shift that turned "weak" epidemiological information – because it was deemed hardly relevant for a science-based medicine – into "strong" knowledge that now regulates medical practice and informs governance in the health sector. The increased relevance of statistical thinking and its complex methodologies provided new content for analysing medicine as a science of decision-making, albeit without pushing the discussions towards embracing insights from science-and-technology studies and philosophy of practice. By and large ignoring the societal dynamics underlying the rise of EBM, the discussions in philosophy of medicine disguise the epistemic negotiations that have to be addressed in order to re-construct the rise of EBM from being a framework acknowledging weak knowledge to its status of dominating paradigm. Because it quickly transpired that evaluation is a powerful tool also for legitimising difficult and contested decisions in governance and pub-

---

23 Upshur 2005; Cartwright 2007 and 2011; Bluhm 2007.
24 Most indicative example of this intrinsic dynamic of philosophy of medicine is the massively widened scope between two volumes edited by Thomas Schramme within five years: Schramme 2012 and Schramme and Edwards 2017.
25 Toombs 2001; Meacham 2015; Zeiler and Folkmarson Käll 2014.

lic policy, evidence-based practices rapidly spread from the inner circles of medicine to a massive reform of the health system; they dominate in the education sector and guide public policy in many arenas. In the meantime, EBM has even invaded history and philosophy of science: "Why study the history and philosophy of evidence-based health care? Become a better health-care professional."[26]

5. EBM's defeat by victory: Epistemic hierarchies within the ecology of evidence

Today, Cochrane would have little reason to complain about a neglect of "applied research"; several thousand clinical practice guidelines worldwide recommend treatment procedures for specified conditions, derived from systematic reviews. The pharmaceutical industry spends excessively large amounts on clinical trials, and health services in many countries couple their benefits to evidence of treatment efficacy. The introduction of EBM has simply been a "game changer", as quoted above (Knottnerus and Tugwell 2017, 1). And yet, some of EBM's most vocal proponents recently declared it to be "a movement in crisis", and formed an *EBM Renaissance Group*, arguing that it needed refocusing, as its implementation had resulted in unintended negative consequences.[27] Their criticisms can be summarised into two larger groups, one being the biases of vested interests, the other a standardisation of clinical practice to the detriment of patient-centred approaches (Greenhalgh et al. 2015).

Thomas Frieden, for example, director of the Center for Disease Control under President Barack Obama, recently described, in a prominent review, how the predominant, if not exclusive, reliance on RCTs misguided clinical practice, because study groups hardly represent typical patients with their co-morbidities, cannot capture more rare or more long-term treatment effects and may simply not reflect the complexities of clinical cases (Frieden 2017). Against these well known, though hardly appreciated or embraced limitations, he argued for the specific value of allegedly inferior statistical data from observational studies, as clinical practice had to deal with the complexities of mixed populations and multimorbid patients. Questioning the hierarchy of levels in the pyramid of evidence, he and others thereby re-opened the debate on epistemic hierarchies with the question of whether data should better be statistically sound or more appropriate to real-world conditions (Moreira and Palladino 2011).

---

26 https://www.conted.ox.ac.uk/courses/history-and-philosophy-of-evidence-based-health-care, last accessed 1 January 2019.
27 Greenhalgh et al. 2014, for the Evidence Based Medicine Renaissance Group.

These critical arguments were not new. Already back in 1997, Feinstein and Ralph Horwitz had criticised EBM along similar lines:

Although the proposed practice does not seem new, the new collection of 'best available' information has major constraints for the care of individual patients. Derived almost exclusively from randomized trials and meta-analyses, the data do not include many types of treatments or patients seen in clinical practice. (Feinstein and Horwitz 1997, 529)

Twenty years later (and after Feinstein's death), Horwitz repeated his criticisms under the title "Why evidence-based medicine failed in patient care and medicine-based evidence will succeed" (Horwitz and Singer 2017). What had changed, however, was the environment in which this critique was placed, where EBM now reigned as dominant framework and where its consequences in the form of standardised care have become more tangible. This is certainly one reason why publications on patient-centred approaches have shown exponential growth over the last decade. The changed situation kindles these perspectives, which, in turn, attract greater attention and generate some traction. These voices may agree with Hill that the pendulum favouring RCTs has meanwhile come "off the hook", but the metaphor is misleading, as it is less a matter of changing attitudes, swinging like a pendulum, but of system changes in health care.

Arguments for better clinical care, more individualised treatment decisions and patient-centred medicine will remain a pipe dream, if these system effects are not addressed. As long as EBM functions in smooth alliance with a form of governmentality based upon the powerful imperatives of evaluation and transparency, its intrinsic logic will continue to push in the opposite direction. The current debate on a better inclusion of patients' perspectives and on patient-related outcome measures illustrates this conundrum (Deshpande et al. 2011): even before there was any agreement on how to operationalise this as a study methodology, the Cochrane Collaboration demonstrated how to stabilise its status and maximise the impact of its reviews by integrating the "consumer" branch into its organisation and machinery. Similarly, pharmaceutical companies have shown great skills in presenting and advertising their products as individualised solutions, tailored to the specific needs of patients. But pointing to these tendencies does not imply that industry and systematic reviews would follow the same agenda or share the wrong intentions; on the contrary, across divergent agendas, these actors engage in activities that result in a stabilisation of EBM at systems level.

These problematic system effects are further highlighted with regard to the second set of criticisms. There is general agreement that the aims of EBM have been jeopardised by the vested interests of industry and service purchasers. The issue had been raised by Feinstein back in 1997 and was powerfully re-voiced by John Ioannidis, who had made himself famous with the paper entitled "Why most Published Research Findings are False". In a report posthumously addressed to

David Sackett in 2016, he lamented on how EBM "has been hijacked" in a style reminiscent of Archie Cochrane:

As EBM became more influential, it was also hijacked to serve agendas different from what it originally aimed for. Influential randomized trials are largely done by and for the benefit of the industry. Meta-analyses and guidelines have become a factory, mostly also serving vested interests. […] Risk factor epidemiology has excelled in salami-sliced data-dredged articles with gift authorship and has become adept to dictating policy from spurious evidence. Under market pressure, clinical medicine has been transformed to finance-based medicine. In many places, medicine and health care are wasting societal resources and becoming a threat to human well-being. (Ioannidis 2016, 82)

Because the vulnerability of EBM to vested interests is so well known and generally acknowledged, many measures have been taken to control and counter this, from the declaration of interests, required for publication and special issues on the topic, to prospective trial registration and the retrospective *COMPare Trials Project* (Bauchner and Fontanarosa 2017). The most solid effect of these measures to contain and control vested interest, however, was the development and implementation of stricter and ever more rigid test protocols, allegedly securing quality of data, but moving the spaces of experimentation further away from the complexities of clinical practice. In his railing against the pharmaceutical industry, however, Ioannidis carefully avoided accusing them of bad intentions, but located the problem in the very regulations that had been implemented by the service purchasers and the regulatory authorities to control them: "Corporations should not be asked to practically perform the assessments of their own products. If they are forced to do this, I cannot blame them, if they buy the best advertisement (i.e., 'evidence') for whatever they sell."

Ioannidis' jeremiad inspired the EBM's flagship journal to publish a special issue on the achievements and prospects of the EBM, starting with a reply in the form of a tribute to Feinstein, instead of Sackett, explaining how EBM "was bound to fail" because of its "considerable limitations". Probably inadvertently, this was a perfect illustration of the tensions intrinsic to EBM between epidemiology and clinical decision-making – the unlikely coupling that both Feinstein and Sackett had envisioned as the backbone for reforming medicine to the better: "It is time to substitute the fashionable popularity of a strategy developed outside of clinical medicine with models and research based on the insights of clinical judgment and patient–doctor interaction." (Fava 2017, 3) The journal's invited responses defended EBM in foreseeable ways as either providing statistically sound solutions or as serving the patient – but failed to accommodate the systemic perspective that Ioannidis had taken with his lament.[28] The issue thus provides a fair outlook on the current debate on EBM from the inside, with the actors either defending EBM as the best available approach, or calling for a better integration

---

28 Guyatt 2017; Richardson 2017.

of patient perspectives in the form of a "patient-centred medicine" or "medicine-based evidence".[29] For the time being, EBM will have to live by its own standards and to navigate between the problematical impact of the interests of the various actors and the inapplicability of the evidence generated by these standards.

All the more fascinating is how other quarters in the EBM movement have meanwhile started to embrace a more complex understanding of it. The recently launched "EBM manifesto" for "developing more trustworthy evidence" illustrates this new attitude. For this initiative, the *British Medical Journal* teamed up with the Centre for EBM at the University of Oxford, staging the annual "Evidence Life" conferences, designed to "develop, disseminate, and implement better evidence for better healthcare". The manifesto was a product of this co-operation and a platform also exists on the Internet which invites practitioners to engage in the collective improvement of EBM by working on its agenda in the form of a "living document".[30] Here, the "survival of the fittest" that Ioannidis had located on the side of the pharmaceutical industry has been appropriated by an EBM initiative as a strategy of collective team work:

Through this work and other projects, we know of substantial problems but also progress and solutions spanning the breadth of the evidence ecosystem, from basic research to implementation in clinical practice. [...] The manifesto has been developed by people engaged at all points in the research ecosystem engaging in fixing the problem. (Heneghan et al. 2017b, 120f.)

Evidence, once announced as a new paradigm and thoroughly implemented in medical practice as a reformist thought style, has thus turned into an ecosystem both of and by itself. The reform of the health sector by the introduction of EBM did not follow from the discovery of "evidence" as an objective value to be calculated by RCTs and systematic reviews, but the current state of the health system emerged from the re-negotiation of epistemic hierarchies, assigning each type of evidence its specific differential value of survival. Evidence must be conceived of as a relative concept, determined not only by the different methodologies to establish it, but also by the sociopolitical networks of interaction, debate and regulation.

In an evidence ecosystem, there are also niches, for example, for biomedicine's attempts to discover mechanistic pathways of disease. The introduction of EBM has not led to a situation in which basic biomedical research has lost its importance. On the contrary, research in the life sciences still counts among the most dynamic and productive research areas. The implementation of EBM occurred in a period during which molecular biology, (epi-)genetics and systems biology provided an increasing array of new targets for medical intervention. The

---

29 Bensin 2000; Horwitz and Singer 2017.
30 See http://evidencelive.org/manifesto, last accessed 1 January 2019.

new vision of *precision medicine* mobilises these massive insights from basic research with the goal of replacing the standard approach of treating all patients suffering from a specific disease in the same way by tailor-made therapeutic interventions, defined from highly individualised data and predicted disease trajectories. If EBM were a paradigm, precision medicine is designed to function as its opposite: not a world of medical problems perfectly compartmentalised into treatment groups evaluated by large RCTs, but a world of medical problems perfectly individualised down to the specific fabric of the diseased body. In epistemic terms, precision medicine is the strongest competitor to EBM, directly challenging its approach to group testing and extending physiological explanations down to the level of molecular interaction in individual cases.

At this moment, individualised "biological" treatments are starting to deliver, and precision medicine is beginning to flourish as a high-tech academic research programme. But if precision medicine hinges on trading massive amounts of information with Big Data technologies, the Internet and the new economy may be faster in finding the appropriate solutions by inviting the consumers to take (allegedly) command.[31] Deep-learning algorithms may predict treatment outcomes more reliably than pathophysiological theories, and individual physicians can no longer manage the oceans of relevant information so that the future of medicine belongs to information technology and the companies controlling it, thus replacing the physicians. Perhaps there are more battles to come about weak and strong knowledge in medicine. Perhaps EBM was the last instantiation of physician-based medicine.

References

Ashmore, Malcolm, et al. (1989): *Health and Efficiency: A Sociology of Health Economics*. Milton Keynes: Open University Press.

Atmanspacher, Harald, and Sabine Maasen (Eds.) (2016): *Reproducibility: Principles, Problems, Practices, and Prospects*. Hoboken NJ: Wiley.

Bauchner, Howard, and Phil B. Fontanarosa (2017): "Conflict of Interest." *Journal of the American Medical Association*, 317 (17): 1705–1812. http://compare-trials.org/, last accessed January 1 2019.

Bensin, Jozien (2000): "Bridging the Gap. The Separate Worlds of Evidence-based Medicine and Patient-centered Medicine." *Patient Education and Counseling*, 39: 17–25.

Bernard, Claude (1957): *An Introduction to the Study of Experimental Medicine*. Transl. by Henry Copley Greene, with an introduction by Lawrence J. Henderson. New York: Dover.

---

31 Brown 2015. For a business proposal envisioning the replacement of physician-based medicine, see https://www.youtube.com/watch?v=kbdbpWhBfg0, last accessed 1 January 2019.

Bluhm, Robyn (2007): "Clinical Trials as Nomological Machines: Implications for Evidence-based Medicine." In: Harold Kincaid and Jennifer McKitrick (Eds.): *Establishing Medical Reality: Essays in the Metaphysics and Epistemology of Biomedical Science*, 149–166. Dordrecht: Springer.

Borck, Cornelius (2016): *Medizinphilosophie zur Einführung*. Hamburg: Junius.

Bothwell, Laura E. et al. (2016): "Assessing the Gold Standard – Lessons from the History of RCTs." *New England Journal of Medicine*, 374 (22): 2175–2181.

Bothwell, Laura E., and Scott H. Podolsky (2016): "The Emergence of the Randomized, Controlled Trial". *New England Journal of Medicine*, 375 (6): 501–504.

Brown, Sherry-Ann (2015): "Building Super Models: Emerging Patient Avatars for Use in Precision and Systems Medicine." *Frontiers in Physiology*, 6: 318.

Butterfield, Sir John (1979): "The Contribution of Modern Medicines 1930s to 1970s." In: George Teeling-Smith and Nicholas Wells (Eds.): *Medicines for the Year 2000: A Symposium Held at the Royal College of Physicians*, 26–34. London: Office of Health Economics.

Cartwright, Nancy (2007): "Are RCTs the Gold Standard?", *BioSocieties*, 2: 11–20.

Cartwright, Nancy (2011): "A Philosopher's View of the Long Road from RCTs to Effectiveness." *The Lancet*, 377 (9775): 1400–1401.

Cartwright, Nancy, and Jeremy Hardie (2012): *Evidence-based Policy: A Practical Guide to Doing it Better*. Oxford: Oxford University Press.

Chalmers, Iain (1998): "Unbiased, Relevant, and Reliable Assessments in Health Care." *British Medical Journal*, 317: 1167.

Chalmers, Iain (2003): "Trying to do More Good than Harm in Policy and Practice: The Role of Rigorous, Transparent, Up-to-date Evaluations." *Annals of the American Academy of Political and Social Science*, 589: 22-40.

Chalmers, Iain, et al. (1992): "Getting to Grips with Archie Cochrane's Agenda." *British Medical Journal*, 305 (6857): 786-788.

Chalmers, Iain, et al. (Eds.) (1989): *Effective Care in Pregnancy and Childbirth*. Oxford: Oxford University Press.

Cochrane, Archibald L. (1972): *Effectiveness and Efficiency: Random Reflections on Health Services*. London: Nuffield Provincial Hospitals Trust.

Cochrane, Archibald L. (1984): "Sickness in Salonica: My First, Worst, and Most Successful Clinical Trial." *British Medical Journal*, 289 (6460): 1726–1727.

Conrad, Peter, and Joseph W. Schneider (1980): *Deviance and Medicalization: From Badness to Sickness*. St. Louis MI: Mosby.

Correia, Tiago (2017): "Revisiting Medicalization: A Critique of the Assumptions of What Counts as Medical Knowledge." *Frontiers in Sociology* 2 (14), doi:10.3389/fsoc.2017.00014, last accessed 1 January 2019.

Couto, Joaquim S (1998): "Evidence-based Medicine: A Kuhnian Perspective of a Transvestite Non-theory." *Journal of Evaluation in Clinical Practice*, 4: 267–275.

Cromie, Brian (1979): "Present Problems: The effects of British Regulations." In: George Teeling-Smith and Nicholas Wells (Eds.): *Medicines for the Year 2000: A Symposium Held at the Royal College of Physicians*, 74–83. London: Office of Health Economics.

Cunningham, Andrew, and William Perry (Eds.) (1992): *The Laboratory Revolution in Medicine*. Cambridge: Cambridge University Press.

Daly, Jeanne (2005): *Evidence-based Medicine and the Search for a Science of Clinical Care*. Berkeley CA: University of California Press.

Deaton, Angus (2013): *The Great Escape: Health, Wealth, and the Origins of Inequality*. Princeton NJ: Princeton University Press.

Dee, Cheryl Rae (2007): "The Development of the Medical Literature Analysis and Retrieval System (MEDLARS)." *Journal of the Medical Library Association*, 95 (4): 416–425.

Department of Clinical Epidemiology and Biostatistics, McMaster University (1981): "How to Read Clinical Journals: I–V." *Canadian Medical Association Journal*, 124: 555–558; 703–710; 869–672; 985–990; 1156–1162.

Deshpande, Prasanna R., et al. (2011): "Patient-reported Outcomes: A New Era in Clinical Research." *Perspectives in Clinical Research*, 2: 137–144.

Edwards, Martin (2007): *Control and the Therapeutic Trial: Rhetoric and Experimentation in Britain, 1918–48*. Amsterdam: Rodopi.

Evidence-Based Medicine Working Group (1992): "Evidence-based Medicine. A New Approach to Teaching the Practice of Medicine." *Journal of the American Medical Association*, 268 (17): 2420–2425.

Fava, Giovanni A. (2017): "Evidence-based Medicine was Bound to Fail: A Report to Alvan Feinstein." *Journal of Clinical Epidemiology*, 84: 3–7.

Feinstein, Alvan R (1985): *Clinical Epidemiology: The Architecture of Clinical Research*. Philadelphia PA: Saunders.

Feinstein, Alvan R (1995): "Meta-analysis: Statistical Alchemy for the 21st Century." *Journal of Clinical Epidemiology*, 48: 71–79.

Feinstein, Alvan R. (1963): "Boolean Algebra and Clinical Taxonomy I: Analytic Synthesis of the General Spectrum of a Human Disease." *New England Journal of Medicine*, 269: 929–938.

Feinstein, Alvan R. (1964): "Scientific Methodology in Clinical Medicine. 1: Introduction, Principles and Concepts; 2. Classification of Human Disease by Clinical Behavior; 3. The Evaluation of Therapeutic Response; 4. Acquisition of Clinical Data." *Annals of Internal Medicine*, 61: 564–679; 757–781; 944–965; 1162–1193.

Feinstein, Alvan R. (1967): *Clinical Judgment*. Baltimore MD: Williams and Wilkins.

Feinstein, Alvan R. (1970–1981): "Clinical Biostatistics, Parts I–LVII. *Clinical Pharmacology & Therapeutics*: 11–30.

Feinstein, Alvan R. (1976): *Clinical Judgment*. Baltimore MD: Williams and Wilkins.

Feinstein, Alvan R. (1977): *Clinical Biostatistics*. Saint Louis MI: Mosby.

Feinstein, Alvan R. (1987): *Clinimetrics*. New Haven CT: Yale University Press.

Feinstein, Alvan R. (1996): "Twentieth Century Paradigms that Threaten both Scientific and Humane Medicine in the Twenty-first Century." *Journal of Clinical Epidemiology*, 49: 615–617.

Feinstein, Alvan R., and Ralph I. Horwitz (1997): "Problems in the 'Evidence' of 'Evidence-based Medicine'." *American Journal of Medicine*, 103: 529–535.

Feinstein, Alvan R., and Walter O. Spitzer (1988): "The Journal of Clinical Epidemiology: Same Wine, New Label for the Journal of Chronic Diseases." *Journal of Clinical Epidemiology*, 41: 1–7.

Field, Marilyn J., and Kathleen N. Lohr (Eds.) (1990): *Clinical Practice Guidelines: Directions for a New Program*. Washington DC: National Academy Press.

Fleck, Ludwik (1979): *Genesis and Development of a Scientific Fact*. Chicago IL: University of Chicago Press.

Frieden, Thomas R. (2017): "Evidence for Health Decision Making – Beyond Randomized, Controlled Trials." *New England Journal of Medicine*, 377: 465–475.

Gerber, Andreas et al. (2005): "Evidence-based Medicine is Rooted in Protestant Exegesis." *Medical Hypotheses*, 64 (5): 1034–1038.

Gifford, Fred (Ed.) (2011): *Philosophy of Medicine*, (Handbook of Philosophy of Science, Vol. 16). Amsterdam: Elsevier.

Glover, Jan, et al. (2006): "Pyramid Schemes: The Fusion of Evidence Levels and Information Resources." Poster session presented at the Medical Library Association Annual Meeting, Phoenix, May 2006.

Grady, Mary L., and Kathleen A. Weis (Eds.) (1995): *Cost Analysis Methodology for Clinical Practice Guidelines*. Rockville MD: US Dept. of Health and Human Services, Public Health Service, Agency for Health Care Policy and Research.

Greene, Jeremy A., et al. (Eds.) (2016): *Therapeutic Revolutions: Pharmaceuticals and Social Change in the Twentieth Century*. Chicago IL: The University of Chicago Press.

Greene, Jeremy A., and Scott H. Podolsky (2012): "Reform, Regulation, and Pharmaceuticals – The Kefauver-Harris Amendments at 50." *New England Journal of Medicine*, 367(16): 1481–1483.

Greengross, Peter, et al. (1999): *The History and Development of the UK National Health Service 1948–1999*. London: DFID Health Systems Resource Centre.

Greenhalgh, Trisha, et al. (2015): "Six 'Biases' against Patients and Carers in Evidence-based Medicine." *BMC Medicine*, 13: 200.

Greenhalgh, Trisha, et al. for the Evidence Based Medicine Renaissance Group (2014): "Evidence Based Medicine: A Movement in Crisis?", *British Medical Journal*, 348: g3725.

Guyatt, Gordon (2017): "EBM has not only Called out the Problems but Offered Solutions." *Journal of Clinical Epidemiology*, 84: 8–10.

Guyatt, Gordon H. (1991): "Evidence-based Medicine." *ACP Journal Club*, 114: A16.

Guyatt, Gordon H. (2008): "Preface." In: Gordon H. Guyatt et al. (Eds.): *Users' Guides to the Medical Literature: A Manual for Evidence-based Clinical Practice*. 2nd edition, New York: McGraw-Hill Medical.

Guyatt, Gordon H., and Drummond Rennie (1993): "Users' Guides to the Medical Literature." *Journal of the American Medical Association*, 270 (17): 2096–2097.

Hardy, Anne, and E.M. Tansey (2006): "Medical Enterprise and Global Response, 1945–2000." In: William F. Bynum et al. (Eds.): *The Western Medical Tradition [2]: 1800 to 2000*, 405–533. Cambridge: Cambridge University Press.

Haynes, R. Brian (1991): "The Origins and Aspirations of ACP Journal Club." *ACP Journal Club*, 114: A18.

Heneghan, Carl, et al. (2017a): "Evidence Based Medicine Manifesto for Better Health Care." *British Medical Journal*, 357: j2873.

Heneghan, Carl, et al. (2017b): "Evidence Based Medicine Manifesto for Better Health Care." *Evidence Based Medicine*, 22: 120–122.

Hill, Austin Bradford (1965): "Reflections on the Randomized Controlled Trial." *Annals of Rheumatic Diseases*, 25: 107–113.

Holmes, Dave, et al. (2006): "Deconstructing the Evidence-based Discourse in Health Sciences: Truth, Power and Fascism." *International Journal of Evidence-Based Healthcare*, 4 (3): 180–186.

Horwitz, Ralph I., and Burton H. Singer (2017): "Why Evidence-based Medicine Failed in Patient Care and Medicine-based Evidence will Succeed." *Journal of Clinical Epidemiology*, 4: 14–17.

Howick, Jeremy (2011): *The Philosophy of Evidence-based Medicine*. Chichester: Wiley.

Illich, Ivan (1975): *Medical Nemesis: The Expropriation of Health*. New York: Pantheon Press.

Ioannidis, John P.A. (2016): "Evidence-based Medicine has been Hijacked: A Report to David Sackett." *Journal of Clinical Epidemiology*, 73: 82–86.

Jewson, Nicholas D. (1976): "The Disappearance of the Sick-Man from Medical Cosmology, 1770–1870", *Sociology*, 10: 225–244.

Jones, David S., and Scott H. Podolsky (2015): "The History and Fate of the Gold Standard." *The Lancet*, 385 (9977): 1502–1503.

Jorland, Gérard, et al. (Eds.) (2005): *Body Counts: Medical Quantification in Historical and Sociological Perspectives*, Montreal: McGill-Queens Press.

Knottnerus, J. André, and Peter Tugwell (2017): "Evidence-based Medicine: Achievements and Prospects." *Journal of Clinical Epidemiology*, 84: 1–2.

Kuhn, Thomas S (1962): *The Structure of Scientific Revolutions*. Chicago IL: University of Chicago Press.

Lambert, Helen (2006): "Accounting for EBM: Notions of Evidence in Medicine." *Social Science and Medicine*, 62: 2633–2645.

Leibovici, Leonard (2001): "Effects of Remote, Retroactive Intercessory Prayer on Outcomes in Patients with Bloodstream Infection: Randomised Controlled Trial." *British Medical Journal*, 323 (7327): 1450–1451.

Marks, Harry M. (1967): *The Progress of Experiment: Science and Therapeutic Reform in the United States, 1900–1990*. Cambridge: Cambridge University Press.

McKeown, Thomas (1976): *The Role of Medicine: Dream, Mirage or Nemesis?* Oxford: Blackwell.

Meacham, Darian (Ed.) (2015): *Medicine and Society, New Perspectives in Continental Philosophy*. Dordrecht: Springer.

Medical Research Council (1948): "Streptomycin Treatment of Pulmonary Tuberculosis: A Medical Research Council Investigation." *British Medical Journal*, 2: 769–782.

Moreira, Tiago, and Paolo Palladino (2011): "'Population Laboratories' or 'Laboratory Populations'? Making Sense of the Baltimore Longitudinal Study of Aging, 1965–1987." *Studies in History and Philosophy of Science Part C: Studies in History and Philosophy of Biological and Biomedical Sciences*, 42: 317–327.

Peckham, Michael (1991): "Research and Development for the National Health Service." *The Lancet*, 338: 367–371.

Podolsky, Scott H. (2014): *The Antibiotic Era: Reform, Resistance, and the Pursuit of a Rational Therapeutics*. Baltimore MD: Johns Hopkins University Press.

Rennie, Drummond (2008): "Foreword." In: Gordon H. Guyatt et al. (Eds.): *Users' Guides to the Medical Literature: A Manual for Evidence-based Clinical Practice*. 2nd edition, New York: McGraw-Hill Medical.

Richardson, W. Scott (2017): "The Practice of Evidence-based Medicine Involves the Care of Whole Persons." *Journal of Clinical Epidemiology*, 84: 18–21.

Rosenberg, Charles E. (1977): "The Therapeutic Revolution: Medicine, Meaning and Social Change in Nineteenth Century America." *Perspectives in Biology and Medicine*, 20: 485–506.

Sackett, David L., et al. (1985): *Clinical Epidemiology: A Basic Science for Clinical Medicine*. Boston MA: Little Brown & Co.

Sadegh-Zadeh, Kazem (2012): *Handbook of Analytic Philosophy of Medicine*. Dordrecht: Springer.

Schramme, Thomas (2012): *Krankheitstheorien*. Berlin: Suhrkamp.

Schramme, Thomas, and Steven Edwards (Eds.) (2017): *Handbook of the Philosophy of Medicine*. Dordrecht: Springer.

Smith, Richard (2015): "David Sackett: Physician, Trialist, and Teacher." *British Medical Journal*, 350: h2639.

Solomon, Miriam (2007): "The Social Epistemology of NIH Consensus Conferences." In: Harold Kincaid and Jennifer McKitrick (Eds.): *Establishing Medical Reality: Essays in the Metaphysics and Epistemology of Biomedical Science*, 167–177. Dordrecht: Springer.

Solomon, Miriam, et al. (Eds.) (2017): *The Routledge Companion to Philosophy of Medicine*. London: Routledge.

Spitzer, Walter O. (1996): "The Future of Epidemiology." *Journal of Clinical Epidemiology*, 49: 705–709.

Spitzer, Walter O., et al. (1975): "What is a Health Care Trial?". *Journal of the American Medical Association*, 233 (2): 161–163.

Starr, Mark, et al. (2009): "The Origins, Evolution, and Future of The Cochrane Database of Systematic Reviews." *International Journal of Technology Assessment in Health Care*, 25 (Suppl. 1): 182–195.

Sturdy, Steve (2011): "Looking for Trouble: Medical Science and Clinical Practice in the Historiography of Modern Medicine." *Social History of Medicine*, 24: 739–757.

The Lancet, Editorial (1992): "Cochrane's Legacy", *The Lancet*, 340 (7): 1131–1132.

Thomas, Hugh F. (1997): "Some Reactions to Effectiveness and Efficiency." In: Alan Maynard and Iain Chalmers (Eds.): *Non-random Reflections: on the 25th Anniversary of Archie Cochrane's Effectiveness and Efficiency*, 21–27. London: BMJ Publishing Group.

Timmermans, Stefan, and Marc Berg (2003): *The Gold Standard: The Challenge of Evidence-based Medicine and Standardization in Health Care*. Philadelphia PA: Temple University Press.

Toombs, S. Kay (Ed.) (2001): *Handbook of Phenomenology and Medicine*. Dordrecht: Kluwer Academic Publishers.

Tröhler, Ulrich (2000): *"To Improve the Evidence of Medicine": The 18th Century British Origins of a Critical Approach*. Edinburgh: Royal College of Physicians of Edinburgh.

Upshur, Ross E.G. (2005): "Looking for Rules in a World of Exceptions: Reflections on Evidence-based Practice." *Perspectives in Biology and Medicine*, 48: 477–489.

Valier, Helen, and Carsten Timmermann (2008): "Clinical Trials and the Reorganization of Medical Research in Post-Second World War Britain." *Medical History*, 52: 493–510.

Walsh, John (1963): "AMA: Convention Accents Positive by Announcing Research Institute, Reshaping Scientific Sections." *Science*, 140 (3574): 1382–1383.

Wennberg, John, and Alan Gittelsohn (1973): "Small Area Variations in Health Care Delivery." *Science*, 182 (4117): 1102–1108.

Wennberg, John, and Alan Gittelsohn (1982): "Variations in Medical Care among Small Areas." *Scientific American*, 246 (4): 120–134.

White, Kerr L., et al. (1961): "The Ecology of Medical Care." *New England Journal of Medicine*, 265: 885–892.

White, Kerr L. (1997): "The Ecology of Medical Care: Origins and Implications for Population-based Healthcare Research." *HSR: Health Services Research*, 32: 11–21.

Wolstenholme, Gordon (Ed.) (1963): *Man and his Future*. London: J. and A. Churchill.

Zeiler, Kristin, and Lisa Folkmarson Käll (Eds.) (2014): *Feminist Phenomenology and Medicine*. Albany NY: SUNY Press.

Weak Knowledge in Medicine:
A Comment

Mitchell G. Ash

In one respect, the story these chapters tell appears to be quite simple: as all of our authors tell us, the standard tale of the triumph of "scientific" over traditional medicine as a victory of "hard" (and therefore "strong") over "weak" knowledge needs to be challenged, in a number of ways.

In the eighteenth century, according to Suman Seth, medicine that is now described as pre-scientific, that is as epistemically "weak", because it was based on doctrinal tradition and/or clinical experience rather than experimental natural science, was nonetheless socially strong, to the extent that its practitioners were certified through membership in the Royal College of Physicians and Surgeons, and the practitioners shared prejudices with the ruling colonial and commercial élites. In the nineteenth century, according to John Warner's account, laboratory-based "experimental" medicine did not become universally accepted as "strong" knowledge across the board. Rather, intuitive clinical medicine maintained considerable epistemic strength and social robustness, not only on the margins of medical research and clinical practice or among older practitioners, but as part of basic medical education. In the courts, according to José Brunner, something comparable happened: "scientific" medical claims failed to achieve the credibility amongst judges and juries that the triumphalists allege that they acquired amongst medical scientists and practicing physicians. In this field, "strong" knowledge appears to have been weakened in what Andy Pickering once called "the mangle of practice" (Pickering 1995) – perhaps even to the detriment of the very expert status physicians and their interlocutors in the courts wanted to claim. One hundred years later, according to Cornelius Borck, a rather different and yet in one sense comparable tale has played itself out: the alleged strength of both "scientific" ("basic" laboratory based) and intuitive clinical medical knowledge have been undermined by so-called evidence based medicine (EBM), grounded mainly in metastudies of large numbers of double-blind clinical trials. Summarised in this way, we have before us a fascinating revisionist tale indeed. Shall we accept this story as offered to us? Before answering this question, I would like to query some of the categories that have been employed in these essays in various ways.

First of all, it seems clear that, on methodological grounds alone, "weak" knowledge, being relational by definition, cannot be historicized without also historicizing "strong" knowledge. One hundred twenty years may seem like a long time, but in the long history of medicine it is actually rather brief. So we need to clarify for each of the case studies what was considered to be "strong" and "weak" knowledge at the time and in the context in question.

In addition, since we agree that medical science, like other sciences, is a social project, we must also ask: What or who decides what is "strong" knowledge, and on what basis? One way of approaching an answer to this question is to distinguish explicitly between the epistemic and the social robustness of knowledge claims, as scholars in social studies of science have been doing for some time.[1] Of course, this distinction doesn't work perfectly, especially if we agree that scientific research is itself a social process. This implies that there is a social component to the claim of "epistemic" robustness, as suggested by references to a consensus of scientific opinion. This implies in turn that such claims cannot be adjudicated on philosophical grounds alone, though philosophers of science might wish that this were possible. On the other hand, socially based claims about the impact or success of scientific knowledge claims cannot escape having to examine the epistemic dimensions at work, since one, albeit not the only factor that unifies scientific communities within which such claims are decided is the presence of commonly accepted criteria for deciding whether knowledge claims are credible or not. Whether the acceptance of such criteria derives from abstract "reason" or from the common institutional contexts of medical training would appear to be a moot point, since precisely such modes of reasoning are part of what is supposedly inculcated in medical training. A similar argument applies to decisions about what is "weak" knowledge. Seen from this perspective, "weak" knowledge might be defined as knowledge claims lacking in both epistemic strength and social acceptance, either in the scientific community or amongst wider publics, not least including patients.

Yet assessments of the strength of knowledge also relate to social positions of the actors. As Suman Seth writes, in the late eighteenth century, "the medical knowledge of both abolitionists and pro-slavery writers was strong enough to command attention", due to the status of the debating physicians as educated men or to the claims of other participants to medical knowledge, "but too weak to command assent".[2] This was so because it was not clear what was to be regarded as "strong" medical knowledge when it came to deciding whether the obvious decline in slave populations in the Caribbean was to be attributed to diseases contracted during the voyage, before the so-called "seasoning" of black men in their new locations to the brutal climate of the region, or to the customs

---

1 For a brief discussion of the relation between the notion of "social robustness" of knowledge, coined by Helga Nowotny, Peter B. Scott and Michael T. Gibbons (2001) and the approach to "weak knowledge" explored in this volume, see the chapter by Moritz Epple.

2 See Suman Seth's contribution to this volume, 378.

of the slaves themselves. In such circumstances, Seth argues, epistemic "weakness" was defined in large part by lack of consensus, that is, in social terms. Neither physicians who claimed to have treated thousands of slaves nor abolitionist medical men were able to convince their opponents or the public at large, in large part because the participants could not even agree on the terms of the debate, nor could closure be achieved by other means. And yet even the epistemically weak knowledge of British medical practitioners was socially stronger than that of the enslaved themselves, although former slaves' reports could be and were cited by abolitionists.

I turn now to the question of whether the introduction of experimental methods into medical research altered this dynamic. Let me briefly introduce here a parallel example from psychology, a discipline considered by many even today as a paradigmatic case of "soft" science, and therefore of "weak" knowledge. Two reasons are or have been traditionally advanced for this attribution: the invisibility of psychical processes, or "the mind" itself, and the corresponding inaccessibility of mental processes to direct mathematical treatment. The traditional account of the history of psychology is a triumphalist tale of efforts to overcome this dual challenge, which runs not only chronologically but also discursively parallel to the triumphalist tale of the success of "scientific" medicine. As the story goes, Gustav Theodor Fechner's Psychophysics showed the way to the mathematical treatment of psychological processes (here, judgement of sensory differences). In addition, the story continues, the mobilisation of instruments from experimental physiology, including some of the same ones that John Warner names, made it possible to "objectify" and control the presentation of stimuli in psychological experiments. To make this regime work, experimenters and subjects had to discipline themselves, thus creating what Henning Schmidgen has called human-machine ensembles (Schmidgen 2014). In a series of studies, Jill Morawski has shown how experimental psychologists' commitments to strict natural-scientific methods of observation led to the abstraction of their procedures from their own (psychological) selves, to whom the knowledge derived was in theory also supposed to apply (Morawski 2007). Peculiar "scientific selves" – or scientific personae, as Lorraine Daston and Otto Sibum (2003) have called them – resulted. Experimenting psychologists were carefully trained to observe "objectively", to avoid the errors and biases common in "lay" observation, and to prefer laboratory subjects similarly capable of exercising such an "objective" gaze, i.e., of simply reporting sensory experiences with no emotional or judgmental colorings.

One might well argue that a similar separation of the scientific persona from the subject being treated took place during the rise of experimental medicine, even though medical scientists understood that their knowledge claims would apply to themselves if they became patients. In his famous introduction to experimental medicine, which John Warner cites, Claude Bernard exemplified this discourse when he claimed that the pain or even death of thousands of laboratory animals was a necessary price to pay for "objective" medical knowledge. Bernard was not a proponent of instrument-based research, as his German counterparts were. By entering into the regime of "mechanical objectivity" – if indeed they did so – physicians, like experimental psychologists, actually became not so much masters, but rather components of the human-machine ensembles they had assembled. We might conclude from all this that the "strength" of "scientific" medical knowledge came at a rather high price.

But was supposedly "scientific" (meaning laboratory-based) knowledge or the clinical practice allegedly, though perhaps not actually, based on such knowledge already as "strong" in the period John Warner describes as it became decades later? Famous anatomical atlases of the nervous system were being created just at this time, and were by no means complete as yet. On the functional side, actual pathological processes *in* or among nerves corresponding to what physicians were pleased to call "nervous illness" had yet to be observed. One might even ask if we are dealing with "strong", meaning precise knowledge at all in this field, or rather with a passionately advanced programme for obtaining such knowledge – that is, with a strong *belief* that such knowledge would be forthcoming, if only medical scientists would get with the programme. Social robustness, it would appear, preceded epistemic robustness in this case, and not the other way around.

What happened to the status of practical clinical knowledge, derived from long experience? Diagnostic geniuses figure prominently in doctor movies from the 1920s onward. Such apparently magical skills are of course not inborn, but founded on intensive and extensive clinical training and experience – "tacit knowledge" as Cornelius Borck nicely puts it. This is the kind of knowledge that Sir William Osler meant when he asserted that the practice of medicine was both an art and a science, or, more precisely, "an art based upon science" (Bean and Bean 1950, No. 259). Obviously, there is an élitist dimension to this story: physicians with upper class patients tended to emphasize such intuitive skills, along with their carefully cultivated "bedside manner", whereas clinic physicians may have had less time for such things; whether the turn to machine medicine made social mobility into the profession easier in this period is perhaps a relevant issue. However, we should remember in this context that Lorraine Daston and Peter Galison claim that scientists soon realised the problematic character of "mechanical objectivity" and shifted to a new ideal or epistemic virtue, based on supplementing "mechanical objective" data with "trained judgment" (Daston and Galison 2008, Chapter 6). Whether less well educated medical students could make such a combination of skills work might be an important issue, if we agree that the "strength" of knowledge has something to do with its social robustness.

The situation of expert testimony is rather different from that of testimony by experimental subjects, or patients in clinics, who tended to be situationally defined as non-experts (as they were in experimental psychology as well). José Brunner retells in his paper the story of what came to be called "railway spine". This is also part of the history of psychoanalysis, since Freud cited such cases in his papers on male hysteria in the 1890s. As Brunner shows, this was a difficult struggle at the epistemic level – perhaps it is more exact to say that the epistemic issues were inseparable in this case from social relationships. The reality of "subjective" injuries proved difficult for judges or juries to accept, despite obvious physical evidence or impact of seemingly psychically caused traumata. During the period Brunner examines, it appears to have been easier to accept Herbert William Page's "political" interpretation of symptoms over John Erich Erichsen's. Progress was nonetheless evident in the sense that even Page did not claim outright that patients were engaging in deliberate deception, although he did note a suspicious tendency of symptoms to disappear once compensation had been awarded. Perhaps it is not surprising that the dispute was not resolved at the time. Indeed the issue is still very much alive today, for example in claims of traumatic injury allegedly suffered by automobile accident victims due to so-called "whiplash". The tension between the sophisticated interpretations of experts and the yes/no answers demanded by judges and juries, i.e., the logic of the legal system itself, based as it is on the need to award damages or not, appears to be baked into the system, so to speak, or as Americans would now say, to be part of its DNA.[3] So which knowledge was "weak" and which was "strong" in this case; and are we discussing epistemic or social robustness here?

Cornelius Borck brings us into the present. His is the story of an alleged "paradigm shift" that wasn't. If I read him right, the shift to EBM is a clear case of social robustness in a new key – more precisely, of epistemic standards being adapted rather blatantly to the requirements of the health care system, more precisely, to the requirement of efficiency in the provision of care. Indeed, as Borck shows, new work in so-called "philosophy" of medicine appears not to have stimulated, but rather to have been stimulated by this shift, though it is not clear exactly what arguments are advanced in this literature. One way or the other, Borck argues convincingly that the turn to EBM has brought with it a shift away from causal models of explanation in medicine. The efficacy of treatment regimes is apparently being measured here purely statistically, following an input-output model that I would regard as a classic example of what might be called administrative reason. Spectacular or even routine cures of single patients involving long hospital stays and thus incurring enormous costs might be of scientific benefit according to the previous medical regime, but now they apparently quite literally "count" for less – or do they? Here, too, we might note an analogy from the psychical realm; the emergence of short-term psychotherapy, in preference to long-term classical psychoanalysis, accompanied by severe methodological cri-

---

3 For discussion of this issue see Golan 2004.

tique of psychoanalysis coming from philosophy of science, as well as an entire
literature claiming to evaluate the "success" of short- and long-term psychother-
apies, showing, it was claimed, that there was little difference.

Unfortunately, Borck has not provided us with any detailed examples of how
EBM actually works in clinical practice or health care administration. Not having
a concrete picture of just what sorts of statistical reasoning are being employed
here makes it difficult to decide what exactly accounts for the apparent epistemic
"strength" of EBM – more sophisticated statistical methods, or measurably
higher "cure" rates, however these might be defined? Critics of EBM have alleged
for some time that more efficient use of institutional resources, i.e. shorter hospital stays, has now been redefined as medical success. If this is the case, then
perhaps we might say that "strong" knowledge in this case is knowledge that
effectively employs tools and provides results in conformity with managerial priorities, i.e., with administrative reason. If so, then this is obviously a triumph of
social robustness, one so far-reaching that it has transformed or overcome previously accepted criteria for epistemic robustness. Whether this is so is a question
that would surely repay further study.

References

Bean, Robert. B., and William B. Bean (1950): *Sir William Osler: Aphorisms from his bedside
teachings and writings*. New York: Henry Schuman.
Daston, Lorraine, and H. Otto Sibum (2003): "Introduction: Scientific Personae and their
Histories." *Science in Context*, 16: 1–8.
Daston, Lorraine, and Peter Galison (2008): *Objectivity*. New York: Zone Books.
Golan, Tal (2004): *Laws of Man and Laws of Nature: The History of Scientific Expert Testimony
in England and America*. Cambridge MA: Harvard University Press.
Morawski, Jill (2007): "Scientific Selves – Discerning the Subject and the Experimenter in
Experimental Psychology in the United States, 1900-1935." In: Mitchell G. Ash and
Thomas Sturm (Eds.): *Psychology's Territories: Historical and Contemporary Studies from Dif-
ferent Disciplines*, 129–148. Mahwah, NJ & London: Lawrence Erlbaum.
Nowotny, Helga, et al. (2001): *Re-Thinking Science: Knowledge and the Public in an Age of Un-
certainty*. Oxford: Polity Press.
Pickering, Andrew (1995): *The Mangle of Practice: Time, Agency, and Science*. Chicago: Univer-
sity of Chicago Press.
Schmidgen, Henning (2014): *The Helmholtz Curves: Tracing Lost Time*. Translated by Niels
Schott. New York: Fordham University Press.

Authors

Mitchell Ash is Professor Emeritus for Modern History at the University of Vienna. His research focuses on general history of science, especially the relations of science to politics, society and culture in the 19th and 20th centuries, science emigration and the history of psychology.

Nitzana Ben David is a Research Fellow at the Buchman Faculty of law at Tel Aviv University. Her scholarly interests focus mainly on the social and professional history of the Juvenile Court in Palestine and Israel.

Cornelius Borck is Director of the Institut für Medizingeschichte und Wissenschaftsforschung at the University of Lübeck. In addition to brain research between media technology and neurophilosophy, his areas of research include the contemporary history of medicine and man-machine relationships in art and science.

José Brunner is Professor Emeritus at the Buchmann Faculty of Law and the Cohn Institute for the History and Philosophy of Science and Ideas at Tel Aviv University. He works on the relationship between law, memory and identity, the history and politics of psychoanalysis, the politics of the mental health discourse, and psychological theories of Nazism and genocide.

Sven Dupré is Professor of History of Art, Science and Technology at Utrecht University and the University of Amsterdam. His research in art history and the history of science and technology focuses on the link between art and knowledge in Pre-Modern Europe.

Corinna Dziudzia is an Assistant Professor at Catholic University Eichstätt-Ingolstadt. She is a literary scholar focusing on conceptual history and processes of canonisation.

Moritz Epple is Professor for the History of Modern Science at Goethe University, Frankfurt/Main. He works on the history of the mathematical sciences of the 18th to the 20th century in their scientific, cultural and political context.

Rivka Feldhay is Professor Emerita at the Cohn Institute for the History and Philosophy of Science and Ideas at Tel Aviv University. Her research area comprises the relations between knowledge, religion, and politics in the early modern period, with a focus on intellectual currents in the Renaissance, Galileo Galilei and Jesuit scientists.

Orna Harari is Professor at the Department of Classics and the Department of Philosophy at Tel Aviv University. Her research combines ancient logic, proof theory, and mathematics, with topics such as the logical role of geometrical constructions, ancient philosophical accounts of constructions and diagrammatic reasoning and the epistemic status of the principles of proof.

Matthias Heymann is Professor for the History of Technology at the Centre for Science Studies at Aarhus University. He works on the history of environmental science and technology, including the history of energy technologies, the history of atmospheric and climate research, and the history of engineering design.

Martin Herrnstadt is a Post-Doctoral Research Fellow at the Centre Marc Bloch at Berlin and at the Leibniz-Institute for European History in Mainz. He works at the intersection between the history of the human sciences and the history of administrative knowledge.

Annette Imhausen is Professor for the History of Sciences in the Premodern World at Goethe University, Frankfurt/Main. She studies the history of ancient Egyptian mathematics, its contexts, developments and uses within Egyptian culture, as well as its historiography.

Lukas Jäger was a PhD student and Research Fellow in the CRC 1095 "Discourses of Weakness and Resource Regimes" at Goethe University, Frankfurt/Main. He works on the historical beginnings of the sociology of scientific knowledge and Karl Mannheim's tradition in sociology.

Daryn Lehoux is Professor of Classics at Queen's University in Kingston, Ontario. His research interests include ancient sciences (astronomy, astrology, life sciences), epistemology, observation, and astrometeorology.

Natalie Levy is a PhD student at the Sociology and Anthropology department in Tel Aviv University and a Research Fellow at the Van Leer Institute. Her scholarly interests focus mainly on ethnic relations and identifications of Jews and Arabs, and integration in education.

Anne Marcovich is a Research Fellow at Sorbonne University, Paris. She works on the relations between human body representations and representations of the social body, the history of ideas and theories concerning cancer, the human brain, and the processes and mechanisms of the mental development of children.

Falk Müller is Lecturer in the History of Science at Goethe University, Frankfurt/Main. His research focuses on physics and engineering in the 19th and 20th centuries, experimentation, industrial research, the interaction between science and technology in the 20th century, and the history and historical epistemology of materials research.

Dominique Pestre is Director of Studies at the École des Hautes Etudes en Sciences Sociales, Paris. His scholarly interests include the history of modern scientific and technological practices and, more broadly, on the social and political history of modern science.

Andrew Pickering is Emeritus Professor at the Department of Sociology, Philosophy and Anthropology at the University of Exeter. His research in modern history of science focuses on cybernetics, alternative forms of life, especially those spanning science, technology, the arts and spirituality.

Hans-Jörg Rheinberger is Emeritus Scientific Member of the Max Planck Institute for the History of Science in Berlin. The main focus of his research lies in the history and epistemology of experimentation in the life sciences.

Linda Richter is Assistant Professor in the History of Science Working Group at Goethe University, Frankfurt/Main. She researches the history of meteorology and climatology in the eighteenth and nineteenth century.

Sebastian Riebold was a PhD student and Research Fellow in the CRC 1095 "Discourses of Weakness and Resource Regimes" at Goethe University, Frankfurt/Main. Being a trained sinologist, his research interests lie in the reception and adaptation of so-called "Western knowledge" in late nineteenth-century Imperial China.

Suman Seth is Professor at the Department of Science and Technology Studies at Cornell University. His scholarly interests include the history of medicine, race, and colonialism, the physical sciences (particularly quantum theory), gender and science.

Terry Shinn is Honorary-Emeritus Research Director at the CNRS, Paris. His research covers relations between social structure and educational hierarchy in the sciences and the place of "generic instrumentation" in the growth of 20th century scientific knowledge in the physical sciences.

Richard Staley is Rausing Lecturer in the History and Philosophy of Science at the Department of History and Philosophy of Science at Cambridge University. He works on the history of the physical sciences (broadly construed) from the 19th century to the present.

Laurence Totelin is Senior Lecturer in Ancient History at Cardiff University. Her research entails the history of pharmacology and botany with a focus on gynaecological treatments, aphrodisiacs, and the properties of milk.

John H. Warner is the Avalon Professor of the History of Medicine at Yale University. His scholarly interests focus mainly on the cultural and social history of medicine in 19th and 20th century America.

Monika Wulz is Assistant Professor for Science Studies at the ETH Zürich. She works on the French philosophy of science and historical epistemology and on the history of social and economic epistemologies in the 19th and 20th century.

Index